THE ROUTLEDGE COMPANION TO INTERNATIONAL CHILDREN'S LITERATURE

Demonstrating the aesthetic, cultural, political and intellectual diversity of children's literature across the globe, *The Routledge Companion to International Children's Literature* is the first volume of its kind to focus on the undervisited regions of the world. With particular focus on Asia, Africa and Latin America, the collection raises awareness of children's literature and related media as they exist in large regions of the world to which 'mainstream' European and North American scholarship pays very little attention.

Sections cover:

- Concepts and theories
- Historical contexts and national identity
- Cultural forms and children's texts
- Traditional story and adaptation
- Picture books across the majority world
- Trends in children's and young adult literatures.

Exposition of the literary, cultural and historical contexts in which children's literature is produced, together with an exploration of intersections between these literatures and more extensively researched areas, will enhance access and understanding for a large range of international readers. The essays offer an ideal introduction for those newly approaching literature for children in specific areas, looking for new insights and interdisciplinary perspectives, or interested in directions for future scholarship.

John Stephens is Emeritus Professor in English at Macquarie University, Australia.

Section Editors:
Celia Abicalil Belmiro is Professor in the Faculty of Education of the Federal University of Minas Gerais, Brazil and researcher at the Centre of Literacy, Reading and Writing (CEALE/UFMG).

Alice Curry is the founder of Lantana Publishing, an independent publishing house in the UK specializing in multicultural children's books.

Li Lifang is Professor and Vice-Dean of the School of Literature, Lanzhou University, Gansu, China.

Yasmine S. Motawy is Senior Instructor in the Department of Rhetoric and Composition at the American University in Cairo, Egypt.

For further information on this series visit: www.routledge.com/literature/series/RC4444

THE ROUTLEDGE COMPANION TO INTERNATIONAL CHILDREN'S LITERATURE

Edited by John Stephens with Celia Abicalil Belmiro,
Alice Curry, Li Lifang and Yasmine S. Motawy

LONDON AND NEW YORK

First published 2018
by Routledge
2 Park Square, Milton Park, Abingdon, Oxon OX14 4RN

and by Routledge
711 Third Avenue, New York, NY 10017

Routledge is an imprint of the Taylor & Francis Group, an informa business

British Library Cataloguing-in-Publication Data
A catalogue record for this book is available from the British Library

Library of Congress Cataloging-in-Publication Data
Names: Stephens, John, 1944– editor.
Title: The Routledge companion to international
children's literature / John Stephens.
Description: Abingdon, Oxon; New York: Routledge, 2017. |
Series: Routledge companions |
Identifiers: LCCN 2017006088 (print) | LCCN 2017024787 (ebook) |
ISBN 9781315771663 (Master) | ISBN 9781317676072 (pdf) | ISBN 9781317676065 (ePub) |
ISBN 9781317676058 (Mobi/Kindle) | ISBN 9781138778061 (hardback: alk. paper) |
Subjects: LCSH: Children's literature–History and criticism. | Children–Books and reading.
Classification: LCC PN1009.A1 (ebook) | LCC PN1009.A1 R69 2017 (print) |
DDC 809/.89282–dc23
LC record available at https://lccn.loc.gov/2017006088

ISBN: 978-1-138-77806-1 (hbk)
ISBN: 978-1-315-77166-3 (ebk)

Typeset in Times New Roman
by Out of House Publishing

Printed in the United Kingdom
by Henry Ling Limited

CONTENTS

ILLUSTRATIONS

Tables

CONTRIBUTORS

Faraj Dughayyim Addhafeeri is a writer of children's comic strips and animated cartoons. He has acted as editor in chief for two children's magazines and attended several regional and international conferences where he presented papers. He has also published a number of picture books for children as well as essays for different magazines. Aldhafeeri is an MA candidate in curriculum design and teaching strategies at King Saud University, KSA. He works as a secondary school teacher and was a member of the Arabic studies national examination committee in 2015–2016.

Sabah Abdulkareem Aisawi is an Associate Professor at the Department of English/ College of Arts, University of Dammam, Kingdom of Saudi Arabia where she teaches Western children's literature among other courses in English literature. Dr Aisawi was the first researcher to gain a PhD in the field of children's literature in Saudi. Her research has been presented at international conferences and published in refereed journals. Among her academic activities is the design of two children's literature courses. Dr Aisawi is the writer of *Fostering Children's Minds* and a contributor to the *Guide to Children's Writers and Illustrators in Saudi Arabia* (in Arabic). As a visiting research fellow, she conducted research at ICRCL, University of Worcester in 2010, CRYTC, University of Winnipeg in 2012 and the College of Education, University of Glasgow in 2016. Her principal research interests are Arabic children's literature, cultural diversity and the portrayal of disability in children's literature.

Ilgım Veryeri Alaca is an Assistant Professor at Koç University, Department of Media and Visual Arts in Turkey. She obtained an MFA in Art and Design from the University of Illinois at Urbana-Champaign, and a PhD from Hacettepe University, Department of Fine Arts. She contributed to *The Routledge Companion to Picturebooks* and *The Routledge International Handbook of Early Literacy Education*. Her publications appeared in *Bookbird, Leonardo* and *International Journal of Education Through Art*. She received an International Youth Library Fellowship in 2016, and a Turkish Cultural Foundation Post-Doctoral Fellowship in 2013. Her artworks are included in collections such as Butler Museum of American Art, Zimmerli Museum and Southern Graphics Council. Picture books, art and cultural heritage are among her research interests.

Maria Inês de Almeida is Associate Professor at Universidade Federal de Minas Gerais (UFMG) Faculdade de Letras (Teachers College) coordinator of Literaterras Research Transdisciplinary Center: writing, reading, translation, where books and magazines are produced, organized and edited with indigenous communities from all regions of Brazil. She was coordinator of Course for Intercultural Training of Indigenous Educators, at UFMG (2006–2011) and director of UFMG Cultural Center (2011–2014). Since 2013, she has organized the international and itinerant exhibition MIRA – Indigenous Peoples Contemporary Visual Arts, involving twenty-five indigenous peoples from five Amazon countries. She is author of: *Doze Trabalhos de H* (Twelve Labours of H], *22 Arcanos* (22 Arcana) and *Desocidentada – Experiência Literária em Terra Indígena* (De-occidentalized: Literary Experience in Indigenous Land). She has also published articles and chapters concerning literary theory, Brazilian literature, publishing, translation and indigenous education and intercultural experience.

José Hélder Pinheiro Alves is an Associate Professor at Universidade Federal de Campina Grande (UFCG), in the State of Paraíba, where he has taught Brazilian literature, popular literature and children's literature since 1992. At present he is a professor at the MA Course of Language and Education and his research area is on Literature and Education. He is also a research advisor on themes related to the teaching of poetry. He has published *Poetry in the Classroom* and *String Literature in Daily School Life* (2012), with Ana Cristina Marino Lucio.

Salinee Antarasena is an Assistant Professor in the Department of English at Chiang Mai University, Thailand. She holds an MA and a PhD, both in Creative Writing, from Macquarie University, Sydney. In addition to her continuing interest in creative writing, her research has dealt with color perceptions and color categorization in advertising created by the blind, and with individual differences in language acquisition especially in those with hearing impairment and hearing loss. She also researches Asian literatures and films, and Australian and Asian picture books. She received a Young Alumni Award for an outstanding Thai alumnus who has made a significant contribution to relations between Thailand and Australia in 2009 through to 2010.

Suchismita Banerjee is an Executive Editor with a publishing firm based in Girgaon, India. She has an MPhil degree from Jawaharlal Nehru University, New Delhi. The focus of her research is the idea of childhood in contemporary Indian English fiction for children, specifically the impact of globalization on the construction of the child and the formation of childhood identities as represented in Indian English children's literature.

Mônica Correia Baptista is a Professor in the Faculty of Education at the Federal University of Minas Gerais (UFMG). She is a member of the Centre for Literacy Reading and Writing (CEALE), Coordinator of the Research Group on Reading and Writing in Early Childhood (LEPI) and Coordinator of Studies and Research in Early Childhood Education and Childhoods (NEPEI). Currently her research directions are: reading and writing in early childhood, early childhood education and public policy and teacher training for early childhood education.

Frieda Liliana Morales Barco is a freelance researcher into children's and young adult literature and reading habits in Guatemala. She is co-editor of *Era uma vez na escola... formando educadores para formar leitores* (Once upon a time at school... training teachers to shape readers), which received an honor award from Fundação Nacional do Livro Infantil e Juvenil, Brazil. She has published books and essays about Guatemalan CYAL, literary reception and reading habits in several magazines and in the edited volumes of *Diccionario de autores de la literatura infantil y juvenil iberoamericana Latin American* (Dictionary of Latin American Children's and Young Adult Literature Authors); *Diccionario de ilustradores de Iberoamerica* (Dictionary of Latin American Illustrators); *Hitos de la literatura infantil y juvenil de Iberoamérica* (Milestones of Latin American Children's and Young Adult Literature). She was awarded the BID Cultural Development Prize in 2006.

Celia Abicalil Belmiro is a Professor in the Faculty of Education of the Federal University of Minas Gerais, Brazil, with a post-doctorate at University of Cambridge, UK, and researcher at the Centre of Literacy, Reading and Writing (CEALE/UFMG). She coordinates a research group on literary literacy and has published several articles and book chapters on picture books for children and young readers, as well as on the development of teachers' literary competence. She is editor of *Livros e Telas* (Books and screens) and *Onde está a literatura: seus espaços, seus leitores, seus textos, suas leituras* (Where is the literature: its spaces, its readers, its texts, its readings).

Lijun Bi is a lecturer at Monash University, Australia. After early study at Nanjing Normal University, she completed a doctorate at the University of Melbourne in which she identified and documented the role of moral-political education in early modern Chinese children's literature and its link to the nationalist sentiment. A specialist in Chinese children's literature, she is the author of *Chinese Children's Literature in the 20th Century: Its Political and Moral Themes* and has published articles on the social role of children's books in China. Lijun has also built a strong nexus between her teaching practice and her research interests in pedagogy, especially the experiential interactive and co-operative learning approach. Her other research interests include moral education in China and Chinese intellectual history.

Alma Carrasco Altamirano is full Professor at Benemérita Universidad Autónoma of Puebla, Mexico, where she teaches educational theory and management. She is a member of the National System of Researchers in Mexico and co-coordinator of a research group on training trajectories of young scientists, focusing on academic literacies and institutional organization of doctoral programs. She develops at the Consejo Puebla de Lectura AC (CPL) programs for literacy, particularly for babies, and literacies for family practices.

Silvia Castrillón is a library expert of the University of Antioquia. She was a founder of the Colombian Association for Children's Books, Fundalectura, and Asolectura, the National Association of Reading and Writing. She is the author of books: *Flexible Model for a School Library System* (Bogota: OAS, 1982); *The right to read and write* (Mexico: Conaculta, 2005; Buenos Aires: Argentina 2006 and Brazil 2011), recognized in Brazil as highly recommended by the National Foundation for Children and Youth Book in the category of theory books; *A look* (Bogota: Asolectura, 2010); and co-authored with Didier Alvarez Zapata *School library* (Bogotá, Asolectura, 2013).

Stuart Ching is an Associate Professor of English at Loyola Marymount University. His doctoral dissertation, completed at the University of Nebraska, Lincoln, investigated memory in composition studies and K-12 literacy education. His research interests are in writing instruction, the politics of literacy, literary and ethnic studies, multicultural education and creative writing. He publishes both research papers and creative writing, and thus his scholarship has appeared in journals such as *The New Advocate* and *Language Arts*, while his essays and stories have appeared in publications such as *The Best of Honolulu Fiction* and *A Voice for Earth: American Writers Respond to the Earth Charter*.

Alice Curry is founder of and Publisher at Lantana Publishing, which specializes in diverse and multicultural picture books for children. Alice is passionate about the vital role local stories can play in improving literacy, cognition and self-esteem in young readers, and has edited a range of multicultural books for children for various international organizations, including the Commonwealth Education Trust (UK) and Lift Education (New Zealand). Following a degree in English Literature from Oxford University and a PhD in Children's Literature from Macquarie University in Sydney, Alice has published *Environmental Crisis in Young Adult Fiction: A Poetics of Earth*, along with articles in leading international journals. An active member of international children's literature organizations, Alice channels her academic energies into producing books that can be loved by children wherever they are in the world.

Fanuel Hanán Díaz is a graduate in Literature and Magister Scientiarum in Science and Applied Arts. He coordinated the Department of Selection of Books for Children and Young People of Banco del Libro and he has been a member of the jury for the Hans Christian Andersen Award, for the Bologna Ragazzi Award, and for the Bratislava Biennal of Illustrations. He received the Internationale Jugendbibliothek Scholarship. He is author of *Leer y mirar el libro álbum: ¿un género en construcción?* (Bogotá: Norma, 2007); *Panorama breve de la literatura infantil en Venezuela* (Caracas: BBVA, 2013); *Temas de literatura infantil* (Buenos Aires: Lugar, 2015); and *Visti da lontano* (Novara: Interlinea, 2015). He has given lectures and workshops in several Latin American and European countries.

Yasuko Doi is a senior researcher at the International Institute for Children's Literature, Osaka (Japan). She is also a member of the Japanese Board on Books for Young People (JBBY) and is on the jury of the Hans Christian Andersen Award organized by the International Board on Books for Young People (IBBY). She researches Japanese historical periodicals and devises workshops on children's books for children. She is an associate editor of *100 Questions and Answers About Children's Books* (Osaka: Sogensha, 2013) and of a booklist called *Children's Books on War and Peace* (Tokyo: Iwasakishoten, 2016).

Jaqueline S. du Toit is Professor in the International Studies Group at the University of the Free State (South Africa). She has an interest in cross-generational production and transfer of information in religious collectives. Her focus is on the Bible in late nineteenth and early twentieth century Afrikaner folk religion as represented by children's Bibles and religious literature for the young, travelogues, sermons, early Afrikaans literature, and the like. This project is entitled, "Children of a Jealous God: The Bible and the Apartheid State." Her books include *Canada's Big Biblical Bargain* (2010) with Jason Kalman (Hebrew Union College-Jewish Institute of Religion) and *Textual Memory: Ancient Archives, Libraries and the Hebrew Bible* (2011).

Nadia El Kholy is a Professor of English Language and Literature at Cairo University. She served as Director of the National Council for Children's Culture, was a member of the jury for the Hans Christian Andersen International Award for Children's Literature, was a member of the IBBY Executive Committee from 2012–2014 and is President of the Egyptian Board of Books for Young Readers (EBBY). Her research interests include writing and translation for children, Comparative and Postcolonial Literature, and Gender Studies. She has contributed to the *Oxford Encyclopaedia of Children's Literature*, was co-editor of the *Women Writing Africa* series published by the Feminist Press in New York, and the ASTENE publication *Egypt in the Eyes of Travellers*. She has published several articles on the modern Arabic and English novel, children's literature and has translated *Alice in Wonderland* into Arabic.

Fatemeh Farnia is a PhD candidate in English Literature at Shiraz University, Iran. She gained her BA and MA both in English Literature at Shiraz University. Her PhD dissertation explores a comparative model for studying empowerment in young adult novels. She is an active member of the "Picturebooks Group" at Shiraz University Centre for Children's Literature studies, which is working on the *Encyclopedia of Iranian Picture Books* project. For over eight years she has been teaching general English, ESP and literature courses at various institutes and Payame Noor university campuses.

Atiyeh Firouzmand is an MA graduate in Children's and Young Adult Literature from Shiraz University. Her research deals with intertextuality, decentralization and empowerment in Iranian and non-Iranian picture books. She is an active member of the "Picturebooks Group" at Shiraz University Centre for Children's Literature studies, which is working on the *Encyclopedia of Iranian Picture Books* project. She lectures in children's literature, storytelling, creative drama, and scriptwriting at the University of Applied Sciences, Technical and Vocational University, the National Intellectual Foundation and other institutes. She is author of the picture book *An Imaginary Fear* (Elmi-Farhangi Publications).

Patricia Glinton-Meicholas is a poet, a writer and a folklorist: she has written eighteen books and numerous essays on Bahamian history, art and culture. She was a lecturer at the College of The Bahamas (now University of The Bahamas [UB]) for seventeen years, and is the president of BACUS (The Bahamas Association for Cultural Studies) which has published, in association with Guanima Press Limited, several volumes of the journal *Yinna*. She is also Vice President of Creative Nassau, which secured and maintains for The Bahamas capital membership in the UNESCO Creative Cities Network. Her monograph on Bahamian folktales, *Talkin' Ol' Story: A Brief Survey of the Oral Tradition of The Bahamas*, was published in the Encuentros series of the IDB Cultural Centre, Washington, DC. Her essays also appear in the *Grove Dictionary of Art* and the *Dictionary of Caribbean and Latin America Biography* (OUP). She was the first winner of the Bahamas Cacique Award for Writing and recipient of a Silver Jubilee of Independence Medal for Literature and a Lifetime Achievement Award for Culture and Literature from UB.

Supriya Goswami Supriya Goswami teaches courses in children's literature in the Honors Program at George Washington University, Washington, DC. She is the author of *Colonial India in Children's Literature*, which is the first book-length study to explore the intersections of British, Anglo-Indian and Bengali children's literature and defining historical moments in colonial India. Her research interests include colonial and post-colonial children's literature and culture. She has published in the *Children's Literature Association Quarterly* and *Wasafiri*.

Anna Katrina Gutierrez gained a PhD in Children's Literature from Macquarie University, in which she explored conceptual blending and glocalization in East-West literary exchanges. She subsequently held fellowships at several international research centers, including the Hans Christian Andersen Centre, the Swedish Institute for Children's Books, and the International Youth Library in Munich. Her publications include *Mixed Magic: Global-local dialogues in fairy tales for young readers* and numerous articles and book chapters. She is Communications and Project Manager with Lantana Publishing.

Iman Hamam teaches in the Department of Rhetoric and Composition in the American University in Cairo. Her research interests include Egyptian film and popular culture. She writes mostly across the disciplines, looking at visual culture in medicine, film and urban studies. She has written about Egyptian mainstream comedy films, Arab satellite television, representations of ancient Egyptian mummies in science, film and fiction, and the ways in which the 6th of October War has been commemorated in the city of Cairo.

Lalita Pandit Hogan is a Professor in the Department of English at the University of Wisconsin at La Crosse, and Affiliate faculty of the South Asia Center at the University of Wisconsin-Madison. She is the co-editor and contributing author of three scholarly books: *Criticism and Lacan: Essays and Dialogue on Language, Structure, and the Unconscious* (Georgia University Press, 1990); *Literary India: Comparative Studies in Aesthetics, Colonialism, and Culture* (SUNY Press, 1995) and *Rabindranath Tagore: Universality and Tradition* (Fairleigh Dickinson University Press, 2002). She is also contributing author and co-editor of three special issues of journals: *Comparative Poetics: Non-Western Traditions in Literary Theory* (*College Literature*, 1996); *Cognitive Shakespeare: Criticism and Theory in the Age of Neuroscience* (*College Literature*, 2006); and *Hindi Cinema:* (*Projections: A Journal of Movies and Mind*, 2009), and has authored many articles and book chapters on Shakespeare, Rabindranath Tagore, cognitive approaches to literature, emotion studies, Indian literature, Indian cinema and comparative aesthetics. She has also published poetry and fiction online and in print outlets in English, as well as in Hindi. Currently, Lalita Pandit Hogan is an editorial board member of Ohio State University Press's Special Series on *Cognitive Approaches to Culture*.

Ying Hou is Professor and PhD Supervisor at the School of Literature, Northeast Normal University, China. She has been the Director of the Research Center of Children's Literature at NENU. She is actively involved in the affiliation with China Redactological Society (CRS), Chinese Association of Allegorical Literature, and Chinese Association of National Normal Schools for the Study of Children's Literature. Her major research field is children's literature and its application in teaching Chinese. Her books, all written in Chinese, include *A Multiple Approach to Children Literature* (2009); *On the Educational Function of Children's Literature* (2012); *Sense and Sensibility in Children's Literature: Hou Ying's Literary Theory Set* (2013); and most recently, a modern fairy tale *La Laqi and La Laguai: The Coolest Inventors* (2013).

Siti Rohaini Kassim was an Associate Professor in the Department of English, Faculty of Arts and Social Sciences, University of Malaya, Kuala Lumpur. She was also a Researcher at the Asia-Europe Institute, University of Malaya. In the twenty-five years she with the Department of English, she taught undergraduate as well as postgraduate courses in stylistics and literature in English, and was also involved in various research projects on language and literature. Her areas of interest include literature for children, Malaysian and Asian literatures in English, and literature and culture.

Morteza Khosronejad is Assistant Professor in Philosophy of Education at Shiraz University, Iran. He is author of *Innocence and Experience: An Introduction to Philosophy of Children's Literature* and editor of *Greats of Children's Literature Theory and Criticism*, along with about twenty articles. He has also written more than twenty picture story books for children, all in Persian. He is founder and president of Shiraz University Centre for Children's Literature Studies (SUCCLS).

Helen Kilpatrick is a Senior Lecturer in the School of Humanities and Social Inquiry, University of Wollongong, Australia. After finishing degrees in Japanese (Hons.), Sociology and English Literature, Helen Kilpatrick completed her doctorate at Macquarie University in the field of English literature with a focus on Japanese literature for young people and picture books. Helen has published in the areas of literary and cultural studies, gender and the visual arts. She is the author of *Miyazawa Kenji and his Illustrators* (Brill Academic Publishing, 2013), which explores Buddhist ideologies in modern Japanese picture books of the early twentieth-century narratives of Miyazawa Kenji (1896–1933). In 2013 she received The 7th Inoue Yasushi Award for Outstanding Research on Japanese Literature in Australasia.

Edgar Roberto Kirchof is Professor of Literature and Cultural Studies at the Lutheran University of Brazil (ULBRA). He is the editor of *Novos horizontes para a teoria da literatura e das mídias: concretismo, ciberliteratura e intermidialidade* (New horizons for the theory of literature and the media: concrete poetry, cyberliterature and intermediality) (2013) and author of *Estética e biossemiótica* (Aesthetics and biosemiotics) (2008), *Estética e semiótica: de Baumgarten e Kant a Umberto Eco* (Aesthetics and semiotics: from Baumgarten and Kant to Umberto Eco) (2003) among others. His current project on digital literature is partly published in a series of articles.

Sung-Ae Lee is a Lecturer in Asian Studies in the Department of International Studies at Macquarie University, Sydney. Her major research focus is on fiction, film and television drama of East Asia, with particular attention to Korea. Her research centres on relationships between cultural ideologies in Asian societies and representational strategies. She is interested in cognitive and imagological approaches to adaptation studies, Asian popular culture, Asian cinema, the impact of colonisation in Asia, trauma studies, fiction and film produced in the aftermath of the Korean War, and the literature and popular media of the Korean diaspora.

Li Lifang is Professor and Doctoral Supervisor at the School of Literature, Lanzhou University, China. She has focused on development of theories about Chinese early modern children's literature, as well as studies on western Chinese children's literature. Her books include *Studies on the Localization of Chinese Children's Literature in the Early*

Period (2007), *Criticisms of Western Chinese Children's Literature Writers* (2013), and *A Conversation with Childhood* (2013).

Maria Zélia Versiani Machado teaches and researches in Literature and Literacy Studies. She is an Associate Professor in the School of Education at the Federal University of Minas Gerais and a researcher at the Research Center on Literacy, Reading and Writing (CEALE). She is also a member of GPELL – Research Group for Literary Literacy – she coordinates the research group that focuses on literature genres for children and youth. She also has voting rights with the National Foundation for Books for Children and Youth (FNLIJ), as well as the Brazilian section of IBBY – International Board on Books for Young People – in the selection process of literary works for children and youth that receive the "Highly Recommended" seal. Her edited books on literature and reading practices include: *A criança e a leitura literária: livros, espaços, mediações* (Children and literary literacy: books, spaces, mediations).

Anuja Madan is Assistant Professor in the Department of English, Kansas State University, where she teaches courses in Postcolonial Literature and Cultural Studies. She received her BA, MA and MPhil in English from Delhi University and her PhD from University of Florida. She is co-author of *Notes of Running Feet: English in Primary Textbooks* (2013) with Rimli Bhattacharya, Sreyoshi Sarkar and Nivedita Basu; the book analyzes contemporary English textbooks used in Indian schools. Her major research areas are Indian children's literature and media as well as Indian comics. Her research investigates post-millennial Indian comics, graphic novels and animations that draw on Hindu mythology, paying special attention to cross-cultural influences and processes of nation-building within these texts. She has published articles on an Indian graphic novel, English-language picture book adaptations of *Mahabharata* and Jean-Luc Godard's films.

Alice Áurea Penteado Martha graduated in Language Arts at the Penápolis College of Philosophy Sciences and Languages (1969), has a master's degree and PhD in Language Arts at the Paulista State University Júlio de Mesquita Filho. She is a Brazilian Literature teacher at the Maringá State University, working on the following themes: reading, children's literature, literature and Monteiro Lobato. She is a voter, since 2005, on the National Children and Teenage Books Foundation (FNLIJ); coordinator at the Center for Literature, Reading and Writing Studies: history and teaching (CELLE), certified by CNPq/UEM; and takes part in the Reading and Literature at School Research Group, which brings together teachers from several universities in the country.

Aracy Alves Martins has graduated in Language and received her MA and PhD degrees in Education from the Federal University of Minas Gerais (UFMG). She was awarded a Doctoral Sandwich grant to study in the INRP – Institut National de Recherche Pédagogique, Paris, France. Her post-doctoral studies were conducted at the University of Minho, University of Campinas and University of Coimbra. She is currently Associate Professor at the Faculty of Education at UFMG and researcher of CEALE (Center of Literacy, Reading and Writing) and NERA (Center for Studies and Research on Race Relations and Affirmative Action). She has extensive experience in language and education with a focus on literary reading, teacher training, education, textbooks, tensions between languages and ethnic-racial relations.

Yasmine Motawy teaches Rhetoric and Composition at the American University in Cairo and is a translator of, among other things, many Arabic children's stories. Her doctoral dissertation at Cairo University was titled "Ideology in Selected British and Egyptian Children's Literature: A Comparative Study". Her other scholarly interests include Sufi poetry and life narratives. Yasmine has been involved in the promotion of reading in the Arab world and the revival of the Egyptian section of IBBY in 2011. She served on the 2016 Hans Christian Andersen Award Jury.

Manuel Peña Muñoz is a writer, Spanish teacher, specialist in literature for children and young adults, lecturer, feature writer, university professor and writer of numerous works of literary critique, essays and narrative books on children's oral poetry. He is a winner of the Gran Angular Prize in Madrid with *Mágico sur* (Ediciones SM, 1998 and author of scholarly literature such as *Historia de la Literatura Infantil en América Latina* (History of children's literature in Latin America) (Fundación SM Madrid, 2009). A distinguished teacher of seminars on literature for children and young adults in Chile, he has lectured on literary themes in Spain and various Latin American countries. He has been a member on three occasions of the jury panel for the Paris-based UNESCO Prize in children's literature in support of peace and tolerance. Working in Santiago, he is a dedicated author, teacher of courses in children's literature, and a collaborator in different programs to encourage reading.

Robert Muponde is Full Professor in the Department of English, University of the Witwatersrand (Wits), South Africa. He holds a PhD (Wits) in literary and cultural studies from the same university. His publications include: *Some Kinds of Childhood: Images of History and Resistance in Zimbabwean Literature*; *No More Plastic Balls: New Voices in the Zimbabwean Short Story*, co-edited with C. Chihota; *Versions of Zimbabwe: New Approaches to Literature and Culture*, co-edited with Ranka Primorac; and *Manning the Nation: Father Figures in Zimbabwean Literature and Society*, co-edited with Kizito Muchemwa. He served for several years on the Editorial Board of *Sankofa: A Journal of African Children's and Young Adult Literature*. His current interests are in researching Cultures of Representation (which includes studies of narratives – visual and textual – and knots in critical practice in the Global South, with specific reference to Southern Africa).

Mickias Musiyiwa is Associate Professor in the Department of African Languages and Literature, University of Zimbabwe, in which he teaches literary theory, African literature, and oral literature. He holds a master's degree in African languages and literature from the University of Zimbabwe and a PhD in discourse analysis of popular songs from Stellenbosch University, South Africa. He has published over twenty journal articles and book chapters in the fields of children's literature, children's songs, popular music, Zimbabwean literature, politics and oral literature, Shona oral narratives, and gender and literature. In 2009 he was awarded the International Youth Library Fellowship, Munich, Germany, and in 2011 the African Doctoral Academy Scholarship to pursue his doctoral studies at the University of Stellenbosch, South Africa.

Shalini Nadaswaran is currently a Senior Lecturer with the English Department, University of Malaya. She completed a PhD in English specializing in African Women's Literature at the University of New South Wales, Sydney, Australia. Her research interest considers the constant evolving representations of women in local and global spaces. She has published in the field of African literature and women's literature in journals such as *African Literature Today*, *Matatu*, *Wasafiri* and *Tulsa Studies in Women's Literature* and in various essay collections. While her primary focus falls under the remit of African (women's) literature, she also has additional interests in research that explores modern day slavery, literature and injustice, and the figure of the "child" in postcolonial literature.

Sharifah A. Osman is Senior Lecturer at the Department of English, Faculty of Arts and Social Sciences, University of Malaya, Kuala Lumpur. Her research interests are nineteenth-century British literature, romantic Orientalism and children's literature in Malaysia. She has published on Lord Byron, Mary Shelley and Felicia Hemans, and is currently involved in a research project on feminist ideas in Malaysian children's literature.

Jann Pataray-Ching is a Professor in the College of Education and Integrative Studies, California State Polytechnic University, Pomona. She holds a doctorate from Indiana University in Language Education/Literacy Studies. She has published widely in such areas as children's play; Asian-American children's literature; assessing multicultural books in the context of authenticity, insider and outsider perspectives, and equitable representation; and exploring moral and ethical understanding with children.

Bahia Shehab (Beirut, 1977) is an award-winning artist, designer and scholar based in Cairo. Her artwork has been on display in museums, galleries and streets around the world, and was featured in the 2015 documentary Nefertiti's Daughters. She is the recipient of many international recognitions and awards, which include the UNESCO-Sharjah Prize for Arab Culture (2016), Prince Claus Award (2016), TED Senior fellowship (2016), and BBC 100 Women list (2013 and 2014). Bahia is Associate Professor of Design and founder of the graphic design program at the American University in Cairo where she has developed a full design curriculum mainly focused on visual culture of the Arab world. Her publications include *A Thousand Times NO: The Visual History of Lam-Alif*.

Soudabeh Shokrollahzadeh is an instructor in museum education at Shiraz Art University and a PhD candidate in Philosophy of Education at Shiraz University, Iran. She is a member of the "Picturebooks Group" at Shiraz University Centre for Children's Literature Studies. She gained her BA in English Literature and MA in Philosophy of Education. Her research interests are philosophy for children and adolescents, picture books, YA fiction and dialogism.

Aisha Spencer is a lecturer in Language and Literature Education at the University of the West Indies, Mona Campus, in Kingston, Jamaica. She has been teaching language and literature for over eighteen years and is especially passionate about finding innovative forms of pedagogy to help children and young people better connect with and enjoy all genres of literature. She is the co-editor of an anthology of Caribbean poetry, entitled *"Give the Ball to the Poet": A New Anthology of Caribbean Poetry*. Her areas of research interest are in gender and nationalism, postcolonial literatures, literature education,

Caribbean children's literature, and the Caribbean female-authored short story. She is Associate Editor for the *Journal of Education and Development in the Caribbean* (JEDIC). and acts as Cultural Adviser and Editorial (Caribbean) with Lantana Publishing.

Sandra Stadler teaches English Literature and English Didactics at Regensburg University. She gained a PhD in English Literature from Regensburg University, in which she documented for the first time how post-millennial South African young adult novels in English decipher South Africa's complex cultural landscape. She is author of *South African Young Adult Literature in English, 2000–2014* (2017), while further articles have appeared in *Bookbird* and *AfrikaSüd*. Her subsequent research focus involves the analysis and evaluation of digital reading practices and habits of young adults in secondary schools.

John Stephens is Emeritus Professor in English at Macquarie University. He is author of *Language and Ideology in Children's Fiction*; co-author of *Retelling Stories, Framing Culture* and *New World Orders in Contemporary Children's Literature*; editor of *Ways of Being Male* and of *Subjectivity in Asian Children's Literature and Film*, and author of about a hundred articles and two other books. He is a former President of the International Research Society for Children's Literature and Editor of *International Research in Children's Literature* (2008–2016). In 2007 he received the 11th International Brothers Grimm Award and in 2014 the Ann Devereaux Jordan Award, both in recognition of his contribution to research in children's literature.

Cuthbeth Tagwirei is Professor of English at Midlands State University and a postdoctoral fellow in the Department of English, University of Johannesburg. His research interests include the "behaviours" of literary and cultural systems. He has published on children's texts in journals such as the *Journal of Literary Studies* and *Children's Literature in Education*. His other publications may be found in *Critical Arts: A Journal of South-North Cultural Media, Latin American Report* and *The Journal of Commonwealth Literature*. He has written articles on Latin American literature and Zimbabwean children's literature. His research interests include Zimbabwean literature, gender, nationalism and discourse analysis.

Fengxia Tan is a Professor of Literature in the Department of Chinese at Nanjing Normal University, China. Her research areas are children's literature, comparative literature and modern Chinese literature. She is author of *Poetic Pursuit at the Margin: A Study of Writings about Childhood in Modern Chinese Literature; A History of Chinese Children's Films*; and *Comparative Study on Chinese and Western Children's Literature* (forthcoming). She has published a novel and collections of essays, and translated some English children's novels into Chinese. Her research focuses on children's literature written by ethnic Chinese in the Western world.

Lai Suat Yan is Senior Lecturer in the Gender Studies Program, Faculty of Arts and Social Sciences, University of Malaya, Kuala Lumpur. She was the lead consultant on the working conditions of female and male lawyers in Kuala Lumpur and Selangor commissioned by the Association of Women's Lawyers and the Malaysian Human Rights Commission in 2013. She has published locally and/or internationally on the topic of gender violence, the women's movement, gender equality and the legal profession as well as on Buddhism and gender issues. Her research interests include gender, religion and social change, violence against women, and gender equality in various issues including work and the provision of public facilities.

Andrea Mei-Ying Wu is an Associate Professor in the Department of Taiwanese Literature at National Cheng Kung University. Her research interests include children's and young adult literature, boyhood studies, childhood studies, and cross-cultural/transcultural studies. She is author of *Discourses of Subject, Gender, Place, and (Post)modern Childhood in Postwar Taiwanese Fiction for Young People* (in Chinese). Her other publications include "Toward a (Re)signification of Cultural Hybridity: *Guji Guji* and *Master Mason*" (*IRCL* 2013) and "Model Children, Little Rebels, and Moral Transgressors: Virtuous Childhood Images in Taiwanese Juvenile Fiction in the 1960s" (*Ethics and Children's Literature* 2014). She was awarded a Fulbright Senior Research Scholar fellowship in 2014–15 and served as a Board member of the International Research Society for Children's Literature (IRSCL) in 2013–17.

Vivian Yenika-Agbaw is Professor of Literature and Literacy in the Department of Curriculum and Instruction at Penn State College of Education, where she teaches courses in children's and adolescent literature. Her research and scholarship centres on children's and young adult literature/texts and is informed by theories of critical multiculturalism, postcolonialism and reader response. She publishes and presents primarily on topics related to social justice and the representation of populations that have been historically marginalized and under-represented in children's texts and culture (with particular concern toward race, class, gender and disabilities). She is the author and/or co-editor of numerous books including *Adolescents Rewrite their World: Using Literature to Illustrate Writing Forms*, (with Teresa Sychterz) and *Fairy Tales with a Black Consciousness: Adaptations of Familiar Stories* (with Ruth McKoy Lowery and Laretta Henderson). She has also published numerous articles in major international journals, such as *Children's Literature Association Quarterly* and *Sankofa: Journal of African Children's and Young Adult Literature*.

Xu Xu is a former Assistant Professor of Children's Literature in the Department of English Language and Literature at Central Michigan University, where she taught courses such as children's literature, multicultural children's literature and international children's literature. She is now an independent researcher, whose research focuses on the entangled relationships between the construction of the Chinese nation and childhood in modern China. She has published articles and chapters on constructions of childhood, gender and translation. Her article, "'Chairman Mao's Child': *Sparkling Red Star* and the Construction of Children in the Chinese Cultural Revolution," was the runner-up in the Children's Literature Association Best Article Award for 2011.

Regina Zilberman is a graduate of Letters from the Federal University of Rio Grande do Sul, and a PhD in Romanistics from the University of Heidelberg (Germany), with postdoctorates at University College (London) and Brown University (USA). Some of her publications are: *A literatura infantil na escola* (Children's Literature at School); *Estética da Recepção e História da Literatura* (Aesthetics of Reception and History of Literature); *Como e por que ler a literatura infantil brasileira* (How and Why Read Brazilian Children's Literature); *A leitura e o ensino da literatura* (Reading and the Teaching of Literature).

INTRODUCTION

Western culture has a big mouth and very small ears. Even when it condescends to listen to other cultures, it does so within the framework of 'searching for spices' and specifies both what it wants to hear and how it should be said. So it often ends up hearing only an echo of its own voice.

Godfrey B. Tangwa

The essays in this collection were commissioned by an international editorial team whose members are situated in five different continents. Our purpose was to leave the well-worn path of Anglophone and European scholarship and to explore some of the scholarship that concerns itself with children's literature and media in the Majority World – principally Africa, Asia, the Caribbean and Latin America, and to commission essays from "insider", embedded scholars. This conceptualization of the project incorporates not only local insights but also the methodologies produced within particular academic cultures. The collection thus describes children's literatures not from a global perspective but as local (sometimes glocal) products characterized by local concepts of childhood and of the purposes underpinning children's literature, and then more particularly by local genres, styles, registers and applications. Local literatures are repertoires that are grounded in local sociolinguistic systems and take shape in relation with, and sometimes in opposition to, social and cultural ideologies and political systems. Critical description of particular literatures is apt to be culturally embedded, but to varying degrees influenced by practices of outside academic cultures, which in turn become glocalized.

As scholars in an international field, regardless of geographical or academic locality, we must understand how colleagues in other parts of the world go about what they do, and we accordingly need, to develop Godfrey B. Tangwa's aphorism, mouths and ears of much the same size everywhere. What are the particular constraints of other scholarly domains, and what do we learn about our own constraints by asking this question? What are the assumptions and presuppositions we make about the bases of our own and other scholarship? In posing these questions we bring our own positionality and the critical discourses associated with it into fuller consciousness. In trying to think about a regional scholarship, much as with regional literatures, we are generally taking an etic position toward an emic entity. An emic entity refers to a scholarly practice both *as it is* and as it

1

perceives itself (that is, an insider's perspective or the *perspective from within*). In contrast, the etic viewpoint, which perforce any scholars take toward literatures and criticisms that are not their own, is a perspective *from outside*. Both positions can be, but need not be, self-reflective.

Of the many factors that constitute an emic entity, four have a major function for this collection of essays. These elements overlap and point to a need to recognize a critical process that focuses on local practices and enables discussion of sociolinguistic embeddedness, flows of influence, glocalization and preferred textualities. We have appropriated the term *ethnopoetics* to describe this process, shifting the term away from its original application to oral performances. One of the first proponents of this term, Dennis Tedlock, sketched some principles pertinent to our aim when he described ethnopoetics as "a decentered poetics" outside the Western tradition, but also contemporary and no less complex than Western or metropolitan poetics. He also argued that any poetics is an ethnopoetics, and that is a position we find particularly important.

Embeddedness within a particular language context limits the flow of influence in and out, so that, for example, Latin America's 600 million inhabitants possess a local aesthetic, with particular forms of expression in music, dance, arts, crafts, literature and other cultural forms. Latin American children's literature and criticism in Spanish, for example, circulates throughout Latin America (including Portuguese-speaking areas), on Europe's Iberian peninsula, and to some extent in the USA. However, few children's literature scholars in other parts of the world could name (m)any authors or illustrators from the region. They might vaguely know that the concept of magical realism originates in Latin America as a mode of resistance against the various military forces that prevented freedom of expression in the mid-twentieth century; and they may know, as Teya Rosenberg puts it, that "most works termed magical realism ... have a 'gritty' tone or a liberal political stance ... [and] critique tyranny or oppression" (2002: 77). Rosenberg is one of the few Anglophone scholars who refers to the writing of Latin American scholars – others usually define magical realism on the basis of Wendy B. Faris's "Scheherazade's Children: Magical Realism and Postmodern Fiction" (1995). Her point that, "In early discussions, Latin American writers defined the form [magical realism] in terms of the geography and culture of their countries," but as the concept was borrowed elsewhere definitions shifted to the formal qualities that constitute magical realism, discloses an important ethnopoetic contrast.

Such conceptual modifications reflect how the repertoires of genres and forms utilized by children's authors differ between regions. The temporal relationship between the emergence of children's literature and the impact of modernity varies widely across the world. Animal stories, for example, begin to appear in Chinese children's literature in the 1980s, whereas they had existed in England at least since the "autobiography" *Dick, the Little Pony* (1799). This difference of almost two centuries entails an almost unbridgeable dissimilarity, if only that, in the West, the genre had diversified and the criticism had begun to absorb animality theory before the genre emerged in China. The difference also highlights an issue for ethnopoetics which concerns the availability, generation and impact of various concepts and theories. Is it possible to effectively identify – or even see – a textual phenomenon if the critical language lacks a word or concept that defines it?

In *Literary Conceptualizations of Growth* (2014), Roberta Trites contends that Anglophone Young Adult fiction (the corpus of her study) is focused literally and metaphorically on narratives of growth and that the concomitant literary criticism likewise focuses on metaphors of growth. This conjunction – not previously observed – is underpinned not only by the preoccupations of the fiction but also by a cultural and critical assumption that the world shares a common taken-for-granted objective reality *of a particular kind* whereby agentic individualism is a primary life objective. Such an aspect of social ideology underpins ethnopoetics and is reflected textually by the two preferred narrative modes that had come to dominate Anglophone children's fiction by the 1960s: first person narration and narrative focalization by a single protagonist. Both modes characteristically produce characters who are subjective individualists.

Many parts of the Majority World – China, Japan, Sub-Saharan Africa, for example – offer different ethnopoetic structures, which are grounded rather in communal or collectivist values. African critical wisdom, Cuthbeth Tagwirei suggests in this volume, needs to be reassessed for its relevance to contemporary critical theory. To this end he invokes *unhu*, also known as *ubuntu* – an Afrocentric theory of communalism and solidarity. *Unhu* is not just a quality of being, but also a mode of seeing: a gaze that is predetermined and holistically focused on the whole person and not the parts that make up the person. An *unhu* literary gaze would therefore draw attention to characters' experiences of community and the several connections that are created in order to make the community possible. An *unhu* gaze sees the human first, and race, class, gender and so on second.

Ethnopoetics and local pressures: China and Iran

Tagwirei's argument exemplifies how children's literature and its associated scholarships are, or ought to be, challenged by local knowledges. Iran and China are distinctive examples because the possible ethnopoetics of both countries are framed by processes of exclusion and of generation of local expectations. Both countries have a strong centralized ideology, which has been sustained through varying kinds of coercion, which is to a great extent internalized (but sometimes resisted) by populations, but which is also in a state of constant modification. Change occurs in a bottom-up kind of way, but at certain points meets resistance from above. Both countries experienced huge change at the end of the 1970s: for China, it was the implementation of the reform and opening-up policy in 1978; for Iran, it was the Islamic revolution of 1979. For China, this change began a process whereby eventually, in the early twenty-first century, there occurred a boom in publication and consumption of local children's literature, which overtook the high consumption of translated foreign literature through the 1980s.

Tang Sulan (2014: 116) has argued that a child-oriented approach in contemporary Chinese children's literature has "a special historic mission" that consists of four facets. First, it aspires to change and improve the attitudes of the general population toward children; second, its mission is to "protect children's dispositions and inspire the development of their talents"; third, it helps children enjoy their childhood and live happily; and fourth, it makes use of the aesthetic functions of children's literature to modify the "rigid and oppressive" system of school education. Underlying this mission is a belief, held by contemporary Chinese writers, as by their predecessors, "that children's growth holds the key to the development of a modern Chinese nation" (Xu Xu, 2013: 78). Tang Sulan (114) contends that "children's writers in China always shoulder responsibility for society and the nation as a whole" (114), and this is more important than entertaining readers.

What constitutes childhood and children's literature is a recurrent theme in the various essays from China that appear in this volume and that, we think, will intrigue our readers. What underlies such scholarship is a century-long engagement – advocated by intellectuals since the 1919 May 4th movement – with conceptions of childhood as "natural" but eventually corrupted by experience and education. Thus an obvious contrast with scholarship in other parts of the world is the continuing influence of the writings of the New Culturalists of the early twentieth century, and especially Zhou Zuoren's theory of a Chinese children's literature that appealed to the kinds of thing that naturally pertained to childhood – a theory that is like, but not the same as, the idea of "the romantic child" in Western criticism. This project of reform seems to be always unfinished business and continually has renewed or new challenges to confront.

In contrast to China and its expanding children's literature, the impact of major change on Iran's literature and its ethnopoetics has been more negative. A top-down push to impose authority and dominance by means of ideological narratives has depressed local fiction and prompted audiences to turn to imported and translated literature, which may contain themes and motifs excluded from Iranian literature. Taking a more etic perspective in their essay in this volume, Morteza Khosronejad, Fatemeh Farnia and Soudabeh Shokrollahzadeh explain that Iranian YA fiction excludes numerous problematic issues: abuse, sexual violence, acceptance of difference, suicide, challenges of dating, confrontation of emotional problems, pregnancy, parenthood and abortion, sexual desire, multiculturalism, and queer themes. In general, representation of otherness has been excluded from this literature, and it follows that local critical writing will be constrained according to what the creative literature itself deals with.

In practice, the list of issues excluded from Iranian literature is not unique to Iran, but can be identified in other parts of the Majority World, including China. What is not written about, for whatever reason, has a profound effect on a country's ethnopoetics, because the literature and its concomitant scholarship are socioculturally embedded in ways that promote particular ideologies and textualities and restrict some flows of external influence. A simple example emerges from the essay in this volume about Iranian picture books. It is argued that interactive picture books are very rare in Iran and consequently, in comparison with picture book criticism in other parts of the world, there is a relative absence of criticism grounded on an assumption of interactivity.

Children's literature in Africa and the Caribbean

Africa is a continent with a long and rich oral past. The trans-Atlantic slave trade from the sixteenth to nineteenth centuries ensured that West African cultural and spiritual practices have also made an indelible mark on the Caribbean. As folklorist Patricia Glinton-Meicholas notes in this volume, the similarities in story structure and type between folktales and oral narratives in Africa, the United States and the Caribbean, have created a shared cultural grammar, sealed by shared African bloodlines, ethos and customs, even while the literatures of each country bear unique territorial markers. From the evangelicalism of the earliest missionary crusades and the limitations imposed by colonial language policies and censorship, through to the recouping of indigenous oral traditions and the reclaiming of a nationalist consciousness in the aftermath of independence, each continent's literatures have emerged and grown as a consequence of their dialogue with colonialism.

Africa and the Caribbean have seen a relatively recent emergence of modern children's literature. As Killam and Rowe's *Companion to African Literatures* makes clear, several factors have nurtured this development, but three factors in particular. First, the introduction of Western systems of education, with their emphasis on reading and writing, and the redefinition of schooling as a formal process outside the immediate jurisdiction of the tribal community. Second, the shift from community-led oral storytelling as a mode of social and moral instruction to a growing prioritization of written modes of narrative communication. Third, the dominance, through colonialism, of European languages and their literary and aesthetic paradigms.

This latter point is one of concern to many of the contributors to this volume. As Ashcroft, Griffiths and Tiffin have made clear in their foundational work on postcolonialism (1989), colonial languages were the medium through which conceptions of "truth", "order" and "reality" became established (7). Consequently, literature in indigenous languages was relegated to inferior status, thought unable to equip African children with the requisite knowledge to become productive members of their societies. An African writer's social commitment to communicate a sense of cultural heritage to African children becomes complicated because such a literature also seeks recognition by the metropolitan center, and not solely by its African audience – a problem also experienced by Caribbean authors whose native patois or Creole was widely rejected by the literary establishment of the metropolitan west.

The context of conflicted cultural and linguistic practices within which both African and Caribbean children's literatures have emerged poses a challenge for the identity of these literatures. What would an African or Caribbean ethnopoetics look like given a cultural heritage that is, by virtue of imperialism, fragmentary and at least partly illusory? African literary culture, particularly as it pertains to children's literature, is neither completely Western nor African rooted, but straddles the two cultures to form a cultural consciousness in a kind of middle position. In *Caribbean Literary Discourse*, Barbara Lalla et al. remark that the Caribbean is similarly "multicultural, multilingual, hybrid, and creolized" and can be "characterized by its very complexity, its multiplicity of origins, its elusive boundaries, and its defiance of fixity" (2). What is perhaps clearest in reading the essays from this region is that the history of colonialism has left bodies of work and critical discourses that are both paradoxical and hybridized – neither fully embracing nor wholly rejecting colonialism's continuing legacy.

Perceiving and erasing borders: understanding children's literature in Latin America

The variety of academic and artistic productions in children's and young people's literature in Latin America is the result of how much this region is shaped by diversity, in every sense of the word: first, in the language – Spanish in the majority of countries, Portuguese in Brazil, and also French, Dutch and English in Guyana and in some other islands; second, in terms of the constitution of its population – with a mixture of Amerindians, blacks, and immigrants from European and Asian countries; third, in its harsh stories of political independence and struggles against military dictatorships, with severe economic and social consequences; fourth, in its luxuriant nature – which includes a wide range of temperatures and forests that help to maintain the balance in the global climate; finally, fifth, in the variety of religions and religious syncretism in different countries.

The history of catechism in the Catholic church, enforced by both the Spanish and the Portuguese, led to the official erasure of other indigenous and African religions, considered to be the worship of sin and the devil. These different religious manifestations were legitimated only after a considerable time and due to the many struggles by minorities, such as Amerindians and blacks, for recognition of their cultural origins. In Brazil, for example, an increased distribution of books themed on ethnic-racial relations has resulted not only in a great number of books by authors of African origin (mostly in English and French) but also books translated into Portuguese, books in the local languages of African countries, books in the Portuguese of Portugal with its lexical and syntactic peculiarities, texts by black Brazilian authors, and finally texts with "black" themes by black and non-black Brazilian authors (Belmiro and Martins, this volume).

The diverse and numerous elements outlined above define this vast region of the planet, with its countries connected (or separated, depending on one's perspective), by the Andean Massif, the world's longest mountain range, extending 8,000 kilometers along the western coast of South America from Patagonia on the southernmost tip of Argentina to Venezuela in the north. Throughout the region children's literature presents multiple characteristics, depending on the experiences of each country. More recently, the development of homegrown printing presses has fostered the production of works by domestic authors and illustrators and weakened the competition from translations of foreign books.

The unique circumstances of Latin America have contributed toward local and regional versions of ethnopoetics. An example that encapsulates many of the available characteristics is the famous, or perhaps notorious, Mexican picture book, *La Historia de los Colores* (1996) by Subcomandante Marcos (Rafael Sebastián Guillén Vicente) and illustrated by Domitila Domínguez. The story is a retelling of a Mayan creation myth about how colors came into the world, which both affirms the vitality of indigenous cultures and beliefs and advocates tolerance and respect for diversity. "Marcos" – storyteller, poet, novelist, philosopher and Zapatista guerilla and spokesperson – epitomizes popular struggle against oppression. Domi (Domínguez) is an eminent indigenous artist and sculptor renowned for her vibrant postmodern paintings. Doris Seale and Beverly Slapin summarize the themes of *La Historia de los Colores* as "about the joy of seeing the world around us with new eyes. It is about the way that very ancient peoples can often see very far. It is about the holy power of harmony and balance among the many forms of life on our planet" (2006: 301).

Children's literature scholars across the world valorize creativity and experimentation, so that the various constraints and sociocultural restrictions that literature is subject to can go unnoticed or be deemed not to exist. We accept – implicitly or explicitly – that literature belongs to a community's sociolinguistic system, and we assume that within this expression of a system we will find combinations of social, cultural, cognitive, emotional, affective and aesthetic elements. What an ethnopoetic analysis might attempt is to disclose culturally embedded ways of nuancing those elements within an emic entity. *La Historia de los Colores* is perhaps one of the best places for beginning to expand our ears and explore what ethnopoetics can teach us all.

Bibliography

Ashcroft, Bill, Gareth Griffiths and Helen Tiffin (1989) *The Empire Writes Back: Theory and Practice in Post-Colonial Literature*, London: Routledge.

Faris, Wendy B. "Scheherazade's Children: Magical Realism and Postmodern Fiction," in Zamora and Faris, 163–90.

Lalla, Barbara, Jean D'Costa and Velma Pollard (2014) *Caribbean Literary Discourse: Voice and Cultural Identity in the Anglophone Caribbean*, Tuscaloosa: University of Alabama Press.

Rosenberg, Teya (2002) "Genre and Ideology in Elizabeth Goudge's *The Little White House*," *Children's Literature Association Quarterly*, 27(2): 77–87.

Seale, Doris and Beverly Slapin (2006) *A Broken Flute: The Native Experience in Books for Children*, Lanham, Maryland: Rowman Altamira.

Tang, Sulan (2014) "The Multiple Facets and Contemporary Mission of the Images of Children in Chinese Children's Literature," in *Representing Children in Chinese and U.S. Children's Literature*, ed. Claudia Nelson and Rebecca Morris, Farnham, Surrey and Burlington, VT: Ashgate.

Tangwa, Godfrey B. (1996) "Bioethics: An African Perspective," *Bioethics* 10(3): 183–200.

Trites, Roberta (2014) *Literary Conceptualizations of Growth. Metaphors and Cognition in Adolescent Literature*, Amsterdam and Philadelphia: John Benjamins Publishing Company.

Xu Xu (2013) "Imagination: Imaginations of the Nation – Childhood and Children's Literature in Modern China," in *(Re)imagining the World: Children's Literature's Response to Changing Times*, ed. Yan Wu, Kerry Mallan, Roderick McGillis, Heidelberg, New York, Dordrecht, London: Springer.

Zamora, Lois Parkinson, and Wendy B. Faris, eds. (1995) *Magical Realism: Theory, History, Community*, Durham: Duke UP.

PART I

Concepts and theories

1

GLOBALIZATION AND GLOCALIZATION

Anna Katrina Gutierrez

Children's and young adult literature have been understood and interpreted through, if not shaped by, the effects of economic, political, cultural, social and technological processes on theoretical perspectives. Globalization is a term synonymous with the acceleration of such processes in the late twentieth century and the development of infrastructures in support of transnational connectivity and mobility, albeit with varying degrees of intensity across the world. It establishes a "network society" (Castells 1994, Lorrigio 2004) between First and Third world nations, the hegemonic West and North and developing East and South, and dominant and minority cultures, and foregrounds operations of integration and exchange across disparate spaces. The impact of global connectivity upon representations of subjectivity in narratives for young readers, and indeed upon child and youth culture as a whole, has drawn considerable interest from critics in the field, but critical discourse for non-Western texts has mainly been grounded on Western theories of globalization, culture and subjectivity. Theoretical perspectives from non-Western domains are rarely brought to bear because of the assumption that subjectivity, like globalization, is a Western invention. This essay anchors its overview of research regarding globalization and children's literature on the development of subjectivity from within a global network society in order to illuminate the critical exchanges between hegemonic/West and non-hegemonic/non-West spaces in the construction and transformation of representations of childhood and adolescence. In viewing globalization as a dialectical process – often uneven but a dialogue all the same – it seeks to elevate the participation of non-Western nations as more than a passive recipient of information and images.

As a phenomenon, globalization is hardly new. Globalizing pressures have existed alongside colonialism and structures of modernity, which explain why it is generally understood as an extension of Western imperialist strategies, which homogenize (and in particular Americanize) economies and cultures. However, others point out that in early international relations until perhaps the age of industrialization, "Oriental" cultural influences heavily flowed into Europe (Pieterse 2000; Tu 2000). Globalization is thus historically a multidimensional and polycentric process that comprises "multiple intentionalities and criss-crossing projects on the part of many agents" (Pieterse 2000: 70). Still others argue that globalization has entered a new phase in which progressive technologies facilitate global relationships across different platforms at an increased rate, creating the sense that time and space have been compressed into a single place (Harvey 1989; Giddens 1990; Robertson 1992), that boundaries are blurred and borders are porous, and promoting the "intensification of the consciousness of the world as a whole" (Robertson 1992: 8). The term began to define an age only after the fall of the Berlin Wall in 1989 (Robertson and White 2008), when the literal and metaphorical breaking of barriers between capitalism and communism foregrounded a common desire for increased flows of money, markets and populations across varying spaces. Advancements in communication and information technologies coincided with the end of the Cold War, which contributed to the increased rate of economic and cultural globalization. The internet, satellite television, cellular communication and the like enabled the infiltration of globalist values into the routines of communities and individuals irrespective of national belonging (Tomlinson 2003). These fundamental transformations in sociocultural, trade and industry structures result in new communities and hybrid identities.

Castells's image of a global network society brings to the forefront the interactions and interdependency of global signs and concepts of nation, and thus is able to show that all three perspectives overlap while remaining distinct from one another. It demonstrates the depth of globalization and the multiple levels it operates on. A matrix of commercial and cultural relations can simultaneously acknowledge Western dominance, move away from Eurocentric viewpoints, and show that informational flows of influence are multidirectional and collaborate in transformative ways. The idea of a network of exchanges further illustrates that distinct localities and cultures are linked via elements of sameness, yet the spaces themselves are not the same, making the impact of globalization uneven across the world. The interplay of differences and similarities concerning globalizing structures and involved nations discloses existing paradoxical pressures between homogeneity and diversity, unification and fragmentation, global and local, modern and traditional flows.

Although the global network was initially based on assumed similarities in consumer behavior, over time its facilitation of capitalist enterprises led to a complex exchange of images, ideas, information and populations that led to the mutual reconstitution of cultural formations in all directions. The belief, then, that globalization creates a homogenous "global culture" is untenable. What occurs is a global localization, or "glocalization", in which the blending of terms describes the adaptation of a global outlook to local conditions, and the reciprocal reinvention of global signs and local meanings. Robertson (1995) devised the term to internationalize the practice of *dochakuka*, a Japanese business model that evolved from an agricultural principle of adopting farming techniques to specific landscapes. The glocal encompasses and moves beyond Bhabha's concept of hybridity (1994), which is too difficult to separate from the hierarchy of colonial power. Such a reading of cultural globalization, and for our purposes child and youth culture specifically, would yield reductive conclusions. With the glocal as the focal point, a more nuanced view of global-local negotiations emerges in which the flows do not simply counter or copy one another but are each a set of multifaceted relations (inclusive of but not limited to gender, age, class, ethnicity, ecology and technology) that achieve transformative effects through a complex dialectic. The boundaries between spaces blur and from their negotiations arise glocal concepts that enrich both spaces.

Global-glocal imaginaries

Literature is a significant space from which to assess cultural shifts caused by socioeconomic and political processes related to globalization and it serves as a place wherein the network society can unfold and be represented as a glocal imagined community. The global-local dialectic also impacts upon the development of subjectivity, such that identity and the self take on global, local and glocal dimensions. Child and youth culture as a whole has been susceptible to the internationalization of trades and markets (Bradford et al. 2008), which have mainly been driven by trends in book, film and toy production in the US and the UK. New technologies have also led to innovative modes of storytelling that pivot around connectivity and reflect the increasing intersectionality of the world. Among these are "hypertextual" and multimodal fiction, web-based forums (such as fanfiction sites), e-books and interactive book apps and toys and, in the gaming world, MMORPGs or massively multi-player online role-playing games (the most famous is *World of Warcraft*). These types of stories span multiple spaces and split the sense of self so that subjectivity is developed and restructured along several planes at the same time, an experience that Giddens describes as "disembeddedness" (1990: 21).

Subjectivity is defined within the boundaries of the nation state but is also compelled to align with images representative of internationally shared values and qualities. Anchored on a sense of "sharedness" (Strauss and Quinn 1997), these global images are fluid and neutral even when they originate from a specific culture. But Stuart Hall concludes that the global-local dialectic is continuous, and that "what we usually call the global, far from being something which, in a systematic fashion, rolls over everything, creating similarity, in fact works through particularity, negotiates particular spaces, particular ethnicities, works through mobilizing particular identities" (1997: 62). Because of the economic dominance and cultural potency of Anglophone nations, images from many of their franchises, such as the Disney and Pixar films and the Harry Potter books, have come to represent global childhood and adolescence. The national meanings embedded within remain but are refined, and some even stripped away, in order to be relevant to a universal experience. But the last twenty years have witnessed counterhegemonic movements through local adaptations and glocal blends that, as the boundaries between source and destination are blurred and negotiated, reinvent the original and its copies. From these interchanges emerge glocal subjects that potentially enrich child and youth culture, literature and media on national and international levels. Hence, Stephens and McGillis argue for:

> a criticism aware that its objects of attention are contingent with historically specific relations to place, history, politics, and aware that the local is now also the 'glocal', whereby pressures from globalization for institutional change and social adaptation encounter pressures to preserve local identity and customs. These tensions are especially apparent in sites of cultural diversity and economic inequality.
>
> (2006: 367)

Countercultures can in turn become globalizing forces, as exemplified by the popularity of Japanese anime and manga, led by the development of Asian media markets in the 1990s. Manga and anime are both products and agents of globalization. Tezuka Osamu, hailed as "the Father of anime and manga", combined techniques from Disney animation and ancient Japanese picture scrolls (Yoshida 2004) to create a unique graphic style able to narratively express the nation's glocal position. Anime and manga are among the most important cultural exports of Japan and, like Disney cartoons, have been localized in many countries. In effect, these terms can also refer to visual narratives that have been inspired by the Japanese style and yet are stripped of the original national and cultural markers. When non-Japanese manga and anime (labeled "Original English-language", "international" or "global"), such as Nickelodeon's *Avatar the Last Airbender* (2005–2008) and the Canadian manga series *Scott Pilgrim* (2004–2010), are set beside their Japanese inspirations, it is evident that stylistic modifications had been made to support the themes, ideologies and genre boundaries of the producing nations. Anime and manga, then, are narrative mediums that represent shifts in the perception of childhood, subjectivity and culture from monolithic and stereotypical to glocal and boundless.

Glocalizing subjectivity

Readings that examine the effects of international connectivity on children's texts need to consider whether or not these narratives can be analyzed from outside the framework of the nation state and national literatures, and what might be learned from the possibilities and problems that arise from taking multiple vantage points. Contemporary texts for young readers generally center on the infiltration of capitalism into developing spaces and the effects of modern technology, urbanization, commodification and consumerism on local environments and public and private histories (Bradford et al. 2008; McCallum 2009). The approaches these narratives take range from a binary logic to one that fosters integration. The former is based on a self-Other spectrum that advocates nationalism and segregation, while the latter promotes diversity, adaptation and hybridity often portrayed as a utopian multiculture or a glocal blend. As postcolonialism, multiculturalism and postmodernism are discourses concerned with heterogeneity, these have become the main tools through which these relationships are addressed (Stephens 2008; Gutierrez 2013; Eoyang 2007, 2012). Through these lenses, subjective agency emerges intersubjectively from the dialectic between the self and the impersonal systems that operate through it, mimic its functions, and ultimately fragment it.

The Australian picturebook *Old Magic* (Baillie and Wu 1996), for example, demonstrates the pressures children face when negotiating the global and local images that inform their lives. Omar and his kakek (Bahasa for grandfather) exemplify extreme and opposite reactions to the Western modernity of Australia, their new home country. Omar responds with an eager and indiscriminate assimilation. He scolds his grandfather for clinging to the "old magic" of Indonesia. When kakek, clad in turban, a sarong over wide trousers, and a jacket marked with a star and crescent, offers his grandson a spinning top that signifies his connection to their native land, Omar rejects it. His trendy baseball cap and football uniform and the skateboard and basketball he carries signify his preference for fast-paced modernity over memory and tradition. Di Wu's blend of Chinese and Western illustration techniques gives a foreign, dreamy cast to the Australian habitus. The effect makes Omar feel as unanchored to the landscape as his grandfather even though his appearance locates him in Western culture.

His kakek's despair prompts Omar to remember the night markets, shadow puppets and provincial tranquility of Indonesia in light of the availability of TV, pizza and computer games. The neutrality of modern youth culture pales in comparison to the local color of his memories. Omar realizes that the answer is not in forsaking one over the other, as that would lead to homogenization without depth or cultural isolation, but to develop an identity from within a balanced dialogue. He creates a dragon kite with Western materials (including wire, ribbons and table tennis balls) that "would never be seen in a jungle village...but perhaps they would allow the magic to work here" as an expression of glocal innovation. Omar invites his kakek to fly the kite with him, whose reply "Let's swallow the sun" affirms the ability of children and youth to blend and empower their global and local affiliations. The isomorphism of their bodies as they "played the great kite" across the sky underscores the connectedness they achieved. That Omar still wears his head-phones while his *kakek* remains in traditional clothing visualizes the multiple flows that enrich their interrelation and the unifying effect of glocalization.

Philip Reeve's *Hungry Cities Chronicles* (2001–2006), although from outside the focused countries of this collection, is worth a critical look for its representations of the changing complexities of the network society and the impact of global-local and West-East exchanges on subjectivities. Globalizing processes and their emergent dichotomies are embodied in the tensions between mobilized and static cities. The relationships between the cities are metonymic of the evolution of social formations in response to contradictory pressures towards the preservation of the nation state and towards decentered internationalism. Because of a geological cataclysm caused by a devastating war between the American Empire and Greater China, cities west of Eurasia become "Traction Cities" that trade with, but more often prey upon, one another in order to survive in a world with depleted natural resources, while the Indian sub-continent and China continue to be separate and static. Reeve's cities are cyborgian entities that arose from the blended concept "Municipal Darwinism". Their technological ecosystems caution readers against the increasing interdependency of people and processes, with the endless mobility of the "hungry cities" forming homologies with deterritorialized global market and capitalist models of the USA and Britain (McCallum 2009). In *Mortal Engines*, the first book in the quintet, the traction city London intends to breach the Shield Wall that protects the "anti-tractionist" cities with the superweapon MEDUSA, and "gobble up" Batmunkh Gompa, a static city characterized by Eastern pacifism. That the Shield Wall is reconstructed along West-Orient demarcations revives colonialist relations between both spaces. White imperialist London defines itself against the "strange" and "uncivilized" Batmunkh Gompa. "Batmunkh" is a Mongolian name that means "powerful" and "everlasting" and "gompa" a Buddhist fortification of learning and enlightenment. London intends to reenact the colonization of a society peopled with those who have been historically oppressed or labeled minorities (Reeve 2001: 275–276), but the novel instead cultivates a perspective of tolerance and syncretism, and as the series unfolds moves towards models of subjectivity reflective of postmodern and glocal hybridity.

Cross-cultural reconfigurations: Introducing non-Western perspectives

Recent studies argue that the anti-hegemonic tendencies of Western discourses of heterogeneity are still reliant on a Western binary opposition, whereby hybridity is judged according to liberal humanist ideals and legitimates neocolonial aspects of globalization (Lebra 2004; Yoshimoto 2006). Eoyang observes that postmodernism vaunts pluralism but "envisions fragmentariness as wholeness truncated" and "claims to be revolutionary in its eclecticism, but is ignorant of East Asian syncretism" (2007: 109). Such statements can be extended to postcolonial hybridity and weak multiculturalism, anchored as they are on self-Other power relations. Hence, recognition of the transformative influence that non-Western and minority flows can have on the global network society calls for a comparative criticism of child and youth narratives grounded on a cross-cultural dialogue between Western *and* non-Western discourses of subjectivity (Stephens 2013; Gutierrez 2013). Western binary logic collapses when applied to non-Western texts wherein subjectivity is negotiated relationally, partly because its strategic concept hinges upon the absence or presence of a constant "I", and partly because this "I" will not accommodate a non-Western construct as subject (Lebra 2004; Yoshimoto 2006). For instance, Mauss' research foregrounds that identity images in Hindu, Chinese, Pueblo and Native American literatures are amalgams composed of connections with place, sociocultural structures and other selves (1985). Rosaldo reached a similar conclusion in her study of Philippine indigenous tribes, by which identities are not defined according to an ideal subject but are forever negotiated in multiple contexts (1980). The Japanese concept of *wakon yōsai* (Japanese spirit, Western techniques), conceptualized in the Meiji Era when Japan opened its gates to the Western world, provides an example from the context of globalization. *Wakon yōsai* sought to infuse modernization with a sense of national continuity, such that the consumption of the West simultaneously reinforced connections to Japanese roots (Wood 2009), resulting in hybrid goods that in turn gave inspiration to Western modernity (Iwabuchi 2002; Day 2007).

Eoyang's proposal for a cross-cultural analysis that focuses on glocal relations interpreted through the overlapping lenses of postmodernism and the Chinese principle of *maodun* (矛盾: spear-shield) as representative of East Asian syncretism is of particular interest because *maodun* literally brings together and balances contradictory states. Alluding to a fable about an "impenetrable shield" and an "invincible spear", the concept is based on Chinese "four-cornered logic" that allows both dualities to be true, for one to be true and the other false, or for both to be false (2012: 120–128). *Maodun*, then, encompasses more than is indicated in its English translation, "contradiction". A more precise rendering would be "paradoxical opposites" or a "contradictory unity", whereby the fusion of contrasting images opens up pathways of meaning not available to binary logic (2007; 2012). A combination of postmodernism and *maodun* deepens our understanding of global-local relations by allowing us to perceive glocal manifestations outside the realm of Western rational thought and accept that syncretism and dichotomy can occur simultaneously in all things (2012: 135).

Hans Christian Andersen's fairy tales afford an excellent example. They are popular world-wide, but dimensions of meaning unfold when a dual lens of postmodernism and *maodun* is applied to non-Western adaptations. Andersen's scripts and schemas influence cultures, but what happens is also an Africanization, sinicization, Filipinization, and so on, of Andersen. The general themes that run through his fairy tales – emancipation, the search for identity, the desire to cross borders, the rise of the middle class, the omnipotence of God, noble intellect versus noble blood, the recognition of natural beauty and magic – reflect Andersen's and his nation's twin struggles for recognition in an increasingly modern Europe (Zipes 2005; Frandsen 2014). Andersen's works are entwined with Danish romanticism and the national imaginary, such that Andersen *is* Denmark. He integrated Scandinavian folk motifs, religious themes and vernacular idioms into the literary fairy tale genre, the blending of which provided a global outlook to personal and national concerns. The international popularity of his fairy tales, however, indicates that the embedded themes are also global concerns. To the non-Western world, his fairy tales are representative of a more general Western culture and children's literature. This dampening of Danish nationalism is largely an effect of the English translations, wherein the nuances of Andersen's language were simplified to target a young upper class readership rather than maintain the wider and more inclusive audience of the originals, given that nineteenth century Britain and America considered fairy tales and fantasy the realm of children and women (Frandsen 2014). The universal themes explored in Andersen's tales, retold in English, transform them into globalizing images, but these are in turn reconfigured by local landscapes. A multidirectional analytical framework of Andersen retellings, then, is grounded on a reciprocal dynamism that includes and moves away from a central binary relation and understands that cultural icons are organic and take their shape and meaning from interactions with other ideologically charged artifacts. Because the Andersen source texts and the global idea of Andersen and his tales are reconfigured locally and vice versa, the glocal meanings that arise can be contradictory and integrative at the same time.

Sindiwe Magona's retelling of *The Ugly Duckling* (2010) is a straightforward example. Magona grounds the Ugly Duckling's narrative in an African *vlei* (a shallow lake) and creates a glocal atmosphere by interlacing African signifiers into the global imagery of the narrative. A blue crane, a hadeda, and other birds native to the region surround the Ugly Duckling, as do the ducks, swans and hens typical to the tale. The South African habitus as a glocalized space is further established when the Ugly Duckling is taken in by an African farmer and his donkey. The windpump – so vital to the country's agriculture – and the mix of native huts and Western-style housing in the background support the global-local framework of the retelling and indicate that glocalization is a historical and continuing process. In situating the global coming-of-age script (ugly chick to beautiful swan) in a glocal space, this retelling foregrounds the fluid and mutual reconstitution of global and local domains. The migratory nature of swans strengthens the universal and transferrable quality of the tale, as it allows readers to imagine the porous borders between the source text and the African retelling and maintain a contradictory unity through an analogous yet mutable swan schema.

In China, Andersen is known as "An Tusheng" or "born into a poor family" (Ye Rulan 2014). Translations, retellings and reversions of his tales reflect the political ideologies of specific periods in Chinese history, but the image of Andersen as a wise storyteller who exposes society's ills prevails, which says more about China than it does about Andersen's tales, the man himself, and what he was trying to achieve in and for Denmark. Two reversions of "The Emperor's New Clothes" demonstrate the ways the globalized scripts and schemas of the tale and Chinese political ideologies negotiate and affect global and local subjectivities. "The Emperor's New Clothes" was China's introduction to Andersen, but it was not the Danish original that first reached Chinese shores but rather a Japanese adaptation (Zhu 2014). In 1914, Liu Bannong translated the Japanese play, *The New Clothes*, which adapted the vanity motif into a critique of Western modernity. His chosen title, "A Sketch of a Fetishist of the Western World" (洋迷小影), aligns with the anti-foreign sentiment and resurgence of cultural heritage that characterized the 1911 Republic of China (established following the downfall of the Qing Dynasty and the Boxer Rebellion in 1899) (Zhu 2014). In this reversion, a student infatuated with Western goods to the point of wishing some magic would transform him into a Westerner takes the place of the Emperor. He is swindled by "great weavers from the West" who present him with a magical fabric that becomes more beautiful when seen by a good person but turns invisible when seen by a bad person. The student proudly shows off his imported clothing but is ridiculed for his nakedness. Liu writes in classical Chinese to emphasize his rejection of Western sociopolitical formations and a return to literary traditions and cultural purity on a linguistic level (Zhu 2014). But this device also underscores that since the student clings to signs not grounded in local landscape and language, his identity has no substance – he is naked. That Liu advocates an anti-imperialist stance through an adaptation of a Western fairy tale is contradictory, but also demonstrates *maodun*. The self-Other binary it mirrors simultaneously upholds and fragments the Western subject by declaring its adoption by the non-West irrational. But Liu's version also develops Chinese subjectivity on two fronts: through a return to nationalism and through glocal adaptation.

In 1930, Ye Shengtao wrote a sequel to Andersen's "The Emperor's New Clothes" as a commentary on the clash between the Nationalist Party and Communist Parties amid the threat of a rising Japan. Bearing the same title as the source text, Ye Shengtao adapted Andersen's playful script on upper class vanity to explore the power relations between a people who deride their leader and an Emperor who reacts with tyranny. Humiliated and angry, the Emperor chooses to continue to wear the magic clothes and declares that any who says that he is naked shall be executed. Yet the jokes and comments continued, which led to the death of thousands. His people revolted, demanding "freedom of speech and freedom of laughing and joking" and tearing at his flesh to rip off his "non-existent clothes". They replaced him with the child who first spoke the truth about the Emperor's foolishness (Ye Shengtao 1930, tr. Ye Rulan 2014). Because of the political climate at the time this tale was published, scholars believe that Ye Shengtao modeled the Emperor after Chiang Kai-shek and that the tale was a subversive critique of the dictator's anti-Communist agenda that plunged China into civil war (Farquhar 1999; Zhu 2014). Ye Shengtao inverts power structures by putting the child on the throne, favoring truth and the common people over the self-deception of the Emperor. His subversion aligns with that of Andersen and transforms it to reflect local ideologies, thus enriching global and local imaginaries by presenting variations of the Emperor and child schemas that simultaneously complement and contradict the original. Both Ye Shengtao's and Liu Bannong's versions use the "vain and foolish Emperor" schema to call for a China that stands strong against imperialist influences and support this with the image of Andersen as a writer for the oppressed albeit under different sociopolitical circumstances.

A final example is *Rosamistica* (Bellen and Flores 2004), a picturebook from the Philippines that fuses elements of Andersen's "The Little Match Girl", the Cinderella tale type and an apparition of Mary Mother of God called the Rosa Mystica. Bellen retells a tale originally written by Severino Reyes, who was called the "Hans Christian Andersen of the Philippines" for the way he syncretized Western, Asian and Filipino folktale scripts and schemas, religious motifs and the fairy tale genre to subvert colonial rule. Embedded in each of Reyes' fairy tale blends is a "triumph of the underdog" script, wherein the ingenious, creative and resilient underdog represents the Filipino people (Gutierrez 2009). The story begins by showing an orphaned girl named Rosamistica in a Cinderella role. Her aunt and uncle force backbreaking chores upon her until Christmas Eve, when they give her twenty-five centavos to spend on whatever she wishes, not out of kindness but to remove her from their festivities. Hungry and alone, she walks towards the church and looks longingly at the toys and food that the vendors are selling. In the illustrations, a white space around Rosamistica keeps her separated from the cheerful families and busy vendors. It signifies that she is an outsider and alludes to the Little Match Girl, who envisions scenes of physical and emotional nourishment with each match she lights. Instead of matches to warm her soul, Rosamistica imagines the joys she can purchase with her coin. Rather than buy something for herself, she gives her coin to a beggar woman and her baby. The grateful woman offers her a pouch in return, which Rosamistica finds is filled with coins. The woman and her baby disappear, and when Rosamistica reaches the church she sees their likeness in the image of Mary and the Christ Child.

The story ends with a statement that Rosamistica never returned to her cruel aunt and uncle. Her disappearance after seeing an apparition of the Rosa Mystica, adorned with a rose and thorns that symbolize the beauty that comes from great suffering, links with the Match Girl's vision of her grandmother's spirit and their flight to heaven. Rosamistica does not die, but is liberated through an altruistic nature that suggests she is a Filipino version of her holy namesake. She is the ideal Filipino child, created from the fusion of suffering, hardworking and good-hearted Match Girl and Cinderella schemas, and the infusion of Catholic symbolism in the religious motifs of the Andersen pretext. Rosamistica's pilgrimage to the church, the *parols* (Philippine Christmas lanterns) that decorate the Spanish-style plaza, the colonial era clothing, and the emphasis on Catholic values negotiates with global ideas of the Match Girl and Cinderella as well as with the colonial past and the Western influences of the present, which highlights the glocal dialectic. The negotiation of flows is further visualized through an illustration style that draws from the stylized "cuteness" of manga and imbues the Philippine retelling with the combination of sweetness and independence that characterizes Japan's cute culture, further strengthening the emancipation of Rosamistica. The appropriation of Western and Japanese influences to empower Rosamistica exemplifies the glocal paradox, in which interactions with hegemonic signs antagonize representations of national subjectivity while liberating them from both Western or traditional molds. The result is a fragmented unity free from the constraints of tradition or hegemony.

Conclusion

Glocal perspectives of children's literature and culture that include non-Western theories such as *maodun* move us to consider subjectivity and childhood as a product of multidirectional relations without a fixed center. Focusing on the transformative conversations between dominant and minority flows, in which West and non-West interactions accommodate more than oppositional binaries, enriches virtual and symbolic spaces and physical landscapes. It allows us to look at childhood and subjectivity in exciting new ways wherein boundaries give way to blends, and subjectivities are ever-changing constructs that are rooted in local traditions but have a global outlook. Glocal children especially empower non-Western spaces, for they demonstrate through their existence the complex interchanges between domains and possess the ability to further these dialogues and make a difference throughout the global network.

Bibliography

Baillie, Alan and Wu Di (1996) *Old Magic*, Sydney: Random House Australia.

Bellen, Christine and Liza Flores (2004) *Rosamistica*, Mandaluyong City: Anvil Publishing House.

Bhabha, Homi K (1994) *The Location of Culture*, London and New York: Routledge.

Bradford, Clare, Kerry Mallan, John Stephens, and Robyn McCallum (2008) *New World Orders in Contemporary Children's Literature: Utopian Transformations*, Basingstoke and New York: Palgrave Macmillan.

Castells, Manuel (1996) The Rise of the Network Society, The Information Age: Economy, Society and Culture, vol. 1, Malden MA: Blackwell.

Day, Tony (2007) "'Self' and 'Subject' in Southeast Asian Literature in the Global Age," in Kathryn Robinson (ed.) *Asian and Pacific Cosmopolitans: Self and Subject in Motion*, New York: Palgrave Macmillan, 19–36.

DiMartino, Michael Dante and Bryan Konietzko (2005–2008) *Avatar the Last Airbender Books 1–3*, Burbank, CA: Nickelodeon Animation Studios.

Eoyang, Eugene Chen (2007) *Two-Way Mirrors: Cross-Cultural Studies in Glocalization*, Lanham, MD: Lexington Books.

———— (2012) *The Promise and Premise of Creativity: Why Comparative Literature Matters*, New York: Continuum International Publishing Group.

Farquhar, Mary Ann (1999) *Children's Literature in China: From Lu Xun to Mao Zedong*, Armonk, NY, and London: M.E. Sharpe.

Frandsen, Johs. Nørregaard (2014) "Hans Christian Andersen and His Chinese Dreams," in Johs. Nørregaard Frandsen, Sun Jian and Torben Grøngaard Jeppesen (eds.) *Hans Christian Andersen in China*, Odense: University Press of Southern Denmark, 13–28.

Giddens, Anthony (1990) *The Consequences of Modernity*, Stanford, CA: Stanford University Press.

Gutierrez, Anna Katrina (2009) "Mga Kwento ni Lola Basyang: A Tradition of Reconfiguring the Filipino Child," *International Research in Children's Literature* 2(2): 159–176.

———— (2013) "Metamorphosis: The Emergence of Glocal Subjectivities in the Blend of Global, Local, East and West," in John Stephens (ed.) *Subjectivity in Asian Children's Literature and Film*, New York and London: Routledge, 19–42.

Hall, Stuart (1997) "The Local and the Global: Globalization and Ethnicity," in Anthony D. King (ed.) *Culture, Globalization and the World-System: Contemporary Conditions for the Representation of Identity*, Minneapolis: University of Minnesota Press, 20–39.

Harvey, David (1989) *The Condition of Postmodernity*, Oxford: Basil Blackwell.

Iwabuchi, Koichi (2002) *Recentering globalization: Popular culture and Japanese transnationalism*, Durham and London: Duke University Press.

Lebra, Takie Sugiyama (2004) *The Japanese Self in Cultural Logic*, Honolulu: University of Hawai'i Press.

Liu, Bannong (1914) "A Sketch of a Fetishist of the Modern World,", *Chinese Novel (Zonghua xiaoshuo jie)* 7th issue.

Loriggio, Francesco (2004) "Disciplinary Memory as Cultural History: Comparative Literature, Globalization and the Categories of Criticism," *Comparative Literature Studies* 41(1): 49–79.

Magona, Sindiwe and Natalie Hinrichsen (2010) *The Ugly Duckling*, Johannesburg: Jacana Media.

Mauss, Marcel (1985) "A category of the human mind: the notion of person; the notion of self" (translated by W.D. Halls), in Michael Carrithers, Steven Collins, and Steven Lukes (eds.) *The Category of the Person*, Cambridge: Cambridge University Press, 1–25.

McCallum, Robyn (2009) "Ignorant Armies on a Darkling Plain: The New World Disorder of Global Economics, Environmentalism and Urbanisation in Philip Reeve's Hungry Cities," *International Research in Children's Literature* 2(2): 210–227.

O'Malley, Bryan Lee (2004–2010) *Scott Pilgrim*, Vol.1–6, Portland, OR: Oni Press.

Pieterse, Jan Nederveen (2000) "Globalization North–South: Representations of Uneven Development in Interaction Modernities," *Theory, Culture and Society* 17(1): 129–138.

Reeve, Philip (2001) *Mortal Engines*, London: Scholastic.

Reeve, Philip (2006) *A Darkling Plain*, London: Scholastic.

Robertson, Roland (1992) *Globalisation*, London: Sage.

———— (1995) "Glocalization: Time – Space and Homogeneity – Heterogeneity," in Mike Featherstone, Scott M. Lash and Roland Robertson (eds.) *Global Modernities*, London: Sage, 25–44.

Robertson, Roland and Kathleen E. White (2008) "What is Globalization?" In George Ritzer (ed.) *The Blackwell Companion to Globalization*, Singapore: Blackwell Publishing Ltd., 54–66.

Rosaldo, Michelle (1980) *Knowledge and Passion: Ilongot Notions of Self and Social Life*, Cambridge and New York: Cambridge University Press.

Stephens, John (2008) "'They are always surprised at what people throw away': Glocal Postmodernism in Australian Picture Books," in Lawrence Sipe and Sylvia Pantaleo (eds.) *Postmodern Picturebooks: Play, Parody, and Self-Referentiality*, New York and London: Routledge, 89–102.

———— (2013) "Introduction: The Politics of Identity: A Transcultural Perspective on Subjectivity in Writing for Children," in John Stephens (ed.) *Subjectivity in Asian Children's Literature and Film*, New York and London: Routledge, 1–18.

Stephens, John and Roderick McGillis (2006) "Critical Approaches to Children's Literature," in Jack Zipes (ed.) *The Oxford Encyclopedia of Children's Literature*, Vol.1, New York: Oxford University Press Inc., 362–367.

Strauss, Claudia and Naomi Quinn (1997) *A Cognitive Theory of Cultural Meaning*, Cambridge: Cambridge University Press.

Tomlinson, John (2003) "Globalization and Cultural Identity," in David Heid and Anthony McGrew (eds.) *The Global Transformations Reader*, Cambridge: Polity Press, 269–277.

Tu, Wei Ming (2000) "Multiple Modernities: A Preliminary Inquiry into the Implications of East Asian Modernity," in Lawrence E. Harrison and Samuel P. Huntington (eds.) *Culture Matters*, New York: Basic Books, 256–267.

Wood, Chris (2009) "The European Fantasy Space and Identity Construction in *Porco Rosso*." *PostScript* 28(2): 112–121.

Ye, Rulan (2014) "Hans Christian Andersen in China: An Overview," in Johs. Nørregaard Frandsen, Sun Jian and Torben Grøngaard Jeppesen (eds.) *Hans Christian Andersen in China*, Odense: University Press of Southern Denmark, 75–94.

Ye, Shengtao (1930) "The Emperor's New Clothes," *Education Magazine* 22(1).

Yoshida, Kaori (2004) "Issues in Children's Media in Glob/calized Cultural Industry". Paper presented at the Graduate Student Research Conference "Asia Pacific: Local Knowledge versus Western Theory," The University of British Columbia, 5–7 February 2004. www.iar.ubc.ca/centres/cjr/publications/grad2004/index.htm (accessed 25 September 2007).

Yoshimoto, Mitsuhiro (2006) "The Difficulty of Being Radical: The Discipline of Film Studies and the Post-Colonial World Order," in Dimitris Eleftheriotis and Gary Needham (eds.) *Asian Cinemas: A Reader & Guide*, Honolulu: University of Hawai'i Press, 27–34.

Zhu , Jianxin (2014) "A Discussion on Political Appropriation of Andersen's Fairy Tales in China," in Johs. Nørregaard Frandsen, Sun Jian and Torben Grøngaard Jeppesen (eds.) *Hans Christian Andersen in China*, Odense: University Press of Southern Denmark, 123–132.

Zipes, Jack (2005) *Hans Christian Andersen: The Misunderstood Storyteller*, New York: Routledge.

2

THE *UNHU* LITERARY GAZE

An African-based mode of reading Zimbabwean children's texts

Cuthbeth Tagwirei

One of the tragedies of criticism in Africa is its philosophical open-check syndrome. It seems there is no limit to how much criticism in Africa borrows from the opulent West whose theories have travelled farther than most as a result of its histories of writing, imperialism and slavery. Because Europe long dominated the medium of print and was involved in expansionist projects into distant parts of the world, it managed to promote its philosophies and thus enable their wider circulation and appeal. Although "the nuancing and/or adaptation of some Western theoretical concepts can illuminate and enliven certain aspects of [...] Zimbabwean experience, tradition and culture as re-presented in fiction" (Mhlahlo 2013: 10), African wisdom, which has remained relatively preserved within more provincial texts – including local songs, proverbs and folklore – needs to be released. One of the challenges this article poses to African-based critics is the need to excavate and cultivate philosophical gems that resonate with set values, beliefs and goals of specific communities. New patterns of voluntary migration, where individuals from former European colonies are now able to penetrate the former metropoles, and developments in information communication technologies provide opportunities to recast African modes of speaking in wider contexts and consequently curtail what Vambe (2005: 89) has called "a poverty of theory in Zimbabwean literature."

This article posits an African-based mode of reading children's texts in Zimbabwe. It argues for a reading that frees African texts from the ideological limits of Western philosophy, which pursues experiences of class, ethnicity, race and nationality in children's texts while remaining oblivious to the human factor rendered in these texts. The reading of children's literature the world over owes much to feminist, Marxist, poststructuralist and postcolonialist paradigms, among others. African criticism of children's texts approximates Western criticism in this regard. Some African-based perspectives also obsess over race, colonialism and class. It is argued that these pursuits are essentially *negative readings*. Their objective is merely to draw attention to divisions at the expense of unities. Their pursuits of individual predicaments eclipse the attendant communal anguish that results from any crisis to the individual. Negative reading thrives on the magnification of divisions and turns a blind eye on the linkages that characterize human existence. The movements thus pursued are movements away from the community rather than movements towards the community even where texts do contain both forms of movement.

While these modes of reading are important in drawing attention to some of the injustices in the world, they fail to equally point out the importance of foregrounding the human against secondary identities of race, gender, class or ethnicity. I propose the conceptualization of *unhu* as not just a quality of being, but also a mode of seeing; a gaze that is predetermined and holistically focused on the whole person and not the parts that make up *munhu* (person). The *unhu* gaze does not entirely abandon nuances of gender, race or class. It remains aware of people's individuality but subsumes these within the ambit of humanness. In Shona we are told that "murombo munhu" (someone poor is also human). The lesson to be gained from this saying is that idiosyncrasies do not diminish one's humanness. The *unhu* gaze sees past idiosyncrasies towards humanness. In this regard, "*unhu*" refers to the quality of being whereas "*unhu* gaze" refers to a mode of seeing, and so I proffer the *unhu* gaze as an alternative, African-based conceptualization of African literature, in this case Zimbabwean children's literature. Just as nouns and pronouns are not gendered in the Shona language from which the philosophy of *unhu* derives, the *unhu* gaze sees human before gender, race or class. Its gaze rests upon the code that can subsume differences and therefore make possible the co-existence of people with different racial, class or ethnic backgrounds. As the reading of texts will show, the *unhu* gaze is a positive gaze. I argue that most Western theories are negative gazes that pull apart (one gender from another and one class from another) whereas *unhu* draws together (one person to another).

In the reading of texts, the possessor of the *unhu* gaze rewrites the text along the lines of *unhu*, a relational philosophy that centers human relations in all things. In conventional understanding, *unhu*, the Zimbabwean/Shona variant of an African-based philosophy of communalism – variously deployed as *ubuntu* in Xhosa and Ndebele, *umundu* in Yawo, *umunthu* in Chewa, *bunhu* in Tsonga, *botho* in Sotho or Tswana, *umuntu* in Zulu and *vhutu* in Venda – is a set of moral attributes and beliefs. *Unhu/ubuntu* expresses "our interconnectedness, our common humanity and the responsibility to each other that deeply flows from our deeply felt connection" (Nussbaum 2003: 2). Among its core values are "compassion, reciprocity, dignity, harmony and humanity in the interest of building and maintaining community with justice and mutual caring" (2). *Unhu* can therefore be considered "a sense of collective solidarity that is internalised and manifests in activities and attitudes such as love, caring, tolerance, respect, empathy, accountability, responsibility, fairness, justice, compassion, unity, compromise, etc" (Museka and Madondo 2012: 259). Samkange and Samkange (2013: 458) add "brotherliness, togetherness, sharing, caring for one another, kindness, courtesy and good relations" to the list of *unhu* attributes.

The *unhu* literary gaze draws attention to characters' experiences of community and the several connections that are created in order to make the community possible. Rine's "Small Flowerings of *Unhu*: the Survival of Community in Tsitsi Dangarembga's Novels" (2011) is a good example of how the *unhu* literary gaze can be applied to literature. Even where elements of *unhu* do not seem apparent, she affirms the existence of these elements, whether on a small or larger scale. Any text can therefore be subjected to the *unhu* literary gaze, since the reader only needs to direct attention to those aspects that "[set a] premium on human relations" (Samkange and Samkange 1980: 34). *Unhu* also governs how texts are seen as participating in the creation of *munhu* (person) and in the creation of a humane environment.

In Zimbabwe, the Ministry of Primary and Secondary Education set the stage for the utilization of *unhu* through its vision "of united and well educated Zimbabweans with

Unhu/Ubuntu," although it did not follow up its vision with strong support structures that would enable the translation of vision into actual practice. Following a presidential inquiry into the education curriculum in 1999, the government adopted an education agenda that sought to create patriotic citizens who valued and adhered to the principles of *unhu*. Even then, *unhu* was not clearly defined and the government did not clearly spell out how this *unhu* was to be achieved. In reaction to this discrepancy, a somewhat *unhu* renaissance has emerged in Zimbabwe since the year 1999. This development is seen in the incorporation of *unhu* in mission statements and values of some institutions of higher learning in Zimbabwe. For example, Great Zimbabwe University and Gweru Polytechnic College have *ubuntu/unhu* among their lists of core values; and Ezekiel Guti University strives to "inculcate knowledge, skills, and attitudes that develop learners into solution-driven, innovative, enterprising, and patriotic members of society who fully subscribe to the values and philosophy of *unhu/Ubuntu*." An *ubuntu* clothing line was also established by Simbarashe Simbabrashe as a way of extending *unhu/ubuntu* to other cultural areas of life in Zimbabwe.

Samkange and Samkange (1980) were the first to bring *unhu* into critical discourse in Zimbabwe, followed by two decades of ideological latency. Since 1999, scholars have applied *unhu* in several disciplines and discursive domains and toyed with the possibility of making *unhu* a philosophy of choice in several facets. Twenty years after the Samkanges expressed the hope that *unhu* would "guide and inspire thinking," it now seems that the hope is coming to fruition. There are calls in Zimbabwe to make *unhu* the philosophy of education in Zimbabwe (Magudu 2012, Chitumba 2013, Muropa *et al.* 2013, Ndondo and Mhlanga 2014); explorations of the significance of *unhu/ubuntu* in African morality (Ramose 1999); calls to make *unhu/ubuntu* the ethical code guiding social networking (2014); calls to make it part of Zimbabwe's philosophy of environmental preservation (Mawere 2012); moves towards the reaffirmation of *unhu* through a re-reading of Shona proverbs (Mandova *et al.* 2013); and proposals to revisit the policy of reconciliation in Zimbabwe within the framework of *unhu* to cherish values and attitudes found in other cultures (Hapanyengwi-Chemhuru and Shizha 2012). These deployments of *unhu* are very encouraging especially for the ways in which they enable the concept to appreciate in ideological currency.

Critics of children's literature in Zimbabwe need to consider the significance of the *unhu* gaze in the understanding of texts. There still appears to be a dearth in the philosophy's application to literary studies. As mentioned above, Rine (2011) focuses on how "small flowerings of *unhu*" characterize Tsitsi Dangarembga's *Nervous Conditions* (2004) and its sequel *The Book of Not* (2006). She contends that the concept of *unhu* is implied to a large extent in Dangarembga's novels, although it is not explicit in either text, and has thus received less attention than other aspects of the novels. Mabura (2010) demonstrates how Tsitsi Dangarembga and Yvonne Vera's "combined feminine gaze" (110) in works such as *Nervous Conditions*, *The Book of Not* and *The Stone Virgins* (Vera 2002) borrows from the principles of *unhu*. She argues that gender relations in these texts exhibit *unhuism* at various levels.

This essay differs from existing criticism of *unhu* in literary texts in two ways. First it focuses on children's literature. The choice of children's literature is by no means accidental. The importance of developing a philosophy for children's literature cannot be understated (Ndondo and Mhlanga 2014). Any reaffirmation of African values has to consider children, who are an important resource to any community's growth. Secondly, the paper does not pursue instances of *unhu* in texts. Rather, it makes *unhu* the framework of analysis; the lens through which children's texts are read. In other words, my primary objective is the proposition of a theory of Zimbabwean children's literature, one that is not necessarily in opposition to Western modes of reading, but one that makes the reading of children's texts culturally specific and relevant.

Defining the *unhu* literary gaze in respect to children's literature

The *unhu* literary gaze is characterized by positive reading. Three broad tenets may be posited for this gaze. Firstly, the gaze identifies the presence of *unhu* (love, caring, tolerance, respect, empathy, accountability, responsibility, fairness, justice, compassion, unity, compromise, kindness, courtesy and good relations) at various levels in texts and makes them the subjects of analysis. These instances of *unhu* are magnified and foregrounded in the discussions of texts. Texts for children everywhere attempt to promote what are considered universal virtues of love, kindness, compassion and respect. Samkange and Samkange (1980: 39) advise us that "traits or attributes of unhuism are not exclusive to the Bantu even though, in its entirety, the concept is." Any text can therefore be subjected to the *unhu* literary gaze. Zimbabwean texts for children invariably contain these virtues and it is up to the reader and critic to make them the subjects of literary discussion. The motive of such a reading is to promote *unhu* as a way of guaranteeing the survival of communities. Fixating on the absence of *unhu* is bound to reinforce a myopia that seems inherent in negative reading.

Secondly, the gaze sees individual problems as communal problems. The hero or protagonist's experiences epitomize the experiences of the larger community. There is no experience that is cut off from the community, however personal it may appear. This is consistent with the dictum "your pain is my pain, my wealth is your wealth, and your salvation is my salvation" (Nussbaum 2003: 2). The Zimbabwean texts for children, like most African texts, emphasize the importance of empathy. Characters in these texts are not an indifferent lot who find amusement in the suffering of others. There is always awareness that the loss of an individual is a loss to the community where the individual is a mere link within a system.

Thirdly, the gaze focuses on primary and end motives of being human and not on dynamic motives of being male/female, poor/rich, black/white. At the birth of a child, the Shona send their blessings, which are usually accompanied by the question "munhui"? At the basic level this question enquires after the sex of a new born child but it is possible to extend this to other markers such as class, ethnicity, health etc. Okot p'Bitek (1986: 19) explains that "man is incapable of being free. For only by being in *chains* can he be and remain 'human'" (emphasis in original). In African culture, one is born with predetermined roles as an uncle, a nephew, an aunt, a brother and an in-law, among other identities. The new born whose humanness is guaranteed is therefore marked in other identity nuances whose value is only guaranteed within a community of people, for the human being "has a bundle of *duties* which are expected from him by society as well as a bundle of *rights* and *privileges* that the society owes him" (ibid, p. 19; emphases in original). Significantly, that one is born *munhu* (a person) is a given. It is something society owes to the individual. Secondary markers of identity are only ascribed onto one's essential humanness. Sadly, the moment one's humanness is established, negative reading commences the pursuit for peculiarities for their own sake or in conflictual terms. Positive reading, on the other hand, asks how a peculiarity contributes to communal existence.

For a community to exist, there is need for difference so that each individual can give to the community what the next person cannot. A community needs farmers, artisans, hunters and rulers but even a king is a king because of other people as the Shona saying "Mambo vanhu" illustrates. Race, gender, class and ethnicity are recognized as individualities that mean nothing outside the framework of being human. They are utilitarian idiosyncracies. Outside the community, one's individuality is a negative force as the discussion of texts will show. This is not to suggest that there is an essence to humanness. *Munhu* is not a static category. It changes as the community changes.

Zimbabwean children's literature is a literature of forging relations, of creating bonds with the natural and spiritual world. The texts are therefore suitable for this preliminary discussion because of the ways in which they enable an *unhu* reading. Belonging, as they do, to a cultural polysystem that tries to make *unhu* the locus of cultural life, they make useful case studies. Even before the Nziramasanga Presidential Commission's recommendations to revise school syllabi to foster *unhu* in Zimbabwean children in 1999, efforts had already been put in place to revise history textbooks along the lines of "a nationalist, Africa-centred and Marxist-inspired" ideology (Barnes 2007: 263). Literature set books in schools also reflected this need as examinable texts for children published in the 1980s and 1990s would testify. Not only are the texts revisionist documents about the past, Gascoigne's *Tunzi the Faithful Shadow* serves to construct ideal citizens (Tagwirei 2013a) while Chater's *Crossing the Boundary Fence* encourages a reconciliation of races precicated on silences about certain aspects of the colonial past (Tagwirei 2013b).

As can be imagined, children's texts read in Zimbabwean schools are carefully selected so that they can propagate the values and ideals of the postcolonial nation. Zimbabwean texts for children are therefore by and large didactic and their didacticism is one that resonates with the values of *unhu*. I therefore use Hanson's *Takadini* (1997), Chater's *Crossing the Boundary Fence* (1988), Gascoigne's *Tunzi the Faithful Shadow* (1988) and Mucheri's *Friend Billy and the Msasa Avenue Three* (1989) to illuminate how an *unhu* literary gaze may be employed in the study of Zimbabwean children's texts. These texts have a wide circulation in Zimbabwean secondary schools because they have been part of a set of examinable texts in Zimbabwe at some point. *Takadini* narrates the story of an albino child and her mother who are forced to escape stigma and find accommodation in another community; *Crossing the Boundary Fence* is about a black girl who befriends a white girl during Zimbabwe's nationalist war; *Tunzi the Faithful Shadow* is an adventure about a boy and his dog who are both kidnapped by bandits and later rescued by the community; and *Friend Billy and the Msasa Avenue Three* is about four friends who are kidnapped by criminals who are hatching a plot to destabilize the government.

I make three postulations that derive from reading these texts from an *unhu/ubuntu* gaze, albeit in a non-exclusive sense:

Postulate one: The hero/ine is a link in the chain of human communion

Zimbabwean texts for children more often than not depict child protagonists who forge alliances and create links with other people in order to create communal ties. This aspect is easy to miss in feminist, Marxist and post-structuralist readings for various reasons. A feminist reading of *Takadini* would focus on Takadini's mother who ostensibly suffers because she gives birth to an albino after years of barrenness. The absence of girl characters in *Friend Billy and the Msasa Avenue Three* would obviously irk the feminist reader. The *unhu* gaze provides a different dimension to the texts whereby the hero/ine (whether male or female) is a link in the chain of human communion. Protagonists in all four texts embark on a journey into the community. This journey follows forced removal from the community by forces that seek to destroy communal existence.

Both Takadini, the albino child, and her mother, Sekai, are ostracized by a community whose adherence to prejudicial traditions is acute. Thus disengaged from other people, the two find themselves struggling to survive until they discover a traditional healer who leads them towards restoration/integration into another community. In this new community, Takadini is initially rejected. Nevertheless, the novel's final resolution is the rehabilitation of both mother and daughter into the community. *Crossing the Boundary Fence* demonstrates the movement towards other people through the advances a white girl and a black girl make towards each other in breach of the racial barriers erected to separate them. Despite the challenges they face, both girls are able to cultivate a bond that sees them enter a new Zimbabwe as friends. Through a reconciliation agenda consistent with calls made by the new Prime Minister Robert Mugabe at independence, the text is able to foreground the importance of moving towards each other as opposed to moving apart. Similarly, the four boys in *Friend Billy and the Msasa Avenue Three* endear themselves to an old widow who lives alone and cannot find an opportunity to visit her relatives and friends. Setting themselves the task of helping her with domestic chores and thus enabling her to visit her family, the boys epitomize *unhu*'s values of compassion and respect. The abduction of the boys by criminals marks the severance of communal ties, which nevertheless does not persist to the end. The boys are later rescued and honored by the President at a communal function to reaffirm the virtues they have demonstrated. Even *Tunzi the Faithful Shadow*'s Temba, who is kidnapped by bandits, is eventually rescued by the villagers and restored to the community. There is a sense in which the adventures/journeys are symbolic renditions of spiritual journeys akin to initiation whereby the individual is made to suffer individualism in order to appreciate the importance of community.

Postulate two: *Differences are resolved through recognition of a common humanity*

Although it is not true that all differences end amicably in children's texts, those in which they do owe much to individuals' recognition of a common humanity. In explaining *unhu/ ubuntu*, Ramose (1999) observes that the recognition of another's humanity is the basis of one's own humanity. Such recognition fosters respect for the other. The reader of children's texts is encouraged to see past the peculiarities of individuals and focus on their humanness. Following the birth of the albino child in *Takadini*, the old midwife, Ambuya Tukai, tells the prejudiced father: "His hair is like yours, only it is of a different color, like pale honey. Yes, he is strange, different from the rest of us. But he is more like you than different from you" (17). Even the mother ponders:

> [...] was her son not human? True, he was somewhat different but only in his colour. He had no more fingers and toes than his father, and the same number of eyes and ears – she had counted them all. When everything was put together he was more like the others around him than he was unlike them (28).

Despite his different skin pigmentation, Takadini is eventually accepted by the Musasa community. Initial impulses to reject him are eclipsed by the fear of transgressing against a *human* being and consequently incurring the wrath of the ancestral spirits who warn against the ill-treatment of strangers (41). When Takadini proves to be a gifted mbira player, the community becomes blind to his perceived disability and begins to see him "not as *musope* [albino], but as a musician, a person sharing a common interest with them" (110). At this point negative difference is transformed to positive difference.

In *Crossing the Boundary Fence*, a black nationalist explains "we're not fighting against white people [...] We're fighting to end racial discrimination" (120). The humanity of both whites and blacks is underlined. Diana is compelled to question her brother's racism against blacks thus: "Weren't they human beings like whites" (28)? Individuals from both races are seen as people who have something to contribute to Zimbabwe. This is why the interracial friendship between Diana and Musa is a significant factor in the narrative. Nuttall (2009) approximates the recognition of the other as human through the notion of entanglement. She defines it thus:

A condition of being twisted together or entwined, involved with; it speaks of an intimacy gained, even if it was resisted, or ignored or uninvited. It is a term which may gesture towards a relationship or set of social relationships that is complicated, ensnaring, in a tangle, but which also implies a human foldedness. It works with difference and sameness but also with their limits, their predicaments, their moment of complication.

(1)

By focusing beyond differences, both girls are enabled to see the other as a part of oneself. The white character, in particular, becomes increasingly aware of the colonized's status as human and commences to treat him with respect. Both Diana and her sister begin to learn Shona, one of the languages of blacks, as a commitment to co-existence.

Postulate three: Community, and not self-determination, is the critical feature of humanness

Community disequilibrium is always certain in Zimbabwean children's texts. This appears in the form of characters moving out of the community for whatever reason, although in most cases this disengagement is forced. Disequilibrium enters the text through the actions of individuals bent on destroying the spirit of *unhu*. In *Tunzi the Faithful Shadow* poachers, dissidents and bandits undermine the balance of society through their actions. Child readers of the text are therefore cued to reject these elements, which do not embody the values of *unhu*. *Friend Billy and the Msasa Avenue Three* has criminals and dissidents who seek to undermine the country's sovereignty. Likewise in *Crossing the Boundary Fence* we encounter racists such as Diana's brother, who threatens her not to fraternize with blacks and is determined to preserve colonialism at all costs. Cultural fundamentalists and misogynists are the agents of disequilibrium in *Takadini*. In children's texts, both villain and hero/ine are clear. The child reader does not travel a winding route to align him/herself to the hero/ine and develop a dislike for the villain. The *unhu* gaze recognizes the villains as the antithesis of *unhu*.

The agent of equilibrium in Zimbabwean children's texts is the community and not individual genius. A saying "varume ndivamwe, kutsva kwendebvu vanodzimurana" (men are all the same, when their beards catch fire they help each other to extinguish the fire) tells us that one person's problems are resolved through communal effort. It is therefore not surprising that as part of its restoration of balance the community caters for the welfare of individuals. Community-initiated equilibrium is usually part of a text's resolution. There is an explicit realization that the community needs to remain intact in order to survive. In *Tunzi the Faithful Shadow*, the community comes together to rescue kidnapped Temba so that they can restore him to the community. Temba is told by his father: "A family needs to stay together. When it can't, it grows weak. When the family is weak, then the whole village is weak" (23). It is therefore in the community's best interest to restore Temba to the community. Takadini's stigmatization is redressed at a *dare*, a communal gathering, where it is resolved that he be accepted as a member of the community. The name "Takadini" translates as the question "what did *we* do?" Its singular form would have been "Ndakadini?" The name therefore suggests that Takadini is the community's problem, which the community should therefore address. A nationalist war, characterized by the involvement of every member of the community, facilitates the reconciliation of blacks and whites in *Crossing the Boundary Fence*. Finally, it takes group effort to rescue the four boys in *Friend Billy and the Msasa Avenue Three* and foil an attempted destabilization of the government. The resolution is one that almost always involves the reconvening of community forces, group efforts that serve to reaffirm the principles of *unhu*. The lesson children's texts carry is that the society takes care of its own. Ideally, the community also rehabilitates those who go against the principles of *unhu*. The *unhu* literary gaze therefore pays attention to the ways in which texts represent communities engaging individuals and the multiple ways through which fall-outs are rehabilitated into the community.

Conclusion

The *unhu* literary gaze has great lessons for the study of Zimbabwean children's literature and obviously other literary categories that are almost-always infused with didactic elements. This approach is not only a powerful tool for those who teach literature to children, but also for critics of literature. What the *unhu* literary gaze postulates is not childhood innocence but positive reading – which is not entirely blind to the cracks in communities but zooms in on the movements to mend these cracks. Literary studies stands to benefit from pursuing gender, race, class and ethnicity in literature not for their own sake but as elements required in the service of the larger community. Less and less attention should be paid to cracks and more and more to linkages; the bonds that *unhu* fosters and makes possible for the survival and success of communities.

Bibliography

Barnes, T. (2007) "History has to play its role: Constructions of Race and reconciliation in secondary school historiography in Zimbabwe, 1980–2002," *Journal of Southern African Studies* 33(3): 633–665.

Chater, P. (1988) *Crossing the Boundary Fence*. Harare: Quest Publishing.

Chitumba, W. (2013) "University Education for Personhood through Ubuntu Philosophy," *International Journal of Asian Social Science* 3(5): 1268–1276.

Dangarembga, T. (2004) *Nervous Conditions*. Emeryville: SEAL.

——— (2006) *The Book of Not: A Sequel to Nervous Conditions*. Oxfordshire: Ayebia Clarke.

Gascoigne, M. (1988) *Tunzi the Faithful Shadow*. Harare: College Press.

Hanson, B. (1997) *Takadini*. Harare: Fidalyn Productions.

Hapanyengwi-Chemhuru, O. and Shizha, E. (2012) "Unhu/Ubuntu and Education for Reconciliation in Zimbabwe," *Journal of Contemporary Issues in Education* 7(2): 16–27.

Mabura, L. G. (2010) "Black Women Walking Zimbabwe: Refuge and Prospect in the Landscapes of Yvonne Vera's *The Stone Virgins* and Tsitsi Dangarembga's *Nervous Conditions* and Its Sequel, *The Book of Not*," *Research in African Literatures* 41(3): 88–111.

Magudu, S. (2012) "Citizenship Education in Zimbabwe: Challenges and Prospects," *Journal of Educational and Instructional Studies in the World* 2(4): 179–187.

Mandova, E., Chingombe A. and Nenji, S. (2013) "The SHONA Proverb as an Expression of *UNHU/UBUNTU*," *International Journal of Academic Research in Progressive Education and Development* 2(1): 100–108.

Mawere, M. (2012) " 'Buried and Forgotten but Not Dead': Reflections on 'Ubuntu' in Environmental Conservation in Southeastern Zimbabwe," *Global Journal of Human Social Science, Geography and Environmental Geo Sciences* 12(10): 1–9.

Mhlahlo, C. L. (2013) "Subalternity Revisited: *unhu/ubuntu*/Existentialist Intersubjectivity and Ancestral Silence in Yvonne Vera's *Nehanda*," *The Criterion: An International Journal in English* 4(4): 1–13.

Mucheri, M. G. (1989) *Friend Billy and the Msasa Avenue Three*. Harare: Longman.

Muropa, B. C., Kusure, L. P., Makwerere D., Kasowe R. and Muropa, Z. (2013) "Unhu/Ubuntu and Its Relationship with Civics and Citizenship Education," *Journal of Emerging Trends in Educational Research and Policy Studies (JETERAPS)* 4(4): 658–661.

Museka, G. and Madondo, M. M. (2012) "The quest for a relevant environmental pedagogy in the African context: Insights from *unhu/ubuntu* philosophy," *Journal of Ecology and the Natural Environment* 4(10): 258–265.

Ndondo, S. and Mhlanga, D. (2014) "Philosophy for Children: A Model for Unhu/Ubuntu Philosophy," *International Journal of Scientific and Research Publications* 4(2): 1–5.

Nussbaum, B. (2003) "African Culture and *Ubuntu*: Reflections of a South African in America," *Perspectives* 17(1): 1–12.

Nuttall, S. (2009) *Entanglement, Literary and Cultural Reflections on Post-Apartheid.* Johannesburg: Wits University.

P'Bitek, O. (1986) *Artist the Ruler: Essays on Art, Culture and Values.* Nairobi: East African Publishers.

Ramose, M. B. (1999) *African philosophy through ubuntu.* Harare: Mond Books.

Rine, D. (2011) "Small Flowerings of Unhu: the Survival of Community in Tsitsi Dangarembga's Novels," M.A. Thesis, University of Florida.

Samkange, S. and Samkange, T. M. (1980) *Hunhuism or ubuntuism: A Zimbabwean indigenous political philosophy.* Harare: Graham Publishing.

——— (2013) "Philosophies and Perspectives in Education: Examining their Roles and Relevance in Education," *Greener Journal of Educational Research* 3(10): 454–461.

Tagwirei C. (2013a) "Fictions, Nation-building and Ideologies of Belonging in Children's Literature: An analysis of *Tunzi the Faithful Shadow*," *Children's Literature in Education* 44(1): 44–56.

——— (2013b) "Significant Silences and the Politics of National Reconciliation in Chater's *Crossing the Boundary Fence* (1988)," *Journal of Literary Studies* 29(4): 20–35.

Vambe, M. T. (2005) "The Poverty of Theory in the Study of Zimbabwean Literature." In Primorac, R. and Muponde, R. (eds) *Versions of Zimbabwe: New Approaches to Literature and Culture.* Harare: Weaver Press, 89–100.

Vera, Y. (2002) *The Stone Virgins.* New York: Farrar, Straus and Giroux.

3

REALISM AND MAGIC IN LATIN AMERICAN CHILDREN'S BOOKS

Fanuel Hanán Díaz

Magical realism is an extensive and complex concept and it may seem ambitious to explore it deeply in a brief paper. I therefore offer a large framework that will allow me to contextualize the development of a type of narrative in Latin American children's books where a symbiosis between magic and realism is attained. To talk about magical realism as a Latin American literary movement it is necessary to probe into the considerations about the identity and the historical process that produced multicultural nations with common roots; it implies the need to recognize the power of faith as part of a deep and racially mixed religiousness; and to admit the powerful presence of nature, impressive and boundless, in everyday life.

Latin America represents almost 14 percent of our planet's continental space. Throughout its extensive area eighteen Spanish-speaking countries are distributed, in addition to other non-Spanish speaking countries such as Haiti, Brazil and innumerable islands that form Dutch, French and US overseas territories. Large regions mark notable differences in this part of the planet, the Caribbean with its clear waters, its idyllic beaches and its afro-descendent population also covers a part of the coasts of the continental countries. The Andean region, with its colossal mountains, its perpetual snow and its lunar landscapes, is inhabited by communities that descend from the first native people. The Amazonas, for its part, with its thick rainforests, exotic landscapes and ancient rock formations, still preserves an ancestral and unknown memory.

This generous geography, irrigated by enormous and boundless rivers, interspersed with rainforests where trees grow like giants and where planet Earth's greatest biodiversity is concentrated, also harbors a fertile melting pot of tales that have their origins in the indigenous cosmogony, the different historical inter-oceanic voyages, and legacies that time has fused together. Latin America is also the kingdom of crossbreeding. A slow and laborious process has permitted the fusion of three great cultural components. First, there is the indigenous substratum with its worldview, its mythology, its aesthetics of synthesis, its ancient languages, its connection to the natural world, its restraint. Second, the Spanish conqueror contributed a sense of astonishment, a particular religion, scientific knowledge, ambition, an expansive language, cruelty and poetry. Finally, slaves from Africa, who were forcibly brought here as a workforce, have bequeathed to us their rhythm and musicality, their zeal for the supernatural, their profound lamentation, their rebel spirit, their animistic perception, their beliefs.

This outlook, somewhat subjective and simple, shows elements that define our cross-bred cultures, and determines this permanent coexistence between the center and the periphery, the hegemonic discourses and the subordinated ones, between rational thought and magical thought, conflicting emotions, the presence of the supernatural in everyday life, and a very strong connection with the natural world, which in Latin America is characterized by its lushness, its excess and its exoticism.

During the 1940s there arose, amidst the coordinates of this geographic and social context, a literary trend that breaks the ties to a descriptive tradition and to foreign models such as surrealism. Authors such as Cuban Alejo Carpentier, Venezuelan Arturo Uslar Pietri and Guatemalan Miguel Ángel Asturias generate a consciousness of this new way of looking with which reality is observed, and which assumes crossbreeding, indigenous heritance and elements of popular religiousness, that together with the untamed natural world, the history of conquest still warm in its ashes, and hilarious and absurd episodes related to the political classes of remote Latin American countries, make way for a different scene where magic penetrates reality as part of everyday life. In literature this idiosyncrasy, this cultural fusion, leaves deep and very distinctive marks. A new and different discourse appears and a new literary trend that flourishes with its entire splendor would surprise the world during the decades to come. Children's books also fall under the influence of this hybrid vision of the world and of the coexistence between magic and reality in the everyday dimension.

Where does magic come from?

One of the most controversial dichotomies in Latin American children's literature has to do with the presence of fantasy and reality in the discourses of children's books. Since Antoniorrobles, a Spanish poet exiled in Mexico, offered a cycle of conferences in 1941 with the curious title of *Did the Wolf eat Little Red Riding Hood?* a controversial discussion about the appropriateness of magic, of fairytale's violent and terrifying contents, the harm or benefit of offering fantasist contents to children, and the origins of fairytales and their kingdoms as counterfeit and not autochthonous universes in children's books discourses, has been taking place. This is not the place to delve into the nuances of this discussion, but the important point to grasp is the fact of the existence, in Latin America, of other roots, other seeds, from which magic, its beings and its marvel emanate.

In this context, the indigenous worldviews represent an endless source, with their gods, protectors of the natural elements, their sacred mountains, their mythical characters that undergo marvelous transformations into animals or plants; with their dualities that expose the terrible and the luminous sides of the psyche, with their countless explanations for the understanding of an overwhelming and gigantic natural world. Then the encounter with the New World also produced another seed for magic: the astonishment in front of an untamed landscape full of wonders and images never seen before awakened the fading European fantasy, which had been fed by chivalric novels where superhuman knights accomplished great feats amidst the tricks of alchemists and wizards. Somehow, the influence of chivalric novels such as *Amadís de Gaula* and *Belianís de Grecia* extended, during the years of the conquest, the imagery full of dragons, hags, witches, unicorns and sirens that the conquerors and chroniclers thought they had found in the new American fauna. The terrible crocodiles, the majestic condors, the gentle manatees, the huge snakes and the strange tapirs nurtured this imagery and gave it a new unexpected surge.

In the opening of his Nobel Prize acceptance speech in 1982, Gabriel García Márquez describes such unexpectedness as it was recounted in the journal of Antonio Pigafetta, the Florentine navigator who accompanied Magellan on the first circumnavigation of the world. Márquez suggests that what Pigafetta recorded in South America "also seems to be an adventure into the imagination". Pigafetta writes that, "There are also some pigs which have their navel on the back, and large birds which have their beak like a spoon, and they have no tongue" (1874: 46). His description of a guanaco encapsulates the attempt to relate otherness to familiarity: "This beast has its head and ears of the size of a mule, and the neck and body of the fashion of a camel, the legs of a deer, and the tail like that of a horse, and it neighs like a horse" (1874: 50). His long account of the Patagonian native populace dwells on their difference, for example, when the explorers played host to a man described as a giant, "The captain caused food and drink to be given to this giant, then they showed him some things, amongst others, a steel mirror. When the giant saw his likeness in it, he was greatly terrified, leaping backwards, and made three or four of our men fall down" (1874: 50).

When confronted with the other, the idea of that which is monstrous appears. To the European eye, the American indigenous people represented very different races: naked, copper toned skin and plentiful hair, with ornaments on their bodies and painted skins. They embodied the enemies of a battle that was justified because of religion; they were seen as impious, Satan and pagan idol worshipers, cannibals. Such a perception was necessary if the exploitation of these new races was to be rendered morally acceptable, and representations of cannibalism played a central role, as exemplified in engravings included in the voluminous works of popular geographer Theodor de Bry. Drawing on reports by travelers, he depicted Brazilian indigenous people busily feasting upon human flesh (Bucher 1981: Chapter 6).

Representations of deformed human beings then proliferate. These already had their precedents in European imagery, as we can see in the engraving *Chosmographia*, by Sebastian Müster in 1544. In the center of the picture there is a headless being, whose eyes and mouth are located in his chest – that is, the mythical *Ewapainoma*, who would later be described by Sir Walter Raleigh during his voyage through the Venezuelan Guayana rain-forests in search of the mythical El Dorado. In another map of 1599 by the Dutch cartographer Jodocus Hondius, we can once again see an image of this character (Ewapainoma) beside an athletic Amazon, one of the mythical women who gave their name to one of the greatest rivers on the planet and who were thought to dwell somewhere amongst the New World's intricate jungle. Chimeras, products of a prolific imagination, were thus adapted to this new fantastic geography, nurturing the first tales about America, of the so called "Chronicles of the Indies", which, from this first moment, drew the stories about this territory under the magnetic charm of marvel. Nor did this fantastic bestiary represent the only merging point between reality and fantasy.

The image of the cross section of a slave boat that appears in an anti-slavery pamphlet issued by Thomas Clarkson in London, 1798, emphasizes the inhuman way in which the bodies were laid out in the hold of the ship. The image depicts hundreds of slaves, men and women, who are being transported in ruthless conditions. Stacked up like sacks, naked, in foul and suffocating spaces, they were starting on an endless voyage towards unknown and strange lands. When they got there, they were sold like animals, branded as cattle, and forced to work through exhausting working days.

As a way of exorcising this feeling of excision, they find refuge in rites. The Catholic religious practices blended in with the religious systems of the transplanted people, such as the Yoruba, in an exceptional syncretism that gave way to Santería. The *orishás*, or deities, find their representation in the images of Catholic saints, which acquire an animist aura and are worshiped by rituals linked to magic. Soothsaying, the world of the dead in relation to the earthly world and the reinterpretation of that which is sacred, are some of the elements that penetrate the magic flow in Latin America.

How do these traditions affect children's literature? They have a lot to do with this literature, as they have to do with life itself, with the way we conceive the world, and more closely, with the world of childhood, because in this dimension of wonder is of vital importance; and when we talk about magic, we are not referring to the European tradition of fairy tales, nor to the type of spells that flow from a magic wand, nor to the transformation of a pumpkin into a carriage, nor to the flying carpets of the oriental stories. Our magic comes from other sources; it forms part of our daily life, of that which is called Latin American magical realism.

Magical realism in Latin American children's literature

Magical realism represents a literary current that symbolizes the most authentic American literature. The term was first coined in 1925 by the German reviewer Franz Roh, in regard to post-expressionist painting, referring to a generation of painters who attained a new view of reality, painting everyday objects from the starting point of contemplating the world as if it were emerging from emptiness, a magic recreation. Even though the term hardly had any impact in the European plastic arts, due to the influence of avant-garde movements, it was subsequently adopted by a generation of Latin American writers, who constituted the first generation of "magicrealists" during the 1940s and the 1950s, a period when the so-called boom of Latin American literature emerges. We owe Venezuelan writer Arturo Uslar Pietri the appropriation of this term in an essay of 1947 (published in 1948), in which he refers to that literary generation's awareness of man as a mystery in the face of reality.

In the essay "De lo real maravilloso Americano" (On the Marvelous Real in America), first published in 1967, the Cuban writer Alejo Carpentier advances this condition inherent to Latin America's deepest essence.

> Y es que por la virginidad del paisaje, por la formación, por la ontología, por la presencia fáustica del indio y del negro, por la revelación que constituyó su reciente descubrimiento, por los fecundos mestizajes que propició, América está muy lejos de haber agotado su caudal de mitologías. ¿Pero qué es la historia de América toda sino una crónica de lo real maravilloso?
>
> [And it is because of the landscape's virginity, the formation, the ontology, because of the fortunate presence of the indigenous and the negro, because of the revelation that constituted its recent discovery, because of the fertile cross-breeding that it brought about, America is far away from having used up its wealth of mythologies. But what is all of American history if not a chronicle of the marvelous real?]
>
> (7–8)

Magical realism has the real and marvelous, and other influences, among its first precedents; these slowly germinate until they bloom dazzlingly into a new literary model.

Many critics recognize the influence of surrealism as one of the primary catalysts, and also a literature of fantastic style that expands in southern Latin America with Jorge Luis Borges as its main representative. Nevertheless, the magical realism that emerges into a more authentic vision of Latin America has its roots in more remote and ancient soil.

What defines magical realism, its essence, is the way it perceives and shows reality. If surrealism shows the distortions of the world of dreams, and fantastic literature deals with supernatural events that invade reality, in magical realism it is reality itself that has the power of being exceptional. At a stylistic level, this representation is attained through resources that show, on the one hand, everyday events as if they were amazing, and on the other, prodigious incidents described as part of common life. Undeniably, the metaphor of this unusual geography is Gabriel García Marquez's legendary town of Macondo.

In order to explain this concept in a more graphic way, I here recount two memories from my childhood. The first has to do with my grandmother. We used to spend vacations in a little town in the Venezuelan Llanos in a farm that was very far away from civilization. I remember one night that I couldn't fall asleep, because an owl was desperately hooting outside. The farmers say that the hooting of owls attracts the dead, so obviously I was afraid. My grandmother slept deeply beside me until I woke her up to tell her about the owl. She simply told me "place your shoes the other way around so it will leave". Said and done, I turned my shoes around under my bed and the night bird ceased to sing. Another memory has to do with nature's force, the image of a winter night with the sky unleashing a tropical rain storm. And in the corridor of that house in the middle of nowhere, a lamp showed a curtain of light with millions of insects fluttering around it. The strange act of turning around a pair of shoes in order to drive a bird off is assumed to be part of the simplest daily life, while a natural event like a storm can give way to the supernatural, like the image of a cloud of insects that surprises us in the middle of the night.

These two evocations allow me to engage with magical realism, from certain coordinates that are linked with telluric force, a return to origins, ancestral magic and the presence of the astonishing in everyday life. To do so, I will talk about three works that are representative of Latin American children's literature. The first is *Zoro* by Colombian author Jairo Aníbal Niño, written in 1976, which tells the story of an indigenous boy who, accompanied by an old man, travels through the rainforest in order to find his town. The second, *Mo*, written in 1991 by Lara Ríos, tells the story of a teenage girl of the Cabécar ethnic group in Costa Rica, who goes through a growing process to reach the maturity that will allow her to turn into a *Sukiu* (that is, a shaman), with the awareness of the magic powers and ancient knowledge of her people. Finally, the novel *Tres buches de agua salada* (*Three Mouthfuls of Salt Water*), written by Chilean author Verónica Uribe in 1992, deals with the world of Santería seen through the eyes of a little boy who isn't able to walk well.

These three works are linked to each other in the spirit of magic realism, and have the following aspects in common: nature's prolific force, phenomena that in the tropics reach disproportionate dimensions, the never-ending rain, the impenetrable and dense rainforest, the permanent presence of animals and plants, rivers so wide they seem to be seas, the noises of the night in the mountains. It all simply exists and there is no need to invent anything. Each of the main characters, in their own way, starts on a journey of understanding, of learning, that could be classified as a *Bildungsroman*. However, the characteristics that define this narrative framework are others; it is the search for origins, and they embark on metaphoric journeys in search of identity, which is an eternal and recurrent Latin American question. What are our roots? Where are our roots?

In *Zoro*, the rainforest takes on a leading value within the adventure, with its imminent danger: a crystal tiger, an eagle of ice and anacondas that seem to be lianas hint at a fantastic zoology that has a strong hold on reality. For example, the space of a house in the middle of the rainforest expands, as a resource that gives supernatural value to an ordinary event:

> Suddenly, behind a reddish cloud, the big house appeared. It was a disproportionate house. So big that it filled the whole space, and inside it, through the rooms and corridors ran stormy rivers. Some of the rooms harbored strange ponds of calm waters, and to go from one wall of a room to another, you had to ride a horse.

This very realistic description doesn't generate doubt as in fantastic literature. The unreal becomes believable, because this is how the tropics invade life – penetrating houses through cracks, with thousands of insects, plants and larvae, and birds that make their nests on the balconies.

Mo goes through an initiation process. On the one hand, she equips herself with the necessary courage to defeat the forces of evil, embodied by the wicked sorcerer. On the other, she obtains the knowledge that will allow her to become shaman of her clan, spokesperson of her ancestors and with their power to heal. The passage through different planes establishes the coexistence between real events and solutions that involve intuition, the emission of signals from natural surroundings and sudden messages from the spirits.

Finally, in *Three Mouthfuls of Salt Water* the emphasis is on Santería and the power of African magic. Here, Yemayá, the goddess of the waters, represents the character who articulates the experiences that Juan has during his vacations. Important transformations are brought about by following the ritual of drinking three mouthfuls of salt water during a day when the sea is charged with beneficial energy, or *aché*. When he returns, Juan is healed and finds love.

The close coexistence between magic and reality, the presence of a system of beliefs that blends the indigenous worldview and African animism, a sense of permanent wonder in front of the small and big miracles the tropics offer, as well as the stylistic resources, make it possible to give literary beauty to magic reality and make it an object of fiction. In a great part of our children's literature both dimensions coexist, but the boundaries between them aren't determinate nor is it necessary to identify resources to move from one to another. Not only has magical realism in children's literature developed within the same coordinates as in literature for adults, but it has also inherited that unique and particular way of approaching the world, inseparable from its primal enchantment.

Conclusion

The magical realism movement had late derivations in Latin American children's literature, and its manifestations tend to camouflage themselves within diverse forms of coexistence between reality and fantasy, which pertain to literature for childhood. However, visible influences of this trend can be traced in contemporary children's narrative.

The wonders and marvelous elements amidst a boundless geographic framework find their place in works such as *El valle de los cocuyos* (The Firefly Valley) (1985) by Colombian author Gloria Cecilia Díaz, a tale that also combines the journey with the search for identity. In this adventure, which also becomes a rite of passage, the elements of nature act as opponents and helpers of Jerónimo, the protagonist, moved by a cosmic strength that enshrines the immeasurable power of the very nature of magical realism. In the end, Jerónimo can defeat the Spirit that holds captive a mysterious woman, and that embodies a supernatural force. The recovery of ancient knowledge often takes the characters through initiation journeys, as is the case of *Sueño Aymara* (Aymara Dream) (1995) by Peruvian writer Aníbal Eduardo León Zamora. In this book, a group of indigenous children start out on a journey to the Aymara hell where they are able to find part of their identity. The eternal question of who we are and the inverse journey to our origins, our roots, give the protagonists of these voyages a special impetus. The relationship with the world of the dead as beings that cohabit with us in everyday life, without raising any surprise, reaches aspects of dark humor in *Los muertos andan en bici* (Dead People Travel by Bike) (2012) by Mexican author Christel Guczka. In this story, a boy who is repremanded at school because of his overflowing fantasy experiences an unforgettable vacation when his grandfather, who had been dead for two years, suddenly appears.

Children's and young people's narrative offers new opportunities for that strange reality to have a main place in literature, for the fictional universe to be imbued with the fruit of crossbreeding among that group of beliefs, and for those tiny and surprising events to coexist with quotidian life. The attitude toward surroundings that attain marvelous aspects in everyday life, or that give ordinary qualities to incredible events in order to integrate them to common life, guarantee the continuation of magical realism in children's books. If there is a space in fiction where that hybrid condition can still project itself, or where exists that particular world view where surprise emerges from the unexpected or flows with spontaneous naturalness, that territory belongs to children's literature.

Bibliography

Abate, Sandro (1997) "A medio siglo del realismo mágico" (A Half Century of Magical Realism), in *Anales de Literatura Hispanoamericana* (Hispanic American Literature Annals). Madrid: Universidad Complutense.

Becco, Jorge (1992) *Historia real y fantástica del nuevo mundo* (Real and Fantastic History of the New World). Caracas: Biblioteca Ayacucho.

Bucher, Bernadette (1981) *Icon and Conquest: A Structural Analysis of Illustrations of de Bry's GREAT VOYAGES*. Chicago: The University of Chicago Press.

Carpentier, Alejo (1976) "De lo real maravilloso americano" (On the Marvelous Real in America), in *Tientos y diferencias*. Buenos Aires: Calicanto.

Díaz, Gloria Cecilia (1985) *El valle de los cocuyos* (The Firefly Valley). Madrid: SM, 1993.

Flores, Angel (1954) "El realismo mágico en la narrativa hispanoamericana" (Magical Realism in Hispanic American Narrative). Conferencia (Conference).

Guczk, Christel (2012) *Los muertos andan en bici* (Dead People Travel by Bike). México, D.F.: Ediciones El Naranjo.

Márquez, Gabriel García (1993 [1982]) "Nobel Lecture: The Solitude of Latin America," in *Nobel Lectures, Literature 1981–1990*, ed. Sture Allén. Singapore: World Scientific Publishing Co. Also available at: www.nobelprize.org/nobel_prizes/literature/laureates/1982/marquez-lecture. html.

Niño, Jairo Aníbal (1976) *Zoro*. Bogotá: Carlos Valencia Editores.

Oviedo Pérez, Rocío (1999) *Huellas de vanguardia: Realismo mágico/literatura fantástica. Esbozo de una relación* (Magic Realism/Fantastic Literature. Outlining a relationship). Madrid: Universidad Complutense.

Pigafetta, Antonio (1874) "Pigafetta's Account of Magellan's Voyage," in *The First Voyage Round the World, by Magellan*, trans. Lord Stanley of Alderley. London: The Hakluyt Society, 35–163.

Ríos, Lara (1991) *Mo*. San José: Farben.

Uribe, Verónica. (1992) *Tres buches de agua salada* (Three Mouthfuls of Salt Water). Bogota: Grupo Editorial Norma.

Uslar Pietri, Arturo (1948) "Realismo mágico," reprinted in *Godos, insurgentes y visionarios* (Goths, rebels and visionaries). Barcelona: Seix Barral, 1986.

Zamora, Aníbal Eduardo León (1995) *Sueño Aymara* (Aymara's Dream). Medellín: Universidad Pontificia Bolivariana.

4

POLITICS AND ETHICS IN CHINESE TEXTS FOR THE YOUNG

The Confucian tradition

Lijun Bi

Introduction: the Confucian tradition

The Chinese term for politics, 政治 (*zheng zhi*), consists of two characters. The first character 政 (*zheng*) in ancient times was a synonym for 正 (*zheng*), which had a very broad range of moral connotations and could be used as a noun, a verb and an adjective: the obverse side, to rectify, to correct, to mete out punishment to a criminal, straightforward, unbending, honest, virtuous, original, just, unbiased, and formal. The second character 治 (*zhi*) is mainly a verb, and occasionally a noun. The basic meaning of this character is to administer, to control, to rule, to regulate, to harness (a river), and to treat (a disease). As a noun, it denotes stability, peace and order. From the lexicological perspective, the combination of 政 (*zheng*) and 治 (*zhi*) strongly denotes the use of what is righteous and just to govern, to rule and to administer.

When Confucius was alive (551–479 BC), the imperial rule of the central government of the Zhou dynasty (1046–256 BC) was weak, and the feudal princes vied for supremacy. There were constant wars. Thus, Confucius dreamed of restoring the social order according to the rules of propriety in the early Zhou dynasty. The teachings of Confucius were concerned with practical ethics: the ways in which human beings might live together in harmony and good order. He envisaged man as a social creature who was bound to his fellows by 仁 (*ren*), a term meaning either sympathy, human-heartedness, benevolence, mercy or kindness. This *ren* is believed to be expressed through the five human relationships – sovereign and subject, parent and child, elder brother and younger brother, husband and wife, and friend and friend. Each person has a role to perform. If everyone performs their role properly, social order would be sustained. Correct conduct cannot be forced by compulsion, but rather it can be performed out of a sense of virtue that is obtained by observing learned models of deportment.

Books, as an educational tool, are to hold the absolute truth, the highest degree of morality, as reflected in the traditional Chinese phrase 文以载道 (*wenyizaidao* – writings/books are for conveying *dao* – the Path). Training in Confucian Classics was essential to ensure that the educated man would acquire the moral qualities that would enable him to fulfil his duties, both as a filial son at home and as a loyal subject in society. This ancient Chinese stress on the moral educability of men has persisted to the present, and continues to inspire both writers and the government to pursue moral education of the young.

Before 1911: Filial piety to parents, loyalty to emperor

For thousands of years there had been a concept of an intellectual elite, who were entitled to rule by virtue of their knowledge and moral qualities. Generally speaking, their elite status, distinguished from that of commoners, was gained not by virtue of hereditary status or economic wealth, but by virtue of their educational qualifications, gained through passing a series of strict imperial civil service examinations. These educated men of dynastic China had a monopoly control of power at all levels of civil administration.

Training in Confucian Classics started at a young age with an emphasis on filial piety. One of the world's oldest texts expressly created for children is a Chinese exposition: *An Essay of a Thousand Characters* (*Qian zi wen*). This text uses vivid metaphors to illustrate how to show reverence to one's parents: "As if treading on the brink of a deep gulf or on thin ice, a filial son has to be apprehensive and cautious" (my translation)

The application of filial piety is a life commitment and was also expected to extend beyond the immediate family to relatives, the clan, and finally to senior members of society and the state. Indeed, the dynastic rule was fully justified as being as natural as the parent-child relationship. The traditional term in the Chinese language for the government officials representing the ruler is thus 父母官 (*fumuguan* – parent-official), and the term for the ruled 子民 (*zimin* – child-people). Confucius formulated the following for a youth, which conveys his core political and moral message:

> A youth, when at home, should be filial, and, abroad, respectful to his elders...
> When he has time and opportunity, after the performance of these things, he
> should employ them in polite studies.... People, having perfected their studies
> of these writings, have to apply themselves to the official management of the
> state affairs
>
> (Fang and Bi, 2013: 131).

As a filial son at home and as a loyal subject in society, a youth was expected to have a high sense of respect for public responsibilities, and was even anticipated to commit suicide and perish with his Emperor if the dynasty were defeated. Indeed, whilst many shifted their allegiances with the fall of the Empire, some did choose to die. Likewise, for familial relationships, disobedient offspring were regarded with particular revulsion, and there are many recorded instances of undutiful and disrespectful adult sons and daughters being thrown down wells to their deaths by angry relatives.

Confucianism has been the most successful of all conservative systems in human history. This success explains why passivity, compliance, submissiveness, acceptance of fate and maintenance of the *status quo* were always highly valued in China. Such a demanding concept of filial piety and social discipline may help to explain the lack of individualism and the veneration of obedience and conformity that has been a continuous feature of Chinese culture. Thus, these features continue to be main attributes of Chinese culture, with its notable characteristics of alertness to hierarchic differences and the demand of obedience to proper authority.

From 1911 to 1949: Educate children, save the nation

From the mid-nineteenth century onwards, China began to suffer from a number of humiliations, being defeated by Western powers and Japan and having to cede territories such as Hong Kong, Macau and Taiwan. After the Qing dynasty collapsed in 1911, young intellectuals began to challenge the long-standing Confucian value of holding one's elders in high esteem. They claimed that filial piety, loyalty and righteousness were nothing but slavish morality (Bi and Fang 2013: 58). These iconoclastic intellectuals turned to a fresh area of children's education, hoping that the new generation would eventually break with the feudalistic past and shoulder the task of building a new China.

A modern literature for children and youth in a newly promoted vernacular emerged in the May Fourth New Culture Movement. This movement takes its name from a mass patriotic demonstration in Beijing in 1919 against the national government's agreement with a term of the Treaty of Versailles after World War I that saw China cede the Shandong Province, previously held by Germany, to Japan. Ostensibly, this new literature was to liberate children from the Confucian cult of ritualized subordination, but in reality it also had the purpose of constructing new political and moral content to involve the young in the politics of adults. For example, in the story "White Flags" (*Bai qizi*) by Cheng Sheng, published in *Weekly Review* on May 26 1919, three weeks after the May Fourth patriotic demonstrations, five characters are depicted to represent "typical" attitudes of that time. Erer and his big brother are portrayed as children with an innate sense of righteousness, both having a clear-sighted outlook as to what was right or wrong for the nation. Both characters are supportive of older students who took part in the demonstration at Tiananmen on May Fourth. These two boys, a primary school pupil and a secondary school student, are thus positive characters who represent the future and are the hope of the nation. In contrast, their father, a government official, is negatively depicted as someone who represents a "heartless and shameless traitor." The mother and the house servant reflect the "ignorant" and indifferent majority of the Chinese population: people who felt that the demonstration at Tiananmen or the threat of the nation's extinction had nothing to do with them. Other stories, like Lu Yin's "Two Pupils" (*Liang ge xiao xuesheng*, 1926) and Dai Pingwang's "Xiao Feng" (1928), also focus on children's participation in political demonstrations that concern the fate of the nation. Such stories ironically affirm the traditional Confucian notion of political-moral training for the common good, but in a chronological reversal of Confucianism, because in this political ideology Chinese youth were to lead and educate both their elders and parents.

Typical of the early phase of this new literature is the common goal of ensuring children understood that the future of the nation was linked to the well-being of all Chinese citizens. Some authors tried to connect *social realism* to *patriotism* by exposing social ills to the young readers. Ye Shengtao's "Scarecrow" (*Daocao ren*, 1923) is an example. This work, focussing on the destitute lives of peasant women, depicts the scarecrow as a creature with human motivations and the ability to reason. Authors like Ye Shengtao tackled the issues of social ills that many patriotic intellectuals regarded as the roots of the nation's weakness – a kind of erosion of a waning and sick nation. These works of patriotic exposé were descriptive, but many impatient writers felt that China's problems urgently needed something much more prescriptive.

The success of the Russian Bolshevik Revolution in 1917 seemed to provide a blueprint to Chinese intellectuals for solving China's problems quickly. The Marxist doctrine and the Leninist vanguard theory provided an instant program of political action, definite goals and a historically determined role for the elite. It was in this context that the school of revolutionary literature emerged. These writings duly reflected their hostility towards privileged foreigners, their contempt for wealthy Chinese and their determination to awaken the poor workers and peasants. The concept of equality – of people, gender, class and nation – was their essential argument. Jiang Guangci was one of the first Chinese literary figures to attempt to embody the theme of revolution in literature for young Chinese readers. In his poem "Infants of the October Revolution" (*Shiyue gemingde yinger*), the family background of these Russian youngsters is emphasized to highlight that their revolutionary spirit derives from their proletarian class upbringing. The poem reveals the harshness and the poverty that characterized Soviet life in the early years of the revolution, which Jiang witnessed firsthand. But rather than being depressed, Jiang was uplifted by the poor living conditions, for it seemed to him that a kind of new nobleness graced the Soviet Russian children.

Zhang Tianyi's fairytale *Big Lin and Little Lin* (*Dalin he Xiaolin*, 1933) perceives Chinese society as an arena of conflict between the rich and the poor. Although the poor were commonly identified as Chinese, while most of their oppressors were foreign, the conflict in *Big Lin and Little Lin* is less a national struggle between Chinese and foreigners than a clash between the exploited and the exploiting classes. The characters simply play the role in which the Marxist view of society casts them. The capitalist is depicted as a monster eating a hundred children each day, and thus presents a burning sense of urgency to save children. The protagonist, as symbolic of the emerging proletarian children, organizes militant anti-capitalist activities. Stories like this became a pedagogic instrument to project values concerned with the pursuit of a new nation based on the Marxist ideal of an egalitarian society.

The national crisis caused by the Japanese invasion in the late 1930s and early 1940s became a complete justification for a more pragmatic and utilitarian function of literature for the purpose of national defense. In this political and moral context, Mao Zedong made his famous speech at the Yenan Forum on Literature and Art in 1942 "to ensure that literature and art fit well into the whole revolutionary machine as a component part, that they operate as powerful weapons for uniting and educating the people and for attacking and destroying the enemy." For children's literature, the implication of such a call of purpose only exacerbated the trend to return to fusing the worlds of adults and children. Revolutionary children's literature blended *social realism* with an *active militant romanticism*, and protagonists of this era were all fighters ready to sacrifice themselves for the noble cause.

From 1949 to 1976: Gratitude to the Party, devotion to Chairman Mao

When a "new China" was finally established with the Communist victory in 1949, Maoist cultural guidelines governed and controlled literature to propagate a singular statist ideology. China's traditional ancestral reverence, family-clan cohesiveness and filial piety had long been eroding, and the Communist victory furthered this demise. In children's books of the 1950s, children were praised for denouncing their "backward" parents, thus spectacularly reversing the ancient stress on filial piety as the highest virtue. In order to represent the new political inspiration and ethical value, stories for children had to shift their focus to the space of the adult world, where there was more "socialist revolution," "socialist reconstruction" and "class struggle."

The politicization of children's literature was set in motion in the early 1950s, to ensure the cultivation of children's gratitude and loyalty to new institutions like "the new society," "the motherland" and "the Communist Party." Authors of children's literature were obliged to create stories to praise young people for criticizing the "traditional feudalistic ideas" of the older generations of parents and grandparents, as these ideas were shown to hinder the social progress of the Communists. For example, Ma Feng's 1954 story, *Han Meimei*, tells how a seventeen-year-old girl applied new scientific farming to boost the output of the village. She is depicted as firmly believing that she could contribute to the socialist motherland by answering the Party's call to participate in agricultural work. At the end of the story, Han Meimei's parents and grandmother had to admit that they had been wrong to doubt that the new socialist countryside could be a vast arena for the development of the young people.

However, to foster children's loyalty to such abstract identities is inherently difficult. In the dynastic periods, loyalty to the emperor was built upon the idea of filial piety, which was based on the natural bond between children and parents. The influence of parents or family now in this new Communist society was often analyzed in terms of class background and, consequently, such influence was believed to be class influence. Children were no longer regarded as heirs to the family but to the proletarian revolutionary cause.

In order to bridge these ideas and cement the newfound loyalty, many children's books cultivated fear: fear of deprivation of food, shelter and clothing, as well as humiliation and maltreatment, and only Mao and the Party could provide an end to these fears. Further radicalization of texts for children and youth gained momentum in the early 1960s, as Mao turned to the young people for his continuous revolution. When he was more and more conscious of his estrangement from other Party leaders, especially in regard to the assessment of the disastrous Great Leap Forward, Mao felt that it was the youth of China who were less corrupted by the influences of the old society and more amenable to his radical ideas, because "they were clean sheets of paper on which the newest revolutionary words could be written" (Meisner 2007: 149). Mao needed youths, full of class hatred and ready to fight against his enemies, real or potential, within the Communist Party.

One of the major works that fostered the emotion of class hatred (*jieji chouhen*), which is the rationale for class struggle, is Lo Kuang-pin and Yang Yi-yen's novel *Red Crag* (*Hong yan*, 1963), which graphically describes the brutal tortures and coldblooded executions of underground Communists at the hands of former Nationalist secret agents before they fled to Taiwan. The novel is based on real lives of many people, among whom Jiang Zhuyun is the best known. In 1947, Jiang's husband, a fellow underground Communist, left the city of Chongqing and led a group of Communist guerrillas. Twelve months later, she went to join him for an armed uprising. On her way she saw some wooden cages hanging on the gate tower of the city wall. It was a display of the heads of her comrades captured and killed by the enemy. She read the notice and found her husband's name was the first. Later, she was also arrested, tortured and eventually executed. She is also celebrated as the protagonist of the well-known 1964 opera, *Sister Jiang*.

To be full of class hatred is still not enough. A true good child of Chairman Mao had to be ready to die for his cause. He Yi depicts such a brave boy as a role model in the book *Liu Wenxue* (1965). Based on a true story of a fourteen-year-old Young Pioneer member, the story tells of his death, as he was killed by a former landlord when he found the class enemy stealing capsicums that belonged to the people's commune. To die for the interests of the people is extolled, even if these interests are almost insignificant in terms of material substance, such as a basketful of capsicums.

In the Cultural Revolution from 1966 to 1976, the cult of Mao allowed Mao to stand above the Party and to impose his personal political supremacy. Tens of millions of teenagers called themselves "Red Guards" and listened only to Mao, their supreme leader. Their activities were socially chaotic and culturally destructive, attacking whoever they regarded as a class enemy, including many teachers and writers. Almost all writers for children were severely attacked and suffered physical maltreatment, which these writers had vividly depicted in their works to foster children's "class hatred." Children's literature became "cannibalized by a distortion of the educational theory that had nurtured it" (Farquhar 1999: 301).

From 1976 to 2000: Love money, love China

The Cultural Revolution came to an abrupt end when Mao Zedong died in 1976. China, under the leadership of Deng Xiaoping, adopted policies of *gaige kaifang* (reform and open door) in 1978. The focus of the nation shifted to the program of "four modernizations": in industry, agriculture, science and technology, and national defense. It was the beginning of the renaissance of Chinese children's literature.

Notably, the first major work was Liu Xinwu's "The Class Teacher" (*Banzhuren*, 1977). It exposes the failure of education during the Cultural Revolution, as embodied in the dynamics of a secondary school classroom. The female student, Xie Huimin, blindly refuses to wear a colorful skirt to shun the decadent "bourgeois influences." The story reveals a childhood distorted by political dogmatism and extreme puritanism. The writer, like many writers of the time, did not oppose the Communist educational system but instead had faith in the system to rectify the past extremism. The process of rectification relied heavily on the classroom teacher, who once again took up the task of providing moral guidance to students.

In this new period of modernization, to encourage children to be ordinary laborers, like Han Meimei, appeared to aim too low. The new trend was to encourage them to climb the peaks of science and technology, as presented in Wei Binhai's long poem, "Worry and Confidence" (*Danyou he xinxin*, 1984):

> The pearl on the crown of mathematics has already been picked;
> The moon and Mars have already been left with some footprints;
> The mystery of UFOs, which I am fascinated with,
> will also soon be solved, I am afraid.

(my translation)

Ke Yan's poem "If I Became the Mayor" (*Jiaru wo dang shizhang*, 1988) lists all the problems urgently needing attention in the town. The poem concludes:

> The most important thing is to open the door of my office
> and my secretary will arrange visits of the masses to my office
> so that they can tell me
> what I haven't thought of
> and what I have overlooked.

(my translation)

The poem criticizes the reality by means of a long list of existing problems, whilst also criticizing the current mayor, who obviously did not open the door of the office to listen to the masses. This poem encourages children to develop a political ambition on the moral grounds of democracy, which duly reflects the political atmosphere before the 1989 students' democracy movement. However, ultimately, Deng Xiaoping's rule only allowed economic growth, not a change in ideology.

Deng Xiaoping's slogan "to get rich is glorious" has made its presence felt in children's literature, as it does everywhere in China. "Money" was no longer a dirty word. Zhuang Zhiming's "Little Fortune God" (*Xiaocaishenye*), published in the prestigious *Children's Literature* (*Ertong wenxue*) in 1985, is a good example of this new development. It is about a secondary school student Shen Hong, who was full of wonderful ideas to make his home village rich. He convinced the chief of the village to spend a thousand Yuan on an advertisement in the major newspaper for the beautiful scenery around their village to attract tourists. The following is the conversation between Shen Hong and his friends, two village boys:

> "Da Shan," said Shen Hong confidently, "don't you worry about that. All you need to worry about is handling the money, which will be like a flood, swamping our village."
> "What shall we do with that much money?" Xiao Quan became alarmed.
> "To build houses and to get married. Everything needs lots of money," Da Shan said.

This newfound hunger for money can be found even in *Good Children* (*Hao ertong*), a magazine for lower primary school children under eight years of age. Yan Zhenguo's story "Two Grocery Stalls" (*Liangge zahuopu*, 1990) depicts how two bear brothers run grocery stalls in competition across the road, and how they engage in a price war. They start from 10 percent discount and finish at 40 percent discount. When Detective Monkey orders Elephant to dig up the road between the two stalls, citizens of the animal town are shocked to find that there is a tunnel between the two stalls. The two bear brothers are running the same business. All the fuss of fighting and price war are just their marketing strategies. This story reflects the reality of a highly commercialized society, as well as a decline of moral standards in this same society. Ostensibly, it attacks the lack of moral principles in business, but it also subtly admires the smartness of the two bears. The most amazing feature of this story is the use of highly sophisticated marketing strategies in a story targeting children under eight.

The slogan "to get rich is glorious" caused problems for the Party as the moral authority. It was difficult to simultaneously encourage people to become rich whilst also advocating noble ideas such as self-sacrifice for the socialist modernization. Writers, too, were affected by this new ideology, as they also wanted to become rich quickly. They could achieve this by meeting the demands of the market for children's books: a lucrative market indeed for the only-child generation. However, the most powerful decision-making people in this market were parents. After their own experience of the rigid revolutionary political indoctrination, they became tired of politics and sick of the explicit politicization of children's books. As a result, the demand for children's books containing explicit political rhetoric to support the leadership of the Communist Party was rapidly shrinking.

Meanwhile Deng Xiaoping's slogan "to get rich is glorious" stimulated the growth of small private enterprises. When these small private enterprises sought to expand, they needed approval from the local government. Local officials were also among the first group of people, together with those private entrepreneurs, to become rich. Corruption became serious and widely spread. It was this issue of corruption, plus a bout of soaring inflation in the late 1980s, that made students of Beijing feel that it was their historical mission to speak on behalf of the masses in 1989.

After the 1989 students' pro-democracy movement, in which young people revealed absolute contempt for government authority, the state, once again, resumed its role as the absolute moral authority in regulating human relationships. In doing so, the lost ground of using children's books for political and moral education was reclaimed. In the mid-1990s, a new ideological system of Neo-Confucianism began to take shape, filling the vacuum left by the decline of faith in Marxism and Maoism in China. Another category of chil-dren's books, "stories of moral education" (*deyu gushi*) was established, in addition to "chil-dren's literature." This realignment attempted to clarify the role of "children's literature," which was now understood to meet children's needs for entertainment and development. Although the contents of both categories were still highly didactic and political, "children's literature" was relatively free of explicit political slogans, but, in contrast, authorities could now blatantly pour their political and moral messages into "stories of moral education," which once again drew heavily from the Confucian canon. For example, in 1995, Beijing Children and Juvenile Publishing House re-published the major Confucian Classics. The moral values of "filial piety" and "fraternal submission" were restored to fundamental importance. Also in 1995, Jiangsu Juveniles and Children Publishing House published a set of ten volumes entitled *The Golden Treasure House of Stories for Moral Education* (*Deyu gushi dajinku*). The core value advocated in these volumes is to "love the nation" (*aiguo*), but each volume covers two more focused political and moral topics:

Volume 1: To love the nation and her people;
    To establish ideals
Volume 2: To devote to the public and be selfless;
    To seek truth from facts
Volume 3: To be independent and self confident;
    To study assiduously
Volume 4: To be modest and prudent;
    To be hardworking and thrifty
Volume 5: Solidarity and mutual help;
    Sense of responsibility
Volume 6: To respect elders;
    Harmony in family and love between friends
Volume 7: To be upright and kind;
    To be honest and faithful
Volume 8: To be well disciplined and obey laws;
    To be civilized and polite
Volume 9: To be brave and fearless;
    To be determined and resolute
Volume 10: To practice what one preaches; and
    To admit one's mistakes and correct them

(in Fang, 2003, 20)

Towards the end of the twentieth century, theoretical debates on the role of children's literature have become vibrant, and a new generation of theorists is determined to make Chinese children's literature compatible with the rising status of China in the international community. "Like their predecessors, contemporary Chinese writers also believe that children's growth holds the key to the development of a modern Chinese nation" (Xu Xu 2013: 78).

Conclusion

The unconcealed didactic nature of Chinese texts for the young stemmed from a pragmatic goal: for the rulers of China, whoever they might be, to utilize the education system as part of political indoctrination that strengthened their reign. Writers, Confucian or Communist, all considered themselves as educated moralists and moral educators. It can be said that there were three uniquely Chinese factors reinforcing this common goal and theme in Chinese children's books. The first was Chinese writers' *obsession* with the nation's fate. In spite of their attack on the Confucian tradition as spiritual lethargy, they retained the conviction that their historical epic mission was to launch China onto the path of modernity through educating the young.

Another contributing factor to the strength of the didactic theme in Chinese children's literature was the unique collective consciousness of these writers, as opposed to personal subjectivity. Collective social reality, not individual experience, was both the primary inspiration, as well as the main subject matter of their writings. The authors were convinced that they *collectively* represented the quintessential spirit of the time. Their writings, regardless of their different political persuasions, shared a faith in youth: improve yourselves and you can improve China.

Finally, many emotional young intellectuals, when facing national crises in the early twentieth century, had tended to be impulsive. These patriotic writers all had a commitment to a strong and independent China. But, instead of glorifying China's native past, many of them chose to draw attention to the burden of China's heritage, such as Confucianism, as an obstacle to the nation's rejuvenation. Their tone was bombastic, their language was invested with strong emotions, and their condemnation of the tradition was simplistic. In the end, their impatience with the established and impulse to create the new led to their hasty embracing of the Western ideology of Marxism and a Leninist-influenced Communist revolution, which they believed to be an instantaneous social-political remedy. Their persistent use of what children read for political persuasion and moral cultivation is nevertheless a strong confirmation of the continuity of the traditional Confucian past, and not a departure from it, as they believed.

In the mid-1990s, Confucianism made a spectacular comeback. The fundamental difference between traditional Confucianism and Neo-Confucianism, however, is that the former traditional construction of children's moral character derives from a long-term value-oriented ideology, which aimed at achieving a tranquil and happy world of benevolence, whereas the latter contemporary form aims at strengthening the subject-sovereign relationship through emphasizing obedience in the child-adult relationship so as to maintain a stable social order without political upheavals.

Acknowledgements

I wish to thank Fang Xiangshu for his generous assistance with the preparation of this essay. His deep knowledge of Confucianism and Chinese intellectual history has been an invaluable resource for me.

Bibliography

Bi, Lijun (2013) "China's Patriotic Exposé: Ye Shengtao's Fairytale, *Daocao ren* [Scarecrow]," *Bookbird, A Journal of International Children's Literature*, 51(2): 32–38.

Bi, Lijun and Fang Xiangshu (2013) "Childhoods: Childhoods in Chinese Children's Texts – Continuous Reconfiguration for Political Needs," in *(Re)imagining the World: Children's Literature's Response to Changing Times*, ed. Yan Wu, Kerry Mallan, Roderick McGillis, Heidelberg, New York, Dordrecht, London: Springer.

Fang, Xiangshu (2003) "Neo-Confucianism in Chinese Children's Books," *Papers: Exploration into Children's Literature* 13(2): 17.

Fang, Xiangshu and Lijun Bi (2013) "Confucianism," in *Handbook of Research on Development and Religion*, ed. Matthew Clarke, Cheltenham and Northampton, MA: Edward Elgar Publishing, 125–137.

Farquhar, Mary (1999) *Children's Literature in China: From Lu Xun to Mao Zedong*, New York: M. E. Sharpe.

He, Yi (1965) *Liu Wenxue*, Shanghai: Shaonian ertong chubanshe.

Ke, Yan (1988) "Jiaru wo dang shizhang" (If I became the mayor), originally in *Bashiniandai shixuan* (Selected poems of the 1980s) (Nanchang: Jiangxi shaoer chubanshe), reprinted in *Zhongguo ertong wenxue daxi, shige II* (The great anthology of Chinese children's literature, poetry 2), ed. Feng Jiang, Taiyuan: Xiwang chubanshe.

Liu, Xinwu (1977) "Banzhuren" (The class teacher), Renminwenxue, vol.11, www.rain8.com/article/class6/2232_2.htm (accessed June 15, 2014).

Lo, Kuang-pin and Yang Yi-yen (1963) *Hong yan* (Red crag), Beijing: Zhongguo qingnian chubanshe.

Mao, Zedong, "Talks at the Yenan Forum on Literature and Art," www.marxists.org/reference/archive/mao/selected-works/volume-3/mswv3_08.htm (accessed June 2, 2014).

Meisner, Maurice (2007) *Mao Zedong*, Malden, MA: Polity Press.

Perry, Elizabeth J. and Mark Sheldon (2000) "Introduction: reform and resistance in contemporary China," in *Chinese Society: Change, Conflict and Resistance*, ed. Elizabeth J. Perry and Mark Sheldon, London and New York: Routledge.

Wei, Binhai (1984) "*Danyou he xinxin*" (Worry and confidence), *Ertong wenxue* (Children's literature), 11: 17.

Xu, Xu (2013) "Imagination: Imaginations of the Nation – Childhood and Children's Literature in Modern China," in *(Re)imagining the World: Children's Literature's Response to Changing Times*, ed. Yan Wu, Kerry Mallan, Roderick McGillis, Heidelberg, New York, Dordrecht, London: Springer.

Zhuang, Zhiming (1985) "*Xiaocaishenye*" (Little Fortune God), *Ertong wenxue* (Childrens literature), 1: 74.

5

EGYPTIAN CHILDREN'S LITERATURE

Ideology and politics

Nadia El Kholy

A children's story, however trivial it might be, is more than just a story. Because stories grow out of particular cultures and societies at particular points in time, they reflect the values of these societies, "to imagine a story…is to imagine the society in which it is told." (Dowling 115). Therefore, stories that are woven out of the imagination of their writers are part of a larger body of stories, which together form a kind of national allegory that gives expression to the dreams, desires and fears of a particular culture. Since children are the future of any society, the literature adults write for them is a conscious effort to shape the ideology of its readers. The socialization and politicization of children's literature has been and still is a reality in children's books. Roderick McGillis has argued that "Children and their books are ideological constructs" (106) and that the publishing industry is continuously "perpetuat[ing] the values and cultural conceptions of the ruling group" (112). The role of children's texts is to help acculturate children into society and to teach them to behave and believe in acceptable norms.

The existence of children's literature as a genre has, to a large extent, depended on its function as a force of social manipulation, rather than on any concern with literary value. Certainly one can speak about a specific literary fairy tale for children as a symbolic act infused by the ideological viewpoint of the individual author. Almost all critics who have studied the emergence of the literary fairy tale in Europe (Soriano 43) agree that educated writers purposely appropriated the oral folk tale and converted it into a type of literary discourse about mores, values and manners so that children would become civilized according to the social code of that time

The fairy tale hence is designed to both direct as amusement and inculcate ideology as a means to mold the inner nature of young people. Like other types of literature, works written especially for children are informed and shaped by the authors' respective value systems, their notions of how the world is or ought to be. The promulgation of these values through publication is a political act. In well-written books, an author's narrative skill, imaginative brilliance and ability to create engaging characters and plot lines tend to mask the ideologies being expressed. But if ideologies have potential powers of persuasion, they are no less persuasive because they are hidden. The perspectives and positions assumed by members of society toward the dominant activity amount to a configuration. The configuration designates the character of a social order since the temporal-corporal arrangement is designed around a dominant activity that shapes the attitudes of people toward work, education, social development and death. Hence, the configuration of society is the pattern of arrangement and rearrangement of social behavior related to a socialized mode of perception. In the folk tale the temporal-corporal arrangement reflects whether these are perceived to be new possibilities for participation in the social order or whether there must be a configuration when possibilities for change do not exist. This is why, in each new stage of civilization, in each new historical epoch, the symbols and configurations of the tales are endowed with new meaning, transformed, or eliminated in reaction to the needs and conflicts of people within the social order. The writers of fairy tales for children act ideologically by presenting their notions regarding social conditions and conflicts, and they interact with each other and with past writers and storytellers of folklore in a public sphere. For Jameson, the individual literary work is a symbolic act "which is grasped as the imaginary resolution of real contradiction" (5). Such a definition is helpful in understanding the origins of the literary fairy tale for children because through it is immediately perceived the process of writing as part of a social process, as a kind of intervention in a continuous discourse, debate and conflict about power and social relations. Jameson sees ideology not as something "which informs or invests symbolic production; rather the aesthetic act itself is ideological, and the production of aesthetic or narrative form is to be seen as an ideological act in its own right, with the function of inventing imaginary or formal 'solutions' to unresolvable contradictions" (6).

This interaction led to an institutionalized symbolic discourse on the civilizing process that served as the basis for the fairy tale genre. The importance of the term "institutionalization" for studying the origins of the literary fairy tale can best be understood if we turn to Peter Bürger's *Theory of the Avant-Garde* (7). Bürger argues that "works of art are not received as single entities, but within institutional frameworks and conditions that largely determine the function of the works. When one refers to the function of an individual work, one generally speaks figuratively; for the consequences that one may observe or infer are not primarily a function of its special qualities but rather of the manner which regulates the commerce with works of this kind in a given society or in certain strata or classes of a society. I have chosen the term 'institution of art' to characterize such framing conditions" (8). In fact, literary fairy tales were constantly employed in the seventeenth century to reinforce the Western civilizing process and their discourses on manners and norms has contributed to the creation of social norms. This "symbolic act of writing" marks the birth of the historical rise of the literary fairy tale for children. Perrault and his predecessors rearranged the motifs, characters, themes, functions and configurations of oral folk tales in such a way that they would address the concerns of the educated and ruling classes of late feudal and early capitalist societies. Therefore, the adaptation of folk material, as an act of symbolic appropriation, was a re-codification of the material to make it suitable for the discursive requirements of French court society and bourgeois salons. Implicit pedagogy and didacticism characterized the writing of fairy tales with the aim of molding the manners and mores of the young to reflect the standard mode of socialization at that time. Fairy tales were a functional vehicle advocating exemplary models of child behavior patterns. Similarly, in Germany the Brothers Grimm constantly endeavored to link the beliefs and behavioral patterns of the characters in the tales to parallel, enhance and cultivate bourgeois norms. The Grimms' fairy tales were a vehicle for the common people to make themselves heard in folk tales that symbolically represented their needs and dreams. They were literary products voicing the German bourgeois quest for identity and power. Therefore, in the tales, the Grimm Brothers cultivated a value system that advocated an objectified, standard way of living that encapsulated the values of work and productivity at its core and was popular not only in Germany but throughout the Western world. Based on this hypothesis that folk tales and fairy tales have always been dependent on customs, rituals and values in the particular socialization process of a social system, the same applies to the Arab world. As in the West, tales have always symbolically depicted the nature of power relationships within a given society. They are thus strong indicators of the level of civilization, that is, the essential quality of a culture and social order. The effectiveness of emancipatory and reutilized tales has not only depended on the tales themselves but also on the manner in which they have been received, their use and distribution in society.

Children's literature is a social product and a social force, and this is exemplified by how fairy tales and folk tales were never originally invented for mere pleasure but were always a response to some need from the surrounding environment and society; they were the offspring of a dialogic situation with nature, human beings and animals. Jack Zipes has rightly stated that fairy tales "are historical prescriptions, internalized, potent, explosive, and we acknowledge the power they hold over our lives by mystifying them" (1983: 11). The essence of our lives has been prescribed and circumscribed by common cultural discourses and filled with artifacts that we can never really bypass. A complex relationship exists between fairy tales and society, the nature of which is understood in radically different ways from one discipline to another and from one investigation to the next. Furthermore, the apparent relationship of fairy tales to society shifts according to whether one regards the fairy tale as a record and reflection of society, as a normative influence on its reader or listener, or a combination of both. Within the context of fairy tales as social rewards, the existence of specific themes informs us that a given society recognizes and addresses certain topics that eventually became part of our common cultural heritage. Egyptian children's literature is also a product of the socialization of society and at certain turning points in Egyptian history stories have been politicized in order to comply with specific agendas. Moreover, writers were commissioned to create stories that propagated particular ideas and value systems. Fairytales and their reception through history indicate the hidden power of the common place, a power we forget or tend to repress.

Arabic children's literature

The Arab World has been, and is still referred to, by the West as the Orient, the land of *The Arabian Nights*, with its connotations of magic and glamour. The famous tales of Aladdin, Ali Baba and Sindbad were circulating in the Arab World for centuries, long before they were translated and exported to the West. Throughout history, tales have been told and retold orally, attesting to the phenomenon that oral tradition exists at the roots of every civilization and children adopt adult literature that they find diverting. Likewise, storytelling played an important role in the lives of the Ancient Egyptians. The deeds of gods and kings were not written down in early times and only found their way through oral tradition into the literature of a later date. This treasury of popular tales, myths and legends was transmitted orally until finally set down in writing, examples of which are the first Egyptian *Cinderella*, written on papyrus under the name

Radoubis, and a black and red twenty-four page collection of children's stories made out of papyri.

In pre-Islamic Arabia origins of children's literature can be identified in popular stories, songs and legends that mostly recounted the valor of various heroes and the wars between the tribes. With the advent of Islam there was a shift in the storytelling tradition to more serious and religious topics drawing from the Koran and the Prophet Muhammad's life. Other famous narratives that were popular with children were *Hayy ibn Yakzan*, written by the medieval philosopher Abu Bakr ibn Tufayl (d.1185) (which inspired the much later *Robinson Crusoe*), and the *Sirat of Sayf Ibn dhi Yazan*. Storytelling was popular throughout the Arab World, fueled by the rich and diverse folkloric tradition. Stories about *Clever Hassan*, buffoons like *Goha* and the popular *Arabian Nights* were part of the Arab cultural fabric. Epics about brave warriors such as Abu Zaid al-Hilali, the *Sirat of al-Amira Zat al-Hima*, the saga of *Banu Hilal*, the romances of chivalry like *Sayf ibn Dhi Yazan* and *Sirat 'Antara* have all contributed to the formulation of the Arab identity through concepts of Arab "Shahama" (chivalry), courage, love for one's country and the sacredness of honor. This rich repository of narratives was shared from one generation to the next and is still popular in the present. Animal stories also found their place in *Kalla wa Dimna*, whose origin goes back to the Indian *Panchatantra*, and which was Arabized by ibn al-Muqaffa' from its Pahlavi translation.

Egypt, the oldest cultural center of the Arab World, was the origin of modern Arabic children's literature. Early interest in children and their development goes back to the intellectual enlightenment witnessed at the end of the nineteenth century under the reign of Muhammed Ali, who sent scholars on study missions to France. Sheikh Rifa'a al-Tahtawi was extremely impressed by the French educational books for children and so he published his *Guide for Boys*, a book about child education and development, in 1870. An immediate follow up on that was the appearance of *The School Children's Meadows* (1870), the first school journal for children by Ali Mubarak, which was a channel for the pupils' own creative literary works in addition to adult contributions from professional writers. Ahmed Shawqi (1868–1932), the Egyptian poet laureate, who had also been to France and studied French literature, wrote a volume of poems in a simple, direct and humorous style suitable for children under the title *Shawqiyaat Saghirah* ("Shawqi's Verses for the Young"), strongly influenced by La Fontaine's *Fables*. In response to Shawqi's call to other Arab writers, in 1897 Ma'aruf al-Rasafy from Iraq and Ibrahim al-Arab responded by producing a number of poems specifically for children. In 1927 a collection of animal fables in verse form similar to La Fontaine called *Adab al-Arab* ("Arabian Ethics") was distributed to all primary schools in Egypt. Later, in 1894, Muhammad Othman Jalal translated Aesop's *Fables* into Arabic. Although these books were important in the development of interest in children's readings, they would not be considered suitable for children by modern standards. Their language was difficult, the tone was often didactic, and the topics were not chosen with children's interests and needs in mind. A more appropriate direction was offered by the prolific Egyptian writer Mohamed al-Harawy (1885–1939), who wrote songs, poems and musical one-act plays especially for children. In 1922 he produced an illustrated collection of poems, *Children's Companion for Boys*, in three parts, followed by *Children's Companion for Girls* in two parts. He also wrote five plays for children, three of which were in verse form and two in prose. In 1931 he published two collections of stories: *Goha and the Children* and *The Pie Vendor*, both of which were very popular at the time. Al-Harawy dealt with a wide range of topics: the didactic, the religious, the nationalistic, the social, and the moralistic. However, the real revolutionary movement in children's literature in the Arab world started with the pioneer Kamil Kilani (1897–1959). During the 1930s, Kilani gained prominence as a publisher by translating, adapting and simplifying more than 200 foreign titles for children. Kilani's dedication to children's literature is evident in the works he produced in a span of approximately thirty years. His first book, *Sindbad the Sailor*, was published in 1927. He translated, re-wrote and Arabized nearly all the children's classics and Western fairy tales for Arab children. Inspired by Kilani, a number of writers were encouraged to translate children's stories from both English and French, for example, Hamid Al Kassaby and Boulos Effendi Abdel Malek, who translated eight of Hans Christian Andersen's stories. This opened the way to more creative writings such as Mohamed Said al-Eriyan's *The Sindbad Stories*, and Ateya al-Ibrashi's series *The Green Library Children's Stories*. Longer fiction in the form of novellas for teenagers were the contribution of Mohamed Farid Abu Hadid, who wrote stories influenced by *The Arabian Nights* (for example *Amrounshah*), and they were all part of the well-known series, *Awladouna* ("Our Children"). All these works contributed to the modernization of Arabic children's stories until the end of British rule in Egypt in 1952. In the 1960s the entire Arab World underwent dramatic changes with their gaining of independence and this was in turn reflected in the field of children's books.

Heroism as ideology in Arab children's literature

Maria Nikolajeva argues that "children's literature has from the very beginning been related to pedagogics" and that children's literature has always been considered "a powerful means for educating children" (3), is ideologically biased and has didactic tendencies. If this applies to children's literature in general, in the Middle East there is an underlying tendency to make children aware of the political and military challenges that face the Arab Nation. The fear of chaos and the fear of losing power was the main motive behind not establishing democratic regimes of one kind or another in most Arab nations. Instead the hierarchical societies across the Middle East, whether in the form of kingdoms or military regimes, were insistent on their desire for certainty, security and the total obedience of their subjects. They propagated the ideology of total surrender to the ruling system, since it was feared that without hierarchy, without mastery, all would dissolve into chaos – physical, political and personal dissolution. Consequently, this ideology gave rise to the popularity of stories that revolve around heroism as a main theme. Different types of hero stories were created all based on the structure of the hero narrative. Hero stories are primarily quest stories. The hero sets out to achieve a certain goal and the success of his mission depends upon the realization of what he initially set out to do.

Historically the hero opposes the forces of darkness. He symbolizes the power of reason, and the transforming strength of human intellectual energy. In early legends the hero's task is to defeat the forces of evil, fear and ignorance and to ensure the survival of the state, the realm of civic order and rational behavior. Within the Arab oral tradition there are numerous legends about popular heroes like Abu Zayd al-Hilali and Antara ibn Shadad. Courage and prowess are projections of childhood and adolescent fantasies of invincibility. The hero is completely dedicated to his cause in an image of youthful idealism that is quite admirable. His struggle against evil (in whatever shape or form) invests his aggressive instincts with dignity and purpose. He is full of energy and purpose. Also, the hero is a man of action and this is expressed in his skill, courage, dominance and determination. He is constantly moving forward in his quest to defeat evil.

Types of heroes

There are four types of hero found in Arabic children's literature: the archetypal or mythic hero, the religious, the romantic hero, and the national and historical hero. The archetypal hero conforms to Jung's argument that all myths, including the hero myth, are transcultural and transhistorical because they emerge from the collective unconscious and are common to all peoples in all times. He states that "the hero figure is an archetype, which has existed since time immemorial" and "the universal hero myth…always refers to a powerful man or god-man who vanquishes evil in the form of dragons, serpents, monsters, demons, and so on, and who liberates his people from destruction and death" (73, 79). Building on Jung's theory, Joseph Campbell's influential work *The Hero with a Thousand Faces* (1975) reaches the conclusion that although hero myths vary enormously in detail they are structurally the same, in what he refers to as the "monomyth." He says that the heart of the classical monomyth is "a magnification of the formula represented in the rites of passage formula: separation – initiation – return" (31). This corresponds exactly to the "basic plot" of children's fiction, identified as home – away – homecoming (Nodelmann and Propp). In continuation of the relationship between hero, myth and history, Marina Warner concurs with Roland Barthes that "myths are not eternal verities, but historical compounds which conceal their contingency, changes, and transitoriness" (xiii). Barthes' definition of myth "can give rise to newly told stories, can sew and weave and knit different patterns into the social fabric" (xiv). Warner goes on to show how the fictional heroes of twentieth-century popular culture embody the qualities of the epic superhero of ancient myth. Examples are Superman, Spider-Man and Batman, who all possess some secret superhuman powers.

This mythic hero typically encounters a force in the world that threatens to bring destruction or bondage and it is his task to overcome it and defend the status quo. It is mandatory for the archetypal hero to maintain security and stability and to defend humanity at large. This is why many Arabic stories revolve around this type of hero endowed with superpowers that enable him to overcome all sorts of difficulties. Early on, countless stories were inspired from *A Thousand and One Nights* as retold by Kamel Kilani, such as the story of *Sindbad the Sailor* (1928) and *Abu Sir and Abu Qir* (1927), *The Adventures of Antara* (1968) by Abraham Azzouz, and the Hilal Series for Boys and Girls (1983). All of these narratives depict their characters as representatives of absolute evil or absolute goodness in very obvious binary oppositions, and follow a linear plot in which the archetypal hero triumphs over all evil powers. The social and political climate in the Arab world encouraged this kind of writing that promoted the ideology of total surrender to the authority of the ruler in order to safeguard the security and stability of the people. In the early days of the 1952 revolution by the Free Officers, hundreds of stories were published in Egypt commemorating the character of President Gamal Abdel Nasser as a hero of Arab Nationalism and freedom. Within this framework writers compared the image of Saladin, the defeater of the Crusaders, to that of Nasser, the legendary hero who freed the country from the British.

Many writers for children in the Arab world see spreading Islamic moral values as the main purpose of literature and express this in narratives whose protagonist is a religious hero. The prophet Muhammad holds a central and major position in the tales about Islam. Another genre of narratives is the retelling of tales from the Koran about outstanding Islamic figures, such as the prophet Muhammad's companions and the heroes of the Islamic conquest, for example, Khalid ibn al-Walid, Ubeida ibn al-Jarrah, Ali ibn Abi Talib, and many others.

In contrast, romantic heroes are usually ordinary human beings who do not have supernatural powers. This type of hero is usually oppressed, lonely and a victim. But his success lies in his intelligence, resourcefulness and skill, which enable him to overcome difficulties and obstacles. He is often favoured with a magical tool (for example, a magic wand, a flying carpet, a magic lamp, etc.), which enables him to triumph over his enemies by defeating time and overcoming distance, which is a common feature in fairy tales such as "Cinderella" or "Aladdin" (and more recently in the Harry Potter series). The basic feature of the romantic hero is his purity, his innocence and naivety. It is his goodness that makes him triumph over evil forces.

Finally, historical and national heroes are numerous because historical fiction is a major part of the literature written for Arab children. The writer of historical fiction strives to join the fact of a particular historical event with his own vision of the meaning of that event and finally create a successful melding of fact with fiction and thus help the child/reader to feel the overwhelming presence of the recreated past. When a seamless blending of history and imagination is achieved, the work can capture the essence of the specific historical period represented. This genre encompasses political themes such as the commemoration of the glorious Arab past, with stories about heroic Arab figures, just caliphs, major Islamic conquests and, more recently, victorious Arab wars. The main trait of this type of hero is the glorification of all the qualities of the invincible warrior: the hero of war, the brave soldier, the patriotic civilian, the loyal and faithful leader who sacrifices his life for his country. We also find children's literature about local political leaders like presidents and kings. This strong political trend in children's literature in the Arab world could, understandably, be explained by the tumultuous political events the region has experienced and the challenges the Arab countries have had to face. Moreover, children's literature in the Arab world is a powerful political propaganda tool in the hands of politicians and decision-makers who exploit it in the political socialization of children.

Conclusion

The contemporary popular figure today is a superviolent hero who destroys his enemies with maximum bloodshed and dramatic effects. The camera lingers on the details of shattered and mutilated bodies. The enjoyment of vicarious violence has become an end in itself, although it is part of a wider structure of audience engagement that includes, for example, scopophilia (the pleasure in looking at images) and visceral response (physical reactions of fear, disgust, triumph, and the like). Examples are many, ranging from the popular Harry Potter films, *The Lord of the Rings*, *Spider-Man*, *Troy*, and so on. Watching real torture, killings, bombarding of civilians and bulldozing their houses has become an ordinary scene on television, recorded and transmitted live. Why the threshold of tolerance seems to go on increasing is a complex puzzle. On the one hand, special effects and computer-generated imagery create an audience expectation of increasing spectacle, which often involves blowing things (and people) up. On the other hand, major changes have been occurring in global society, politics and culture since the end of the Cold War, many of which stem from what Michael Gross (2010) terms "asymmetrical conflict" – that is, conflict between powerful and weaker nations, which takes the form of guerrilla warfare, terrorism, targeted assassination, and other non-conventional forms of conflict. Responses to such situations of apparent randomness seem to produce a weak-ening or erasure of altruistic moral restraints and open the way to uninhibited violence. Nancy Cheever points out that violence in some form appears in two out of three televi-sion programs on US screens, while in children's television violence occurs in seven out of ten programs (2009: 30). The impact of global events is reflected in the fact that "The incidents of torture scenes on television rose from just four a year before the September 11th attacks to more than 100 after the attacks" (Mayer 2007). Whether such changes are scripted or intuitive, they indicate an increased tolerance of violence in the name of world order. The question for children's literature is whether gestures of mastery will become its pre-eminent cultural ideal and message. Although children's literature has long been imbued with ideology and didacticism, there has also been a great interest in writing a literature for children that they could read for mere pleasure. This tendency is becoming stronger in Arab children's literature in recent years, although I acknowledge that this literature will remain permeated with ideology, didactics and morality because it is a true reflection of Arab societies, which are facing so many challenges, and there is a sound conviction that children should not be spared such challenges since they will be the future decision-makers.

Bibliography

Barthes, Roland (2000 [1957]) *Mythologies*, New York: Vintage Books.
Bürger, Peter (1984) *Theory of the Avant-garde*, Manchester: Manchester University Press.
Campbell, Joseph (1968 [1949]) *The Hero with a Thousand Faces*, 2nd. ed., Princeton, NJ: Princeton University Press.
Cheever, Nancy (2009) "The Uses and Gratifications of Viewing Mixed Martial Arts," *Journal of Sports Media* 4(1): 25–53.
Dowling, William C. (1984) *Jameson, Althusser, Marx: An Introduction to the Political Unconscious*, Ithaca: Cornell University Press.
Gross, Michael L. (2010) *Moral Dilemmas of Modern War: Torture, Assassination, and Blackmail in an Age of Asymmetric Conflict*, Cambridge: Cambridge University Press.
Jameson, Frederic (1982) *The Political Unconscious: Narrative as a Socially Symbolic Act*, New York: Cornell University Press.
Jung, Carl G. (1964) *Man and His Symbols*, London: Aldus Books.
Mayer, Jane (2007) "Whatever It Takes: The Politics of the Man behind *24*," *The New Yorker*, February 19 Issue.
McGillis, Roderick (1996) *The Nimble Reader: Literary Theory and Children's Literature*, New York: Twayne.
Nikolajeva, Maria (1996) *Children's Literature Comes of Age: Towards a New Aesthetic*, New York: Garland.
Nodelman, Perry (1996) *The Pleasures of Children's Literature*, 2nd ed., New York: Longman.
Propp, Vladimir (1968 [1928]) *Morphology of the Folktale*, Austin: University of Texas Press.
Soriano, Marc (1977) *Les Contes de Perrault: Culture Savante et Traditions Populaires*, rev. ed., Paris: Gallimard.
Warner, Marina (1994) *Managing Monsters. Six Myths of Our Time*, New York: Vintage.
Zipes, Jack (1979) *Breaking the Magic Spell: Radical Theories of Folk and Fairy Tales*, Austin: University of Texas Press.
Zipes, Jack (1983) *Fairy Tales and the Art of Subversion: The Classical Genre for Children and the Process of Civilization*, London: Heinemann.

6

"THE TREES, THEY HAVE LONG MEMORIES"

Animism and the ecocritical imagination in indigenous young adult fiction

Alice Curry

Young adult fiction is evolving. Readers of best-selling dystopian novels such as Meg Rosoff's *How I Live Now*, Suzanne Collins' *The Hunger Games* and Veronica Roth's *Divergent* are by now familiar with the imaginary devastated post-apocalyptic landscapes of the United Kingdom, United States and other western nations and the radically ruptured societies of our imagined future. Yet a recent subset of this popular genre that one might label "ecological dystopias" has recently emerged from the margins of the Anglo-American publishing superstructure with ideologies rooted not in western environmentalism but in indigenous and animist belief systems. Canadian Métis author Catherine Knutsson's *Shadows Cast by Stars* (2013) and Australian Aboriginal author Ambelin Kwaymullina's *The Interrogation of Ashala Wolf* (2012) are two exemplary novels of this genre. Where Knutsson's and Kwaymullina's novels differ from western best-sellers is in their indigenous protagonists' deep spiritual connection to their roots – roots that are culturally *and* ecologically entwined. The capacity of the novels' teenage heroines to enter into an intersubjective relationship with the spirit world to achieve social and environmental change is an ontological recourse unavailable to Rosoff's, Collins' and Roth's western heroines. More specifically, the protagonists' explorations of their human relationships with the natural and supernatural world by means of an animist discourse that invests "spirit" in the more-than-human, provides a transformative response to environmental estrangement centering on poiesis, autopoiesis and ecopoiesis that may have significant implications for ecocriticism as it is currently practiced.

Spirit, a concept with a critical history in both western and eastern academic traditions stretching back to the dawn of philosophical and theological enquiry, is in the main conspicuously absent from the majority of western-produced dystopian novels. In both Knutsson's and Kwaymullina's novels, by contrast, a pre-modern understanding of spirit as deeply embedded in human relations with the environment renders the ontological separation of human and nonhuman reductive. *Shadows Cast by Stars* is a novel set 200 years in the future, in which a plague ravages the human population after devastating earthquakes, tsunamis and floods have destroyed much of what was left of the old world. Aboriginal peoples throughout North America and Canada, whose blood is being harvested to cure the plague, take refuge on an island where powerful creatures of the spirit world exert their capricious influence over the human population. In *The Interrogation of Ashala Wolf*, a single continent has emerged following a cataclysmic redistribution of landmasses, and Ashala, a young Aboriginal girl, must draw on the stories of the spirit world told by her ancestors in Australia to protect a group of individuals who have emerged with paranormal abilities. In both novels, spirit worlds exist as physical spaces bordering, and on occasion penetrating, the post-apocalyptic landscapes of the living. In the former, the spirit world is an eerie place of perpetual twilight where lost souls wander and spirit creatures – Raven, Sisiutl (the double-headed serpent), Dzoonokwa (the woman of the woods) – and other gods of the Métis pantheon "writhe and twist and meld together" (426). In the latter, the spirit world is a contrastingly utopian space of transformation and renewal – a vast forest equivalent to a "world soul" where "[e]verything was brighter than it should be, the colors so vivid it almost hurt to look at them" – that corrects the social and ecological imbalances found in the world of the living (111).

In what follows, I shall explore Knutsson's and Kwaymullina's varying literary instantiations of an animist discourse by means of three critical paradigms: the "animist materialism" developed by Harry Garuba, the "animic ontology" explored by Tim Ingold, and the "poet-shaman aesthetics" coined by Gloria Anzaldúa and elaborated by AnaLouise Keating. These four theorists, spanning various geographic locations and disciplines, are alike in critically analyzing the place and function of animism in human relationships with our wider environment. Each acknowledges the fraught critical history of animism, with its roots in the pejorative association of animist beliefs with "primitive" peoples, yet argues for a new animist discourse that counters the ontological separation of humans and nature that has been at the heart of western development and formed the bedrock of industrialized society. Alf Hornborg terms this pervading dichotomous relationship a crisis of modernity:

> It is by drawing a boundary between the world of objects and the world of meanings that the "modern" project has emerged. By, as it were, "distilling" Nature into its material properties alone, uncontaminated by symbolic meanings or social relations, modernists have been freed to manipulate it in ways unthinkable in pre-modern contexts.
>
> (2006: 21)

Approaching this deeply ingrained sense of environmental estrangement from a variety of perspectives – from anthropology to literary analysis to women's studies – each of these theorists takes as his or her model societies in which an alternative animist ontology has been constructed through the dismantling of culture-nature binarisms and a converse re-inscription of "symbolic meanings and social relations" into environmental understanding. In their examination of non-western belief systems and sociocultural practices, these theorists provide a useful critical framework through which to analyze the ecological dystopias of Knutsson and Kwaymullina and the challenge posed by animist ideologies to the hegemonic images of culture-nature segregation common to much contemporary young adult fiction.

Ecopoiesis: animist materialism and spirit

Harry Garuba, whose research centers on West African societies, questions the applicability of western-derived ecological paradigms to non-western cultures where animist beliefs and practices inhere in a still extant belief in other-than-human forces. Where such forces – both natural and supernatural – are believed to have a material impact on society, an animist mode of thought, Garuba argues, becomes "embedded within the processes of material, economic activities and then reproduces itself within the sphere of culture and social life" (2003: 269). A tendency to assimilate new sociocultural developments into an inherently animist framework, Garuba notes, leads West African societies to "continually spirituali[ze] the object world, acknowledging and appropriating recent material developments and discoveries and animating them with a spirit" (2012: 7). This practice renders West African societies in a continual state of becoming whereby new scientific, technological and socio-political developments are deliberately incorporated into a flexible animist system. This non-dialogical approach to the more-than-human provides a useful model for ecocritical reappraisal since an animist frame of reference can "elide the either/or orientation of monotheistic religions and their logic of binarism and exclusivity" (Garuba 2003: 271 n. 21; see also Curry 2013). Animism, as it is thus understood, is not a regressive instantiation of a "primitive" worldview antithetical to modern science and technology, but rather a future-facing discourse in continuous evolution in which human and more-than-human are ontologically inseparable.

In both *Shadows Cast by Stars* and *The Interrogation of Ashala Wolf*, the protagonists' ability to spirit walk by means of shamanic ritual or dreaming allows the girls to recognize and respond to those intangible aspects of spirit that manifest themselves in a voiced and agential natural world. Both Cassandra and Ashala communicate the messages of the spirit creatures to their human communities via a form of ecopoiesis, here used in the sense coined by Jonathan Bate as a discursive practice designed to "give voice" to nature's self-realization (2000: 75). Such relaying of information demands an extension of care, empathy and compassion towards an agential environment – often at direct cost to the protagonists' own physical and mental health; Cassandra in particular struggles to keep the visions, premonitions and lies of manipulative spirit creatures at bay in her attempts to maintain the fragile balance between human community and its spiritual counterpart. As Piers Vitebsky argues, shamanic practices "are generally regarded by the communities in which they occur, not as part of some extraordinary sort of mystical practice, but as a specialized development of the relationship which every person has with the world around them" (2000: 55). Cassandra and Ashala's development of a tri-partite relationship between human, non-human and more-than-human allows for the establishment of a relational, rather than separatist, ontology that dismantles western binarisms in favor of the animist materialism examined by Garuba.

In *Shadows Cast by Stars*, the village healer, Madda, offers a mythological rendition of human history that posits the ontological separation of humans from their environment as a direct consequence of a prior separation of the world of the living from its spiritual counterpart. In such a separation, most humans have been "cut off" from the more-than-human world, with the exception of healers and shamans (127):

A few, like you, like me, can still travel to the spirit world. Most people, though, just have that little piece of spirit in them. Not everyone, mind you. Some people have given their spirit away, to greed or crime, to addiction or to just something as simple as forgetting that us and the earth are one. And that's when you see a person get really sick. If your spirit's healthy, if you walk in harmony with the

world, then you're healthy too. That's one of our jobs as healers, to bring that
piece of spirit back.

(127)

In this perceived shift away from an animist mode of being towards an anthropocentric
"forgetting," estrangement from spirit manifests itself in "greed," "crime," "addiction"
and other human abuses such that walking "in harmony with the world" is equivalent to
the maintenance of normative social values (127). The "shades," or spirit animals, that
accompany those who have retained their "little piece of spirit" reveal the intertwined
nature of environmental and spiritual wellbeing; Bran, the son of the missing rebel leader,
for instance, retains the memory of his former alcohol addiction in the matted feathers of
his kingfisher "shade." The sickness of the earth itself is personified in a hybridized god
known as the sea wolf – "a creature that's part wolf, part whale, and something else that
has no name" – that steals the totems, or souls, of Aboriginal peoples and thus enacts the
violent separation of body and soul, human and spirit, human and non-human in a crude
depiction of the "modern project" as defined by Hornborg (224). Cassandra's role as healer
and shaman for her community centers on her capacity to journey into the spirit world to
protect those in her care by bringing back those lost pieces of spirit and enacting a rejoin-
ing of human and more-than-human on behalf of a besieged natural world: *"Earth's lent
you some of her power, because she needs your help"* (310, italics in original).

In *The Interrogation of Ashala Wolf*, the roots of spiritual crisis extend backwards
into the pre-apocalyptic past to a similarly troubled relationship between human, non-
human and more-than-human. When Ashala seeks shelter amongst the trees of the First
Wood – an ancient forest of towering Tuart trees – with her band of paranormal Illegals,
she receives the forest's blessing only after acknowledging the destruction wrought by her
human ancestors:

> Images poured into my mind, nightmarish pictures of things I'd never seen
> before. Strange vehicles with metal jaws, weird saws with teeth that roared, and
> humans, always more humans, cutting and hacking and slashing and killing.
> [...T]he pictures kept on coming, filling my body with pain and my mind with
> the shocked confusion of dying forests. I realized the trees wanted to know why.
>
> (193)

Such images of environmental destruction prompt Ashala's realization of the uneven
power dynamic that has structured old world relations, leading her to promise an agential
natural world that "I won't hurt you or anyone else because I think you don't count as
much as me" (194). Ashala's Aboriginal blood, making her "the last to carry the blood-
line of those who [the Rainbow Serpent] created, in the world that was," gives her the capacity to spirit walk in the "greater Balance" where souls of the deceased are believed to
exist as energy before reincarnation (121). In paving the way for a reciprocal relationship
between the human, non-human and more-than-human world, Ashala's band of Illegals
and the forest become bound by a pact that creates new kinship bonds; while the forest
shelters the Illegals from government patrols, the Illegals protect the forest from harm by
working with its reptilian guards, the saurs, to deter government presence, aligning the
paranormals more strongly with their nonhuman counterparts than with the humans
from whose society they are marginalized. Thus, Ashala nurtures her connection to spirit
to establish a respectful and reciprocal relationship with her natural environment.

Autopoiesis: animic ontology and embodiment

Tim Ingold, whose anthropological field studies have centered on indigenous societies of the circumpolar regions, notes some common misconceptions about animist societies. The attribution of "life" to natural objects, he argues, does not constitute a retrospective "infusion of spirit into substance, or of agency into materiality," but rather indicates that life is already "immanent in the very process of that world's continual generation or coming-into-being" (2006: 10). Adopting a critical stance that resembles Garuba's, Ingold locates such a distinction within an ontology of becoming:

> [W]e are dealing here not with a way of believing *about* the world but with a condition of being *in* it. This could be described as a condition of being alive to the world, characterized by a heightened sensitivity and responsiveness, in perception and action, to an environment that is always in flux, never the same from one moment to the next. Animacy, then, is not a property of persons imaginatively projected onto the things with which they perceive themselves to be surrounded. Rather…it is the dynamic, transformative potential of the entire field of relations within which beings of all kinds, more or less person-like or thing-like, continually and reciprocally bring one another into existence.
>
> (2010: 10)

In the animic ontology, beings of all kinds perform a reciprocal autopoiesis – described by John Stephens as "self-fashioning and self-disclosure" (2010: 210). Contrary to the western-derived culture-nature dichotomy that situates humanity outside, or apart from, nature, animist belief systems embed such self-disclosure in a wider notion of ecopoiesis. Through a discourse of interconnectedness and becoming, the animic ontology thereby challenges western ideologies of culture-nature segregation by placing responsibility for social and biosocial wellbeing within "the entire field of relations" of which human, non-human and more-than-human are a part.

Both Knutsson's and Kwaymullina's novels envision autopoiesis as physical metamorphosis in the liminal space "where spirit and flesh merge" (*Shadows* 3). Cassandra's journeys into spirit see her assume the characteristics of spirit animals and elemental forces; she grows the wings of a crow and the tongue of a serpent and abandons her human form entirely "until I am the sky, I am the air, I am the fire of stars and the water of rain" (284). Her almost total disembodiment in her movement into the spirit world is experienced as a segregation of mind and body that critiques pervading notions of defined and finite selfhood: "My head is light, fuzzy, like it always is when spirit comes to call, as if a veil has descended in my mind, detaching me from my body" (14). In "hat[ing] this feeling, like I'm no longer part of myself," Cassandra calls into question the spiritual wisdom of a mind-body duality, gesturing instead towards a reintegration of both through a reclamation of spirit (14). The theft of Bran's father's shade, or soul, is experienced by Cassandra as the ultimate segregation of human from spirit: "I can…feel the wound left behind, a raw, gaping hole in his being, a wound that must be stanched before it bleeds him dry" (418). A reclamation of spirit thus becomes a way to re-inscribe lost values of spiritual wholeness into a world where body and mind, human and spirit, human and nonhuman have been torn asunder.

Where Cassandra reveals her affinity with the natural world in the animal characteristics she assumes when spirit walking, the Illegals of the First Wood in *The Interrogation of Ashala Wolf* undergo a form of "animal bonding" through which they develop a similar affinity with an animal species (99). As Ashala notes of the enforcer whose experiments on detained Illegals resemble the violence perpetrated on the trees of the First Wood, "Neville would never understand what it was like to run with wolves the way I could. Or call crows from the sky like Ember, or have the night vision of a treecat like Briony" (99–100). Ashala's experience with spirit at the crux of the novel, in which she calls on the Rainbow Serpent to bring Connor, the boy she loves, back to life, demands her complete disembodiment as she is transformed into an "empty" vessel ready to receive the "life-giving song" gifted to her by the Rainbow Serpent (379; 380). Her experiences with spirit are sensory and immersive (the Rainbow Serpent's song "sank into my flesh"; "flared throughout my body") until her subjectivity, like the song, expands from being "part of" a wider whole to becoming "the whole world" (379). Both protagonists' complete surrendering of body and mind to spirit in their shamanic movement between worlds reunites the triad of human, nonhuman and more-than-human necessary for social and environmental wellbeing within the transformative space of their own bodies.

Poiesis: poet-shaman aesthetics and language

AnaLouise Keating, in analyzing the *mestizaje* writings of Gloria Anzaldúa, draws on indigenous worldviews, and particularly shamanic practices "in which words, images, and things are intimately interwoven," to create a "poet-shaman aesthetics" grounded in a "metaphysics and ethics of interconnectedness" (2012: 52; 63). Like the animic ontology explored by Ingold, such an ethics provides an alternative vantage point from which to question human responsibility towards the environment in contrast to that underscored by western binarisms. In noting the intertwined nature of "words" and "things," Keating adds language as a category of analysis to animist enquiry: "words have causal force; words embody the world; words are matter; words become matter…and the intentional, ritualized performance of specific, carefully selected words *shifts* reality" (2012: 52, italics in the original). Keating bases her aesthetics on Anzaldúa's "poet-shaman analogy" which links the shaman and poet in their ability "to preserve and create cultural or group identity by mediating between the cultural heritage of the past and the present everyday situations people find themselves in" (Keating 2012: 51; Anzaldúa 1990: 99). This constructivist focus on poiesis, or the capacity of language to bring ideas into being, works not in opposition to the self-realization of the natural world but in service of it. Such mediation between past and present by means of an ongoing animist discourse is testament to the importance of generational storytelling to Aboriginal peoples and argues for the contemporary relevance of an animist ontology to authorial renderings of our imagined future.

Both Knutsson's and Kwaymullina's novels enact a return to the "old stories" of their Aboriginal ancestors to establish an animist mode of being-in-the-world that can sustain a new and more caring world order. In *The Interrogation of Ashala Wolf*, Ember tells an old story of the Rainbow Serpent that embeds hope in the Illegals for a more just and equitable society to come. As members of the Tribe retell the story to each other they transform it so that soon "there was this rumor going around the Tribe that there was some special Illegal with the power to make a new world" (294). Such a whispered progression of words from the mind of one to the imaginations of many, rooted in the "ancient story" of an old world creator god, demonstrates the capacity of stories to preserve and create cultural identity (294). Not only does the "special Illegal," known as "the Serpent," inspire the paranormals in their fight for justice but he also becomes integral to Ashala's premeditated attack on the government detention center; the importance of this literary construct as stimulus for change ("power to make a new world") outweighs and outlives its mythical origins. *Shadows Cast by Stars* likewise invests "the old stories" passed down through generations of "witching women" with the capacity to affect healing; as Madda tells Cassandra, "stories are living things, as alive as you and me. Just in a different way, that's all," and the body that houses them is created by words and sustained by retelling (452). Where stories have souls and are invested with spirit, the practice of embodying them with words and passing them on from one generation to the next is simply one further facet of ecoconscious engagement with the natural world to enable social and ecological flourishing. Such a practice resembles that undertaken by the Rainbow Serpent in *The Interrogation of Ashala Wolf* after the cataclysmic events of the Reckoning: "I sang, reminding life of its shapes, strength and its many transformations. Until life remembered its nature, and grew" (121).

This overarching focus on creativity – singing, storytelling, dancing, dreaming – as a positive force for autopoiesis and renewal sees both novels embody what Sian Sullivan terms the "uncynical ontology" that characterizes animist worldviews (2013: 56). Where the apocalyptic futures so common to the contemporary literary imagination are a consequence of uneven power structures, inequalities and prejudices found in the present – as indeed they are in the novels in question – Knutsson's and Kwaymullina's reclamation of an older spiritual connection between people and place counterbalances any residual cynicism. Garuba and Ingold come close to describing such an "uncynical ontology" in their respective exploration of "enchantment," on the part of Garuba, and "astonishment," on the part of Ingold. For Garuba, the animist unconscious operates "through a process that involves...*a continual re-enchantment of the world*" (2003: 265, italics in the original). Countering the much-theorized modernist disenchantment first propounded by Max Weber in the early twentieth century, a *"re-enchantment"* of the world conversely results in "the rational and scientific [being] appropriated and transformed into the mystical and magical" (2003: 267). For Ingold, this process allows one to regain "the sense of astonishment that is so conspicuous by its absence from contemporary scientific work" (2006: 19). Surprise, he suggests, "exists only for those who have forgotten how to be astonished at the birth of the world"; astonishment, by contrast, allows "those who are truly open to the world...at every moment to respond to the flux of the world with care, judgement and sensitivity" (2006: 19). If enchantment and astonishment are indicators of a modern and future-facing animist discourse, their enactment in Knutsson's and Kwaymullina's futuristic fantasies in service of such "care, judgement and sensitivity" indicates the ongoing relevance of an animist ontology to current ecocritical enquiry.

Conclusion: social and environmental wellbeing

Whether in its exploration of poiesis, autopoiesis or ecopoiesis, an animist discourse in both novels serves to counter social and environmental estrangement and develop a non-oppositional ontology that invests value in social and environmental health. Anzaldúa notes the creative impulse behind the healing of sickness:

> [T]hrough my poet's eye I see "illness," *lo que daña*, whatever is harmful in the cultural or individual body. I see that "sickness" unbalances a person or a community. That it may be in the form of disease, or disinformation/misinformation

perpetrated on women and people of color. I see that always it takes the form of metaphors.

(1990: 91)

Sickness, as it is thus understood, describes any harm that is perpetrated on those who are vulnerable to dominance and oppression; the "metaphors" it can take are representative of a power dynamic that situates one category in a position of control over another thus damaging the mind, spirit or collective subjectivity of a people. In Canada and Australia – countries in which colonial relationships with the indigenous populations still have ongoing repercussions – such a power dynamic is of particular resonance. The literary instantiation of a future-facing animist ontology in Knutsson's and Kwaymullina's novels both widens the scope of contemporary young adult fiction and honors the cultural and spiritual roots of the authors' indigenous communities.

Garuba's argument for the importance of an animist "re-enchantment" gives particular weight to this celebration of non-western environmental ontologies:

> For the mass of ordinary people, animism cushions the movement into modernity by providing cultural certainties, which create the "illusion" of a continuum rather than a chasm, thus giving an imposed subjective order to the chaos of history. [...] Animist culture thus opens up a whole new world of poaching possibilities, *prepossessing the future*, as it were, by laying claim to what in the present is yet to be invented. It is on account of this ability to prepossess the future that continual re-enchantment becomes possible.

(2003: 270; 271, italics in the original)

Where Knutsson and Kwaymullina *"prepossess"* the future they do so through the absorption of human, nonhuman and more-than-human actors into a relational animist framework. Envisioning, thus, an apocalyptic future rooted in western ideologies of culture-nature segregation, these authors lay claim to an alternative mode of being-in-the-world that can engender autopoietic and ecopoietic flourishing. In so doing, these novels flag the importance of widening one's critical viewpoint to take into account the various "invisible forces" that animate non-western belief systems and practices (Tangwa 2004: 389). If such forces can challenge hitherto ineffective parameters for human-nonhuman interaction, they may prove particularly useful for ecocritical theory and praxis.

Bibliography

Anzaldúa, Gloria (1990) "Metaphors in the Tradition of the Shaman" in James McCorkle (ed.) *Conversant Essays: Contemporary Poets on Poetry*, Detroit: Wayne State University Press 99–100.

Bate, Jonathan (2000) *The Song of the Earth*, Cambridge, MA: Harvard University Press.

Curry, Alice (2013) *Environmental Crisis in Young Adult Fiction: A Poetics of Earth*, Critical Approaches to Children's Literature Series, Basingstoke: Palgrave Macmillan.

Delbanco, Nicholas and Laurence Goldstein (eds.) (1991) *Writers and Their Craft: Short Stories & Essays on the Narrative*, Detroit: Wayne State University Press.

Garuba, Harry (2012) "On Animism, Modernity/Colonialism, and the African Order of Knowledge: Provisional Reflections," *e-flux journal* 36: 1–9.

——— (2003) "Explorations in Animist Materialism: Notes on Reading/Writing African Literature, Culture, and Society," *Public Culture* 15(2): 261–285.

Harvey, Graham (ed.) (2000) *Indigenous Religions: A Companion*, London & New York: Cassell.

Hornborg, Alf (2006) "Animism, Fetishism, and Objectivism as Strategies for Knowing (or not Knowing) the World," *Ethnos* 71(1): 21–32.

Ingold, Tim (2006) "Rethinking the Animate, Re-Animating Thought," *Ethnos* 71(1): 9–20.

Keating, AnaLouise (2012) "Speculative Realism, Visionary Pragmatism, and Poet-Shamanic Aesthetics in Gloria Anzaldúa – and Beyond," *WSQ: Women's Studies Quarterly* 40(3 & 4): 51–69.

Knutsson, Catherine (2013) *Shadows Cast by Stars*, New York: Atheneum Books for Young Readers.

Kwaymullina, Ambelin (2012) *The Interrogation of Ashala Wolf*, London: Walker Books.

Stephens, John (2010) "Impartiality and Attachment: Ethics and Ecopoeisis in Children's Narrative Texts," *International Research in Children's Literature* 3(2): 205–216.

Sullivan, Sian (2013) "Nature on the Move III: (Re)countenancing an Animate Nature," *New Proposals: Journal of Marxism and Interdisciplinary Inquiry* 6(1–2): 50–71.

Tangwa, Godfrey B. (2004) "Some African Reflections on Biomedical and Environmental Ethics," in Kwasi Wiredu (ed.) *A Companion to African Philosophy*, Malden, MA: Blackwell Publishing Ltd.: 387–395.

Vitebsky, Piers (2000) "Shamanism," in Graham Harvey (ed.) *Indigenous Religions: A Companion*, London & New York: Cassell: 55–67.

7

GROUNDS FOR "RIGHTS READING" PRACTICES

A view to children's literature in Zimbabwe

Robert Muponde

Introduction

This essay is written within the context of what Jack Donnelly (2003: 223–224) calls the modern state's "awesome powers to bring individuals to their knees; if necessary, to break their minds as well as their bodies" (a description that snugly fits the character of the Zimbabwean postcolonial state). It responds to the comparable tremendous powers of conventional folk narratives to stipulate for children an unquestioned curriculum for moral and intellectual development. Folktales, especially, constitute the common sense of society. They convey taken-for-granted wisdoms and truths, which form the basis and rationale for the continuity of society/community. In the folk narratives, children are presumed to double up as the audience as well as the future of a society.

In order to overturn the generalisations that stand in place of critique, I propose a "rights reading" of the Zimbabwean folktale tradition as masterfully retold by Charles Mungoshi in *Stories from a Shona Childhood* (1989). A "rights reading" is a critical enquiry aimed at instilling the virtues of questioning as the very basis of democratic, rights-driven, ethical citizenship. It promotes reading and thinking risks and conditions for re-reading community as well as the kinds of narrative we retell when we perform tradition. As a critical approach, it illuminates the inequities, discrepancies and potential of certain conventional narratives. Beyond the usual understanding of the imaginative benefits of the make-believe world of folktales, it suggests "other worlds" beyond conventions and forms.

A rights reading practice enables me to question, for instance, the fetishisation of cultural enfreakment of individuals and the simultaneous despising of non-conformity and dissidence in the much retold story about how animals decided to dig a well during a life-threatening drought. In this story, "The Hare and the Animals of the Jungle" (Mungoshi 1989: 3–20), contrary to received truths and interpretations, collective rights to a well in a situation of drought strengthen forces of repression (cf. Donnelly 2003: 224); the well turns out to be a source of fundamentalism and virulent resource nationalism (think of postcolonial conflicts around this); group or individual rights impede the development of a diverse society and individual talents; a story of communal preservation has the seeds of destructive tyranny; and the trickster and the despised freak become central to new modes of community regeneration. By changing the lens on the same body of narratives, through "rights reading", it is possible to locate the possibilities of a "local" literary/cultural theory; critique ideology as common sense; and question certain concepts of social identity as conveyed in children's stories.

What's in a drought? Contexts for rights reading

"The Hare and the Animals of the Jungle," the story that I intend to base my reflections on, has variants in other parts of the continent. In one Shangani account recorded by Stockil and Dalton (1987) it is titled "The Waterhole," and in East Africa it is retold by Pamela Kola (1980) as "The Cunning Tortoise." Whatever the version, the story centres on how a long time ago a group of wild animals was threatened by a drought and, against all animal sense, decided to dig a well together. Lion, the King of the Jungle, shows some leadership by calling the community to put aside its differences for the common good. Whoever refused to dig the well was not allowed to drink the water. One animal, the Hare or the Wolf (the East African villain), declined to participate and is ostracised and refused access to the well. The Hare used his honey to trick and then tie up the animals guarding the well; and the Wolf enticed the guards into a wild dance that caused untold exhaustion and ultimately deep sleep. The tricksters are brought to justice through the ingenuity of underrated animals such as Tortoise and Frog, those whose humility and perseverance found the water in the first place when the big animals failed. The story, as in "The Hare and the Animals of the Jungle," begins in one of these predictable ways: "Once upon a time, there was a severe drought in the land where all the animals of the jungle lived" (3). It is a powerful, ominous and striking opening line which, while frugal in the way it frames the dire setting, is capacious and subtle enough to insinuate archetypal possibilities and epochal energies surging in the ancient tale. It provides the grounds for the normative reading of common sense.

The drought as a literary motif can be understood in at least four ways: as a natural environmental occurrence; an archetypal experience of social stress; a barometer of social consciousness; and a catalyst for anti-colonial as well as other social struggles. First, on a physical level, the frequency and severity of drought is determined by the unfortunate climatic conditions of Southern Africa, of which Zimbabwe is a landlocked part. Zimbabwean writers cannot avoid representing its impact on food security, social relationships and political cultures. Second, the drought is archetypal, transformed from a physical experience to a literary motif that expresses not only how well a writer reflects the truthfulness of his people's recurrent experiences and fears, but also the individual's ideological and ethical proclivities. This reflection segues with the third point, but may be illustrated by referring to how in "committed" literature writers are expected to articulate their class and ideological positions in relation to those who are vulnerable. In *Waiting for the Rain* (1975), Charles Mungoshi invites us to condemn Lucifer who had "become something that is not the colour of this soil" by rejecting his drought-stricken roots. Dambudzo Marechera in his poem "Oracle of the Povo" (1984: 106–107) rages against a kleptomaniac postcolonial elite who abuse "The most vulnerable and hungry of citizens" by hijacking Drought Relief grain trucks.

Third, as well as being an existential condition within and with which to judge character and resilience, the drought illuminates social relationships as well as power dynamics among the society of animals and human beings. All four beautifully retold stories in

Stories from a Shona Childhood are inspired by drought. In "The Pumpkin that Talked," "All the trees in the forest were dry and there were no leaves or fruit on them. So Nzou [Elephant] had nothing to eat. Each time he passed Tsuro's [Hare's] field and saw the pumpkins, his mouth watered" (22). The desperation that the drought induces transforms Nzou the Elephant from a majestic protector of the weak to a common thief as he starts to covet and steal Hare's pumpkins. He is killed by Hare, his protégé, who now wields power over his erstwhile protector because he possesses the ingenuity that physical might alone cannot displace. In "The Slave who became Chief," Kakore [Little Cloud] the ill-treated and reclusive slave became a messiah and gained a chieftainship by playing his haunting *mbira* [thumb piano] music and "singing the rainmaking songs of his now distant land" and causing rain to fall when drought struck Chief Chisvo's country. Just as Hare used his pumpkins to alter his situation of inexorable dependence on Nzou the Elephant, Kakore's sacred power of rainmaking is a weapon in the hands of the weak. In a drought condition where "The only food available was lean meat from the cattle that were dying in their hundreds" (32), mere hereditary influence without the power of rainmaking, or the allure of honey, is exposed, shifts and crumbles. "The Spirit of the Ashpit" inverts the figure of the man of the house as an altruistic protector. Kuruta, the man, faced a situation: "That year many people died from hunger and thirst" (41). When he came across some honey, his character experienced a metamorphosis for the worst: "If six people can feed on this honey for a week, how long can I feed on it?" He began to hate the fact that he was to share the honey with his wife and children, and hid the honey under an ashpit. "After all, they have been sitting at home doing nothing while the bees stung me. Why should they eat my honey?" (43). His dependable and anguished wife discovered the deception, and turned the tables against him, but only to kindly remind him to resume his unchallenged position as the man of the house. The power shift is momentary as Kuruta is restored to patriarchal normalcy, confirming Margery Hourihan's (1997: 205) warning that "inversion is not the same as subversion" and that inversions may fail to subvert the material they deride.

Fourth, the experiencing of drought is related to undergoing social consciousness of oppression and lack. The metaphorical drought and hunger is the seed-bed of Zimbabwean anti-colonial nationalism, which gave rise to adult literary works with titles such as *The House of Hunger* (Marechera 1978); *Coming of the Dry Season* (Mungoshi 1972); *Waiting for the Rain* (Mungoshi 1975); and *Those Years of Drought and Hunger* (Zimunya 1982). The "drought" and "hunger" are related both to the loss of land and culture. Above all, the drought intensifies the awareness of land as "the land of rising bones," where "the power of the land is more than the power of any other miracle that can cheat the eye" (Hove 1988: 58), and without which we cannot dream (Vera 1994: 32–34). However, in adult literary works, the interpretation of this collective experience of drought and the land of rising bones will be shaped by literary technique and the author's ideological predilections. There is little chance of an individualistic authorial rendering of the common sense of drought in retellings of the traditional folktale. So, in the reading of the children's folktales based on the archetypal drought and hunger there is an unacknowledged impetus of anti-colonial nationalism derived from the express need to reclaim stolen land and liberties and reverse the effects of a pervasive material and spiritual drought. There is no attempt to link the experience of postcolonial dictatorship and violent resource nationalism to, say, a new reading of Mungoshi's "The Hare and the Animals of the Jungle." Consequently, behind the need to have forms of these foundational stories retold is a nationalist project, a project that, in line with new sets of experiences and circumstances in the postcolonial situation, advances a cultural revival that does not revive social critique.

While we can appreciate the isolated, and seemingly remote, non-recurring setting as an estranging formulaic device, we should consider how ideology is embedded in the way in which the rendition of the story of drought seems to be uninterrupted by current social and political contexts while the narrative itself is a direct product of social upheavals in the pre-colonial *anciens régimes*.

The absence of a reading that might transform the significance of the drought from being the basis of an anti-colonial political imaginary to a permanent sense of agitation against any form of cultural and material lack and social emergency is because readers are expected to draw insinuations when confronted by the postcolonial regime and its knack of repeating colonial experiences. These extrapolations are made on the basis of intuition and assumed universal moral equivalences, rather than a particularised critique invented for the purpose. However, the catch-all approach (used much like a biblical verse to every situation or a master key to every door) does not reorient understanding if the culture of reading the traditional children's story is not questioned and reset.

There are two main reasons why the modes of reading may remain unaltered, both of which justify and reinforce the pedagogical thrust and ideological preferences of post-colonial nationalist culture. One reason the reading culture and its critical tropism is not rearranged is that there is a firm belief in those who set up "Reading Tents" and embark on "books for African children" expeditions and galas that African children "love animal books." No attempt is made to interrogate this assumption and to ask, as does Maria Nikolajeva, whether there has been "any empirical research about real children's attitude toward animals, nor about young readers' preferences for animals in their stories" (Nikolajeva 2010: 156). Pedagogically, this is perhaps because there is something invariable about wild animals who are the protagonists in these traditional stories. It makes it easier for the culture to transmit constant "timeless" values. Ideologically, society is safer with its thoughts and yearnings sewn into the bodies and shapes of the unchanging animals that survived an archetypal menace in a distant time, giving itself the sense of depth, continuity and perpetuity with which it reassures those of its children who adhere to its common sense.

The other reason is that most of the "Reading Tent" initiatives assume that oral narratives are the unquestionable backbone of African children's literature. They embark on an indiscriminate pillaging of oral traditions. There is therefore a supposition that converting oral stories into written literature is all there is to constructing a reading culture in Africa. In the case of Charles Mungoshi's two widely celebrated anthologies *Stories from a Shona Childhood* (1989) and *One Day, Long Ago: More Stories from a Shona Childhood* (1991), the emphasis is on the virtuosity of recreating an oral tradition, rather than the meaning and times of the subject of artistic creativity. A comment on the blurb of the latter book reads: "Once again Charles Mungoshi brings to readers of all ages the delights of folklore at its finest, with a literary elegance that is entirely his own." Pedagogically, his interests lie in bridging the gap between reading and listening as well as the inequities of literary production where the oral tradition is viewed as primitive and communal, and the written tradition as the *sine qua non* for cultural maturity and modernity. His project is therefore largely more about cultural renovation and embellishment than resuscitation and reinvention.

Questions arise from the unchallenged wholesale plundering and dispersal of stereotypes that come pre-packaged in the common sense of oral narratives. These stereotypes may be around gender, religion, race, sex, age, justice and community. In *One day, long ago*, a collection of four folktales, freaks of culture such as in "The Prince and the Leper," "The Blind Man and the Lion" and "The Lazy Young Man and his Dog" are acknowledged as such, and the only way they can succeed in society is by performing miraculous feats in order to get a wife, or secure a social advantage. The women themselves are estranged and objectified as deaf-mutes or lepers awaiting a male suitor or saviour who is blind to their infirmity. How might alternative interpretations of old stories be constructed in such a way that the continued fetishisation and enfreakment of marginalised characters and social groups is critically revoked? What kinds of literacy changes critical lives and in which direction? How can folk narratives be quarried in order to ascertain how children have an instinctive, undiluted and uncritical love of animal stories without evading the significance of the pedagogical and ideological fraudulence that the use of animal characters in children's stories might mask? Maria Nikolajeva uncovered the duplicity and concluded that: "The use of animals allows circumventing some aspects inevitable in a narrative with human characters, such as age and social status" (2010: 156), and I add, sexual orientation, religion, difference and voice. For the purposes of my essay, how may a rights reading approach cater for new cultural common sense and new reading politics?

Community, difference and voice

In "The Hare and the Animals of the Jungle," fantasy suspends quotidian animal common sense. Community is reconvened on new, though tenuous terms. The Lion, who called himself King of the Jungle, called a meeting of all the animals:

> "Friends, we are in danger. If it doesn't rain soon, then all of us, big and small, will die. So I suggest that we put our heads together because we must find water to drink. I know we don't all like one another, but this is not the time to let our differences show. Instead, let us unite and find a way to save ourselves. What do you think?".
>
> (3)

Usually, the "danger" alluded to would be Lion himself. Lion converts from being the "danger" to being the opportunity and the salvation. The drought calls for community action and community cohesion, and suspension of habitual modes of thinking and doing social business. Difference, which ensured that each animal was allotted its own unchangeable place in the wild, and lived its life based on fate and not choice, is both a source of friction and strength in so far as the maintenance of the normalcy of jungle life goes. In the absence of water, difference kills, and is killed. Lion champions the need for an overriding common sense that dissolves difference into one undivided voice.

Certain habituated rights are called into question: for example, the Lion can no longer just pounce. To insist on its right to eat other animals as per its nature, or as per nature, will imperil the community project, which was necessitated by a community emergency. In fact, to assert nature-given rights at all would be to ensure self-destruction. Similarly, for Hare to maintain his quiddity as the typical unreformed trickster would also jeopardise the community. In the same vein, for the Lion to claim being King and director of operations in the Jungle on the basis of might and the fear it inspires in other animals also proves detrimental to community justice. When, for example, "All the animals thought Lion's idea was a good one. There were, however, certain animals like Zebra and the Hare who thought that Lion wanted to play a trick on them so that later he could kill and eat them. But they were afraid to say so." (3). It is a false consensus that produces fakery and saboteurs.

The community that Lion invents in order to find water is intolerant of dissent and individual choice. It is the reason why the water is a source of woe, as the animals now concentrate their energies on guarding the well against Hare instead of flourishing, that is enjoying the goods that one has a right to benefit from (cf. Lewis 2012: 220). They are slaves to the well, much in the same way they are haunted and tormented by the drought.

Marginal characters like Hare (who refused to dig the well because of inherent fear of treachery) and Frog (who actually finds the water against all expectations) are actually overlooked systematically. Lion ends up stealing Frog's bragging rights by intimidating the other animals into chanting a ditty: "King Lion dug the deepest! King Lion dug the deepest!" when it was all clear that he only raised dry dust with his unfit-for-purpose claws. So, the "danger" that Lion has always been to the animal society has only been hidden to avoid showing "difference," but it ripples on the surface at the slightest provocation. Hare, who entertains critical doubt, albeit misplaced, is hunted down like a criminal and condemned to death by strangulation or thirst even before he is tried.

Yet the marginal characters hold the key to society's survival in this story. They function as checkpoints to social arrogance and unbridled optimism. In other words, the lack of guaranteed minority rights almost threatens the community project. It is Hare's much unappreciated corrective laughter that spurs the animals to not fail and consider every contribution from their midst.

Reaction to individualism by community is violent and intolerant of diversity. Refusal to acknowledge and respect the talents of those at the fringes of society ensures that society is ruled via a monologic that insists on Big-ism and Might-is-Right. The Lion speaks, innovates and leads, and the Elephant endorses and modulates his power. Small is viewed as last resort. The established hierarchy and protocol of digging and guarding the well recuperates the differences that characterise a society that reveres the normativity of asymmetrical power relations. However, as we see at the end of the story, the ability of retold cultures to "describe situations in which established power structures are interrogated without necessarily being overthrown" (Nikolajeva: 9) is highlighted when a stark dualism represented by the Lion (Water) and the Hare (Honey) is inverted in such a way that it substitutes Hare normativity for Lion normativity.

The symbolic and practical meanings of the WELL

The WELL, which I capitalise here because of the absoluteness of its influence in the animals' lives, is developed more as a common sense alternative to death, while promising certain death to those who laughed at its conception.

> It is the ONLY thing to be done.
> It becomes all there is to do and to think.
> It is the reason one is alive or will be alive.
> The WELL is LIFE.
> Anyone not part of the WELL should not LIVE.

The WELL lays firmly the grounds for lack of tolerance much as it advances the interests of the "majority," but then it is not the majority of the animals that speaks at the WELL.

Not even Frog, who rescued operations at crucial moments, is allowed to air his views on what should happen to Hare after he is caught. It is Frog who found the water and who trapped Hare when all the animals had been fooled by him. The Lion speaks. He makes and unmakes rules. And when he suggests that anyone who allows the water to be stolen again by Hare will be killed, and he allowed Hare to drink the water (when he was fooled by him) and he has to be killed, that ruling is deferred because it is contrary to his personal interests.

The WELL lays the ground for fundamentalism built around the need to protect a hard-won resource. Hare, a certain category of animal, draws the wrath of the "community" because he did not dig the WELL and must be condemned to death before he has been tried. While, as Jack Donnelly (2003: 222) argues, a group can be justified to protect its natural resource against plunder by another group, here resource nationalism comes across as a vengeful form of protectionism and self-interest. It epitomises and replays the same awesome powers that the modern state exercises to bring non-conforming individuals to their knees (223). Dissention is criminalised and, in turn, because it is not allowed independent creative existence, it indeed becomes criminal as we see in Hare.

However, Hare's own version of individualism creates destructive freaks out of marginal characters, the very grounds of social exclusion. Tricking and tying up fellow animals, robbing them of their water, and bathing his whole body in the very WELL they toiled for while he laughed at them, illustrates how through excessive individualism an individual can in fact crush society. Hare's story allows us to debunk Jack Donnelly's romanticisation of individual human rights discourses. In Donnelly's words, "Every day we see individuals crushed by society. Rarely, if ever, do we see society torn apart by the exercise of individual human rights. Social disorder and decay are instead usually associated with the violation of individual human rights by the state or some other organized segment of society" (Donnelly: 224).

Possibilities occluded by the WELL

The obsession with drought and water, just like the blind fixation with the retelling of the story, is all-consuming. No connection is made at all in this story to Hare's legitimate self-interest. His competencies are elsewhere. The WELL society does not allow for mutually beneficial social trade-offs. Hare could have been considered skilled at finding honey, instead of water, and a legitimate honey-for-water deal could have been struck, but alternative avenues of aspiration (such as honey-gathering) are closed. Yet animals cannot live by water alone. The honey, just like the dance by the Wolf in the East African version of the story, is an essential life good that the WELL underestimates. Court Lewis argues that, "Too often, *tangible* life goods dominate discussions of justice; but in cases of extreme vulnerability, nontangible life goods such as comforts are just as (if not more) important" (2012: 228). They are inalienable symbolic and material accessories and necessities of a flourishing life (spiritual or economic). Inflexible obsession with water rights thus impedes the development of society. It is the reason why, when the animals finally "roared in one voice as Lion threw Hare as hard as he could on to the ashheap" in accordance with Hare's request, only to find after Hare escaped unhurt that they had been tricked again, "The animals looked at each other and never said a word either then or ever again" (19). They regress to their dumb state of nature, which the fantasy of a thinking collective had ambitiously ameliorated.

The WELL discourse forecloses possibilities of creative plurality as it denies choice and voice to individuals (cf. Berger & Zijderveld 2009: 5–17). Even when Frog, who captured the Hare, felt they should forgive him, "he dared not say it aloud" (Mungoshi: 19). The charge sheet as crafted by Lion reads: "You all know what a nuisance Hare is becoming. He lives alone, doesn't want to work with us when there's work to do together, like digging this well. On top of that, he has the cheek to laugh at us as if he knew everything and we are just fools. I, for one, wouldn't mind wringing his neck" (7).

Instead of being constructed to serve the whole society, the WELL and its system of justice turn out to be strictly tailored against a particular individual, who must "DIE!" It is more like retributive justice based first on an injustice (no real trial of Hare ever takes place before execution). A society based on retributive rights is bound to turn violent and consume itself in shame. Hare also learns from this experience as he had tried to revenge himself on the animal community that had denied him access to a community-owned good which he believed he had a right to benefit from. Hare had flourished not because he had deserved the water that he stole and dirtied, but because he thought little of his victims and the needs of others and was oblivious to the concept of justice and compassion that Court Lewis (2012) argues is inseparable from an ethical conception of the good life.

In Shona society, at the community courts, convicted offenders are often asked to suggest more appropriate punitive measures against themselves to show that they really appreciate their predicament. So are children. Hare of course abuses this leeway when he asks that he be killed by being thrown hard on to the ashheap, and his captors readily grant him his request. But it points to right of choice even for the condemned or convicted, which same right of choice is denied to Hare as regards the digging of the WELL. So, here, at the end of the story, we have a situation that questions the hypocritical and selective application of "choice" as a right. In fact, at the end, the WELL becomes a site of community failure and shame as well as abuse of individual and collective rights. It seems disappointing that what is traditionally lauded in this story turns out to be the recycled normativity of violence, tautology and regression both in the republic of children's books and the common sense of the postcolonial state.

Conclusion

Rights reading illuminates the inequities, discrepancies, and potential of certain narratives. Even though the architecture of conventions might be a form of prison demanding normative conformity, and the tendency of children's genres to recuperate critique are enhanced (cf. Eisenstadt 2012: 193), there is a way in which a reading revamped and reoriented by rights reading practices could subvert outright the political project of cultural common sense and, in the words of Peter Costello (2012: xv–xvi), shape children's literature into a "valuable tool to further self-awareness and social justice."

When applied to folk narratives, rights reading sanctions creative and imaginative thinking beyond the constraints of a given genre or explanation of events and certain narrative structures. It also tolerates critical and imaginative possibilities of "other worlds" within certain conventions.

Bibliography

Berger, P. L. and Zijderveld A. C. (2009) *In Praise of Doubt: How to Have Convictions Without Becoming a Fanatic*, New York: HarperOne.

Costello, P. R. (ed.) (2012) *Philosophy in Children's Literature*, Lanham and New York: Lexington Books.

Donnelly, J. (2003) *Universal Human Rights in Theory and Practice*, New York: Cornell University Press.

Eisenstadt, O. (2012) "The things that are not among the things there are to do: *Harriet the Spy* and Maurice Blanchot's passivity," in P. R. Costello (ed.) *Philosophy in Children's Literature*, Lanham and New York: Lexington Books, pp. 191–204.

Hourihan, M, (1997) *Deconstructing the Hero: Literary Theory and Children's Literature*, London and New York: Routledge.

Hove, C. (1988) *Bones*, Harare: Baobab Books.

Kola, P. (1980) *The Cunning Tortoise*, Nairobi: Heinemann.

Lewis, C. (2012) "*The cricket in Times Square*: Crickets, compassion, and the good life," in P. R. Costello (ed.) *Philosophy in Children's Literature*, Lanham and New York: Lexington Books, pp. 219–233.

Marechera, D. (1978) *The House of Hunger*, London: Heinemann.

——— (1984) *Mindblast*, Harare: College Press.

Mungoshi, C. (1991) *One Day, Long Ago: More Stories from a Shona Childhood*, Harare: Baobab Books.

——— (1989) *Stories from a Shona Childhood*, Harare: Baobab Books.

——— (1975) *Waiting for the Rain*, London: Heinemann.

——— (1972) *Coming of the Dry Season*, Nairobi: O.U.P.

Nikolajeva, M. (2010) *Power, Voice and Subjectivity in Literature for Young Readers*, New York and London: Routledge.

Stockil, C. and Dalton, M. (1987) *Shangani Folk Tales: A Collection of Shangani Folk Stories*, Harare: Longman.

Vera, Y. (1994) *Without a Name*, Harare: Baobab Books.

Zimunya, M. (1982) *Those Years of Drought and Hunger: The Birth of African Fiction in English in Zimbabwe*, Gweru: Mambo Press.

8

THE CONSTRUCTION OF A MODERN CHILD AND A CHINESE NATIONAL CHARACTER

Translating Alice

Xu Xu

In January 1922, the Commercial Press in Shanghai published the first Chinese translation of Lewis Carroll's *Alice's Adventures in Wonderland*. The translator was the prominent Chinese linguist, Zhao Yuanren, who had returned to China in 1920 to teach at Tsinghua University after ten years' study and teaching in the United States. The book was a great success. Zhou Zuoren, Zhao's eminent contemporary and often hailed as the forefather of Chinese children's literature studies, praised the for its "unparallelled and unprecedented brillance" as a children's book ("Alice's Adventures in Wonderland"140). The book's characteristic imaginative nonsense would be "naturally appreciated" by children as "inborn poets," as Zhou stated. Even for adults, Zhou further argued, the book is a must. Zhou lamented: "Too many adults who were once children themselves lost their child-hearts, just as caterpillars have transformed into butterflies, [the former and latter becoming] completely two different stages" (140). Because those "unfortunate" adults forget their childhood selves, according to Zhou, they are unable to understand, nourish and educate children. Zhou was worried that if these adults become parents or teachers they would impede children's natural development. Therefore, Zhou strongly recommended the book to Chinese adults and also urged them to let their children read it.

The importance of Zhao's translation of the Alice book is not so much its vivid portrayals of children's natural characteristics, as Zhou believed, as its intricate connection with the May Fourth nation-building project of transforming the flawed Chinese national character. Rather than an inconsequential children's book, Zhao's translation took on a national significance in the Chinese context. It was imagined to be capable of transforming the degenerate Chinese, including both adults and children, into a modern citizenry. It is important to note that Carroll's *Alice* was not directly consumed by Chinese readers, but mediated through translation. The book's success in China was greatly indebted to Zhao Yuanren's skillful translation. Zhou Zuoren expressed in his book review that he "greatly admired" Zhao, particularly praising him for adopting vernacular Chinese and using John Tenniel's illustrations from the original. Even the most valued quality of the book—"playful nonsense"—would be merely nonsense were it not for Zhao's creative adaptation. I argue in this essay that Zhao's translation constructs a modern child that came to embody the May Fourth imagination of an ideal modern Chinese citizen, a child that both originates and deviates from Carroll's Alice.. But in order to better understand the important role Zhao's translation played in the May Fourth nation-building project, the entangled relationship between the construction of the modern child and the modern Chinese nation needs first to be traced back to late Qing, when the door of the thousand-year-old Chinese empire was forced open by foreign guns and cannons.

Inventing the Chinese national character

Until the mid-nineteenth century, China had perceived itself as the "Middle Kingdom"—the center of the world. Yet China's encounters with aggressive foreign powers and its devastating military defeats in the second half of the nineteenth century led late Qing intellectuals to reflect on the cause of the country's degeneration from a powerful empire to a subaltern nation on the periphery of the world. Some Chinese believed that the root of the problem lies in the negative nature of the Chinese race. The prominent late Qing reformist, Liang Qichao, for example, proposed in *The New Citizen*, originally published as a series of essays in the *New Citizen Journal* from 1902 to 1906, that the most urgent mission for China was not to learn advanced technologies or political systems from the West, but to forge the masses into new citizens. To illustrate what makes a modern Chinese citizenry, Liang discussed five racial groups in the world—black, red, brown, yellow, and white—from a social Darwinian perspective, which, since Yan Yu's 1898 translation and exposition of T. H. Huxley's *Evolution and Ethics*, had been a major theoretical framework for the Chinese to understand why China had lagged behind Western powers. Based on the evolutionary principle of the survival of the fittest, Liang presented in his Five Races Chart the white race as the strongest and the black weakest. The Chinese race, the yellow race, was placed next to the white, as the second strongest race. Liang employed this essentially racist discourse only to make a point that a renewal of the Chinese people would lead China to catch up with the white race. Liang then analyzed the different national characteristics of the five races seen as the deciding factor in the racial composition. Based on the comparison, Liang concluded that the ideal Chinese national character should possess traits such as progressiveness, adventurousness, self-respect, physical prowess and gregariousness. Sadly, Liang noted, the reality is that the Chinese people had acquired exactly the opposites.

In her important work *Translingual Practice*, Lydia Liu insightfully suggests that the concept of the Chinese national character was imported to Asia by Westerners, mainly Western missionaries, but appropriated by progressive Chinese for nation-building projects. One influential work on this subject in late Qing was Arthur Smith's *Chinese Characteristics*, published first as a series of essays in the *North-China Daily News* of Shanghai in 1889. Smith, an American missionary who lived in North China for many years, vividly described the characteristics of the Chinese race as a whole with elaborate anecdotes, such as a disregard for accuracy, a talent for misunderstanding, an absence of public spirit, conservatism, an absence of sympathy and an absence of nerves. The homogenous and essentialist nature of Smith's descriptions of the Chinese race hardly reflected the reality of a highly stratified Chinese society, but these so-called national characteristics/weaknesses nevertheless shaped "reality" and how the Chinese perceived themselves and were perceived by the West. As Liu states, "Smith's book belongs to a special genre of missionary and imperialist writings that made a huge difference in modern Western perceptions of China and the Chinese, as well as the self-perception of the Chinese and the Westerners themselves" (58). While Smith invented a China for the

Orientalist gaze of the West, Liu suggests, he also introduced a totalizing but enabling discourse about the Chinese to the elite Chinese who tasked themselves with the mission of "saving the nation" and mobilized the discourse for nation-building projects in both late Qing and the Republican period (1912–1949).

Liang Qichao was among the first generation of Chinese intelligentsia who closely connected reforming the national character of the Chinese to the establishment of a modern nation-state. As noted earlier, Liang lamented in *The New Citizen* the absence of the desired characteristics in the Chinese. Yet unlike his Western contemporary who held a totalizing view on the Chinese, Liang suggested that those ideal national characteristics are in fact characteristic of the young, and the negative nature of the Chinese race is limited to the old. As early as 1900 in his essay "On Youthful China," Liang both provided a rationale for and repudiated the then popular saying among the Westerners and Japanese that China is an "old"—declining—empire. Liang first argued that the answer to the question whether a country is old or young depends on whether its people are old or young. Old people were described as indulgent of the past, conservative, pessimistic, cowardly and timid, whereas young people were seen as future-oriented, progressive, optimistic, heroic and adventurous. Since the Qing empire was governed by the old, corrupt and weak, Liang reasoned, China was indeed an old and dying empire. But Liang also refuted this idea by associating the young with a modern Chinese republic in the making. Liang argued that China of the past is not a true nation, for it originated as clans and primitive tribes and was then ruled by feudalist nobles and despotic emperors. The development of a democratic nation, Liang stated, resembles an embryo's development into an adult. China was at the embryonic stage before it entered infanthood of the Shang and Zhou Dynasties (before 771 BCE). From the time of Confucius (around 551 BCE–479 BCE) to the present, Liang wrote, China had been in childhood but was now about to become a youth. Liang reasoned that China had developed so slowly because past rulers had obstructed its natural growth, which then explains why China, only in its childhood now, already *looked* old and dying. In this light, China was mistaken for an old empire, when it was in fact a sick child. As for how China can develop into a "true" nation, Liang turned to the youth of China. As he wrote, "It is the responsibility of Chinese youth to create a youthful China in the future."

The ideal Chinese national character therefore came to conflate with an ideal modern Chinese childhood supposedly possessing those "innate" positive potentials, and the key to the national rise lay in the education of children. The successful cultivation of children's "natural" characteristics thus fundamentally influenced the fate of China. Nevertheless, while Liang made it clear that a youthful China was in the process of becoming, the Chinese youth Liang so passionately spoke of was not an existing demographic group but another social category, like the nation, waiting to be made. Liang's thinking had a tremendous impact on the Chinese imagination of a modern nation in the following decades. As Liu states, "Liang's theory [on new citizenship] exerted a profound influence on Chinese intellectuals that by far exceeded the exigencies of any particular political agenda in the years that followed" (48). Liang's association of national salvation with the young drew the attention of more Chinese to the importance of the issues of children. A theory of the modern child did not become crystalized, however, until the May Fourth period.

May Fourth imagination of a modern child

In 1911 Chinese revolutionaries overthrew the Qing Dynasty and founded the Republic of China in the following year. But as Peter Zarrow suggests, "The new 'Republic of

China' was not republican; many of the old Qing bureaucrats simply stayed in their jobs. Nor did culture, society, and the economy appear to change, even with the collapse of the imperial political structure" (30). Transforming China into a modern nation was still the urgent mission for the educated Chinese. The concept of the Chinese national character continued to be a major discourse during the period and was effectively incorporated into the May Fourth movement. In the narrow sense, the May Fourth movement refers to student demonstrations in Beijing on May Fourth, 1919, against the terms of the Treaty of Versailles, which allowed the transfer of territorial rights in Shandong peninsula from Germany to Japan, instead of returning the sovereignty to China as promised by the Entente Powers as the condition for China to join the Allied axis during World War I. This incident led to a series of nation-wide protests against Japanese imperialism as well as Chinese warlords who had fragmented and weakened the nation to a point where it was forced to sign the treaty to appease Japanese interests (Denton 114). Denton characterizes the movement as "one of the first large-scale expressions of Chinese nationalism" (114). The May Fourth movement is also referred to, in a broad sense, the cultural-intellectual activities preceding and following the incident, also dubbed the New Culture movement. This movement covers a period from the mid-1910s to mid-1920s and is generally seen as the broad cultural dimension of the political protest movement. The New Culture movement was led by progressive (usually Western-trained) Chinese intellectuals and characterized by radical anti-traditionalism aimed at transforming China from a Confucian society into a modern democratic nation through borrowing advanced Western cultural, political and scientific knowledge.

The beginning of the New Culture movement was signaled by the launch of the magazine *New Youth* in September 1915 by Chen Duxiu. Chen opened the first issue with an essay "To Youth," which strongly echoed Liang Qichao's concept of Chinese youth discussed earlier and named the imagined ideal force of a new nation. Like Liang, Chen imagined the ideal youth to be progressive, energetic and fresh. "Youth" was defined not only by age but also, more importantly, by spirit according to Chen. Chinese youth, Chen argued, are youthful in age but old in character, and had been poisoned by Chinese traditions that had made them stale, conservative and incompetent in comparison with Europeans defined in exactly the opposite terms. Believing that China's future belongs to the young, Chen urged Chinese youth to shed tradition and become independent, progressive, aggressive, cosmopolitan, utilitarian and scientific. While Chen's idea of Chinese youth is a further development of Liang's concept, Chen's stance is fundamentally different in his uncompromising anti-traditionalism, a signature gesture of the New Culture movement, which sited the root of the negative nature of the Chinese national character in Chinese "tradition"—encompassing the moral, cultural and political systems of imperial China. The term "tradition," sometimes used interchangeably with "Confucianism," came to represent all social evils and stand in opposition to Western modernity. Inventing a new culture therefore fundamentally rests on constructing a binary between the old (Chinese tradition) and new (Western modernity). To establish a new culture and new nation is to dismantle the old that had supposedly obstructed national development, the core mission of the New Culture movement. Importantly, the self became a crucial site of the battle between the new and the old.

Zhou Zuoren, also a leading New Culturalist, for example, published an influential essay in *New Youth* in 1918, titled "Literature of Man," in which he contended that "Now we should promote a new literature, simply put, 'a literature of man'. What should be discarded is inhuman literature" (100). Zhou argued that Europe discovered the truth of "man" first in the Renaissance and next in the French Revolution, and that women and children were discovered relatively late in the nineteenth century, whereas China had never touched on the issue of man, let alone that of women and children. Zhou urged his countrymen to "discover 'man'" and to "open up the wasteland of man," although "it sounds ridiculous" because man in fact came into existence 4,000 years ago (101). But in China Confucian rituals repress human nature and promulgate asceticism. Especially important is Zhou's idea that children were most dehumanized in imperial China: as part of the human race, children had never been "discovered." In other words, children's "true" nature had not been recognized (1918: 101; 1923: 186). This failure was because the ancients had evinced an incorrect understanding of children in treating them as "miniature" and "incomplete" adults. That is, children were indoctrinated in Confucian classics, and their physical and psychological needs were completely ignored. In reality, Zhou believed, children are "complete individuals," although "physiologically and psychologically different from adults" (1920: 122). What Zhou was suggesting is that Confucianism cruelly ignores children's nature and prematurely indoctrinates them in Confucian morals such as "filial piety, respect for seniors, self-restraint, and compliance" (Zhou Yiqun 339). While the Confucian child represents repressive Confucianism, the implied natural child incarnates a future modern China. The task for May Fourth intellectuals was thus to "discover"—invent—the modern child. The "true" self would emerge once the child, or man in general, is freed from Confucian shackles.

For New Culturalists, the best means to "liberate" man is literature, as Zhou Zuoren suggested in "Literature of Man." Since the problem lay in the minds of the Chinese, learning advanced political theories, sciences and technologies from the West would not fundamentally and thoroughly remedy the sickness of the country. To create a new literature that celebrates "human nature" was thus indispensible to the May Fourth nation-building project to transform the national character. Chinese children's literature, a new form of literature emerging during the same period and allegedly appealing to children's natural interests, was thus also an integral part of the May Fourth movement. But as Li Li argues, "modern Chinese children's literature traveled a path beginning with translated foreign children's literature and then followed by local creation. Translated foreign children's literature had a great impact on the formation and development of Chinese children's literature" (1). One such influential foreign children's book during the period is Zhao Yuanren's translation of *Alice's Adventures in Wonderland*.

The child as the model citizen

The act of translation is not simply a transparent process of rendering a source text into a linguistic equivalent within the target culture, but a process of making new meanings in the local context. Zhao's translation of the Alice book acquired a national status in the sense that it was both producing and produced by the kind of "new culture" May Fourth nationalists were forging. As discussed earlier, the modern child supposedly freed from Confucianism came to embody the May Fourth imagination of a modern China. But what exactly this modern child looked like was at issue, as both Chinese children and adults had already been "contaminated" by Chinese tradition according to May Fourth intellectuals. Yet Zhao's translation of the Alice book provided the May Fourth generation with a concrete form of the modern child. This does not simply mean that the Alice of the original text represents a "liberatory" childhood from the West, which was absent from a backward and tyrannical China nevertheless trying hard to "copy" the West in order to modernize itself, as May Fourth intellectuals themselves believed. The modern child was presupposed and created through translation. While the discourse of the modern child vis-à-vis the repressed traditional child was a product of the New Culture movement, the modern child effected through Zhao's translation epitomized and further produced such nationalist imagination. That is, Alice was made into a "natural" child in the Chinese translation. And one of the "natural" characteristics the modern child was supposed to possess is the so-called "children's natural language"—vernacular Chinese.

Zhou Zuoren's book review particularly stressed that one crucial factor in making Zhao's translation outstanding is his use of vernacular Chinese (142). As early as 1918 Zhou wrote an essay on the problem of translating foreign fairy tales into Chinese, using the translation of Hans Christian Andersen's fairy tales published in the same year as an example. Zhou criticized the translators for using traditional literary Chinese to preach morals and thereby depriving Andersen's tales of their innate value. Zhou perceived Andersen as an "old kid" capable of producing the kind of language used by primitive people, which is also the language of children, Zhou argued. Zhou's understanding of fairy tales reflects his belief in recapitulation theory, which was a popular discourse at that time. Based on the principle that ontogeny recapitulates phylogeny, childhood is to adulthood as primitive society is to advanced civilization. Zhou thus suggested that children's natural characteristics correspond to those of primitive people. Accordingly, since fairy tales were products of primitive civilization, they should also be enjoyed by children.

Zhou proposed that in sharp contrast with Andersen's original stories, the translation is a thin mask of Confucianism. Traditional literary Chinese, the choice of the translators and language of traditional Chinese literati, mediates Confucian morals that repress human nature. As commonly known, the language revolution—replacing traditional literary Chinese with vernacular Chinese—is integral to the literary revolution as part of the New Culture movement. Like Zhou Zuoren's "Literature of Man," Hu Shi's "Some Modest Proposals for the Reform of Literature," published in 1917 in *New Youth*, was a rallying call for the literary revolution, followed in the next year by a series of supporting articles, including Chen Duxiu's "On Literary Revolution," Liu Bannong's "My Opinions on the Reform of Literature," and Hu Shi's "On Instructive Literary Revolution." The literary revolution is essentially a language revolution. In "Some Modest Proposals for the Reform of Literature," for example, Hu Shi called for an end to imitation, allusiveness, floweriness and pedantry characteristic of the classic literary tradition and advocated a new lively language closer to the spoken language. According to Hu, for a long time the spoken and literary languages in China have been turning their backs on each other, whereas the rise of European literary giants began with a "living literature" written in their own "vulgar" language to replace a dead literature in Latin (138). Hu thus advised Chinese writers not to avoid "vulgar diction," two imitable examples of which are *The Water Margin* and *The Journey to the West*, two popular vernacular novels derided as "vulgar" by traditional Chinese literati. In 1919, Hu Shi, Zhou Zuoren and Liu Bannong proposed to the Republican government that China should adopt a unified "national language" (guoyu), and this campaign to unify the pronunciation of myriad Chinese dialects should start from elementary schools. That is, they saw elementary school textbooks as a means to promote the new national language—standardized vernacular Chinese, Mandarin. They suggested that all schools replace textbooks written in the literary language (guowen) with those written in Mandarin (guoyu). The proposal was approved by the Ministry of Education, with the result that the school subject "guowen" (traditional literary Chinese) was officially renamed as "guoyu" (vernacular Mandarin Chinese) in 1920. In the same year Hu Shi published *The Experimental Collection*, the first collection of poems written in vernacular Chinese. One year later, Zhao Yuanren, Hu Shi's close friend, finished his translation of *Alice's Adventures in Wonderland*.

Zhao stated in the preface that his translation is a test for the ongoing language reform and the success of the book indicates the success of the reform. To put it another way, the invention of a standard national spoken language had enabled the translation, and the successful translation justified the creation of a standardized national language. Translating *Alice* was indeed a challenge. As Hu Rong observes, "It looked like a mission impossible to put such a book full of 'nonsense' into Chinese, the vernacular Chinese particularly, since no one had succeeded in the last half century" (430). But Zhao did it beautifully, as shown by the enthusiastic acceptance of his work by his contemporaries. Zhao's success lies in his ability to make it "vibrant" (Zhao 11). As suggested earlier, the traditional literary language is a site of Confucian ethics and dismissed by May Fourth nationalists as pretentious, moribund, decadent and unintelligible to all but the elite literati. Vernacular Chinese came to represent the opposite: lively, popular, natural and devoid of didacticism. "Vibrancy" is precisely what Zhao saw as the nature of vernacular Chinese. Zhao's "vibrant" translation was achieved not only through using vernacular Mandarin Chinese but also through adopting a particular dialect—the "living dialect" of Beijing, as Zhao put it.

Zhao explained in the translator's note that while the narration is translated into vernacular Mandarin Chinese, he used Beijing dialect to translate the conversations. This is because Beijing dialect is "very rustic," "easily understandable," and suitable for lively conversations (15). Zhao included a glossary of "special words" used in the book—local expressions in Beijing. For example, Zhao translated the English word "snake" into Beijing dialect, "changchong" ("long worm" literally), rather than "she" ("snake") in Mandarin. Zhao also heavily used the rhotic vowel "er" ("儿") characteristic of Beijing dialect. Zhao's use of Beijing dialect changed the formal language style of the original text into a colloquial one. One telling example is the moment when Alice finds herself growing after she eats up a cake at the beginning of the story. Since Alice's head and feet grow so far from each other, she wonders if she would be able to put on shoes and stockings for her feet. In Carroll's text, Alice addresses her feet "dears" (20). Zhao did not translate it literally into "qin'ai de" ("亲爱的"), but used "baobao" ("宝宝") (15), meaning "baby." The different styles of the original and translation are not merely a linguistic difference. In Carroll's text Alice's style of expression reveals her upper-middle class identity and trained propriety. As Alice finds herself growing, she "was so much surprised, that for the moment she quite forgot how to speak *good English*" (Carroll 20; emphasis mine). But Carroll's book was written in "good English." Alice tries hard to speak politely and properly despite the fact that she easily loses control of herself in the seemingly arbitrary Wonderland. In the same scene Zhao's translation reads differently: "because Alice was so surprised she quite forgot how to speak" (15). Alice's concern with speech refinement was completely dropped here, a change that foregrounds the translation's "rustic" style, transforming Alice into an uncultivated child. But it is exactly this "vulgar" child that represents the May Fourth "natural" child.

The above example also suggests that Zhao tended to suppress the cultural specificity of foreign words and use words that were more familiar to Chinese readers. Such examples abound in the text. In the chapter "Pig and Pepper," for example, Alice meets the Duchess and her baby. While nursing the baby, Alice finds that it "had a very turn-up nose, much more like a snout than a real nose" (Carroll 63). The baby turns out to be a pig. Zhao translated the word "snout" into "ba jie" ("八戒"), not the literal equivalent in Chinese "zhu bizi" ("猪鼻子"). "Ba jie" is the pig character from *The Journey to the West*, which Hu Shi mentioned in "My Opinions on the Reform of Literature" as a model of vernacular Chinese literature. Zhao in fact emphasized the importance of indigenization in translation in the translator's note: "The translation method of the book is that after I read a sentence in the original text, I first think about how we say it in Chinese and how to make it sound authentically Chinese; and then write it down and check it against the original. I try my best to reach the standard of 'word-to-word accuracy' and keep revising it. But I stop right before it begins to sound like a foreign language, and this is an extremely dangerous moment" (16). Zhao believed that semantic accuracy should not outweigh the natural flow of the translation. Doubtlessly, Zhao's rule to make the foreign text "sound authentically Chinese" had a strong nationalist effect. By effacing the foreignness of the original, Zhao made the translation extremely fluent and immediately recognizable to Chinese readers. As Lawrence Venuti suggests, "The easy readability fosters an illusion of transparency where the second-order status of the translation is effaced and the reader comes to feel as if he or she were reading, not a translation, but the original" (182). Such transparency invited Chinese readers to identify with a national culture defined by every-day and commonsensical knowledge rooted in a specific geographic location. But the national culture Zhao attempted to forge through the translation was still in the process of becoming. It came to embody the antithesis of the thousand-year-old Confucian tradition—vernacular culture closely associated with children.

The vernacular Chinese-speaking Alice thus embodies a new social order; she is what the submissive Confucian child is not. She is curious, active, brave, playful and adventurous, the characteristics associated with the ideal Chinese citizen discussed earlier. Furthermore, Alice is also innocent—innocent of Confucian tradition. Just like the iconoclastic image of May Fourth intellectuals themselves, she is anti-traditional. But Alice's uncompromising radicalism is also the effect of Zhao's translation. In the original text Alice's identity is more ambiguous, straddling both conventional Victorian England and rule-breaking Wonderland. This can be illustrated by a scene in the second chapter "The Pool of Tears." After Alice finds that she has grown abnormally large, she becomes uncertain about who she is and tries to retrieve her old self. Her way is to distinguish herself from Mabel, who, Alice believes, knows very little. Alice first tries to recall what she knows about multiplication and geography, and then to recite a poem "how doth the little—," whose words, however, "did not come *the same* as they used to do" (Carroll 23; emphasis mine). Zhao's translation made two changes to the scene. The first is the title of what Alice tries to recite. In the Chinese version Alice tries to recite "*Elementary Mandarin Chinese*" (*Xiaoxue yu*) (20), not "How Doth the Little Crocodile." The second change is that the words Alice tries to say "seemed to come out *involuntarily*" ("字说出来亦好像不由自主似的") (Zhao 20; emphasis mine).

The two seemingly small changes made a significant change to the identity of Alice. Instead of Isaac Watts' "How Doth the Little Busy Bee," a popular didactic poem about industriousness, the words spoken by Carroll's Alice become a nursery rhyme about a sluggish crocodile luring fish into its mouth with a welcoming smile, a parody of the original poem. That Alice recites the poem in a "wrong" way represents the clash of two contrasting worlds, Wonderland and Victorian England. As her performance contains elements of both worlds, Alice herself also traverses the boundaries between them and, as Jenkins suggests, "resorts to applying familiar scripts to what she discovers there" (80). As the above scene illustrates, when Alice finds herself growing into an abnormal size after eating the cake, she tries to use the knowledge acquired in her own world—Victorian England—to clear up the confusion, but nevertheless fails. Thus, Alice also performs an unconventional self in Wonderland, signified by her "false" memorization of the poem. But Alice's ambiguity is lost in Zhao's translation. Rather than being a parody of social convention, the poem from *Elementary Mandarin Chinese* is a reference to the undergoing language education reform discussed earlier. That Alice recites a poem about a crocodile from *Elementary Mandarin Chinese* signifies her radicalness, rather than conventionality. Zhao skillfully rendered the original crocodile poem into vernacular Chinese, successfully maintaining the form of the original poem. The poem's simplicity, rhythm and entertaining nature made it a perfect example of "natural" children's literature in contrast to didactic Confucian texts. That Alice recites a piece of "modern" children's literature precisely positions her in a new social order imagined by May Fourth intellectuals. In this light, it is not surprising that in the Chinese version the words of the poem "seemed to come out *involuntarily*"—that is, spontaneously, unbound by tradition. Therefore, unlike Carroll's Alice who discloses traces of social convention, Zhao's Alice becomes a radical modern child who embodies a new China.

In the book review Zhou Zuoren suggested that the Alice book would help those adults who had not been completely "poisoned spiritually" reconnect to their childhoods and rediscover their child-hearts. While the "child-heart" is a signifier for childhood innocence closely associated with a new China, the "spiritually poisoned" refers to the adult indoctrinated in Confucianism. That is, the adult had already been molded by Confucianism and seemed irredeemable. But there is a way to transform him into a modern citizen, as Zhou suggested above—to reconnect to childhood and retain the child-heart. For the May Fourth intellectuals, fortunately, there were model adults in the other parts of the world who still regain their child-hearts, like Lewis Carroll. In his preface to the translation, Zhao Yuanren saw Carroll as "a friend of children" (7). Although he did not have his own children, Zhao stressed, Carroll "had many intimate child friends and thus understood children better than their own parents" (7). It is therefore precisely because Carroll retained his child-heart as an adult that he was able to write a book appealing to children. In this light, *Alice* was not merely an entertaining read for Chinese adults and children, but also performative in nature, capable of transforming the degenerate Chinese, especially adults, into idealized citizens.

Bibliography

Carroll, Lewis (2000) *The Annotated Alice: Alice's Adventures in Wonderland & Through the Looking-Glass*. Definitive ed. Introduction and Notes by Martin Gardner. New York: Norton.

——— (1922) *Alisi manyou qijingji* (Alice's Adventures in Wonderland). Trans. Zhao Yuanren. Shanghai: Commercial Press.

Chen, Duxiu (1915) "Jing Gao Qingnian" ("To Youth"). *New Youth* 1(1): 1–24.

Denton, Kirk A. (1996) *Modern Chinese Literary Thought: Writings on Literature, 1893–1945*. Standford, CA: Standford University Press.

Hu, Rong (2010) "Zhao Yuanren's Translation of *Alice's Adventures in Wonderland* and Its Significance in Modern Chinese Literary History." *Frontiers of Literary Studies in China* 4(1): 425–41.

Hu, Shi (1917) "Some Modest Proposals for the Reform of Literature," in Kirk A. Denton (ed.) *Modern Chinese Literary Thought: Writings on Literature, 1893–1945*. Stanford, CA: Stanford University Press, 1996. 123–39.

Jenkins, Ruth Y. (2011) "Imagining the Abject in Kingsley, Macdonald, and Carroll: Disrupting Dominant Values and Cultural Identity in Children's Literature." *The Lion and the Unicorn* 35(1): 67–87.

Li, Li (2010) *Shengcheng yu jieshou: zhongguo ertong wenxue fanyi yanjiu (1898–1949)* (Production and Reception: A Study of Translated Children's Literature in China 1898–1949). Wuhan: Hubei changjiang chubanshe.

Liang, Qichao (1900) "Shaonian zhongguo shuo" ("On Youthful China"), in *Liang Qichao quanji* (Complete Collection of *Liang Qichao's Works*). Vol. 2. Beijing: Beijing chubanshe, 1999. 409–11.

——— (1994) *Xin min shuo* (The New Citizen). Shenyang: Liaoning renmin chubanshe.

Liu, Lydia H. (1995) *Translingual Practice: Literature, National Culture, and Translated Modernity – China, 1900–1937*. Stanford, CA: Stanford University Press.

Venuti, Lawrence (2005) "Local Contingencies: Translation and National Identities," in Sandra Bermann and Michael Wood (eds.) *Nation, Language, and the Ethics of Translation*. Princeton, NJ: Princeton University Press. 177–203.

Zarrow, Peter (2005) *China in War and Revolution, 1895–1949*. New York: Routledge.

Zhou, Yiqun (2009) "Confucianism," in Don S. Browning and Marcia J. Bunge (eds.) *Children and Childhood in World Religions: Primary Sources and Texts*. New Brunswick, NJ: Rutgers University Press. 337–92.

Zhou, Zuoren (2012) "Andesen de *Shi zhi jiu*" [1918] (Andersen's *Nine out of Ten*), in Liu Xuyuan (ed.) *Zhou Zuoren lun ertong wenxue* (Zhou Zuoren's Discussion on Children's Literature). Beijing: Haitun shubanshe. 94–99.

——— (2012) "Ren de wenxue" [1918] (Literature of Man), in *Zhou Zuoren lun ertong wenxue*. 100–08.

——— (2012) "Ertong de wenxue" [1920] (Children's Literature), in *Zhou Zuoren lun ertong wenxue*. 122–30.

——— (2012) "*Alisi manyou qijingji*" [1922] (*Alice's Adventures in Wonderland*), in *Zhou Zuoren lun ertong wenxue*. 140–43.

——— (2012) "Ertong de shu" [1923] (Children's Books), in *Zhou Zuoren lun ertong wenxue*. 184–88.

9

VIOLENCE AND DEATH IN BRAZILIAN CHILDREN'S AND YOUNG ADULT LITERATURE

Alice Áurea Penteado Martha

Suffering and death are very common themes in children's and young adult (YA) literature if the embedding of the genre in popular narratives, which normally contain violence of all sorts, is taken into account. Macabre stories and bloody scenes, including the deaths of human characters, are recurring episodes in fairy tales. Many readers still feel shaken after reading Andersen's *The Red Shoes*, due to the cruelty suffered by the heroine Karen, enchanted by a pair of red shoes she received when still a very young girl, and which were destroyed by the old lady who adopted her after her mother's death. When the girl's christening day arrived, the rich old lady gave her a new pair of red shoes in which she constantly danced without stopping. To end the non-stop ballet, the executioner amputated Karen's feet but her pain continued until her death. However, according to Vera Teixeira de Aguiar, death episodes in fairy tales do not constitute death as a central narrative theme. It is "not even an issue to be solved or a suffering that should be overcome since it is dealt with naturally: the tale presents the child with the information that death is a fact of life and its presence may create or solve conflicting situations" (Aguiar 2010, p. 37). It is necessary, according to the author, considering its function within the narrative construction.

However, conditions of violence and death gradually vanish from children's and young adult books as they become appropriated by the school, a bourgeois institution, with strict mental hygiene principles, whose aims are generally bound to Christian and moralizing values. A host of images of an idealized world, inhabited by perfect and immortal beings, exempted from struggling for survival, replace the darker motifs and secure a place in texts for children. Bloody tales were also rewritten to insert them within the new social, political and economic reality.

The erasure of the theme of death from children's literature has been part of a wider historical process, whereby during the first half of the twentieth century death became a taboo area and replaced sex as the principal forbidden subject (Ariès 1974, p. 92), although in children's and YA literature the taboo on sex remained in place. Ariès shares a view that in modern society the suppression of mourning also produces suppressed trauma (p. 90). Even though avoided or masked, death was for a long time an absent theme in children's literature, which reflected the control adults exercized over the literature written for young people. It may also be the product of adults' fear at life's passage. In Brazil, during the 1970s, children's and YA literature was thoroughly renewed so that readers would be shown realistically "life as it is." This aim was carried out by the *Coleção do pinto* [Chicken Stories Series], published by the Editora Comunicação of Belo Horizonte, Brazil. The most emblematic book of the series is *O menino e o pinto do menino* [The boy and the boy's chick] (1975), by Wander Piroli. Although the chicken dies at the end, the story underscores the tensions experienced by a family living in a big city. However, as Regina Zilberman argues, the causes of the depicted problems were not clarified, events causing stress were generally insoluble – such as the conflicts in urban areas that are described in Wander Piroli's book– and the point of view was that of the adult, so the issue, although innovative, ended up generating a series of unresolved conflicts. (Zilberman, 2005, p. 199).

In the wake of the so called real-life literature, contemporary production of Brazilian children's literature began problematizing with more frequency and quality the notion of childhood as a period of unconcern and happiness. In fact, this conception was highly useful for such institutions as the school and the family, interrogating a literary decadence in whose creative or adaptive process there was every effort to eliminate suffering and cruelty. Idealized and perfect characters, reared in unpolluted milieus, are replaced by children and adolescents that are in the midst of psychological maelstroms, live in inhospitable environments and experience violent feelings and emotions. Provoking themes, understood as confrontations that fictionally comprise evolutionary stages lived by humans, gather forces and may be important catalysts for young readers to acknowledge their worries. In fact, such distress represents the fears that they meet on a daily basis: death, separation, violence, identity crisis, choices, relationships, losses and others.

Several possibilities exist for approaching "violence and death" as a thematic pair, ranging from that which causes the outcome in an unjust, irresponsible and frivolous way, to the death of civilizations, cultures, beliefs, fauna, flora, people. It is crucial to discuss the substance derived from any of these issues with young readers "in a sincere, honest and open way, as events happen and how they may not occur ... Understanding death as the natural closing of a cycle, not excluding pain, suffering, nostalgia, feelings of loss" (Abramovich, 1989, p. 114).

Analysis of the methods many contemporary Brazilian authors employ for the symbolic construction of the real turns on the presupposition that literature reflects, transfigures and, at the same time, triggers reflections of the world and people's experience. It is a complex textual process and requires fine sensitivity in the narrative strategy to maintain a balance between feelings and emotions and moral perspective. So that, to express the world as a whole, the works need to get away from clichés, should work with the language in all its nuances and meaning possibilities, and valorize its sound, semantic and syntactic resources, among other items.

The discussions of the types of manifestations of violence and death in contemporary Brazilian production for children and young adults try to recognize whether such literary works can express, translate and shape the emotions and feelings that, frequently at the same time, enchant and torment people of all times and places. It is also asked whether they give priority to the ways narrative is constructed, which may reveal degrees of closeness and alignment between readers and fictional characters.

As previously commented, controversial themes from the 1970s to the present are not rare in children's and YA Brazilian literature. For instance, Lygia Bojunga employs negative affect in various narratives: loneliness in *Bolsa amarela* [Yellow Bag] (1976), in which Raquel's desires may not receive any responses within the traditional family; tense family relationships and loss in *Corda bamba* [Tightrope] (1979), in which Mary experiences a difficult circus apprenticeship and witnesses the death of her parents; and suicide in *Meu amigo pintor* [My friend the painter] (1987), in which ten-year-old Claudio's reflections on the death of a neighbor lead to a meditation about the meaning of death, art and politics. Marina Colasanti also deals with the theme of death in the short story "Onde os oceanos se encontram" [Where the oceans meet], published in *Doze reis e a menina no labirinto do vento* [Twelve kings and the young girl in the labirinth of the wind] (1978). The short story narrates events in the life of two sisters who, moved by passion and jealousy, try to conquer the love of a man and finally cause his death. Although at different times there is a deepening vision of childhood and adolescence as periods of intense vulnerability in the family and the school, contemporary literary works, following the footsteps of Lygia Bojunga, Marina Colasanti and others, have found within the force of the language of the imaginary the road towards the subjectification of young readers. In fact, they deal beautifully and with delicacy with several themes that may scare unprepared parents and teachers rather than young people.

A contemporary and emblematic story that deals with the theme of death is Graziela Hetzel's *O jogo de amarelinha* [The Game of Hopscotch] (Manati, 2007). The story narrates the overcoming of the trauma produced by the death of Letícia's mother and the acceptance of the step-mother, a character fraught with symbolism derived from fairy tales. The third-person narrator focuses on Letícia and narrates the story of a girl who, in the children's game of hopscotch, refuses to reach the home base called Heaven. In Heaven live all those people she loved and lost forever. "In Heaven lies her small dog Xerife; her guinea pig Joaninha ... Clara, Letícia's mother is there too. Has no one the sense to understand why she never reaches it?" (Hetzel, 2007, p. 8). Although the narrative voice is in the third person and maintains a distance between the narrator and the events, the slipping into character focalization shortens the distance. In the first part of the enunciation of the passage, one may easily recognize the narrator's voice referring to the young girl and her losses. In the harrowing question "Has no one the sense to understand why she never reaches it?" readers cannot determine the speaking voice with certainty, but will assume it is probably Letícia. The use of free indirect discourse mingles the voices and reduces the distance between the voice that narrates and that of the child character. The same linguistic resource also promotes the alignment of readers and the events narrated.

Another interesting aspect is the deconstruction of the evil image of the step-mother. Primordial narratives are full of its high symbolic meaning, the cause of so much suffering to orphan girls. According to Bruno Bettelheim, "the fantasy of the wicked step-mother not only preserves the good mother intact, it also prevents having to feel guilty about one's angry wishes against her" (Bettelheim, 1976, p. 86).

In her picturebook *O guarda-chuva do vovô* [Grandfather's umbrella] (2008), Carolina Moreyra, whose style is characterized by a minimalist narrative, does not employ niceness and platitude to write on the theme of death from the point of view of children. Colloquial language, short, simple and objective phrases valorize the voice of the child, which narrates the clear-cut idea of gradual distancing and absence of trauma in the period leading up to the death of the grandfather: "One day I perceived that grandpa was somewhat different and asked my father why he was shrinking" (Moreyra, 2008). The text's simple structure brings about an uncomplicated connection with the narrative demise, or rather, after a period of illness, grandfather dies, which provides readers with the natural stages of life, and makes easy the assimilation of loss, and the awareness of gain, such as being given grandfather's umbrella after his death. "I glanced at grandpa's house, which is his no more. I was given his umbrella as a gift" (Moreyra, 2008). The chaacters, even the narrator, lack names: they are named by their kinship, such as the young girl, the grandmother, grandfather, father; in fact, it is a strategy to insert the readers within the narrated world, who align themselves with the people thus named: "Grandma used to bake a chocolate cake for teatime and so we used to call grandpa. But he never came" (Moreyra, 2008).

Two distinct narrative manners are underscored when the theme of death and violence is presented to young people. Lygia Bojunga describes interiorized conflicts; rather than violent episodes, she presents the great fissures that events cause to the characters. On the other hand, Luís Dill gives priority to the brutishness of events and explicit physical viclence mainly committed by young people against young people.

Although the above-mentioned themes in Lygia Bojunga are not precisely new, so many conflicts have never been dealt with in a single narrative such as *Sapato de salto* [High-heeled shoes] (2006). Its discourse simultaneously highlights vehemence, courage, sensitivity and artistic care. The eleven-year-old Sabrina is taken to a home for children's care by her mother before the latter commits suicide. In the orphanage she experiences sexual abuse and is hated by the matron of the house. As if these events are not enough, the saga of her sufferings is just starting. When she is returned to her aunt, she receives the news of her mother's death: she had tied a stone to her body and thrown herself into the river. Living with her grandmother is torture: broken by a life of hardships and sufferings, the old woman wallows in an imaginary world filled with clotheslines where she hangs the motifs of her madness. In spite of the numberless problems surrounding her, the girl feels happy in the family house until she witnesses the murder of her aunt. Survival pushes her towards a pathway suggested by her former employer who, in their encounters in the bedroom, does not give her presents but tips. Sabrina solves her daily hunger problem by eventual encounters with the butcher in a wood on the banks of the nearby river. This is also the place where the boy who enchanted Sabrina has a love affair with an older lad. After so many misfortunes, Sabrina and her grandma are received into the house of the boy's mother.

The narrative is organized into fourteen titled chapters, some of which are subdivided into topics. The first chapter, "O segredo azul fraquinho" [The light blue secret], comprises a multiplicity of perspectives to narrate sexual abuse, one of the strongest and most painful events in Sabrina's life. The event is highlighted by the oscillation of points of view, between showing and hiding the feelings of the narrator and the characters that witness the episode. The first few lines of the text reveal three contrasting perspectives: on the arrival of Sabrina at the house of the Gonçalves family, the matron Dona Matilde is introduced to the reader with the narrator's not so favorable comments; on the other hand, the matron reveals a lack of sympathy with the unlucky girl and anticipates her future bad relations with her, whereas her husband, Mr Gonçalves, Sabrina's future seducer, treats the newcomer with the greatest kindness.

The attitudes and feelings of the characters and the narrator intertwine in opposing focuses and form the network of the narrative's perspectives. When focusing on Dona Matilde, the narrator is always direct and the reader is left with no doubts about her: she is wicked, lacking every feeling and does not tolerate the girl. In the case of Mr. Gonçalves, the tension between adult seduction and the child's naivety is revealed in slow motion, as the silent and cold crawling of the snake towards the victim. Actions trigger the seduction game marked by cunning in planning vis-à-vis the enchantment of the girl who, for the first time ever, receives care and attention. The game produces its secret: for the male, hunting the prey; for the girl, a game of hide and seek.

A new perspective occurs when Sabrina traces a flower on paper. She remembers a girl who used to escape from the orphanage to seek her father. One day the girl did not come back and Sabrina concluded that she had met her father. The carefully prepared trap by the landlord also makes the girl believe that she had also met her father to whom she offered the picture. After such a gesture, the landlord "wanted to know whether other lessons were also learned as that one. He entered her room and lay on her bed, as if he were inventing a new game" (Bojunga, 2006, p. 20). The secret "enlivened his life but brought heavy shades on hers." Henceforth Sabrina did not pay attention to her studies nor did she think about the colors of her feelings and emotions; light blue gave way to black.

With the arrival of Aunt Inês, Sabrina's existence is perceived from the girl's point of view and from that of her demented grandmother and her dead mother. The suicide event is introduced by the aunt, directly and without any roundabout ways: mother, hugging a huge stone, drowned in the river, immediately after leaving the newly born child in a home for infants. Further, the grandmother's gaze is directed towards the objects she received together with the news of her daughter's death, reminding her daily of that final touch. She hangs stones on the clothes lines as the marks of the tragedy.

Sabrina's history is also reconstructed through the mother's eyes by the mementos left by her: the escape; the report to her friend Marlene on the difficulties to survive after being abandoned by the child's father; the message written on the birth of the child; the farewell to dear life. The other message is left on the child when she is left at the Home for Abandoned Children, giving her an identity. The messages fulfill their revealing role: they explain the mother's decisive moments and border situations, also crucial in Sabrina's life. It seems that by osmosis the girl had already crossed these frontiers before her birth.

In *Sapato de salto*, Sabrina's mother, still a young woman, goes beyond the frontier of the unnameable and the unknown, and, through the ritual of note writing, explains life and death from the young woman's perspective. The solution of the adolescent mother's conflicts is translated by escapism, by sexual promiscuity, by aggressive behavior and, at last, by suicide. Materializing "psychological autopsy," the notes reveal the angst of the young mother with regard to the forfeiting of her illusions and of Dona Gracinha's hopes for a better life for her daughter. Death, within the context of Inês's cold-blooded murder, witnessed by the young girl and by Dona Gracinha, is also a theme. After a violent struggle, the aunt takes hold of the revolver in the man's pocket but is herself killed when he deflects the shot.

Characterized by different formal and thematic marks, proper to the age bracket of the readers and inherent to the social and cultural context of authors and receptors, Dill's narratives *Todos contra Dante* [All against Dante] (2008) and *Beijo mortal* [The fatal kiss] (2009) feature a problematizing language and complex narrative techniques. They comprise themes previously prohibited to younger readers, among which death, kidnapping, disappearances, separations, identity crises, choices, relationships, losses, sexuality, affectivity and others may be mentioned.

The protagonist in *Todos contra Dante* creates a blog in which a dialogue is maintained with his namesake, Dante Alighieri, the author of the *Divine Comedy* (written between 1307 and 1321), to whom he narrates his dreams and the violence committed by his peers against him. The boy, hailing from a poor borough and, therefore, belonging to a different social class, is harassed every day by his classmates since he does not meet the standard beauty type and shuns the consumer life style of the group. Besides undergoing psychological aggression, he is beaten and finally murdered. Bullying is currently an emerging theme in society and fiction, with constant reports of violence in Brazilian schools and worldwide as the book's *post-scriptum* "The dark motif" reveals. In the paratext, Dill narrates the story of a 13-year-old girl who was beaten to death by her peers, close to the school she attended. The author informs the readers that the story was based on a real event and thus makes one think of the strategy to transform the real thing into an aesthetic product. He builds a close tie between the two worlds since the theme of violence among young people and the school milieu are the daily experience of young readers.

It is highly relevant to underscore the way the narrator inserts violence into the structure and organization of the narrated world of *Todos contra Dante*. Through this strategy, there is an intertwining of attitudes and feelings of narrator, protagonist and other characters. The narrator's point of view may be divided into multiple perspectives, as that of Manuela's and Dante's:

> Manuela sat at the table set for dinner. Light from the street easily penetrated the room through the wide L-shaped windows. The glare seemed to enhance the colors of things and the texture of the plates: soufflé vegetables, red lettuce salad with cubes of cheese and celery, chicken meat with cream and rosemary sauce. He struggled to control his dizziness …
>
> (Dill, 2008, p. 8).
>
> […].
> Hello, my Florentine namesake. Here I am once more. Through how many tortures did you have to pass to reach Paradise? Inferno, then Purgatory, right?
> (Dill, 2008, p. 15).

Diversified textual structures, such as links, chats, blogs, items which are very close to young readers, are the stuff of the narrated matter. In the several links (1, 2, 3, 5, 6 and 7, for instance), placed on the left-hand pages, the third-person narrator knows the feelings and the thoughts of the characters: "Owing to the insistence of his colleague and neighbor, David kept the timetable he had on the pitcher's mound. Already in the warm-up, he realized the error: he just couldn't play as usual" (Dill, 2008, p. 12).

In other links (4, 8 and 12, for instance), some passages from Dante's *Divine Comedy* bring forth the dialogue with the young protagonist whose voice is inserted in a blog on the pages at the right. The boy confides to the writer his feelings for Geovana and compares them to the poet's pain on his lover's death (Dill, 2008, p. 15). He even describes the torments suffered at school and thus enhances explicit intertextuality with the *Divine Comedy*, as noted above.

In the pages with the title *dialogue*, several conversations ensue, in direct discourse between characters, on a mobile telephone, and also, face to face, with the consequent restriction of the narrator's voice. In other conversations, there are several commentaries of the community around an internet site under the heading *I screw Dante*, in which colleagues discuss such issues as: "Define Dante's nose," "Disease or sheer ugliness?", "Did u fuck the ugly one this week?", where the narrative voice vanishes:

> Description: community of Dante's colleagues, that slim urchin, shrunk guy, with the look of a beggar, a nose that seems more like a trunk, two bloodshot eyes. Type of guy working as an extra in a terror film, sort of creature that gives the greatest fright to the gang, it's the authentic ugly one.
>
> (Dill, 2008, p. 11).

Beijo mortal [The fatal kiss] (2009) is another representation of a violent world in which Dill's characters are active. The different mode of the narrative construction results from the layout of events at two different instances. They are narrated in the present as if the readers were following the events in real time. On the one hand, the narrator has Guilherme's actions in focus; he is the ringleader behind every tragedy, along with his friends Betinho and Cabeça: "Guilherme, Betinho and Cabeça walk naturally through the streets of the borough. Although they carry weapons and in spite of their arrogance, they do not cause any suspicion or fear in the people who eventually cross their path [...]" (Dill, 2009, p. 40). On the other hand, here is also shown the interest of Francisco, a younger man, who tries to understand how the massacre occurs, so that, six months later he undertakes some research and interviews people involved (Dill, 2009, p. 21).

The narrative unit is maintained by the event of the lads' massacre and by motives that go through the construction of the narrated environment, inhabited by adolescents who experience feelings and emotions lived by young people of all social strata, such as immature love, jealousy, family relationships, identity issues, self-knowledge, losses and loneliness.

The characters receive their psychological outlines not merely by the narrator's voice but through attitudes and actions in rapid dialogue among themselves. Frequently they are identified by changes in the focalization level, a resource that exposes their feeling in discourses that mix the voice of the narrator with that of the young people. This may be seen in the passage in which Francisco reveals his emotions when he meets his dream-girl Elisa: "She knows my name, he concludes near the love circle. Better still: she does not call me by my nickname" (Dill, 2009, p. 81).

The readers follow the growth of the inner tension that the massacre developed in Cabeça's psyche brought about by the near erasure of the boundary between the voice of the narrator and that of the character. This aspect favors easily his introduction into the fictional world and consequently the relationships between literature and reality:

> Cabeça, the only boy standing up, is close to the window in Guilherme's room, and looks persistently outside, Don't know, chap, don't know, he mumbles in a low voice; the persisting pain in his stomach which started during the last hour is torturing him even though he had not eaten anything since the night of the crime. It was not hunger
>
> (Dill, 2009, p. 73).

Besides the internal factors that make up the aesthetic construction of the text, the publishing house also invests in the book's external aspects and in the graphic design to bring the readers closer. By the end of the narrative, Francisco Müller Moreno gives details about the massacre which, in his opinion, was provoked by a simple exchange of kisses, in a blog written in the jargon of police journalism. Blog insertion in the plot (an interesting communication and updated strategy at the instance of writing the text) and the use of a new and objective style of language filled with items employed by young people in their daily life, are resources that really engage the readers: "All started at the government-run school, many days before the shooting. After dating G.P.W., 15, in a come-together, the girl T.J.M., 14, exchanged kisses with F.S.S., 14. Caught red-handed by G.P.W., a terrible strife ensued between the boys" (Dill, 2009).

The literary works presented in this essay corroborate statements by Antonio Candido (1976) on the types of representation of society within the textual structure or, more precisely, the internalization of themes, such as death and violence, in the narrative organization. In real life, violence is responsible for social disorder and family rupture, among other factors, whereas in the construction of the artistic object it may manifest itself in the destabilization of literary rules of language, genres, structured elements and others. As aesthetic objects, these literary works mirror the real thing and even though they do not always represent the good and the beautiful, they show situations and feelings that acknowledge basic truths to the readers. While reading the narrative, the readers simulate experimenting with similar situations to those experienced by the characters. However, distancing makes the readers, also the objects of disorder in their daily activities, reflect on their own experiences, opting or not for their rejection.

Bibliography

Abramovich, Fanny (1989) *Literatura infantil: gostosuras e bobices*. São Paulo: Scipione.

Aguiar, Vera Teixeira de (2010) "A morte na literatura: da tradição ao mundo infantil". In: Aguiar, V.T.De; Ceccantini, J.L.; Martha, A.A.P. *Heróis contra a parede*. Estudos de literatura infantil e juvenil. São Paulo: Cultura Acadêmica; Assis: ANEP.

Ariès, Philippe (1974) *Western Attitudes toward Death: From the Middle Ages to the Present*. Translated by Patricia M. Ranum. Baltimore and London: Johns Hopkins University Press.

Bettelheim, Bruno (1976) *The Uses of Enchantment: The Meaning and Importance of Fairy Tales*. New York: Alfred A. Knopf.

Bojunga, Lygia (2006) *Sapato de salto*. Rio de Janeiro: Casa Lygia Bojunga.

Candido, Antonio (1976) *Literatura e sociedade*. 5th ed. São Paulo: Duas Cidades.

Dill, Luís (2008) *Todos contra Dante*. São Paulo: Cia das Letras.

Dill, Luís (2009) *Beijo mortal*. Porto Alegre: Dulcinéia.

Hetzel, Graziela B. (2007) *O jogo de amarelinha*. Rio de Janeiro: Manati.

Moreyra, Carolina (2008) *O guarda-chuva do vovô*. Illustrated by Odilon Moraes. São Paulo: DCL.

Zilberman, Regina (2005) *Como e por que ler a literatura infantil*. São Paulo: Objetiva.

PART II

Historical contexts and national identity

10

INDIGENOUS AND JUVENILE
When books from villages arrive at bookstores

Maria Inês de Almeida

> Consideré que aun en los lenguages humanos no hay proposición que no implique el universo entero, decir el tigre es decir los tigres que lo engedraron, los ciervos y tortugas que devoró, el pasto de que se alimentaron los ciervos, la tierra que fue madre del pasto, el cielo que dio luz a la tierra.
>
> (J. L. Borges)

While researching how books recently produced by indigenous peoples enter the Brazilian publishing market and educational scene, I came across an intriguing observation: in general, books by indigenous authors are placed in the section dedicated to juvenile literature. What characterizes them as such seems to be, at first sight, the attractive covers, the profusion of illustration, the colors, the economy of words, the apparent lightness of themes. It is also evident that marks of orality persist in these texts and hence they are suitable for reading aloud. Also apparent, in most cases, is a strong relation with the traditional narratives and ancestral voices which contribute to the structuring of communities. Books for children, in general, contain teachings about citizenship, which connects them with principles that govern civilization.

How and where are these voices expressed within the texts? In order to better understand so-called "indigenous literature", and perhaps, to a great extent, "juvenile literature", beyond limiting labels, it is necessary to see in them, at least in the national pedagogic effort, a tradition that evolves in consonance with history, seeking to rescue the lived experience – a re-writing of the world of books – but which is finally recognized as a suppression of individual memory.

From that suppression of memory comes a necessary emphasis on reading, a practice able to restore to words their primordial resonance, which would allow access to the language of the other and to a renewed knowledge of the art of narrating, because it is grounded in an absence of narrator self-consciousness. In general, contemporary forms of narrative, not just those of Indians and children, bring modern concepts of authorship and narration into conjunction with a creative instance, once a text can be understood as an actualization or transmission of voices that are manifested in acts of reading. Literary writing may then be subsumed into orality, because, as an activity not limited to the two-dimensionality of books, orality extends its foundational structure into virtual space, in infinite connections with the outside. Because the text's fruition, even when contained in a book, is increasingly tied to vocal performance, the literary construction comes into being as a repetition and reception of external discourses: the text is expressed as a comment and a listening.

Thus, the decentered reading position to which certain texts lead the reader refers to the anonymity and to the impersonality of a writing that lets itself be possessed by the memory of the other. Reading and writing are conditioned by these texts to the practice of "self-nonidentification" (Blanchot 1993 p. 384) in favor of a narrative demand, and are invested with ubiquity by the conjunction of seeing and saying. They are therefore governed by what Blanchot called "narration that is governed by the neutral" (384), a voice always different from the one who pronounces it, absent in the one who transports it, not creating a center. Literature, then, is made within the community of a text, that is, in writing and reading processes where incompleteness and experimentation lead to thinking, to the interchange between body and word. While the simple act of reading is an actualization of voices, it restates the precariousness of the text and the risk of thinking.

Indigenous authors and writing procedures

To what extent are the writing procedures of indigenous authors and the outcomes of these procedures similar to those in contemporary literary production in general? Over 500 works of indigenous authorship were published in Brazil in the decades after 1980.[1] Most were written by young teachers still in training, who represent their ethnic community and seek to reinforce, revitalize, or even invent their ancestral marks and signs, either making explicit or legitimating the belongingness to a certain territory, which has often been subject to questioning by national authorities. While mediating between village and city, these young writers become political leaders as well. Through linguistic and iconic marks, and recognizing the importance of illustrations, they work as writers to ensure that the public will hear their ancestral stories. It is very significant for the Brazilian educational scene that it has been officially acknowledged that there are still around 200 indigenous languages spoken in Brazil. From these, around half are already the object of reading in village schools, thanks to the efforts of these indigenous teachers – a category created by the Brazilian Estate in 1988, when a new Constitution was promulgated, legally ensuring to each of the indigenous peoples a differentiated and specific school education:

> Art. 210. Minimum contents will be established for the primary education, so as to ensure a common basic instruction and respect to national and regional cultural and artistic values.
>
> (my translation)

> § 2.nd The regular primary education will be administered in the Portuguese language, while indigenous communities are also ensured the use of their native languages and their own learning processes.
>
> (my translation)

The acknowledgement that a literary corpus is emerging from the different ethnic groups, that different oral traditions are being transformed into writing, and that the experience of authorship does not erase the multiple voices of a community, points back to the very origin of books. Unconventional forms and techniques, through which this literature is established, provide their producers and receptors with activities and experiences in which oral speech and writing are so much entangled that voice and letter are faces of a poetics that is only manifest in an explicitly non-silent reading. This situation is in turn mimicked in procedures and formulae of composition and publication, which over time may perhaps become less and less conscious. As Michel de Certeau states: "To read without uttering the words aloud or at least mumbling them is a 'modern' experience, unknown for millennia. In earlier times, the reader interiorized the text; he made his voice the body of the other; he was its actor" (1984 pp.175–76).

What is evident in the materiality of these new published texts and books is that they are a result of education, and have generated a written dissemination, in literate environments, of the oral tradition of some different social or ethnic groups in Brazil, and their forms mark an editorial procedure concerned with not breaking with such oral traditions, including by announcing new forms of writing and reading literature, because, for one thing, their target public, the communities, is not very familiar with written verbal expression. Production and consumption of literature would then be tied to the work by the voice, the preferred material form of these writings. Here I explicitly refer to books authored by representatives of indigenous communities and published in the last three decades. These books are usually edited in workshops to produce teaching material for their own schools. Most of them are written in indigenous languages or are bilingual (Portuguese/Indigenous language). However, some language communities, such as Pataxó, have almost entirely lost their indigenous language and communicate in Portuguese, albeit in a form that incorporates local words – especially names of things – and local nuances, which in books, in combination with expressive illustrations, eloquently convey a local sense of place. In *A ciência do dia e da noite* (2012, The Knowledge of the Day and Night), for example, the phases of the diurnal cycle are sharply realized by activities and the senses. Mid-afternoon (14.00–16.30) is marked by the perceptible changes in the heat of the sun and the strength of the breeze, by the calls of particular birds (chororão, tururum, jacu), and by the characteristic activities of this time of day.

The accompanying illustration – as with the other illustrations in *A ciência do dia e da noite* – could be characterized as "Naïve" or "Primitive" art, in its many characteristics that resemble children's drawings (see Figure 1): it pays no regard to (Western) perspective, so that the objects furthest from the viewer are also the largest, and both color saturation and precision of detail do not decrease with distance. The use of "X- ray perspective", which, depicting what is seen by the mind rather than by the eyes, allows viewers to see inside houses and the canopies of trees, seems a deliberate strategy to disregard realism in order to show what is important to the community. The chosen palette – dominated by cool greens – contrasts with the previous, heat-of-the-day illustration, while a pervasive canting of objects toward the right suggests a kinetic energy as the villagers move into another, active phase of their day. While the illustration seems primarily to confirm the value of the villagers' everyday life, right down to the recognizable depictions of the oversized and colloquially referenced jacu[pemba] birds toward the top right corner, it is also effective in conveying this value to outside readers.

Among new oral tradition writers, such as the team of teachers and students who produced *A ciência do dia e da noite*, the act of narrating functions also as a deconstruction of literary representation as the texts cut through the appearances of discourse to express beingness. By means of a textual expression of "I always speak of another place" the narrator confesses his non-knowledge, the empty space of the enunciation that, because it is marginal, lends substance to the presence of the other, his material body, his voice. In this practice of literary collective production, narrator and reader are dissociated in separated acts, as if they both belonged to different, remote practices, when reading and writing were not assigned to the same individuals. This dissociation leads to old reading

Figure 10.1 Mid-afternoon in *A ciência do dia e da noite*, p. 20.
Source: Reproduced with kind permission of FALE/UFMG.

and writing procedures, when writing was the act of inscribing, marking a surface with signs that didn't always carry clear meanings, and reading was to decode signs so that listeners could finally attribute meanings to them.[2]

Indigenous writers, while translating their oral poetic forms into written language, forge a literature in which the reading, with their voices, is superimposed upon the writing and visual expression. They are, after all, privileged authors for a study of the forms assumed by literature in post-modernity and also in the way that, starting from a notion of community, contemporary narratives have been structured: readers, on one side, and scribes, on the other, who continually act as transcribers of an already existing text – as carriers of the letters, but not owners of the meaning.

When edited into book form, representations of the indigenous universe, in which myth, science, art, life and history all coincide, contribute to enlarge the concept of literature as such. In order to understand how the insertion of this new literature into the contemporary market occurs, editors and educators alike need to consider the semiotic implications of a mode of writing in which impersonalism is an outstanding feature. A new approach to a new literature, to expand this concept to a literary explosion, will reshape the boundaries of Brazilian literary history. The texts of so-called minorities, spaces for a new configuration of voices and authorships – but always alien – are offered to history, even though at its margins. The understanding of textuality expressed by

Portuguese writer Maria Gabriela Llansol offers the productive possibility of employing the term "textualities" rather than indigenous literature (or juvenile literature):

> But what can give us the textuality that narrativeness does not (and, strictly speaking, never did) (…) I have stated that we are created, far away, distant from ourselves: textuality is this unlikely and unpredictable geography of creation; the body of textuality is creative imagination, sustained by a puissant function – the swing of intensity. It allows us, at each one's costs, risks and joy, to approach the strength, the real that will come to our body of affections[3]
>
> (my translation).

To obtain a better understanding of our literary system in its relations with Brazilian society would require an investigation into the way historiography has addressed, since their beginnings, both indigenous cultural production and popular literature, and how these have been mediated to schools and to middle readers. Therefore, it would be useful to determine what approaches have been taken to oral and popular traditions, and to understand why oral literature has been excluded from literary, theoretical and critical studies, to be present only in ethnographic and sociological studies, under the umbrella of folklore. In this historical process, literary production and consumption in Brazil have apparently become practices restricted to a socio-cultural elite. The alienation of voices has then resulted in the alienation of readers from popular classes and ethnic minorities.

With the new schooling and cultural diffusion policies brought with the democratization of the country, and with the arrival of new audiovisual media that by and large dispenses with the traditional skills of linguistic performance (knowledge of the standard written language), reading and writing possibilities are so much expanded that a new concept of literature is required to comprehend most of those texts whose readers and writers, historically marginalized, have not yet found a place in the world of books.

Literary education and criticism have not effectively recognized the need for this semiotic expansion of writing and thus exclude the majority of the Brazilian population from the literary system, even though this majority, in their own way, has always consumed and produced literary art. Perhaps because there has been a lack of theoretical conceptualization sufficient to endow oral production with a status equivalent to writing, critics and historians have ignored it. With the advance of studies in language, cognitive processes, linguistic sciences and with the re-approximation of art and science, it now seems timely to attempt to theoretically unite these two ends of the cultural universe: writers from the erudite, literary tradition, and writers in progress, scribes of the oral tradition. After all, the gesture that originates the two types of works represents the contradictory attempt to annul the individual act of writing in favor of the community. In the absence of adequate theoretical parameters, both critical instances in their different ambits and the school instances in their different levels contribute to establish labels which, though didactic, are also unfavorable to the expansion of worlds to which these same texts are directed.

A practice implemented at Universidade Federal de Minas Gerais, in Núcleo Transdisciplinar de Pesquisas Literaterras (Transdisciplinary Center for Literature Research), has brought an opportunity to work on the expansion of the Brazilian literary space. "Intercultural workshops" with indigenous researchers as participants explore reading, writing, illustration, translation, layout development, and publication practices, and thereby establish a dialogue amongst quite different languages and cultural traditions. The language and speech forms of the conqueror (that is, Portuguese) are interrogated, broken, and become precarious when they are appropriated in Indian writing. A totalitarian narrative can no longer be built in Portuguese, whereas indigenous writing finally grasps the discourses it has inherited and traces timeless stories.

The workshops at UFMG with indigenous teachers/writers, which by 2014 had produced and published twenty-seven books, were inspired by the work of Maria Gabriela Llansol, and particularly her call for "peasant voices" rather than a "Portuguese literature", with its imposing representation of a colonizing people. It is now possible to see indigenous books written in languages that are lexically and syntactically filled with obscure terms, not found in dictionaries, precarious forms never before read, as, for example, the title to the first book by Krenak teachers: *Coisa Tudo na Língua Krenak* (1997) (approximate translation: All Things in Krenak language). The book was written by five Krenak teachers who met with researchers from UFMG in an intercultural lab at the Parque Estadual do Rio Doce, Atlantic Forest reserve in upper Doce river, Minas Gerais. The Krenak or Borun people are descendants of one of the indigenous groups commonly named *Botocudos* by the Portuguese in the late eighteenth century. Today they live in a reservation of 4,000 hectares assigned to them by the Brazilian Department of Justice. *Coisa Tudo na Língua Krenak* is a bilingual work (Portuguese-Krenak), in which, for the first time in history, the indigenous language, spoken fully only by elderly members of the community (five women and one man), but understood by almost all members, was given literary form, a Krenak textuality. The Krenak teachers have grasped the writing instruments, the Latin alphabet letters, and used them to "stain" the Portuguese language with the structure and resonance of the wild indigenous language. In this process of literary creation, those who had not mastered or understood the prevailing language, but heard it and feared it, now take possession of its instruments and transmission techniques to attempt to possess it and provide answers to what we could not yet ask. The "whites", the colonizers, those who have named the native peoples "Indians", did not know (and we still don't know) how to read what each people, in their own way, have been writing for at least 10,000 years (on their bodies, on stones, on utensils, on the forest), and that now, even in books filled with words written in the Latin alphabet, they keep on writing, insidiously. Graphisms (expressions of cognitive processes in material symbols) are, for those who will read them, systemic traces that compose complex semiotic systems, which only recently have been an object of attention by literature experts.

So, the Indians who learn the language and the alphabetic writing technology leave their textualities in traces. They modulate, with their "Portuguese mistakes" and silences, a performance visible in graphic projects and gestures, on the pages of their books, because they interrogate the assumptions of modern language, and, even more deeply, Western concepts of time: as Menezes de Souza puts it, "mythical time is not seen as a distant and already occurred past time, but as an omnipresent time which has constant and continuous effects over the present with which it coexists simultaneously" (2015: 80). The evocation of pre-history in this way affirms the perspective of those who seem to have been positioned on the margin of Western historiography. The lack of knowledge about the writing of the other is the basis for discovery, as much for the Indians who create books as for the children who consume them. As Oswald Andrade expresses it:

> The language without archaisms, without erudition. Natural and ecological. The millionaire contribution of all mistakes. As we speak. As we are. (…) Only Brazilians of our time. The necessary in chemistry, mechanics, economy and ballistics. Everything digested. Without cultural meeting. Practical. Experimental.

Poets. No bookish reminiscences. No supporting comparisons. No etymological research. No ontology.

Barbarians, credulous, picturesque and sweet. Newspapers readers. Pau-Brasil. Forest and school. The National Museum. Cookery, iron ore and dance. Vegetation. Pau-Brasil.[4]

(my translation)

In this context, another history of Brazilian literature would begin with the sentence: indigenous peoples are discovering Brazil. Their textualities, their barely traced lines, their assemblages of letters and drawings, pages composed in an unconventional way for our occidental parameters – for example, books produced with Maxakali teachers, which can be read from right to left, or whose pages are ruled in circles – come to show how intuition and radicalism in Brazil are appropriated.

At a tangent to the Brazilian literary tradition, which maintained an idealistic relation with Indians, literary modernism opposed the "whitening" of the Brazilian nation and sought instead to capture colloquial speech (rather than "correct" Portuguese) and to represent local themes, which drew on native folklore and legend. Amerindian (and African) voices, in their materiality, would thus become audible/visible in written poetry and prose, legible in the Brazilian language, rather than appearing as enigmas (to be deciphered in long explanatory notes, as in José de Alencar's indianist romances).

A further step in the historiography of Brazilian marginal literature occurred with the emergence in contemporary indigenous literature of a radicalized modern movement. When Berta Ribeiro organized the publication of a book by a Desana author, *Antes o mundo não existia* (1980) (The world did not exist before), she was, maybe inadvertently, from the editorial point of view, opening a way for this new literary movement. In the same way as the Desana world, other worlds started to be discovered in the nation.

Why, among all possibilities of relations with national society, did the writing experience become so urgent for indigenous peoples? Perhaps it is due to the power of writing in history, and with the winning of a space in the social dialogue network, made possible in the country's democratization process. A stronger explanation, however, is that literature brought an opportunity to concretely introduce life in the villages, including ways of life strange to Western civilization – writings that we others still cannot read but can learn how to read. Writing in indigenous languages, now realized by Indians, not only serves to register other ways of life but also initiates an exchange. This is the reason for the large investment by indigenous teachers and leaders in translation, in the intercultural labs made available by some Brazilian universities since the creation of the Indigenous Major Program (PROLIND) by the Department of Education, in 2006.

The new words and images emerging from indigenous books enable new local, national, continental stories or, indeed, stories of humankind. On the other hand, these textualities challenge conventional Western linear reading and thinking because of the multiplicity they introduce, a web always subject to expansion due to the countless signs of the unknown with which indigenous authors mark their works. The reader of an indigenous book may be captured by the "much that it didn't contain" and, abandoning a critical position, leap to the wish to know the worlds inside the world. The archaic language, the new language, the unknown language, the abundance of icons and indexes, the indeterminacy, are the material for this new fragmented literature, made from leftovers, however strong in its movement. Indigenous textualities place time and space in an absolute contemporary shape. Here, where aged voices can be read, one must not seek the bottom, but the surface, the literal. The story is an experience. Characteristic literary processes, such as figurations in ways of telling stories or adaptations of already told stories are joined by the effort of a reading that surrenders to literature in its literal dimension.

To produce books with Indians has been a transforming experience because it displaces and changes our conception of teaching and literature. The new understanding of this cultural phenomenon called "a book", in a country where its circulation is scarce, leads to the object, to the body of the text, to its useful vitality. To create a book would then be a process that involves an occupation of the territory as a landscape (the land as far as the eye can see), "authorship experience", as this practice was called by a pioneer entity, Comissão Pro-Índio (Pro-indigenous committee) in Acre. The literary experience is based on singularity, difference, but what is about to be printed is something very common to all, that is, the experience itself.

To listen, transcribe, draw, translate, edit. With the creation of each book, Brazilian literature unfolds not as a system but as multiple voices. The gesture of writing inaugurates the different and points to the countless translations that will transform and re-write the text, so that, in paper or on the web, the text will be valued to the same degree that has made it remain in oral tradition.

It is no longer a matter of thinking in language from a specialist point of view, or even from the perspective of the disciplines that compose Modern Languages curricula. The concreteness of indigenous literary language requires us to think of words as of the earth. At the same time, we are also taken to the spirits who infuse vitality into things. To listen to a story told by the elder and make it legible to a white man, even in a strange language (Portuguese, in this case), takes the indigenous writer to the distilling of the language in a page configuration, where the listened and the dreamed, the word and the drawing will be printed. So, even without the sense inferred by reason, the reader sees and listens.

The being of language, in indigenous and non-indigenous writers' contemporary literature experience, becomes the elision of the subject, reflection, memory, escaping from the classical representation and becoming a landscape to the outside, dispersion, no-ownership, making the space, the village, the ethnic group appear through a language that intends to be neutral, anonymous. When a chief or a shaman speaks, what speaks is not a subject, or a *cogito*, but a neutral entity that he would call people, ancient times, ancestral, "tronco véi" (old trunk), as Xacriabá Indians would say.[5]

This road of theoretical investigation may lead us to a better understanding of the literary phenomenon that is the production of indigenous books. It would be useful to think of the processes of collective authorship, listening to oral narratives, production and circulation as starting from the translation practice. Our methodological investment is in the production of texts in different media and forms, by increasingly heterogeneous groups, which are usually composed of university students and indigenous people from different schooling levels, therefore, different domains of techniques and languages. The result is multidimensional indigenous textualities, which we can regard as hypertexts, or a constellation of signs in the theater of the page, with infinite exits.

Indigenous script finally replaces ethnography, when indigenous persons participate in Brazilian social life. With alphabetic writing, and print culture, indigenous peoples have entered an epistemological debate, because the technological domain, throughout human history, has always produced great developments. This is a dimension that Claude Lévi-Strauss neglected when reflecting on the writing he took to the Nambikwara (1979). He did not think, because he was European, in terms of the anthropophagic metaphor suggested by Oswald Andrade, which took "the cannibal trope", used to justify the annexation of peoples, cultures, and natural resources to the logic of empire (Castro-Klarén 2000: 295; see also Madureira 2005), and turned it upside-down. Oswald's "Manifesto antropófago" (1928) is seen as a metaphor that produced "the nation" for Brazilian *modernismo*, in the sense that "The nation" stands for "that entity capable of integrating the fragments, oppositions, and contradictions inherited from the dislocations of peoples, cultures, and languages that the regime of coloniality brought about" (Castro-Klarén: 297). Maybe Brazilians should also read Florestan Fernandes more, on Tupinambás education, to better understand Amerindian ways of thinking.

If Nambikwara persons do not reveal their names to strangers, as Lévi-Strauss tells us, it is perhaps because genealogy, or history, as well as the passage of time, or narrative, are engraved/written in some sacred place. But might not what we now want to read, from Indians, and what we call thinking, be engraved in some space that, somehow, is shown in rituals? Because it is already written, it would be natural. What we call nature is culture and, chiefly, a form of writing.

In this sense, authors like Oswald de Andrade, Haroldo de Campos, Florestan Fernandes, Viveiros de Castro, have a lot to inform the reader interested in indigenous literature. After all, they point to the path for a new understanding of Brazilian culture as a difference, different from itself. Before the arrival of Europeans in America, indigenous people already wrote in countless forms. Today, its writers, scribes, illustrators, translators, mingle their ancient forms with the new alphabet letters. The Maxakalis, for example, help us read the *Mĩmãnãm*, or *pau-de-religião* (religion stick), erected at the village center, besides the *Kuxex*, or *casa-de-religião* (religion house) where boys learn chants: there is written the history of how they become persons. Today, as always, indigenous peoples continue to practice their rituals and transitions from one space to another: the body, the paper, the computer, so that their different forms of writing are realized.

Notes

1 For a comprehensive survey of this literature, see the Master's degree dissertation by Amanda Machado Alves de Lima, submitted at UFMG Faculdade de Letras (Teachers' College): *O livro indígena e suas múltiplas grafias* (2012) (The indigenous book and its multiple scripts), in which the author lists 538 indigenous authored works published between 1980 and 2011.

2 Arns (1993) "Entre o ditado feito pelo autor e o texto que nos é transmitido, há uma dupla etapa a ser percorrida: primeiro, a passagem do ouvido à mão dos taquígrafos, que se substituem alternadamente, em obras fixas, junto ao autor; depois, a segunda etapa, do olho à mão dos escribas, que reconstituem a taquigrafia em escrita comum; enfim a passagem do olho ou do ouvido à mão dos calígrafos, que transcrevem definitivamente a cópia." Between the author's dictation and the text transmitted to us, there are two stages to be completed: first, the transition from hearing to the hand of the stenographer, which is then turned into a final version, in consultation with the author; then, the second stage, from the written text to the scribe's hand, who re-creates shorthand in common writing, and finally the transition from the written or heard text to the calligraphist's hand, who finally transcribes the copy (my translation).

3 Mas que nos pode dar a textualidade que a narratividade já não nos dá (e, a bem dizer, nunca nos deu?) (…) Eu afirmei que nós somos criados, longe, à distância de nós mesmos; a textualidade é a geografia dessa criação improvável e imprevisível; a textualidade tem por órgão a imaginação criadora, sustentada por uma função de pujança – o vaivém da intensidade. Ela permite-nos a cada um por sua conta, risco e alegria, abordar a força, o real que há-de vir ao nosso corpo de afectos (Llansol 1994: 12).

4 "A língua sem arcaísmos, sem erudição. Natural e neológica. A contribuição milionária de todos os erros. Como falamos. Como somos. (…) Apenas brasileiros de nossa época. O necessário de química, de mecânica, de economia e de balística. Tudo digerido. Sem meeting cultural. Práticos. Experimentais. Poetas. Sem reminiscências livrescas. Sem comparações de apoio. Sem pesquisa

etimológica. Sem ontologia. Bárbaros, crédulos, pitorescos e meigos. Leitores de jornais. Pau-Brasil. A floresta e a escola. O Museu Nacional. A cozinha, o minério e a dança. A vegetação. Pau-Brasil." *Manifesto da Poesia Pau-Brasil.* (*Pau-brasil* (*Caesalpinia echinata*) is a species of Brazilian timber tree, and the premier wood used for making bows for stringed instruments. The wood also yields a red dye called brazilin. The name of Brazil is shortened from *Terra do Brazil* "land of brazilwood". The term expresses a Brazilian essence.)

5 The Xacriabá are an indigenous people living in the North of the state of Minas Gerais, with whom Núcleo Literaterras has produced the Xacriabá Literature box, containing four books and one CD, from the teachers' researches with the elders in their villages.

Bibliography

A ciência da noite e do dia (2012) by Professores e alunos indígenas Pataxó da aldeia Muã Mimatxi. Belo Horizonte: Literaterras – FALE/UFMG.

Almeida, Maria Inês and Sonia Queiroz (2004) *Na captura da voz. As edições da narrativa oral no Brasil.* Belo Horizonte: Autêntica e FALE/UFMG.

Almeida, Maria Inês (2009) *Desocidentada. Experiência literária em terra indígena.* Belo Horizonte: Editora UFMG.

Almeida, Maria Inês (Ed.) (1997) *Conne Pãnda – Ríthioc Krenak: coisa tudo na língua krenak.* Belo Horizonte: SEE-MG; Brasília: MEC/UNESCO.

Andrade, Oswald (1970) *Do Pau-Brasil á Antropofagia e às utopias.* Obras Completas VI. Rio de Janeiro: Civilização Brasileira.

Arns, Dom Paulo Evaristo (1993) *A técnica do livro segundo São Jerônimo.* São Paulo: Imago.

Blanchot, Maurice (1993 [1969]). "The Narrative Voice (the 'he', the neutral)" in *The Infinite Conversation.* Trans. Susan Hanson. Minneapolis: University of Minnesota, pp. 379–87.

Borges, Jorge Luis (1974) *Obras Completas.* 4 vols. Buenos Aires: Emecé Editores.

Castro-Klarén, Sara (2000) "A Genealogy for the 'Manifesto antropófago,' or the Struggle between Socrates and the Caraïbe", *Nepantla: Views from South* 1(2): 295–322.

De Certeau, Michel (1984 [1980]) "Reading as Poaching" in *The Practice of Everyday Life.* Trans. Steven F. Rendall. Berkeley: University of California Press, pp. 165–76.

Fernandes, Florestan (2012) *A Função Social Da Guerra Na Sociedade Tupinambá.* São Paulo: Biblioteca Azul.

Lévi-Strauss, Claude (1979) *Tristes Trópicos.* Trans. Jorge Constante. Lisboa, Edições 70.

Llansol, Maria Gabriela (1994) *Lisboaleipzig 1. O encontro inesperado do diverso.* Lisboa: Rolim.

Llansol, Maria Gabriela (2000) *Onde vais, Drama-Poesia?* Lisboa: Relógio D'Água.

Madureira, Luís (2005) *Cannibal Modernities: Postcoloniality and the Avant-Garde in Caribbean and Brazilian Literature.* Charlottesville and London: University of Virginia Press.

Maxakali, Professores (2000) *Geografia da nossa aldeia – Uxuxet Ax, Hãm Xeka Ãgtux.* Belo Horizonte: SEE – MG/MEC.

Menezes de Souza, Lynn Mario T. (2015) "The Ecology of Writing among the Kashinawá: Indigenous Multimodality in Brazil" in *Reclaiming the Local in Language Policy and Practice*, ed. A. Suresh Canagarajah. London and New York: Routledge, pp. 73–95.

Monte, Nietta (1997) *As escolas da Floresta. Entre o passado oral e o presente escrito.* Rio de Janeiro: Multiletra.

11

THE BRITISH EMPIRE AND INDIAN NATIONALISM IN RABINDRANATH TAGORE'S HISTORICAL POEMS AND *THE LAND OF CARDS*

Supriya Goswami

Although largely overlooked as a children's author, the Nobel laureate Rabindranath Tagore (1861–1941) not only produced an impressive and diverse body of writing for children, but he also played an active role in shaping the field of Bengali children's literature in the late nineteenth and early twentieth century.[1] From the nostalgic reminiscences of his childhood in *Boyhood Days* [*Chhelebela*] (1940), a memoir written for young readers shortly before his death, to poems, plays, and short stories which celebrate, in Romantic fashion, Nature and the imagination of the child, Tagore's immense contribution to the development of Bengali children's literature has yet to receive the critical attention that it deserves. I will here focus on how Tagore's complex and evolving views on the British Empire and the Indian national movement are represented in his writings for younger audiences. While it has been well documented by Ashis Nandy, among others, that Tagore's works repeatedly address his reservations about nationalism, especially the more violent and revolutionary manifestations of it in early twentieth-century India, there has been very little emphasis on how he approached the idea of Indian nationalism and the impact of British rule in his children's texts. I will begin with a brief examination of some of his historical poems for children, penned in the late 1890s and compiled in *Legends and Tales* [*Katha o Kahini*] (1908), and then focus on *The Land of Cards* [*Tasher Desh*] (1933), a musical drama for young adults, in which Tagore's views on the oppressive nature of colonial rule and the importance of political, intellectual, and spiritual freedom are clearly articulated.

Historical context and the poems from the 1890s

Born a few years after the Revolt of 1857 into a well-to-do family that had made its fortune by furthering the interests of the East India Company, Tagore was both appreciative and critical of the colonial encounter. In the tradition of the early nineteenth-century Bengali reformist, Raja Rammohan Roy, who had looked to Western ideas and modes of thought as a means to emancipate the eastern Indian state of Bengal from superstition and ritualism, Tagore, like many Bengalis of his generation, was never fully dismissive of British presence in India.[2] In fact, in *Boyhood Days*, Tagore describes his growing up years in "old-time" Calcutta, the capital of the British Raj, with great fondness as he brings to life for his young readers the "leisurely pace" (7) of a city lit up at night by castor-oil lamps. These seemingly happy years, as described in his memoirs, are unmarked by any antipathy toward the British. Interestingly, the 1860s and 1870s, the decades that coincide with Tagore's boyhood years, have been viewed by historians such as Francis Hutchins and Thomas Metcalf as a phase marked by mutual suspicion and mistrust during which there was also a systematic effort by the British to establish a more permanent and authoritarian empire in India. Sandwiched between the uprising of 1857 and the establishment of the Indian National Congress in 1885, the organization that eventually led India to freedom, this period also witnessed the gestation of a new national consciousness that was to emerge among Indians from the 1880s onward. However, far from being anti-British in his stance, Tagore ends *Boyhood Days* with a brief description of the time he spends in England as a young man (from 1788 to 1880) where he is sent by his father, Debandranath Tagore, to study law in order to eventually join the Indian Civil Service. Although he leaves England without a degree, he describes his short stint there in glowing terms; he regards it as a place where the "process of [his] character formation began to acquire the stamp of foreign craftsmanship" (89) and where his "intimacy with the English heart" had enabled him to absorb within himself "the fusion of East and West" (90).

However, despite his apparent lack of rancor toward the British and their presence in India as a boy, Tagore's return to Bengal as a young man in 1880 coincided with the emergence of an organized Indian national movement, which looked to glorify an Indian past, and his early writings for children reflect the patriotic zeal of his times. He thus argues that, "the [Indian National] Congress has not merely been memorializing the rulers year after year without any result—Congress has also ... planted the seed of a new consciousness in our minds" (quoted in Bhattacharya 69). However, instead of focusing exclusively on a Hindu past, as imagined by such early Congress leaders as Bal Gangadhar Tilak, Lala Lajpat Rai, and Aurobindo Ghosh, who regularly deployed Hindu mythology and symbols to evoke a nationalistic sense of pride among Indians, Tagore's vision of a bygone India for his young readers is a more inclusive one. In "History of India" (*Bharatvarsher Itihas*), an essay written in 1902, Tagore emphasizes what he considers is India's ability to "establish unity amidst differences, to bring to a convergence different paths, and to internalize within her soul the unity of severalty" (quoted in Bhattacharya 70), and his celebration of the country's religious and cultural diversity is evident in the poems he writes in the late 1890s. These poems, based on historical legends and tales, draw on many different traditions: ranging from religious sources (such as the life of Buddha) to more secular sources, which highlight the deeds of India's warrior-kings.

"The Representative" [*Pratinidhi*] (1897), for example, recounts an encounter between Shivaji, the seventeenth-century Maratha ruler, and Ramdas, his spiritual mentor, in which the former is willing to lay down his "kingdom in entire" at the latter's "lotus-feet" (*Selected Writings* 188). While Shivaji is willing to give up his kingdom and follow his *guru* around like an ascetic, Ramdas makes the case for the importance of good governance by asking the warrior-king to rule selflessly as a "beggar's representative" (189). It cannot be a coincidence that Tagore validates this kind of homegrown leadership, which is spiritually enlightened, altruistic, and, in many ways, the very antithesis of the exploitative nature of British rule in India. In "The Magic Stone" [*Parashpathar*]

(1899), Tagore returns to the theme of spiritual wisdom trumping material wealth as Jiban, a man who has lost all his material possessions, realizes after meeting Sanatan Goswami (a saint of the *Bhakti* movement, a reformist spiritual movement in medieval India) that a magic stone that can turn all things into gold is of far less value than the feeling that comes from being free of such worldly objects. In the "The Beggar's Bounty" [*Nagarlakshmi*] (1899), Tagore narrates an incident from the life of Buddha, which, once again, has a moral thrust. When famine strikes the town of Shravasti and Buddha asks his disciples, "Who will take on the load/To give the hungry food?" (*Selected Writings* 191), its wealthy citizens profess an inability to undertake such a daunting task. It is a young woman of few means who readily volunteers to use her begging-bowl to collect alms for the famine-stricken population of her town. It is significant that Tagore uses the metaphor of a famine—and highlights the unwillingness of well-to-do citizens to alleviate the situation—to make a moral point. India (and Bengal in particular) was wracked by catastrophic famines several times during British rule and the disinclination of the British to take timely administrative measures seems to mirror the actions of the wealthy townspeople of Shravasti.

In *Talking Back*, Sabyasachi Bhattacharya writes that the "British discourse on India's history was by and large a monologue for the greater part of the nineteenth century" (1). Beginning with publication of James Mill's multi-volume *History of India* (1817), which had a considerable impact in shaping the somewhat derogatory perceptions of India's past during the nineteenth century, the British—scholars, civil servants, and historians alike—continued to generate a vast body of textual knowledge about India's history. The nationalistic project of reclaiming and rewriting this history by Indians began in the late nineteenth century when the first graduates (such as Bankimchandra Chatterjee and R.G. Bhandarkar) of the newly established universities in Calcutta and Bombay began questioning British interpretations of India's past. Tagore, in keeping with the spirit of the times, also displays a keen interest in Indian history and, more significantly, understands the value of communicating this history to the youth of the country. In "History of India," for instance, he emphasizes the importance of writing history for young people as it would enable them to develop a sense of self-esteem and have pride in their country: "In a country favoured by fortune, people perceive in their histories, their own country, shaped by its past and *in their childhood reading history introduces them to their own country*. It is just the opposite in our country. Books of history [written by the British] hide from us our country" (quoted in Bhattacharya 70; my emphasis). In fact, Tagore's first historical essay, on the Rani of Jhansi (the fiery leader of the 1857 rebellion who, as legend goes, died fighting the British on horseback with her small child strapped to her back), was written when he himself had barely attained adulthood, at the young age of seventeen. While he made it his mission to publish essays and poems on historical themes for his young readers, unlike some of his contemporaries he attempted to be objective and did not lionize or sugarcoat every aspect of India's past. In fact, he points out several of its less-than-glorious moments in poems such as "The Fake Fortress" [*Nakal Gar*] (1899) and "The Captive Hero" [*Bandi Bir*] (1899). In "The Fake Fortress," Tagore narrates an incident from fourteenth-century Rajput history that highlights the mendacious actions of the Rana of Chittor, the supreme Rajput ruler of the day, and his powerful army. "The Captive Hero" describes a violent early eighteenth-century encounter between the Sikhs and the Mughals which, ultimately, results in the brutal and senseless death of a young child. In this poem, the captive Sikh leader, Banda, is forced to kill his own son with a knife, after which he is tortured to death as a "hushed" Mughal court watches on (*Selected Writings* 186).

Tagore's early writings for children also reveal the social and economic inequities that existed in colonial India and, although he belonged to a landowning family himself, he was particularly sensitive to the plight of peasants. In many ways, the Bengali peasant had become a symbol of suffering under British rule as one of the earliest decrees passed by the East India Company to consolidate its rule in Bengal was a land revenue measure which, as historian Ranajit Guha has described, had terrible consequences for the subjugated peasant. The Permanent Settlement Act of 1783, which was in effect in Bengal through much of the nineteenth century, gave ownership of land to the *zamindars* (landowners) who, in turn, paid a fixed amount of revenue directly to the British, largely by collecting rent from the tenanted peasants who tilled the land. This system of revenue collection proved to be tremendously burdensome to the peasant and Tagore, who, ironically, was a landlord himself for a few years (as he managed his family estates in Shilaidaha in Eastern Bengal in the 1890s), had a lot of sympathy for the poor and exploited peasants of Bengal. Most famously, in his poem "Two Bhigas of Land" [*Dui Bigha Jami*] (1895), Upen, who has lost almost all of his land to pay his debts, is "trapped ... by a false decree" (*Selected Writings* 176) into giving up the two remaining *bhigas* (two thirds of an acre) he possesses so that his landlord can have a perfectly square garden. After having wandered homeless and landless for fifteen years, Upen returns to his village and seeks out the shade of the mango tree that had once belonged to him. When two ripe mangoes fall beside him, overcome with emotion, he sees them as a "sign" (177) that he (the child) has found his long-lost mother (the tree). His elation is short lived as the landlord calls him a "brazen thief" (178) and threatens to kill him for stealing the fruit. The poem ends on an ironic note with Upen musing upon his fate: "You, lord, are a moral man today, and I a thief indeed!" (178). The theme of social injustice is one that Tagore continually returns to in his poems for children; for example, four decades later, in "Madho" (1937), Tagore presents his young readers with a character who is doubly oppressed: initially, as a child, by the local landlord (who threatens him with a public whipping), and then, as an adult, by British jute-mill owners (who unleash police violence on striking workers).

No analysis of Tagore's post-1905 writings can be complete without consideration of two events in early twentieth-century India that had an enormous impact on his literary output for both children and adults: the *Swadeshi* movement and the Jallianwala Bagh massacre. The partition of Bengal in 1905 by Lord Curzon, viceroy of India, for so-called administrative reasons resulted in the *Swadeshi* (of our country) movement (1905–11), which essentially called for a boycott of British products and institutions in favor of Indian ones. The protracted period of civil disobedience, which included marches, demonstrations, strikes, and the picketing of government offices, schools, courts, and shops, as Sumit Sarkar outlines, took an extremist and revolutionary turn by 1908 and ultimately alienated the more moderate supporters of the movement. Tagore, who was initially one of the main advocates of the *swadeshi* cause, began to distance himself from it (and from the national movement in general) when, in 1908, Khudiram Bose, an eighteen-year-old, accidently killed a woman and child during a failed attempt to assassinate the magistrate of a town in the Indian state of Bihar. The irrationality of such acts and the senseless violence and terror generated in the name of *swadeshi* left Tagore questioning the basic principles of a national movement based on revolutionary tactics, and his disillusionment is perhaps best reflected in such novels as *The Home and the World* [*Ghare Baire*] (1916) and *Four Chapters* [*Char Adhyay*] (1934). In fact, so troubled was Tagore by the bloody imaginings of *swadeshi* that he remained skeptical of all nationalistic calls for civil disobedience and economic boycotts, including the non-violent Non-Cooperation Movement launched by Mahatma Gandhi in the 1920s.

Up until 1919, one can argue that Tagore had some faith in the British Empire and even in his most nationalistic and anti-colonial phase was somewhat conciliatory toward the British. In fact, in 1915, a couple of years after he received the Nobel Prize in Literature, Tagore was knighted for his literary achievements, an accolade which he accepted without any reservations. However, that was to change when on April 13, 1919, a peaceful and unarmed crowd of people at a political meeting in Amritsar, a city in the Northern Indian state of Punjab, were fired on, without warning, by troops under the command of a British military officer, Brigadier-General Dyer. The gathering had taken place in response to Gandhi's nation-wide call for non-violent protest against the Rowlatt Acts of 1818, which greatly threatened civil liberties. While an official inquiry stated that 379 people were killed and over 1,000 wounded, the body-count, as estimated by the Indian National Congress, was higher. As historian Stanley Wolpert puts it: "Dyer's troops fired for ten minutes, pouring 1,650 rounds of live ammunition into the unarmed mass of trapped humanity at point blank range. Some four hundred Indians were left dead, and twelve hundred wounded, when the brigadier and his force withdrew at sunset from the garden they had turned into a national graveyard" (299). Tagore, dismayed by the lack of any real remorse on the part of the British government in India over this massacre, decided to renounce his knighthood. In a letter dated May 31, 1919, and addressed to Lord Chelmsford, viceroy of India, Tagore writes:

> The enormity of the measures taken by the government in the Punjab for quelling some local disturbances has, with a rude shock, revealed to our minds the helplessness of our position as British subjects in India. The disproportionate severity of the punishments inflicted upon the unfortunate people and the methods of carrying them out, we are convinced, are without parallel in the history of civilized governments ... Considering that such treatment has been meted out to a population, disarmed and resourceless, by a power which has the most terribly efficient organization for destruction of human lives, we must strongly assert that it can claim no political expediency, far less moral justification.
>
> (*Essential Tagore* 108)

He goes on to chide "our rulers" for ignoring and "possibly congratulating themselves for imparting what they imagine as salutary lessons" and, on a patriotic note, proclaims that "the very least that I can do for my country is to take all the consequences upon myself in giving voice to the protest of the millions of my countrymen, surprised into a dumb anguish of terror" (108). He ends the letter by declaring that the "time has come when badges of honor make our shame glaring in the incongruous content of humiliation" (108) and asserting that he wishes to "stand, shorn, of all special distinctions, by the side of those of my countrymen who, for their so-called insignificance, are liable to suffer degradation not fit for human beings" (109). Thus, while dissatisfaction with colonial policies had prompted Tagore to initially support (and then distance himself from) *swadeshi* based modes of resistance in the early years of the twentieth century, the Jallianwala

Bagh massacre ultimately led to his complete disillusionment with colonial rule, which is reflected in *The Land of Cards*.

In a land of cards

The Land of Cards opens with a young prince who is so restless and dissatisfied with the state of affairs in his country that he declares to his companion, a merchant: "We are fenced in with falsehoods. Languishing in the cage of safety, our wings have grown stiff. Everything here is a farce, from beginning to end" (79–80). It is telling that Tagore casts, as his central character, a prince who feels imprisoned and fettered by the "cage" that he lives in. So unhappy is he by what he views as his shackled condition that he decides to leave home and sets sail on a ship in search of a treasure that he calls "Nabina" (newness) (82). The rulers of princely states in India were among the staunchest supporters of British rule and, in the wake of a largely middle-class led national movement, showed tremendous loyalty to the Raj. Wolpert, for instance, writes that even "during the most turbulent eras of … nationalist agitation, the British could always call upon their aristocratic lobby in every region of the subcontinent to defend the imperial cause with vigor and conviction" (240). Ian Copland contends that the "princely alliance connected British rule, however tenuously, with Indian tradition" and the support of the native princes "gave the Raj a much needed touch of legitimacy" (9). Thus, by deploying a prince as the mouthpiece of discontent, Tagore deliberately reverses the pattern of loyalty and seems to suggest that even the most steadfast subjects of the Raj, who were greatly reliant on the British for their privileged existence, are also ultimately stifled by colonial rule.

The prince, accompanied by the merchant, soon finds himself shipwrecked on an island inhabited by cards that are lifeless, rule abiding, and lacking in any emotion. The land of cards, a concept clearly inspired by Lewis Carroll's *Alice* books, is undoubtedly meant to represent colonial India; a joyless country whose residents show a zombie-like obedience to the law. From a national anthem which requires the cards to "*Just follow the leader,/Ever-docile*" (97; emphasis in the original) to a law that ensures that they "dare not turn to look south-west" (96), it is a state that is immensely controlling of its citizens. As one of the cards says, when asked to explain the meaning of all the rituals they follow: "There are no meanings, only rules" (111). In fact, the frightening lack of civil liberties and individual freedoms in this land are presented by Tagore as a cause of tremendous concern and the merchant, on first seeing the cards, darkly describes their movements as "a dance of corpses possessed by spirits!" (87). Mirroring aspects of life in colonial India, Tagore creates for his young readers a moribund society in which newspapers are censored, education is strictly controlled, and a small ruling class has absolute power over the masses. Thus, the periodic clamp down on Indian newspapers by the colonial state for "seditious" activities, the lack of any real opportunities for Indians who had gone through the grid of a colonial education, and the authoritarian nature of imperial rule that is unresponsive to the basic needs, aspirations, and desires of its colonized subjects are all touched upon in this play.

The *Land of Cards* also displays Tagore's skepticism of the Indian national movement and the tactics employed by Gandhi to dismantle the British Raj. While Gandhi and Tagore had fairly similar visions of an ideal and free Indian society— self-reliant and modeled on the small village communities of India's past—they differed in their methods for achieving it.[3] While Gandhi's strategy for unyoking India from British rule was based on *satyagraha* (truth force), which proposed that tyrannical colonial laws could be vanquished if enough people collaborated peacefully to resist them, Tagore, as a result of the excesses he witnessed during the *Swadeshi* movement, was opposed to the very idea of civil disobedience and mass agitations as a means of achieving self-sufficiency and freedom. The Non-Cooperation Movement launched by Gandhi in 1920 in response to the government's "light-hearted treatment" (quoted in Copland 102) of the Jallianwala Bagh massacre, among other grievances, was unequivocally denounced by Tagore. The campaign, as Gandhi put it in a letter to Lord Chelmsford, dated August 1, 1920, was a "remedy of non-cooperation" which was meant to "compel" the government to "retrace its steps and undo the wrongs committed" (quoted in Copland 103). In a letter to Gandhi, written in March 1921, Tagore, however, called it an "orgy of frightfulness" and "an attempt at spiritual suicide" which found "a disinterested delight in any unmeaning devastation" (quoted in Raychaudhuri 141). Tagore continued to display his skepticism about subsequent *satyagrahas* initiated by Gandhi and was not above taking a dig at the latter's non-violent methods in *The Land of Cards* by showcasing how ineffective the cards are at displaying any dissent. To begin with, the cards gather in large crowds, not unlike the followers of the Non-Cooperation Movement, and are unarmed and peaceful. When asked by the merchant what type of weaponry is used in battle, a card proclaims proudly: "*No arms we bear,/No battle gear*," (92; emphasis in the original) which is clearly a reference to Gandhi's call for peaceful resistance to British rule. As Michael Collins writes: "Tagore's argument was that despite naming freedom as his ultimate aim, in essence Gandhi's *satyagraha* was motivated by negative intentions, even hatred in some cases. It would naturally bring out violent and dark forces" (84).

However, despite its function as a disquieting allegory of empire, *The Land of Cards*, in the tradition of children's literature, presents Tagore's young readers with a hopeful and happy ending. The cards, initially unable to display any emotions or feelings beyond subservience to the law, gradually begin to wake up from their stupor under the guidance of the young prince who is determined to free them intellectually, spiritually, and emotionally. As he tells the cards, "When the law of the fence is broken, the law of the open road reveals itself" (95). One by one all the cards realize that the time has come for them to give up their old ways and embrace a new and rejuvenated way of life. According to one of the cards, "a new birth is in the air" (108), which enables them to dream, sing, laugh, and talk together as they had never been able to do in the past. The play concludes with all the cards, rulers and subjects alike, singing a victory song about setting their "*captive spirits free*" and fearlessly embracing the "*new life*" that beckons them (123–4; emphasis in the original). Thus, by foregrounding the essential oneness and unity of mankind, Tagore validates for his young readers a vision of an ideal world which is all-embracing and does away with artificially constructed boundaries that separate the rulers and the ruled.

Tagore was thus as much a critic of British colonialism as he was of Indian nationalism, especially in the aftermath of the *Swadeshi* movement and Jallianwala Bagh massacre. In fact, he considered the ideology of nationalism the principal reason for British (and European) territorial aggrandizement which, in his opinion, led to self-destructive wars and the subjugation of non-European peoples. As Tagore declares in 1917, at the height of World War I: "The political civilization which has sprung up from the soil of Europe ... is over running the whole world ... It is carnivorous and cannibalistic in its tendencies, it feeds upon the resources of other peoples and tries to swallow their whole future" (*Nationalism* 60). More importantly, he warns against the pitfalls of Indians embracing the creed of nationalism—which he refers to as a "great menace" (112)—as a mode of resistance to British rule and, instead, calls for "[Indian] civilization [to] take its firm stand upon its basis of social co-operation and not upon that of economic exploit-ation and conflict" (130). Even some of his more patriotic early poems, as I have shown, exhibit an inclusiveness that attempts to transcend divisions of caste, creed, and religion, and his later works, as is evident in *The Land of Cards*, become increasingly critical of both the British Empire and the Indian national movement. Significantly, however, he never loses his faith in the essential goodness of mankind. As he proclaims in "Crisis in Civilization" (1941), his last birthday message to the world: "I shall not commit the griev-ous sin of losing faith in Man" (*Essential Tagore* 215).

Notes

1 Tagore was immensely influential in sparking an interest in folklore in late nineteenth- and early twentieth-century Bengal. He viewed folk tales and rhymes as authentic transmitters of Bengali culture, especially valuable for children who were exposed to an Anglicized colonial education; he not only wrote and collected them himself, but also actively encouraged others to do so as well. Among those influenced by Tagore were his nephew, Abanindranath Tagore, who wrote "Khirer Putul" ["The Condensed-Milk Doll"] (1896), the first original fairytale in Bengali, and Dakshinaranjan Mitra Majumdar, who published *Thakumar Jhuli [Grandmother's Bag]* (1907), a beloved collection of folktales.
2 Rammohan Roy established the Brahmo Samaj, a reformist organization that had a pro-found impact on nineteenth-century Bengali thought and culture, in 1828. Tagore's father, Debandranath Tagore, an ardent follower of Roy, was one of the main leaders of the Brahmo Samaj. Not surprisingly, Roy's utopian belief in a world without disparities, segregation, and dogma resonated strongly with Tagore.
3 Tagore's vision of a *swadeshi samaj* (community) based on traditional Indian villages and his notion of *atmasakti* (self-strengthening) as a means of attaining individual self-sufficiency are not very different from Gandhi's core beliefs found in *Hind Swaraj [Indian Home Rule]* (1909).

Bibliography

Bhattacharya, Sabyasachi (2011) *Talking Back: The Idea of Civilization in the Indian Nationalist Discourse*, New Delhi: Oxford University Press.
Carroll, Lewis (2000) *Alice's Adventures in Wonderland and Through the Looking-Glass*, New York: Signet Classic.
Chaudhuri, Sukanta (2002) "Introduction." *Selected Writings for Children: Rabindranath Tagore*, Ed. Sukanta Chaudhuri. New Delhi: Oxford University Press.
Collins, Michael (2012) *Empire, Nationalism and the Postcolonial World: Rabindranath Tagore's Writings on History, Politics and Society*, New York: Routledge.
Copland, Ian (2001) *India 1885–1947: The Unmaking of an Empire*, London: Longman.
Gandhi, Mohandas Karamchand (2010 [1909]) *Hind Swaraj*, Delhi: Rajpal & Sons.
Guha, Ranajit (1996) *A Rule of Property for Bengal: An Essay on the Idea of Permanent Settlement*, Durham: Duke University Press.
Hutchins, Francis G. (1967) *The Illusion of Permanence: British Imperialism in India*, Princeton, NJ: Princeton University Press.
Metcalf, Thomas R. (2005) *Ideologies of the Raj. The New Cambridge History of India*, Vol. 3, 4. Ed. Gordon Johnson. New Delhi: Foundation Books.
Mill, James (1975) *The History of British India*, Ed. William Thomas. Chicago: The University of Chicago Press.
Mitra Majumdar, Dakshinaranjan (1907) *Thakurmar Jhuli* [Grandmother's Bag], Calcutta.
Nandy, Ashis (1994) *The Illegitimacy of Nationalism*, New Delhi: Oxford University Press.
Raychaudhuri, Tapan (1999) *Perceptions, Emotions, Sensibilities: Essays on India's Colonial and Post-colonial Experiences*, New Delhi: Oxford University Press.
Sarkar, Sumit (1973) *Swadeshi Movement in Bengal, 1903–8*, New Delhi: People's Publishing House.
Tagore, Abanindranath (1896) *"Khirer Putul"* ["The Condensed-Milk Doll"]. Calcutta.

Tagore, Rabindranath (2005 [1916]) *The Home and the World*, Trans. Surendranath Tagore. New York: Penguin.

———— (1918) *Nationalism*, London: Macmillan.

———— (2010 [1933]) *The Land of Cards*. In *The Land of Cards: Stories, Poems and Plays for Children*, Trans. Radha Chakravarty. New Delhi: Penguin.

———— (2002 [1934]) *Four Chapters*, New Delhi: Rupa & Company.

———— (2007 [1940]) *Boyhood Days*, Trans. Radha Chakravarty. New Delhi: Penguin.

———— (2002) *Selected Writings for Children: Rabindranath Tagore*, Ed. Sukanta Chaudhuri. New Delhi: Oxford University Press.

———— (2011) *The Essential Tagore*, Ed. Fakrul Alam and Radha Chakravarty. Cambridge, MA: Harvard University Press.

Wolpert, Stanley (2000) *A New History of India*, 6th ed. New York: Oxford University Press.

12

"BREAKING THE MIRROR"

Reshaping perceptions of national progress
through the representation of marginalized
cultural realities in Caribbean children's stories

Aisha Spencer

> So, friend of my childhood years
> One day we'll talk about
> How the mirror broke
> Who kissed us awake
> Who let Anansi from his bag...
> > Olive Senior, "Colonial Girls School"[1]

As the first "site of European colonization" (Puri 2), the Caribbean region has been scarred by experiences of oppression, dehumanization, and fragmentation. Both the history and literature of the region have therefore been shaped by an amalgamation of cultural realities emerging out of their own historical beginnings prior to the Caribbean's contact with the West, their previous colonizer-colonized relations and systems, which were framed by the presence of the British, Spanish, French and Dutch, and the cultural realities which were crafted out of the creative energies of a people determined to survive and to reclaim an indigenous sense of identity and culture in a postcolonial environment.

Having been labelled "uncivilized" by the West and having longed for the experience of freedom, Caribbean territories such as Trinidad, Jamaica, and Guyana highly anticipated independence during the nationalistic years of the 1940s to 1950s, particularly after the region's experience of World War II. Through emergent leaders of this period such as Eric Williams from Trinidad, Norman Manley and Alexander Bustamante from Jamaica, and Cheddi Jagan and Linden Forbes Burnham from Guyana, citizens approached their post-independent years (as early as 1956 to 1962) with great hopes of social equality and freedom, yet these hopes were often crushed because the social, economic, and political conditions desired were often not achieved. Franklin W. Knight asserts that "[v]ery few of the new leaders had ideas incompatible with the old status quo" (148). Additionally, disunity and barriers to social justice often occurred as a result of the racial, class, and gender prejudices inherited from the preceding colonial regimes.

The birth of literature within the Caribbean region, with particular focus on Trinidad, Jamaica, and Guyana, paralleled the period of nationalism for these countries and so often represented the nationalistic conditions during the 1940s to the 1980s. At its outset, the Caribbean literary tradition, like other postcolonial new literatures, faced the problem that it inherited literary forms from the colonizer, such as traditional British forms of verse and prose, heroic and romantic elements in the novel, and the dominant use of formal English. As the Caribbean literary tradition grew, however, writers began to provide a new Caribbean aesthetic, which powerfully represented the continuing journey away from a colonial way of life to the experience of their own newly established societies. Writers such as C.L.R. James and V.S. Naipaul in Trinidad, Victor Stafford Reid, Louise Bennett-Coverley (popularly known as "Miss Lou"), and Roger Mais in Jamaica, and Guyanese writers such as Wilson Harris and Martin Carter have played a major role in the development of contemporary Caribbean literature.

Although the history of children's literature begins with the first set of folk tales of West Indian cultures written by "foreigners" over a century ago, Cynthia James (2005) argues that a distinct form of Caribbean children's literature emerged in the 1950s and 1960s through the production of various anthologies as well as in the writing of Philip Sherlock and Andrew Salkey, from Jamaica, and later in the 1970s and 1980s, in the works of Trinidadian Paul Keens-Douglas (who helped to maintain an effective balance between the oral and the written) and those of John Agard and Grace Nichols, from Guyana.

Caribbean children's stories, however, lag behind Caribbean children's poetry and the popular folk tale tradition in their readership and the critical attention they receive, with the consequence that the Caribbean children's books that tend to be more commonly discussed both locally and internationally are those that present Caribbean folklore, such as the popular Anansi stories, rather than the more contemporary and recent books written for children. There is thus a need for more critical exploration of Caribbean children's literature, not simply as it relates to literacy and children's education (which tends to be the main focus in the region), but to enable a deeper understanding of its aesthetics and thematic concerns. More specifically and significantly, contemporary Caribbean children's literature has represented new positions on nation-ness and notions of belonging, and a deeper understanding of the intricate complexities of this "Other" space and of the importance of carving out new methods for resisting dominant stereotypes rooted in a colonial past. Ideas about national progress are thus reshaped, even with the dominant presence of globalization. Post-colonial readings of particular Caribbean children's literature texts will enable what Gyan Prakash defines as a "radical re-thinking and re-formulation of forms of knowledge and social identities authored and authorized by colonialism and western domination" (8), whether these forms of domination are connected to the United Kingdom or the United States of America.

Over the past half century a new form of Caribbean children's literature has emerged, which attempts to represent a balance of the older forms of Caribbean culture (for example, folk tales and proverbs) with newer modes of cultural practices and ways of thinking (for example, sports and reggae music). Central to this representation has been the figure of the child as an independent, valuable source of energy for the perpetuation of growth and development in the community and an agent of unity and transformation within his or her society.

Further, these Caribbean children's books prompt continued interrogation of the influence of the West on post-independent Caribbean nations, particularly as this influence has been advanced by the very leaders of these Caribbean territories. The international, and sometimes the local, assumption tends to be that with the end of slavery and colonialism the nations of the Caribbean became completely free from the influence of the Western world. However, emergent models of Caribbean children's literature have demonstrated that Caribbean societies are still negatively affected by colonial attitudes deeply embedded in the fabric of the region's social life through race, class, and gender. Nowhere is this more evident than in the society's poorer classes and those who do not match the traits matching the status quo. Joanne Gail Johnson, Diane Browne, and Sherlina Nageer represent, through their children's stories, the role marginalized cultural realities might be able to play in the process of reshaping Caribbean identity and progress, and – to come to the principal focus of this essay – in "the breaking of the mirror".

In the prophetic final stanza of her famous poem "Colonial Girls' School" (as quoted in this essay's epigraph), Olive Senior creatively presents the effects of colonialism on a people, and specifically its powerfully negative effect on the child, through colonial education. The symbol of the mirror, which this essay draws from Senior, speaks of the reflected notions of self and belonging, which were based on the ideals and ideologies of European cultures and systems, and the breaking of that mirror suggests that this colonial reflection must be shattered in order for once-colonized people to embrace new reflections of diverse and complex, yet rich and productive forms of identity and experience, such as those presently represented within Caribbean children's literature. The representation of marginalized cultural realities in the nations of the Caribbean region are usefully exemplified in three books for middle grade readers: *Sally's Way* by Joanne Gail Johnson, *Every Little Thing Will Be Alright* by Diane Browne, and *Thumbelina* by Shaleem Nageer. My analysis is informed by specific concepts articulated by Frantz Fanon, Benedict Anderson, and Homi Bhabha, as well as by post-colonial critics such as Padmini Mongia, Elleke Boehmer, and Ashcroft, Griffiths, and Tiffin. The three children's books provide representations of national progress in the twenty-first century through the presentation of distinct marginalized cultural realities faced by Caribbean people. These subaltern cultural realities reveal that the Caribbean region remains tainted by colonial perceptions and systems that have permeated the region either through past systems of slavery and colonialism or through colonial influences that form the root of the racial and class prejudices present in the attitudes and institutions of these post-independent nations. On the other hand, Caribbean children's books for middle grade readers, through their narration of these marginalized cultural realities, have forged a new kind of *poetics* and *politics* for representing and reading the nations of the Caribbean. The *poetics* and *politics* embedded within these literary works, evident through both the narrative strategies these writers employ and the depiction of the thematic concerns raised through their child protagonists and the situations they encounter, reposition the nations of the Caribbean in an alternative space, and promote the need for Caribbean nations to be *Other* than the dominant, capitalist, racist, classist, and sexist classifications so heavily associated with the West and its influence both prior to and after independence. Additionally, through the recurrent trope of rediscovery, each of these children's stories promotes the imperative for Caribbean nations to respond to the marginalized in their societies, not simply in terms of addressing the negative treatment they often receive but also as a means of exploring how these groups are able to offer further solutions to the situation of growth and development in the Caribbean.

Representation in children's literature is highly significant. According to Stuart Hall, "we give things meaning by how we represent them…the stories we tell about them" (3). The representation of marginalized cultural realities in the writings of Johnson, Browne, and Nageer is fundamental to the depiction of the process of reshaping Caribbean national identity and consciousness. Each writer depicts a number of marginalized cultural realities, but three predominate: the experience of the child in an adult world; the stereotypical notions attached to the geographical space of the rural community, based on Western notions of progress and advancement; and the situation of poverty.

Each of the stories focuses on the world of the child and the ways in which that child attempts to negotiate the spaces she occupies. What becomes important in the representation of these child protagonists, however, is the independence they acquire as a result of the restrictive realities imposed on them based on a "particular hierarchy of value" (Ashcroft, Griffith, Tiffin 94) which renders them insignificant, particularly in terms of their ability to contribute positively to the nation's development. Although explored by only a few Caribbean writers and critics, such as Derek Walcott, Velma Pollard, and Olive Senior, childhood sensibility is highly significant in the depiction of Caribbean identity and consciousness for, as Sandra Pouchet Paquet affirms, meaning as attached to the representation of a nation's history in literature is often acquired "through the scenes and conditions of childhood" (155). By "writing through" the stages of childhood in the literary text, many writers have attempted to reconstruct both selfhood and nationhood in Caribbean societies. This strategy is critical because of the fragmentation and brokenness that has limned the history of the Caribbean people and the numerous gaps that therefore exist in the representations of their individual and national histories. The child therefore becomes a symbol of the growing nation. Through the character of the child, the Caribbean writer is able to reconfigure and rework the images and practices that were once projected as negative and "uncivilized" by colonial dictates and practices. Additionally, the innocence associated with the figure of the child enables a realistic and effective projection of the creativity and processes of rebirth used by Caribbean writers to affirm the worth and value of the culture in their societies and to suggest possibilities for further growth.

Until the late twentieth century, the figure of the child occupied a highly marginal space. Children were "to be seen and not heard". Patterned on Western traditions, which determined the place of the child in the family, children in the Caribbean were viewed merely as "miniature adults" who needed to be trained to become adults, rather than children with distinct experiences and voices of their own. In a number of ways, children in the Caribbean are still seen as being inferior and powerless, though presently, due to the influence of particular children's programs in the media and the growing presence of children's books on the shelves in many bookstores, this reality is beginning to change.

In *Sally's Way*, Johnson introduces us to a female child protagonist, Sally, who is from a rural area and whose family does not have immediate access to modern plumbing fixtures or water facilities. Through her own innovativeness, determination, and hard work Sally is able to find various ways of saving money to purchase a much-needed tank that will be able to supply water for her and her grandmother. Sally cannot achieve this unassisted, however, and the figure of the child is used here to depict the kind of unity needed to enable growth in the Caribbean, as the child protagonist marshals help from various individuals across different sections of the society: from Marvin, the fruit vendor; from Mr. Dindial, an Indian man, who owned a hardware store; from the Dindial girls, Crystal and Sharon, who Sally at first avoided because they were materially richer than her; and from Rasta Dan, the Rastafarian taxi driver. Sally thus brings together the various ethnicities and social classes that make up Trinidad, demonstrating how even with their differences, everyone is able to contribute to the social advancement of others.

Such confluence is also evident in Browne's story "Louisa Jane and The Street of Fine Old Houses", where the child protagonist, Louisa Jane, is able to convince a local archi - tect to assist in the restoration of houses on the street on which she lives, even in the face of the political decision to "knock down the houses" (56) because of their poor, dilap - dated condition and to replace them with new and advanced infrastructure based on what Chatterjee terms a "bourgeois rationality" (164). Once again, through her persistence and fearlessness, the child is depicted as playing a major role in the provision of a solution for a problem experienced by adults. In an attempt to save her grandmother's house, Louisa Jane heads to an architect's house because she has learned at school about the importance of restoring old buildings as part of her country's heritage. She remains undaunted by the brash, uninviting response of the architect's secretary when she arrives at his office, and insists that she speaks with him. Though at first her request for the restoration of her grandmother's house is turned down, eventually the architect finds Louisa Jane's grand- mother, Miss Eliza, and explains to her that it was her granddaughter's idea that helped him to envision the prospect of restoration for the houses on her street. Through the experience of Louisa Jane and her community, Browne represents an opportunity both to recover the past and to enable restoration for the future. Through the child, the normative expectations that maintain the societal status quo are questioned and challenged. The *outsiders* of the *broken down* neighborhood, through Louisa's intervention, move into an "inside" space as they become a major part of the nation's productivity, through the use of their neighborhood as part of a scheme to help preserve the architectural frame- work of the past to showcase to tourists. Through the experience of Louisa Jane, Browne demonstrates that rather than simply binding ideas of progress to the general and abso- lute tenets of globalization and eliminating supposedly *non-progressive, useless* aspects of Caribbean culture in the attempt to preserve an ideal of the nation deeply connected with socio-economic processes aligned to globalization, the Caribbean region needs to look to itself and focus much more closely on answers that lie within its borders, rather than merely accept supposedly progressive solutions from without or from "the global North" (Reddock 188).

The emotional response of the child to the situation highlights for the reader the great injustice perpetrated by the dominant social groups in society who continue to devalue the lives and experiences of the impoverished. This home is all Louisa Jane has known, having been left in the care of her grandparents by her mother who now lives abroad. It is also the sacred place of memories and happiness for her grandparents, and so whereas it is just another remote area of insignificance for those managing the country, it is an area of great signification for its inhabitants. Through Louisa Jane's determined efforts to prevent the government from demolishing her grandparents' home, Browne offers the important perspective that present identities are shaped by understanding the past and cultivating a sense of history as a sense of the possible, as a new culture emerges from among the diverse peoples of the Caribbean. Louisa Jane's creative outlook, as is so often present in children, allows her both to see and share ways in which past elements of the society can be appropriated in the present to create a more sustained future for her society.

In *Thumbelina and the Yarrow*, Nageer also uses her female child protagonist to help a community of people in Guyana to move beyond the psychological and social frag- mentation that has for so long framed their lives. Through her use of intertextuality, Nageer invokes the European fairy tale child character of Thumbelina and rewrites the script through the context of her Guyanese society. Nageer thereby also rewrites the story of her people, and through her representations of their social conditions subverts the Eurocentric, colonial stereotypes that have been used to label their identities and behavior. Nageer's Thumbelina does not begin in a space of belonging as does her European counterpart, but is instead neglected by her Aunt Maude who "missed her husband very much" after his sudden death, and so spends more time drinking than nurturing Thumbelina. As opposed to the frog in the Thumbelina fairy tale, Nageer's Thumbelina encounters a yarrow fish, a popular fish in certain villages in Guyana, but rather than attempting to rob Thumbelina of her freedom (as the frog does in the Western version), the yarrow offers Thumbelina psychological freedom from her sadness by offering her comforting words and playful experiences. Nageer seems to suggest that territories considered "Other" need to look inside rather than outside of their nations for solutions to their problems. The yarrow too points Thumbelina towards that which is inward rather than outward, so that by the time she is rescued from the well she has attained a certain level of independence and becomes more empowered to survive, despite the odds. Her fall into the well has prompted the adults in her community to intervene in Thumbelina's situation, and causes the village leader, the toshao, to chastise the villagers for their failure to properly lead the future generation, and for their choice instead to succumb to the harsh circumstances surrounding them. Each of these writers therefore seems to be proposing the same line of argument as Franklin W. Knight when he suggests that "[t]he challenge of the future will be to produce new and creative solutions to local problems, not to import, mimic, and adapt" (212).

In the twenty-first century, nations are predominantly configured through achievement in technological advancement. A major feature of this type of advancement involves the use of land, which has always played an important part in colonial and postcolonial discourse. In Caribbean literature, land has often paradoxically represented both a site for exploitation and a site for productivity. More specifically, distinction between rural and urban landscapes has been used to characterize both individual and national identity. The rural space in the Caribbean often occupies a marginal and inferior position and is usually characterized by a sense of invisibility, particularly due to the association of the rural space with the plantation system during the period of slavery.

In the stories of Johnson, Browne, and Nageer, the rural is represented in different ways. By illuminating some of the day-to-day realities of this space, these writers have sought to restore the way the rural space has tended to be characterized when subjected to the dominant mode of discourse, privileging the urban space as the space reflecting the concept and experience of modernity.

In *Sally's Way*, as Sally enjoys an early morning bath by the village stand pipe, at the start of the story, she imagines being at a waterfall and begins to dream about what it would be like to have her "very own shower!" (3). According to the Pan American Health Organization's assessment of Trinidad and Tobago in 2012, only 7.8 percent of the population in Trinidad and Tobago are without water piped directly to their houses. On the other hand, 50 percent of households "own their own water storage tanks" because of the unreliability of piped water supplies. Through her representation of the cultural realities of this rural community, Johnson helps to shed light on the ways in which members of society continue to experience inequality at the hands of what Fanon terms the "national bourgeoisie" (116) of the country. This national bourgeoisie replaced the old colonial regime but, rather than eliminating the values and systems of colonialism, has merely perpetuated many of them in order to secure their own interests in wealth and power by promoting "party politics", which continue to promote social injustices of varying kinds.

Although a great portion of the nation's heritage is connected to rural space, rural spaces in the Caribbean have tended to be associated with backwardness and stagnancy, and governments very rarely invest in these communities in the same ways in which they invest in the urban areas of their countries. Through the actions of both Sally and the members of the community, who assist her in purchasing her water tank, Johnson offers an alternative depiction of the value of rural space as a space of creativity and productivity. As Gordon Lewis argues, "[t]he overpowering cultural image of Britain, reinforced by the West Indian mimetic process, and which permeates nearly every nook and cranny of West Indian social psychology, must give way to new concepts of national and even personal identity rooted in West Indian experience itself" (513).

The rural community is also heavily represented in Nageer's *Thumbelina and the Yarrow* through the village setting she creates. She uses features of the environment to construct the plot of her story and to establish her major and minor characters. Cultural realities connect the child with the environment and as a result make a powerful statement about this significant relationship. The well into which Thumbelina falls, the practice of drinking kari (a drink made out of cassava), which is associated with village life in Guyana, the yarrow which helps to keep the drinking water clean, all help to shape village identity and all play a role in sustaining the people. Nageer seems to offer this rural space as an alternative to the individualistic power struggles associated with city life. Additionally it again provides a way of finding solutions within the space of the nation, rather than through intervention from outside Western powers or through migration. For, as Rhoda Reddock asserts, "many of the characteristics of globalization have been part of the historical experience of this region" (185), and have perpetuated in various ways experiences of oppression and victimization for the people of the Caribbean. Whereas rural space is often projected as offering limited social and economic experiences for the members of its community, Nageer demonstrates how, through the coming together of people, regardless of their differences, balance can be attained to provide what is needed for the nation's children. In addition, by reinserting the importance of the oral tradition of the village, a major feature of Caribbean rural space, through the act of story-telling by the village toshao who admonishes his people to become more productive in their communities, Nageer reminds readers of the importance of the nation's cultural beliefs and practices to provide self-knowledge and to enable both individual and communal progress.

Cultural realities associated with poverty in the Caribbean region raise questions about the ideologies of power that frame nations. According to Boehmer, in her discussion of those territories once colonized by various European powers, "[n]ationalists…reached for that which was progressive, 'modern' and improving in a Western sense as vehicles of political mobilization" (111). This action inadvertently produces a moral superiority attached to dominant social groups, which reduces the value of those who are impoverished, both in terms of how they are viewed and in terms of how they are expected to participate in the nation. What also occurs as a result of the displacement of those who are impoverished is a negative stereotyping of the identities and experiences of this group of people. The nation thus becomes defined through a series of class struggles, as progress and development of and in the nation becomes articulated through "commercial pursuits and social climbing" (Knight 162). The condition of poverty and the reality of these class struggles are evident in the Caribbean children's stories of Johnson, Browne, and Nageer.

The way of life and work ethic of Sally in *Sally's Way* celebrates the hard work of centuries of Caribbean people who have had to experience and endure conditions of poverty.

Sally is determined to buy the water tank for her household because she conceives of a time when she might be able to have her own shower in her own home. She works very hard to attain the money she needs for this venture, but there are moments in the book when the fatigue she experiences because of all the tasks she has to do to accomplish her goal becomes a bit overwhelming for readers to internalize. Though the hard work is commendable, the narrative prompts us to critique a society in which a child has to work to possess what she should really be entitled to, as a citizen of the nation – a basic water supply to meet even the most basic hygienic needs. Though Sally creates a sense of agency for herself through her determination to achieve her goal, Johnson also critiques the lack of equity present in the society, especially for a group such as children, who in many ways have no control with regard to the spaces into which they are born. Despite this, however, Sally seizes her destiny and shapes it for herself, and Johnson makes much of this within the narrative.

Browne's "Louisa Jane and The Street of Fine Old Houses" and Nageer's *Thumbelina and the Yarrow* both also depict the condition of poverty through the setting, the characterization, and the experiences of the characters. Although the cultural realities endured by impoverished people in each story is different, both child protagonists experience varying degrees of sorrow and oppression as a result of their social status. Louisa Jane at first feels the effect of poverty through the hopelessness prompted by the government's decision to destroy their homes. Thumbelina, likewise, experiences loneliness and sadness as a result of the "many days ... [at] home, in dirty clothes, without any food in her belly" (7). The representation of the cultural realities of poverty as experienced by these children challenges the ways in which such impoverished groups in society are treated, but at the same time each of these writers reveals ways in which their child protagonists are able to forge a pathway through the problems they encounter. Once again, these writers demonstrate that the solution to the problem of poverty in the nation rests in the psychological or spiritual state of the character, rather than in the material. This of course rests in deep opposition to Western principles internalized by postcolonial societies, which assign rank and respectability based on one's material possessions and social status.

The cultural education Browne's Louisa Jane receives from her teacher at school transforms her mental state and attitude and prompts her to change her situation. Likewise, the cultural education received from the yarrow and the village leader prompts positive transformation for both Thumbelina and the members of her community, including her once neglectful Aunt. Sally too acquires her cultural education from the street "corner" through the gathering of neighbors and friends who eventually all help to bring her own dream of progress to fruition. Education is therefore not restricted to "book knowledge", but is instead a fluid concept, which can be attained through various ways of knowing. It is therefore promoted as a major tool needed to secure the authenticity of the nation's character.

With different degrees of intensity, each of these children unashamedly stands against the accepted norms that govern codes of behavior based on who they are as children, as girls, and as members of the poorer class in their societies. Through a representation of their marginalized cultural realities, Johnson, Browne, and Nageer revisit the nation's past, reconstruct the nation's present, and reframe the epistemological foundation of the nation, all of which have tended to privilege Western, colonial ideologies over the cultural customs, beliefs, and experiences of the Caribbean people.

Note

1 "Colonial Girls' School" is taken from Olive Senior's poetry collection *Talking of Trees* (1985)
   © Olive Senior 1985, used by kind permission of the author.

Bibliography

Ashcroft, Bill, Gareth Griffiths and Helen Tiffin (1989) *The Empire Writes Back: Theory and Practice in Post-Colonial Literatures*. London: Routledge.

Boehmer, Elleke (2005) *Colonial and Postcolonial Literature*, 2nd ed. Oxford: Oxford University Press.

Browne, Diane (2003) *Every Little Thing Will Be Alright*. Kingston: Carlong Publishers.

Chatterjee, Partha (1993) *The Nation and its Fragments: Colonial and Postcolonial Histories*. New Jersey: Princeton University Press.

Fanon, Frantz (2004 [1961]) *The Wretched of the Earth*. Trans. Richard Pilcox. New York: Grove Press.

Hall, Stuart (1997) *Representations: Cultural Representations and Signifying Practices*. London: Sage Publications Ltd.

Health in the Americas (2012) Pan American Health Organization. www.paho.org/saludenlasamericas/index.php?option-com

James, Cynthia (2005) "From Orature to Literature in Jamaican and Trinidadian Children's Folk Traditions," *Children's Literature Association Quarterly* 30(2): 164–178.

Johnson, Joanne Gail (2002) *Sally's Way*. Oxford: Macmillan Education.

Knight, Franklin. W. (1978) *The Caribbean: The Genesis of a Fragmented Nationalism*. New York: Oxford University Press.

Lewis, Gordon (1996) "The Challenge of Independence in the British Caribbean," in Hilary Beckles and Verene Shepherd (eds) *Caribbean Freedom: Economy and Society from Emancipation to the Present*. Kingston: Ian Randle Publishers.

Nageer, Sherlina (2013) *Thumbelina and the Yarrow*. Raleigh, NC: Lulu.com.

Pacquet, Sandra Pouchet (2002). *Caribbean Autobiography: Cultural Identity and Self-Representation*. Wisconsin: The University of Wisconsin.

Prakash, Gyan (1992) "Postcolonial Criticism and Indian Historiography," *Social Text* 31/32: 8–19.

Puri, Shalini (2004) *The Caribbean Postcolonial: Social Equality, Post-Nationalism, and Cultural Hybridity*. New York: Palgrave Macmillan.

Reddock, Rhoda (2004) "Caribbean Masculinities and Femininities: The Impact of Globalisation on Cultural Representations," in Barbara Bailey and Elsa Leo-Rhynie (eds) *Gender in the 21st Century: Caribbean Perspectives, Visions and Possibilities*. Kingston: Ian Randle Publishers.

Senior, Olive (1985) *Talking of Trees*. Kingston: Calabash.

13

POSTCOLONIALITY, GLOBALIZATION, AND TRANSCULTURAL PRODUCTION OF CHILDREN'S LITERATURE IN POSTWAR TAIWAN

Andrea Mei-ying Wu

Introducing *The Cambridge Companion to Postcolonial Studies*, Neil Lazarus cogently argued that the notion of "postcoloniality" had ceased to be designated as "a historical category," a mere indicator of a historical moment that can be clearly perceived or understood as "*after* colonialism" (2004a: 3; original emphasis). Rather, "postcolonial" is a "fighting term" and a "theoretical weapon" which, on the one hand, goes beyond the ideological assumptions and articulations of "modernity" so often associated with postcolonial discourses, and, on the other hand, resists any attempt to consolidate or concretize its meanings with "all forms of nationalism" (Lazarus: 4). Ania Loomba similarly avers that "postcolonial" is "a descriptive [and] not an evaluative term" (1110). As such, postcoloniality is better understood as a critical term featuring "migrancy, liminality, hybridity, and multiculturality" as some of the major tropes and terrains for describing and investigating the complex cultural contacts and crossings, and its approaches are aptly those marked with indeterminacy and ambivalence, instead of moving toward a holistic and systematic analysis of social changes (Lazarus 4). Timothy Brennan further argues that what have been considered the "states of virtue" in postcolonial studies are the dynamics of "mobility and mixedness"—not so much for the accentuation of contingent historical experiences, as for the articulation and signification of common modes of being (2004: 133).

Such arguments neither negate nor disregard the critical changes of political regimes in the historical trajectory of Taiwan, in particular, in the post-World War II era. The contour of the contemporary history of Taiwan, as Fangming Chen shows, derives "not only from the period of Japanese occupation but also from the political authoritarianism of the postwar period" (2007: 27). After Japan's defeat in World War II, Taiwan was in 1945 ceded to China (specifically, the Kuomintang, aka KMT, the ruling party led by Chiang Kai-shek). What was subsequently introduced and enforced was not only the mandates of traditional Chinese language and culture but also the prevalence and incorporation of American culture, primarily in and through the practices of military, economic, and educational aids. Such "aids" in Neil Lazarus's delineations are "the direct, active, and sustained support of the

United States, self-proclaimed 'keeper of the peace' in the post-1945 period" to function as effective, and sometimes evasive, apparatuses for global dispensation and cultural expansion (2004b: 20). Ann McClintock, on the other hand, points out that the global expansion of the United States since the 1940s and the concomitant flow of commodities, armaments, and media information generates an impact "as massive as any colonial regime" (2004: 1189). Given the "greater subtlety, innovation and variety of these forms of imperialism," she continues, the term postcolonialism is subject to (re)negotiations and reinterpretations, as the historical rupture it implicitly or explicitly associates is no longer warranted or cannot be easily grasped (1189). Thus, with the rise of the political and economic power of the United States in the latter half of the twentieth century, postcoloniality may take a new appearance in relation to globalization which, in effect, functions as a synonym of Americanization.

In analyzing the divergent development and yet interrelated conceptualization of postcolonial discourse and globalization theory, Timothy Brennan, however, suggests that globalization, analogous to postcolonialism, is a term characterized by "a fundamental ambiguity" (122). One of the main factors lies in the opposing views the term evokes. On the one hand, it is claimed to accelerate the formation of new communities and create chances for (cross) cultural collaboration and coalition, and thence to generate a new hope for social advancement and transformation; on the other hand, it signals a threat or a danger in hegemonizing cultural differences, making the localities invisible or unidentifiable by (re)configuring the world into a single social space (Brennan 122; Ashcroft et al. 111). The binary logic of these polarized contentions, however, fails to recognize the plurality and the multi-dimensional transmutations that globalization often indicates. The possibility of permutation and renovation in (re)defining the local, as well as the global, speaks to the dynamics of globalism, as Timothy Brennan enthusiastically explains: globalization theory "looks rather to a 'new' dynamic forged by the happy chaos of an infinitely mobile citizenry, a constantly self-defined subjectivity, a terrain of virtual space consisting of multi-faceted niches of an always malleable and morphing freedom" (124). Such a freedom, marked by an ongoing and irrepressible propensity for change—in nuanced alteration or vibrant modification of the dominant—is manifest in all forms of cultural contacts and negotiations, some latent and some overt, whether in the colonial, the postcolonial, or the globalized contexts.

Bill Ashcroft, Gareth Griffiths, and Helen Tiffin add a warning against any easy acceptance of the assumption that globalization is an all-encompassing force working in a uniform dimension:

> In some respects, globalization, in the period of rapid decolonization after the Second World War, demonstrates the transmutation of imperialism into the supra-national operations of economics, communications and culture. This does not mean that globalization is a simple, unidirectional movement from the powerful to the weak, from the central to the peripheral, because globalism is **transcultural** in the same way that imperialism itself has been.
>
> (2000: 112; original emphasis)

It is thus appropriate to regard globalization as a process embedded with transcultural formations and practices, instead of casting it as something governed by a top-down and one-dimensional dominance. If globalization is to be understood as a process infused with dynamic and multi-dimensional interactions, communications, negotiations, and at times tensions and confrontations, then it is significant to see how the local subjects (re)imagine, (re)define, and represent themselves in the global context and how they react to and (re)appropriate the norms of the dominant in the transcultural process. It is from this perspective that this essay examines the transcultural production of children's literature in postwar Taiwan, with a focus on the establishment of the *ertong duwu bianji xiaozu* (Editorial Task Force for Children's Books[1]), as well as the impact of Americanization, not so much to valorize the American cultural norms, as to see the nuanced alterations and (re)appropriations of the dominant forms on the production of children's literature texts for young readers in Taiwan. Two of the initial and representative publications of the Editorial Task Force for Children's Books are discussed: Liang Lin's *Wo yao da gongji* (I Want a Big Rooster) and *Xiao yaya huijia* (Little Duckling Gets Back Home).

Ertong duwu bianji xiaozu as a site for transcultural practice

In the field of children's literature in postwar Taiwan, the establishment of *ertong duwu bianji xiaozu* (Editorial Task Force) in the mid-1960s can be regarded as one of the monumental events indicative of transcultural practice. With the sponsorship of the United Nations Children's Fund in a five-year project to develop *guomin jiaoyu* (national education), the Editorial Task Force was set up, in 1964, as an official organization to create, produce, publish, and distribute children's books to elementary schools for the supplementary reading of young learners. In a span of thirty-eight years (1964–2002), it produced almost 1,000 children's books, as well as children's encyclopedia and magazines, with various subjects and genres. Those children's books were published under the series title *zhonghua ertong congshu* (Sino-Children's Book Collection), which consisted originally of three categories, literature, health, and science, and was later increased to five to include arts and social sciences. The genres they deal with embody those typical of children's literature, such as picture books, short stories, fairy tales, folktales, myth, poetry, fiction, non-fiction, and songs and rhymes for children. Given the copious and high-quality children's books it has created and produced, as well as the writers, illustrators, editors, and other professionals it recruited, nourished, and built up later to take up the leading roles in the field of children's literature, it is fair to say that the Editorial Task Force operated significantly as a vital cultural site for the institutionalization and canonization of children's literature in postwar Taiwan.

In *Taiwan ertong wenxueshi* (The History of Taiwanese Children's Literature), Wen-Chiung Hong notes:

> Compared to those practiced in the past, the writing techniques and editorial concepts of children's literature in Taiwan did make a great advance in and after 1964, the first year that Taiwan experienced its economic take-off. [...]. In 1965, the Editorial Task Force released its first set of *zhonghua ertong congshu* (Sino-Children's Book Collection). If we compare the collection of children's books with all other children's books published at that time, we can see that they are far more revolutionary and innovative, whether it is in terms of format, layout, printing, writing, or illustrations.
>
> (4–5)

The establishment of an editorial task force with a goal to publish children's books in an unconventional scope and with novel ideas and skills as such, in particular in the early postwar decades, would have been unlikely to take place were it not for the economic aids from the United Nations Children's Fund—and, I would argue, with the United States as the major supporter and facilitator. Economic aid, as previously mentioned, works not only for the advancement of local societies but also for some purposes of cultural expansion. Negotiating in between various kinds of power structures and struggles—politics, economics, and language policy, etc., the Editorial Task Force functioned also as a crucial site for the contestations, as well as the conflation, of the ideologies dominated by, for instance, American culture and Chinese culture. Suffice it to say that the "foreign" power manifest both in American culture and Chinese culture would make the production of children's literature in Taiwan in the early postwar period inextricably transcultural.

Americanization and the production of children's literature in Taiwan: colonial or transcultural?

The way that the United States becomes the "model" for the production of children's literature in the postwar era is succinctly described by Liang Lin, an eminent writer and critic of children's literature in Taiwan:

> When the Second War World was over, the powerful United States became the model of a "successful country" admired by all mankind. People were interested in studying American culture. American children's literature also exercised a great influence on all other countries. The contact between our country and the United States with regard to children's literature was natural, in that we did not pursue it on purpose, nor did we avoid it.... The achievement of American children's literature was conspicuous. By means of translation, it almost became the new source for the development of children's literature in our country.... Translation was flourishing greatly during the 1960s, and the targets for translation were mostly children's literature texts from the United States.
>
> (*"Taiwan diqu"* 3)

Based on Lin's observation, the crosscultural contact in the production of children's literature in postwar Taiwan is evident. It is not uncommon for writers (and quite a few also work as translators; Liang Lin is one of them) in the field of children's literature to adapt, rework, or appropriate children's literature texts from foreign countries as legitimate sources to write for children in the early postwar period. American children's literature texts and presumably those classical and canonical texts from the English-speaking societies served as major sources, or "models," for the buildup of children's literature in postwar Taiwan.

Optimistic and affirmative as Lin's remarks may sound, they are, in an ironic sense, resonant with what Roderick McGillis identifies as the expressions of a particular mind-set in the colonial context:

> Colonialism is not only a political and economic activity, but it also affects cultures and it assumes a certain mind-set: a colonial mentality. The colonial mentality assumes that the colonizer represents a more advanced state of civilization than the colonized does, and therefore that the colonizer has a right to assume a position of dominance.
>
> (xxii)

It would be far too simplistic and erroneous to interpret Lin's remarks on the cultural development of Taiwanese children's literature in the early postwar period as a mere reflection of the quasi-colonial mentality. Nevertheless, what Lin delineates encapsulates the shared ideology, or the common mind-set, of those working in the field of children's literature in the early postwar decades. Liang Lin is certainly not the only one who discloses such a mentality—a willingness and an openness to embrace American culture, without signs of doubt, critique, or resistance. As a leading figure of children's literature in Taiwan, Liang Lin is highly revered and his reflections on and reaction to the American cultural effects on the formation of Taiwanese children's literature in the early stages can be indicative and representative of the common ethos and politics from that particular era and thus deserve our attention.

If considered from a different perspective, however, Lin's comment on the early impact of American children's literature on the production of Taiwanese children's literature might point to a common cultural practice in the transcultural context of the dynamic (re)negotiations and (re)appropriations of the dominant cultural forms for the renovation of the local cultural formation, not in the sense of replacement or repression, but in the promise and possibility of cultural mobility and mixedness. As Bill Ashcroft, Gareth Griffiths, and Helen Tiffin argue,

> By appropriating strategies of representation, organization and social change through access to global systems, local communities and marginal interest groups can both empower themselves and influence those global systems. Although choice is always mediated by the conditions of subject formation, the belief that one has a choice in the processes of changing one's own life or society can indeed be **empowering**.
>
> (114; emphasis mine)

It could have been in this kind of "empowering" mindset that Liang Lin wrote two children's books for the initial publication of the Editorial Task Force in the 1960s: *Wo yao da gongji* (I Want a Big Rooster, 1965; hereafter referred to as *I Want a Big Rooster*) and *Xiao yaya huijia* (Little Duckling Gets Back Home, 1966; hereafter *Little Duckling Gets Back Home*). Both are significant in that they are not only exemplary of the early publications of the Editorial Task Force, but also enlisted in *Taiwan (1945–1998) ertong wenxue 100* (One Hundred Children's Literature Texts from Taiwan, 1945–1998), the result of a formal and massive endeavor endorsed by the Council for Cultural Affairs at the turn of the century to classify and identify representative children's literature texts produced in postwar Taiwan. *I Want a Big Rooster* is identified as the first among the twelve debut publications of the Editorial Task Force and generally regarded as the first distinctive "picture book" published in postwar Taiwan (Lin and Zhao 65), while *Little Duckling Gets Back Home* is one of the earliest fairy tales produced in the postwar period for young readers.[2] Classified as a "fairy tale," the book is akin to a picture book in terms of format and rich illustrations; whereas the narrative is replete with signs of (re)appropriations, or, to put it in another way, intertextuality, of several Western classical children's tales, such as Beatrix Potter's *The Tale of Peter Rabbit* (1902) and Marjorie Flack's *The Story about Ping* (1933).

Transcultural literary production: *I Want a Big Rooster* and *Little Duckling Gets Back Home*

Narrated in terse phrases, rhythmic sentences, and child-like language, *I Want a Big Rooster* depicts the lively and amusing interactions between a little boy and a big rooster. The story opens with the unexpected encounter of Pang Pang, the boy protagonist, with a big rooster, while the boy dozes away in the breeze under a tree. Below is my tentative translation of the first few lines:

In the shade	樹蔭下，
Grows the grass,	有青草，
No sunshine	大太陽，
Can reach there.	晒不到。
Pang Pang feels sleepy	微風吹過來，
In the breeze.	胖胖想睡覺。
One two one	一二一，
Here comes a big rooster	來了一隻大公雞，
In a red cap	戴著大紅帽，
How proud he looks!	樣子真神氣！
Big Rooster	大公雞，
Feels no shame	不客氣，
Stretching his neck	伸伸脖子，
To snitch peanuts away from Pang Pang's hand.	搶走胖胖手裡的花生米。
Pang Pang is awakened in a fright.	胖胖嚇醒了。
Wow!	呀！
What a Big Rooster!	好大好大的一隻公雞！

The language demonstrates what Liang Lin has advocated for decades about the ideal narrative style for children. He maintains that one of the aesthetics of children's literature lies in the beauty of *qianyu* (plain language), which characterizes the language pattern and structure children can truly grasp and appreciate. The major task for children's literature writers is hence to craft and master such a narrative skill so as to "use and capture the language and words that children can savor and comprehend" ("*Lun ertong*" 102). For Liang Lin, "plain language" does not necessarily mean simple sentences or simplified contents, but a narrative art form carefully and creatively fashioned and practiced to embody the merit of children's language and to invigorate the imagination of childness. The deployment of "plain language" to cater to the need of child readers may not suggest something new but a common literary practice—locally and globally, for instance, in the creation of picture books. However, by advocating and insisting on the practice of plain language, Liang Lin has established a hallmark in the terrain of children's literature and such a notion has shaped the norm of literary production for young readers in Taiwan for decades.

In addition to language arts, what is characteristic of Lin's creation is the accentuation of the dynamic interaction between a child and an animal. The depiction of child-animal relationships is likewise a common motif that can be found in numerous classical children's literature texts from both the East and the West. While such a motif can be universal in the literary rendition for children, the employment of a rooster, rather than other creatures commonly found in Western children's literature texts, such as dogs, cats, rabbits, and little mice as household companions or personal pets, may speak to distinct local experiences and social realities. In the early decades of postwar Taiwan, it was not unusual for a family to keep chicks, hens, or roosters in the countryside, as well as in urban areas, as Taiwan was in the stage of transforming from an agricultural country to an industrial society. The close relationship between a child and a rooster is thus not odd or arbitrary but a familiar and relevant life experience for child readers. The proclamation "I Want a Big Rooster," as the book title illustrates, is registered with a genuine sense of childhood activities and memories. The positioning of a rooster as the key animal character in the story is therefore not purely imaginative, but indicative of a hybrid representation of the conventional mode of child-animal narrative for young readers with a subtle twist and presence of local character.

The way that the rooster is positioned not as a tender and submissive domestic creature, but a robust and aggressive competitor to the boy protagonist, is both hilarious and unsettling. Unlike the classical animal tales for children in which the major animal characters are described as either "runty" (e.g., the pig in *Charlotte's Web*) or "naughty" (e.g., the monkey in *Curious George*), the Big Rooster is portrayed as a self-confident and yet confrontational other at the outset of the story. The transgressive acts of the Big Rooster are clearly marked in his inadvertent escape from his master, his aggressive attempt to take away Pang Pang's peanuts, and his persistent pursuit of the little boy in search of more treats. The delineation of an alternative animal character as such makes the story exceptional, for it explicitly or implicitly disrupts and subverts the conventional representation of animal subjects in children's tales and recasts, from the outset, the child-animal relationship not in a foreseeable loving companionship but in an unexpected encounter registered with contestations and dynamic negotiations. The competing relationship of the two comes to a halt when Pang Pang and his brother decide to keep the rooster. The boys' decision, nevertheless, counters their mother's will—to keep a clean house without animals. While it might be stereotypical to position children and adults in opposition in terms of their polarized attitudes and reactions toward animals, the subjective agency of the two boys is meticulously highlighted in the portrayal of their "good behavior" at dinner, as well as at bedtime. The image of a "good boy" is, at this juncture, ironically reinforced, as the good demeanors of the boys are meant to impress their parents so as to keep the rooster in secret. In comparison to the Western canons of children's literature where "wild boy" images predominate—for instance, Huck in *Adventures of Huckleberry Finn* and Max in *Where the Wild Things Are*, the discourse of "good boy" is by and large underscored in the narrative for children, particularly in the 1960s when the society is relatively restrictive due to political conservatism.

The story ends with a happy reconciliation by means of the adults' agreement to Pang Pang's keeping the rooster on condition that he collect fifty stamps in exchange (for the owner of the rooster, their neighbor Mrs. Chang). Such a deal might appear peculiar to modern child readers, as the once popular childhood activity of stamp collecting has rapidly diminished with the technological advances that have made the world globally digitalized. However, the rare combination of the boy's determination to keep a rooster with an enthusiasm for stamp collecting paradoxically and yet profoundly makes the story exceptional in terms not only of local expression but of global imagination. Arguably, the mechanism of stamp collection functions not simply as a fun activity for children but a significant way for them to learn and identify self and others, as well as to connect the local with the global. Such a message is evidently communicated, perhaps right from the beginning, on the book cover where signs of crosscultural contacts and a doubleness of transcultural formation are epitomized and highlighted in the juxtaposition of two images: the exultant fusing together of the boy and the rooster and an image of the globe covered with a medley of stamps featuring various aspects of the social developments of Taiwan and its international relationships, in particular, with the United States

Figure 13.1   Cover of *I Want a Big Rooster*, Liang Lin.

[see Figure 13.1]. Such doubleness, as Clare Bradford suggests, is typical of "transnational textuality" in that it characterizes "transnational identities and lived experience" (24). Liang Lin's *I Want a Big Rooster* appears to be imbued with emerging signs of transcultural representation and (re)appropriation of the common mode of child-animal narration with an embedding of novel subjects and native implications.

Unlike the story of *I Want a Big Rooster*, which centers on a child-animal relationship, *Little Duckling Gets Back Home* is an anthropomorphic tale of a defiant little duck and his eventful adventures. Analogous to the child protagonist in Beatrix Potter's the *Tale of Peter Rabbit*, the little duckling is positioned as a nonconformist. While Peter Rabbit is distinct from his three docile sisters in his unruliness and individualistic acts to seek adventures, the little duckling is dissimilar to his ten obedient brothers in his willfulness and waywardness. As can be imagined, the little duckling refuses to follow his mother's order to stay home and, instead, sets out for some exciting excursion, while she is absent. Not knowing the danger in the water, the little duckling gets into serious trouble and the expedition turns out to be a calamity. He then drifts away to a remote town where he encounters an old ox, a big yellow dog, and a big wild cat who nearly swallows him up. Devoid of all hope, the little duckling is eventually captured, only to discover that it is his master, Mr. Ke, who comes to his rescue and gets him back. Like Peter, the duckling has a blissful reunion with his siblings and his mother who welcomes him home with loving care. Didactically significant, the little duckling has learned a good lesson, just like his literary counterpart.

Both stories are resonant with didacticism in the end, but that the little duckling is rescued by his master, instead of finding a resolution on his own, may suggest a disparate cultural imagination and representation of the child subject. As a canonical figure of children's literature from the West (typically, the United Kingdom and the United States), Peter represents the idea of individuality and the spirit of autonomy commonly valued and valorized in Western societies. However, although the little duckling is depicted as a nonconforming character, his proclivity for individualism is somewhat hampered in the process and his subjectivity is not one that accords with the "model" in the Western literary canon, but one resonant with traditional Confucian didacticism: to obey one's parents. As such, the narrative closes with a candid description of the little duckling's rueful repentance as he cries bitterly in front of his siblings [see Figure 13.2]: "Good Mother! Good Mother! From now on, I surely will listen to you" (Lin, *Xiao yaya* 35). The moralistic messages are effectively communicated in the little duckling's open confession of his wrongdoings, as well as a promise of his conversion into a good boy who will "listen and obey"—by way of self-regulation and self-discipline.

The story of *Little Duckling Gets Back Home* is reminiscent of another classical children's tale, *The Story about Ping* (1933) written by Marjorie Flack and illustrated by Kurt Wiese—both are award-winning authors and illustrators in the United States. Both stories draw on a duckling as the central character who lives in a large family. While the main character in the story of *Little Duckling Gets Back Home* embarks on a solitary journey out of a sense of willfulness and ignorance, the protagonist of *the Story about Ping* becomes a loner wanderer because of a moment of inadvertence and timidity. Away from home, both encounter a series of life-threatening mishaps. Both stories close with a happy ending, as the two loners are eventually reunited with their families. The storyline may seem parallel; the subject formation of the two main characters in the respective tales however differs significantly. Ping is positioned as a self-contented little duck who follows the command of his master, just like everyone else in his family. His vagrant life in the wild is initiated not by his determination to get away, as is the naughty duckling in *Little Duckling Gets Back Home*, but by his negligence and a failure to follow suit. The subjectivity of the two characters remains in sharp contrast.

Albeit *The Story about Ping* is set against the backdrop of Yangtze River and is accordingly infused with Oriental cultural implications, the subject formation of the protagonist Ping is still largely situated in the Western/American context, as he is eventually ordained to be punished by his master—something he dreads the most from the beginning. An exemplification of male toughness and a valorization of individualistic self-autonomy of the juvenile subject are clearly articulated and consolidated. Ping is ultimately (re)configured as a conventional (Western) hero who dares to pit himself against his misfortune. By contrast, the little duckling in Lin's narration looks audacious in the beginning and yet lacks all the courage and capacity to stand on his own feet in the long run. He is after all a little one in need of an other's protection.

The reference to the two classical Western children's tales not only imbues Lin's creation of *Little Duckling Gets Back Home* with a mixed sense of cultural hybridity but also

Figure 13.2   From *Little Duckling Gets Back Home*, Liang Lin (34).

intertextually significant in that it "offers insights into the representation of subjectivity," as John Stephens argues in another context (2000: 19). The subject formation of the little duckling diverges from that of the protagonist either in *The Tale of Peter Rabbit* or in *The Story about Ping*. Peter is positioned as a typical "wild boy" who nimbly escapes danger by his own wits, while Ping is fashioned as a common boy in the beginning but eventually finds the courage to go through the ultimate test. Both illustrate the culturally sanctioned and expected ideal of boyhood with an accentuation of individualism and self-autonomy. The subject position of the protagonist in Lin's fairy tale *Little Duckling Gets Back Home*, by contrast, remains passive and demonstrates a vacillation between the audacious and rebellious and the submissive and powerless. The subjectivity of a juvenile character constructed as such is problematic and may suggest a dilemma in transcultural negotiations and adaptations. Given that the little duckling is miraculously protected and saved by a superior (foreign) power, the story is evocative of a "colonial" sentiment and metaphorically speaks to the juvenile and peripheral identity of Taiwan as a nation at a time when the rubrics of the Cold War divide are in place.[3]

Notes

1 I adopt Shu-Jy Duan's translation of *"ertong duwu bianji xiaozu"* as "Editorial Task Force for Children's Books" (154). It will be referred to as the Editorial Task Force hereafter. All other translations from Chinese into English are mine, unless otherwise indicated.
2 Prior to the publications of the Editorial Task Force, translations of classical fairy tales from the West and adaptions of traditional Chinese literature and folktales are some of the common modes of literary production for children.
3 This paper is part of the result of the research project "Mapping the Canons and Transcultural Production of Children's Literature in Postwar Taiwan" (MOST 103-2410-H-006-068-MY2) sponsored by the Ministry of Science and Technology in Taiwan.

Bibliography

Ashcroft, Bill, Gareth Griffiths and Helen Tiffin (2000) *Post-Colonial Studies: The Key Concepts.* New York: Routledge.

Bradford, Clare (2011) "Children's Literature in a Global Age: Transnational and Local Identities," *Barnboken: Journal of Children's Literature Research*, 34(1): 20–34.

Brennan, Timothy (2004) "From Development to Globalization: Postcolonial Studies and Globalization Theory," in Neil Lazarus (ed.) *The Cambridge Companion to Postcolonial Studies.* Cambridge: Cambridge University Press, 120–138.

Chen, Fangming (2007) "Postmodern or Postcolonial? An Inquiry into Postwar Taiwanese Literary History," in David Der-wei Wang and Carlos Rojas (eds.) *Writing Taiwan: A New Literary History.* Durham: Duke University Press, 26–50.

Duan, Shu-Jy (1997) "Text and Context: Factors in the Development of Children's Literature in Taiwan, 1945–1995, and the Emergence of Young Adult Literature," in Sandra L. Beckett (ed.) *Reflections of Change: Children's Literature Since 1945.* Westport: Greenwood, 153–160.

Flack, Marjorie (1933) *The Story about Ping.* Illus. Kurt Wiese. New York: Scholastic, 1933.

Hong, Wen-Chiung (1994) *Taiwan ertong wenxueshi* (A History of Taiwanese Children's Literature). Taipei: Chuan-Wen. (In Chinese)

Lazarus, Neil (2004a) "Introducing Postcolonial Studies," in Neil Lazarus (ed.) *The Cambridge Companion to Postcolonial Studies.* Cambridge: Cambridge University Press, 1–16.

——— (2004b) "The Global Dispensation since 1945," in Neil Lazarus (ed.) *The Cambridge Companion to Postcolonial Studies.* Cambridge: Cambridge University Press, 19–40.

Lin, Liang (1965) *"Lun ertong wenxue de yishu jiazhi"* (On the Aesthetic Values of Children's Literature). *Ertong duwu yanjiu* (Studies on Children's Reading Materials). Taipei: Xiao Xuesheng, 99–109. (In Chinese)

——— (1965) *Wo yao da gongji* (I Want a Big Rooster). Illus. Kuo-Tsung Chao. Nantou: Department of Education of Taiwan Provincial Government. (In Chinese)

——— (1966) *Xiao yaya huijia* (Little Duckling Gets Back Home). Illus. Ying-Wu Chen. Nantou: Department of Education of Taiwan Provincial Government. (In Chinese)

——— (1991) *"Taiwan diqu sishiwu nian lai de ertong wenxue fazhan, 1945–1990"* (The Forty-five Years of Development of Children's Literature in Taiwan, 1945–1990), in Hong Wen-Chiung (ed.) *Huawen ertong wenxue xiaoshi, 1945–1990* (The Concise History of Sino-Children's Literature, 1945–1990). Taipei: The Children's Literature Society of the Republic of China, 1–4. (In Chinese)

Lin, Wen-Bao (ed.) (2000) *Taiwan (1945–1998) ertong wenxue 100* (One Hundred Children's Literature Texts from Taiwan, 1945–1998). Taipei: Council for Cultural Affairs. (In Chinese)

Lin, Wen-Bao and Xiu-Jin Zhao (2003) *Ertong duwu bianji xiaozu de lishi yu shenying* (The History and Silhouette of the Editorial Task Force for Children's Books). Taitung: Graduate Institute of Children's Literature. (In Chinese)

Loomba, Ania (2004) "Situating Colonial and Postcolonial Studies," in Julie Rivkin and Michael Ryan (eds.) *Literary Theory: an Anthology.* 2nd ed. Oxford: Blackwell, 1100–1111.

McClintock, Anne (2004) "The Angel of Progress: Pitfalls of the Term 'Post-colonialism'," in Julie Rivkin and Michael Ryan (eds.) *Literary Theory: an Anthology.* 2nd ed. Oxford: Blackwell, 1185–1196.

McGillis, Roderick (2000) "Introduction," in Roderick McGillis (ed.) *Voices of the Other: Children's Literature and the Postcolonial Context*. New York: Garland, xix–xxxii.

Potter, Beatrix (1902) *The Tale of Peter Rabbit*. London: Frederick Warne.

Rey, H.A. (1941) *Curious George*. New York: Houghton Mifflin.

Sendak, Maurice (1963) *Where the Wild Things Are*. New York: HarperCollins.

Stephens, John (2000) "Children's Literature, Text and Theory: What are We Interested in Now?" *Papers: Explorations into Children's Literature* 10(2): 12–21.

Twain, Mark (1995 [1885]) *The Adventures of Huckleberry Finn*. New York: St. Martin's.

White, E.B. (1952) *Charlotte's Web*. New York: Harper Trophy.

14

THE PARADOXICAL NEGOTIATION OF COLONIALITY AND POSTCOLONIALITY IN AFRICAN CHILDREN'S LITERATURE WITH PARTICULAR REFERENCE TO ZIMBABWE

Mickias Musiyiwa

Introduction

In this chapter I interrogate the creative process of African children's literature in order to evaluate the invariably complex and ambivalent role by which the African writer endeavors to assist juvenile audiences negotiate colonial and postcolonial conditions. Various factors influence a creative process in which the transposition and/or revival of the African oral tradition and its blending with modern literary strategies has become the dominant creative aesthetic trend. Within a context fraught with cultural tensions such as the African and Western cultural interface, African society expects its writers to engage with the endlessly dynamic and ever complicating African modernity and interpret it for children. Writers therefore aspire to use literature to teach, inform and entertain children relative to the social turbulence of their audience's world of experience. In order to fully conceptualize such a creative process located in a socio-historically volatile political and cultural context, in which both a multiplicity of scores with imperial centers are still to be settled and intra-postcolony complexities attended to, a multi-theoretical perspective is required. I therefore situate my analysis within Afrocentric and postcolonialist frameworks. I argue that whereas African writers have tended to strategize their social commitment around the aesthetic technique of blending African and Western literary traditions in order to negotiate coloniality and postcoloniality, a multitude of complex questions relating to language of expression, the use of oral literary styles and themes and audience may impede the accomplishment of their purposes. If any success is to be measured, it is limited and paradoxical.

Theorizing and defining the African creative process

Any attempt to conceptualize African children's literature will inevitably draw upon theories of Afrocentrism and postcolonialism. Afrocentrism provides an ideological inspiration for the African writer with which to counter the imperial power and attempt to assert social and cultural autonomy. Consciously or unconsciously a great number of African writers demonstrate a clear obsession with the foregrounding of the African past and its values, a strategy to respond to the conditions of coloniality and postcoloniality. Postcolonialism enables one to fully comprehend the nature of the complex drama that constitutes the interplay between African and Western culture in the context of imperial domination and its aftermaths. African literature emerged and grew consequent to its dialogue with colonialism. From a postcolonial perspective therefore, modern African literature is an example of postcolonial literatures, which, according to Ashcroft, Griffiths & Tiffin (2002: 2)

> emerged in their present form out of the experience of colonization and asserted themselves by foregrounding the tension with the imperial power, and by emphasizing their differences from the assumptions of the imperial centre.

However, this definition raises some complex questions with implications for the identity and function of African literature. In the absence of an ideal but hybridized African culture, what identity does the new literature assume? How feasible will it be for the African writer to assert complete Africanness through that literature? As regards function, what does it function to teach in a world in which exhibition of complete Africanness is by and large practically impossible, as is also the total embrace of Western culture? Generally there are two categories in the African creative activity. On the one hand there is an interface whereby a writer attempts to blend both the African and the classical Western canons, and on the other hand the two canons stand more or less autonomously. These are the oral literary creative process of the pre-European era and the modern, colonially-induced written creative activity. The orientation of children into clan or tribal cultural and moral ideologies was considered a serious responsibility left especially to storytellers. When modern African children's literature rose in the 1950s and 1960s, African writers were putting themselves in the shoes of the traditional oral artists before them. They saw themselves as the modern or neo-oral artists extending the role of their predecessors. Partly but strongly inspired by the African nationalist ideology, pioneer African writers championed the Afrocentric perspective and argued that their writing ought to be conscious of the role their societies have historically placed upon them – to educate their societies in the most sensitive issues concerning life. It is this consciousness that makes African writers exhibit "the sense of utilitarian obligation … towards the societies that have nurtured them" (Killam & Rowe 2000: 64). As expected, one such obligation is the (re)teaching and entertaining of children. Chinua Achebe, Africa's first novelist, confirms this role in his essay "The Novelist as Teacher" when he states that: "The writer cannot expect to be excused from the task of re-education and regeneration that must be done." In another essay, "The Writer and his Community," he justifies this role by reference to how the traditional African artist was obligated to serve society without claiming personal ownership of the art they would have produced. He thus finds himself bound to inherit and perpetuate this traditional obligation in the modern context.

However, the emergence within a predominantly oral creative process of written literature, intended to perform the same function as oral literature, that is, teaching children, is an avant-garde trend. The combination of letters of the alphabet to construct words, phrases and sentences as literary expressive modes is a modernist tendency in relation to African traditional aesthetics. The transposition of the expressive medium (of art) defamiliarized how African audiences perceived the same reality: what was once easily perceived through the verbal and bodily artistic images of oral performances was now being delivered through an unfamiliar modality which required the skills of literacy to decipher. While some writers merely transposed oral literature into the written form, others went further to produce a new written African literature which fused Western and African literary styles. This arose after the realization that the new world of experience had been significantly transformed and required experimentation with new images in order to comprehend the dynamic reality. For other writers it was mere imitation of Western literary models, glorifying metropolitan values as beneficial to Africans. However as Ashcroft *et al.* (2002: 220) rightly observe, the literature, philosophy and art "produced by post-colonial societies are in no sense continuations or simple adaptions of European models." Rather, through such new creative endeavors the African writer is making fundamental remarks pertaining to his culture and to the domineering imperial culture which has transformed him into a new consciousness. Unfortunately, the new consciousness is neither completely Western nor African rooted, but straddles the two cultures to form a cultural consciousness in a kind of middle position. Achebe (2009: 5) admits to his own orientation into this new cultural consciousness which views "events from neither the foreground nor the background, but the *middle* ground." He further substantiates the paradoxical consciousness saying:

> The middle ground is neither the origin of things nor the last things; it is aware of a future to head into and a past to fall back on; it is the home of doubt and indecision, of suspension of disbelief, of make-belief, ... of the unpredictable, of irony
> (Achebe 2009: 6).

Clearly the modern African creative process has twists and turns as well as somersaults in its mediation of modernity, a problem that, as I stated before and will illustrate later, emanates from its contradictory origins. This critical realization thus necessitates the logic behind the adoption of post-colonialism as a theoretical framework to further comprehend how, why and the extent to which the African writer "writes back to the centre," to borrow Salman Rushdie's phrase. The complex duality and subtlety of postcolonial culture as a mongrelized culture invariably entails "a dialectical relationship between the 'grafted' European cultural system and an indigenous ontology, with its impulse to create or recreate an independent local identity" (Ashcroft *et al.* 2002: 220). But as I questioned before, in view of this complex hybridity, is the pursuance of an autonomous African identity possible? Many African writers, including Chinua Achebe, as noted above, think this is possible – they have to resuscitate Africa's cultural past.

The rise of modern African children's literature

The emergence of written African children's literature emanates from Christian missionaries' evangelical-linguistic efforts. The missionaries' primary intention was to harness strategies that would aid their evangelical activities. Africans would understand the Bible (or Christian salvation) better if it was translated into their own mother tongues. Working in harness with their African converts, they designed orthographies for native languages and proceeded to translate hymns, biblical stories and passages and other liturgical material into native languages. They also introduced Christian literature meant to broaden African converts' conceptualization of Christian life and salvation. Missionaries were the first to introduce European children's literature, although it was later to be expanded in colonial schools. It is precisely for this reason that the Western literary and Christian sensibilities are so resonant in modern African literary texts. Later African independence and subsequent attempts at nation building marked the onset of a new aesthetic trend in which celebrating African independence and revivifying Africa's cultural and historical past were the major thematic preoccupations.

Before delving into the content of this new literature, with its expected function in mind, it is crucial to stress its elitist origins and thus its double-edged role in responding to coloniality and post-coloniality. The language issue is here crucial within the African creative process. That the new literature appeared in both colonial and native languages and was written by an African elite class envying European privileges resulted in two categories of children's literature with unequal status. By using a language symbolizing the prestige and power of the metropolitan culture, African literature in European languages naturally assumed a privileged status as compared to that written in local languages. "By the very fact of writing in the language of a dominant culture," the new African writers signified that "they have temporarily or permanently entered a specific and privileged class endowed with the language, education and leisure necessary to produce such works" (Ashcroft *et al.* 2002: 220).

Against the backdrop of social commitment, the new literature had a problem of audience. The majority of African children and indeed adults remained illiterate or semi-literate. Even the literature in indigenous languages had the same problem of audience when the limited access to literacy by African children is again taken into consideration. In colonial Zimbabwe for instance, like elsewhere in colonial Africa, a screening mechanism was effectively employed to allow only a small minority of black children to learn beyond primary school (see Kadhani & Riddell 1981). Although African children continued to be entertained by their oral literature, in the face of being deprived of literacy the literature produced by old storytellers in the villages was largely deficient in the symbols and images that could assist African children's mental cognition of the social change that was taking place. Whereas simply written literature in indigenous languages would be deciphered by an African child with primary school literacy level, it did not fare well in relation to its intended function in light of the linguistic context in which it was being produced. Writing and speaking (the privileged) colonial languages was the expectation and the norm. As a strategy to exert their power and values among the colonized, metropolitan centers imposed in their colonies language policies that promoted "the metropolitan language as the norm," meanwhile marginalizing the languages of imperial subjects "as impurities." Colonial languages were "the medium through which conceptions of 'truth', 'order', and 'reality' become established" (Ashcroft *et al.* 2002: 7). Consequently, literature in indigenous languages was not considered to have adequate cognitive parameters to equip the African child with the requisite knowledge to perceive society. Bakhtin (1980: 271) has theorized that the "victory of one reigning language ... over others," results in the incorporation of the lower social classes (or the colonized in our case) "into a unitary language and truth, the canonization of ideological systems," and this would determine "the content and power of the ... unitary language in the linguistic and stylistic thought...." Having been introduced into that linguistic mind-set, the African writer developed a negative attitude towards African languages and their literatures.

Thus colonialism's linguistic consciousness was of unequal relations. "Far from being merely a system of abstract grammatical categories," the centralized European languages were " 'ideologically saturated,' embodying a worldview, a particular set towards behaviour and action in the social world" (Bolland 1996: 3). It is against this linguistic fact vis-à-vis the Afrocentric role of African literature that Ngugi wa Thiong'o (1987: 16) contends that: "The domination of a people's language by the languages of the colonizing nations was crucial to the domination of the mental universe of the colonized." The social commitment to regenerate and rehabilitate African children culturally becomes ambivalent for the reason that such a literature also seeks recognition by the metropolitan culture, and not solely by its African audience. It is a literature that now participates with vigor in imperial glory and its popular culture. Elevating a language to higher status does not only give power to the language, it also gives power and prestige to the culture it embodies. As a result the culture and values of African children's traditional literature, whether written or oral and in colonial or native languages, were perceived as inferior. The cultural-linguistic element is so domineering that whether African writers demonstrated their mastery of the colonial language writing about African culture and its environment, it is Western children's literature with its Christian and Western historical, cultural and environmental images – snow, ships, trains, knights, etc. – that was considered superior. Of course there are other African writers, such as Zimbabwean writers, for example, who have decided to make their creative processes emollient by ignoring the sticky language debate. They write in both African and European languages, but that still does not escape the entrapment because their works "follow an implicit hierarchy" in which the colonial language matters because it is the language of creative recognition (Ricard 2004: 133).

A Zimbabwean case study

Although I now refer to specific texts of Zimbabwean children's literature to illustrate my argument concerning the paradoxical social commitment of the African writer, in many respects I have already made the argument. Zimbabwean writers of juvenile literature were pre-occupied with reviving African tradition. Hence, their works draw heavily from oral tradition to revive African people's history and culture (Veit-Wild 1992: 79). It is important to state that Zimbabwean children's literature in indigenous languages, like elsewhere in Africa, straddles the boundary between what is generally called children's and adult's literature because both adults and literate children could read it.

Zimbabwean writers have combined modern and traditional stylistics in fascinating ways. *Feso* (1956), the first Shona novel, written by Solomon Mutswairo, experiments with African and Western literary styles to comment on colonial oppression. It blends the *ngano* (folktale) devices of Shona storytelling and characterization and the Christian quest from (evidently) John Bunyan's *Pilgrim's Progress*, to produce an allegorical indictment of colonial repression, and of suppression and land alienation. The narrative's eponymous character, Feso, embarks on a precarious journey to the neighboring Pfumojena's kingdom in search of a wife for his newly installed chief, Nyamombe. He is an ideal ruler – he provides for and respects his subjects, who are living in harmony. He is contrasted with Pfumojena who rules with an iron fist to the effect that his subjects are in constant lamentation. The contrast between the two kings' governances symbolizes the colonizer-colonized relationship. The inclusion of the Nehanda legend in the narrative through a poetics fashioned out of a Shona religious poem is a reaffirmation of African culture and history, which the metropolitan center had denied existed. The writer thus endeavors to counter Eurocentric stereotypes about Africa. In a sense Mutswairo was therefore writing back to such metropolitan echoes, to teach the African child that Africa had culture and history to be proud of.

It is because of such a subtle and sharp attack on the colonial value system through the use of Shona metaphor and idiom that the novel became so popular with African readers. The wide reception extended to political activism. The poem in the novel was recited at African nationalist rallies resulting in the book being expunged from the school curriculum and subsequently banned. The same fate was to follow Ndabaningi Sithole's Ndebele novel, *Umvukela wamaNdebele* [*The Ndebele Uprising*] (1956). Based on Ndebele military history, the narrative incorporates Ndebele war songs and, like its Shona counterpart, is an attempt to revive African history to inculcate pride and confidence among the colonially subdued Africans. Its title was, however, viewed as seditious, bent on evoking anti-colonization violence such as the British had encountered in the 1890s when colonizing Zimbabwe. The book's militant title was thus removed and it was re-titled *AmaNdebele ka Mzilikazi* [*The Ndebeles of Mzilikazi*] to conform to tribal consciousness, which was part and parcel of colonialism's survival strategy of divide and rule. Ndebele children should contend with their identity as followers of Mzilikazi and not imagine any shared experiences with their Shona neighbors or the possibility of a union, which might challenge colonial domination.

Such literature reflects two challenges for the role of the African writer. First was that of censorship by the colonial authorities. How could the African educate the African child about their history and cultural values without antagonizing the powers that be? Indeed some African writers, such as Mutswairo, had employed subtle idiom and metaphor to allegorize the essential message of their works to evade censorship, but the messages were eventually detected with the help of comprador African reviewers and readers. Second was a challenge of a philosophical nature, which I earlier alluded to. If the African writer was committed to the project of cultural regeneration, how was this possible to a people whose mind-sets had been culturally hybridized? Some less educated writers simply enjoyed the activity of converting oral literary forms into the written form without deploying their subjectivities in case they ruffled the feathers of colonialism.[1] Although arousing nostalgia with these representations of an idealized Shona past, they were not emotionally combative in their response to colonialism, dealing as they did with nature, African marriage, taboos, hunting, etc. – topics colonial authorities felt were not provocative. Iyasere (1982: 20) contends that Western critics wanted African literature to deal with "non-literary elements in African creative writings …the socio-anthropological details, the quaint, and, to them, the exotic aspects." Therefore, such literature merely taught children about how life was in the past so that they could compare it with the present.

A combination of censorship, alienation and inferiority complex prompted the majority of Zimbabwean writers in local languages to produce writings that glorified Eurocentric values, and perpetuated and validated such colonial stereotypes as the invincibility of the whiteman, the whiteman's burden, the supposed primitiveness of the blackman, the blackman's propensity for tribal warfare, Africa as the "Dark Continent," and many others. Because the majority of critical voices influencing the African writer were non-African, a dangerous situation arose in which writers "come to emphasize the values which they think their foreign readership demands" and this led "to an expatriate literature, and false artistic values" (E.D. Jones cited in Iyasere 1982: 20). In the same literature the city as a symbol of modernity and whiteman's culture is to be envied and the rural space, symbolizing tradition and retrogression, ought to be despised by the African child. Ironically, in the same literature the African who has ventured into the urban space is depicted as a figure of comic buffoonery. To the African the city environment is sophisticated and untameable. Its technology and structures – tall buildings, bright street lights, tapped water, trains, fast-moving and hooting vehicles, crowded people and the general sonic urban environment – are a marvel. But the African lacks the knowledge to conceptualize its images and fit into this unprecedented environment. It confuses him. In Marangwanda's *Kumazivandadzoka [Journey of uncertain return]* (1959), the naïve and rural dweller, Saraoga, enters the city but it baffles him. He sees people fetching water at a tap but does not know how the tap is operated. He whips the tap thinking it is stingy or just too lazy to give him some water. The writer ridicules the African as lacking the knowledge and consciousness required to comprehend modernity.

Western education is therefore a must if an African needs to be at peace with the fast changing and complicating environment. As a result, formal education is celebrated in children's literature. In Ntabezihle Sigogo's poem "Bongani amakhiwa" ("Be thankful to the Europeans"), the Ndebele writer pays homage to Europeans for bringing formal education to Africa. The poem's authorial ideology is merely an affirmation of other forms of literature such as plays, songs and stories, which were an important component of the colonial school curriculum, which considered education as the light coming to illuminate the "Dark Continent." I personally recall the song "This little light of mine" which we sang in primary school in eulogy of Europeans' presumed benevolence in bringing education to Africans. We vowed in the song that "we will not put it under a bushel/But let it shine, let it shine, let it shine." Therefore in reading this literature and singing such songs we were in a process of self-denigration; alienating ourselves from our culture. This brings back the crucial question in this chapter – the paradoxical function of this kind of children's literature. The pursuance of Christian themes is a common trend in Zimbabwean children's literature in which the African polygamous marriage is always condemned as adulterous and ancestral veneration as pagan worship. The priest and Shona writer Patrick Chakaipa sees nothing good in the African past and its marriage and religious institutions. In *Karikoga gumi remiseve* (*The-lonely-one: Master of Ten Arrows*, 1959) Africans are depicted perpetually engaged in tribal warfare, with tribal groups raiding each other for cattle, women and grain and in the process committing horrendous bloodshed. The book's title is an epithet meaning someone who, like Karikoga, the eponymous protagonist of the narrative, has expertise in shooting with a bow and arrow.

After independence in 1980, a plethora of children's works by African writers emerged. The new creative tendency was inspired by independence with literature adopting a nationalist thrust of foregrounding African customs and traditions for cultural rehabilitation. With obstacles of colonial censorship removed, new publishing houses opened and the new government calling for imaginative writing to participate in the process of cultural restoration and national identity, writers wrote nationalist literature extolling the liberation war, pre-colonial history and the new nation's cultural past. Literature that had been banned during the colonial period, like Mutswairo's *Feso* and Sithole's *Umvekela wamaNdebele*, were republished. As Killam & Rowe (2000: 64) have noted, such literature demonstrates a "desire to provide African children with an Afrocentric view of the world, one that may balance and rectify the cultural, ideological and other content of non-African texts." Although the transposition of oral to written literature continued, there was a notable stylistic shift in which the syncretisation of oral and English literary techniques became a trend to many writers. Children's poetry, drama and prose were fashioned out of some piquant traditional stories such as myths, legends, historicizing narratives, dilemma and trickster tales, among others, with such elements that enthrall children as humor and make-belief included. Such a stylistic trend emanates from the Zimbabwean writer's realization that despite independence, the legacy of the imperial center was permanent. African culture had been diluted, and to resuscitate the African pre-colonial culture was a complex task riddled with contradictions.

Charles Mungoshi's *Stories from a Shona Childhood* (1989) and *One Day Long Ago: More Stories from a Shona Childhood* (1991) resuscitate the scintillating storytelling tradition of the Shona, bringing African cultural life of the pre-colonial period to the fore. They attempt to achieve the Afrocentric assertion that African oral literary tradition constitutes "the historically indisputable core of the canon of African literature" (Chinweizu, Jemie & Madubuike, 1980: 13). In their anthology of folktales Stephen Alumenda and Roger Harmon include aetiological myths, traditional stories which children find fascinating because they try to explain some complex mysteries in their physical and social environments. Alumenda's *Yemurai and the Talking Drum and Other Stories* (2008) includes stories about why the pig's snout is blunt and why the chameleon walks slowly, while Harmon's *Hare, Baboon and their Friends* (1987) introduces children to the animal world. It also includes the pourquoi stories, explaining how animals came to live with human beings and why the hippo has short hairs. In her book *The First Ones: Nehanda and Chaminuka* (2001), Margaret M. Tredgold revives the most influential legends of Shona political and religious history, Nehanda and Chaminuka. The legend of Nehanda is of particular significance because of Nehanda's courage in inspiring armed resistance to British colonization in the 1890s. It is the same legend which Mutswairo incorporated into his narrative *Feso*, nearly half a century earlier, and which led to the narrative's censorship. Her refusal to be baptised into Christianity just before she was executed and her words that "my bones are going to rise" greatly inspired the armed struggle for independence in the 1960s and 1970s which culminated in Zimbabwe's independence in 1980. Today she stands as the nation's foremost female icon. Chaminuka is famous for his supernatural powers, which baffled the Shona neighbors, the Ndebele, and incoming Europeans. His prophecy "I see men without knees invading the land" has been immortalized in Shona folklore and nationalist myth-making.[2] Tredgold is obviously in search of relevant cultural icons and models for African children as alternatives to the Western and biblical heroes and heroines imposed on them through English and Christian literatures. However, with the new Zimbabwean government inheriting colonial educational institutions and making superficial or no reforms at all to disentangle the education curriculum from the cultural legacy of the imperial center, such works remained hierarchically lower in status than English children's literature. English literature continued to be imported by the Ministry of Education and donated by Western philanthropists. Meanwhile speaking in English was being enforced in schools and speaking in local languages punishable. Although Shona and Ndebele are now recognized as official languages on a par with English in the newly introduced 2013 Constitution, English still maintains a more prestigious status as the constitution recognizes it as "the language of record."

Conclusion

In my interrogation of African children's literature the intention was to illustrate and evaluate the ambivalent outcomes African writers endeavor to accomplish against the contradictory cultural milieu in which they write. The history of modern African literature in general and children's literature in particular is laden with emotive arguments, and in particular the call for the African writer to be socially committed. They have to identify with Africa in their writings if they want to assume the respected traditional role of the African storyteller of the past. To (re)construct Africa's cultural and historical identity in order to help their audiences negotiate their colonial and post-colonial experiences, they should not only have the relevant linguistic consciousness to enable them to resist the imposed linguistic power of the imperial center, but also should adopt a suitable stylistic stance. I have demonstrated that the aesthetic stance of African children's literature is influenced by a horde of factors including the initial missionary evangelical crusades, Christian and colonial education, the colonial language policy, colonial censorship, the African oral tradition and African nationalist ideologies and independence. The desire, on one hand, to be culturally germane and carry out the responsibility of educating children and, on the other hand, to simultaneously engage with the center to resolve certain African grievances, necessitated recourse to the Afrocentric and post-colonial theories in order to attain a broader and deeper conceptualization of the nature and concerns of African children's literature. My contention is that although African writers strategized their approaches to coloniality and postcoloniality by adopting various aesthetic ideologies, their literary works are entrapped in a complex and antagonistic cultural interface that renders their function paradoxical.

Notes

1 Such is the case with anthologies of Shona folktales such as Jane Chifamba's *Ngano dzePasichigare* [*Folktales of the Pre-colonial Era*] (1964), Aaron Hodza's *Ngano dzeMatambidzanwa* [*Traditional Folktales*] (1982) and Shamuyarira's *Madetembedzo Akare Namatsva* [*Shona Traditional and Modern Poetry*] (1959).
2 The prophecy was spoken in 1883 when Chaminuka was about to be executed by Ndebele warriors. "Men without knees" refers to the fact that the Europeans' knees could not be seen because they were wearing trousers.

Bibliography

Achebe, C. (2009) *The Education of a British-Protected Child*, London: Penguin Books.
Achebe, C. (1988) *Hopes and Impediments*, New York: Anchor Books.
Alumenda, S. (2008) *Yemurai and the Talking Drum and Other Stories*, Gweru: Mambo Press.
Ashcroft, B., Griffiths, G. & Tiffin, H. (2002) *The Empire Writes Back: Theory and Practice in Post-colonial Literatures*, 2nd edn., London: Routledge.
Bakhtin, M. (1980) *The Dialogic Imagination: Four Essays* (trans. C. Emerson & M. Colquitt), Austin and London: University of Texas Press.
Bolland, J. (1996) *Language and the Quest for Political and Social Identity in the African Novel*, Accra: Woeli Publishing Services.
Chakaipa, P. (1958) *Karikoga gumi remiseve*, Harare: Longman.
Chimweizu, Jemie, O. & Madubike, I. (1980) *Toward the Decolonization of African Literature*, London: KPI.
Harmon, R. (1987) *Hare, Baboon and their Friends*, Gweru: Mambo Press.
Iyasere, S. O. (1982) "African Critics of African Literature: A Study in Misplaced Hostility," *African Literature Today* 7: 21–27.
Kadhani, M. & Riddell, R. (1981) "Education," in Colin Stoneman (ed.), *Zimbabwe's Heritage*, London: Macmillan.
Killam, D. & Rowe, R. (2000) *The Companion to African Literatures*, Oxford: James Currey.
Marangwanda, J. (1959) *Kumazivandadzoka*, Salisbury: Longman.
Mungoshi, C. (1989) *Stories from a Shona Childhood*, Harare: Baobab.
Mungoshi, C. (1991) *One Day Long Ago: More Stories from a Shona Childhood*, Harare: Baobab.
Mutswairo, S. (1959) *Feso*, Salisbury: Longman.

Ngugi wa Thiong'o (1987 [1981]) "The Language of African Literature," in *Decolonising the Mind: The Politics of Language in African Literature*, Harare: Zimbabwe Publishing House, pp. 4–33.

Ricard, A. (2004) *The Languages & Literatures of Africa*, Asmara: Africa World Press.

Sigogo, N. (1959) "Bongani amakhiwa," in Literature Bureau (ed.), *Imbongi Zalamuhla Layizolo*, Salisbury: Longman.

Sithole, N. (1956) *Umvukela wamaNdebele*, Salisbury: Longman.

Tredgold, M. M. (2001) *The First Ones: Nehanda and Chaminuka*, Gweru: Mambo Press.

Veit-Wild, F. (1992) *Teachers, Preachers and Non-Believers: A Short History of Zimbabwean Literature.* Harare: Baobab.

15

"IMPERIAL GOSPEL"

The Afrikaans children's Bible and the dawn of Afrikaner civil religion in South Africa

Jaqueline S. du Toit

In the Afrikaner civil religion, God imbues all history with ultimate meaning. He rules sovereign over the world and works His will in the affairs of nations – most visibly of Afrikanerdom

(Moodie 1975: 1).

The 1873 publication of the first children's book in nascent Afrikaans anticipated the *terminus a quo* of the so-called First Language Movement by two years. *Die Geskiedenis van Josef voor Afrkaanse Kinders en Huissouwens. In hulle eige taal geskrywe deur een vrind* (The History of Joseph for Afrikaans Children and Households. Composed in their own language by a friend)[1] was written as an elaborate retelling – not translation – of the Old Testament story of Joseph by C.P. Hoogenhout (1843–1922). The booklet was produced at the urging of Hoogenhout's friend and mentor, Dr. Arnoldus Pannevis. Like Pannevis, Hoogenhout was a teacher of Dutch birth who arrived in the Cape in 1860.

The impetus for "Joseph" in Afrikaans was Christian mission to the mixed-race "colored" community of the Cape who predominantly constituted the servant class. At the time Islam was already firmly established in this community. The first Islamic school in the Cape dates from 1793 with Malay, the language of the Cape slaves, as medium of instruction. By the mid-nineteenth century this changed to Afrikaans as the religious leadership found the local populace unable to understand religious instruction otherwise (Du Plessis 1986: 30–31 and Ponelis 1993: 46–47).

By 1872 Pannevis passionately urged the translation of the Bible in "Afrikaans-Dutch" for the purpose of making it accessible to the "colored" community as well as the "simpler (childlike/innocent/naive) segment of society" (het eenvoudiger gedeelte der bevolking, cf. Nienaber 1934: 16). The use of language and code switching as signifiers of social and economic status is important in this context, as Isabel Hofmeyr (1987: 96) explains:

Linguistically … social differentiation expressed itself in an upper and middle class who spoke English. Included in their number were wealthy Dutch families who manipulated a variety of linguistic registers. These stretched from what passed for High Dutch, through more informal discourse to a language for servants, workers and farm labourers. These workers, along with *Statenbijbel*, were rapidly accumulating in jumbled racial communities, in which the language "Afrikaans" was emerging quite clearly.

Hoogenhout responded to this perceived need first with a proof translation of the Gospel of Matthew, chapter 28, from the Dutch Authorised Version ("Statebybel"). The choice of this chapter is pertinent to the context, as it includes Jesus' commission to his disciples in vv. 16–20, which is interpreted by Christians as a call to mission. The translation was submitted to the editor of the Dutch Reformed Church journal, *De Kerkbode*, but never published. The Afrikaans literary historian, P.J. Nienaber (1934: 7), has suggested that the editor's lack of enthusiasm for an Afrikaans translation of the Bible indicated a reluctance to see the "Word of God" disgraced by use in what was considered by the colonial establishment to be a crude and vulgar vernacular. This seems to be supported by the response of the British and Foreign Bible Society. Pannevis had also urged the Society to consider the translation of the Bible into Afrikaans (explained as "a kind of bastardized Dutch"). He claimed that already "many thousands" at the Cape are unable to speak Dutch or English, but speak Afrikaans exclusively (cf. a reprint of this letter in Nienaber 1975: 121). The Society's response was that it was not interested in legitimizing a patois (Nienaber 1934: 19). Apart from what Nienaber suggests is a conviction that Afrikaans would lack the sophistication of expression required for elevated religious discourse, Hofmeyr (1987: 96–97) perhaps points to the more obvious objection by established religious functionaries in the Cape and in Britain to an Afrikaans translation. Namely, that the terminology associated with Afrikaans at the time "pointed to a strong association with poorness and 'coloredness'." This included "'hotnotstaal' (Hottentot language), 'griekwataal' (Griqua language), 'kombuistaal' (kitchen language), 'plattaal' (vulgar language) and 'brabbeltaal' (patois/lingo)."

When Hoogenhout's "Joseph" is published later the same year, the audience included children and the "household" in its titular dedication. It pointed to both the perception of the child as convert and the domestic inclusion of the servant in the eighteenth and nineteenth century imperial conception of the family unit. It also perpetuated the image of the "domestic servant as a child to be taught" (Straub 2009: 19).

Five hundred copies of "Joseph" were printed in 1873 by Smuts & Hofmeyr of Cape Town. The booklet consisted of thirty-six pages with a red, faux leather cover and no illustrations. Ten years later a revised second edition of 1,000 was published to reflect both the popularity of the book and the standardized spelling that had since been adopted by the Fellowship of True Afrikaners (Die Genootskap vir Regte Afrikaners or GRA), founded in 1875 to promote Afrikaans as a language. A third edition published by J.L. van Schaik followed in 1922, shortly after Hoogenhout's death. This was the first edition to include illustrations. In 1940 and again in 1975, the book was reprinted, without illustrations, by Human & Rousseau and combined in a volume with the first Afrikaans novel, Hoogenhout's *Catharina, die dogter van die advokaat* (Catharina, the daughter of the solicitor), originally published in 1879 (Hoogenhout 1975). The reprint included an extensive introduction and contextualization by P.J. Nienaber.

In 1974, in anticipation of the centenary of the defunct GRA, the first edition of "Joseph" was reprinted by Perskor (Hoogenhout 1974). Established in 1971, Perskor acted as mouthpiece for the northern, conservative wing of the National Party. The reprint of "Joseph" was supplemented by a brief introduction by Nienaber and a modern

Afrikaans "translation" on each of the facing pages, absent from Human & Rossouw's reprint. The purpose of this publication, which seems excessive in light of a limited audience and Human & Rossouw's contemporaneous reprint, was to remind the juvenile reader of Afrikaans literature (two years before the Soweto Uprising, read: "white") of what the GRA, according to Perskor, had accomplished, namely, "to gain recognition for Afrikaans as language of the Afrikaner" (Hoogenhout 1974: 1). The inclusion of a modern Afrikaans version trumpeted the extent to which the language had evolved in a century but also featured as religious propaganda: one of the first products in Afrikaans was a biblical morality tale for children, the future of the Afrikaner *volk* ("nation").

The pietistic and retroactive inclusion of "Joseph" as part of the First Language Movement served for Afrikaner civil religion as divine approval of Afrikaans as exclusive voice of Afrikaner nationalism. The first to neatly incorporate "Joseph" in this fashion as a kind of "anticipation of" or "preparation for" the First Language Movement, is Dutch Reformed Church minister and founding member of the GRA, S.J. du Toit, in his early history of the language movement. Du Plessis (1986: 37–38) points out that this assumption, including the existence of clearly demarcated First and Second Language Movements, was never seriously challenged by subsequent scholarship. Much of Du Toit's turn of the twentieth century exposition has been taken for granted by later scholarship and included into a broader and undifferentiated "Afrikaans literary history" or "Afrikaner history": "The entire history of the Afrikaans language movements were simply incorporated into Afrikaner history. This situation would subsequently lead to inevitable mythologizing of both the overarching history and in particular mythologizing within a specific ideological framework" (Du Plessis 1986: 1).

The story of Joseph

The story of Joseph, favored son of the patriarch Jacob, derives from the Old Testament book of Genesis, chapters 37–50. It constitutes a free standing diaspora novella (Lang 2009: 24)[2] which seemed to have been inserted by the post-exilic Jewish redactors of the Hebrew Bible as a link or bridge between the patriarchal (ancestral) narratives of Genesis and the book of Exodus. In essence, the story of Joseph functions as an elaborate editorial plot device to explain the presence of the people of Israel in Egypt in anticipation of the biblical exodus. It also signifies the transition from the history of a family (Abraham, Isaac, Jacob and their descendants) to that of a nation (Israel). In short, the biblical story of Joseph is an example of revisionist mythologizing in aid of the creation of a national *raison d'être* by early diaspora Judaism.

Joseph is the beloved son of Jacob, the well-to-do grandson of the arch-patriarch, Abraham. Joseph's mother is Jacob's favored wife, Rachel, who dies giving birth to Joseph's younger sibling, Benjamin. With his father and siblings, Joseph resides in Canaan, where the nomadic family moves from place to place in search of pasture for their large flock. His doting father's evident partiality and Joseph's precociousness (telling tales to his father about his brothers; relating dreams in which his superiority over his parents and brothers are evident) alienates the young Joseph from his ten older brothers who become jealous. Plotting to kill him, the brothers eventually sell Joseph to itinerant merchants who in turn sell him on as a slave in Egypt. His father is told that he was killed by a wild animal. In Egypt, Joseph ends up in the household of a wealthy Egyptian functionary, Potiphar, where he rises through the ranks of servants because of his virtuous traits. However, Potiphar's wife tries to seduce him and Joseph, ever honorable and loyal to Potiphar, resists by running away from her. In a fit of pique, she accuses Joseph of attempting to seduce her and he is sent to prison. In prison, Joseph's moral character again makes of him a model prisoner. He is asked to interpret the dreams of two of the Egyptian king's (Pharaoh) imprisoned servants. Later, based on the recommendation of one of these servants, Joseph is called upon to interpret the dreams of the Pharaoh. Joseph's interpretation predicts an impending famine and Pharaoh appoints Joseph to high office and in charge of anticipating the coming food shortage by storing grain. When the drought becomes severe, Jacob sends his ten older sons from Canaan to Egypt to purchase food. Joseph recognizes them immediately but they do not recognize their brother. What follows is an exchange in which Joseph manages by subterfuge to entice them to bring his younger brother, Benjamin, to Egypt. Subsequently, Joseph reveals himself to his brothers, they repent and his father is brought to Egypt where they all settle in the land of Goshen and become the nation Israel.

Historically, this story's structural independence from the rest of Genesis, its hero as moral exemplum, its exciting plot twists, and its potential for transmitting religious-ethical object lessons and social commentary have made Joseph popular in the European milieu from which Hoogenhout and his contemporaries came. Already by 1687, the Joseph story is recommended as a basic text for children's education (Lang 2009: 66). Though no evidence could be found for direct derivation or translation of Hoogenhout's "Joseph" from an extant version, existing Joseph stories fashioned for educational purposes are clearly what Hoogenhout recalls when he explains his choice of subject matter in the foreword: "Each person has their own preferences, but for me the most beautiful story in the Old Testament is without a doubt 'The history of Joseph'. If I think back to my youth, I recall this as one of my school textbooks; yes, the book that I could best understand" (Hoogenhout 1974: 8). Although Hoogenhout's "Joseph" might not derive directly, this retelling incorporates the same social directives that a tradition of early modern European transmission of this tale (cf. Lang 2009: 55–111) has already established.

In accordance with similar practice in European retellings, Hoogenhout subdivided the story into nine subsections with descriptive titles: 1) Joseph's Family; 2) Joseph is Sold by His Brothers as Slave; 3) Joseph in Prison in Egypt; 4) The Butler and the Baker of King Pharaoh; 5) Joseph Leaves Prison and Becomes Deputy Ruler of Egypt; 6) Joseph's Ten Brothers Come to Egypt to Buy Wheat; 7) The Second Journey of Joseph's Brothers; 8) Joseph Tests His Brothers One More Time and Reveals That He is Joseph; and 9) Jacob Hears that Joseph is Alive and Moves to Egypt. The author as social commentator proves a lively, meddlesome and active participant in the story. He does not shy away from evoking emotion and using narrative expansion to involve the reader in the tale. When Joseph lands in jail after the incident with Potiphar's wife, for example, he comments: "And, as you know, he was entirely innocent. Yes, my child, you're welcome to cry; I won't be mad, because I realize that you also love Joseph and feel sorry for him. But even though Joseph is in jail, his conscience is clear and God won't forget him. God can also help him in prison" (Hoogenhout 1975: 24). Dismissive of the my and he uses dream interpretation sequences, Hoogenhout treats these sections as mere mechanisms to move the story forward. "Joseph", for Hoogenhout, is a cautionary tale using the end of each subsection for social commentary cloaked in anticipation of what is to come.

The societal virtues espoused fall within an existing thematic range for children's Bibles of the time: the sanctity of the family (Bottigheimer 1996: 70–90); respect for the existing social order; the "enshrinement of agricultural virtues" (Bottigheimer 1996: 92) as foil for the evils of urbanization and industrialization; and the "injunction to work" (Bottigheimer 1996: 91–102) or propagating a work ethic.

The first section, "Joseph's Family", is an unusual elaboration. Retellings of children's Bible stories, with their strong emphasis on narrative, as a rule dispense with the biblical belaboring of genealogy. But Hoogenhout uses this section to remind his audience that this story is about a family and to situate the story in an agrarian environment familiar to his Afrikaans audience. Ruth Bottigheimer explains that using stories such as Joseph doing "his work" (Gen. 39) and the people of Israel laboring in Egypt (Ex. 1), "provided examples that fit the social organization of communities such as American Mormons" (1996: 92). She notes that their "civic enshrinement of agricultural virtues" resulted in an inclination for these American pioneering communities, not dissimilar from the Afrikaner rural communities, to expand on these attributes when retelling Bible stories to their children.

In his discussion of western European retellings of Joseph, Bernhard Lang (2009: 57–64) makes much of the idealized setting for the telling of such stories depicted in the frontispieces of educational volumes. A 1707 version, for example, shows a mother and father, "as primary agents of education", teaching the children in an idyllic parlor setting with two servants in the background. Subsequently, the Swiss Reformed pastor, Johann Kaspar Lavater, evokes similar scenes: "By exposing one's family and servants to the biblical story and by recommending Joseph as a model to emulate, one may inculcate the proper social order and prevent it from dissolving. In other words, Lavater considers the biblical story the perfect antidote to the destabilizing forces of the French Revolution, intended as it is to promote traditional order in both the home and wider society" (Lang 2009: 80).

Hoogenhout's depiction of Joseph foregrounds the same values. For most of the story, Joseph is either somebody's child, or servant. In these roles Joseph is presented as obedient, patient, accepting of his fate, hard-working, trustworthy and non-retributive. God, explains Hoogenhout in the second section, acts as the memory of wrong-doing. Joseph must forgive and forget. Not only would God compensate Joseph for his misfortune by looking after him while he is in slavery, but God will also punish the wicked brothers. Unfair and unjust servitude, Hoogenhout suggests to his audience, is therefore not something to be railed against, but something to accept. Joseph the servant excels as worker and caretaker. Because he proves himself trustworthy, Potiphar entrusts him with all his affairs, "both inside and outside the home" (Hoogenhout 1975: 22). And because of Joseph, the good servant, God blessed Potiphar.

Women do not feature prominently in the Joseph tale. Rachel has died by this time and Potiphar's wife does not fare well in the interpretive history of the text (cf. Kugel 1990). By the time of Hoogenhout's "Joseph", the seduction scene has been largely censored from children's Bibles (Bottigheimer 1996: 116–127). But Hoogenhout faces the quandary that the event cannot be excised in its entirety as the incident is the impetus for Joseph's subsequent imprisonment. Hoogenhout therefore explains no more than that Pothiphar's wife was evil ("godless" or *goddeloos*) and that because Joseph did not want to "sin with her" she accused him of "doing all kinds of bad things at home" when Potiphar was away. These "bad things" are never explained although Hoogenhout assures his audience that it was not for "stealing", clearly a particularly heinous crime for a servant. Potiphar's willingness to believe his evil wife sends Joseph to prison. Again, although Joseph's innocence is emphasized, it is clear that the behavior expected of the virtuous is patient acceptance that God is in charge and would intervene. Joseph's "obedience" is offered as reason why, even in prison, the warden eventually puts Joseph in charge of the prisoners.

After the subsequent interpretation of the Pharaoh's dreams, Joseph is appointed to the position of deputy to the Pharaoh. Again, Hoogenhout emphasizes Joseph's exemplary qualities: although he is in this exalted position, Joseph is not "lazy", but immediately executes his plan to store grain for the famine to come. Thus, even in a position of relative power, Joseph is the model underling. It should be noted that in this respect Hoogenhout follows a specific strain of a two-tier tradition of children's Bibles. Whereas no children's Bible before 1750 seemed to "praise work" (Bottigheimer 1996: 94), during the eighteenth century children's Bibles for the poor responded to the rise of workhouses for orphans. Here great emphasis was placed on a work ethic: "For the first time in the history of children's Bibles the concept of work emerged as a practice to be justified and a virtue to be inculcated" (Bottigheimer 1996: 96).

The "most beautiful part of the history", to Hoogenhout, is told from section 6 onwards, when Joseph "hears from his family". Although the author is clear that vengeance is not the object of the exemplary Joseph's actions, the comedy of errors to follow does leave at least one brother in prison for a time. However, Hoogenhout is quick to remind his audience that, just as Jesus did, his audience is expected to "forgive their enemies" and "forget those who sinned against them". This forgiveness, Hoogenhout suggests, includes the sin of murder.

The denouement returns to the earlier emphasis on family: Joseph requests his brothers to bring their families and their father to Egypt and live with him. The moral object lesson is forgiveness and the pre-eminent importance of family. In the elaborate detail expended to explain the intricacies of what is required to move Joseph's family to Egypt and, upon arriving, where to settle them best as nomadic cattle farmers, the preference for the agrarian lifestyle as an idealized life choice is again evident. Joseph's closing promise is to look after his family: "He was hundred-and-ten years old when he died and his soul went to heaven. Before he died, he predicted that his family would one day return to Canaan to own that land as their property" (Hoogenhout 1975:64).

Idealized womanhood

The rise of Afrikaner nationalism in the early part of the twentieth century relied upon the successful retrospective fashioning of a unifying history of origins and a common foe, the British Empire/English. In this endeavor religion, most particularly, neo-Calvinism (Moodie 1975, Hexham 1981, and De Gruchy 2011)[3] and language (Afrikaans) proved important political instruments. The success of this approach led to the adoption of the "central myth" of Afrikaner nationalism (Marx 2008: 182), the so-called "Great Trek". It functioned as an exodus narrative, a physical enactment of a symbolic journey from Egypt (the Cape Colony under British rule) to Canaan (the Boer Republics) to divest the Afrikaner of the shackles of imperial rule. Hence a series of divergent migrations by the predominantly Dutch-speaking pioneers ("Voortrekkers') from the Cape Colony in the 1830s were mythologized as a "deliberate political movement": "Only with their exodus from the Cape Colony had the Voortrekkers 'laid the foundation for a new nation in South Africa'. The epic of the Great Trek imbues the exodus myth with an anti-colonial context", writes Christoph Marx (2008: 183–184).[4] And, if the Great Trek symbolized the Afrikaner's synchronicity with biblical Israel, then the death of 26,000 Afrikaner women and children during the South African

War (1899–1902) became a symbol of purification – a proverbial slaughtering of the innocents at the hands of the evil British imperialists, Milner and Rhodes. Past suffering created the moral justification for subsequent salvation history encapsulated in Afrikaner nationalism. It also elevated the Afrikaner woman and mother as example of enduring resilience. In Afrikaner myth she became the idealized "mother of the nation" (*volksmoeder*). Much of the responsibility for the Afrikaans literary propagation of the *volksmoeder* ideal falls on the shoulders of J.D. du Toit and his brother-in-law, Willem Postma (Brink 1990: 279).

In 1913, J.D. du Toit, leader in the so-called Second Language Movement and son of S.J. du Toit, published his third collection of poetry, *Rachel*. The titular reference to Rachel, mother of Joseph, is derived from an obscure passage in Jeremiah 31:15: "Thus saith the Lord; A voice was heard in Ramah, lamentation, and bitter weeping; Rachel weeping for her children refused to be comforted for her children, because they were not" (KJV). Biblical allusion permeated the work of the early Afrikaans poets but none more so than that of theology professor, Totius (J.D. du Toit), who is best known for his subsequent translations of the biblical Psalms, and who would have been raised with "Joseph". The influence of the Bible on his work is described by Cloete as "all-encompassing": "Especially our earlier national poetry speaks biblical language. Clearly our earlier poets saw a parallel with the ancient Israelite struggle in the Holy Land. This parallel would later be taken up by coloured poets and used to describe their people. This therefore is deeply embedded in Afrikaans poetry" (1989: 875, 876). *Rachel*, the second in Totius' collection of "national" or "war" poetry, is of negligible literary quality but emblematic of the role the Afrikaans woman and mother would come to inhabit in Afrikaner mythology and of the extent to which this mythology would be informed by biblical symbolism. Willem Postma, in turn, would pen *Die Boervrouw: Moeder van Haar Volk* ("The Boer Woman, Mother of her Nation") (1918), a treatise on the Afrikaner woman and her virtues. Brink (1990: 275) sees in the work of Totius and Postma, "a clear convergence between the development of the ideal of the *volksmoeder* and the rise of Afrikaner nationalism". *Rachel*, together with Totius' earlier collection of poems, *By die Monument* ("At the Monument"), sanctified the Afrikaner women and children's suffering during the war in poetry with overt reference to the biblical slaughter of the innocents by King Herod.

The hitherto primarily Victorian ideals of female domesticity, what Hofmeyr (1987: 100) refers to as the "imperial gospel of the family", came to merge in the work of Totius and Postma with an idealized conception of the virtues of the Afrikaner woman: her primary role as homemaker, as mother and educator of a future generation of Afrikaner children in Afrikaans. The extraordinary privileging of the family and household, already present in Hoogenhout's "Joseph", would come to dominate the social and political constructs of Afrikaner nationalism and apartheid. By the 1920s and 1930s, the so-called "poor white" question, resultant urbanization, as well as rapid post-war industrialization, meant the breakdown of the idyllic agrarian family unit. This proved a grave concern to Afrikaner nationalists who mobilized around the emphasis on the traditional and domestic virtues of the *volksmoeder*. As McClintock (1993: 72) explains:

> The family household was seen as the last bastion beyond British control, and the cultural power of Afrikaner motherhood was mobilized in the service of white nation-building. Afrikaans was a language fashioned very profoundly by women's labors, within the economy of the domestic household.

Concluding remarks

Among a nineteenth and early twentieth century South African rural populace with little access to formal education and with limited access to Afrikaans literature, "Joseph', like most children's Bibles of the time, "served a further potentially valuable purpose among relatively uneducated adults" (Punt 2012: 75). The influence the Bible would have on the populace resonates in the names they gave their children and the land they settled. Concomitantly, their Protestant, Reformed disposition fetishized and objectified the Bible as moral authority, legitimator of world view and source of social conformity (cf. e.g. Hexham 1981).

The biblical story of Joseph is a story of a family and the anticipation of an unfolding national history. This appealed to the sensibilities of Afrikaner civil religion. Although the purpose in retelling this particular biblical story in Afrikaans was clearly far removed from a later Afrikaner nationalist agenda, the biblical subject matter and the acuity of its resonance made the story useful to later political operators. Its emphasis on family and the implicit respect for the existing social order spoke to the angst of a society in which the "traditional web of authority" (Hofmeyr 1987: 100) was unravelling.

Postscript: In 1955 the 32nd General Synod of the Reformed Church (*Gereformeerde Kerk*) in South Africa, the most conservative of the three Afrikaans churches and the church of Totius and Postma, declared the designation "children's Bible" and the use of such Bibles in conflict with the Reformed understanding of the Bible.[5] Nonetheless, children's Bibles remain popular among an Afrikaans readership to this day (Du Toit & Beard 2007).

Notes

1 All translations are mine, unless indicated otherwise. "Joseph" is not the first South African children's Bible. The Dutch *De Kinder-Bijbel* (The Children's Bible) by "a minister of the Reformed Church in South Africa" was published in 1853. It proved extremely popular (fifteen editions by 1898) and was reputedly written by the Reverend John Murray of Burgersdorp. *De Kinder-Bijbel* served as manual to parents and to supplement Sunday school (cf. Roux 1983: 9–10).
2 Other examples include Ruth, Esther, Daniel and Jonah. The parallel with Daniel, including the dream interpretation sequences, is particularly pronounced.
3 However, André Du Toit (1983 & 1985) cautions incisively against overestimating the influence of neo-Calvinism.
4 This appropriation of the story is especially poignant in light of the significance of the self-same biblical narratives for the liberation struggle. Compare, for example, the title of Albert Lutuli's autobiography, *Let My People Go* (1982).
5 My thanks to Dr. Wymie du Plessis of the Reformed Church Archives in Potchefstroom for his assistance in locating this information.

Bibliography

Bottigheimer, R.B. (1996) *The Bible for Children: From the Age of Gutenberg to the Present*, New Haven: Yale University.

Brink, E. (1990) "Man-made Women: Gender, Class and the Ideology of the *Volksmoeder*", in C. Walker (ed.) *Women and Gender in Southern Africa to 1945*, Cape Town: David Philip.

Cloete, T.T. (1989) "Die Boek wat Laaste Uitgepak word: Oor die Bybel in die Afrikaanse Digkuns", *Hervormde Teologiese Studies*, 45(4): 874–893.

De Gruchy, J.W. (2011) "Calvin(ism) and Apartheid in South Africa in the Twentieth Century: The Making and Unmaking of a Racial Ideology", in I. Backus and P. Benedict (eds.) *Calvin and His Influence, 1509–2009*, Oxford: Oxford University Press.

Du Plessis, L.T. (1986) *Afrikaans in Beweging*, Bloemfontein: Patmos.

Du Toit, A. (1983) "No Chosen People: The Myth of the Calvinist Origins of Afrikaner Nationalism and Racial Ideology", *American Historical Review*, 88: 920–952.

Du Toit, A. (1985) "Puritans in Africa? Afrikaner 'Calvinism' and the Reception of Kuyperian Neo-Calvinism in Late Nineteenth Century South Africa", *Comparative Studies in Society and History*, 27: 209–240.

Du Toit, J.D. (1913) *Rachel*, Potchefstroom: Koomans.

Du Toit, J.S. & Beard, L. (2007) "The Publication of Children's Bibles in Indigenous South African Languages: An Investigation of the Current State of Affairs", *Journal for Semitics*, 16(2): 297–311.

Hexham, I. (1981) *The Irony of Apartheid: The Struggle for National Independence of Afrikaner Calvinism against British Imperialism*, New York: Edwin Mellen.

Hofmeyr, I. (1987) "Building a Nation from Words: Afrikaans Language, Literature and Ethnic Identity, 1902–1924", in S. Marks & S. Trapido (eds.) *The Politics of Race, Class & Nationalism in Twentieth Century South Africa*, London: Longman.

Hoogenhout, C.P. (1974) *Die geskiedenis van Josef*, Johannesburg: Perskor.

Hoogenhout, C.P. (1975) *Josef en Catharina*, Cape Town: Human & Rossouw.

Kugel, J.L. (1990) *In Potiphar's House: The Interpretive Life of Biblical Texts*, Cambridge, Mass.: Harvard University.

Lang, B. (2009) *Joseph in Egypt: A Cultural Icon from Grotius to Goethe*, New Haven: Yale University.

Luthuli, A.J. (1982) *Let My People Go: An Autobiography*, London: Collins.

Marx, C. (2008) *Oxwagon Sentinel: Radical Afrikaner Nationalism and the History of the Ossewabrandwag*, Berlin: Lit Verlag.

McClintock, A. (1993) "Gender, Nationalism and the Family", *Feminist Review*, 44: 61–80.

Moodie, T.D. (1975) *The Rise of Afrikanerdom: Power, Apartheid, and the Afrikander Civil Religion*, Berkeley: University of California.

Nienaber, P.J. (1934) *Die Geskiedenis van die Afrikaanse Bybelvertaling en 'n Hoofstuk oor die vertaling van die Psalm- en Gesangboek en die Formuliere*, Cape Town: Nasionale Pers.

Nienaber, P.J. (1975) *Eerste Sooie*, Johannesburg: Perskor.

Ponelis, F. (1993) *The Development of Afrikaans*, Frankfurt am Main: Peter Lang.

Postma, W. (1918) *Die Boervrouw: Moeder van Haar Volk*, Bloemfontein: Nasionale Pers.

Punt, J. (2012) "The Other in South African Children's Bibles: Politics and (Biblical) Systems of Othering", in C. Vander Stichele & H.S. Pyper (eds.) *Text, Image & Otherness in Children's Bibles: What Is in the Picture?* Atlanta: Society of Biblical Literature.

Roux, C.D. (1984) "Perspektiewe op Aspekte van Afrikaanse Kinderbybels", MA thesis, Stellenbosch University.

Straub, K. (2009) *Domestic Affairs: Intimacy, Eroticism, and Violence between Servants and Masters in Eighteenth-Century Britain*, Baltimore: Johns Hopkins University.

16

CHILDREN'S LITERATURE IN THE GCC ARAB STATES

Sabah Abdulkareem Aisawi and Faraj Dughayyim Addhafeeri

Children's literature in the Gulf region is part of a larger entity: Arabic children's literature. Although the Gulf states have their history, traditions and economy that differ from other Arab countries, yet GCC (Gulf Cooperation Council) states share Islamic and Arab culture with the rest of the Arab region. Children's literature in the Gulf continues to benefit from the literatures written for Arab children, which preceded it by more than half a century. Although it developed in the second half of the twentieth century, it has flourished within a relatively short period of time to become a fresh addition to contemporary Arabic children's literature. With globalization and the information technology which have opened channels among different cultures, GCC children's literature has broadened its scope beyond its culture while retaining its characteristic identity.

Even though the GCC consists of six separate political regions, similarities among those regions in language, history, culture, economy, traditions and beliefs constitute them as a unit, which encouraged the declaration of what came to be called the Gulf Cooperation Council for the Arab States on May 25, 1981. Those states that overlook the Arabian Gulf (also known as the Persian Gulf) are: Saudi Arabia, the United Arab Emirates (UAE), Oman, Kuwait, Qatar and Bahrain. The Council aims to achieve further solidarity among those neighboring states. Gulf children constitute about 50 percent of the population (Abderrahman 95)[1] and they are regarded as the core of human development for the future.

The GCC states share a unique history that shapes their contemporary culture. Different Gulf states were colonized by First World countries due to the importance of the location of the Arabian Gulf on the trade route between the east and the west. The discovery of oil in the region added to its importance. It also opened the path for economic prosperity and modernization for the inhabitants who were originally bedouins and pearl divers. The oil boom had a great effect on the area; it also attracted people from different parts of the world who came to work. Religion is an integral part of Gulf society that governs its beliefs and daily life.

After their independence, the Gulf states turned into fast developing countries that took care of education and childhood among several other pillars of modern society. Children's education turned from memorizing the Holy Quran (at what was called *katatib*) to the establishment of formal schools. Consequently, Arab teachers from Egypt, Iraq, Syria and Lebanon came to work in the Gulf and made a palpable change in Gulf society and its intellectual atmosphere. Scholarships to Arab states as well as different parts of the world helped the area make contacts with the outside world.

Tracing the development of children's literature in the GCC states is not easy, as the size of the area covered poses a hindrance. Additionally, academic studies and literary histories of children's books in the area are scarce, and it is difficult to find helpful publications as the process of classification and documentation has only been introduced in some states recently. Problems in distribution also continue to hinder research. Children's literature in the area does not revolve around a number of well-known authors, but depends on several writers of merit some of whom have stopped writing for children. This continues to be the condition of writers in the Gulf region.

Studies of the history of books for children that first appeared in each state reveal various similarities among the Gulf states in the time of appearance of different genres, the publication of books and in the topics dealt with. Whereas in other Arab states such as Egypt, Iraq, Lebanon and Syria books for children began to appear in the late nineteenth and early twentieth centuries, printed children's literature in the GCC did not start until the 1950s. The oral literature available then consisted of myths and legends, not specifically told for children (Ahmad et al. 217). These forms of traditional literature were common in different dialects depending on the various areas of the Gulf region. Folk songs were usually in the form of lullabies, which often began with the mentioning of God and Prophet Mohammed (Albilushi et al. 49). Songs accompanying common children's games, such as hide-and-seek, feature as an important component of traditional heritage in the Gulf region, although they varied slightly from one area to the other.

In the 1950s and 1960s, the number of reading children was still limited. Children were not used to buying books before the oil boom; the hardships of life made books and reading a luxury (Ahmad et al. 217). The reading material available was the magazines published in Egypt such as *Sameer*, *Sindibad* and storybooks by Kamil Kilani—the pioneer of children's books in Egypt. The few storybooks available to children were in the form of detective stories, comics such as *Tarazan*, scientific books, historical and religious stories (217).

Translation has played a major role in Arab children's literature both in the Gulf and in other Arab states. Storybooks as well as TV programs that were translated, mainly from English children's books and programs, constituted up to 95 percent of what was then produced for children until the 1970s (Ahmad et al. 218). Kilani and other major children's writers in Egypt translated European literature for children, which travelled to the Gulf and made an important current of stories (Bataweel 200); fables of Aesop and La Fontaine in addition to classics such as *Robinson Crusoe* and *Gulliver's Travels* were translated and adapted. At the same time, translations of commercial adventure and police stories were common, though educators and parents objected to the foreign content (201). However, translated books and TV programs have helped open new horizons to the child in the Gulf (Ahmad et al. 219).

The international and regional interest in childhood has affected views of the child in the Gulf. The different states started to join international and regional associations and councils—such as UNICEF, ACCD (The Arab Council for Childhood and Development), AGFUND (The Arab Gulf Program for Development)—in order to achieve the care and wellbeing of the child on all levels. The Gulf states are parties to the CRC (Convention on the Rights of the Child). Conferences held in the Arab region during the 1970s and 1980s drew attention to children's literature as part of the program for the child's development.

That children's literature was not formerly regarded highly can be attributed to the intellectual, economic and social atmosphere when writers for children were not considered to be as important as those who wrote for adults (Aisawi 89). The economic boom of the 1970s brought about a change of attitude towards children and children's literature. Caregivers were able both to realize the importance of books for children and to afford to buy them. On the other hand, the number of writers for children increased as the making of children's books was taken more seriously. As a result, there appeared publishers who wholly or partially specialized in children's books. A gradual shift of conception of the child from a person in need of education to an individual capable of thinking influenced both form and content of books. It dictated an observation of literary and artistic merit in children's stories, which appeared in the shift in story topics to the child's everyday life and a change of tone ensued. Additionally, books began addressing a larger audience including two age groups that had been overlooked, namely, preschoolers and teenagers.

A study of the content of GCC children's literature shows that it does not reflect political or social undercurrents of meaning. Since the Gulf society continues to be prosperous and peaceful to a great extent with no ethnic struggle or major political strife, its children's literature reflects that type of life.[2] The researchers could only trace one story that deals with the Iraqi invasion of Kuwait on its surface level (Thuraya Albagsami, *Fattoma*, 1992). This event is regarded as the major political event in the modern history of the region. While other parts of the Arab region reacted to communism, capitalism and democracy, such movements have had little effect on Gulf people due to the dire circumstances of survival in the region in the early part of the twentieth century (Abderrahman 55). Furthermore, Gulf children's writers do not seem to regard such serious topics as suitable material for literature addressed to young readers.

Such restrictions, however, do not entail a lack of openness to the world; the Gulf states took the initiative to convene partnerships for the development of children's literature. The annual book fairs in the region are international events that include rich cultural programs in children's literature such as talks by both local and western speakers. UAE has become a member of IBBY (International Board on Books for Young People) and it hosted the 2013 IBBY regional conference. English, French and German translations of children's books can also indicate the open channels with the rest of the world.

The rising importance given to children's literature by the states of the GCC is also reflected in the big annual awards assigned for distinctive books. These awards are not limited to nationals but are open to all Arab writers. The most renowned are found in UAE: Sharja Award for Children's Books, Abderrahman bin Hamid Award for Culture and Science (Children's Literature Branch), Etisalat Award for Children's Books (UAEBBY—the UAE IBBY Section), Sheik Zayid Book Award (Children's Literature Branch). The Etisalat Award, established in 2009, is one of the world's most generous children's literature awards, offering rich prizes, totaling about $266,000, in five categories. Qatar's State Award for children's literature is another big award in the region.

Children's stories

The story is the most popular form of printed children's literature in the Gulf region (Albilushi et al. 190). The beginnings of locally published stories for children were in different forms. Children in the region read and still read retellings of universal folktales ("Cinderella", "Sleeping Beauty", "Snow White", among other well-known titles). As with children's literature worldwide, animal stories have proved to be enjoyable to children. Religion features as a source of different forms of stories taken from Islamic heritage or propagating the teachings of Islam. Retellings of stories mentioned in the Holy Quran and the sayings of Prophet Mohammad usually appear in story series. Among these stories, biographies of prophets and important Muslim figures are common. As Muslims are proud of their past civilization, stories about caliphs, battles and achievements make good historical fiction as well as nonfiction. However, writers are also open to other cultures and civilizations, as appears in the translation and localization of western children's classics. Other forms include scientific stories, biographical stories about internationally recognized figures and nonfiction such as alphabet, numerical and concept books, atlases, math and science books.

The first known children's storybooks found in Saudi Arabia are a series of three adventure tales co-written by two educationalists, Abdallah Bogus and Mohammad Awwad, dating back to 1959 (Bataweel 246). The same year, the first magazine for children was printed under the name *Arrawdah* [Kindergarten]. The second collection appeared in 1979 when a well-known author, Abdelkareem Aljuhaiman, wrote ten stories in the folktale form. In Bahrain, the first story appeared in 1977 when Abdelgader Aqeel published *Man Saraq Qalama Nada?* [Who Stole Nada's Pen?] (Ma'awda 33). Emirati Ibrahim Assabbag subsequently published five stories under the general title, *Jazeeratu Alkanz* [Treasure Island] (1981), derived from Arab folktales (34). Abderrahman comments on the literature of that period:

> The stories written during the eighties and nineties reflected the style of life in pre-oil Gulf society and its prevailing morality. Obviously, those stories were a natural reaction to the sudden developments in intellectual and social life as a result of the economic boom in the Gulf region. The stories reflected the change of values and the ensuing moral dilemma that people in the Gulf went through having their roots in the past with its morals and values while watching the present with caution.
>
> (76)

Children's stories flourished in the Gulf during these two decades. Saudi author Yaqoub Is'hak published more than 200 titles in two series: one is a combination of two forms— a scientific encyclopedia about animals followed by a story dealing with each animal; while the second is in comic strip form, written in a highly didactic tone. In Qatar, Latifa Assileiti wrote *Hanan wa Adhafeera* [Hanan and the Braid] and *Ushu Alusfoor* [The Sparrow's Nest] in 1983. Kuwaiti writer, Teiba Alyahia wrote a series of stories under the title, *Attiflu AlMuslim* [The Muslim Child] in 1985. In Oman, the National Committee for Child Welfare published two stories by Tahira and Fatima Allawati in 1989. The literary quality of these early stories was not always high and illustrations were of limited artistic value (Ahmad, et al. 237). Choice of story topics can be seen in the light of the intellectual atmosphere at that time. Views of children as subjects of instruction were still dominant, and so stories written for entertainment still had a clear educational tone. Retellings of folktales and animal stories probably achieved both aims. Several authors wrote on the teachings of religion and used stories and poems to instill morality into the young and teach them acts of worship.

Several social and political developments in the region affected children's literature positively, hence it entered a new phase. Globalization offered new generations of authors a chance to be exposed to children's stories and attitudes towards children's literature worldwide. The awareness of the importance of children's literature in the development of the child became well recognized, and writers for children started to be appreciated and acknowledged. Consequently, publishers either making children's books as a line of production or specializing in such books for the young increased in numbers and their books achieved international standards. Further, communication between the children's book industry in Arab countries and in the West resulted in improved literary styles, fresh ideas as well as high artistic standards of design and illustration. Such development flowed on into the 1990s, which became an important period for children's stories in the GCC states as it heralded what can be seen as the onset of the golden age of Arab children's literature. Collaboration with foreign artists was a common practice in this period. Competitions and awards for quality storybooks have encouraged writers, illustrators and publishers to improve their books for children. Furthermore, academic study of children's literature in the region has reflected positively on its development and created links with its study abroad.

With the rise of feminism in Gulf society, female children's writers now outnumber male writers in the Gulf region (Aisawi 90). The effect is also seen in the increase of female characters and their depiction – for example, renowned Emirati writer Asma' Alzaro'uni deals with the aspirations of a village girl to become a doctor in her story, *Salama* (2000). The protagonist is empowered by her determination, and through her strong will she begins to achieve her dream.

As mentioned earlier, a major development in GCC children's literature at the end of the twentieth century is the change in both its tone and topic to become more suitable for child readers. The obvious tendency towards moralizing has given way to addressing the child reader's daily life, problems and aspirations (Aisawi 92). At the same time, books began to appear that addressed young children between 3 and 5 years old, who previously had no literature of their own. Kuwaiti Naif Almutawa' wrote two stories on difference; the first was on the Honour List of the 1997 UNESCO Young Children's Literature Prize for Tolerance. *To Bounce or Not to Bounce* deals with difference metaphorically showing how the protagonist proves to be useful despite being a half ball in a city inhabited by balls. In her prize-winning *Hikayat Ammona* (2005) [*Ammona's Tales*], Saudi Wafa' Assubail deals with several early childhood issues such as the first day at school, sibling rivalry, and sense of ownership among other problems (see Figure 16.1). The illustrations by Osama Mizhir, from Syria, are a good example of the collaboration between Gulf writers and artists from other parts of the Arab world. It also reflects the high artistic standard of books for children in the GCC states at the close of the 20th century. The illustrator does not accentuate any ethnic features of the protagonist to indicate Gulf or Arab identity, a practice which is a characteristic of the majority of contemporary children's stories' illustrations.

Despite the influence of globalization and the communication with other cultures, GCC children's stories never lost their cultural roots. According to Albilushi et al, Emirati story authors write on both local as well as universal topics (192). The same can be said about authors in the rest of the Gulf states. They choose topics related to traditions and customs to acquaint the child with national heritage (191) while dealing also with basic human issues shared by writers of children's literature around the world. This produced both local and glocal literatures. An excellent example is *Ommi Jadida* [*My New Mother*], written by Mariam Alrashidi and illustrated by Reem Almazroui. The story deals with a child's management of sorrow over the loss of a beloved step-mother. Details of background and plot are also taken from the local environment of the early

Figure 16.1   Hikayat Ammona [Ammona's Tales]. Ill. Osama Mizhir. Riyadh: Maktabat Almalik Abdelaziz, 2005.
Source: Reprinted with kind permission of King Abdul Aziz Public Library.

Gulf society (see Figure 16.2): for example, the illustrations depict the characters wearing the traditional women's costumes in the Gulf (which are little worn today, especially by children, except on national and cultural festivals). The artist shows small details of women's dress (called *daffa*), which is always black in color, and *bukhnug* for girls, which comes in different colors. Such interest in Gulf heritage is a rising trend in contemporary Gulf children's literature. The book won both the 2012 Award of Made in UAE (as a manuscript before its publication in 2013) and the Etisalat Award for the category of best text.

Children's poetry

Even though poetry is an integral part of Arabic literature, there are few poets for children in the Gulf region. This dearth may be partly responsible for the allocation of poetry to a subsidiary position in children's lives today. Apart from poems that are made into songs, children only come across poetry in their language textbooks. According to Abdelrazak Jafar, poetry selected or especially written for educational purposes lacks the

عِندما كُنت طِفلةً صَغيرةً كنت
أظن دومًا بأنّ أُمّي جَديدة هِيَ
جَدّتي، إلى أَن قالَ لي أَبي يَومًا
إنّها زَوْجَتُه الأولى! وإنّ لديّ
أُمّيْن، أُمّي وأُمّي جَديدة.

Figure 16.2   Ommi Jadida [My New Mother]. Dubai: Dar Alaalm Alarabi, 2013.
Source: Reprinted with kind permission of Alaalm Alarabi Publishing and Distribution.

capacity to show the fun of poetry (cited in Ahmad et al. 228), another reason why it is
not popular among children.

Unlike story production that flourished in the Gulf and continues to develop, poetry
emerged as a strong presence during the 1980s but did not continue to do so. Bahraini
poet, Ali Ashargawi, published more than eight collections of poetry for children, beginning with *Aghani Alasafir* [Songs of Sparrows] in 1983. The same year, poet, dramatist
and storywriter Hessa Alawadhi from Qatar published *Unshudati* [My Song] followed
by several other collections. Emirati poet, Aref Asheik published *Anashid min Alkhalij*
[Songs from the Gulf] in 1986 while Saudi poet, Ibrahim Abu-Aba'a published *Anasheed
Attufula* [Childhood Songs] the same year. In Oman, two collections of children's poetry
appeared in 1991 by Sa'eeda Alfarsi under the title *Ughniyat Littufula wa Alkhudra*
[Songs for Childhood and Greenery] and by Ali Alkahali *Unshud Maei* [Sing with Me].
In Kuwait, children's poets preferred to write songs for TV programs and the theatre.
Topics addressed by poets ranged from the religious, national, social, and educational.

While some poets tried to offer children fun, the majority saw poetry as a means for instruction. Some poets wrote in classical Arabic while others chose everyday language (Ahmad et al. 222).

Children's theatre

Children's theatre in the GCC Arab states preceded other forms of literature. It began in the form of what is known as school theatre and coincided with the beginning of formal education in Bahrain at the start of the twentieth century; the first school play dates back to 1919 and it was used as an effective educational and recreational tool. Schools competed in giving performances during national occasions and at end-of-year celebrations. In Kuwait, children's theatre began in 1922. Thanks to the efforts of Hamad Rejeib, a school theater department at the Ministry of Education was established in 1959. As for the other states, different dates are given by literary historians to indicate the beginning of school theatre.

The period from the end of the 1970s to the mid-1980s can be regarded as the golden age of children's theater in the Gulf; TV helped by broadcasting the plays and radio aired the songs and thus made them popular. Saudi Abdullah Alabdelmohsen, Kuwaiti Awatef Albadr, Qatari Majed Almarzougi and Bahraini Ali Asharqawi are pioneers in this field. Plays of this period were mainly adapted from folk literature. The subsequent recession opened the way for commercial theatre that was based on clowning. It also relied on folktales but mainly drew from American TV cartoons which offered ready-made characters such as Mickey Mouse, Donald Duck and Tom and Jerry.

Theatre subsequently regained its place in the Gulf region, but only on a limited scale since theatre-going is not considered a common practice for children in the Gulf. Literary competitions and awards encouraged writers and producers to specialize in children's theatre. While classic fairytale characters continue to appear on stage both in Arabic and English versions in some Gulf states, western hegemony may at times be more discernible in Gulf children's culture. For example, in *Winter's Concert*, the 2016 winning dramatic performance in the Annual Competition of Children's Theater arranged by Dammam Culture and Arts Society/KSA (see Figure 16.3), the main character (a ballet dancer), some costumes, and details of stage setting (such as snow)

Figure 16.3 Scenes from *Winter's Concert*. Director, Iman Attawil; performance scriptwriter, Khadija Attalhi.
Source: Reprinted with kind permission of the Dammam Society for Culture and Arts.

evoke a western atmosphere which shows both the influence of globalization and appreciation of different cultures as a source of inspiration. The play deals with the universal theme of friendship. Furthermore, bilingual schools as well as schools administered by foreign embassies organize different theatrical performances which feed children's theatre in the Gulf.

Children's press

Children's press appeared in the Gulf states through the pages designated for children in the daily newspapers, which devoted pages—often weekly—geared to children. The content of these pages was mostly activities, such as puzzles, calculations, mazes and spotting the difference between two images. Photos of children occupied a large area of the page, in addition to some occasional interviews with distinctive or talented children. These press pages also published some stories; the comic strip form of story featured in those publications. As for early children's magazines in the GCC states before the 1950s, some were produced for commercial reasons to promote products while others targeted child awareness. Various magazines were short-lived.

The real beginning of a children's press in the GCC came on September 17, 1959, with the first issue of *Arrawdah* in Saudi Arabia. It was published weekly, but stopped after issue 27 because of financial difficulties. *Arrawdah* can be considered a leading magazine for children, as it included illustrated stories, comic strips and use of color. By contemporary standards, the magazine enjoyed good printing and design but the stories were of limited quality and often tended to moralize.

In 1969, the second most important children's magazine in the Gulf states, *Sa'ad* appeared in Kuwait. Its stories were mainly in comic strip form. It published translations of *Tintin* for a period of time, then it changed to stories written and illustrated by Arab writers and artists. *Sa'ad* continued to be published until 2010. *Hasan* magazine, which appeared on 20 April 1977 in Saudi, was regarded as one of the best periodicals at the time. Well-known authors and illustrators in the Arab region, mainly from Egypt, helped give the magazine its high standard. However, it ceased publication in 1980 due to financial difficulties.

The Emirati contribution to a children's press came on February 28, 1979, when the first issue of *Majid* came out. This is a landmark in children's literature since within a few years it became the leading children's magazine in the Arab region from the Arabian Gulf to the Atlantic Ocean. The financial support the magazine receives from the Government of Abu Dhabi (UAE) is an important factor in the spread of the magazine and its continuation. Today *Majid* is read by millions of Arab children both in hard copy and online.

Two other magazines continue to be produced in the Gulf: *Alarabi Alsaghir* (The Little Arab) sponsored by Kuwaiti Ministry of Information, and *Basim*, which was first issued on September 15, 1987 and competes with *Majid* in its sales. Other magazines in Qatar, Bahrain and Oman were unsuccessful. Today, both *Majid* and *Basim* have attained international standards in children's magazines.

Children's TV programs and satellite channels

Children's programs began on the radio and then the TV. Like many TV corporations around the world, main channels allocated specific times for children's programs on TV in the mornings or late afternoons. They showed cartoons dubbed into Arabic. On weekend mornings, a special children's program was also shown; it included storytelling, songs and conversations with children in the studio and later on the phone. A popular TV program for children is shown during the month of Ramadan (fasting) which consists of 30 daily questions usually accompanied by songs. Radio programs for children were similar.

Due to lack of specialists in animation, cartoons have been imported from western and Far Eastern companies and these are usually dubbed for the Arab child. Cartoons like *Mickey Mouse*, *Popeye the Sailor* and *Tom and Jerry* are enjoyed by generations of Gulf children. GCC states produced an Arabic version of *Sesame Street* called *Iftahya Simsim* [Open, Sesame], which was aired in 1979. Its second, third and fourth parts appeared in 1982, 1989 and 2015.

The advent of satellite channels drew children away from programs on television and from books. The number of foreign channels that children in the Gulf can watch is high and parents show concern over the quality and content of those channels. They also practice control over local channels that appeared at the turn of the century. In 2000, the satellite channel *Space Toon* (Bahrain) started broadcasting and it initiated other child-oriented channels across the Arab region. The most famous are *Ajial*, which is sponsored by Saudi TV, *Cartoon Network* (UAE), *AlJazeera Kids* (Qatar), which later branched into *Baraem* for preschoolers and *Jeem* for children aged 7–12. These channels provide high quality programs produced in the station or sourced from global production companies.

MBC3 has developed into a versatile and evolving children's satellite channel address-ing different age groups from preschoolers to teenagers. However, it is subject to criticism from some sectors of society due to its content, which at times does not coincide with society's values and traditions. On the other hand, *Almajd* channel aims to preserve the Muslim identity of its young viewers through focusing on an Islamic content. Kuwait pioneered the production of children's TV programs as well as songs in the 1970s and 1980s, which circulated among children in the other Gulf States. The spread of satellite channels and internet has also provided Gulf children with easy access to Arab and for-eign channels, which connect them with world children but, in the view of some educa-tors and parents, constitute a threat that Gulf children may be foreignized.

The internet, apps and games

With the advent of contemporary information technology, satellite channels have started to lose their place in children's lives in the Gulf states. Computers, video games and elec-tronic gadgets such as iPods and iPads have become the main source of entertainment and culture. They can also give easy access to applications of satellite channels as well as favorite children's classics. However, e-games continue to attract the majority of children.

The internet and electronic devices are perceived as another threat. Most children and young adults in the Gulf states own electronic devices and get access to the internet. The situation is similar to that in other parts of the world where the internet allows easy access to electronic books, websites addressed to the young, film versions of classical novels, but it also makes harmfully unsuitable material available at the click of a button. Before the turn of the twenty-first century, there was little on the internet offered in the Arabic language. A 2013 study of the electronic stories in the Gulf region revealed other problems such as lack of creativity, poor design, absence of sound effects and few inter-active options (Addhaferi 20). An example of a successful app produced in the Gulf is Pink and Blue, *Qissati* [My Story], a free app that deals with the daily life of two siblings, a brother and sister.

Children and young adults spend many hours on social media to communicate with friends and young people around the world and play online games with them. The boys' favorite games are *Minecraft* and *FIFA* while the girls' are the various dress-up apps.

Illustration

In comparison with GCC children's writers, the number of illustrators is still limited. Artists from Egypt, Lebanon and Syria usually collaborate with the GCC writers to produce books. Even though artists are found in the GCC states, few take illustrating children's literature as a profession. According to illustrator and publisher Thuraya Batarji, "illustrators of children's books neither receive the recognition nor the profit expected: it is the writer whose name is often linked to the book; awards also go to writers; illustration is not considered a profession in the Arab region" (Facebook message dated June 21, 2014).

Apart from the illustrations that show characters in national dress and background depicting the past, characters appear in modern day dress and common surroundings, which do not distinguish them from children in many parts of the world. Ethnically, Gulf children do not have starkly distinctive features that clearly mark their identity. Modern artistic techniques adopted in children's books emphasize this worldliness in illustrations.

Young adult literature

Books written especially for young adults only began to appear in Arabic at the turn of the twenty-first century, although they remain scarce. What is present in the Gulf region is often written by Arab writers from outside the region. Young adult theatre and poetry are almost nonexistent. Adolescents usually attend plays and read poetry written for adults. They also watch adult TV series and films. Most cinemagoers are teenagers and they often choose to watch action, horror and comic films.

Foreign satellite channels have recently started to address this age group. Recent releases of American films produced for young adults (and children) are often shown in cinemas in the Gulf almost at the same time as their US debut. TV and DVD versions of those films, often subtitled in Arabic, make them more popular. Young people in the Gulf waited for the final *Harry Potter* film with the same anticipation shown by youth worldwide. Again, this is a matter of concern for many parents as they believe programs and films will Americanize the young generation.

Conclusion

Children's literature in the GCC states had a late start yet it developed in a relatively short time to occupy a noticeable place on the map of children's literature regionally and internationally. While sharing several aspects with the literatures of the rest of the Arab region, it has its own identity that reflects both the traditions and history shared by its states as a geopolitical unit. Two important elements have contributed to its development: Arab writers' expertise, and translation from world literature. Today, several GCC stories are translated into other languages and appear in international book fairs. Kalimat Publishers (UAE) was shortlisted for the Best Asian Publisher at Bologna in 2013.

However, GCC children's literature still needs to fill gaps and manage its weak points. Some writers still have a limited view of literature as a tool for instilling morals and values they write educational stories, poems and plays that are in demand by a group of care-takers. Gulf writers need also to give some depth to their writings and to address young adults. Stories are the main achievements of GCC children's literature. The importance of illustrators has still to be recognized and more local artists are to be encouraged to venture into children's book illustration. While TV channels and programs have flour-ished in offering Gulf and Arab children entertainment and intellectual nourishment, yet producers need to preserve the identity of the child in the Gulf. Poetry remains a genre of secondary importance, despite the fact that verse publications are increasing. Theatre continues to develop and is expected to achieve success, although the process is slow. Cinema, websites and apps need expertise to give children the joy and personal devel-opment expected of such forms in the home culture. Additionally, more magazines are needed to achieve variety and address different age groups.

Notes

1 References used in this article are in Arabic. They, along with titles of primary works, have been transliterated then translated for easier reference for non-Arabic speaking readers.
2 Political tension with Iran and military conflict in Yemen, which began in 2014 between some allied Gulf states and *Houthis* to reinstate the government of President Abdrabbuh Mansour Hadi, have not featured in children's books.

Bibliography

Abderrahman, Suad (2011) *Qisas Alatfal fi Aladab Al Emirati* [Children's Stories in Emirati Literature]. Assharja: Daerat Althaqafawa Ali'alam.

Addhaferi, Faraj (2013) "Qisas Alatfal Alelectroniya" [Children's Electronic Stories], *Mu'tamar Aludaba' Alsu'udyeen Alrabi'*, 27–29.

Ahmad, Mohammad, Hasan Annasir and Mohammad Annokhatha (1996) "Foreword: Adab alat-fal fi Alkhaleej" in *Adab Alatfal fi Alalam Almua'asir ma' Alishara Li a'dab Alatfal fi Alkhaleej Alarabi* [Contemporary Children's Literature with Reference to Children's Literature in the Gulf States]. Manama: University of Bahrain, 215–220.

Aisawi, Sabah (2007) "Adab Altifl Alarabi: Ila Ayn?" [Developments in Arabic Children's Literature], *Almarifa* 150: 88–93.

Albilushi, Laila, Aisha Asshehi and Muneera Albilushi (2007) *Adab Altifl fi Dawlat Alimarat* [Children's Literature in UAE]. Assharja: Marakiz Alatfal wa Alfitian; Daerat Althaqafa wa Ali'alam.

Al-Mutawa, Naif (1996) *To Bounce or Not to Bounce*. Kuwait: Naif Al-Mutawa.

Alrashidi, Mariam (2013) *Ommi Jadida* [My New Mother]. Dubai: Dar Alaalm Alarabi.

Assubail, Wafa' (2005) *Hikayat Ammona* [Ammona's Tales]. Ill. Osama Mizhir. Riyadh: Maktabat Almalik Abdelaziz.

Bataweel, Huda (1993) *Alintaj Alfikri lmatbou' Liltifl fi Almamlaka Alarabiya Alsu'udiya: Dirasa Tahliliya* [Children's Publications in Saudi Arabia: An Analytical Study]. Riyadh: Maktabat Almalik Fahad Alwataniya.

Ma'awda, Aisha (2007) *Adab Alatfal fi Albahrain* [Children's Literature in Bahrain]. Bahrain: Aisha Ma'awda.

Majid magazine. Abu Dhabi: Emirates Media, Inc.

PART III

Cultural forms and children's texts

17

IMAGOLOGY, NARRATIVE MODALITIES AND KOREAN PICTURE BOOKS

Sung-Ae Lee

Picture books produced in South Korea or in the large Korean diaspora in the USA invite an imagological analysis because of their intense focus on identity and the social circle of contemporary society within which children are growing up, and because of the differences of emphasis between the two areas. The corpus selected for this essay, which takes an imagological approach, samples the major themes of Korean and Korean American picture books: experiences of everyday life; identity within a conflicted country; the impact of a traumatic past; migration; and trans-national adoption. The essay argues that the reception process is structured by a net-work of schemas and scripts, and through this network specific images are endowed with cultural power.

Imagology, as described by one of its leading exponents, Joep Leerssen, is "image studies, which deals with the discursive and literary articulation of cultural difference and of national identity" (2000: 268–69). Leersen argues that imagology is especially evident in creative narrative: "The question of cultural, national, and ethnic identity is particu-larly noticeable in the field of literature, which of all art forms is most explicit in reflecting and shaping the awareness of entire societies and which often counts as the very formu-lation of that society's cultural identity" (2000: 268). Multi-modal texts such as picture books have been key purveyors of cultural and national identity within both South Korea and the Korean diaspora.

The focus of this essay is representations of attitudes, perceptions, and representa-tions that shape Korean social groups. How people envisage others (that is, construct *hetero-images*) and fashion self-perceptions (*auto-images*) is the core business of imagology. Picture books about Korea or Koreans present an unusual imagological situation in that although images of the "other" and the "self" may feasibly be con-structed with respect to the nearest international neighbors, Japan or China, the pri-mary others against which it sets itself are North Korea and, in the case of diasporan books, the United States. There is neither a long history nor, in reference to North Korea, an ethnic distinction through which to assert alterity. Construction of stereo-types thus entails a variation from the common type of definition of "imagology" such as offered by Ton Hoenselaars and Joep Leerssen in their description of national othering:

> Imagology is based on, but not limited to, the inventory and typology of how nations are typified, represented, and/or caricatured in a given tradition or corpus of cultural articulations. On the basis of the analysis of texts or cultural artefacts, it raises questions about the mechanism of national/ethnic "othering" and its underlying self-images. Questions raised concern the relation between "character" and "identity"; historical variability; genre, canonicity, and irony; and intermediality.
>
> (2009: 251)

In her imagological study of eighteenth-century British literature, Birgit Neumann makes the useful observations that the purpose of stereotypes is to influence their recipients and that the stereotyping of others can have intra-national pragmatic dimensions in addition to serving as "powerful catalysts of national consciousness" (280), or, to put it more simply, what constitutes a subject's context and how does she or he fit into it? Thus citizens who do not belong to majority groups may be stereotyped as always already other, and hence are always apt to be excluded, and may be labelled with the national stereotypes applied to hostile nations. For example, in *We Adopted You, Benjamin Koo* (1989) the author, Linda Walvoord Girard, invokes stereotypes to describe the teasing directed at the protagonist in elementary school:

> A few kids call me "Chink" when they tease. Some people don't want to know anything about me. They just think I'm from Afghanistan or Hawaii or Timbuktu
> "I don't like him," I heard a girl say. "He's Japanese."
> "Yeah, but watch out – he probably knows karate," said the other kid.
> I don't know karate, and I'm not Japanese.
>
> (Opening 13)

Someone who is different is thus categorized in generic terms, or historical suspicions and clichéd attributes are evoked as a schema which positions the other as a threat.

Stereotyping serves to fulfil functions in specific historical, cultural, and aesthetic contexts. The North-South Communist-Capitalist divide of the Korean Peninsula has generated a large amount of strategic stereotyping, which can serve to demonize the other or, as in many national stereotypes, belittle the other. In her account of the ideological contexts and functions of children's literature in South Korea, where anti-Communism was mandated social ideology from 1958 until the end of the 1980s and the production of children's literature persistently reproduced the myth of childhood innocence, Dafna Zur concludes that, "Literature for children inscribed an uncompromising anti-North Korean position for its young readers" (197). The image stereotypes that underpin such a position are also referred to in imagological discourse as *schemas*. According to schema-theory, socio-culturally determined motifs are grouped into structures which operate during both the production and reception of a text. Understanding is thus a product of the text's own discourse and a reader's prior knowledge. Three crucial aspects of this understanding are that a reader accesses prior knowledge in the form of schemas whose meanings are already largely socio-culturally determined, that a schema instantiates a much richer web of meaning than is textually visible, and that a schema hence implies default values for the normal ways of filling out a partially indicated schema. A schema is then invoked either by naming it or by naming symptomatic components: in the above example – "He's Japanese … he probably knows karate" – the added components, "dislikable" and "knows karate," help stipulate the kind of schematic field to be evoked. Similarly, visual schemas, referred to as *image schemas*, ask viewers to assemble the components, identify the schema, and finally instantiate a fuller version than the visible data provide.

Because the picture books about the Korean diaspora mostly deal with a limited range of topics – minority identity within a multicultural community, the experience of migration, transnational adoption, and, rarely, postmemory of the impact of a traumatic past – they are underpinned by particular common scripts. The concept of *script* is here derived from Roger Schank and Robert Abelson's account of the function of scripts in everyday life as a stereotyped sequence of actions that is part of a person's knowledge about the world: "Specific knowledge exists in detail … with respect to every standard situation that [a person] has been in many times" (38). Scripts are also a recognizable narrative form, that is, as "a knowledge representation in terms of which an expected sequence of events is stored in the memory" (Herman 2003: 10). The (re-)telling of a story may thus seem familiar but may reproduce a script rather than stemming from a particular printed source, or a common script may be discerned as the narrative frame of a bundle of texts. *We Adopted You, Benjamin Koo* is a useful example because this relatively early example of a Korean adoptee narrative is a "standard situation" rather than a "recognizable narrative form," even though it is a work of fiction. This focus on the script is perhaps because transnational adoption stories tend to have a bibliotherapeutic function, most evident in this case in the direct address on the final page to readers who are adoptees. The script of *We Adopted You, Benjamin Koo* comprises: the circumstance surrounding Benjamin's birth and abandonment; infancy in an orphanage; journey to America; realization at around the age of seven that he is racially different from his parents, and resulting conflict and resolution; adoption of a second child (optional component); conflict at school; and optimistic anticipation of the future. Like a schema, a script has both core and optional elements, and thus the retelling of a familiar or predictable narrative prototype, such as a story of transnational adoption, will involve a choice amongst possible variants of a familiar story, and the coexistence of multiple possibilities creates a script, although a script may also blend different components of stories and will not necessarily be narratively equivalent to any particular version. A script may be represented by both a pattern of action sequences, as here outlined, or by a single action sequence within a larger pattern (for instance, Benjamin's recognition and resolution of his racial difference).

The script may thus be truncated, as in *Jin Woo* (2001) by Eve Bunting, illustrated by Chris Soentpiet, which revolves around the adoption of a second child and is blended with an unrelated script that informs numerous picture books, the anxiety experienced by a child about the imminent birth of a second child (see, for example, Anthony Browne, *Changes* (1990) and John Burningham and Helen Oxenbury, *There's Going to be a Baby* (2010)). Narrated by David, the existing child, the script is only taken to the point where Jin Woo has been collected at the airport, brought to the house, and happily accepted by his new big brother, but is doubled by assurances that the joy of the adopting parents was equally great when David was adopted. The book is rather naïve and simplistic: while picture books about adoption are characterized by images of broadly smiling adults, this one employs the motif to excess and so tends to undermine its theme that transnational adoption is simple and problem free. From an imagological perspective, transnational adoption offers a significant comment on South Korean auto-images, but it does not enter picture books. In 2007, within a few years of the publication of *Jin Woo*, South Korea moved to gradually phase out foreign adoption, as have most other countries. However, internal adoptions remain rare, as few Koreans are willing to resist the taboo on adoption, which arises from the emphasis placed on ancestors by Korean Confucianism and a consequent reluctance to raise children from outside the family blood-line. From the beginning of the twenty-first century these assumptions have conjoined with equally strong taboos on pregnancy outside marriage and single parenting to produce a substantial increase in orphanage populations. There is thus a contrast implied by the ebullient auto-image in *Jin Woo* of an open, welcoming society eager to offer love to "a baby … from a different country who needed parents," although Jin Woo's Korean origin is not imbued with significance in itself. Picture books about Korean adoptees appear to have become a defunct sub-genre within a couple of years of the turn of the century.

Most diasporan books produced in the USA focus on the experiences of migration, and where these are written and illustrated by authors and illustrators from the Korean diaspora they have often needed to research Korean culture and history, which have already become "other" to the second generation. The visit of a grandmother from Korea is a frequent script, which enables exploration of the otherness of origins and the production of stereotypes. A symptomatic text is *Halmoni's Day*, written by Edna Coe Bercaw and illustrated by Robert Hunt. Although Bercaw is a member of the Korean diaspora, she admits to knowing very little about Korea, while Hunt is an outsider to both homeland and diasporan cultures. The child protagonist, Jennifer, is apprehensive when her grandmother (*halmoni*) visits from Korea at a time corresponding with Grandparents' Day at school, but what she has to deal with is constituted as a set of stereotypes. Halmoni ("a small woman in an elaborate silk gown") is only ever dressed in a *hanbok*, the traditional clothing of Korea, which is now usually only worn on special occasions. Her visit to America and her day at Jennifer's school are special occasions, but the *hanbok* marks Halmoni as different: "Jennifer couldn't help but notice how different she was from the other grandparents, dressed in their running shoes and casual clothes" (Opening 8). In addition, her voice "chimes softly" when she speaks, a common schematic attribute in diasporan picture books. These simple attributes are part of a halmoni schema, or stereotype, and recur in diasporan picture books. The child is placed in an ambiguous position: she is herself a stereotype, ethnically Korean, enculturated to American life and speaking no Korean, so that the arrival of Halmoni foregrounds questions of subjectivity which concern Jennifer throughout the book. This effect is intensified by Hunt's illustrations, which are very high modality and approach photorealism (See Figure 17.1).

Modality refers to the truth value or credibility of (linguistically realized) statements about, or representations of, the world (see Kress and van Leeuwen 2006: 155ff). Highest modality is expressed verbally by factual expressions of actuality, with lower modalities expressed by suppositions, hypotheses, future possibilities, and the like. The same principle applies to truth value or credibility of visual images, and thus the level of visual modality plays an important role in imagological representation, since we all learn at an early age to associate photonaturalism with the real and the authentic. The normal reference point – that is, the base modality – for picture book images is not photorealism, however, but some degree of abstraction: a modality somewhat lower than photographic naturalism is here the norm for visual representation. The lower modality of representations is produced in a variety of ways: cartoon-type figures; absence of ground; flat colors; low saturation; restricted palette; soft focus; or multiple modalities within a single image (Stephens 2000: 47). The numerous combinations of such elements that an artist

Figure 17.1 Halmoni and her daughter, from *Halmoni's Day* by Edna Coe Bercaw, illustrated by Robert Hunt.
Source: Illustrations copyright © 2000 by Robert Hunt. Used by permission of Dial Books for Young Readers, an imprint of Penguin Young Readers Group, a division of Penguin Random House LLC.

may use ensure that there is a great range along the spectrum from highest modality to lowest, but in general picture books from Korea and the diaspora are grounded more or less in the middle. A key implication of this convention as a social practice is that truth value or credibility inheres in such medium modality images, so that when illustrations are closer to photonaturalism the meanings they convey will appear to have an intensified truth value or credibility and thus represent the world as it actually is rather than as it is conventionally represented. In many picture books, the use of medium modality has the effect that Korean people are depicted as generically Asian (broad faces and buttonhole eyes, for example) and characters whose appearance is specifically Korean are very rare. Robert Hunt is one of the very few illustrators to have painted Korean figures with a high level of verisimilitude. His practice of painting with reference to photographs he has taken of models is reflected in the high modality of *Halmoni's Day*, especially in the evident decision to reproduce skin tones and to allude to (without reproducing) the shading and texture of how light falls on the contours of a human face. He thus maintains a higher modality than observed in the picture books of, for example, Chris Soentpiet, an adoptee from Korea, whose process is to ask models to play the parts of the main characters. Soentpiet makes the costumes and fixes each model's hair and makeup, and then takes photographs to use as reference tools during the painting process, but his figures are clearly *painted*, not photographed, and less specifically Korean than Hunt's. Hunt's images seem closer to photonaturalism, but are softer in focus than found in the normally hard edges of a photo, to the extent that bodies or objects may be left incomplete in order to direct viewer attention to salient elements of the scene, such as facial expression.

A further element of *Halmoni's Day* that has significant implications for an imagological approach is its narrative structure as a frame story and a *thematically* parallel embedded story. When Jennifer takes her Halmoni to school, all of the grandparents are invited to speak and share a special family memory, and Halmoni tells of her father's return after a five year absence during the Korean War and its immediate aftermath. Physically broken and suffering from chronic illness, he is at first unrecognizable and the nine year old girl Halmoni then must get to know this transformed person. The thematic relationship with the frame story pivots on recognition and acceptance of otherness/difference. The same narrative structure, also embedding a story of the Korean War, is employed in Haemi Balgassi and Chris Soentpiet's *Peace Bound Trains*. In this postmemory narrative the embedded story is based on the actual experience of Balgassi's mother. In the fictive version, Sumi, a young girl separated from her widowed mother who has joined the army to earn a good salary and qualify for funded higher education, yearns for the coming of the train which will bring her mother home. To solace her, Sumi's grandmother tells her the story of her train journey south to Busan with her two children to escape the North Korean and Chinese armies advancing on Seoul; her husband stayed behind to fight, and was never heard of again. The two stories are structured contrapuntally: the grandmother's loss is permanent and irreversible, both an intensely personal loss and a metonym of all the separations and losses that occurred during the half-century of occupation and civil war, which has been a major factor in the production of diasporan Korean communities since 1950. Sumi's loss is temporary, however, now metonymic of successful immigration, as her mother draws on the resources of American society to overcome loss and deprivation. The story's final page, by counterpointing Sumi's euphoric imagining of the day of her mother's return with a portrait of her grandfather, lost decades before she was born, encapsulates the boundary between past and present, loss and recuperation. Drawn into a reciprocal gaze with this handsome man, determined and compelling, readers are drawn into the unfinished business of divided Korea and the hopes of its diasporan communities. As the theory of *postmemory* proposes, when memory of what has not been directly experienced is passed on to the second generation, they are enabled "to establish affective links to a traumatic past that they did not personally experience" (Stone 454).

Women are more likely to function as "kin-keepers" than men, and hence the prominence of familial and female roles in narrative is central to the reconstruction of the past and an affirmation of its personal meaning. While it has been suggested that *Halmoni's Day* and *Peacebound Trains* "tend to shift reader attention away from the War itself, which does not occupy a central place in the characters' lives" (Dahlen 2007), an imagological reading might suggest instead that the Korean War occupies a central place in diasporan experience as a core cause of a subsequent dystopian situation, which has in turn led to one of the world's largest modern diasporas as a percentage of the total ethnic group. Emotional engagement, of the kind promoted by this narrative structure of thematically parallel stories, does not necessarily preclude critical engagement with or moral reflection on the underpinning events. On the contrary, the thematic connection maximizes what can be thought of as high emotional modality.

The narrative structure of *Halmoni's Day*, *Peace Bound Trains*, and *Jin Woo* expresses what Leerssen describes as "the idea of the motivation of behaviour," and binds narrativity to images and national schemas. The process of narrative analysis most apt for imagology is a critical discourse analysis that incorporates a complex of scripts, schemas, and intertextuality. Teun Van Dijk's large project on discourse, context, and ideology offers a conceptual base for identifying and interpreting the properties attributed to social groups by means of the following questions about the discourse of the group (2008): who constitutes the group (gender, ethnicity, appearance, origin, etc.)? What kinds of actions characterize the group? What motivates the group? What are the group's norms and values? What relationships exist with other groups? These are pervasive assumptions that inform the schemas and scripts underpinning narrative structures. An excellent example of how these processes function in a picture book is Gwon Jeong-Saeng's *Gomi wa Opundori Ajeossi* (*Gomi and Uncle Opundori*, 2007),[1] illustrated by Lee Dam, probably still the most significant picture book about the Korean War published in South Korea. The eponymous characters of the book awaken one spring night on Chiak Mountain, and it is quickly disclosed that both died there thirty years previously during the war. Readers will assume that they are *jibak ryeong*, Korean traditional ghosts who haunt the place where they died, and whose attachment to the objects, places, and events that caused their death is a constant reminder of its problematic causes. Gomi, a child, died when North Korean planes bombed refugees as they attempted to escape the conflict; Opundori, a North Korean soldier, died in an ambush. But the cause runs deeper. The conversation that ensues challenges South Korean ideology by affirming that the opposing sides in the conflict have the same ethnicity and origin, the same desire to protect their country, and the same norms and values:

"Who were you at war with, Uncle?" Gomi asked.
"I fought against the South Korean army."
"What kind of people were the South Korean army?"
"They were people who guarded their country."
"What country did the people guard?"
"They were people just like me, protecting exactly the same country, only by a different name."
"What do you mean by 'exactly the same'?"
"Because we are all the descendants of Dan Gun [the legendary founder of Gojoseon, the original Korean kingdom] …"
"…."
"There was no other difference except that I lived in the North and they lived in the South."

(Opening 6, My translation)

The catalyst for the conflict lay rather in external forces – the USSR and the USA – which used the peninsula as a site for struggle between their opposed ideologies. The point is made by means of an intertextual relation between a depiction of a small country laid waste by a struggle between large foreign powers and an adaptation of a well-known folktale, "Sun and Moon," about a brother and sister who escape from a marauding tiger which has disguised itself as their mother, and ascend into the heavens where they turn into the sun and moon. In *Gomi and Uncle Opundori*, however, there are two tigers and the children do not escape (see Figure 17.2). The picture book challenges the auto-images projected by both the South and the North, particularly through its representation of the failure of the brother and sister to find a united form of resistance to the rival deceits of the tigers: each is (self-)deceived. As Dafna Zur

Figure 17.2 The tigers that devastated the Korean peninsula. From *Gomi and Uncle Opundori*, illustrated by Lee Dam, Seoul: Bori Publishing Co., 2007.
Source: Reproduced with kind permission of the publisher.

argues, the cultural authority of the folktale "is enhanced by realistic artwork that supports the assumption that the version unfolding in the pages of the picture book is not just traditional lore" (2009: 200). In other words, the photorealistic, high modality representations of the tigers, now in black and white rather than the previous sepia palette, impart a high truth value to the visual images of the tigers and the effect of their destruction of the children's cottage as a metonymy for the destruction of Korean culture and tradition.

The early twenty-first century saw a blossoming of South Korean picture books in international awareness, and many of these books now affirm the strength of Korean tradition and culture. Characteristic of many of these books is a mingling of several levels of modality, as seen in *Cloud Bread* (2004), by Korean author/illustrator Baek Hi-Na, winner of the 2005 Bologna Illustrator of the Year Award. The characters and many of the artifacts in *Cloud Bread* are two-dimensional paper cutouts or collages, often positioned to emphasize their two dimensionality, whereas other objects in a scene – curtains, furniture, raincoats, umbrellas – have been pasted in from photographs by Kim Hyang-Su. The result is a playful disruption of any illusion of the real. A comparable mixing of modality is found in Lee Ho Baek's *What on Earth Happened During That Time?* (2000; paraphrased in English as *While We Were Out* (2003)), with which I conclude this essay.[2] *What on Earth Happened* is a fascinating imagological challenge, which also exemplifies the kind of problem that can occur in transferring auto-images into hetero-images in the process of translation. The story and images illustrate how cultural practices are enacted by habituation and repetition, and hence may go unnoticed, but may be highly visible and mysterious to an outsider, for whom they represent hetero-images. Alternatively, an outsider perspective may activate scripts and schemas that erase the significance of the original work's images. *What on Earth Happened* tells how when a family goes away on a brief overnight trip their pet rabbit slips into the house and lives as a human, eating human food, watching a video, experimenting with make-up and dressing up, looking at books, playing with toys, and sleeping in a human's bed. The rabbit has observed human society from the outsider perspective of its home on the verandah, and now for a few hours enters that foreign culture. One function of the book is to offer a humorous celebration of modern Korean family life, as the rabbit experiments with the half-familiar domestic space it has invaded, where readers find that "authentic" contemporary Korean culture may incorporate traditional dress and artifacts (as often represented in diasporan picture books), but is not defined by them. The English paraphrase seems to miss this point, presumably for two reasons. First, the underlying script the author identifies is the familiar anthropomorphic animal story found in myriad picture books, in which human behaviour is attributed to animals. There are, to my knowledge, very few books of this kind in which the animal protagonist is shown on most pages to drop faeces pellets, as here, so readers assuming the anthropomorphic script are asked to perform a mental backflip when these are foregrounded on the final page and the rabbit's animality affirmed. The script Lee Ho Baek is rather working with is the "foreign visitor" or "stranger in a strange land" script, including the stranger's propensity to commit social solecisms. The difference between original and paraphrase is sharply evident in several places, but one of the more extreme is when the rabbit watches a video. The original reads, "Rabbit always wanted to watch interesting videos and this is a good chance. After considering what to watch, Rabbit chooses a video which is about 'The Snowman.' Watching an animation while eating biscuits – this is really the best"; the paraphrase is simply, "Now is her chance to watch a movie." The video, the 1982 animated version of Raymond Briggs' *The Snowman*, doubles the theme of *What on Earth Happened* in that much of it involves the magically brought-to-life Snowman exploring the house of his human maker and its cultural artifacts. For readers who recognize the reference the theme of culture contact is emphasized.

Second, the long history of picture books in the West and the critical assumption that a picture book is (at least potentially) an interaction between two semiotic codes neither of which is self-complete produces a greater expectation of reader gap-filling and schema instantiation than in South Korean picture books. The book is thus experienced differently in the different languages. Where the paraphrase selects a different informing script the gap-filling will take a different form, as when in Opening 6, in which the rabbit dresses up in a child's *hanbok*, the Korean version represents this act as a cultural encounter which might need to be explained to outsiders. In *Jin Woo*, for example, the baby's escort hands the new parents a box and explains, "This is his hanbok to wear on his first birthday. It is traditional." *What on Earth Happened* details the significance of the clothing as "something wonderful … the party clothes the mother of the house made for the youngest child's first birthday party" and thus in combination with the illustration invokes the specific cultural script. In contrast, the English paraphrase invokes a "dressing up" script, whereby the rabbit "finds a colorful costume. The youngest in the family

Figure 17.3 The family tableau from *Peacebound Trains*, by Haemi Balgassi and Chris K. Soentpiet, Clarion Books (Houghton Mifflin Harcourt), 1996.
Source: Text © Haemi Balgassi; illustrations © Chris K. Soentpiet. Reproduced with kind permission of the publisher.

wore it to her first birthday party." Here, the conjunction of "colorful," "costume" and "party" suggests fancy dress rather than the traditional cultural practice readers of the Korean text will identify. Further, the facing pages of this opening offer a strong visual contrast between a higher modality *rabbit-ness* of the rabbit in the conté sketch on the left-hand page and the anthropomorphic appearance on the full-color, but lower modality, right-hand page, thereby foregrounding the rabbit's status as an intruder upon the culture of the human occupants of the house.

In *Peacebound Trains* (pages 16–17) the grandmother is depicted as a young wife at home sharing a meal with her husband and children in around 1950 (see Figure 17.3). The scene is like a museum tableau. The wife wears the iconic *hanbok*, and the others also wear traditional clothes; they kneel or sit cross-legged on a rug, using chopsticks to eat from a small, low table; behind them to one side is an inlaid cabinet on which sits several artifacts, including a green celadon vase and a white porcelain jar with blue ornamentation; behind the family to the other side is a folding screen painted with a birds and flowers motif. The only one of these artifacts to appear in *What on Earth Happened* is the *hanbok* made for the baby – Lee Ho Baek's world is simply modern, no longer defined by traditional visual images and cultural practices.

Picture books produced in South Korea and the diaspora in the USA engage with different perspectives on questions of cultural, national, and ethnic identity. Some themes are shared by the two bodies of literature, such as experiences of everyday life, the impact of a traumatic past, and issues of identity, although the latter faces different pressures in South Korea and in the diaspora. A substantial literature dealing with migration and, until the early twenty-first century, transnational adoption has been particular to the diaspora. These thematic differences add extra nuances to images of "other" and "self," which are inherently particular from an imagological perspective. Diasporan children may occupy an ambiguous position, stereotyped as Korean but culturally American, and contact with the land of origin is depicted as a source of potential conflict. A narrative form that may effectively deal with this conflict is the structure of frame story and thematically related embedded story, which can express both an historical context and a sense of purpose and thus has the potential to reflect a child's own sense of a dual being. The threat posed by origins as hetero-images marks how a diasporan child is positioned as an outsider to two cultures, whereas picture books in South Korea affirm modernity and innovation in contemporary culture.

Notes

1 All Korean names appear in the order of family name followed by given name. RR (Revised Romanization) system has been used unless names or titles have been otherwise specified in a source.
2 The argument here draws upon a longer analysis of the picture book in John Stephens and Sung-Ae Lee (2006).

Bibliography

Baek, Hi-Na (2004) *Gureum Ppang* (*Cloud Bread*), Illustrated by Baek Hi-Na with Photograph Images by Kim Hyang-Su, Paju, Korea: Hansol.

Balgassi, Haemi (1996) *Peacebound Trains*, Illustrated by Chris K. Soentpiet, New York: Clarion Books.

Bercaw, Edna Coe (2000) *Halmoni's Day*, Illustrated by Robert Hunt, New York: Dial Books for Young Readers.

Bunting, Eve (2001) *Jin Woo*, Illustrated by Chris Soentpiet, New York: Clarion Books.

Dahlen, Sarah Park (2007) "Illustrating the Unspeakable: The Korean War and Children's Picture Books," SHCY Newsletter (Society for the History of Children and Youth), 9: unpaginated. www.history.vt.edu/Jones/SHCY/Newsletter9/park.html.

Girard, Linda Walvoord (1989) *We Adopted You, Benjamin Koo*, Illustrated by Linda Shute, Morton Grove, Illinois: Albert Whitman & Company.

Gwon, Jeong-Saeng (2007) *Gomiwa Opundori Ajeossi* (Gomi and Uncle Opundori), Illustrated by Lee Dam, Paju, Korea: Bori.

Herman, David (2003) "Introduction," in David Herman (ed). *Narrative Theory and the Cognitive Sciences*. Stanford: CSLI, 1–30.

Hoenselaars, Ton, and Joep Leerssen (2009) "The Rhetoric of National Character: Introduction," *European Journal of English Studies*, 13(3): 251–55.

Kress, Gunther, and Theo van Leeuwen (2006) *Reading Images: the Grammar of Visual Design*, 2nd Edition, London and New York: Routledge.

Lee, Ho-Baek (2003) *While We Were Out*, La Jolla, California: Kane/Miller Book Publishers.

——— (2000) *Dodaeche Geudongan Museuniri Ireonaseulkka?* (*What on Earth Happened During That Time?*), Seoul: Jaimimage.

Leerssen, Joep (2000) "The Rhetoric of National Character: A Programmatic Survey," *Poetics Today*, 21(2): 267–92.

Neumann, Birgit (2009) "Towards a Cultural and Historical Imagology: The rhetoric of national character in 18th-century British literature," *European Journal of English Studies*, 13(3): 275–91.

Park, Sarah (see Dahlen)

Schank, Roger, and Robert Abelson (1997) *Scripts, Plans, Goals and Understanding: An Inquiry into Human Knowledge Structures*, Hillsdale: Erlbaum.

Stephens, John (2000) "Modality and Space in Picture Book Art: Allen Say's *Emma's Rug*," *CREATA*, 1(1): 44–59.

Stephens, John, and Sung-Ae Lee (2006) "Diasporan Subjectivity and Cultural Space in Korean-American Picture Books," *Journal of Asian-American Studies*, 9(1): 1–25.

Stone, Katherine (2016) "Sympathy, Empathy, and Postmemory: Problematic Positions in *Unsere Mütter, unsere Väter*," *The Modern Language Review*, 111(2): 454–77.

Van Dijk, Teun A. (2008) *Discourse and Power*, Basingstoke: Palgrave Macmillan.

Zur, Dafna (2009) "Whose War Were We Fighting? Constructing Memory and Managing Trauma in South Korean Children's Fiction," *International Research in Children's Literature*, 2(2): 192–205.

18

ETHNIC-RACIAL RELATIONS IN LITERATURE FOR CHILDREN AND YOUNG PEOPLE IN BRAZIL

Celia Abicalil Belmiro and Aracy Alves Martins

Introduction

The history of Brazil has revealed the influence of the traditions of its constituent peoples: the white Portuguese, the Brazilian Indian and the black African among others. The strong features of these cultures in our daily lives, our imagination and in our different ways of being can be recognized whether in dance, food, the arts or literature.

On the other hand, social movements, and human rights struggles for the dignified status of women and for healthy childhoods, permeate the trajectories of black people in Brazil, indicating the necessity to highlight issues of their own. Shared with other groups, the importance of the formation which the Brazilian anthropologist Darcy Ribeiro calls the "Brazilian people" creates a relatively ambiguous situation, which allows, at least, for dual understanding. Jacques Rancière examines the concept of the "distribution of the sensible" and reflects on a point of view that is pertinent to the current discussion:

> For the term aesthetic constitution, what must be understood here is the *distribution of the sensible* which forms the community. *Distribution* means two things: participation in something in common and, conversely, separation and distribution into portions. A distribution of the sensible is, therefore, the way in which it determines, in the sensible relationship between a sharing of something in common and the division of the exclusive parts.
>
> (1995: 7)

The consideration that is necessary to admit the existence of different cultures, including African, as something that is shared in common goes some way towards the recognition of the exclusive parts of the multicultural mix that is Brazil. These exclusive parts are, for the most part, constructed by tense relations that inhibit the presence of the sectors which do not have control over their participation – that is, they tend to be snuffed out by those who assume the determining voice. These tensions have presented severe repercussions in terms of public policies, popular demands and artistic manifestations, which have resulted in new interpretations of Brazil and in the reconstructions of several collective subjectivities which were born here and which seek greater visibility, that is to say, acceptance by the hegemonic strata in order to take its place as one of the pillars of our society.

The insertion of diversity, Gomes (2007) argues, involves understanding the political, economic and social causes of phenomena such as ethnocentrism, racism, sexism, homo-phobia and xenophobia. In each of these phenomena, the difference becomes evident, with a tendency towards the superiority of some over others. Gomes further contends that to speak of diversity and difference implies positioning oneself against processes of colonization and domination.

From a cultural standpoint, diversity can be understood as the historical, cultural and social construction of differences that exceed the biological characteristics visible to the naked eye.

> The differences are also constructed by social citizens throughout the historical and cultural process, in the processes of adaptation of men and women to the social environment and in the context of power relations. Thus, even the typically noticeable aspects, which one learns to see as differences from birth, only begin to be perceived in this way because we, as human beings and social citizens, in a cultural context, name and identify them.
>
> (Martins and Gomes 2010: 145)

In terms of cultural and media communication, Van Dijk (2008: 21) argues that both newspapers and television end up contributing in their own ways to the discursive rep-resentation of racism in society. Since racism is not innate but learned, there must be some means for this process of ideological acquisition and practice. The majority of what the white supremacy groups "know" or think they know regarding ethnicity of Others was therefore formulated more or less explicitly, in countless conversations, stories, news-paper reports, textbooks and political discourse.

The discourse can be considered in this text from the point of view of CDA – Critical Discourse Analysis – as an instrument of the *social construction of reality*, as Van Leeuwen calls it (1993: 193), summarizing Berger and Luckman (1973), whereby everyday social reality is learned in continuous classifications, which become progressively more anonym-ous as one moves away from the here and now of the face to face situation. To this end, the focus of this work will be the analysis of children's literature that emphasizes the social construction of the Brazilian reality of the Afro-descendants.

Images of black people

It can be observed that the black community has been ignored or portrayed in a nega-tive or stereotypical way in fiction until the twenty-first century. In the current historical moment, more than ten years after the enactment of Law 10,639/2003, which mandates studies of Afro-Brazilian history and culture, the book *A decade of affirmative action*, which includes a thorough investigation of the developments of this law, records:

> Databases of theses and dissertations are increasingly housing works that dis-cuss the issue, providing data and statistics for intellectuals who study the theme and also for militant black movements which are now in universities building specific spaces made possible by the enactment of these policies
>
> (Costa et al. 2012: 8–9).

Indeed, it can be seen that the debate widens further, not only in the education networks, in relation to the processes of continuing training for teachers, eager to know how to work in school, in compliance with the law, but also society itself has already outlined new perspectives and actions. Thus, viewers find it less strange when in soap opera plots black characters get other spaces and less menial professions such as medicine or law, or less servile positions such as artists, coordinators or department heads.

Offering another perspective, Duarte (2014) discusses the place of black people in literature and denounces their absence as characters and above all as *authors*:

> The black person occupies a **minor place** in Brazilian literature. In prose, it is a place which is often expressionless, almost always in a supporting role or, more markedly in men, as a villain. In the Brazilian literature file constructed by canonical books, the presence of the black man is **rarefied and opaque**, with few characters, verses, scenes or stories set in the national literary repertoire or present in the memories of the readers. (…) And from the beginning it unequivocally configures something fundamental for this observation: the fact that the negro is present much more as a *theme* than as an ***authorial voice***.
>
> (Duarte 2014: 151, emphasis added).

In Brazil, many studies have sought to identify the use in today's production of literature for children which could fulfill the requirements of Law 10,639/2003, updated by Law 11,645/08 to include the indigenous peoples. Paulo V. B. Silva (2007), for example, makes the important observation that black characters in stories are regularly treated as the object of action of another, in contrast to white characters who are depicted as acting autonomously.

Many studies have focused on reviews of books produced for children and young people in order to indicate the works of better quality, such as didactic or informative literature, for example textbooks. Quality is publically identified in three main ways. First, the distribution of textbooks is subsidized by Programa Nacional do Livro Didático – PNLD (National Textbook Program), conducted by the Ministry of Education, for Elementary students. Second, Programa Nacional de Biblioteca da Escola – PNBE (National School Library Program) sends selected books to every public school library in Brazil. Third, Fundação Nacional do Livro Infantil e Juvenil – FNLIJ (National Foundation of Children's and Young Readers' Books), a non-governmental organization, promotes an award system for those works most nominated by invited voters, and thus provides a reference point for the formation of library collections. Voters represent different forums and regions of the country, and thus a diversity of evaluation criteria is assured in the determination of what quality means in works from various categories. The books in this essay have been subject to at least one of these three evaluations.

In contrast, more than ten years after the enactment of Law 10,639, another study (Martins and Belmiro 2012) analyses the presence of black and indigenous characters as protagonists in narratives that tell us about their history and culture.

Ethnic-racial relations in works of children's and young readers' literature

Within the production of works for children and young readers, the treatments of ethnic-racial relations in the construction of characters are diverse in their approaches, as are the proposals for graphic-editorial projects. Such a wealth of perspectives is justified by the long history of struggle that black communities have waged since the period of colonization, in some cases individually and in others as a large population critical of inequality.

Due to interchange between Brazil and Portuguese-speaking countries and the increased distribution of books themed on ethnic-racial relations, as a result of the Law 10,639/2003, there are a great number of books by authors of African origin (mostly in English and French). Furthermore, there are books translated into Portuguese, books in local languages of African countries, books in Portuguese of Portugal, with its lexical and syntactic peculiarities, texts by black Brazilian authors, and finally texts with "black" themes by black and non-black Brazilian authors.

For these reasons, the quantity and quality of the materials have varied widely, from a strictly ideological perspective, conceived by the struggle for affirmation of African peoples and their descendants, to texts that tell the story of these populations in picture book format. Others are explicitly informative regarding the history of Africans in Brazil, works that develop the black theme, with black characters, even black characters whose themes are far from the fight or the development of the African peoples. The latter is much more recent, replacing the theme of black leadership with that of black people as protagonists in various themes. Thus, the wealth of production in children's and young readers' literature that deals with this field allows for a more intense and complex dialogue on the current Brazilian reality. The *corpus* selected for our discussion thus presents only a select collection of production in the area, owing to the impossibility of totally encompassing the many nuances that are represented and that enrich the reading and understanding of black people.

In further compliance with Law 10,639/2003 these literary books invest in the use of visuals that highlight and explore concepts, developing a visual aesthetic based on the ethics of recognition of customs and values of a culture that had been destroyed by cultural prejudice and by economic power. One such element is the importance given to the aesthetic of the bodies of the black man and woman, appreciating the hair, mouth, teeth, the body shapes of certain ethnicities, and the strong facial features. Unlike the discourse of the colonizer, which saw the slender and firm body of the female black slave as a justification for the libidinous attitudes of the white Portuguese, or the body of the African as purely an instrument of work, a contemporary representation of their beauty emphasizes the treatment of the hair as a rite of passage, a generational symbol and a union with their peers. As Rancière claims with regards to the distribution of the sensible, its aesthetic constitution is what shapes the community and, in this case, the assertion of groups that maintain the sharing of something in common. Books like *Chico Juba, Nikkè Entremeio sem babado, Palmas e vaias* [*Chico Juba, Nikkè, Frills without an embroidered strip, Applause and boos*] among many others, explore the hair, whether of a child, or a teenage boy or girl, as something which must be cultivated and treated with pride and as a form of group distinction. It can be plaited, long, short or voluminous, but is always representative of Africanness. The book *Nikkè*, which is the name of the young African female character, has two stories: the first is the history of hair (blond and black), and the second is of a girl who dreams of putting an end to world hunger. As usual, someone tells the story of the girl, who wanders around the world also telling stories, in a reminiscence of the *Arabian Nights*. In *Chico Juba*, the discussion is about the decision the boy wants to take regarding his hair. The result is an awareness of the beauty of his hair.

This characteristic of oral transmission recurs in many books and brings back a character from the tradition of the African nations that keeps alive the memory of his deeds. This "guardian of the word" is a storyteller (*griot*), so very frequent in oral societies, who echoes the soul of the people through his narratives. The language of the griot conveys the knowledge of his people and guards the people's traditions through the power of word. He produces and maintains the ancestral memory of the community of which he is a part, composing oral literature which enhances the extent to which he values his culture.

There are several books that feature this legendary character in recounting stories from different regions of Africa. In *Toques do Griô: memórias sobre contadores de histórias africanos* [Touches of the Griot: Memoirs of African Storytellers], Brazilian authors present different stories, varying situations and characters; for instance, an important era for Northwest Africa, and the thirteenth-century Mali Empire. There is also one of a sovereign who had sailed to the New World before its Discovery, and finally the apprentice griots living between Mali and Paris in the twenty-first century. In *Nina África: contos de uma África menina para ninar gente de todas as idades* [Nina Africa: tales of an African girl to lull people of all ages to sleep], many narratives deal with the creation of things, the goddess of the river, and the stars. They are stories adapted or created for the Brazilian public. Thus, in some cases there presides a visual uniformity of ethnicities and narrative structure in order to help the Brazilian reader understand, as if he were a "foreigner" in relation to African cultures. This can be seen in the illustrations that are similar throughout the book, the characters are maintained with the same traits, unifying and emphasizing a mythical dimension. The tale "O Fogo de Deus" [The Fire of God] admirably portrays the enchanting nature of the griot's teachings about the fire that came to Earth: "Kintu was proud of his grandfather, who was the chief of the council of elders. After all, he knew everything about nature. He told many stories. Fantasies and lessons for everyday life" (2010: 44). In *Lendas da África moderna* [Legends of modern Africa], the authors understand that modern-day Africa continues to produce its own stories and these arrive in Brazil in the form of legends. This work contains a collection of tales from Mali, Kenya, South Africa and Ghana, prepared with a narrative structure of myth. In contrast to the former work, the illustrator is the same for all of the tales in this book, but the illustrations are suggestive and connotative, with graphic work that leaves room for the reader to relate the visual language to the verbal in a significant pairing. One of the highlights is the story about the griot Fassekè, "who travels through time and to anywhere on the planet: China, Cuba, Madagascar and Brazil. It is said that he lives between Burkina Faso and Paris" (2010: 13). In other books, even if he is not the center of the narrative, the character of the "storyteller" is cited as an element that marks the cultural context of that people. Such is the case, for example, with *Madiba*, who "also loves the stories told by his grandmother, at dusk" (Barbosa 2011: 13).

Another trend that is assuming a marked presence in contemporary Brazilian production has been the choice of exemplary figures in the history of Africans in Brazil. Remembering Chico Rei, Zumbi dos Palmares and Esperança Garcia (King Chico, Zombie of Palmares and Esperança Garcia) as protagonists indicates the importance of recovering the history of slave resistance. However, many of these books, albeit well produced, are tangential to the literary language and yet are fundamentally informative, preoccupied with the introduction of the context of slavery in the school environment. In Renato and Graça Lima's *Zumbi* [Zombie] (2009), the ploy of the story is to present a boy, the son of an African man and a "Nisei" (a child of Japanese parents), who learned "capoeira," a cultural expression of African slave descendants, which is a mixture of martial arts and music. His master nicknamed him Zumbi because of his rebelliousness. A friend expresses interest in the name and so the boy tells the story of Zumbi dos Palmares, the leader of the slave resistance who fled to hidden settlements within the forests known as "quilombos." Zumbi was the leader of the Quilombo dos Palmares. Alternatively, *Chico Rei* (2006), also by Renato and Graça Lima, also presents a child character who asks his grandmother to tell him the story of the African king, who became a slave in Brazil, and who collected gold nuggets from mines and finally bought his freedom and freedom for many other African slaves. *Chico Rei* is a mixture of history and legend. The illustrations in both these books are by Graça Lima and some paint solutions she uses give her the freedom to create an environment of contrasts and tensions. For example, the images are in black and white, with significant contrast produced by the light against the black. Further, the naïve representation of Africanness, apparently simplified, is similar to the way artisans of northeastern Brazil make dolls of people by immersing their hands in local clay. The freedom of representation in contemporary illustrations of that era was based on the Brazilian imagination of how life was for Africans and on the drawings of European artists who visited Brazil on missions in the centuries that followed. Thus, the myth survives in history and in the illustrations that built it.

It is worth noting that these two protagonists of African literature in Brazil are literate, having learned Portuguese and Latin with the catechism of Jesuit priests. It is also the case with the protagonist Esperança Garcia, in *Quando a Esperança Garcia escreveu uma carta* [When Esperança Garcia wrote a letter] by Sonia Rosa and Luciana Justiniani Hees. The first part of the story is narrated in first person, denouncing the forced separation of her family after the Jesuits were expelled from Brazil in the eighteenth century. The narrator recounts the difficult life that a slave woman led: "I was very lucky! Here, in this place, almost all of the women are illiterate. The female slaves, then, I won't get into this...they can't recognize their own names." She decides to write the first ever petition letter by a literate Afro-Brazilian slave in Brazil, detailing the mistreatment suffered at the hands of Captain Antônio Vieira de Couto's administration. Giving a voice to a female African slave in that era reinforces the need, nowadays, for a more specific discussion of ethnicity and gender, illuminating this subject that has been overshadowed by the culture of the white man. In the second part of the book, the third-person narrator takes over the plot in order to praise the courage of the African woman and to keep her spirit alive within us. This is actually a true story, and the original petition can be found in Portugal.

The illustrations in this last book are distinctly different from those that have been produced in Brazil (See Figure 18.1). The book is written by a Brazilian woman who lives in Brazil and is illustrated by another Brazilian woman who has lived in Mozambique since 2003. It can be assumed that Hess is working under the influence of Mozambique African art, since the figure of the protagonist is close to the visual profiles and faces that Mozambican artists have produced. Malangatana Ngwenya is one such Mozambican artist who has not given up his cultural roots in order to make art.

Another recurring theme in a great deal of literature originating in Africa is the tambor or "talking drum" and its significance. As the symbol of mother Africa, this instrument is the theme of so many stories, revealing the deepest feelings of African emotion. The context of Guinea-Bissau echoes the subject in the tale "A Lua, o macaco e o tambor" [The moon, the monkey and the talking drum] in the book *Nina África*, and tells the reader that "This story happened when Africa was still an immense Forest, and man and animals lived in harmony" (2010: 26). The monkey is given a beautiful musical instrument by the moon, which she herself had received when she was small, a million light years away. After some mischief, the little animal arrives at his village, and everyone is delighted with the sound of the instrument. The villagers then begin to make new talking drums, and consequently it becomes the symbol of great mother Africa. Another book that explores the

Figure 18.1 Quando Esperança Garcia escreveu uma carta [When Esperança Garcia wrote a letter] by Sonia Rosa; illustrations by Luciana Justiniani Hees. Rio de Janeiro: Pallas, 2012. Source: Reproduced with kind permission of Pallas Editora.

talking drum as the center of feelings and emotions is *O Menino coração de tambor* [The boy with the talking drum-like heart] (See Figure 18.2). Set in Minas Gerais, a Brazilian state with a strong tradition of the rhythms of African slave culture, the book covers the story of a child still in the womb, whose heart already beats, signaling, in different ways, his expression of affection. The music that the mother hears, particularly in Congado[1] (Afro-Brazilian) parties, the roots of samba,[2] and the father's saxophone, resonates with the unborn child's heartbeat. Once grown, the boy becomes a dancer and "his body energetically and nimbly accompanies the drum beats." It is the time when all hearts beat as one, to the rhythm of the talking drums. The presence of this musical instrument definitely marks the importance of this representation, since by such oral communication, by the body and by the music, African cultures come to be recognized.

Many tales echo the imagery of African people, in different instances of their culture, in which the fictional representation of the narratives serves to reconstruct the imagery of the African peoples for the Brazilian reader. *Madiba* tells the story of the life of Nelson Mandela, romanticizing the story of the boy who grew up, suffered and fought for freedom, becoming the first black president of South Africa. *África Eterna* values the expressions of different African regions, with their fauna, flora, agriculture, religions and dance etc. Hence, so many informative and argumentative books, such as *Agbalá, a continent* where every person would have the seed and memory of the place within themselves, or *Brasil em preto e branco* (Brazil in black and white), which tells stories of the past, of the present, of traditions and of beliefs. It recovers texts of a Brazilian romantic poet who portrays the life of Africans on board slave ships and adds a final text, as a battle cry. This book is not, as a whole, composed of fictional or informative texts, but is argumentative in essence.

Figure 18.2   O Menino coração de tambor [The boy with the talking drum-like heart] by Nilma Lino Gomes; illustrations by Maurício Negro. Belo Horizonte: Mazza.
Source: Reproduced with kind permission of Mazza Edições.

Not all African-themed books focus on diversity, but may bear features of works that are effectively literary (Amâncio et al., 2008:167). In recent years a trend in picturebook projects has been to highlight African protagonists in narratives whose themes are not those of blackness or traditional Afro-Brazilian cultural values, but of the everyday life of an African woman, a cleaner in urban regions of the country, who returns to her house in the slum at the end of the working day (Graça Lima, *Luzimar*); or of a child who lives on the bank of a river and who will become part of the community through the bonds of friendship and collective sense of community where he lives (José Marinho, *O Príncipe da Beira*) (The Prince of the Bank); or a black child, in a book for very young children, who imagines household objects turning into animals which live in his imagination (Graça Lima, *Cadê?*) [Where?]; or also of a very talkative black girl who eventually learns that silence makes us more attentive to others (Sonia Rosa, *Lindara*). All of the narratives highlight moments of a simple and unsophisticated everyday life. A notable example by Luís Pimentel and Victor Tavares is *Neguinho do Rio* [Little black boy of Rio] in which the experiences of a little boy constitute a celebration of the city of Rio de Janeiro. Thus, the narrative becomes an informative text, with all of the peculiarities of perspectives of those who like their city. The illustrations in these books make it clear that these characters may live in a simple environment, but they are people of vitality and high self-esteem.

Conclusion

The variety of perspectives presented in books for children and young readers enable us to identify some changes, albeit slow ones. First, editorial production is increasingly attentive to the changes that are taking place in society, owing to the debate regarding

Figure 18.3 From *Obax*, by André Neves. São Paulo: Brinque-Book, 2010.
Source: Reproduced with kind permission of Brinque-Book Editora de Livros Ltda.

ethnic-racial relations, and consequently many books on this topic are published each year. Second, this material is required to satisfy a minimum standard, so that, at least in this case, quantity does indeed lead to quality. Third, the academic field of verbal and visual language experimentation has created some interested discussion of picturebooks, resulting in the development of some bold projects regarding graphic design, the construction of narrative and the plight of the characters presented therein. *Obax*, by André Neves, is an example of artistic refinement combined with quality fiction (see Figure 18.3).

Finally, there is a trend towards a more refined conceptual investigation of diversity. *O Mundo das pessoas coloridas* [The World of colorful people], by Caio Ducca and Thiago Amormino, goes beyond a purely ideological-based direction, and in fact contemplates the acceptance of others: "the blacks, the Indians, the Orientals, Latinos, the Nordics, a plethora of types. And variations within each group…" (22). Alternatively, Alexandre Bersot's *Imagine uma menina com cabelos de Brasil*…[Imagine a girl with the hair of Brazil…] imagines a map made of hair: "each person in this world has their own type of hair: curly, straight, curly blond, brown, red…" (46).

Illustrations in several books emphasize, through color, the vibrant nature of the earth and the forests, portrayed in African art, whether by artisans working in brown, black, green, or red, or in art produced by visual artists who represent, with vibrant shades, the state of mind that is this aesthetic feeling. Further, this aesthetic is present in colorful costumes, with storytellers dressed in brown rags, adult bodies marked by ethnic orientation, and settings by the presence of nature, be it more descriptive – rivers, mountains and plantations – or more imaginary – shrouded in clouds, the heavens, lightning, flying children with plaited hair of gold and black. Thus, there is a series of aesthetic procedures that does not conceal but actually emphasizes the ethical content of speech and both speech and aesthetics work harmoniously together to say something about Africa.

In the midst of these issues, authors such as Duarte are shining a light on this literature of diversity, difference and inequality, not only on the role of black characters, but, above all, on *black authorial voices*, with which young people can build self-esteem that makes them proud of themselves: "hoping that they achieve greater visibility and, who knows, accomplish the *utopia* that moves them: to create an *afro-descendent readership with whom they identify*" (Duarte, 2014: 165, emphasis added).

The *International Decade for People of African Descent*, proclaimed by the General Assembly of the United Nations on 23 December 2013,[3] and scheduled to run from 1 January 2015 to 31 December 2024 with the theme "recognition, justice and development," has strong implications for Afro-Brazilian cultures. In this context, the publication *História e cultura africana e afro-brasileira na educação infantil*[4] [African and Afro-Brazilian history and culture in children's education] invites families and communities to reflect upon the invisibility of African and Afro-Brazilian cultures. This text presents the Capoeira and Griot Space projects, mentioned herein, with whose narratives, whether mythological or literary, other children could feel like *Obax*, "even able to dream of his adventures."

Notes

1 A religious and cultural Afro-Brazilian expression.
2 A rhythm with predominantly black, lower class origins.
3 See: www.un.org/pga/101214_launch-international-decade-people-african-descent/
4 http://unesdoc.unesco.org/images/0022/002270/227009POR.pdf (Brazil-Africa Program: Crossed stories. Cooperation UNESCO/Ministry of Education. Partnership Federal University of São Carlos).

Bibliography

Amâncio, Íris; Gomes, Nilma; Jorge, Míriam (2008) *Literaturas africanas e afro-brasileira na prática pedagógica* [African and Afro-Brazilian literature in pedagogical practice] Belo Horizonte: Autêntica.

Belmiro, Célia Abicalil; Maciel, Francisca; Baptista, Mônica; Martins, Aracy (Orgs.) (2013) *Onde está a Literatura: seus espaços, seus leitores, seus textos, suas leituras* [Where is the literature: its spaces, readers, texts and readings] Belo Horizonte: UFMG.

Berger, P. L.; Luckmann, T. (1973) *A construção social da realidade: tratado de sociologia do conhecimento* [The social construction of reality: a treatise on the sociology of knowledge] Petrópolis: Vozes.

Costa, Hilton; Pinhel, André; Silveira, Marcos Silva da (2012) *Uma década de Políticas Afirmativas: panorama, argumentos e resultados* [A decade of Affirmative Action: panorama, arguments and results] Ponta Grossa: Ed. UEPG.

Duarte, Eduardo (2014) "O lugar do negro na Literatura" [The black's place in Literature], in Belmiro, Celia Abicalil; Maciel, Francisca; Baptista, Mônica; Martins, Aracy (Orgs.). *Onde está a Literatura: seus espaços, seus leitores, seus textos, suas leituras.* [Where is the literature: its spaces, readers, texts and readings] Belo Horizonte: UFMG.

Gomes, Nilma Lino (Org.) (2007) "Diversidade e currículo" [Diversity and curriculum], in *Indagações sobre currículo: diversidade e currículo* [Questions about curriculum: diversity and curriculum] Brasília: MEC/SEB.

Martins, Aracy; Belmiro, Celia Abicalil (2012) "Quem é Protagonista? Relações Étnico-raciais em Livros para Crianças" [Who is the Protagonist? Ethnic-racial relations in Books for Children], in *A criança e a leitura literária: livros, espaços, mediações* [The child and literary reading: books, spaces and mediations] Curitiba: Ed. Positivo, 37–63.

Martins, Aracy; Gomes, Nilma (2010) "Literatura infantil/juvenil e diversidade: a produção literária atual" [Children's and Young readers' literature and diversity: current literary production], in Paiva, Aparecida; Maciel, Francisca; Cosson, Rildo (eds.) *Literatura: ensino fundamental* [Literature: elementary education] Brasília: MEC/SEB, 143–170.

Rancière, Jacques (2005) "A Partilha do Sensível: estética e política" [The division of the sensible: aesthetics and politics], trans. Mônica Costa Netto. *São Paulo Exo Experimental org.* 34; Brasília: MEC/SEB, 2010, 143–170.

Silva, Paulo V. B. (2007) "Desigualdades raciais em livros didáticos e literatura infanto-juvenil" [Racial inequalities in textbooks and children's literature], in Silva, P. V. B.; H. Costa (Orgs.) *Notas de História e Cultura Afro-brasileiras* [Afro-Brazilian Historical and Cultural Notes] Ponta Grossa: UEPG.

Van Dijk, Teun A. (2008) *Racismo e discurso na América Latina* [Racism and discourse in Latin America] São Paulo: Contexto.

Van Leeuwen, Theo (1993) "Genre and Field in Critical Discourse Analysis: A Synopsis" *Discourse and Society*, 4(2): 193–223.

Primary Texts

Barbosa, Rogério A. (2011) *Madiba.* Illustrated by Alarcão. São Paulo: Cortez.

Bersot, Alexandre (2012) *Imagine uma menina com cabelos de Brasil…* [Imagine a girl with the hair of Brazil…] São Paulo: Prumo.

Castanha, Marilda (2008) *Agbalá: um lugar continente* [Agbalá: a continent place] São Paulo: Cosac Naify.

Ducca, Caio (2012) *O Mundo das pessoas coloridas* [The World of colorful people]. Illustrated by Thiago Amormino. Belo Horizonte: Mazza.

Gaivota, Gustavo (2011) *Chico Juba.* Illustrated by Rubem Filho. Belo Horizonte: Mazza.

Gomes, L.; Holanda. A; Gomes, C. (2010) *Nina África: contos de uma África menina para ninar gente de todas as idades* [Nina Africa: tales of an African girl to lull people of all ages to sleep]. Illustrated by Maurício Veneza. São Paulo: Elementar.

Gomes, Nilma Lino (2013) *O Menino coração de tambor* [The boy with the talking drum-like heart]. Illustrated by Maurício Negro. Belo Horizonte: Mazza.

Lima, Graça (2009) *Cadê?* [Where?] Rio de Janeiro: Nova Fronteira.

Lima, Graça (2009) *Luzimar* Rio de Janeiro: Nova Fronteira.

Lima, Heloisa P.; Hernandez, Leila L. (2010) *Toques do Griô: memórias sobre contadores de histórias africanos* [Touches of the Griot: Memoirs of African Storytellers]. Illustrated by Kaneaki Tada. São Paulo: Melhoramentos.

Lima, Heloisa Pires; Andrade, Rosa M. A. (2010) *Lendas da África moderna* [Legends of modern Africa]. Illustrated by Denise Nascimento. São Paulo: Elementar.

Lima, Renato (2006) *Chico Rei* [King Chico]. Illustrated by Graça Lima. São Paulo: Paulus.

Lima, Renato (2009) *Zumbi* [Zombie]. Illustrated by Graça Lima. São Paulo: Paulus.

Marinho, José (2011) *O Príncipe da Beira* [The Prince of the Bank]. Belo Horizonte: Mazza.

Neves, André (2010) *Obax* São Paulo: Brinque-Book.

Oliveira, Rui de (2010) *África Eterna* [Eternal Africa] São Paulo: FTD.

Pereira, Édimo de A. (2011) *Nikkè.* Illustrated by Abu. Belo Horizonte: Mazza.

Pimentel, Luís (2012) *Neguinho do Rio* [Little black boy of Rio]. Illustrated by Victor Tavares. Rio de Janeiro: Palas.

Rochael, Denise (2005) *Brasil em preto e branco* [Brazil in black and White]. São Paulo: Cortez.

Rosa, Sonia (2009) *Lindara.* Illustrated by Marcial Ávila. Belo Horizonte: Nandyala.

Rosa, Sonia (2009) *Palmas e vaias* [Applause and boos]. Illustrated by Salmo Dansa. Rio de Janeiro: Palas.

Rosa, Sonia (2012) *Quando Esperança Garcia escreveu uma carta* [When Esperança Garcia wrote a letter]. Illustrated by Luciana Justiniani Hees. Rio de Janeiro: Palas.

Santana, Patrícia (2007) *Entremeio sem babado* [Frills without embroidered strip]. Illustrated by Marcial Ávila. Belo Horizonte: Mazza.

19

THE CRUCIBLE

Forging a hybrid identity in a multicultural world

Suchismita Banerjee

The simultaneous perpetuation and dismantling of cultural stereotypes has particular shaping effects on the construction of identity in children of multicultural societies. The notion of nation/nativeness is mediated through the institution of the family: specifically, through metonymic interaction between a child and a grandparent. With reference to two novels – *Bringing Back Grandfather* by Anjali Banerjee and *When Amma Went Away* by Devika Rangachari – the essay will show how intergenerational dialogue can negotiate cultural change and continuity, so that child characters' interaction with grandparents grounds their connection with their cultural origins. There are tensions inherent in this process, however, as it is a site of struggle with contested meanings.

The transmission of culture – specifically, of values and traditions – is a primary concern among parents and educators, especially in today's globalized world. While most cultural theorists and educators agree that culture fashions identity, the process of transmission and the aspects of culture considered appropriate for transmission are often contested. Questioning if American society has lost the ability to pass on culture to the youth, Stanton Green comments that it is essential to rekindle the relationship between generations in order to enable the transmission of culture. He notes that the transition from childhood into adulthood occurs at the age when students enter college, hence the role of higher education becomes critical in ensuring the transmission of cultural values:

> One of the functions of higher education in our society—its primary function, some might argue—is to help transmit an ever-changing culture from one generation to the next. Indeed, the transmission of our culture—though not necessarily the uncritical acceptance of its ideas, values, beliefs, and understanding of acceptable behavior—is essential for a society to continue. [...]as we tackle the problems of schooling for the twenty-first century, we rightly are also wrestling with the question of what aspects of our culture we want to pass on to students.
>
> (1998: 31)

This mission of transmitting culture can be viewed from two distinct perspectives, which I will term the "home" (native/domestic) and "away" (immigrant) perspectives respectively. In the former, the native, homegrown culture is concerned with preserving traditional values in the face of "alien" influences (read globalization and mass media) while the latter is characterized by efforts to "import" emblems of the native culture into the adopted land, in order to maintain connection with the roots. In both scenarios, the role of adults in effecting and modulating the process of transmission is critical.

The two novels I have selected for discussion are representative of the home and away perspectives, and the child's identity in each case is molded by the cultural influences to which s/he is exposed. The argument presented here is twofold: first, the opportunity to connect with the child's roots via the presence of the grandparent is viewed differently by the child characters and is strongly influenced by their environment and peer group. Second, there are specific points of convergence and divergence in the idea of "nativeness" between Indian authors based in India and diasporic writers of Indian origin. These differences contribute to the construction of a hybrid identity that strategically combines key elements of the native and adopted culture.

The perception that grandparents and older relatives are the best purveyors of tradition and culture is particularly prevalent in the Asian subcontinent. Discussing the concern of US-based South Asian Muslims about "curtailing the Americanization process", Aminah Mohammad-Arif notes, "The presence of grandparents is seen by the migrants as a definite advantage in terms of the transmission of cultural values. Grandparents are thus endorsed with the function of role-model" (2000: 71). This observation is equally true of diasporic Indian families of all religious denominations as well as of contemporary Indian society. Among all these communities, the primary concern is the aspects of culture that should be passed on to the next generation. The discourse of contemporary children's fiction offers significant insights into the idea of nation/nativeness constructed by community elders, often in response to the "threat" of globalization.

The complex dynamics that underlie the functioning of multicultural societies are decoded in both novels as they explore the construction of shifting identities in response to localized and global events. *Bringing Back Grandfather* focuses on eight-year-old Anu, an American citizen of Indian origin, and his attempts to resist racial stereotyping and discrimination in a post-9/11 world. *When Amma Went Away* traces fourteen-year-old Nalini's efforts to construct a hybrid identity in New Delhi, the cosmopolitan capital city of India, which is dominated by global (western) and local (Punjabi) influence. In both novels, a crisis in the opening chapters puts in motion a series of events that bring intercultural differences and tensions sharply into focus. In *Bringing Back Grandfather*, Anu's grandfather (whom he calls Dadu) suffers a stroke and dies while birdwatching in the woods with Anu. The rest of the book traces Anu's frantic attempts to resurrect his grandfather, ending with his ultimate acceptance of the reality of his Dadu's passing. Anu faces the twin crisis of coping with personal loss as well as with the alienating, often hostile ways he is viewed by peers and adults after the terrorist attack. In *When Amma Went Away*, Nalini's mother's departure for Singapore on a temporary assignment and the arrival of her grandmother (whom she calls Patti) to take her place is a key moment in her life. Eager to establish her independence, the teenager is opposed to the idea of needing a caretaker, and initially resists her grandmother's overtures. Both novels proceed to trace the impact of the grandparent in fashioning the identity of the protagonists.

Whose identity is it anyway? The essentialist trap

Chris Barker points out that identity is a social phenomenon in two ways. First, the notion of what it is to be a person is a cultural question. "For example, individualism is a marker of modern western societies while in many other cultures people conceive of themselves as inseparable from family relations". Second, the very resources that form the material for an identity project are social in nature, for example, language and social practices, so that what it means to be a child, a woman, an Asian, is formed differently in different cultural contexts (2011: 222). In the novels under discussion, the children's identity is necessarily a fragmented one, combining aspects of their native and adopted cultures rather unevenly. If culture is represented through language and social practices, then neither Anu nor Nalini is authentically Bengali/Indian or Tamil/Indian respectively. Anu knows only a smattering of Bengali, his mother tongue, mainly the terms of endearment his grandfather uses and the names of his favorite Bengali dishes. Nalini "understood Tamil well but was too diffident to use it" (2002: 34–35). Both children are, however, fluent in English. With regard to social practices, they are not familiar with the customs and traditions of their native culture, and it is the grandparent who introduces them to some of these practices.

In a discussion of nation states and national identity, Chris Barker points out that Benedict Anderson's concept of national identity cloaks differences of class and ethnicity because national cultural identities are not always coterminous with states, as is evident from the existence of global diaspora like the Indian, African and Jewish communities. Even within a nation, a state does not have ethnically homogeneous populations (2011: 252). Both the home and away perspectives in the two novels are based on essentialist assumptions of a homogeneous Indian and American culture. In *Bringing Back Grandfather*, Anu's identity as an Indian is problematic in that he belongs to the state of West Bengal, but in American society, he is viewed as representative of a pan-Indian culture. This conflicts with his perception of himself as an American. In *When Amma Went Away*, Nalini views herself as a cosmopolitan Delhiite (Delhi being a melting pot of diverse cultures, with the predominant influence of the north Indian state of Punjab), and resists attempts to link her with her ethnic roots in Tamil Nadu, a state in south India.

The depiction of the clash of cultures in fiction is often predicated on such assumptions of homogeneity. As Arjun Appadurai has pointed out, "The central problem of today's global interactions is the tension between cultural homogenization and cultural heterogenization" (1996: 32). An analysis of the cultural encounters in the two books reveals significant disjunctures. Both novels constitute the Other as a homogeneous entity. In reality, however, India and America possess a multitude of diverse communities that makes impossible the concept of cultural homogenization. The identity project of both Anu and Nalini presupposes monolithic categories such as "American" and "Indian", and draws heavily on stereotypes. Historically, American society has been inherently pluralistic, and yet the "American" way of life reflects the dominance of a specific race and class. Contrasting essentialism and anti-essentialism, Stuart Hall notes that the essentialist position from which identity can be understood is based on the assumption of a collective self that is formed out of a common history and ancestry (1990: 223). So an "American" identity would comprise the Stars and Stripes symbol, memories of the Second World War and collective rituals like the Super Bowl. However, this assumption is typically a white, Anglo-Saxon one, excluding blacks and other communities that also constitute America. In *Bringing Back Grandfather*, the identity of Anu's best friend, Unger, is constructed as American from just such an essentialist position in order to set him up as Anu's counterpoint. He is portrayed as the archetypal all-American kid: he makes his entrance in the story wearing a T-shirt with the American flag printed on it (emblematic of the wave of nationalism that swept the US following the 9/11 attacks).

and trades his *Spider-Man* and *X-Men* comics for Anu's *Ramayana* comic. He proudly displays to Anu the money he has made selling his old baseball cards. His father is an insurance salesman and he "wants to be richer than his dad, live in a mansion in Malibu and drive a convertible" (2007: 26).

In a similar manner, the vast multicultural diversity of India is compressed into the dominant symbols with which India is habitually identified in the West: curry and samosas (with the additional inclusion of the Bengali dessert called *payesh*), sitar and tabla, godmen and Hindu mythology. The categories "Hindu" and "Indian" are unproblematically conflated on several occasions, although the Indian demographic comprises significant numbers of Muslims, Christians and followers of other religious denominations. The conflation of Hindu with Indian is more evident in the works of diasporic Indian authors, because it becomes a convenient shorthand to use when the focus is more on the clash of "national" cultures. The monolithic Indian culture thus constructed operates mainly in opposition to an American culture that is avowedly multicultural, but depicted in equally homogeneous terms.

Homegrown narratives are just as susceptible to the essentialist trap. While Anu's troubled search for his identity is set in the global context, Nalini's conflict is more on a national level, focusing on the very real cultural difference between north and south. This cultural disparity is similarly depicted in the form of stereotypical notions that conveniently slot people into either of these geopolitical categories, regardless of the actual differences between communities. It is explicitly stated when Nalini comments on the ignorance of their neighbor, Mrs Anand (who is a north Indian), regarding the distinct cultures of the southern states:

> The lady believed the wildest things about south Indians. She did not know about there being four separate cultures with their distinct languages, and often cheerfully assumed that since the Ramanujans knew Tamil, they knew Malayalam as well.[1] And no amount of correcting made the slightest difference!
>
> (2002: 26–27)

Initially, Nalini appears to be quite comfortable in her "cosmopolitan" identity: attending an English-medium school in Delhi, wearing jeans and shorts and taking sandwiches for lunch. She actively resists attempts by her grandmother to link her with her native culture. When her grandmother gifts her a *pavadai*, a traditional long skirt worn by young girls in Tamil Nadu, she is suddenly shy and quickly hides it in her cupboard. Nalini "had never worn one in her life and felt sure that she would look silly if she did" (27). When Patti suggests that Nalini should take curd rice to school for lunch instead of sandwiches (curd rice, a traditional dish made of yogurt and rice, is commonly consumed in Tamil Nadu as it is believed to cool the digestive system in the hot weather), Nalini reacts strongly to this suggestion: "Nalini almost had a fit. What would the others say ... Richa and the others would not stop laughing if they got to know!" (29)

The conflict arising from cultural disparity and stereotypical ways of viewing the Other is explored through Nalini's consciousness. As Nalini struggles to come to terms with her native culture (represented by her grandmother), which she views as the Other, she questions her father if he faced a similar struggle when he relocated to Delhi. "I just wondered...whether, in the beginning, you felt out of place and people knew you were not from here and whether that made a difference..." (2002: 63).

On the other hand, Nalini's peer group views her as the Other despite her subconscious attempts to blend in with the dominant culture.

Notions of nativeness: the role of the grandparent in fashioning a native identity

Stuart Hall speaks of culture as "the actual grounded terrain of practices, representations, languages and customs of any specific society" as well as "the contradictory forms of common sense which have taken root in and helped to shape popular life" (*Critical Dialogues* 1996: 439). The aspects of culture consciously or unconsciously selected for transmission are indicative of the agenda of the agent of transmission. A study of the notion of "nativeness" as transmitted by the grandparents in both books uncovers significant similarities and differences. The grandparent in each case succeeds in transmitting *emblems* of the native culture in the form of rituals and customs, traditional modes of dress and dietary preferences. Anu's grandfather focuses on familiarizing him with Hindu mythology and religious practices, and tries to establish links with his Bengali roots by cooking typically Bengali meals. Similarly, Nalini's grandmother cooks traditional Tamil dishes, introduces typically Tamil ways of celebrating festivals and encourages Nalini to wear the *pavadai*.

In a discussion of the politics of cultural flows between the South Asian diaspora and the homeland, Dhiraj Murthy (2010) notes: "Both the 'homeland' and diaspora converge in that their shared constructions of an anterior Indian essence(s) are based on an imagined pre-modernity or pre-capitalist India where the populace was in touch with their 'heritage'. For the migrant in the diaspora, the threat to this essence is perceived to be assimilation, while for the elite Delhiites, it is in selected aspects of globalization". (10) The emphasis in *Bringing Back Grandfather* is on fashioning a national identity that has a strong religious base in a foreign country. Murthy terms this a "majoritarian Indian nationalism", which is "secular, but in reality, heavily Hindu-influenced" (3). In *When Amma Went Away*, the focus is more on building a regional identity that can hold its own in a multicultural society in the native country.

The conception of "nativeness" and attention to its performative aspects is more pronounced among the diaspora, and tends to be disseminated by grandparents. This indigenizing project sometimes conflicts with the acculturization project of the parents. Anu's grandfather instills in him an uncritical acceptance of God and Hindu deities, which is an abiding feature of Hindu belief. Anu's parents do not actively oppose this attempt, but adopt a more Enlightenment-inspired world view towards religion that is distinctly western in inflection, as it privileges individual choice regarding religious practices. Puzzled by Anu's attempts to mimic Hindu rituals, Anu's father tells him, "Anu, you can decide to be anything you want—Christian, Hindu, Buddhist, atheist. Eventually, you can make up your own mind". Anu is confused by his parents' neutrality and their refusal to observe rituals:

"Didn't you ever pray to Shiva?" I ask.
Dad shakes his head. "I left for boarding school when I was very little. I never prayed with your Dadu. He was stuck in the old days. Old days and old ways."
"The gods never get old!"
"I'm just telling you to think for yourself," Dad says.

(2007: 51)

That a transplanted culture strives to impose its concept of tradition on the younger generation through traditional attire and observance of festivals is also a concern of *When*

Amma Went Away. Unlike Anu, Nalini does not embrace her native culture with the same enthusiasm. Patti's attempts to acquaint her with her roots are viewed initially with suspicion and met with resistance.

In contrast to Anu's parents, Nalini's father fully endorses the indigenizing process, admitting ruefully that living in Delhi had isolated their children from the influence of the extended family and native culture. Regrettably, there are no non-Hindu characters in *When Amma Went Away*, so the focus is more on transmitting Tamil culture in terms of modes of dress, food and observance of customs.

Hybridity and agency

Homi Bhabha's interpretation of hybridity as "disruptive" and "productive" and its deployment as a strategy for dismantling unequal power relations (Bhabha 1994: 226) has been usefully employed by cultural theorists to negotiate a space for articulation both for and from the periphery, and resonates with the strategy employed by the central characters in both novels to construct a hybrid identity in response to the crisis in their lives. Though Anu thinks of himself as American, his interaction with his grandfather makes him aware of his alternate positioning as a Bengali-Hindu-Indian boy. He does not perceive these identities as conflicting with his sense of self until the 9/11 attack brings his ethnicity into focus (rather erroneously, considering he is neither a Muslim nor remotely connected to the terrorists in terms of nationality). Nalini is similarly not overly conscious of her Tamil roots until the arrival of her grandmother. The internalization of the notion of nativeness is a direct function of their age and environment. Eight-year-old Anu accepts his native culture uncritically and enthusiastically while teenaged Nalini is more skeptical and selectively absorbs only those aspects of her native culture that are validated by her peer group.

The degree to which hybridity confers agency determines the kind of elements the subject will absorb from both cultures. Anu and Nalini both choose to adopt the performative aspects of their cultures because these help them to create a hybrid identity that is compatible with their milieu. As Anu attempts to integrate his Indian and American personae, he is puzzled and hurt by the obvious ignorance of the average American. When he anxiously leads the paramedics through the woods to his grandfather, one of them calls him a "little Islam", to which he responds, "I want to yell that the word is *Muslim*, not *Islam*, and I'm not a Muslim anyway, but I don't have time to explain" (2007: 7). On seeing Anu's grandfather, the paramedic comments, "Like that damned Bin Laden. Check out the beard". He is immediately reprimanded by his colleagues, but Anu is bewildered that anyone could think his beloved Dadu was capable of such evil. His classmate Curtis calls him names as well, sometimes distorting his name to Anus, at others calling him Osama.

"Why don't you go back to Afghanistan?" Curtis says.
"Why don't you learn geography?" I say. I want to punch him in the nose.

Anu's best friend Unger tries to clarify by asserting that Anu is Indian, to no avail.

"Whatever," Curtis says. "Go back to your own country."
"I am in my own country!"

(36)

Tracing the identity formation of young South Asian Muslims in the US, Mohammad Arif notes, "As in the case of other South Asians, religion occupies a significant place in the construction of the identity of Muslims in the US.... this enhanced importance of religion in the lives of South Asian immigrants can also be attributed to the American context: most ethnic minorities in the US (Irish, Greeks, Jews) have traditionally seen in religion an efficient vehicle in their community formation and identity re-composition" (2000: 67). Anu's attitude to his native culture echoes that of his adopted nation: an awed fascination for the exotic element, and a curiosity about its strangeness. When faced with open and subtle racial discrimination that draws attention to his "difference", he subconsciously subverts the attempts to slot him into a stereotype by using that very stereotype to exercise power over those who bully him. He asserts his Indianness and exploits the exoticism of his heritage by showcasing it to his peers, arousing their curiosity and earning their admiration. His naive attempts to use Hindu rituals and customs to bring back his grandfather stem from his refusal to accept the reality of his death, but he is also quick to see their value in rehabilitating him within his school community. Anu announces that like a famous holy man in India, he will shave off his hair and roll to school every day in the hope that this will eventually give him the power to bring back his Dadu. This instantly earns him the curiosity and interest of his classmates, but his selective adoption of those specific aspects of his culture that help create an empowering identity indicate that his grandfather's attempts to instill in him an understanding and appreciation of his heritage amount to mere tokenism: he demands Indian food because his grandfather ate and cooked it, and he performs the rituals he has seen his grandfather doing without really grasping their essence. This tokenism, which is a form of reverse acculturation, is also evident in the way his mother transforms into an "Indian" overnight when they are expecting a relative from India: she shops for Indian rice and spices, changes into a kurta with jeans (a hybrid symbol of Indo-Western sartorial fusion), cooks Indian food and plays Indian music just before their visitor arrives, "like she just now remembered to be Indian" (2007: 65).

Partha Chatterjee observes that nationalism "declares the domain of the spiritual its sovereign territory and refuses to allow the colonial power to intervene in that domain" (2010: 27). This is borne out in Anu's fascination with the mystique and exoticism of Hindu culture. His grandfather's tales fuel his imagination and dominate his inner life. Ironically, the ancient spiritual tradition of India empowers Anu in a way all the technological advancement of America could not. Yet the aspects of Hindu culture that he adopts to empower himself are in themselves hybrid and ambivalent in meaning: the god Shiva is propitiated with cookies and Anu's renunciation of all material things is conditional. He refuses to give away his computer, as he needs the Internet to find ways to bring back his Dadu, and he chooses to continue living with his parents as a matter of convenience (in Hindu tradition, people who embark on spiritual quests generally renounce home and family ties). He attempts to integrate his native culture with his lived reality by adopting the vocabulary and tools of the modern, materialistic world of twenty-first-century America:

> Garuda, the Hindu god of birds, is also the king of bird poop. When he brings finches and nuthatches to our feeders, the droppings fertilize the soil... He flies direct from India to Seattle, and it doesn't matter that the airports have been closed for a week since the planes hit the Twin Towers.
>
> (2007: 1)

In this way, Anu resolves his identity conflict by creating a third space which, in Bhabha's words, "is a mode of articulation, a way of describing a *productive*, and not merely reflective, space that engenders new *possibility*" (Meredith 1998: 3).

However, the appropriation of the Other is not always unproblematic, and there are asymmetries in these intercultural encounters that defy a simplistic East-West opposition. Anu shaves his head in his bid to become a sadhu (holy man), an act that draws attention to his difference from "normal" people, and this defiant act unexpectedly creates a bonding between him and Andy, a cancer-afflicted American schoolmate who is also bald, albeit for a different reason. Similarly, Anu is helped in his attempts to bring his grandfather back to life by his friend Izzy, who is American, yet alienated from the mainstream in her own way. Izzy is a home-schooled child as her mother has no faith in institutionalized schooling.

Power play: influence of dominant culture in framing and validating markers of identity

In a discussion of Stuart Hall's conception of identity, Chris Barker notes that Hall's anti-essentialist position stresses that cultural identity is constituted around points of difference. Identity is thus a strategic positioning which makes meaning possible. Paraphrasing Hall, Barker suggests that, "This anti-essentialist position points to the political nature of identity as a 'production' and to the possibility of multiple, shifting and fragmented identities which can be articulated together in a variety of ways" (2001: 30). Nalini thus resists Patti's forced inscription until her peer group validates her native culture by positioning it as "ethnic" and hence exotic. The markers of difference (attire, food, festivals) that Nalini perceives as threatening because they are likely to alienate her from her peers are ultimately absorbed into her persona once the dominant culture has signified its approval by showing appreciation. When Patti cooks a traditional Tamil meal for her friends, it is a grand success:

> "I have never eaten such wonderful things before," sighed Renuka. "Nalini, your grandmother is great!"
> Nalini felt proud on hearing this.
>
> (2002: 80)

On seeing a self-conscious Nalini dressed in the traditional *pavadai* (she finally plucks up courage to wear it on a visit to the temple), her classmate Richa comments, "Wish I had one like this...All I have are salwar kameezes and jeans and skirts. So boring, isn't it?" (42).[2] Here the author tries to invert the notion of "coolness" by showing Nalini's friend evincing interest in her attire.

In *Bringing Back Grandfather*, Anu feels similarly validated when his friends "adopt" the Hindu deity Shiva at the end of the story, gathering at a makeshift shrine below a fir tree to offer their thanks. Typically, the three American children are thankful for concrete "blessings" (Izzy for passing her exams, Andy for having his hair grow back and Unger for finding money while cleaning the house), while Anu simply thanks Shiva "for bringing together four best friends" (2007: 165).

Conclusion

This essay has traced the effects of culture on construction of identity, and the extent to which dialogues with grandparents are metonymic of cultural dialogues that preserve tradition and fashion a complex subjectivity. The process of shaping children's identity by acquainting them with their native culture is complex and by no means cohesive. As demonstrated above, there is significant congruence between homegrown and diasporic authors with regard to notions of nativeness. However, diasporic writers tend to perpetuate stereotypes that are identifiable to the western reader (multiplicity of Hindu gods and goddesses; the choice of Ganesha, the elephant-headed god, as a favorite deity in many diasporic novels; references to exotic forms of dress and arcane customs) but are often contrary to contemporary lived realities. The politics of publishing is also a powerful factor that contributes to such stereotypical representations. Anjali Banerjee's *Bringing Back Grandfather* was originally published in the US under the title *Looking for Bapu*, and most reviews of the book focus on its value as a multicultural text that can foster better understanding and harmony between cultures. The Indian edition, on the other hand, eschews all associations with Indianness in the cover design and title, including changing "Bapu" to "Grandfather" in its attempt to position the novel as a global product and reach out to the urban globalized middle class readership.

The "home" and "away" trends are evident in other books in this genre as well. Novels written by Indian writers based in India tend to focus on the impact of globalization and the asymmetries of the acculturation process, while diasporic novels are more concerned with what it means to be Indian in a foreign land and to what extent the characters should display their Indianness. Seemi Aziz argues that stories written by authors who are disconnected from the native culture for substantial periods of time run the danger of either silencing significant groups of people or lacking in authenticity (2013: 46). This disconnect is highlighted in Kavita Daswani's *A Girl Named Indie* (aka *Indie Girl*), where Indie evolves from being reticent about her Indianness to developing a sense of pride about her culture in the course of the novel, though she is also forced to acknowledge that her conception of India is quite dated:

> I had known that India was becoming a bona fide fashion capital, that there was even an Indian Fashion Week... And there were plenty of girls here who obviously followed those trends as much as I followed Western ones... Surrounded by women in the latest styles fresh off a Delhi designer catwalk, my outfit suddenly felt dated and boring... Obviously, classic Indian garb just wasn't cool any more.
> (2007: 85–86)

Discussing the problematic category of the term "cultural nationalism", and its "singularizing tendency", Aijaz Ahmed notes:

> Used in relation to the equally problematic category of "Third World", "cultural nationalism" resonates equally frequently with "tradition", simply inverting the tradition/modernity binary of the modernization theorists in an indigenist direction, so that tradition is said to be, for the "Third World", always better than modernity, which then opens up a space for defence of the most obscurantist positions in the name of cultural nationalism.
> (1992: 9)

While contemporary Indian English children's fiction displays such a tendency towards singularization in its conception of native culture, it goes beyond the tradition/modernity binary and makes an honest attempt to explore the complexities and tensions inherent in the process of indigenization and acculturation. By granting the characters agency in fashioning their identity, it holds out the hope that the shaping effects of culture will be tempered by a self-reflexivity and inclusiveness that recognizes and celebrates diversity and hybridity in the constitution of selfhood.

Notes

1 Tamil and Malayalam are the languages spoken in the south Indian states of Tamil Nadu and Kerala respectively.
2 The salwar kameez (an overshirt worn with a pair of drawstring trousers gathered at the ankles) is a form of dress native to north Indian states.

Bibliography

Ahmed, Aijaz (1992) "Literature among the Signs of Our Times," in *In Theory: Classes, Nations, Literatures*, London: Verso, pp. 1–42.
Appadurai, Arjun (1996) *Modernity At Large: Cultural Dimensions of Globalization*, Minneapolis: University of Minnesota Press.
Aziz, Seemi (2013) "The Muslima within American Children's Literature: Female Identity and Subjectivity in Novels about Pakistani-Muslim Characters," in John Stephens (ed.) *Subjectivity in Asian Children's Literature and Film*, New York and London, Routledge, pp. 43–58.
Banerjee, Anjali (2007) *Bringing Back Grandfather*, Gurgaon: Penguin Books India.
Barker, Chris (2011) *Cultural Studies: Theory and Practice*, 4th edition, London: Sage Publications Ltd.
Barker, Chris and Dariusz Galasiński (2001) *Cultural Studies and Discourse Analysis: A Dialogue on Language and Identity*, London: Sage.
Bhaba, Homi (1994) *The Location of Culture*, New York and London: Routledge.
Chatterjee, Partha (2010) *Empire and Nation: Selected Essays*, New York: Columbia University Press.
Daswani, Kavita (2007) *A Girl Named Indie*, Gurgaon: Penguin Books India.
Green, Stanton W. (1998) "Passing on Our Culture to the Next Generation," *About Campus* 3(8): 31–32.
Hall, Stuart (1990) "Cultural Identity and Diaspora," in Jonathan Rutherford (ed.) *Identity, Community, Culture, Difference*, London: Lawrence and Wishart Ltd, pp. 222–237.
Hall, Stuart (1996) "Who Needs Identity?" in P. du Gay, J. Evans and P. Redman (eds.) *Identity: A Reader*, London: Sage, pp. 15–30.
Hall, Stuart (1996) *Stuart Hall: Critical Dialogues in Cultural Studies*. Ed. D. Morley and Kuan-Hsing Chen. London: Routledge.
Meredith, Paul (1998) "Hybridity in the Third Space: Rethinking Bi-cultural Politics in Aotearoa/ New Zealand," Te Oru Rangahau Maori Research and Development Conference, pp. 1–6. http://lianz.waikato.ac.nz/PAPERS/paul/hybridity.pdf (accessed 25 July 2015).
Mohammad-Arif, Aminah (2000) "A Masala Identity: Young South Asian Muslims in the US," *Comparative Studies of South Asia, Africa and the Middle East*, 20(1–2): 67–87.
Murthy, Dhiraj (2010) "Nationalism Remixed? The Politics of Cultural Flows between the South Asian Diaspora and 'Homeland'," *Ethnic and Racial Studies*, 33(8): 1–19.
Rangachari, Devika (2002) *When Amma Went Away*, New Delhi: CBT.

20

CONTEMPORARY POETRY FOR CHILDREN AND YOUTH IN BRAZIL

Maria Zélia Versiani Machado

Multiple targets of "child-youth" poetry

Poetry that targets children and youth began to be published in Brazil in book form during the twentieth century.[1] While there are distinguishable differences between the poetry written for children and that written for young people,[2] this discussion deals with poetry for both groups, children and youth. However, it will also seek to outline some of the unique features of the dual targets it deals with. It should be noted that the expression "child-youth", which is used today in catalogue cards to describe very different types of readers, is inadequate. This grouping no longer works when an assessment of overall poetic works reveals increasing diversification. In the 1980s, Regina Zilberman pointed out the difficulties that resulted from literature being defined by its recipient. The first is the *transience of the reader* since, for this author, readers continue to change and to reject the books presented to them. The second is the *unidirectionality* of literature since it is always produced by an adult, in an asymmetric relationship (1987: 37–38). These problems become more complex when the market for publishing books for children and youth has a greater degree of distinction among the different phases of reader development.

Today, with the publishing market becoming more specialized with respect to the public they wish to reach, particularly the increased production of books for children and youth due to government purchases – which include provision for poetry books[3] – there is a notable strengthening of the trend toward determining the range of readers according to their educational level. Thus, writing is produced that is defined by its public, from small children who are beginning to have contact with books, extending to children who are learning to read, and later to those who know how to read independently the literary books that are offered to them. According to this multi-faceted view of childhood, children's poetry is designed for a public that begins with children who do not yet read on their own, all the way to those who already know how to read. In summary, what in Brazil is now defined as children's literature includes children in preschool – from 0 to 5 years – and children in elementary school – from 6 to 10/11 years. The differences in the interests that separate these age groups are well known.

Next, "youth poetry" includes both readers who are beginning to distance themselves from their childhood and show independence, as well as readers who opt for some adult-oriented cultural poems and products. Thus, such a reader is in the second half of Elementary education (*Ensino Fundamental II* – that is, years 6–9) and is aged betwen 11 and 16 years. Today, in Brazil, poetry seeks a verbal and visual language that wins over these early adolescent readers, and thus moves away from textual and editorial strategies appropriate for children, while seeking distinction from adult books. Youth poetry seeks to represent typical changes in the lives of emerging youth with their new interests, using elements of youth identity, and unravelling the idea of transience or transitioning to the adult world, which has marked this genre for a long time. It is these young readers – and the poetry that is written for them – that will be highlighted in this chapter, alongside the child, the target of what is known as "children's poetry". Further, "youth poetry" is not only a lesser-used expression, but is also a subject that has been studied less in Brazil because youth, particularly in the school setting, have been used to reading poems, in their Portuguese language classes, that were written for and by adults. It is thus important here to revisit, even briefly, poetry and its relationship with the teaching of literature, which – whether positive or negative – taught poetic patterns to children and youth and comprised school literary selections mostly from the first half of the twentieth century.

Poetry and the formation of readers in Brazil: a brief recount of a short history

In the first decades of the twentieth century, poetry was presented to students in a school that was not yet universal, in verses with uplifting content that were imbued with the goal of teaching and that strongly revealed the voice of adults and their educational convictions. Little by little, poets have begun to publish children's poetry books that break the uplifting perspective of poetry by using an aesthetically driven poetic language, whether by playfully apprehending the use of formal and thematic elements, or by perceiving the readers as individuals who are capable of deciding, analysing, feeling and desiring. In the 1940s, *O menino poeta* (The boy poet), a poetry book by Henriqueta Lisboa, was published. Beginning in the 1960s, works emerged that influenced children's poetry in Brazil, such as *Ou isto ou aquilo* (Either this or that) by Cecília Meireles, published in 1964; *Pé de Pilão* (*Pestle Foot*) by Mário Quintana, in 1968; *A arca de Noé* (Noah's Ark) by Vinícius de Moraes, in 1975; and *Poemas para brincar* (Poems for playing), in the 1980s, by José Paulo Paes. Despite the repercussions of these and other works that illustrated the aesthetic possibilities of forming readers, schools continued for a long time to use poetry reading as a means of assimilating thematic or grammatical content, as demonstrated by Marisa Lajolo (1997) in her study of poetry as "the fragile school victim".

Until very recently, poetry circulated in schools not in poetry books, but rather mostly in textbooks. According to Magda Soares (1999), literature education is inevitable and requires adaptation so that it can effectively contribute to the formation of readers in school. Frequently poems were – and often still are – adapted or fragmented to manage the limitations and objectives of textbooks. Therefore, it can be said that many generations of readers had access to a selection of school poems whose objectives were not always the most appropriate for literary development.

Many studies have been dedicated to the understanding and analysis of literature for children and youth in Brazil, also with a focus on poetry. Zilberman and Magalhães (1987) brought attention to the fact that very few children's poetry books were part of Brazilian literature and that there were some founding poets who were responsible for consecrating this genre among us, such as Cecília Meireles, whose work would leave visible marks on future poetry. Cunha (1991) stated that, historically, the most sacrificed part of children's literature is poetry. According to this author, there is a false notion that children do not like poetry and this is due to errors in choosing and working with poems in school where, in general, ethical value has superseded aesthetics in the history of reading in schools. Coelho (2000) recalls that, having emerged at the end of the nineteenth century and spreading in the first years of the twentieth century, children's poetry in Brazil has always been committed to the educational work of schools. The author highlights that, at the beginning of the last century, literary summaries, anthologies and collections adopted in schools revealed the predominance of exemplary poems that sought the development of good feelings (patriotic, familial, fraternal, generous, etc.). Along the same lines, Lajolo and Zilberman (2006) reaffirm the important educational place of poetry for our children when they state that a child's poem is a *privileged vehicle for advice, teaching and rules*. In *Poesia Infantil* (Children's Poetry), which presents the pioneering model study that was necessary to make known Brazilian children's poetry, Glória Bordini (1986) affirms that, in the discussion about the predominance of the adult voice in children's poems, the warning tone represents a betrayal of the child's imagination.

It is clear in many studies that the origins of poetry for children in this country are related to school proprietorship over the genre, which results in the creation of poetic patterns that guarantee circulation in that environment. In addition, the first publications of Brazilian poets emerged at the beginning of the twentieth century under immature graphic design and editorial conditions. For this reason, there was significant dependence upon school content and its concern with student development at that time.

Poets who led the way

Gradually, literature published for children has been diverging from these uplifting precepts with the emergence of poets who primarily explore the fun side of language in their verses. This was done by Cecília Meireles, Mário Quintana, Henriqueta Lisboa, Vinícius de Morais and José Paulo Paes, poets who assumed the role of writing for children and youth, a role that is still undervalued among writers of literature. Other poets, such as Carlos Drummond de Andrade and Manuel Bandeira, while not recognized as having written for these readers, also wrote poems for children and youth or had poems designated as appropriate for these audiences. Some poets thus slowly refined their view with respect to childhood and the initial stage of youth, shifting away from poetry with strictly pedagogical intentions which, for a long time, characterized their work.

While contemporary writing – as well as the reading of poetry in schools – still presents teaching elements, understood as the use of literature to teach school content, there is a great variety of poetic genres in circulation today. Many of these genres resist misappropriation because they lead to unusual aesthetic experiences with the language. An analysis of poetry writing for children and youth discloses that much that is on offer today radically departs from the strictly educational function on which poetry was built in the past, and which was perpetuated through school practices, mainly on commemorative dates when literature teachers always had in their files a poem about the country, about Indians, about mothers, about Christmas, and so on. This group of contemporary works includes haiku poems, quatrains, nursery rhymes, limericks, "cordel" poems, tongue twisters, riddles, narrative poems, as well as other poetic subgenres.

Some trends in Brazilian contemporary poetry for children

In Brazil, poetry books for children primarily bring together poems with themes of interest to children, such as animals, toys and games, typical childhood situations, time at
school or with family, and fairy tales in verse, among others. Narrative poems stand out
by presenting stories with characters and actions that develop in a temporal sequence,
told in verse. For considerable playful appeal, many of these narrative poems create
poetic games with words, promoting new experiences from interactions between sound
and sense; some of these use the "cordel" style, typical in northeastern Brazilian literature. An example of this is the story *O patinho feio* (The ugly duckling) by Hans Christian
Andersen, which is retold by César Obeid in sextuplets of seven syllables each and which
begins like this: "The 'Ugly duckling' in verses / With care the story I will tell. / A very
different style / The story will have, / Because when there is rhyme / It will be all for fun"
(2010: 8).

Other important sources of poetry writing for children are elements of popular culture and the story-telling tradition of children's games. This group includes poems such
as tongue twisters, riddles, nursery rhymes, and shared cultural songs that create up-to-
date versions of poetic texts about our folklore, passed from one generation to the next.
These poems establish links between oral culture and written culture, offering connections between the games of oral culture and the poetic objectives of poetry books. These
similarities are what we find in, for example, *Salada, Saladinha* (Salad, Small salad), a
book of nursery rhymes, arranged by Maria José de Nóbrega and Rosane Pamplona
(2005). The child recognizes the rhymes and repetitions, which combine with gestures and
body movements, that follow the playful objective of nursery rhymes and their various
functions (nursery rhymes to make fun of, to tease, to ask for, to skip rope, to play with
little ones, to play, to bring an end to). In this stream, some poems seem like tongue twisters or actual word games that challenge children more through sound appeal than seman-
tics, as is illustrated by the following fragment of a poem by the writer Ciça (because the
poem plays with the proper name "Lara" and the name of a bird "arara" (macaw), creating a kind of tongue twister, it is here left untranslated): "Arara da Iara / Iara amarra / a
arara rara / a rara arara (…)"(1986: n.p.)

Various poem anthologies use all kinds of animals from Brazilian fauna as their thematic angle. Some explore verbal-visual elements, as in the work coauthored by poet
Ronald Polito and graphic artist Guto Lacaz, in which they present two poems for the
same animal – a visual poem on the left page and a poem on the right page. For example,
using the Brazilian sloth, they offer: on the left page, "p r e g u…" ("s l o…") (2013: 10) as
a visual poem that retrieves the primary characteristics of the animal – it is so lazy that
its entire name is not shown. On the right page, there is another poem about the animal: "Dizem que ela é muito lenta / e que chega sempre atrasada, / ou que nem se movi-
menta, / não pondo o pé fora de casa, / mas a verdade é que a preguiça / não se altera e
nunca enguiça. (…)" ("They say that it is very slow / and always arrives late, / or doesn't
even move, / not stepping out of the house, / but the truth is that the sloth / doesn't change
nor break down. (…)") (2013: 11) In visual poetry, which explores relationships between
names and the animals they represent, another example that can be cited is the book by
Guilherme Mansur (2007) *Bichos tipográficos* (Typographical animals), which includes
word-poems with a hybrid of letters and drawings.

In some children's poetry books, the relationship between verbal and visual languages intensifies. This happens, for example, in the poems about *Bichos da noite* (Night

animals), points of light on the nocturnal pages by Carla Caruso (1998). In this case, it is not possible to reproduce them separately since the verbal text is attached, not only to the drawings, but also to the distribution of the linguistic elements on the pages, which are integrated by the colors that produce the fascinating and mysterious nighttime atmosphere. The interrelationship between the visual image and the poetry in the configuration of the poetry book by Gláucia de Souza (2011), was inspired by *papercuts*, by Hans Christian Andersen. For each of the images created by the Danish writer, the poet created verbal images in *Do alto do meu chapéu* (From the top of my hat).

Another strong marker of contemporary children's poetry is the search for the child's point of view, which is always curious and in a permanent state of discovery, with inquiries that often create a humorous effect. For example, in the anthology *Histórias com poesia, alguns bichos e cia.* (Stories with poetry, some animals and co.) compiled by Duda Machado, the poems' dialogue with black and white drawings by Guto Lacaz, using humorous language in the word games articulated by the lightness of the rhymes, as in the short poem "Curiosidade pura": "Na arca de Noé / Tinha bicho-do-pé?" ("Pure curiosity": "In Noah's ark / Was there a chigoe flea?") (2009: 31) This trend has found many avid readers, reestablishing an equal relationship with the young audience.

Some trends in Brazilian contemporary poetry for youth

Writing that is genuinely directed at the youth has, in recent decades, gained market presence in Brazilian publishing. It has come to address the specific interests of youth who are in the adolescent phase. Poets have sought to explore diction and themes that are appropriate to this life stage, as can be seen in the opening poem of the book *Adolescente poesia* (Adolescent poetry), by Sylvia Orthof: "Adolescência é janela / que se abre em ventania. / Há cantigas nas palavras / ousadas?" ("Adolescence is the window / which opens in the gale. / Are there tunes in the daring / words?" (2010: 7) In this work, Sylvia Orthof presents sixteen poems she has written and illustrated. They are short verses, of one or two stanzas each, which do not always rhyme and which interact with the illustrations and the colors on the pages. Alongside the better known authors for youth, in terms of editorial writings, there has been an investment in anthologies of lesser known contemporary poets, such as Miguel Sanches Neto, who wrote *Alugo palavras* (I rent words). These authors bring poems with a highly imaginative style that appeals to young people: "Do pai herdei / estas roupas (...) / Por elas / tive de ajustar / minhas medidas." ("I inherited from my dad / these clothes (...) / For them / I had to change / my measurements." (2010: 81)

Another venue for publication for youth has been the selection of poems written by different poets who have not necessarily written with this particular public in mind. These works may be the literary work of a single poet or of a group of poets. The collection *A lua no cinema e outros poemas* (The moon in the theatre and other poems) (2011), arranged by Eucanaã Ferraz, is a good example of a writing project that provides young people with a significant poetry reading experience and is also appreciated by adult readers. It offers seventy titles written by twenty-one Brazilian and Portuguese poets of the twentieth and twenty-first centuries, arranged in four parts. The target audience even appears in the peritext of the book – "This book is particularly directed to the young reader of poetry" – and the explanation of how the texts were selected – "But its arranger [...] did not seek out poems especially written for youth. The selection and arrangement were done in such a way that the poems, as a group, make the book one in which a young person will be able to recognise that poetry has a lot to say to him or her"". It can be noted that, beneath this explanation lies the concept that literature for youth – and here we are particularly interested in poetry, more than a literary work written for a certain public – is comprised of texts that can be appropriate for young readers.

The opening section of the anthology is titled "O verbo ser e outros verbos" (The verb to be and other verbs). It begins with the poem "Boas-vindas" (Welcome), by Caetano Veloso, and goes on to present poems full of musicality, in which the lyrical "I" declares a love for life. Next, "A um recém-nascido" (To a newborn), by José Paulo Paes, dialogues with the previous poem as it also has birth as its motto. For the young person and his/her life experiences, childhood, adolescence and old age can also be interesting themes, as well as the topic of love and its doubts. In Cacaso's "*Happy end*" (original title in English), love is explored as a trivial and humorous feeling: "o meu amor e eu / nascemos um para o outro / agora só falta quem nos apresente" ("my love and I / we were born for each other / now we just need someone to introduce us") (52). Then in the sonnet "Diamante" (Diamond), by Antonio Cícero, the feeling of love is compared to a diamond in the polishing process "já que dura e fura e tortura / e fica tanto mais brilhante / quanto mais se atrita, e fulgura" ("since it endures and punctures and tortures / and sparkles even more / the more it is polished, and shimmers") (53).

Questions about life and about the human condition seem to be the selection criteria for some poems in the search for links between poetry and a youthful spirit, such as in the poem "Lembrete" (Reminder), by Carlos Drummond de Andrade, which invites the reader: "Se procurar bem, você acaba encontrando / não a explicação (duvidosa) da vida, / mas a poesia (inexplicável) da vida" ("If you look well, you will end up finding / not the (questionable) meaning of life, / but the (inexplicable) poetry of life") (129). Some poems of the anthology reach the adolescent public with clearly defined precision, even when taken as a theme. This can be seen in "O adolescente" (The adolescent), by Mário Quintana: "A vida é tão bela que chega a dar medo. / Não o medo que paralisa e gela, / estátua súbita, / mas / esse medo fascinante e fremente de curiosidades que faz / o jovem felino seguir para a frente farejando o vento / ao sair a primeira vez, da gruta. (…)" ("Life is so beautiful that it can create fear. Not fear that paralyses and freezes, / a sudden statue, / but / this fascinating fear that rouses curiosity that makes / the young feline move forward, sniffing the wind / upon leaving, for the first time, the cave.)" (25).

In the index, at the end of the book, *A lua no cinema e outros poemas* (The moon in the theatre and other poems), the reader can find all of the poems listed in alphabetical order, as well as the poets and the name of their respective poems. There are also brief biographies of the poets and bibliographical references for their respective poems. Thus, the work exhibits many markings that play a mediating role in the initiation process for youth who are learning to read poetry. These mediation strategies can be identified in many other poetic anthologies that are published today for this reader.

Some poetry books for youth have invested in the graphic-editorial project and in the illustrations as factors that, in dialogue with the poems, constitute the publication. This investment can be noted in *Classificados e nem tanto* (Classifieds and not so much), a book of poems by Marina Colasanti, with xylographs by artist Rubem Grilo. As the title demonstrates, it includes short poetic advertisements (classifieds) that seek to exchange, promote or sell outlandish "articles": "Vendo em leilão / o pouco que resta / do meu coração" ("For sale by auction / the little that is left / of my heart") (2010: n.p.). The graphic design and illustrations allow readers to broaden and recombine the meanings of the verses of the poetic classifieds. The reading of imagery – which presupposes visual and verbal images – aligned with the playful component of the editorial introduction, also makes poetic experiences possible and integrated for young readers, as the example cited above illustrates.

Another significant group of poetry books for youth explores "cordel" literature (see further the essay, in this *Companion*, by José Hélder Pinheiro Alves). There is a strong presence of "cordel" in Brazilian publications directed toward youth. If for the northeastern residents these poems still hold a strong bond with oral practices, they reach readers of other regions in the country through written culture, in books that look like leaflets, with xylograph drawings and the use of fonts that are close to a typographical style. For example, *O lenhador* (The lumberjack, 2011), by Catullo da Paixão Cearense (1863–1946), presents two versions of the poem "O lenhador" (The lumberjack). Besides this poem, there is a collection of passages of other poems by this author, as well as his biographical and bibliographical information, which contextualize the author and his poems for readers who are beginning to read his works. Metaphors, neologisms and oral indices gain primacy in the experience offered by reading "O lenhador" ("The lumberjack").

The poetry genre and public policy regarding the formation of readers in Brazil

It is no longer enough to specify a genre "children's poetry" or a genre "youth poetry" when analyzing the writings that target these publics. The poetry genre does exist, with its various subgenres which target different audiences, as seen by the complex characteristics of the works, including themes, language, graphic design, images, among others. Poetry that is published in Brazil today for children and youth is diversified, however, with respect to the subgenres that are covered, as well as its "older sister" – poetry without an explicit target audience, that is, poetry for adults. The marks of target audiences that can be captured in books for children and youth, in the elements that comprise their editorial plan, in paratexts (considered here as texts that play the role of mediator, such as presentations, biographies, notes, among others), and also in themed texts, point to a growing involvement by publishers in the process of forming readers, motivated by sales expectations and, above all, by government literature book purchase programs for public schools that have been implemented in recent years in Brazil. Such investments have encouraged the production of literature books of various genres. Poetry books are among these, although in a smaller number when compared with other books, whether by Brazilian or foreign publishers, all of whom are attracted by sales potential. It should be stated that publishers register their books, which are directed to a particular public school audience and oriented by a criterion of literary genres, within which the poetry genre is found. Thus, there has been relative growth in the production of poetry books in recent years, which corresponds to the consolidation of these policies. The trends presented here – limited by what is possible within an article – include some of the trends in Brazilian poetry for children and youth as noted today and which exist in a favorable editorial context for the publication of literature for children and youth.

Notes

1 This essay is the result of work undertaken by GPELL – Grupo de Pesquisas do Letramento Literário (Literary Literacy Research Group) – and CEALE – Centro de Alfabetização Leitura e Escrita (Centre for Learning to Read and Write) – in the Faculdade de Educação da UFMG

(Faculty of Education at UFMG), whose work, since being established at the end of the 1990s, has been primarily focused on the development of readers. One of the research avenues of GPELL is dedicated to the comprehension of the genres of literature for children and youth, among which is poetry.

2 Some authors prefer the designation "poetry for adolescents", a psychological category that carries strong implications of transience. The use of this expression for youth, while recognising its wide reach, seems to us more appropriate and in harmony with social applications when used to refer to the formation of readers and its school and editorial implications.

3 The Programa Nacional Biblioteca da Escola (National School Library Program) – PNBE, of the Ministry of Education, buys literary works for distribution among Brazilian public schools and this initiative has resulted in an increase in the production of literary genres for children and youth.

Bibliography

Bordini, Maria da Glória (1986) *Poesia Infantil*. São Paulo: Ática.

Caruso, Carla (1998) *Bichos da noite*. Belo Horizonte: Dimensão.

Cearense, Catulo da Paixão (2011) *O lenhador*. Ilustrações Manu Maltez. São Paulo: Peirópolis.

Ciça (1986) *O livro do trava-língua*. Ilustrações Zélio. Rio de Janeiro: Nova Fronteira.

Coelho, Nelly Novaes (2000). *Literatura Infantil: Teoria, análise, didática*. São Paulo: Moderna.

Colasanti, Marina (2010) *Classificados e nem tanto*. Ilustrações de Rubem Grilo. Rio de Janeiro: Galerinha Record.

Cunha, Maria Antonieta A. (1991) *Literatura infantil: Teoria e prática*. São Paulo: Ática.

Ferraz, Eucanaã (ed.) (2011) *A lua no cinema e outros poemas*. São Paulo: Companhia das Letras.

Lajolo, Marisa (1997) *Do mundo da leitura para a leitura do mundo*. São Paulo: Ática.

Lajolo, Marisa, and Regina Zilberman (2006) *Literatura Infantil Brasileira: História & Histórias*. São Paulo: Ática.

Machado, Duda (2009) *Histórias com poesia, alguns bichos e Cia*. São Paulo: Editora 34.

Mansur, Guilherme (2007) *Bichos tipográficos*. Sabará: Edições Dubolsinho.

Nóbrega, Maria José, and Pamplona, Rosane (2005) *Salada saladinha: Parlendas*. São Paulo: Moderna.

Obeid, César (2010) *O patinho feio em cordel*. Xilogravuras de Eduardo Ver. São Paulo: Mundo Mirim.

Orthof, Sylvia (2010) *Adolescente poesia*. Rio de Janeiro: Rovelle.

Polito, Ronald, and Guto Lacaz (2013) *A galinha e outros bichos inteligentes*. São Paulo: Editora Dedo de Prosa.

Sanches Neto, M. (2010) *Alugo palavras*. Erechim, RS: Edelbra.

Soares, Magda A. (1999) "Escolarização da literatura infantil e juvenil," in Aracy Alves Martins Evangelista, Heliana Maria Brina Brandão, and Maria Zélia Versiani Machado (eds.), *A escolarização da leitura literária – O Jogo do Livro Infantil e Juvenil*. Belo Horizonte: Autêntica.

Souza, Gláucia de (2011) *Do alto do meu chapéu*. Ilustrações de Hans Christian Andersen. Porto Alegre: Editora Projeto.

Zilberman, Regina, and Lígia C. Magalhães (1987) *Literatura infantil: autoritarismo e emancipação*. São Paulo: Editora Ática.

Zilberman, Regina (1987) *A literatura infantil na escola*. São Paulo: Global.

21

EVERY WHICH WAY

Direction and narrative time in
Kaslan Geddan and the *Flash* series

Iman Hamam

Comics writers and artists seeking to address young adult (YA) audiences in the Middle East and North Africa (MENA) region have sought to overcome the dominance of and stereotypes within western media and culture, while at the same time distancing themselves from the medium's common association with young children. One strand of comics concentrating on questions of language, identity and history in their narratives have been performing a kind of cultural diplomacy, battling with mainstream commercial productions in an attempt to bridge and foster understanding and provide culturally relevant protagonists. The characters in Naif al-Mutawaa's *The 99* (Kuwait) and Marwan El Nashar's *Jinn Warriors* (Egypt) play out their differences against a backdrop of global political conflict, each providing less stereotypical heroes and heroines in order to overcome negative portrayals of Arabs in mainstream media (see also Deeb 2012) but at the same time retaining the markedly DC and Marvel style in the drawing of their characters. Mai El Shoush's *Drawn* (Sudan) seeks to construct a character who is not "objectified" like typical female superheroes or even the scantily clad *Jalila* and *Aya* of Ayman Kandeel's *AK Comics* (Kuwait). Joumana Medlej's *Maalak* (Lebanon and published in Arabic, English and French) attempts to counter the more dominant commercial productions of comic book titans produced by Marvel and DC with a "local production" lest YA readers find that they do not have heroes that they can identify with and who "otherwise may feel that their country has nothing valuable to offer" (Gravett 2012). Anxieties about identity are an important component of comic culture in general, with superhero comics in particular offering children "metaphors for their own isolation and longing for power, identity, and acceptance" (Wolk 2007: 72). Such texts are especially appealing among subaltern cultures, where questions of language and the dominance of American and European productions and political turmoil contribute to the feeling of alienation. Consistently, these characters discover or display the richness of their own culture by drawing on Islamic heritage or reconfiguring ancient mythology – with *jinn* characters frequently appearing to offer a non-human being with extraordinary powers as an alternative to the western superhero. In contrast, the two texts discussed in this chapter demonstrate that children's comics can combine fantasy, romance, humor and adventure without defaulting to the popular superhero genre.

Contributing to a landscape of burgeoning art forms – boosted by the bravado of the January 25 youth to speak out, confront taboo subjects and mark their territory – a separate group of artists and writers have sought to distance themselves from the medium's association with children and the cultural mainstream. In 2008, Egypt's first graphic novel for adults *Metro* (by Magdy El Shafae) was banned for "disturbing public morals" and was only rereleased in Arabic in 2013. Meanwhile, a number of collectives have produced several issues of comic magazines – most notably *Tok tok* in Egypt, and *Samandal* (subtitled: "Picture stories from here and there") in Lebanon, *Skefkef* in Morocco and *Lab 619* in Tunisia. In Egypt in 2011 Marwan Imam and Mohamed Reda founded Division Publishing, which in 2012 published a collection entitled *Autostrad* and in 2014 released the first issue of Sherif Adel's *Pass By Tomorrow: Egyptian Satirical Comics from the Future.* Brought up on a staple of television programs and cartoons, including Japanese animation *Mazinger and Grendizer* dubbed into Arabic, *Tintin*, and *Asterix*, and drawing on a rich tradition of caricature and editorial cartoons referencing war and political upheaval (most notably in the work of Palestinian Naji Al-Ali), these artists and writers have celebrated their adulthood and freedom by addressing taboo subjects such as sex, violence, drugs and politics. The titles and covers of these works are indicative of the shift from children to adults: *Tok tok* comes with a warning: "Keep out of reach of children"; comics produced during a 24 jam that took place in Cairo in 2012 was published with the title: *I am Free*; while another workshop resulted in a publication edited by children's author Rania Amin was named *Out of Control*. Most significantly, these publications have opened up a space for artists and writers and develop their own unique individual styles and engage with one another across the region.

While new productions are still experimenting with the medium for YA and adult audiences, an earlier generation of periodicals from Egypt and the United Arab Emirates have sustained their position as a mainstay of children's culture despite market pressures which have seen many others discontinued: *Allaaeddin*, published monthly by the Egyptian state owned Al-Ahram organization; *Samir*, published weekly by the Egyptian state owned Dar El Hilal (and which also publishes translations of Mickey and Donald Duck comics) since 1956 and *Majid* published weekly by the Emirates Media Corporation since 1979. Of the latter, Asmaa al-Hameli (2014) explains that, "The magazine's title, and the name of its main character, was taken from the famous Arab navigator, Ahmed ibn Majid. Its pages followed the Arab navigator on his travels, exploring the world to provide Emirati and Arab children with news, information and tales that would improve their knowledge in a pleasant and memorable way." *Kaslan Geddan* (literally: Very Lazy), illustrated by Egyptian artist Mostafa Rahma and written by Ahmad Omar, is considered the most popular and longest running comic strip published in *Majid*. On the basis of Kaslan's popularity, six stand-alone publications featuring the hero, targeting an audience of 8–15 year olds, were also produced.

One of these publications, *Kaslan Geddan in Night After Night After Night* (UAE) draws on familiar components of children's stories and the fantasy genre. A self-reflexive portrayal of characters and storytelling devices underlines the narrative, and the book foregrounds the character's affiliation with the *Majid* periodical through its comic adaptation of the *1001 Nights* and in the disruption of narrative progress. Through its use of displacement as a narrative device, the comic allows for further consideration of direction, movement and sequence. In contrast, prolific comics book writer and illustrator Khaled Elsafty's *Flash* series – *Pocket Smash, Pocket Flash, Superflash* and *Flash Adventures* (Egypt) – demonstrates little progression of the characters from one issue to the next. Within one strip, the characters might be temporarily displaced, but they end up in much the same place they started, if not ever so slightly better or worse off.

Questions of space are of primary significance in comics, not just in terms of the setting or movement of characters from one place to another, but also in terms of the layout of the page and the movement from one panel to the next. For a medium in which the narrative ordering of the panels and the shape of frames presents endless possibilities, what keeps the narrative flowing in the right direction? Where are the comics set and where do the characters live? What characterizes their surroundings? What other worlds are imagined and what do these worlds and the people that inhabit them offer? Do the characters undergo any change in identity or do they remain as they are? What other comic books and icons of children's culture are referenced? What character duplications and inversions are there? How are superhuman or supernatural characters brought into the narrative? What forms of transportation and mechanical devices are used to facilitate narrative development? Do the heroes act and move freely and independently or is their movement controlled by adults or others? Are the borders of frames respected or do the images, words or figures "bleed" into the gutters? Both popular texts, *Kaslan* and the *Flash* series, draw attention to a crucial component of the comic book medium: the process of movement from one place to the next, whether in a travel or adventure narrative, or in the design and layout of the page.

Throughout the text, *Night after Night* presents a number of self-reflexive devices, including its use of the familiar frame story technique of *1001 Nights*. This self-awareness is carried to such an extent that a significant portion of the two page episodes (titled "Nights" instead of Chapters) are dedicated to sustaining this narrative framing. Before the chapters begin, readers are addressed directly by Kaslan himself who tells us that he ("Yes, I, Kaslan!") has written a story, and that he hopes that his dedicated *Majid* readers will like it. The first episode begins *in medias res*, with Shahrazad telling the young prince a story about a boy called Kaslan (he interjects – "His name is just like mine!" "Yes," she replies, "And he looks like you too"). Kaslan is sailing his boat when suddenly it capsizes and he falls into the sea and "kookoo kookoo" ("cock-a-doodle-doo") the cockerel crows at dawn and marks – through the use of what might be the ultimate archetype of narrative interruptions – the end of the story. As Will Eisner observes, turning a page "permits a change of time, shift of scene, and opportunity to control the reader's focus" (63). In accordance with this principle, the next chapter/night features a dramatic shift in time and place as readers are transported into an office space where Kaslan, dressed in a modern *thub* sits at a desk holding a bunch of papers. His brother, who looks exactly like him except he is bald and named Nasheet Giddan (Very Energetic) cries out: "What happened next?" In this manner, the objection is expressed twice: firstly by Kaslan who is being told the story by Shahrazad, and secondly by Nasheet who is being told the story by Kaslan. We are one and a half pages into the first chapter and there are already three Kaslans (storyteller, hero, and listener) and three frame stories. Kaslan the storyteller asks Nasheet not to interrupt him because he is in the middle of writing a great story and doesn't want to lose his train of thought. If comics are distinguished by their capacity to juxtapose different time frames with immediacy, then *Night After Night* multiplies the effect by making such juxtaposition an integral part of its narrative structure.

Just as the Nights do not begin in one place or frame with any consistency, nor do the characters respect the spatial parameters of the frame stories they inhabit.

For the first half of the narrative, Kaslan is determined to get away from this place under the sea and escape the accusation that he is Hammour (literally, Grouper

Fish), the long lost son of the Fish King and Queen of the undersea world ("but how come I don't have a tail but legs," he asks?). Despite his protestations, he is married to the Princess Mahara (literally: Oyster) and is made an important minister (Kaslan at first objects, "that sounds like a job for Nasheet, not me!"). He is tasked with reforming Education, Finance, and Production. He installs computers in schools, enforces three square meals a day and prohibits corporal punishment. After the wreckage of his boat is discovered, he sends his employees to recover some jewels which he gives to his wife. They find a strange object and tell him about it but it is only months later that he realizes it is a life boat and orders engineers to focus on repairing it. Once they do, he takes off and returns to land, only to feel guilty about the people, responsibilities and world under the sea he has left behind. At the same time that Kaslan the hero has his crisis, Kaslan the storywriter stops to ask his friends whether he should continue with the story. In an inter-textual moment, characters from *Majid* and other well-known comic heroes including Dana from Samira Shafik and Ihab Shaker's series *Shamsa and Dana* tell him he should continue. Kaslan returns to a worried mer-family and wife.

In the second half of the story, Kaslan, now "recovered" (that is, apparently relieved of the torment of two identities), resolves to take his beloved wife to visit the world of dry land, eat ice cream and pizza (which qualify as the best thing about the world of land people) and go to the movies. They check into a five star hotel and Mahara is adorned with the wonders of fashion as she tries on jeans and various dresses. She resolves to go out in her favorite dress of all, until Kaslan explains that it is not appropriate to go out in a wedding dress. They go to the cinema where Mahara is frightened by the image of a shark on the screen. She gets a bad stomach ache and is taken to hospital. A nurse discovers her tail and takes her to the fish market to sell. Having lost Mahara, Kaslan is beside himself with worry. He implores the doctor – "My wife has gone missing! My wife who has a tail!" He is laughed away and left to wander the streets in search of her, mocked and derided as a madman at every turn until he is left standing at the shore, wondering how he will tell Mahara's parents of their loss. Though distraught, he faces up to the responsibility and returns to the sea world, only to find that Mahara herself, after being bought by a kind man at the market and returned to sea, was able to find her way home. They are joyously reunited. But it's not over yet. War is looming. Kaslan goes into battle and is wounded. As he recovers in hospital (there are several incidents involving hospitals in this world and the one above), they are informed that among the captured prisoners is one who has a helmet concealing his identity. The mysterious captive is brought before them. As the helmet is removed, the real Hammour, Kaslan lookalike and true lost son of the Fish King and Queen, is revealed. The only difference between the two boys is that one has red hair and the other has black hair – and one has a tail, and the other doesn't.

The frame stories borrow from each other; as Nasheet asks Kaslan the storyteller to proceed, Kaslan the listener asks Shahrazad and she continues. Each chapter ends in the same way, with the cockerel – or a cockerel substitute – crowing. As an onomatopoeia, this sound is presented as typically free from the constraints of a speech bubble. This feature ultimately becomes a delicate formulaic rupture, which simulates the readers' frustration at the same time that it incorporates it into the story. The story stops and a listener implores the story teller to continue. By including this aspect and reiterating it through the different tales, the story brings together a feature of the *1001 Nights* that the comic medium traditionally exploits: seriality. The characters know what is coming next as much as the reader does. And as quickly as Nasheet grasps the pattern, so too do Kaslan, Shahrazad, and even the cockerel itself. As the chapters progress, each character takes turns in announcing the call of the cockerel and that the story will continue on the next page. On one occasion, three cockerels appear; on another it disappears; when Kaslan endeavours to ask after the cockerel, Shahrazad announces that she has brought an alarm clock instead. As different fish peek into the frames in the undersea story, the cockerel peeks in from the side of the frame as Shahrazad narrates, and in one episode she walks in with another cockerel under her arm and apologizes for being late because she had to go to buy it. All pretexts are gone. Shahrazad asks if Kaslan would like her to continue but then claims she has a headache and cannot. Kaslan gets her a pill and while waiting for it to take effect, he tries to bribe the cockerel into delaying his announcement so he can hear the rest of the story. He later holds on to it as a hostage so that Shahrazad will continue. It doesn't work, of course. On another occasion she brings in a whole cage of cockerels. On yet another, she employs the use of a telephone, which rings to announce, through the receiver, the "kookoo kookoo" we must hear in the final frame of each episode. As Kaslan implores the princess to continue with the story, his interruption gives Shahrazad the opportunity to say she is hungry and thirsty and walk off, leaving Kaslan with no option other than to turn the page himself.

It is notable that the story – which comes in book form and is not part of the *Majid* series where two pages are published every week – sustains the serialism that characterizes the magazine productions of both *Samir* and *Majid* that emerged during the height of comic production. With its parody of the *1001 Nights*, the use of frame stories and the mocking of convention, the story employs familiar narrative devices but – and this might be what makes it good for children and adults alike – it does so knowingly. In effect, the cockerel's announcement emerges to form a narrative thread of its own, marking not only the direct address to the reader, but the movement from one panel to the next, and from one page to another. The stops and starts are captured in the simple turning of a page. What is a feature of the weekly comics – an interruption in time which leaves the reader unable to know what happens next until the following weekly installment or episode – is here used as a device to move the reader through the text spatially. The cockerel's crowing, along with the cock-a-doodle-doo that comes out of the mouths of its substitutes, functions to keeps the narrative flowing in the right direction.

Displacement is also manifest on the narrative level, whereby characters move from one space to another, exhibiting an other-worldly aspect common in children's and YA comics. Early in the story, objecting to the declaration that he is the long lost son suffering from amnesia, Kaslan draws attention to his lack of a tail. This is the one thing that doesn't seem right: How can he breathe? How can he can swim underwater without a tail and how, for that matter, does Mahara manage to wear a pair of jeans on dry land with one? The narrative uses the presence or absence of a tail to foreground these paradoxes, and because it is what potentially undoes the plausibility of the account, it is directly underscored in the narrative. This acclimatization, referred to in *Night after Night* by the elders as "getting used to things," is a prominent element of Elsafty's *Flash* comics: the characters seem to adjust, with relative ease, to their surroundings.

That *Pocket Flash* was part of a series of pocket books published by the Modern Arab Foundation (a publishing house set up in 1960 by Hamdy Mostafa) also underlines the value of portability, which points to the narrative value of "adaptable" comic heroes. Even the characters that are familiar come in exaggerated form – both features of comedy and caricature. This is also underlined by the multiple (and at times duplicitous) nature of the character as shown through the various incarnations of the same figure, the variety of the Flash family types, and in the parodying of well-known stories and narrative forms. Kaslan and the Flash characters continue in the carnivalesque/*1001 Nights* tradition of character inversion and disguise, something that is also an important feature of Hegazzy's *Tanabilat al-Sibyan wa Tanabilat al-Khirfan* (The Lazy Boys and the Lazy Lambs), where "things are seldom what they seem" (Douglas and Douglas 72). Also like Kaslan and the Tanabila, most of the Elsafty characters are children or infantilized adults; they are left to their own devices in an adult world, and often have the same agency as grownups. The adults are frequently pathetic, cowardly, downtrodden, stupid and selfish. Typically, they never age; emphasis is placed on their facial expressions and each episode is like a joke – amusing and forgettable. The issues of *Pocket Smash*, *Pocket Flash*, *Superflash* and *Flash Adventures* are numbered serially but carry no date of publication (they are identified by issue number) and with some strips occasionally serialized. The names of the characters adopt inversions, puns and cultural references that are typical of the comic medium. Hatem Eltaey 2000 watches over his safe; The Stupid Sailor messes up jobs and enterprises whether for himself or his captain (named Captain Drowner) with his dull-wittedness. The Downtrodden Citizen (*Almowatin Elmat-hun*, named Mansy, literally: Forgotten) suffers from such abject poverty that he has become all but a skeleton, with no ears, no nose and no eyes. He meets good fortune with bad luck and is often left starving in an entirely bare room. In November 2013, after making his apologies for another long period of silence, Elsafty writes: "the only character whose situation has not improved is the Downtrodden Citizen – whose hardship has increased, and whose poverty has increased!" (*Pocket Flash* #80)

The value of direction and adaptability are illustrated in a ten-page long episode in issue 2 of *Flash Adventures* entitled "The Fall into the Drainpipe." The strip begins with its main character, Hatem Altaey, walking along one morning on his way back from the bank carrying a suitcase full of cash. His name refers to the early Islamic era Hatem Altaey who was renowned for his generosity, and in a classic case of comic inversion, many of the Hatem Altaey 2000 strips center upon the character's safe deposit box, exposing his greed and selfishness with money in particular. Too stingy to take a taxi, he resolves to ride the bus instead. As he runs to catch it, he falls into an open drainpipe and, refusing to let go of the suitcase, Hatem is unable to save himself. People gather round the site and lament the accident. A journalist named Sameh Goukh (another character from the *Flash Adventures* series and whose name refers to a common phrase for "kiss ass") arrives with his blind photographer. One onlooker exclaims "typical!" We discover just how common the mishap is when Hatem wades through the sewers. As he clutches onto his suitcase, he finds a series of signposts; the first has an arrow pointing left and reads "Welcome," and the next is marked 30km and has an arrow pointing in the same direction. As the reader is guided from one panel to the next, so too is the character within the frame. Hatem meets a group of people who explain that they, just like him, have suffered the same fate. The sewers even feature their own transport system, which is reserved for the wealthy.

Hatem asks about the way out, but the man confesses that they were actually relieved to have fallen into the drainpipe and escaped the toils and troubles of the modern world. Meanwhile, above ground, Sameh Goukh proceeds to investigate the incident, and we see him with tape recorder in hand in the office of a character who is identified (by the name plate on his desk) as simply: Mas'ool (the official in charge, held accountable, or responsible). After dismissing the issue of open drainpipes as unimportant, the official claims that the problem actually lies with the citizens themselves who don't know how to walk properly. He goes on to add that those who do fall into the drainpipes are considered martyrs and go to heaven. On the basis of this fact, he suggests that the journalist "start a campaign for opening up all of the drains in the country. And then it's really down to the citizen whether he falls into it or not. He can fall in ... or he can choose to stay in this world with all of its problems." In the final panel, we see Hatem and his long lost uncle walking along an empty road, having bribed one of the people in the sewer to show them the way out. The final frame reads: "And so ends our imaginary adventure, although the series of children falling into open drains continues."

The *Flash* and *Smash* family characters commonly walk into and out of each other's lives and interact. If the panels are uniform, the characters are not sealed off from one another. In the same issue as that featuring Hatem in the sewers, another popular character named Nazeer asks his father for a pair of Cartier sunglasses as a reward for doing well in his exams and so that he can "give people a break from the power of his eyes." Nazeer is a boy who wreaks havoc and destruction just by looking. Rays are seen to come from his eyes. But these are not laser beams or x-ray vision and Nazeer is no Superman. The idea stems from the belief that the evil eye is able to cause harm when directed at objects of material wealth or physical wellbeing. As the *Nazar* series of notebooks produced by graphic designer and illustrator Mohieddin Ellabbad emphasizes, "seeing" and vision are important features of a medium where it is difficult to control exactly where the reader looks. Nazeer goes to the shop but when he tries on a pair of glasses they shatter. The shopkeeper despairs that they cost over £1,000 and threatens to phone the police unless the money is paid. Nazeer looks at the phone "zeee-yeeew" ("zap") and the line goes dead. Rarely employing his powers with deliberate malice, Nazeer offers to work in the shop to compensate. The next day he returns to see what the work is like before deciding whether to use his powers or not. The shop owner arrives with his son Samy. A caption explains: "Samy was a reader of *Flash* magazine and immediately recognized Nazeer." He whispers something into his father's ear and the shop owner promptly gives Nazeer some cash and sends him on his way. As in *Night after Night*, spatial boundaries are crossed: readers are addressed directly and characters interact with others in the series.

Superflash features a number of strips and splash pages where the characteristics of each of the heroes are highlighted in terms of their preferences or habits. Several features include a selection of *Flash* heroes together: Flash under the sea; Flash on the beach; Flash in a space ship; Flash around the world. This marks a common feature of popular children's magazines and heroes: repetition and familiarity, thus building on characters who do not evolve or develop so much as their habits are recurrent and reinforced. There is very little by way of detailed background or setting; often characters are seen in close up or medium close up. When they are walking in the street the background is often comprised of nondescript brick walls. Interiors are marked by simple windows, door-frames, table tops and the occasional telephone or sofa. But the same applies to the narrative progression. Between the beginning and the end there might be an incident or an event, but little changes for the characters. In strips featuring Allaam, the wall he stands against is so important that it is arguably a third character and is often referenced by Allaam or his conversation partner Mido.

This stasis in the character framing is also featured in the Polaroid style/postage stamp portrait thumbnails used to identify the main characters of the featured strips. But the *Flash* series demonstrates the extent to which comic book authors and illustrators can experiment with layout of images and text. Though setting or background are minimal within any particular panel, in early issues of *Pocket Flash* different sections are framed with a Flash character at the top of the page to identify the specific nature of the section (for example "brain teasers," "games and puzzles," "personality profile" or simply "flash"). The minimalism of the content within the panels is compensated for by the layout of the page itself. At the bottom of the page in *Flash Adventures*, Elsafty provides multiple choice questions about general knowledge or riddles – making it possible for the reader to bypass the comic strips entirely. Light and inconsequential, the *Flash* comics also inform children how to learn about, comment on and critique the world around them.

The *Flash* strips incorporate a variety of other identifiable magazine features – fun facts, riddles, puzzles (with an answer key at the back), coloring pages, prize draw competitions, letters and photos of readers, and so on. The characters comment on other people's stupidity only to expose their own ("can you believe they are still performing *Hamlet* in London, the play that Youssef Wahby did in the 1960s?"). According to Elsafty the purpose of the comic is to help readers estimate their intelligence, make them cultured and their minds active, foster common sense, encourage them to read and research ("it might ask you questions that prompt you to open your dictionary or atlas"), and help pass the time. Above all, *Flash* requires that readers are optimistic, and if they are not, they are offered a "course in optimism." Alongside the various strips, the comics feature profiles of historical figures, short stories, general knowledge and even provide detailed critical commentaries on newspaper clippings. In this, the comics are similar to *Samir* and *Majid*.

The "Fall into the Drainpipe" episode – despite its minimalist style – references specific features of Cairo: overcrowding, public transport, faulty maintenance or negligence of roads and infrastructure. Through its strips, commentaries, short stories and moral tales, the *Flash* series offers an astute insight into the plights of the city's inhabitants in terms of the corruption of city officials and social inequity. Falling into drainpipes is referenced several times in *Flash* strips: for example in issue 2 of *Superflash*, the main hero, Super Allaam ("know it all" who in his ordinary incarnation actually knows nothing but maintains an air of intellectual superiority nonetheless) is heavily reprimanded for trying to save two children from falling into an open drain, accused of trying to kidnap them, and is beaten by their mother with her handbag. Earlier, when patrolling the "City of Chaos" the superhero witnesses a case of bribery in the Ministry of Intermediation. He takes the culprits to the police station only to find seconds later that they have managed to bribe their way out and walk free. Defeated, Allaam laments, "stray and rabid dogs, exposed electricity wires, open drains…there's no point! I did my part but it seems that it is impossible to combat chaos in the City of Chaos."

Such concerns with direction, space and movement and narrative time and progress suggest the importance of "getting somewhere" whether it is leaving the house to look for a job, go to school, or embark on an adventure. These progressions are also rearticulated in the comic medium in terms of how we move from one panel to the next and remain prominent features of contemporary comic book productions. As such, space, place, and the relationship between panels, text, images and frames together offer readers a point to which they can return, even as they themselves change, grow older, and move on.

Bibliography

al-Hameli, Asmaa (2014) "35 years of *Majid* Magic: Reading Becomes Knowledge," *The National*. www.thenational.ae/uae/education/35-years-of-majid-magic-reading-becomes-knowledge (accessed 11 May 2014).

Deeb, Mary-Jane (2012) "*The 99*: Superhero Comic Books from the Arab World," *Comparative Studies of South Asia, Africa and the Middle East* 32(2): 391–401.

Douglas, Allen and Fedwa Malti-Douglas (1994) *Arab Comic Strips: Politics in an Emerging Mass Culture*, Bloomington: Indiana University Press.

Eisner, Will (2008) *Comics and Sequential Art: Principles and Practices from the Legendary Cartoonist*. Revised edition of *Comics and Sequential Art* (1985), New York: W.W. Norton & Company, Inc.

Elsafty, Khaled (n.d.) *Superflash*, Moassasa Alarabiya Al Hadeetha.

———(n.d.) *Flash Adventures*, Moassasa Alarabiya Al Hadeetha.

———(n.d.) *Pocket Flash*, Moassasa Alarabiya Al Hadeetha.

———(n.d.) *Pocket Smash*, Moassasa Alarabiya Al Hadeetha.

Gravett, Paul (2012) "Joumana Medlej: Lebanon's First Superheroine," www.paulgravett.com/articles/article/joumana_medlej (accessed 1 July 2012).

Omar, Ahmed and Mostafa Rahma (n.d.) *Kaslan Geddan in Night After Night After Night*, Abu Dhabi: Emirates Media Incorporation.

Wolk, Douglas (2007) *Reading Comics: How Graphic Novels Work and What They Mean*, Cambridge, Mass: Da Capo Press.

Zitawi, Jehan (2008) "Contextualizing Disney Comics within the Arab Culture," *Meta: Journal des Traducteurs/Meta: Translators' Journal* 53(1): 139–153.

22

OLD/NEW MEDIA FOR MUSLIM CHILDREN IN ENGLISH AND ARABIC

The forest, the trees and the mushrooms

Yasmine Motawy

Muslims are linguistically, ethnically and geographically diverse: fewer than 20 percent of Muslims are Arabs, and one fifth of the world's Muslims live in non-Muslim countries ("Mapping the Global Muslim" 1). Hence the problem of researching the visual depictions of Islamic stories for children lies in deciding which languages or countries to include. New media further problematizes the dilemma; the democratic hybrid nature of these screen— but not strictly "television"—productions are quite often user-generated, not subject to censorship or quality control, are produced relatively cheaply, easily and abundantly and are disseminated widely and quickly. Also, Islamic picturebooks, Young Adult (YA) book series, television and online cartoon productions, online games, apps and websites range in scale from the state-sponsored television series and commercially commissioned comic book series or animations by the Marvel Comics and Disney teams to the Muslim homeschooler blog and self-published paperback. This begs further questions: Which types of stories to study? What level of professionalism in execution or media attention garnered renders productions study-worthy? Are popular user-channels and website material worthy of current academic excavations? Add to this the lack of proper citations and databases of all Arabic language media and the sheer volume of both Arabic and English material, and the results of any critique are limited to the parameters a researcher sets.

This essay therefore attempts to categorize contemporary illustrated books and screen productions for Muslim children in both English and Arabic according to their stylistic approaches, the sources they rely on, the narrative decisions they make as a result of interpretations of religious precepts, and the visual paradigms they adhere to. The decision to include English works recognizes that this is the lingua franca used when Muslims wish to address the world, and choose to operate under the Western gaze. The choice of illustrated books and screen production offers the possibility of the relative permanence—and hence researchability—of the institutions that produce them.

All the digital and traditional media trees seem to tell three main types of stories regardless of the format and language in which they are presented. First, those works that attempt to mainstream Islam and Muslim children by inserting them into the mundane and neutralizing the suspicion associated with those actively practicing the religion, making it more palatable primarily to urban Muslim children themselves, whose identity is besieged by the same images that feed the minds of all other children. Second, those that educate the Muslim child about what Muslims do and think and how they behave. Third, those that retell the stories of Islam within the tradition and rhetorical context of Islamic storytelling.

The motivation for Muslims to "write back," "shape a young Muslim identity," and "counter-represent" in this facile environment is well-documented. In addition, many of the blurbs on the back covers of picturebooks and the descriptions of online apps, games and websites express some variation of the byline, "this is what you have been looking for," and thus indicate a sense of an unmet need. Torsten Janson's rare 2003 doctoral study *Your Cradle Is Green: The Islamic Foundation and the Call to Islam in Children's Literature* traced the *da'wa* (envangelize, mission, call to Islam) theme in the picturebook publications by British Muslim organization/publisher The Islamic Foundation. He also notes "the predicament of Muslim children facing a powerful culture, which is perceived as filled to the brim with greed, secularism and sexual promiscuity. On the other hand, the paratexts emphasise that Muslim parents have the possibility to mould a 'sound' Islamic identity, if they only cease [sic. i.e. seize] the pedagogic means provided by revivalist actors" (215). All three streams identified are not completely separate in terms of content, showing crossover between the categories, but all respond to and thrive on the Muslim parental/societal anxiety Jansen identifies.

Mainstreaming Muslims

This strand, which tries to provide Muslim children and YA with representations of themselves that are both pious and compatible with the values that determine worldly success, yields the least volume of works within the Muslim world, where there is a sharp divide between "regular" and "Islamic" programs, apps, books and films. More works in this area come from Muslims of the West who understand the value of mediating their own images both inside a niche discursive space designed for Muslim children themselves as well as gradually mainstreaming these images into the wider media pool.

These productions invariably react to the dominant visual cultures they are resisting and their defensiveness results in mimicry. Instead of producing characters and plots that are local and inclusive, they actively and urgently compete for Muslim children's contested attention with an uncanny awareness of the competition. The narratives are generally urban and show characters with the same sphere of interests and tone as the mainstream into which they hope to penetrate. Mezba Uddin Mahtab, whose book *Teaching Kids The Holy Quran – Surah 18: The Cave* is a series of Lego dioramas depicting scenes from Islamic verses, best articulates the principles with the widest consensus adoped amongst those working in this category and the next:

1. Keep it as simple as possible. The Holy Quran is meant as a book of lessons and morals, not a book of stories.
2. Keep it clean. … the Holy Quran, even when dealing with some mature subjects, has dealt with them cleanly and sensitively…
3. No portrayal of the Prophets of God. Or of Allah.
4. Keep it contemporary.

The stories produced in the West either focus on the Muslim-ness of the protagonist, such as bestselling YA novel about a young, second-generation immigrant wearing the veil,

Does my head look big in this? by Australian Randa Abdel-Fattah (2005), or YA romance *She Wore Red Trainers* by Na'ima B. Robert (2014), or tell a story where little ado is made about the fact that the heroic protagonist is a Muslim, such as Hassan Radwan's adventure story *Rashid and the Missing Body* (2007) and *Ibrahim Khan and the Mystery of the Roaring Lion* by Farheen Khan (2009), both published by the UK Islamic Foundation.

Understandably, far fewer works of this strand are found in Arabic, although EmariToons production company based in multinational Dubai promises "Action without violence; Excitement without adult themes; Imagination without black magic." Many of their productions seamlessly integrate Islamic precepts into the mainstream and draw attention to the increasing modernization of Muslims themselves. For instance, the humorous *Haamel Elmisk* (the musk seller/bearer) (2011) is set in an American-style summer camp where each 22-minute episode involves a counselor helping campers resolve an issue by conjuring relevant Quranic verses. This models a child-text relationship of ordinary Muslim children drawing from the Quran as a toolbox when necessary. The outward appearance of this mainstreaming group is the fostering of a constant awareness of "what Mohammed would do," and an understanding of the Islamic position on social situations. It proclaims: "I am a practicing Muslim; look how modern I am! Look how well I fit into the modern world!"

Even retelling the stories of Islam – primarily the heroic ones that come from either the "sira" (the life of the prophet Muhammad PBUH) or the twenty-five prophets mentioned in the Quran as well as known hagiographies – are often wrought to uphold this ideological reaction to the West. While these modern productions draw from the repertoire of traditional Islamic stories, they work completely outside the traditional storytelling frame in which these stories were traditionally presented. Instead of addressing a multi-age audience of "believers" with a multilayered narration that is spiritually edifying, these are produced and consumed by subscribers to nineteenth-century modern Islamic reform with its emphasis on the rational and its keenness on following scientific methods to purge Islam of its superstitions and model it on a sober Protestant brand of Christianity. This meant that orally transmitted tales that could not boast a written pedigree of sound transmission were dismissed, as was "foreign" material such as the *isrā'īliyyāt* (in its strictest sense, the collection of narratives and reports coming predominantly from Jewish and Christian traditions (Albayrak 114)). While Imam Al-Shafi'i, the founder of one of the four major Muslim schools of thought, quotes the Prophet PBUH as saying, "Narrate [traditions] from the Children of Israel for there is nothing objectionable in that," the imperative to modernize rejected these stories (Vajda). This decolonization movement, intent on asserting the independence of Islamic accounts from other traditions, dismissed the extra-Quranic literature that was greatly beholden to early Jewish traditions and the body of stories of the early Jewish prophets and thus lost a great deal of their narrative texture once they were "purified."

The "purified" stories have been those most in circulation until today, and the resulting absence of many details that are essential to smooth plot development made them less attractive selections for commercial television productions, and it largely fell to Arab national television to produce animated *sira* and prophetic stories. After a long period of rudimentary claymations and generally low-quality productions, in 2011 a joint Lebanese-Egyptian production house produced an all-star popular retelling, the animated series *Animal Stories in the Quran*, based on the eponymous 1983 classic by Ahmed Bahgat. The new series is framed by an old shepherd narrator whose voice-over is performed by popular Egyptian actor Yahia Elfakharany, and a celebrity guest star appears in each episode. This production received multiple awards and propelled the producers as well as others to follow up with other seasons of Quranic stories with the same winning formula: celebrity casts, a Disney feel and improved writing. The adoption of Disney aesthetics and form is not just where these works step away from traditional storytelling, but they are also modern in their content, presenting only the values that can be understood by the modern urban Muslim and aware of the gaze of the Other to whom they insist: "we are like you, we too have prophets and stories, and in fact, most of them are from the Judeo-Christian tradition." In the series, the shepherd figure is well chosen as a narrator of stories of prophets, as Mohammed (PBUH) said that all prophets were shepherds. The book chapters follow a certain structure, where an animal laments the reputation they have as stupid, evil, harmful or dishonest, when it is in fact mankind that deserves this reputation and proceeds to prove it with a related story from the Quran. The closing of the text is comparable with that identified by Stephens and McCallum in their discussion of retold biblical tales that juxtapose a biblical story with a more contemporary one that mirrors the "salient" features of the story as far as children are concerned (1998 28). For example, the story of a girl who while avoiding the chores her mother assigned is caught in a storm is paired with the story of Jonas, who tries to escape his divine calling and is swallowed by a whale. The determination of meaning begins with the writer's choice of what is relevant to the child reader and continues as the metonymic accessible parallel tale is brought to the same significance as Jonas's.

A tension in the adaptation, that is perhaps already a danger in the conception of the text, it is that while the stories of these animals in the Quran are – like all the stories in the Quran – fit for child consumption, they are not children's stories, and even though the flowing sophisticated language is retained, many of the stories' complexities are by necessity removed. The twentieth-century metaphor of the *palimpsest* is pertinent here. Taken beyond the material figure of traces of the past that are hidden or only glimpsed, the palimpsest alludes to multiple layers or levels of meaning accrued within a text, and hence the possibility of looking beyond surface meaning to perceive a deeper meaning. The layers of meaning of the Quran are best expressed in the recorded saying of the prophet Muhammed (PBUH): "The Quran possesses an external appearance and a hidden depth, an exoteric meaning and an esoteric meaning. This esoteric meaning in turn conceals an esoteric meaning (this depth possesses a depth, after the image of the celestial Spheres which are enclosed within each other). So it goes on for seven esoteric meanings (seven depths of hidden depth)" (Cited in Corbin 1993: 7). The challenge for Quranic adapters is to develop modes of narration that reach into the depths rather than adhering to only the least contentious of the Quran's palimpsests.

Like the anthropomorphic animals in Disney animations, the animals in the stories are all completely humanized. The crows have forelocks and wear a judge's wig. Their dilemmas are essentially human ones: how to administer justice, how their group deals with social problems better than another group, how to study to pass the bar exam. To understand these animals requires an awareness of psychology rather than zoology. The animals all come with background stories with some psychological depth: The whale that swallows Jonas was the son of a cold and severe father and a familiar army-brat-strict-unaffectionate parent psychology is reproduced; Solomon's hoopoe is a workaholic and the ant that stops Solomon's army from trampling her anthill is seeing a therapist to work on her rage against man and her existential crisis. In fact, all of the animals have psychological baggage that makes it of very little consequence that they are animals. Disney also dominates the visualization of the characters: in the Solomon episode, the djinns are blue and look just like the genie from *Aladdin* and the palace of Solomon is not unlike that of the Beast in Disney's *Beauty and the Beast*.

All the animals' dilemmas are thinly veiled human ones, as animals, not humans, are generally more appropriate protagonists for children's productions. Hence the willing suspension of disbelief required to enjoy the story prevents the narrative's impact from transcending the story level; it is only a story, and not even one whose potential complexity ought to be recognized if not completely absorbed. This makes the question of belief in these narratives as spiritual realities all that more difficult, undermining their spiritual value and reducing their function to that of a well-told story with an edifying moral.

In 2012, the English-language animated film *Great Women of Islam* produced by British Badr Productions, which boasts its Disney connections, is set in the time the Muslims are advancing upon Mecca. The film opens with an angry spat between Hend, the wife of the chieftain of Mecca, and her slave girl who blurts out that she is a Muslim. She tells her mistress that her secret conversion was a rejection of the ways of her tribe that placed her as a woman and a slave at the bottom of the social order. When Hend disdainfully tells her that Islam is no different, she responds with the story of how the Quran came to contain a verse on "gender equality." The scene moves to another narrative where Nussiaba bint Kaab, a contemporary of Muhammed PBUH and an excellent archer, complains about the low status of women in Islam and a Quranic revelation is made. Hend is unaffected by the story until her husband tells her that he too has converted and she falls to the ground a shattered woman, and recognizing defeat says "I can resist no more" and resolves to accept Islam herself. The American English that the characters speak is not the only jarring element of this production; the "women's rights" angle, equal opportunity in sports, Islam as a refuge for the underdog, and the falling of the mighty all come from Western-Muslim discourses on Islam, and are modified to run like a fairy tale. As a retelling that is produced under the gaze of the "Other" this type of retelling mainstreams Muslims through the "Disneyfication" of the aesthetics, which can be attributed to the lack of a tradition and a tendency to imitate Western forms. In much the same way that the attractions of a Starbucks venue in a developing country lie in its recreation of a first-world space, making the visitor feel she is a comfortable "world citizen" navigating a familiar branded space, this series replicates many of the same Disney visual *and* narrative formulae. This assumes that the English-speaking audience is trained to absorb the local as long as it can be offered in the same setting they aspire to.

These "retellings" are rightly called "productions," for they are not storytelling at all; they are not narrated to anyone, by anyone. Unlike traditional storytelling that addresses a wide audience at various levels, hence is necessarily sophisticated in its palimpsest, these share a willful lack of dimensionality, and can only become darker when adapted for adults, not multi-layered. Without a conception of a maturing audience, they are caught in a state of extended juvenility as they remain intent on appealing to the lower common denominator and insisting that "we are just like you" in their pragmatic attempt to forge a "cool" Islamic identity to an unknown public.

What a Muslim does

The second type of production exists predominantly in the English language and is made for Western Muslims. It is prescriptive and made to teach Muslim children about their "Muslim-ness" and foster pride in it as an identity, and these works remain the most directly didactic in spite of active efforts to update them. As such, even the logos they include by way of explaining ritual practices, is heavily laced with the pathos necessary to inspire a sense of faith and loyalty to this imagined community.

I will analyze two prominent aspects of these texts, which help the child navigate the logistics of how to keep halal, fast, pay alms, make ablutions before prayer, and so on: first, they reinforce authoritative paradigms, often in spite of their anxiety to do otherwise under the Western gaze; and second, they strive to demystify Islam, including its "mystical" spirituality.

Authority

In programming "edutainment," the question of who acts as the transmitter of [religious] knowledge becomes particularly important. Most of these productions understand the imperative to find formats that break away from the traditional transmission model of information and character development, two tasks entrusted to figures of authority in traditional Islam. This question is dealt with in children's production as variously as t is in the multiple approaches to Islam. On the one hand, traditional Islam focuses on maintaining an unbroken chain of scholars and guides whose spiritual lineage goes back to the Prophet PBUH. The followers of the traditional shaykh will learn the *adab* (manners) of the Prophet from being around him. Hence his authority is high and the teachings he imparts take place in a traditional *halaqa* (circle). On the other hand, there are today two important modern streams of Islam. First, the Wahabbi brand that descends from nineteenth-century Saudi Arabia and derides the authority of those with spiritual lineage and emphasizes rather a return to the literality of the Quranic text. This approach is usually accompanied by an "Arabization" movement that is thought to allow practitioners direct access to the Quranic text, as though language is the only barrier to negotiating this text independently. An example of a production that falls under this influence is the series *Stories of the Prophets* by US-based Yusuf Estes, who replicates the traditional *madrasa* with an interracial group of children sitting in an artificial garden much like the studio sets of the storytelling segments of *Sesame Street* and *Barney and Friends*, in a traditional halaqa around Estes who narrates teaching stories. The second stream, "Reformist Islam," democratizes knowledge of Islam and makes it practical and not only compatible with but conducive to worldly advancement; there are no human repositories of knowledge, only books and good parenting. Children are encouraged to believe in themselves as capable of evaluating information and distinguishing trustworthy sources by measuring the information they disseminate against the democratized school and media curriculum that they have received. Such an approach tends to flatten spiritual knowledge in order to make information accessible to and surmountable by the greatest number of children. Even when programs in this stream change the format of information transmission from the traditional, the exchange of power remains largely symbolic. For example, the five popular 5-minute preschooler episodes of the American *Hurrey for Baba Ali* (2011) features Ali Ardekani, stand-up comedian, miming everyday activities while children's off-screen voices give him instructions for how to get it right, not unlike the maladroit Mr. Noodle from *Sesame Street* – for example, praying before meals and eating with the right hand, being kind to plants and animals, and using time wisely. Online subscription-based channel *Muslim Kids TV*, advertised as "100% halal and interactive" is true to its tagline, "just because you're young doesn't mean your ideas aren't big," and features a children's fatwa show "Ask Aariz" (2011) where a Muppet receives questions that require him to issue a fatwa (religious decision). But before he responds, he forces his viewers to do rounds of physical exercises and other "positive" activities as they wait. While the topics are seemingly triggered by the children on the show, their contributions to how the discussion unfolds is virtual and the agenda is set by the adult who confirms all things with easy answers to their questions.

Simplification

Original "teaching stories" that place children at the center and that do not come from the repertoire of teaching stories from the Islamic tradition can often reveal contemporary urban parenting anxieties. The desire to provide a practical and clear Islam where logical reasons, selected from the rich palimpsest of meanings, are assigned to rituals removes any ambiguity by offering a direct singular meaning to each ritual. These programs also highlight the practical benefits of "character" Islam in navigating the modern world successfully rather than taking on spirituality, which the modern Muslim parent considers "a personal affair."

An example of this is The Misri Bunch's *The Names of Allah* series, which features a cast of five Muslim animal hand puppets, in a Lake District setting, hosted by Abul Waleed, a fox hand puppet sporting a Palestinian keffiyeh. Each episode explains one of the 99 Divine attributes. In one episode, a mother hides cherries in the woods and tricks her daughter into praying to "Al Razzaq" (the Provider) to find them, upon which she nudges her in the direction of the cache. One day when there are no cherries, the mother worries that her daughter's faith will be shaken, but the girl persists in her trust and prayer until she chances upon blueberries. The meaning of provision is flattened to finding fruit when and where one is looking for it, making no accommodations for the complexity with which The Provider provides. The mother is shown to have very little faith in The Provider's reliability, setting up an elaborate ruse to convince her daughter of what she is not convinced of. The purpose of this puzzling episode seems to be to confirm that even if parents have no faith, children should. Or that God and His attributes, like the fairies in *Peter Pan*, are more likely to be believed in by children.

This anxiety about bringing reality to children is also evident in the six-episode show *Enjoying Islam with Zain and Dawud* (2008). The format is a playroom set with a seated boy and girl. In the first episode, Zain talks to them about his trip to South Africa, sings a ditty, become serious and tells them that their time on earth is limited and that they will return to their Creator when they die. Before they can respond, he says that this reminds him of a song and they all sing together again and perform a simple dance. Dawud then comes onscreen and begins to talk about religious diversity in his family and his perennialist philosophy and explains that he chose Islam because he found the Quran to be a clear text that showed him how to keep himself and others safe. He brings out travel souvenirs and says they are all Muslim, and when the children ask how rocks, shells, or flowers can be Muslims he explains that linguistically, Islam means "to surrender to Divine Will," but that the surrender of humans required a series of choices. This segues into other songs that Dawud and Zain sing where the theme of perennialism is strong. The underlying assumption of the pacing of the episodes seems to be that children cannot take too much reality, and that serious ideas need to be thrown out but quickly diluted in a whirlwind of song and dance.

All these productions mushroom in the same forest, unbidden, rootless and tasteless. They may be amusing, entertaining, disturbing but they are all superficial. They resist depth and intellectualism, they fear the symbolic and deeper meanings and interpretations, not unlike new Islamic groups. In the flattening of stories into a single accessible layer, there is a great deal of metaphor; as in religion, as in the stories.

Storytelling: a rare forest

In the midst of these flattened productions, rare works function within the traditional storytelling paradigm and are not confined to the mundane, nor restricted to the known world, and revive the mythical in storytelling by operating as religious constitutive myths that both describe vertical and horizontal relationships in the past and give form to them in the present. For example, Peter Sis's visual rendition of *The Conference of The Birds* takes the verse of Sufi mystic Fariduddin Attar and creates a crossover palimpsestic picturebook with conceptual illustrations inspired by two translations of the Persian poem and a play. The rich plates resist the urge to "decipher" the allegorical poem and dilute its secrets for a child reader. Like traditional storytelling for multiple audience members, this is a non-linear world that can be revisited into adulthood.

In the world of Islamic texts, however, retellings of Quranic stories outsell all other children's books, as the Quran draws attention to itself as a source of stories that remind and teach. The Quranic verse in the chapter titled "Joseph" says, "We relate unto thee the most beautiful of stories, revealing to thee this portion of the Qur'an that thou too was among those who knew it not (12:3)." Instead of accepting the rules of engagement outlined in the previous retellings, in 1999 Azzam and Gouverneur tackle the complexity of the *sira* literature for young adults in the light of Martin Ling's more expansive retelling, and then in 2013, Karima Sperling's *The Story of Moses*, with illustrations by Nabil Ibrahim, abandons prevailing practice altogether for another that is neither proselytizing nor pedantic. The 374-page retelling of the prophetic story most repeated in the Quran seamlessly weaves the fantastical into the natural world, reviving the mythical and fulfilling the function of literature as an "experience" (Sperling 21). The story begins with the story of Joseph, son of Jacob, and expands into a world unconfined to the known world as it flows from the historical genealogy of Moses to the story of the rooster on a pillar of emerald above the throne of God, from the intricate humanizing psychological analysis of the egotistical position of the Pharaoh and the redemption of Moses after wrongfully slaying the Egyptian to miracles, sorcerers and angels in the forms of bulls, lions and falcons. Sperling explains the non-linearity and straying from rationality of the stories by saying: "they contain the things that God apparently feels His creatures need to know. They will help you to balance your joys and to bear your sufferings" (22).

While the circumstances and tribulations of Moses are extraordinary, the first half of the book is a classic *bildungsroman*, a compassionate depiction of a young adult who struggles and develops. Sperling's text thus allows potential for *bildung*, a form that looks at childhood as a station in a trajectory and comprehends the anxieties, cognitive abilities and psychological challenges of growing up. She demonstrates that engagement in an old narrative can enhance current lived experiences in ways that the retellings mentioned above aspire to but fail to accomplish. Following the protagonist well beyond the point where his age corresponds to that of the reader, the complex narrative structure, and the frequent breaking of the fourth wall to offer comments where Abrahamic versions of this story offer different interpretations encourages children to accept non-traditional narratives and rescues it from the banality of a single-layer text.

Stories that are usually event-oriented are here "character-oriented" as the humanity of Moses is underlined in his meditations on his situations, his confusion, and his decision-making. The understanding of the Quranic story as based in plot fails to high-light character development and as such is simplistic. This challenge has a number of key advantages: the narrative is more comprehensible and fully formed to the child audience, which, after all, desires a story rather than a thinly veiled parable followed by a moral. In doing so, it recognizes the humanity of the child reader and character – neither con-descending to nor over-estimating them and holding them to impossible standards. It contends that this is not what stories of heroism are for and recognizes that the texts that do exalt the heroes may also dishearten the reader. As the protagonist approaches the age of the YA reader and then gradually surpasses it into old age, the comfortable distance offers the reader resolutions that can become part of an unlived experience repertoire to be shelved and accessed cyclically.

The story is Islamic in the sense that the values of the religion are at the core of the retelling rather than a separate entity without, much in the same way C.S. Lewis's stories are imbued with Christian values. But this retelling's fantastical elements and weaving of *isrā ʾīliyyāt* and its author's embracing her Jewish roots, Lutheran upbringing and Muslim adulthood make the modern Muslim and Western audience equally slightly uneasy. Nevertheless, the book holds a mature yet accessible opportunity for interfaith dialogue through an analysis of where we diverge and converge.

The chances of survival of these rare productions are, however, probably higher in the medium of the illustrated text within a niche market of Sufi circles than amongst urban-ized globalized Muslims whose desires to know a "practical compatible Islam" continues to drive children's productions.

Bibliography

Albayrak, Ismail (2012) "Reading the Bible in the light of Muslim sources: from *isrā ʾīliyyāt* to *islāmiyyāt*," *Islam and Christian–Muslim Relations* 23(2): 113–127.

Animal Stories in the Quran (2012) Writ. Ahmed Bahgat. Perf. Yahia Al Fakharany. Dir. Mostafa ElFaramawy. Arab Media Associates 2.

Azzam, Leila and Aisha Gouverneur (1999) *The Life of the Prophet Muhammad*, Cambridge: Islamic Texts Society.

Bahgat, Ahmad (1983) *Animal Stories in the Quran*. Illustrations by Ihab Shaker. Cairo: Dar el Shorouk.

Corbin, Henry (1993) *History of Islamic Philosophy*, London: Kegan Paul.

Janson, Torsten (2003) *Your Cradle Is Green: The Islamic Foundation and the Call to Islam in Children's Literature*. Volume 18 of Lund Studies in History of Religions. Lund University.

Mahtab, Mezba Uddin. "Rules," Teaching Kids The Holy Quran. readwithmeaning.wordpress.com

"Mapping the Global Muslim Population" (2009) *The Pew Forum on Religion and Public Life*.

Sperling, Karima (2013) *The Story of Moses*. Illustrations by Nabil Ibrahim. London: Little Bird Books.

Stephens, John, and Robyn McCallum (1998) *Retelling Stories, Framing Culture: Traditional Story and Metanarratives in Children's Literature*, New York: Garland.

Vajda, G., "Isrāʾīliyyāt", in: *Encyclopaedia of Islam*, 2nd Edition. Edited by P. Bearman, Th. Bianquis, C.E. Bosworth, E. van Donzel, W.P. Heinrichs. http://dx.doi.org/10.1163/1573-3912_islam_SIM_3670 (accessed 20 August 2016).

23

BRAZILIAN CHILDREN'S LITERATURE AND BOOKLET LITERATURE

Approximations and distances

José Hélder Pinheiro Alves

In the northeast of Brazil (and especially in Paraíba) there has been a long tradition of oral poetry about various themes. The most prominent diffusers of such rich oral practice were the "violists," who accompanied themselves on a *viola caipira* (country guitar) or *rabeca* as they travelled among small towns, villages and farms giving performances either alone or accompanied by others (Abreu 1999). However, the oral literature did not happen only because of these important folk artists, who used to improvise their presentation, but also for the reason that common people used to recite several stanzas in many ways, such as stanzas of four, six or seven lines, distichs, riddles in verse and other forms. Their singing was a singular event, in which many verses were ornamented, repeated and transmitted orally. The poets themselves tried to memorize some verses created previously during the improvisation, which resulted, later, in several books that registered hundreds of stanzas created/recreated by the singers.[1] As well as the singers, there were many common people who created verses— whether improvised or not – which were recited, passed on and shared in different spaces, often in modified versions. Oral narratives, especially the so-called folk tales, also had great popular penetration and were collected by researchers from different regions of the country.

In this context of rich oral transmission of narratives in verse and prose emerges the image of the *cordelista*, who was referred to as a "workbench poet" – that is, a poet who lacked the "gift" of improvisation, so he had to produce his string booklets on the workbench. Such a poet composed the poems, committed them to memory, and then dictated them to someone who knew how to write. These poets began to publish their poems in simple pamphlets, and to seek ways to disseminate them, especially in street markets of small, medium and large cities. The person who best exemplifies this form of oral transmission of such popular literature is the paraibano Leandro Gomes de Barros. Researchers are unanimous in identifying him as the pioneer in the creation of the booklet model that was subsequently named *cordel* or *string literature*.

The narratives were initially published in 11 cm x 15 cm format. This was a sheet of newsprint (the size of a modern A4 sheet) folded into four and thus resulting in a booklet of 8 pages. It was common to have publications of 8 pages and its multiples – 16, 24, 32, 64. Booklets with 24 pages or more were called novels. The format was established and spread throughout the northeast and was later taken to the north (Bethlehem and part of the State of Amazonas) and to the southeast (especially São Paulo and Rio de Janeiro). There are no statistics on the number of booklets produced throughout the twentieth century, but the work that best documents this production, the *Dicionário Biobibliográfico de repentistas e poetas populares*, by Attila Almeida and José Alves Sobrinho (1978), recorded 4,453 titles of string booklets. The entire publication of the last twenty years of the twentieth century was not included in these statistics, which is quite significant, as well as the numerous pamphlets published in different cities and villages that were neither promoted nor distributed. The circulation of such booklets during the 1960s in northeastern Brazil was so immense that some of these publications had editions of a size comparable with bestsellers. The cheap price of the booklets favored poor people, workers, who went to the market to sell their wares and there met hawkers singing or reciting the string booklets. This phenomenon occurs in the context of a society where most of the people were illiterate; therefore, they used to cultivate their memory in a very rich way.

Oral literature: diversity of topics

One of the striking aspects of the Brazilian booklet literature is the diversity of topics covered, which makes it distinct from the so-called string literature produced in Portugal in the seventeenth and eighteenth centuries. As Marcia Abreu reminds us,

> Unlike the Portuguese string literature, which lacks uniformity, booklets literature produced in northeastern Brazil is quite coded. You can follow the process of constitution of this literary form by examining the singing sessions and booklets published between the late nineteenth century and the last years of the 1920s, a period which defines the fundamental characteristics of this literature, reaching a canonical format
>
> (Abreu 1999: 73).

Abreu also noted that the "proclaimed affiliation of the northeast booklets to the Portuguese string literature, although such affiliation cannot be sustained after a careful comparison, is part of common sense, and [...] is apparently natural" (125). Although many booklets that had great influence among the people came from the Iberian tradition, as shown by Luís da Câmara Cascudo in *Cinco livros do povo* [The five books of the people] (1953), the incorporation of reality in its different nuances remains the great source of poets – both violists and workbench poets. In this sense, any narrower classification or affiliation fails to represent the extent of the phenomenon of creation and dissemination of such production. This diversity has led researchers to speak about cycles, which are nothing more than large thematic groupings. A comprehensive study on the subject is Manuel Diégues Júnior's *Os ciclos temáticos na literatura de cordel* [The thematic cycles in string literature] (2012). For the researcher, there are numerous "possibilities of exploring the themes developed by the string literature, which derives from the existing thematic variety." (2012: 53). In his classification, he has three large groups, each with several subdivisions.

First, there are traditional themes, which include novels and novellas, marvelous tales, animal stories, adventures and mischievousness of anti-heroes, and religious tradition. The second group comprises tales of actual events: physical phenomena, such as floods, droughts, earthquakes; events of social consequences, ranging from parties, sports, soap operas, to astronauts; stories of city and urban life; social criticism and satire; and stories of human existence, which might deal with current or updated figures (for example, Getúlio Vargas, revolutionary and elected President), cycles of fanaticism and mysticism, cycles of banditry, and tales about ethnic and regional types. The third group is about singing and struggles (Diégues Júnior 2012: 53).

Diégues Júnior comments on and exemplifies each of the themes, identifying an important framework for the production of string literature until the 1960s. Symptomatic of these large core themes, and hence the focus for this essay, are animal themes, which Diégues Júnior designates "animal stories," although many of them are also known as *No tempo em que os bichos falavam* (*At the time the animals talked*). These narratives were not considered childlike, nor was their target audience children, although they were very popular among children. The stories were basically about animals that lived in a human-like society, in which they had to face the same kind of conflicts, discriminations, abuse of power and prejudice that a human being has to face, and had to resist and fight against such a hostile society. One feature of almost all these stories is the presence of humor and the exploitation of the animals' particular characteristics as constituent elements of their occupations.

Therefore, parallel to the official children's literature, which had the narratives of Monteiro Lobato, and especially *Narizinho Arrebitado* (1921) as a great paradigm for children's writers, there was another kind of literature highly valued by northeastern people that brought in its scope stories that fed the imagination of both children and adults, without a separation between them, as often happened in classical literature. The folk tales of the oral tradition also had a very wide dissemination, and possibly included versions aimed at children. There are, however, two aspects of string literature that maintain a dialogue – direct or indirect – with Brazilian children's literature: first, string booklets that thematize stories of animals, and, second, string booklets that are frequently retold and published as children's literature.

At the time the animals talked: string booklets of yesterday and now

As already mentioned, the theme of animals in the string literature constitutes an important cycle, highlighted, among others, by Diégues Júnior (2012). Diégues Júnior cites booklets, such as *O Boi Misterioso e o Cachorro dos Mortos* [The Mysterious Ox and the Dog from the Dead], by Leandro Gomes de Barros; *A Vaca Misteriosa* [The Mysterious Cow], by José Costa Leite; and *A História do Papagaio Misterioso* [The Story of the Mysterious Parrot], by Luis da Costa (2012: 55). Some booklets are excluded from this list because they do not incorporate the heroic adventurer character, such as José Francisco Borges, *No Tempo em que os Bichos Falavam* [At the Time when the Animals Talked]; and Manuel Pereira Sobrinho, *No Tempo em que os Bichos Falavam* [At the Time when the Animals Talked] and *Casamento e Divórcio do Calango com a Lagartixa* [The Marriage and Divorce of the Green Lizard and the Gray Lizard]; Leandro Gomes de Barros, *A Noiva do Gato* [The Cat Bride], and *Casamento e Divórcio da Lagartixa*, [The Marriage and Divorce of the Lizard]; Zé Vicente, *A Greve dos Bichos* [The Animals' Strike]; José Pacheco, *A Intriga do Cachorro com o Gato* [The Intrigue of the Dog with the Cat], and countless other booklets. Thus, the folk origins of string booklet literature encompassed a diversity of approaches that included children as one of their possible audiences, for they did not aim to discriminate between children and adults. So, one can distinguish two moments in the history of Brazilian booklet literature: first, the booklets were designed to be appreciated by specific communities of readers – illiterate people and rural communities, who heard the stories and kept them in their memory; later, both older booklets and contemporary creations begin to indicate a target audience – children and, more recently, the school.

In contemporary production, there are two trends: on the one hand, the string litera-ture format of fables and fairy tales predominates among string writers of different states. Some of these works have been published in book form, with the seal of major publishers and national distribution. On the other hand, there are poets who follow the tradition of creating narratives in which animals are presented in the most diverse life situations – conflicts of power, prejudices, and so on, but also staging festivities and having fun. This bias can be seen in booklets such as *Verde-Gaio: o Louro Bisbilhoteiro* [Green-Gaio: The Annoying Parrot] and *Sete dias de forró no reino da bicharada* [Seven days of Dancing in the Kingdom of Animals] by Marcelo Soares. The first is narrated in first person by a parrot who tells of his antics and disagreements because of his habit of sticking his beak into others' business (E se ouço uma conversa / Vou logo metendo o bico). The booklet is an intertextual game between the somewhat roguish Disney-Brazilian com-ics character José "Zé" Carioca and a Green-Jay who meets him at the cinema. Invited by the "Woodpecker, Mr. Know-it-all," to go to Hollywood, he refuses, suspecting that Zé Carioca wants to steal his cousin. The other booklet starts with a situation of sad-ness that involves the animals that want to propose a big party to everyone. The fun and humorous tone is present throughout the entire narrative.

In the booklet *No Tempo em que os Bichos Falavam* [At the Time when the Animals Talked], the poet José Francisco Borges does not develop a continuous narrative, but rather a series of encounters and mismatching situations between the animals and in the end there is a party. The actions of animals are linked to their characteristics in nature. The inclusion of a party is very often a key characteristic of this type of booklet.

Several string booklets present animals as characters in rich plots full of fantasy and inventiveness, as in *O Sabiá da Palmeira* [The Thrush of the Palm Trees] by Antônio Lucena, which tells the beautiful story of a thrush that enchants everyone with his sing-ing. Various animals come to honor the bird. The booklet is an intertextual game with the famous poem "Canção do Exílio" [The Song Of Exile] by Antônio Gonçalves Dias, which begins, "Minha terra tem palmeiras, / Onde canta o Sabiá" [My land has palm-trees / where the thrush sings].

In *A onça e o bode*, [The Jaguar and the Goat] José Costa Leite retells a popular tale in which the two animals begin to build a house; each works on the same site but at a dif-ferent time and, while building the same house, both think they are being helped by God:

A onça chegando viu
o trabalho prosperando
disse assim: 'É Deus do céu
que está me ajudando'

[The Jaguar saw that the work was progressing, and said, "It is God of heaven who is helping me"]. This narrative seems to be a sort of criticism of the differences between social/regional groups. The jaguar might refer to Brazilian southern people who have social advantages over the northeastern because of their economic power. The goat makes an allusion to the northeast because it is their representative animal.

The Cearense poet Sebastian Chicute brings actions and characters of dozens of birds in different situations and spaces in his *Booklet of the birds*. Subsequently, Pedro Costa, a poet from Piauí, wrote his *Booklets for children* in which each six lines is a riddle. Through the rhyme of the final line, the reader, during the oral reading, can guess the animal, as in the following: "Ele gosta de banana / Na destreza não é **fraco** / Se segura pelo **rabo** / Com as unhas coça o **sovaco** / Parece muito com gente / O nome dele é? **MACACO**" [He likes bananas. / He is agile / made secure by his tail / With his nails he scratches his armpit / he looks very like a person / His name is? MONKEY]. More recently the poet Hadook Ezekiel, from Rio Grande do Norte, published *Eleições no reino da bicharada* [Election in the Kingdom of the Animals], which also relates the actions of animals to their characteristic features, whether it be peacock, gazelle, shark or lion, and concludes that entrenched difference produces a disharmonious society. Among the fairy tales that appear in the booklet literature format, *Chapeuzinho Vermelho* [Little Red Riding Hood] is one of the most reproduced. At least three versions of such a string can be found: *Chapeuzinho Vermelho em versos* [Little Red Riding Hood in verse], by Manoel Monteiro; *Chapeuzinho Vermelho* [Little Red Riding Hood], by Geraldo Evaristo da Silva; and *A peleja de Chapeuzinho Vermelho and o grande lobo mau* [The battle between Red Riding Hood and the Big Bad Wolf], by Arievaldo Viana (2011). The three narratives are faithful to Grimm's version that can be found in Brazil through several translations. However, each poet brings something unique to his retelling, to a lesser or greater degree. The version by Manoel Monteiro starts retaking the old meaning of the catchphrase "Once upon a time," addressing the reader/listener: "I'll start slowly / Telling a tale to you." (E – 1) Then, the poet situates the scenario (E – 2) and presents the main character (E – 3–5). Moreover, the poet shows his ability to retell the story using rhymes, as can be seen in the verses below:

A Chapeuzinho Vermelho
Um dia alegre brincava
Atrás de uma borboleta
Que de flor em flor pousava
Nisso ouviu a mãe chamar
E dar-lhe um cesto a levar
Para a vó que o aguardava.

[One joyful day Little Red Riding Hood played behind a butterfly that landed on a flower in bloom ... She heard her mother call and give her a basket to take to her grandmother who was waiting for it]

Like Manoel Monteiro's version, that by Arievaldo Viana is also composed in seven-line stanzas (septilha in Portuguese). Among the three versions, Viana introduces the possibility of a second end, present in the version of the Grimm Brothers, in which Little Red Riding Hood and her grandmother make a trap for the Wolf. The versions written by Evaristo Geraldo da Silva and Arievaldo Viana, in the end, aim at presenting a moral lesson: for Silva it is the value of maternal guidance, which a child should follow; Viana makes a similar point – children need guidance because they may find it difficult to recognize danger and may be easily led astray.

Countless cordelistas have made versions of fairy tales, fables and folk tales into the booklet literature model. Manoel Monteiro also did this with the tale *O gato de botas* [Puss in Boots], *A gata borralheira* [Cinderella], *A cigarra e a formiga* [The Ant and the Grasshopper], and other folk tales like *A Dança das 12 princesas* [The Twelve Dancing Princesses], and *Os três cabelos do diabo* [The Devil's Three Golden Hairs]. The publisher

Queima Bucha published a collection of stories called *12 Contos de Cascudo Em Folhetos de Cordel* [The 12 Short Stories of Cascudo in String Literature Format]. In this collection can be found the *História da Moura Torta* [The History of Moura Torta], by Marcus Aurelius; *A Sorte do Preguiçoso e o Peixinho Encantado* [The Fortune of the Lazy Boy and the Magic Little Fish], by Antonio Francisco Baseado; *Pedro Malazartes e o Arubu Advinhão* [Pedro Malazartes and the Soothsayer Buzzard], by Klévisson Viana, among others. As can be seen, the production is rich and diverse and includes poets from different states of Brazil, which makes it much more difficult for teachers and researchers to have an accurate survey of the collections.

Children's literature, booklet literature

Few scholarly works about children's literature in Brazil have made a deep study of the relations between oral literature and literature produced for children. It is as if children's literature were something indigenous, born in some privileged minds of a few writers. A notable exception is the chapter "Literatura oral" [Oral Literature], in Leonardo Arroyo's *Literatura Infantil* (1990). Arroyo emphasizes the importance of "black cultural currents brought to Brazil during the period of slavery" (45), and the great contribution of many storytellers who nurtured the dreams and the imagination of working class children, slave owners' children, and also the children of free men. One of the sources used by Arroyo was the testimonies collected from the "Livros das memórias" (52), by writers and intellectuals who lived either in the second half of the nineteenth century or during the twentieth century. One of the most significant testimonies was that of Coelho Neto: "for my literary formation, the most important contribution was not that of the authors, but of common people." (Cited by Arroyo 1990: 55.)

Arroyo adduces some influences of oral literature on the works of various writers. Monteiro Lobato, author of the widely read children's book *O Saci* (The Saci, 1932), is thus cited recalling his earliest exposure to knowledge of the *Saci*, the monopedal, magical prankster figure from Brazilian mythology: "My idea of the boy, confesses the writer, was according to what I have heard from some black women on my father's farm, that is, the *Saci* had red eyes like those of drunkards; and made more pranks than malice" (Arroyo 1990: 59). However, although Arroyo engages with writers like Leonardo Mota and Cascudo, the important pioneering scholars of oral literature – and this includes the string literature – are not referred to in his work about the literature in verse that predominated in the northeast of Brazil from the end of the nineteenth century until the early twentieth century.

String literature has been adapted as children's literature. Two notable examples, which will bring this essay to its conclusion, are: *O Pavão Misterioso* [The Mysterious Peacock, 2004] by Ronaldo Correia de Brito and Assis Lima, adapted from *Romance do Pavão Misterioso* [The Romance of the Mysterious Peacock], written by José Camelo de Melo Rezende in the late 1920s; and *A História de Juvenal e o dragão* [The Story of Juvenal and the Dragon, 2011], adapted by Rosinha from the booklet of the same name written by Leandro Gomes de Barros.

The Romance of the Mysterious Peacock, by José Camelo de Melo Rezende, is considered a classic of the booklet literature. It was sung and read by numerous readers and had a great penetration among the people throughout almost the entire twentieth century. It inspired songs, comic narratives and a work focused on children. The booklet written by José Camelo has 32 pages, it is composed of 141 six-line stanzas and tells the story of two brothers – John the Baptist and the Evangelist. They are Turks who inherited their father's large fortune. The first decides to travel to see the world: "My brother, I want to / go overseas / I did not enjoy anything / So, I should spend a year / In a foreign land." The brother leaves and promises, requested by his brother, to bring "a beautiful gift only for a single man." The journey of John the Baptist is summed up in two stanzas. When John is coming back from Greece, he comes to know that the daughter of a count, a beautiful girl who lives isolated from the rest of the world, will be presented to the people – an event that occurs only once a year. The view of the girl, Creusa, is breathtaking, so he decides to buy a picture of her to take to his brother Evangelist. When he comes back home, he gives his brother the gift; Evangelist gloats at first, but when he sees the image of Creusa, he immediately falls in love with her. From this moment on, the focus of the story is on Evangelist – from his trip to Greece until the bringing of his beloved to his own land. In Greece, he manages to convince an old engineer to build a flying machine, in the shape of a peacock, and provide him with a magical scarf which will be crucial for his purpose. After bringing his beloved to Turkey and marrying her, Evangelist is told about the death of the count and becomes the heir of his wealth. The narrative has a happy ending, in a romantic style, which is one of the major characteristics of this type of booklet.

The book by Brito and Lima (2004) is divided into eight small episodes, but unlike the booklet written by José Camelo de Melo Rezende, it has sections variously in either verse or prose. The book begins with the character Antonio Camilo trying, unsuccessfully, to sell his string booklets at the fair in Campina Grande, a city in Paraíba. When a boy gets closer to him, the seller starts to read "The story of the mysterious peacock." In fact, the story told by the character does not transcribe stanzas from José Rezende's booklet *The Romance of the Mysterious Peacock*, but presents parts of its plot in a different way, sometimes summarized and sometimes developed.

The narrative written by Brito and Lima makes no reference to the author of the source booklet, and the brothers are now named João and Luís. Concerning the differences in the plot, for example, there is a shortening of the time João spends in Greece preparing himself to achieve his goal, and there is an addition of a character – a page called Miguilim who accompanies the brothers on the journey. Also, unlike the booklet, the journey of Luís, the first brother, is described in a little more detail. One aspect that stands out in the book is the illustrations. There are numerous pages in which certain scenes are illustrated in red tones. They are either blended with the text or placed on independent pages but always interact with the events or the scenes of the narrative. The framing scene of a booklet seller trying, unsuccessfully, to sell his poems in the fair is a good reference to the situation of such sellers nowadays. The fair or market is no longer a privileged place as before and the target readers are no longer illiterate.

The strength of the two narratives is the romantic plot, led by heroic actions aiming at the attraction of the beloved. The theme of love at first sight – not because of the character itself, but for its image – draws one's attention to the power of fantasy, loving idealization.

The second booklet retrieves and retells *Juvenal and the Dragon*, by Leandro Gomes de Barros, aiming at attracting the attention of the young audience. Within the terminology of the string literature genres, the narrative is classified as a novel as it has 32 pages. It is a story of adventure and heroism. Juvenal, a poor young man, and his sister inherit their father's three sheep and a small house. The sister receives the house, and he inherits the sheep. After the division of their heritage, Juvenal travels around the world "seeking to know what is good and what is evil." On the same day, he sets out, he meets a "weird guy" who offers to exchange the three sheep for three dogs. He is convinced by the unknown man after the following argument: "None of the three is bad / by the time I'm hungry / I can only say this: / Break Iron, get to work / Bring him to me" (3). After a month of journeys, Juvenal finds a carriage and "sees a beautiful girl inside it / she was crying all the way along / and the very sad coachman / who sighed from time to time" (5). He came to know the history of the Dragon that each year carries from the kingdom "one of its prettiest girls." Juvenal, with the help of his dogs, defeats the Dragon. Then he leaves that kingdom and promises to visit the princess three years later. Meanwhile, the coachman threatens to kill the princess if she does not tell people that he was the hero. Warned by a dream, Juvenal returns to the kingdom, reveals the impostor and marries the princess. As can be noted, although it is quite a long, adventurous narrative, it is not directed toward young readers. On the contrary, there are very strong moments, as is evident at the close of the story in the reference to the execution of the coachman.

Rosinha's adaptation of *Juvenal and the Dragon* basically reproduces the episode of the fight between Juvenal and the dragon, and is no longer narrated in verse. The book begins with a problem faced by the people of the kingdom: "In a distant realm, a terrible dragon attacks again." When the time comes for the princess to be taken to the monster, she meets on her journey the "adventurer Juvenal who wants to know what is happening when he sees her crying." In this retelling, there is no mention about the origin of Juvenal, nor anything about the replacement of the sheep by dogs, which are enchanted and transformed into birds in the end. This retelling is suitable for children, since it highlights the climactic episode of the fight, and it is written in accessible language, with short sentences, which are well distributed across the book's pages. A strong point of the work are the illustrations, which resemble the technique of woodcut.

Final considerations

It can be said that in the northeast of Brazil during the twentieth century children's literature, either for the poor children of illiterate parents or, to some extent, for the children of more privileged social origin, was basically this oral literature – fairy tales, folk tales, riddles, popular verses, sung and recited booklets, among other manifestations. They were not thought of as something for children, unlike the writing of La Fontaine in France, who resorted to myths that were frequent in oral tradition. It was something unsystematic, and never reached the very few schools that existed in small towns and villages.

In the late twentieth century and early twenty-first century, many changes occurred: significant decreases in access to the booklets by the most popular groups, since their sales venue is no longer the fair; the emergence of a booklet production more oriented to school, so that the stories become no longer just stories but the content of different disciplines in a booklet (string) literature format. Major publishers started to publish old and contemporary booklets that aim at a new reading audience of private and public schools (through purchases of such booklets by the Brazilian federal government). At the same time, hundreds of poets continue publishing and distributing their booklets outside the circle of the big companies, though with a much smaller audience. One question that arises is: should the publication of the booklets, now in book form, with all the features of children's literature in general, continue to be called booklet literature?

Note

1 The main sources for records of this popular verse are Mota (1925; 4th ed. 1976), Cazuza (n.d.), Linhares and Batista (1976), Alves Sobrinho (2003), and Veras (2004).

Bibliography

Abreu, Marcia (1999) *Histórias de cordéis e folhetos* [Stories of string literature and brochures]. Campinas: Mercado de Letras/ALB.

Alves Sobrinho, José (2003) *Cantadores, repentistas e poetas populares* [Singers, improvisors and popular poets]. Campina Grande: Bagagem.

Arroyo, Leonardo (1990) *Literatura infantil brasileira* [Brazilian children's literature]. 10th ed. São Paulo: Melhoramentos.

Barros, Leandro Gomes de (n.d.) *Juvenal e o dragão*. São Paulo: Luzeiro.

Batista, Otacílio and Francisco Linhares (1976) *Antologia ilustrada dos cantadores* [Illustrated anthology of singers]. Fortaleza: Impr. Universitária da UFC.

Bradesco-Goudemand, Yvonne (1982) *O ciclo dos animais na literatura popular do nordeste* [The cycle of animals in the northeast popular literature]. Rio de Janeiro: Fundação Casa de Rui Barbosa (Literatura Popular em Verso – Nova Série).

Brito, Ronaldo Correia de and Assis Lima (2004) *O Pavão Misterioso*. São Paulo: Editora Cosac Naify.

Cascudo, Luís da Câmara (2000) *12 Contos de Cascudo Em Folhetos de Cordel*. Rio Grande do Norte: Queima Bucha.

Cascudo, Luís da Câmara (1953) *Cinco livros do povo*. Rio de Janeiro: Livraria José Olimpo Editora.

Cazuza, Zé de (n.d.) *Poetas encantadores* [Wonderful poets]. Extracts available on various online sites.

Costa, Pedro (2001) *Cordel para Criança*. Teresina: FUNCOR (Fundação Nordestina de cordel)

Diégues Júnior, Manuel (2012) *Os ciclos temáticos na literatura de cordel* [The thematic cycles in string literature]. Maceió: Imprensa Oficial Graciliano Ramos.

Leite, José Costa (2003) *A onca e o bode*. Prefeitura Municipal de Campina Grande, PB.

Lucena, Antonio (2003) *O sabia da palmeira*. Prefeitura Municipal de Campina Grande, PB.

Marinho, Ana Cristina, and Hélder Pinheiro (2012) *O cordel no cotidiano escolar* [String literature in everyday school life]. São Paulo: Cortez Editora.

Monteiro, Manoel (2008) *Chapeuzinho vermelho: versão versejada*. Campina Grande: Cordelar a Poeta Manoel Monteiro.

Mota, Leonardo (1976 [1925]) *Violeiros do norte: poesia e linguagem do sertão cearense* [Nothern Guitar players: poetry and language of Ceará backcountry]. 4th ed. Rio de Janeiro: Cátedra-MEC.

Pinheiro, Hélder (ed.) (2004) *Pássaros e bichos na voz de poetas populares* [Birds and animals in the voice of popular poets]. Ilustrações/Xilogravuras de Antônio Lucena [Illustrations/Woodcuts by Antônio Lucena]. Campina Grande: Bagagem.

Pinheiro, Hélder, and Marcelo Soares (2011) *Outros pássaros e bichos na voz de poetas populares* [Other birds and animals in the voice of popular poets]. Ilustrações/Xilogravuras de Marcelo Soares [Illustrations/Woodcuts by Marcelo Soares]. Campina Grande: Bagagem.

Rosinha (2011) *A História de Juvenal e o dragão* [The Story of Juvenal and the Dragon]. Porto Alegre: Editora Projeto.

Silva, Geraldo Evaristo da (2006) *Chapeuzinho Vermelho* [Little Red Riding Hood]. Fortaleza: Tupynanquim Editora.

Soares, Marcelo (2006) *Verde-Gaio: o Louro Bisbilhoteiro* [Green-Gaio: The Annoying Parrot]. Timbaúba, PE: Folhetaria Cordel.

Soares, Marcelo (n.d.) *7 Dias de forró no reino da bicharada: um cordel para criança*. Timbaúba, PE: Folhetaria Cordel.

Veras, Ivo Mascena (2004) *Lourival Batista Patriota* [Lourival Baptista Patriota]. Recife: Companhia Editora de Pernambuco.

Viana, Arievaldo (2011) *A Peleja de Chapeuzinho Vermelho com o lobo mau*. Rio de Janeiro: Editora Globo.

24

BRAZILIAN CHILDREN'S LITERATURE IN THE AGE OF DIGITAL CULTURE

Edgar Roberto Kirchof

Digital technology has been increasingly popular and accessible to a broad section of the global population since the final two decades of the twentieth century. Due to the undeniable facilities offered by this type of technology for the production, distribution and consumption of information, contemporary culture is becoming a "culture encoded in digital form" (Manovich 2001: 70). The role played by communication technologies in all processes of globalization renders them ubiquitous in practically every country in the world. This means that the way in which we relate to cultural products – including literature – that we consume today, whether in Europe, the United States, Brazil or any other country, is indelibly characterized by how these technologies and digital media work, transforming many of our practices previously linked to analog media. Brazilian children's literary culture is gradually being transformed owing to its increasingly intense relationship with digital technology. The use of the different types of digital technology transforms the way that these works are produced and consumed, in that it fosters the emergence of new literary forms and new reading media. My focus here is on two new types of literary expression directed towards children: digital poems and digital storytelling.

Children's digital poetry

In the criticism devoted to digital literature, the *digitized literature* concept is commonly used to refer to texts that exist originally in printed form and that are then transferred for the virtual environment with programs such as PDF or EPUB. Specifically *digital literature* (or *electronic literature*), in turn, is produced to be read only on the screens of devices such as computers, tablets and e-readers and usually presents hypertext and multimedia features as integral parts of the package. The first experiments with digital literary works were performed over fifty years ago by Theo Lutz in Germany (Antônio 2008). Although there has been no consensus as to how this literary manifestation is to be referred to – some of the most popular terms are electronic literature, cyber literature and ergodic literature – it is the object of a relatively large body of typologies and theoretical discussions, led by researchers such as Jay David Bolter, George P. Landow, Espen J. Arseth,

Stuart Moulthrop, N. Katherine Hayles, Roberto Simanowski, Jorge Luis Antônio and Alckmar Luis dos Santos, among several others.

In comparison with the production of digital poetry for an adult audience, production intentionally directed towards children is still very limited. This relative lack is not exclusively Brazilian: even in countries where there has been more significant investment in the creation and review of digital works, the number of digital poems for children does not seem to be as extensive as the number of works for adults. In addition, at least until now, the international publishing market is primarily investing in the production of digital narratives for children, mainly to be read on mobile devices, to the detriment of poetry, which thus causes the production of digital children's poetry to remain scarce. Among existing works, many digital poems have their roots in concrete poetry. Others are characterized as adaptations of poems for children which had originally been printed.

The concrete poetry movement, or concretism, refers to a proposal for pioneering poetry which has been successfully practised, in Brazil, from the 1950s. Its main goal has been to extend verbal language towards its phonic (vocal) and iconic (visual) potentials. The Brazilian proponents of this movement used the term "verbivocovisual" to define the advantages of utilizing non-verbal communication for literary purposes, without forfeiting the virtues of the word (Campos, Campos and Pignatari, 1986: 404). Its main Brazilian representatives are the brothers Haroldo and Augusto de Campos and Décio Pignatari. In Europe, the movement was established by the Swiss-Bolivian Eugen Gomringer.

Although it is not a movement directed towards children, the strong presence of visuals and sound in concrete poems in many cases allows it to shrink the boundaries which separate that which is directed towards children from that meant for adults, which results in several of these works being utilized at school, as objects of reading for children and youngsters. Furthermore, from a very early stage, several concrete poems began not only to be scanned but also animated using multimedia and/or hypermedia features. The poem *Bomba* (Bomb) by Augusto de Campos, for example, was originally published in the 1980s and was based on a sound and vision game established between the words *poema* and *bomba* (poem and bomb). In the printed version, the idea of an explosion is constructed iconically through the layout and size of the letters, which seem to be in motion. Even in the 1980s, a holographic version of the same poem was produced, and in 1997, using the Flash program, Augusto de Campos produced a multimedia version (www2. uol.com.br/augustodecampos/bomba.htm).

In addition to concrete poems transformed into digital poems, there also exist in the Brazilian context, albeit small in number when compared to the production directed towards adults, digital poems intentionally created for children. In contrast to poems produced for adult audiences, digital poems for children are clearly characterized as being meant for children, especially with the emphasis on fun, with playful themes related to childhood and a structure reminiscent of games in which it is necessary to achieve some type of objective. A very expressive and successful example of this approach can be found in the work of Angela Lago, an author who is already established in the field of Brazilian children's literature (www.angela-lago.com.br/ABCD.html).

On the home page of her site, there are various figures that refer to a child's imagination such as animals, a lake, a paper boat, an angel and a cloud. The angel and the lake establish a playful dialogue based on the author's own name: Angela Lago. The page contains animated features created using the Flash program, and the figures are actually hyperlinks that refer the reader to different poems or jokes. Furthermore, the site allows the reader to submit to the author not only comments, but also suggestions and even new verses and images, some of which are incorporated by her on to the site.

Among the several possibilities provided on the home page is one in which if the reader clicks on a paper boat this will then sink and in its place rises a bottle with a piece of paper (a letter or a treasure map?), which will end up in the hands of the angel. When clicking on this paper, the reader is referred to a new page, giving access to different poems for children and games with the ability to choose between different languages: English, Portuguese and Spanish. The page in English, as well as the others, features an ideogram inviting the reader to get to know, through new hyperlinks, three other poems (Voodoo; Riddle; Rhyme) as well as printed books by the author (Books). The first link, *Voodoo*, gives access to the poem *The ETs Voodoo*, which combines verses with drawings submitted to the author by two young readers: Bibi and Pedrinho. The structure of the poem is reminiscent of popular songs such as *The Ten Little Indian Boys*, as with every verse one of the characters disappears. In the Angela Lago version, however, the characters are aliens, whose gradual disappearance is not narrated in the verbal text, but from the images shown.

Unlike Angela Lago's work, the page of Ana Cláudia Gruszynski and Sérgio Caparelli is an experiment in adaptation of visual poems for the digital environment (www.ciberpoesia.com.br/). The site has its origins in a book entitled *Poesia Visual* (Visual Poetry), published in 2000 by Editora Global, São Paulo, consisting of 28 visual poems. The authors provided 12 of their printed poems, presented in groups of 4: *Navio, Chá, Van Gogh* e *Babel*; *Cheio, Vazio, Eu/tu, Xadrez, zigue-zague, primavera, gato, flechas* (Ship, Tea, Van Gogh and Babel, Full, Empty, I/you, Chess, zig-zag, spring, cat, arrows). In this case, there is a simple transposition to the screen of the poems contained in the book, which characterize an example of digitized poetry. However, in this digitized version, the reader is able to increase or decrease the size of each poem by clicking on the "zoom" command. Moreover, one can drag the poem to different places within its frame.

On the other hand, not all of these poems were simply digitized: ten were transformed into *cyberpoems*, with the Flash program, and were expanded with hypermedia features, which characterize an example of digital poetry itself. Like the poems of Angela Lago, some of Cappareli and Gruszynski's digital poems are also shown as a type of *game* or *joke*. In *Chá*, for example, the young reader is invited to "make some tea" from the ingredients that are available. The reader is presented with some initial guidance ("Click and drag the ingredients into the cup to prepare your tea" and "When you think you have enough ingredients, click to continue"). From there a new window is opened at the same time as sounds are activated and attract the reader's attention to different "objects" such as a photograph of a couple (when the mouse passes over the image, the sound of a smacking kiss is triggered); three stars which when "activated" trigger playful sounds; hearts which suggest/activate the sound of a heartbeat; a blue teapot (the mouse over the teapot activates the sound of crashing crockery). The spoon, the cup and the tea bag do not emit sounds.

The verses of poetry, in turn, appear graphically, represented by the movement of steam caused by the hot water being poured into the cup. The use of italics, together with the rhythmic movement of the steam/verse, renders the reading more complex. The purpose of the poem seems to be less about the very reading of words than the enjoyment of its graphic layout on the page, which resembles, in part, the aesthetic design of concrete poetry.

Finally, when all the ingredients have been placed in the cup and the reader clicks on the word "ready," the sound of applause emerges, congratulating the child on finishing the reading/joke. This feature also "speaks" in the traditional way of electronic games, in that the child is commended when they are able to overcome an obstacle or pass to the next level of the game. Only after the sound of clapping, hence when the tea is ready, does the following poetic verse appear, merged with the steam: "Deixe a infusão o tempo necessário até que os nossos aromas e os nossos sabores se misturem" ("Leave the infusion for the necessary time for our aromas and flavors to mix"). This then is the reader's prize: a poem resulting from their interactive work with different elements presented earlier. There is, however, more to be said, for the recipe for making a pot of tea is a *script*. The details people learn about particular phenomena are organized within scripts, that is, the pre-stored knowledge representations that we use even in such simple tasks as making tea, and such scripts are in turn comparable to the always already existing plot structures that readers call upon to anticipate the unfolding story logic of creative works (Herman 2002: 89–91; Stephens 2011: 14). From here, it is a straightforward cognitive step to grasp, if only intuitively, that "o tempo necessário até que os nossos aromas e os nossos sabores se misturem" has a metaphorical significance: it refers to the process of understanding and savoring a poem, but also implicates the cognitive process by which scripts are used to comprehend and organize the world. The cyberpoem is not only entertaining, but enacts a top-down comprehension process which may serve to enhance the quality of children's knowledge structures.

Digital narrative for children

In the 1980s and 1990s, especially in the United States, there was intense discussion regarding new narrative forms based on hypertext, which led some authors to even refer to a new artistic and literary movement (e.g. Lister et al.: 2009: 26). *Afternoon, a story* became known as the first hypertext literary work, produced by Michael Joyce in 1987, constructed in a non-linear way to be read specifically in digital media. The hypertextuality of the work configures itself by the links available to the reader, which, by following certain pathways over others, creates a specific reading route and ends up, simultaneously, developing its own storyline with each new reading. Another eminent example of this type of work is *Twelve Blue*, also by Michael Joyce, (www.eastgate.com/TwelveBlue/). After the 1990s, many other forms of digital narrative directed towards adults emerged, in which hypertextuality has not always played such a key role (Hayles 2008).

Recently, the Spanish researcher Celia Turrión (2014) carried out an inventory of digital narratives produced for children in Castilian and concluded that there are predominantly four main types: audiobooks, hypermedia narratives, transmedia narratives and multimedia narratives. Audiobooks had already existed in CD format, and before that on cassette and vinyl. They are comprised of the narration of a previously written story, which can be dramatized by different actors, with sound effects and musical features. Hypermedia narratives, such as *Afternoon, a Story* and *Twelve Blue*, are a development from hypertext narratives and are multi-linear in structure. In this case, the reading pathway will always be defined by the reader's choices, with the possibility of accessing links constructed through verbal text (hypertext) or visual texts (hypermedia). Transmedia narratives, in turn, require the development of a plot through different platforms and may involve animation, electronic games, blogs and fan fiction sites, among others. Finally, multimedia narratives are characterized by adapting or creating a story using different media, usually animation and audiovisual features. In Brazil and the United States, this format seems to be the most predominantly used digital narrative for children.

One of the first narratives for children to be adapted for tablet with multimedia features, making it extremely popular, was *Alice in Wonderland*, produced in 2010 from the 1865 text by Lewis Carroll. This application has 250 pages with numerous original illustrations, fifty-two remastered pages and twenty animated scenes (Borràs 2012: 22). Many universal classics of children's literature have subsequently been adapted with multimedia features, which can mainly be explained by the strong appeal that these features have for a child as a form of entertainment and fun.

Thus, unlike that which happens with narratives directed towards adults, the interest in producing digital storytelling specifically for children is very recent and, internationally, is directly linked to the success in sales achieved by ebooks and other mobile devices. As Yokota (2013: 443) explains, "the rise of e-readers has impacted book sales, with adult ebook sales outpacing those of print books within the first few years that the devices were available." Even though this success has not yet been repeated in the case of books for children, the publishing market immediately identified the immense potential of sales linked to the production of digital works directed towards children and to be used on mobile devices. Thus, an increasing number of narratives for children are available for purchase at online stores such as the App Store, Google Play and Amazon, with the vast majority constructed with multimedia features.

In the international perspective, there are already some initiatives aimed at stimulating the production of digital works for children with high aesthetic quality. In 2012 the Bologna Children's Book Fair created the "Digital Ragazzi" Prize to recognize achievements in digital applications for children. In 2014, the "Bologna Digital" was launched at the Fair, the purpose of which was to encourage technology studios to produce quality applications, product and digital content. In Brazil, a similar initiative was taken in 2015 by the Câmara Brasileira do Livro (CBL) (the Brazilian Book Chamber), which included "children's digital books" amongst the categories that may win the famous Brazilian prize "Jabuti."

Nevertheless, so far, many works available in digital libraries seem to be much more aligned with commercial intent and less with aesthetic elaboration. Due to such a strong subordination to the market – even when the market is based upon projected expectations for the future – the commercial intentions of these narratives are frequently so explicit that they end up obliterating their own aesthetic-literary quality. Many of these are replete with devices seeking to draw the young reader into buying services and other applications, and which are thus superimposed on their literary enjoyment. In the *Alice in Wonderland – Interactive Children's Storybook HD* version, produced by TabTale TLD (2013), for example, the home page itself demonstrates the multimedia aspect of the work, as it allows the child to choose among "Auto Play," "Read It Myself" and "Read to Me" modes. However, what draws immediate attention is a certain visual pollution caused by icons such as "Store," in the upper right of the screen, "More Apps" in the bottom left as well as a banner in the bottom center, which sequentially advertises several other applications, seducing the young reader to instant purchasing.

The narrative itself is an extremely brief summary (eleven pages) of Carroll's work. On each page it is possible to make objects, animals and the central character perform certain movements and sounds by using touch screen. However, what most stands out is that the advertising banner from the home page appears on all of the other eleven pages of narrative. Similarly, the same items offered on the store home page are also present on the other pages, enticing the young reader to play with games and not just read the story. After clicking on this link, child users will receive offers to buy various products: more colors for the coloring game (coloring pages), puzzles, four *match it* type games, and they will also have the option to pay to remove the advertising banners.

The first research regarding production and sales of digital content by the Brazilian publishing sector was carried out in 2011 by Fundação Instituto de Pesquisas Econômicas (FIPE) (the Institute of Economic Research Foundation), commissioned by Câmara Brasileira do Livro (CBL) (the Brazilian Book Chamber) and Sindicato Nacional dos Editores de Livros (SNEL) (the National Union of Book Publishers). According to the most recent results, the selling of ebooks increased 3.5 times from 2011 to 2012, albeit with a total sales value less than 1 percent of the total sector revenues. During the 4th CBL International Conference of the Digital Book, a survey among delegates was carried out regarding themes such as copyright, commercial prospects and relations between the print and digital forms. One piece of data reveals that 58 percent of those editors interviewed still feel insecure about the technical format that they would adopt were they to enter this market, which is characterized as one of the main factors still preventing the expansion of the digital book market in Brazil (CBL Report, 2013). On the other hand, such reticence on the part of editors has not stopped the emergence of some digital narratives created specifically for Brazilian children.

One of the first works for children to be adapted for the tablet with multimedia features was a classic of Brazilian children's literature, Monteiro Lobato's *A menina do narizinho arrebitado* (The girl with the upturned nose). Basically, every illustrated page has some animated and sound feature that requires the interaction of the young reader in order to function. For example, on the second page of the story, the narrator explains, through verbal text, how every day the character Narizinho goes to the edge of a creek to observe the minnows. Practically repeating this information, the background of the page contains the image of a waterscape in which colorful fish continuously move. When a reader touches any of the fish with their finger, the fish move at great speed, as if they are fleeing, and a sound like dripping water emerges.

The remaining pages contain similar features, which generally perform merely an illustrative function in relation to the verbal narrative. On the other hand, to the extent that such features require a certain level of interaction by the reader, they additionally fulfill the function of entertainment and recreation, rendering the children's book to be more similar to a toy or game. On the page in which two insects meet on Narizinho's nose, for example, one of them tickles the main character with its walking stick, making her sneeze. In the illustration, if the reader touches Narizinho's nose, this provokes the character to sneeze, which can not only be heard but also seen in a short animation.

Another very common characteristic of multimedia adaptations is the introduction of small games or playful activities that do not fulfill the function of illustrating the story, but of entertaining the reader. For example, in the Brazilian adaptation of the classic *O pequeno príncipe* (The Little Prince), from the translation by renowned Brazilian poet Ferreira Gullar, the story is interspersed with some activities that interrupt the narrative thread, inviting the young reader to simply play by coloring or drawing. In the one example, the child is challenged to paint an image of the Little Prince, choosing the correct colors for his clothes according to a small model on the top left of the page. In another example, the story is interrupted so that the child can complete the drawing of a sheep, connecting the numbered dots by touching the screen with their fingers.

New scenarios for children's literature

In the field of literary criticism, discussions regarding how this situation is affecting readers have been intense, diverse and often polarized. The main disputes revolve, on one side, around the "future of books" in face of the proliferation of digital books – which were supposedly able to replace the printed book. On the other hand, there have been heated discussions about the "future of reading and literature itself," mainly due to the hybridization of verbal text with multimedia and hypermedia features, as was observed in the poems and the digital narratives presented in the previous sections.

A very brief overview of the first discussion reveals that some authors believe that it is only a matter of time before the printed book completely ceases to exist, giving way to different formats of digital books, while others predict the coexistence of digital and printed media. The main arguments in favor of the first position gravitate around the facilities, comfort and low cost of digital books when compared to printed books. Junko Yokota, for example, suggests that, "It's hard to argue against the appeal of digital reading, given that it is more accessible, convenient, and affordable" (2013: 444). On the other hand, Umberto Eco insists on the superiority of the printed book in contrast to the rapid obsolescence of technologies produced as alternatives to printed media:

> We have seen that modern media quickly become obsolete. Why run the risk of choosing objects that may become mute and indecipherable? It is proven that books are superior to every other object that our cultural industries have put on the market in recent years. So, wanting to choose something easily transportable and that has shown itself equal to the ravages of time, I choose the book.
>
> (Eco, 2012: 36)

Disputes about the future of reading and literature produce even more fierce and polarized discussion. One of the most renowned and popular enthusiasts of new forms of reading connected to the digital domain is the North American George P. Landow. In the third edition of his classic *Hypertext 3.0*, Landow (2006: 125) affirms that hypertext "infringes upon the power of the writer, removing some of it and granting it to the reader." In Landow's view, and those who adhere to his opinion, the reading provided by the culture of printed media is monological and authoritarian since it concentrates all the construction activity of the text in the hands of the author, whereas hypertext transforms the reader into an active participant and thus promotes a more democratic culture.

In contrast to this euphoric perspective on the supposed benefits of hypertext, several studies within the field of cognitive sciences have shown evidence that, unlike sequential and linear texts, hypertext and hypermedia demand higher resources of working memory from the reader, since they make it necessary to simultaneously process information represented in nodes and plan (further) navigation. Due to a natural limitation of the human working memory, this kind of reading (and learning) process is prone to cause cognitive overhead (also referred to as "lost-in-hyperspace"-phenomenon) and cognitive load, which may inhibit learning (Zumbach and Mohraz 2008: 876).

In this context, reading experiments carried out by researchers such as DeStefano and LeFevre showed that increased demands of decision making and visual processing in hypertext impair reading performance (DeStefano, LeFevre 2005: 1616). Studies carried out by Niederhauser, Reynolds, Salmen, and Skolmoski lead to the conclusion that "learners using a sequential and almost linear information retrieval show higher learning success than participants using a non-linear browsing strategy" (cited in Zumbach Mohraz 2008: 876). In addition, studies cited by Fesel et al. (2015: 136) revealed that "rather than 'reading' the digital text features (i.e., embedded hyperlinks in the text or graphical and navigable overviews), readers prefer to 'browse' nonlinearly through the sections, jumping from one text section to another." On the other hand, Zumbach and Mohraz postulate that, in the light of Cognitive Load Theory, the additional cognitive effort demanded by hypertext/hypermedia does not necessarily lead to learning failure. According to these researchers, once readers of hypertext learn how to "reflect upon their prior knowledge in order to make decisions about navigation" (Zumbach, Mohraz 2008: 876), they may even reach more elaborate levels of reading and learning.

It seems, then, that very polarized arguments regarding reading processes, literature and the book run the risk of assuming essentialist and deterministic positions. From this perspective, changes and displacements tend to be either considered as a degrading diversion or as an evolutionary improvement over an archetypal model; a fixed and unchanging essence which would define literature and the book in terms of an idealized scheme. Nevertheless, history has shown that the technology used over time to read and write has never been fixed, having undergone several changes and displacements. The field of children's literature is a relatively recent phenomenon, having only emerged over the seventeenth and eighteenth centuries in Europe.

Furthermore, recent research regarding how culture is received has demonstrated that consumption of any such representation does not have the power to change the consuming subjects in a direct, linear or mechanical way. The way readers effectively take ownership of the various texts at their disposal, producing their own identities, is always regulated by different social forces, power struggles, cultural backgrounds and idiosyncrasies attached to each individual.

According to Fesel et al., research on children's digital text comprehension is still very limited and "there is no consensus on the positive or negative effects of hypertext reading on reading comprehension" (2015: 136). In a study of how children structure their knowledge representations across different digital text types – linear digital text, digital text with overview, hypertext, and hypertext with overview – the researchers examined the similarity of the children's knowledge structures with a sequential model as well as with an expert (hierarchical) model in the four digital text types. It was found among others that "children accomplished the same comprehension scores in all four digital text types, which is consistent with previous research on hierarchical hypertext with adults and children" (Fesel et al., 2015: 141).

Thus, in order to avoid deterministic predictions and premonitions, perhaps the best procedure to analyze what is occurring in children's literature in the world of digital culture is to describe some of the ongoing changes. In this sense, the analysis of digital poems and narratives addressing children allows us to perceive a complex mix of technology and taste, culture and commerce, pointing to what Henry Jenkins has called convergence culture. As Jenkins argues (2006: 235), corporate media soon recognized the potential of cyberspace to expand their consumer base, promoting a specific type of participatory culture, and children's literature is not immune to the same logic.

The ease with which a digitized or digital work can migrate through different media and, furthermore, can hybridize with other texts and pictures from the utilization of relatively easy to use tools, is also producing in the literary field what Henry Jenkins (225) calls convergence between different cultures – in this case, mainly among literary, media and consumer cultures. This phenomenon can easily be observed from the examples of poems for children and digital narratives presented in this article because the very structure of these works reveals a strong hybridization among literature, electronic games intended for entertainment, and consumption.

Jenkins contends that participatory culture promoted by media convergence is revealed in two ways: on the one hand there is participation deliberately produced by corporations, which believe they can (or desire to) control their consumers; on the other hand, however, readers, in some cases, tend to produce their own, often creative dynamic, which may come into conflict with the interests of the corporations.

Within this context, it is possible to conclude that both the book and children's literature are subject to displacements and changes, which are still ongoing. New literary forms and new reading media continue to appear and be changed, and this is a process that has occurred in a context of constant negotiations between artistic and commercial interests, and that seems to be converging ever more intensely in the universe of digital culture.

Bibliography

Antonio, Jorge Luis (2008) *Poesia eletrônica: negociações com os processos digitais*, São Paulo & Belo Horizonte: Veredas e Cenários.

Borràs Castanyer, Laura (2012) "Había una vez una app… Literatura infantil y juvenil (en) digital," *Revista de Literatura Nuevas Tecnologías y LIJ*, 269: 21–26.

Câmara Brasileira Do Livro (2014) *Relatório Anual 2013*, São Paulo: Via Impressa Edições de Arte Ltda.

Campos, Augusto, Haroldo Campos and Décio Pignatari (1986) "Plano-piloto para poesia concreta," in Gilberto Mendonça Teles (ed.), *Vanguarda europeia e modernismo brasileiro*. Petrópolis: Vozes.

DeStefano, Diana, and Jo-Anne LeFevre (2007) "Cognitive Load in Hypertext Reading: A Review," *Computers in Human Behavior*, 23: 1616–1641.

Eco, Umberto, and Jean-Claude Carrière (2012) *This is Not the End of the Book: A Conversation Curated by Jean-Philippe de Tonnac*, London: Harvill Secker.

Fesel, Sabine S., Eliane Segersa, Roy B. Clarianab and Ludo Verhoevena (2015) "Quality of Children's Knowledge Representations in Digital Text Comprehension: Evidence from Pathfinder Networks," *Computers in Human Behavior*, 48: 135–146.

Hayles, N. Katherine (2008) *Electronic Literature: New Horizons for the Literary*, Indiana: University of Notre Dame.

Herman, David (2002) *Story Logic: Problems and Possibilities of Narrative*, Lincoln, NB: University of Nebraska Press.

Jenkins, Henry (2006) *Convergence Culture: Where Old and New Media Collide*, New York & London: New York University Press.

Landow, George P. (2006) *Hypertext 3.0: Critical Theory and New Media in an Era of Globalization*, Baltimore: The John Hopkins University Press.

Lister, Martin, Jon Dovey, Seth Giddings, Iain Grant and Kieran Kelly (2009) *New Media: A Critical Introduction*, London & New York: Routledge.

Manovich, Lev (2001) *The Language of New Media*, Cambridge & Massachusetts: The MIT Press.

Stephens, John (2011) "Schemas and Scripts: Cognitive Instruments and the Representation of Cultural Diversity in Children's Literature," in Kerry Mallan and Clare Bradford (eds.), *Contemporary Children's Literature and Film*, London: Palgrave Macmillan, 12–35.

Turrión, Celia (2014) "Narrativa digital para niños: otras formas de contar," *Literatura em Revista*, 5(Feb.): 47–58

Yokota, Junko (2013) "From Print to Digital? Considering the Future of Picturebooks for Children," in G. Grilli (ed.), *Bologna: Fifty years of Children's Books from around the World*. Bologna: Bononia University Press, 443–449.

Zumbach, Joerg, and Maryam Mohraz (2008) "Cognitive Load in Hypermedia Reading Comprehension: Influence of Text Type and Linearity," *Computers in Human Behavior*, 24: 875–887.

Digital Works

Caparelli, Sérgio and Ana Cláudia Gruszynski. *Ciberpoesia*. www.ciberpoesia.com.br/

Carroll, Lewis. *Alice in Wonderland*. TabTale (App).

Lago, Angela. *O ABCD de Angela Lago*. www.angela-lago.com.br/ABCD.html

Lobato, Monteiro. *A menina do narizinho arrebitado*. Ilustrações de Rogério Coelho. São Paulo: Globo (App).

Saint-Exupéry, Antoine. *O pequeno príncipe*. Tradução de Ferreira Gullar. São Paulo: Agir (App)

PART IV

Traditional story and adaptation

25

"M'RIDDLE, M'RIDDLE, M'YANDAY, O"

Folktales of the Bahamas as signposts of heritage and as children's literature

Patricia Glinton-Meicholas

Oral tradition or orature, encompassing such elements as folktales, legends, beliefs, superstitions, myths, cosmology, songs, proverbs, jokes, riddles and rhymes is a global phenomenon, its advent likely coterminous with humankind's acquisition of language. Folktales and storytelling, the dominant aspect of folklore, are now widely accepted into a more flexible definition of "literature" and rightly so. They are as much inventions of human creativity as any written material. They can also yield valuable information about the origins, ethos and relationships of the peoples who produce such cultural artifacts, especially as regards preliterate societies and those where access to print is limited by poverty or repression. Inevitably, folktales must also play a role in any examination of children's literature; they have delighted youngsters for countless generations across the globe and most certainly throughout the 700-island Bahamas archipelago.

This essay examines the "ol' story" of The Bahamas, which dominated the Bahamian storyteller's repertoire, entertaining and edifying children and adults alike. Such traditional narratives once captured the attention of such eminent folklorists as Elsie Clews Parsons, Zora Neal Hurston and Daniel Crowley. This essay eschews what Gilroy terms "ethnic absolutism" (1995: 1), which has often been central to the rhetoric of nationalist projects of the "black Atlantic." My intention is rather to give due weight to the predominance of the African heritage in the Caribbean area and acknowledge the formative dialectic, however tainted, between Europe and Africa in the regional psyche and creative production. To fail to recognize the reality of "creolization, métissage, mestizaje and hybridity" (Gilroy 1995: 2) is to do a great disservice to the genius of the enslaved scions of Africa and their descendants who forged distinct New World identities despite the countervailing brutalities of bondage and the exclusionary practices of colonialism.

As far as possible, I compare Bahamian folktale tradition to those of Africa and countries within the New World African diaspora, sourced from respected collections. Bahamian references are drawn primarily from my research and first-hand knowledge of the oral tradition. The comparison demonstrates that kinship with places as distant from The Bahamas as Guyana, Belize and Brazil, sealed by shared African bloodlines, ethos and customs, still emerges from beneath the heavy cultural coats imposed by physical distance and colonial compartmentalization. Finally, the folktales will be reviewed to assess how they address the world view, aspirations and entertainment needs of children.

First, a soupçon of the history of the region is needed to explain the origins of the far-flung relationships claimed above. The first European power to dominate and create a Carib-American network was Spain, whose imperium began when in 1492 Christopher Columbus landed on the Bahamian island then called "Guanahaní" and claimed it for the Spanish monarchs. Spain extended its dominion to the entire New World, but by the end of the seventeenth century all the major powers of Northwestern Europe—Portugal, England, France and the Netherlands had gained strongholds in the Caribbean.

By the mid-seventeenth century, Caribbean planters began cultivating agricultural gold— sugar— enslaving millions of West African men, women and children as the labor force, an exploitation that would span two centuries. As Philip Sherlock observed, "Sugar and the slave trade led to the Africanization of the Caribbean" (2005: vi). This sustained African presence and the administrative and social constructs imposed by colonial mandate created a Caribbean culture area, which Donald R. Hill defines as

> All the islands between the Bahamas and Trinidad in the Caribbean, together with certain mainland countries in the Americas where there reside minorities who share cultural features with the peoples of the Caribbean.
>
> (2007: 7)

For The Bahamas, the relationship with the United States is significant owing to proximity and the resettlement in the archipelago of about 8,000 American loyalists, mostly Southerners, white and black, enslaved and free, following Britain's defeat in the American War of Independence.

Caribbean area demographics were further shaped by an influx of uncreolized Africans. Following the abolition of the slave trade in 1807, the British patrolled the transatlantic slave trade routes, interdicting slavers and resettling captives by the thousands in British colonies such as The Bahamas. Despite the trauma of displacement, the imposition of foreign customs and limited access to education, enslaved Africans and, later, the indentured Asians who boosted the post-emancipation labor force, still managed to self-define significantly in the new environment. Among their most powerful tools were the oral transmission of homeland traditions and the creation of New World lore.

Origins of the Bahamian ol' story

For a long time, Western scholarship tended to devalue the genius of the Caribbean imports, especially that of Africans. As they played havoc with the preemptive assignment of inferiority to things African that justified slavery, ol' story and other African oral narratives were often attributed to others such as the Portuguese. Alan Dundes pointed out that early interest among American folklorists in African folk narrative "stemmed from a concern with the possible origins of African-American folktales. ... Racist bias was unfortunately a factor in the arguments that ensued. Some 'scholars' maintained that African-Americans were an 'imitative' people and must have borrowed their tales from either Native Americans or Euro-Americans" (1992: x). Elsie Clews Parsons, while persuaded of Portuguese provenance, remarked nevertheless upon "resemblances between the Bahama and the Cape Verde Islands tales, not only in patterns but in many minor details." (Parsons: xii).

Yet, several Americans collecting or writing about the Bouki and Rabbit stories of the Southern United States in the nineteenth century credited authorship to African-Americans. William Owens observed:

> Travellers and missionaries tell us that...the same wild stories of Buh Rabbit, Buh Wolf, and other Buhs that are so charming in the ears of American children, are to be heard to this day in Africa, different only in the drapery needed to the change of scene
> ("The Folklore of the Southern Negroes," *Lippincott Magazine*, December 1877)

Analysis of folktales he collected in The Bahamas led American biology professor Charles Edwards to conclude that, "The genetic relation existing between the tales and music of the Bahama and of the United States negroes will be readily discerned. Parallels from accessible collections of American, and of native African, folk-lore are indicated" (1942 [1895]: 7). Courlander furthers this perspective with the argument that the folktales of the black Atlantic are "products not only of their African past but of the European cultures on which they have so heavily drawn and, most important of all, of their unique collective experience in the New World" (1976: 2).

The products of this encounter of disparate cultures were not mere calques or amalgams. As with Caribbean creoles, they became new creations, bearing unique territorial markers. This legacy has created a shared cultural grammar or, at least, a mutual intelligibility among the traditional canons of communities where African descendants predominate or are significant. It is equally evident that Bahamian stories are products of a land that has long been a kind of transition/translation node between North America and the Caribbean.

Through the ground-breaking work of William Bascom, African origins are now commonly acknowledged. Alan Dundes called the evidence "incontrovertible" (1992: xv). Bascom identified, widespread in the Americas, twenty-two tale types for which he found cognates nowhere else but in Africa. For "Entering Cow's (Elephant's) Belly," Bascom identified sixty-two versions from Africa, the United States, the Caribbean, including nine from The Bahamas. (83–103). There is remarkable consonance between the Bahamian version of "Entering Cow's Belly" and the Hausa tale "Gizo and the Cow," as retold by Tata Tambai (2014). The Bahamian passwords are: "Open kabunkus, open" and "Close kabunkus, close"; the Hausa: "Saniya-saniya open your vulva for me to enter" and "Saniya-Saniya close your vulva." Bascom also found twenty-five versions of "Agreement to Kill Mothers," linking West Africa, the United States, The Bahamas and Guadeloupe (201–211).[1] Glinton-Meicholas recorded this tale in Crooked Island, Bahamas in 1982. Haiti has produced more than a hundred versions of the story "Mother of Waters," which has cognates in the region and in Africa (Wolkstein 1978: 152 and Glinton-Meicholas 1994: 39–49).

Functions of the Bahamian folktale

Best defined and persistent in places where entertainment was limited, Bahamian storytelling, in its heyday, had a quadruple function—practical, didactic, satirical and

251

aesthetic. In the extended workday of agricultural communities, storytelling invigoratec the evening hours. Michael Craton and Gail Saunders noted:

> The pantomime quality of old stories and their power to enliven and lighten a drab and oppressive existence are obvious. Their richness and adaptability to local conditions and events made them an essentially Bahamian art form.
>
> (2000: 124)

Without being catechetical, Bahamian stories were intended to transmit to children the values and ethos of the community and to warn of the dangers of straying from them. Yet, injecting fun and laughter clearly took precedence in storyteller motivation. The tales underscored an equally profound *raison d'être*. They channeled safe subversion, mocking "ol' massa" during slavery and poking fun at the white elite in the racist societies thereafter.

Ol' story: setting, character, plot, theme and style

The Bahamian ol' story follows basic global conventions. The story setting is what Stith Thompson called a "chimerical world" (1977: 8), peopled by tricksters, obeah women, children good, bad and heroic, ghosts or "sperrits," the devil, shape changers and anthropomorphic animals. Opening and closing formulae create borders that insulate the stories from the intrusion of reality. Yet, in contradiction, verification formulae, spoken in closing, leave audiences in no doubt that the tales are fiction.

Ol' story themes usually address good and evil in stark opposition, reinforcing behaviors that are essential to the preservation of community. Primacy is given to love between parents and children. Respect for elders and kindness to outcasts are richly rewarded, while departure from this ideal is severely punished (Glinton-Meicholas 1994: 39–49). Speaking to their iconic nature, characters are usually activated by a single passion: greed, love, fear, hatred or jealousy. In the settlement of conflict, magic and spirits often parallel the *deus ex machina* of Greek mythology, with the number three as prime operant in the release of magic and in plot development.

Although traditional motifs formed the tale skeleton, creative storytellers added brilliant flesh, incorporating local color and preoccupations, stage props and sound effects, including brief songs (termed "sings" in Jamaica and The Bahamas), which introduced characters, advanced the story action or created dramatic tension. Fundamental to Bahamian tradition is the storyteller's evocation of character by gesture, gait and speech characteristics. Troubled by a variety of speech impediments, "sperrits" in Bahamian lore, like Jamaica's version of Ananse, always speak with a lisp (Jekyll 2005: 2). Bahamian revenants add a nasality that became chilling for those sitting in a well of firelight surrounded by the impenetrable darkness of a moonless night. Without such theatrical devices, storytelling is noticeably bereft. Richard Spears noted:

> There is a considerable difference between a West African folktale told in situ and a simple narrative or storyline…Next to being there in person and participating, only a video recording could provide a satisfactory record of the events that are part of the traditional West African storytelling session.
>
> (in Berry 1991: 2)

Signposts of African and diasporic kinship

Even a cursory examination of folktales from Africa and the Caribbean complex demonstrates similarities beyond coincidence, while revealing sufficient divergence to evidence a dynamic creativity among the Caribbean patchwork of ethnicities. Announced with the formula "M'riddle, m'riddle, m'yanday, O. My father has a thing" in The Bahamas, introductory riddling is shared with Jamaicans (see Tanna 1984: 48). Many of the same riddles appear in the orature of both peoples, a legacy of Africa. On the other hand, the closing and verification statements of the tales are obviously drawn from European tradition. The commonest Bahamian closing is some form of "Be bo ben / My story is en'". From the American South comes: "I stepped on a piece of tin / The tin bended / My story ended" (Hartsfeld 1987: 129). And: "I go around the bend / I see a fence to mend / In it is hung my story end" (Hamilton 1995: 6). A Bahamian example of a verification formula goes: "I was standin' one side listenin', when I catch a blow and it knock me right here to tell you this story/lie"; from Haiti: "And she gave me such a kick in the pants that that's how I got here today, to tell you this story..." (Wolkstein 1978: 21); and from South Georgia: "Of course I couldn't hang around because I had on paper clothes, and I was afraid the wind might blow or it might rain. So, I suppose that he's running yet" (Hartsfeld 1987: 57).

The universal subject of wicked second spouses, guardians and step-parents occurs frequently in Bahamian tales and in Caribbean-area canons. Trials by ordeal, especially at the hands of abusive step-mothers, are common. A Bahamian story (Glinton-Meicholas 1994: 83–90) recounts the sufferings of three young sisters, whose adoptive mother works them hard but withholds food. When the hungry children consume a pot of peas, their angry guardian tries to extract a confession with the aid of the "River of Truth," which will engulf them if they lie. The girls reply with this song:

> *I'n eat no peas*
> *I'n tellin' no lie*
> *'cause if I eat my mama peas*
> *sure the river guh swaller me.*

In the Liberian tale of "Gboloto and the River Demon," the disavowal is:

> *Ma, if that is me eat*
> *the rice and the soup, frypan*
> *must carry me down, and*
> *Gboloto must eat me.*
>
> (Gale 1996: 77)

Stories of a river menacing a character for lying or lack of generosity are also told in Jamaica, as in the following song:

> If a me tief me Muma peas n rice
> Mek de riba wash me way
> If a me tief me Muma peas n rice
> Mek de riba wash me way.
>
> (Tanna 1984: 69–70)

Gruesome in its resolution, another such tale deals with bones or birds, which speak to redress the murder of an abused child. In the Bahamian tale a homicidal step-mother kills her husband's beloved daughter and buries her under the father's favorite pepper tree. When anyone attempts to harvest the chilies, the child's bones sing of the crime.

The motif of this Bahamian story is an example of a European/African connection to New World storytelling. It was collected by the Brothers Grimm and belongs to tale type 780 in the Aarne-Thompson index. The story has cognates in Africa, Louisiana, Cuba, Haiti and Brazil, as inter-territorial relationships are often reflected in tale songs.

In "La Mata de Higo" from Cuba, when the girl is entombed alive by her step-mother a strand of her hair protrudes and a beautiful rose bush sprouts from it, bearing one rose. When her brother tries to pick it, the bush cries:

> *Hermanito, hermanito, no me aranques el pelito*
> *Nicolasa me ha enterrado por un higo que ha faltado*
> (Little brother, little brother, please don't pull my hair,
> Nicolasa buried me for one fig missing from the tree)
> (Hayes 2008: 22–27)

In the Bahamian story the song is almost identical:

> *Do my brother don't pull my hair*
> *Do my brother don't pull my hair*
> *My mother killed me for one fig.*

An analogue also appears in the Brazilian folktale, "The Singing Grasses" (Almeida and Portella 2006: 73–74):

> My father's gardener
> Please don't cut my hair.
> My mother combed me,
> my stepmother buried me,
> for the figs of the fig tree
> that the birds have eaten away.
> Birds, please, go away.

The tale may have different outcomes, however. In the Cuban and Brazilian versions, the child survives her ordeal, but in other versions is killed. In "The Singing Bones" (Louisiana) and "The Singing Bone" (Haiti), the evil step-mother murders the children and feeds their flesh to their father, but her crime is now revealed by the singing bones of the children:

Louisiana	Haiti
Our stepmother killed us	Oh brother mine, come close to me,
Our papa ate us	Oh brother mine, listen now to me:
We are not in a coffin	Stepmother killed me
We are not in the cemetery	Father ate me
Holy, holy, holy	Here I lie
(Reneaux 2005: 158–164)	(Wolkstein 1978: 92–97)

The strong parallel between the two tales, especially in the monstrosity of the father's induced cannibalizing of his own children, is perhaps not unexpected in that Haiti and

Louisiana shared cultural ties in that both were under French colonial domination, a connection that was strengthened with the post-revolution flight of thousands of Haitians to Louisiana and other parts of the United States.

"Sings" can, on the other hand, also reflect unique territorial divergences, affirming community/storyteller creativity. In the Bahamian river trial story (Glinton-Meicholas 1994: 83–89) a goat sings an identification song which has been found nowhere else to date.

> Say man a go, say man a go
> Say man a go, pity man a go
> Some say me de cobbler
> Some say me de seamster
> Some say me de cobbler
> Some say me de seamster.
> (1994: 88)

In a Haitian story a mother searches for her kidnapped daughters and mourns:

> *One cannot come to Mama,*
> *Two cannot come to Mama,*
> *Three cannot come to Mama,*
> *Philamandré is*
> *Where she is.*
> (Wolkstein 1978: 166–170)

In the Bahamian version, the distraught mother who loses two daughters keens:

> *Sintana, muh Jinny, Oh muh Jinny,*
> *I wonder where Sintana gone,*
> *I wonder where muh Jinny,*
> *In this world of sorrow.*

Regional tales are governed by cosmology, powers and a moral code which, while implacable in meting out justice, do not follow Judeo-Christian tenets, a divergence exemplified by the exploits of Bahamian tricksters Bouki and Rabby and the Caribbean-wide Ananse and his dupes. Although all are con artists and thieves, master tricksters Rabby and Ananse are always victorious. What seems unjust can be explained by the fact that trickster and foil are boilerplates for the cleverness and self-preservation prized in subaltern societies, while stupidity and gross intemperance are despised. The trickster and his foil/dupe thus occupied a special place in the liberation mythology of the black Atlantic. Emily Zobel Marshall, like many others who study the tricksters of the African Atlantic diaspora, perceives in Ananse tales a subtext aimed at "undermining the imperial powers, psychologically, culturally and practically" (Marshall 2012: 180)

The same can be said of the Bahamian trickster Rabby, the ultimate survivalist, who laughs scornfully when he defeats antagonists who began with the advantage. Brer Rabbit/Compère Lapin[2] is widely dispersed across the Caribbean and the United States but his dupes vary widely: Zamba (the French Caribbean), Tiger (Dominica and Trinidad and Tobago), Fox (Georgia), Wolf (Virginia), Coyote (Oklahoma), etc. (Bascom 1992: 92–93, #18–24). In contrast, the Rabbit and Bouki (variants Booky/Bouqui/Buqui) combination is a distinguishing feature of Bahamian lore. So far, this pairing has turned up in five other places only: in their homeland, Africa's Senegambia region, as Leuk, le Lievre and Bouki, the Hyena; Haiti where Rabbit is addressed as "Ti Malice"; the Dominican Republic, Louisiana and in Missouri (Carrière 1937: 29–36). The name "Bouki" is retained also in St Lucia as a pejorative, meaning "stupid," "good-for-nothing" [3] and "Bookay" appears as a password in Georgia.

Keith Cartwright has done much to trace the Senegambian presence in the region, and his work suggests that The Bahamas may have been a transmission node for Senegambian culture via Georgia. He notes also: "A close reading of Bahamian folktales shows their closest matches to be the Geechee reworkings of Wolof, Fulbe, and Mande folk reper toires." He further explains that, "The Nassau slave market shared the Savannah and Charleston markets' demand for Senegambians, creating a strong Senegalese presence that was massively reinvigorated by arriving Gullah and Geechee slaves. Since many of the Loyalist whites returned to Georgia after several years with their Geechee slaves and with newly bought slaves from the Bahamas, the circuits of cultural exchange between Senegambia, Georgia, and the Bahamas are indeed complex" (Cartwright 2005: n.p.).

Anthropomorphic beings, all female and fearsome, constitute one of the singularities of Bahamian folklore. Bahamian shape shifters include Pinky Whya, the tiger woman, the Gaulin, and the Hag or "Ole Higue." The latter occurs in tales across the Caribbean area from Belize to Guyana. In former French colonies—Dominica, St. Lucia, Grenada, Trinidad and Tobago, Haiti and Louisiana—she goes by the name soucouyant or loo-garou (loup garou). Human by day, the members of this frightful sorority, vampires all, turn into a skin-shedding creature traveling as a fireball to carry out terrifying nighttime violations. These creatures share a single vulnerability. Their skin, once removed, must be hidden from potential pursuers. If discovered and salted, the bloodsucker cannot don it again and, exposed to the light of day uncovered, she dies. In contrast, the shape shifter "Medeo" in the Louisiana story "Fifolet" (feu follet) (Reneaux 2005: 141–144) is male, but he shares the key weakness—vulnerability to sunlight.

Chief among the shape shifters in Bahamian lore is the Gaulin, who, in her beautiful human form, marries a man to his destruction when he discovers that her true nature is that of a great raptor bird. Glinton-Meicholas' retelling of the tale features Gaulin's self-introductory, chilling song found nowhere else: "When de pond plonga, plonga, meetee B'er Sea Crab, plonga, plonga, meetee B'er Gaulin, plonga, plonga." (Glinton-Meicholas 1994: 137–148). Jamaicans also have a gaulin character, who marries a human being, but diverges sharply from the Bahamian model, and refers to a different bird species. In The Bahamas the bird called "gaulin" is, in all likelihood, the great blue heron (*Ardea herc-dias*), whereas the "gaulin" in Jamaica is the little green heron (*Butorides virescens*). The Jamaican creature is male, is not fearsome and sings an entirely different song:

> My iddy, my iddy Pyang halee
> Come go da river go Pyang, me
> Yahky yahky Pyang me jewahlee Pyang
> (Jekyll: 75–77)

One of the rarest of the fabulous creatures in African diasporic folklore is the guard-ian of the forest, a dwarf with a hairy, yellow-skinned body, red eyes, and backwards-turned feet. He is chickcharnie or Nyancoo in The Bahamas, Tata Duende in Belize (Eberhart 2002: 150–51) and curupira in Brazil (Almeida and Portella 2006: 41–42).

By his distinct body characteristics, he is likely a descendant of abotsia of Fanti tradition or Mmoatia of Asante lore (Reginald Kodjo Awotwe Mensah Yates, personal communication).

Among the greatest distinctions of Bahamian lore were cante fables, all but erased in a general attrition of traditional storytelling. "Miss Annie" centers on a well-to-do widow and the despicable man who woos her. To gain entry to Miss Annie's house and her favor, the cad kills her guard dog. He sings:

Miss Annie, O, Miss Annie, O
Open the door, Miss Annie, O.

The ghost of the dog answers:

Oh, no! Oh, no!
Since my old master died
Nobody dares to come in.

The specter of the Miss Annie's dead husband joins in:

My wife, my wife told me three days ago
That she would not marry no more
But by the light of the key hole I spy
There's a man lying down in my brown cotton, brown cotton drawers.
(Partial transcription, Glinton-Meicholas 1994: 17)

Ol' story as children's literature

Along with tales from Holy Scripture, ol' stories served as the first literature for Bahamian children of African descent. As noted previously, they inculcated the values of the community, provided a rich source of entertainment and that chimerical space, the secret garden, which permits healing retreat from the challenges of reality and bestows power. Ol' story themes elevate elders as sources of wisdom and guardians and purveyors of community power. In the story of Jack and the Magic Eggs, when Jack rides to rescue his sister from B'er Debbil, his mother provides him with the eggs that will release magic to overcome the powerful kidnapper (Glinton-Meicholas 1994: 117–124). Moreover, the elements of laughter-provoking, cartoonish ridiculousness, the Cinderella reward system recompensing good characters and meting out humiliation to the antisocial ones are the stuff of child-salving psychology and satisfaction.

The appeals to children were pronounced in the structure of storytelling sessions and included specific provisions for drawing children into active participation, as with the child-encompassing riddling. Adults would present riddles, mostly as metaphorical statements, some traditional: "Every time the wind blow, Anansy coattail tear" (banana leaf)—others improvised according to the wit of the riddlers. Children would be invited to guess and to offer riddles. Although the child-generated examples were often simple, the older members of the story circle would pretend that they were stumped, miming discomfort, adding to childish glee. As Isidore Okpewho notes, such sessions test children's wit and their knowledge of their people, customs, culture and environment (in Makuchi, 2008: xviii).

Bahamian opening formulae provided a further opportunity for a child's participation and anticipation of delight. One of the favorites of Bahamian lore was

> Once upon a time was a very good time
> Monkey chew tobakker an' spit white lime
> Bullfrog jump from limb to limb
> An' mosquiter keep up the time.

To increase the humor of ridiculousness and fantasy, storytellers would vary the "jumper" and the "timekeeper." Child-entrancing humor is further enhanced with the pratfalls and compromised positions of trickster dupes, such as Bouki. Furthermore, the "sings" of Bahamian stories, rhyming and onomatopoea invite children to join in. A gifted story-teller produces as exciting a folk theatre as any Punch and Judy show, enabling the best of them to insert themselves and their audience, especially the children, into the action of the tale.

Children, firm believers in poetic justice, have no trouble accepting the utter humiliation of wicked stepmothers. Neither do youngsters care much for political correctness, which explains the popularity of the cataclysmic battles of superheroes in films. Bahamian children have derived much enjoyment from the beatings visited upon the intemperate. Many ol' story heroes are clever children, permitting a young audience to gain a psychic measure of control over situations that would normally be hopelessly beyond their influence. In "The Devil Schoolmaster" (Glinton-Meicholas 1994: 69–82) and other Jack tales, the young hero exhibits all the hero's attributes. He is analytical and quick to create a solution that will save him and his fellow captives from the devil's cannibalistic intent. Such narratives usually feature hair-raising chases that are the stuff of childhood fiction.

Highlighted in many Bahamian traditional stories is the bond and love between parent and child, addressing and soothing a number of common fears among children, such as being separated from their parents, suffering abuse or dying. Moreover, the physical connectedness of the storytelling circle echoes the protection of family and community.

It is clear that the Caribbean complex rose above the trauma of its birth from the unshriven marriage between Europe and Africa to endow the world with unique gifts, not least in the realm of orature. Unfortunately, under the impetus of the powerful nationalist thrust which characterized regional decolonization, there tended to be a concomitant promotion of cultural absolutism as the foundation of national identity, denying extraterritorial relationships. Moreover, orature has lost ground to the insistent intrusions of electronic media and global trade. Fortunately, the twenty-first century is witnessing a tentative promotion of regional commonalities and cooperation, together with a more honest view of roots in defining identity. More books are drawing on Caribbean area oral traditions and finding their way into schools and libraries in the region and beyond. It is well worth preserving the folktales of The Bahamas and sister traditions of the Caribbean as artifacts of human endurance and enduring kinship and as validation of the creative contributions Africa and its Atlantic diaspora have made to world patrimony.

Notes

1 See also the discussion of an Nso retelling of this tale in the essay by Vivian Yenika-Agbaw in this volume, 303–4.

2 "La Pain" in Guadeloupe, Martinique, Les Saintes, Marie Galante, Dominica, Trinidad and St. Lucia (Bascom: 86, 99–100) and "Lapen" in the Dominican Republic (Bascom: 96, #37), an obvious, Haitian-influenced hispanicizing of the French "lapin".

3 M. Margot Thomas, National Archivist of St Lucia, conversation with Patricia Glinton-Meicholas, 22 June 2014 at the 44th ACURIL Congress, Nassau, Bahamas.

Bibliography

Almeida, Livia de and Ana Portella (2006) *Brazilian Folktales* (World Heritage Series), ed. Margaret Read MacDonald, Westport, Connecticut and London: Libraries Unlimited, A member of the Greenwood Publishing Group.

Bascom, William (1992) *African Folktales in the New World*, Bloomington: Indiana University Press.

Berry, Jack (1991) *West African Folktales*, ed. Richard Spears, Evanston: Northwestern University Press.

Carrière, Joseph Medard (1937) *Tales from the French Folklore of Missouri*, Evanston: Northwestern University Press.

Cartwright, Keith (2005) "Bugs Bunny Gone Global: The Senegambian Roots of Gullah Culture and 'Hippikat': Migrations to the Bahamas, Trinidad, and Beyond." Paper presented at the Echos Trans-Atlantiques conference, University of Dakar.

Courlander, Harold (2002 [1976]) *A Treasury of Afro-American Folklore: The Oral Literature, Traditions, Recollections, Legends, Tales, Songs, Religious Beliefs, Customs, Sayings and Humor of Peoples of African American Descent in the Americas*, New York: Da Capo Press.

Craton, Michael and Gail Saunders (2000) *A History of the Bahamian People: From the Ending of Slavery to the Twenty-First Century*, Athens and London: The University of Georgia Press.

Dundes, Alan (1992) "Foreword," in William Bascom (ed.) *African Folktales in the New World*, Bloomington: Indiana University Press, vii–xx.

Eberhart, George M. (2002) *Mysterious Creatures: A Guide to Cryptozoology*, Santa Barbara: ABC-Clio, Inc.

Edwards, Charles L. (1942 [1895]) *Bahama Songs and Stories*, Memoirs of the American Folkore Society, Vol. 3, New York: Houghton, Mifflin, and Co. Reprint: New York: G. E. Steckert.

Gale, Steven H. (1996) *West African Folktales*, Lincolnwood, Illinois: National Textbook Company, NTC Publishing Group.

Gilroy, Paul (1995) *The Black Atlantic: Modernity and Double Consciousness*, Boston: Harvard University Press.

Glinton-Meicholas, Patricia (1994) *An Evening in Guanima*, 2nd ed. Nassau: Guanima Press.

Hamilton, Virginia (1995) *Her Stories*, New York: The Blue Sky Press, an imprint of Scholastic Inc.

Hartsfeld, Mariella Glenn (1987) *Tall Betsy and Dunce Baby: South Georgia Folktales*, Athens and London: University of Georgia Press.

Hayes, Joe (2008) *Baila, Nana, Baila*, Bilingual edition. El Paso, TX: Cinco Puntos Press.

Hill, Donald R. (2007) *Caribbean Folklore: A Handbook*, Westport, CT: Greenwood Press.

Jekyll, Walter (2005) *Jamaican Song and Story: Annancy Stories, Digging Sings, Ring Tunes, and Dancing Tunes*, (2nd Dover edition). Mineola, NY: Dover Publications, Inc.

Makuchi (2008) *The Sacred Door and Other Stories: Cameroon Folktales of the Beba*. Foreword by Isidore Okpewho. Athens, Ohio: Ohio University Press.

Marshall, Emily Zobel (2012) *Anansi's Journey: A Story of Jamaican Cultural Resistance*, Jamaica: University of the West Indies Press.

Parsons, Elsie Clews (1918) *Folktales of Andros Island, Bahamas*. Memoirs of the American Folklore Society, vol. 26. Lancaster, PA: American Folklore Society.

Reneaux, J. J. (2005) *Cajun Folktales*, 1st ed. Atlanta, GA: August House.

Sherlock, Philip (2005) "Introduction" in Walter Jekyll (ed.) *Jamaican Song and Story: Annancy Stories, Digging Sings, Ring Tunes, and Dancing Tunes*, Mineola, NY: Dover Publications, Inc.

Tanna, Laura (1984) *Jamaican Folk Tales and Oral Histories*, No. 1 Jamaica 21 Anthology Series, Kingston: Institute of Jamaica Publications Limited.

Tata Tambai (2014) "Gizo and the Cow," in *Press Club Report 30.05.2014: Traditional Hausa Folk Tales*, Kaduna, Nigeria: Najude Pioneer School. www.najude-pioneer-school.org/images/content/pressclub_30.05.14_folktales.pdf

Thompson, Stith (1977) *The Folktale*, Berkeley and Los Angeles: University of California Press.

Wolkstein, Diane (1978) "Mother of Waters," in *The Magic Orange Tree and Other Haitian Folktales*, New York: Knopf.

26

BREAKING AND MAKING OF CROSS-SPECIES FRIENDSHIPS IN THE *PANĆATANTRA*[1]

Lalita Pandit Hogan

Panćatantra: Roots, branches and time travel in brief

Originally composed in Sanskrit approximately in the third century BCE, and based on oral sources, this beast fable comes together in one of its definitive versions in Purnabhadra's *Panćatantra* (CE 1199). An earlier version was translated to Pahlavi in CE 570 by Burzöe and served as the source text for the Syriac translation known as *Kalilag and Dimnag*. Some European translations are based on the Arabic translation, *Kalilah wa Dimnah* (CE 750). Overall, there are nearly twenty-five recensions of *Panćatantra* in India alone, and nearly 200 different versions of this text in at least fifty languages (Olivelle 1997: xliii). Johannes Hertel's *Das Panchatantra*, a German translation of 1914, appeared in the Harvard Classics Series in 1915. The most surprising perhaps is that Thomas North, the Elizabethan translator of Plutarch, made an English translation, *The Fables of Bidpai: The Morall Philosophie of Doni*, in 1570. In a modernized children's literature genre, selected stories have been widely disseminated through the series, *Amar Chitra Katha* in Hindi. Animated versions of *Panćatantra* tales in English can be found in the Appu Series on YouTube; some of these are also available in Indian languages too, such as the animated "The Boy Who Was a Snake" in Telegu.

Because the text has been so widely translated, known and unknown authors have made changes in the stories; however, many constants stay to authenticate a cohesive text. In most instances, it is divided into five books; *pancha* in Sanskrit means five, and Vishnusharman is believed to be the fictional, if not the real, author. An erudite scholar, when asked by the king to educate the three adolescent ignorant princes, he promises to wake up the intelligence of the princes in six months and devises a crash course of beast fable to do so (Ryder 1956:13–16). Book I is titled *Mitrabedhah* (Dissension between Friends); Book II is *Mitralabha* or *Mitrasamprapti* (Gaining Friends); Book III is *Kakolukiyam* (of Crows and Owls); Book IV is *Labdhapranasham* (Losing What One has Gained); Book V is *Aparikshtakarakam* (Hasty Actions). The story structure in *Panćatantra* is organized by an induction constituting the outer frame story, then the inner frame story for each book and embedded stories; embedded tales proliferate into numerous sub-stories, when the listener asks, "Really? And, how did/could this happen," and the teller responds, "this is how." In the first narrator's story, there may be further bifurcations, when characters in his story tell stories to someone. That is how the stories branch off involving many narratees, auditors, story situations and story worlds. The dialogic structure authenticates multiple subject positions, mapping an intricate network of creatures that inhabit generally hostile, unstable environments, but not without possibilities for survival and happiness.

Being human and being animal: *Tantra* as secret knowledge

There is some debate among scholars about the word *Tantra*, which forms part of the title of the book. Olivelle takes it to mean both "book" and "principle," that is, five books dealing with five principles (xiv). The dictionary meaning of the word, Tantra, in Sanskrit refers to weaving, as in weaving of these stories, and the action of spreading out (*tanoti* in Sanskrit) as the frame story in each book is spread out through mazes of stories within stories. Figuratively, Tantra means, "secret knowledge"; and a Tantric is a mystic. Following this meaning, what is of utmost importance for survival in the forest (or allegorically in the *samsara*, the world), is an understanding of *time*. The *present i*s when choices are made and acted upon; *future* is the unknown, towards which one takes a risky leap or a cautious step. *Past* is what one must learn from, and here past is encapsulated in the storehouse of stories. Actors and decision makers are main characters of the frame stories. The characters in the embedded stories are exemplars of action, value, quality and behavior. Thus the term *Kala* in Sanskrit means both time and death as a limit—a possibility, an opportunity for man, woman, bird and beast. The stories spread out like a spider's net, from the brains, minds, quirky personalities of the characters, through events that take place every moment of every day in the great forest, around the beautiful lake, in the vicinity of the gigantic banyan tree, near some city.

As beast fable that maintains a degree of representational realism, *Pañcatantra* provides a glimpse into the social world of animals, which has continuities with the social world of humans. According to Jaak Panksepp, "Our core values arise from the evolved emotions—and incentive-response properties of many ancient networks of our brains—especially those concentrated in the medially situated subcortical brain regions that all mammals share, in homologous networks of complexity, because of their common ancestry. *These primal powers of the mind* become connected to secondary life experiences through learning" (emphasis added, 2012: 480). Following this understanding of what it means to be human and animal, and what it means to be only human and/or only animal, I take the *Pañcatantra* animals to be, first, allegorical humans; second, animals as distinct from humans; and third, emblematic of the *common ancestry* of the *primal powers of the mind*. Uncanny continuity with animal existence is shown in numerous tales, such as the "The boy who was a snake," also known as "The girl who married a snake" (Ryder 432–433). A long-cherished child is born, but turns out to be a snake; his parents raise him secretly, even arrange a marriage for him. To be with his wife, the snake discards his snake body and assumes his human body. One day his father throws the discarded snake body into flames, and all ends well! Splitting of the snake body from the human may resolve a discontinuity and become a site for the Cartesian *cogito*; at the same time tales like this show anxiety surrounding blurred boundaries and fault lines between human and animal. In the following discussion I will focus on the motif of cross-species friendship in the animal kingdom, as depicted in Books I and II, *Mitrabedha* and *Mitralabha*. *Mitra* in Sanskrit means both friend and political ally; *bheda* is dissension or separation, while *labha* means gain. Using insights from cognitive psychology, my focus is on how Book I is organized by Assertion themes, blending natural instinct with social cognition; while Book II, doing the same, is centrally organized by Affiliation and Attachment themes. Keith Oatley, a major researcher in this field says that "the emotional repertoire which humans inherit from evolutionary adaptation is based largely on three social goals, or social motivations" which he classifies as "*assertion* of ourselves against others over conflict of status and power; *attachment*, in which we depend on others whom we trust for protection against danger; and in a generally hostile, unstable environment; *affiliation*, in which we commit ourselves to each other in friendly cooperation" (emphasis added 81). He argues that human desire is at the top of the pecking order and generically similar to what observers of animal behavior call "dominance hierarchy" (82). The focus on cross-species friendships, in my view, speaks not only of animals, but also of India's ethnic and racial diversity that pre-dates colonialism. India was never homogenous; it was always multiple, as can be seen in the epics, *Ramayana* and *Mahabharata*, and other early writings. Book II sets up an ideal of cohabitation in the forest (by suggestion in the social world). Book II also sees amity as possible, but cautions about things that threaten it. Olivelle contends that "the central message of the *Pancatantra*, with the possible exception of Book II, is that craft and deception constitute the major art of government" (xxxv). Rather than a straightforward Machiavellian discourse on *niti* (diplomacy), however, this book should be, more profitably, read as a cautionary tale.

Why the lion killed the bull: vulnerability of cross-species friendship

The main characters in the frame story of Book I are the lion king, Pingalaka, the bull Sanjivaka, two jackals, Damanaka and Karataka; the lion king is named after his tawny color, the bull for his lively temperament. Damanaka is oppressor, or tamer. Karataka means a crow. Crows in *Pancatantra* are often portrayed as clear thinking. The bull is stranded in the forest, having been trapped in mud, and his master, a merchant, abandons him. At first dejected, Sanjivaka survives and thrives in the forest. In time the lion-king and the bull "become the best of friends, their mutual affection growing daily" (Rajan 2006: 44). The jackals are sons of a minister and one of them, Damanaka, sets to work to regain his lost status and sphere of influence. To serve his turn, as an Iago might say it, he turns the lion and bull against each other priming them for a fight in which the bull, inevitably, is killed and the *status quo* in this little dominion is restored. Dominance hierarchy is determined by physical power (of the lion); but the jackal, possessing less physical might and no predatory advantage, defeats and oppresses those mightier than him. This principle is demonstrated in this story, and is time and again reiterated in numerous frame and sub-stories where lions, elephants and snakes are tricked by lesser beings of the jungle. For instance, the hare outwits a lion by convincing him that his reflection in the stirred waters of the lake is another angry lion desiring hegemonic control. To maintain his dominance, the real lion jumps into the lake to fight an imaginary rival and drowns, while the hare saves himself (Olivelle 30–31).

However, Damanaka's victory is of a different kind, as it is not motivated by self-defense. In part it deals with assertion of his own power, while at a deeper level it mandates repression, censorship, of the very idea that friendship can exist (and endure) between a carnivore and a herbivore. In contradiction to the natural law of enmity, the friendship between the lion and the bull begins with mutual trust, as "Pingalaka places his right paw on him—a paw that was stout, rotund, and long, adorned with claws resembling thunderbolts" (Olivelle 21). He asks: "how did you end up in this desolate forest" (21). Friendship, as in Book II, requires exchange of life stories. The bull, being a city dweller is learned, "possessing great intelligence" and "profound wisdom," and in his company the "King of Beasts" transforms from a "creature of the woods, practicing wild ways of the jungle" to a "civilized" ruler "versed in urban ways and manners" (Rajan 44). Ironically, it is Damanaka who had initially brought the bull and the lion together. When he first heard the bellowing of the bull, the lion's reaction was fear of this "prodigious creature" who he thought "must possess a form and strength that matches his voice" (Rajan 29). It is Damanaka who shames the lion for being afraid of a mere sound, listing sounds heard all the time in the forest (Rajan 29). Further, Damanaka convinces the king that Sanjivaka is not an ordinary bull, but "the sacred bull of Shiva," permitted by the Lord "to graze here on the emerald-green meadows bordering the Yamuna" river (Rajan 36). This is the moment when Damanaka seizes an opportunity to move closer to the inner circle of power by taking advantage of the lion's fear of an imaginary enemy in the jungle. Domains of animal and human divide here, in a figurative sense, with the jackal representing human ambition. Mark Twain's well known indictment that human beings are more brutish than animals because language enables dissembling and rationalization is not too far from what this tale unravels. The lion's fear of a voice he has never heard is not a sign of his weakness; a sound unheard before simply activates "anticipatory anxiety" of the fear system (Panksepp 189–190). The evolutionary history that humans share with animals is responsible for scanning by the subcortical brain (for possible dangers), subcortical affect that is modified by cortical appraisals (Panksepp 70–71). In this sense, Damanaka's looking into the cause of anxiety shows cortical evaluation, aligning him more with human cognition.

The persuasion that is required later to tear apart this friendship works its way through argument, counter argument, epigram, counter epigram, story, counter story, with major auditors and narratees as the persons in dialogue. The dialogue continues between the four main characters, and others in the sub-stories. This comprises more than half of Book I as it progresses from the jackal, Damanaka, bringing about a cross-species friendship (for his own reasons), to breaking it up (for his own reasons). The counterweight of what is ethical conduct offered by Karataka has *no* effect on Damanaka, "whose mind worked in crooked ways," and "he quietly slunk away, because these words were sheer poison to him" (Rajan 185). As far as the lion and the bull are concerned, it is important to note that those two had been all this time immersed in *talking* to each other, so much so that other people were excluded and other activities neglected, but in a time of crisis and conflict they don't *talk things out with each other*. Failure of language to restore friendship and amity, and its success in destroying it, is what makes Book I brilliant, though depressing because in the affairs of the world too we see repeatedly how peace talks fail and war lets loose a brute force. In preparation for this denouement, Damanaka instructs them how to read hostile intention in body language, and pointedly dissuades them from conflict resolution through talking through the problem. To the bull he says that though the lion's habit is to "lie at ease on a flat rock," if you see "for the first time he stares at you today, his legs drawn tight, his mouth agape, and his ears erect, then you will know he has hostile intentions" (Olivelle 54). Similarly, he says to the lion, today the bull won't come into his presence in his usual relaxed manner, but "ready for battle with points of horns in a striking position" (Olivelle 37). In a text where every little task is done, every choice is made, and action is performed after reams of stories and counter stories, arguments and counter arguments, the moment of predatory violence is abrupt, expedient, marked by absence of word, story, example and epigram. This is because Damanaka's persuasion has aroused rage as reaction to fear in the grass eater and predatory rage in the flesh eater. Karataka notices that in their murderous rage, the lion and bull "looked like two red palash trees in bloom" (Olivelle 55). Palash trees bloom January to March in big vermillion flowers, making it seem as if there is a forest fire. It is a startling image for the treacherous murder of cross-species amity and friendship in the heart of the forest. At the same time, the image evokes a more upright posture that is unusual for quadrupeds. Paradoxically, as trees they are a lower life form, and in their upright posture more like humans. The site of this murder is the site of *politics*, which is enemy to *friendship* in Baudrillard's words "politics is the site of the exercise of evil, scattered in individual souls and collective manifestations in all forms—privilege, vice, corruption" (2005: 165).

That Sanjivaka has been likened to Shiva's bull, though a fabrication by the deceitful Damanaka, still separates this frame story from the embedded mirror story of the camel that became food for the lion and his retainers. Told by Sanjivaka to Damanaka, it mirrors the former's predicament. In this story too, a cross-species friendship occurs under the same circumstances. Kathanaka, the camel, is left in the forest by a merchant, just as the bull was. The lion king, Madotkata, had never seen such a "comic" creature. One of his servants, the crow, uncovers who this creature is and the lion grants him "protection and safety" (Olivelle 46). Business as usual continues until one day Madotkata is wounded in battle with elephants, and cannot procure food. He asks his retainers to look for food. They can find nothing and the crow hatches a plot. In an impromptu farce they offer themselves as food and the lion declines. Reassured by this, Kathanaka also offers himself and "before the words [are] out of his mouth the leopard and jackal [tear] apart his two sides. He [dies] immediately and [is] eaten" (48). Here too, the lion had to be persuaded (by the crow) that if the camel offers himself it is, then, okay to eat him though he was given protection. The crow's first suggestion had been that they just kill the camel. In the Pingalaka and Sanjivaka story, however, there is no question of food shortage; the bull is only killed, not eaten. The similarity lies in the status of the camel and the bull as outsiders stranded in the forest, as herbivores, not carnivores, fit for predatory scapegoating. There was not a special friendship between lion and the camel, as there was between Sanjivaka and Pingalka. A cross-species friendship that could change the power structure in the forest becomes casualty to puny self-interest.

How the crow became friends with the mouse: affiliation and attachment

In so far as the *Pañcatantra* tales deal with the social world, the focal subject in Book II, in contrast to Book I, is common people, not kings, and their retainers. This book features animals and birds that rank much lower in the dominance hierarchy of the jungle. Still, even though species differences are not so dramatically defined in terms of herbivores and carnivores, there is wariness and anxiety about who can become food for whom. As a counter to this anxiety, the motivational energies of *affiliation* and *attachment* trigger what Panksepp calls the *care system* (286–290). Drawing attention to a *seeking* system that works in tandem with the care system, Panksepp says, "when animals live in social communities," the seeking system urges them "to find nonsexual partners, forming friendships and social alliances" (101). From this perspective, birds and animals in the *Pañcatantra* cannot be taken to stand for humans on the assumption that they are allegorical templates but because the tales reveal secret knowledge, or the mystery of the evolutionary overlap. Threats to survival faced by the creatures in the frame story come from humans (the hunter and the fowler). While impossible distances from cities and towns in Book I is indicated by, for instance, how domestic animals, when stranded, are abandoned there, in Book II too a further movement away from towns and cities, farther into the woods, shows distrust of human habitations. For the crow, the dissatisfaction with proximity to the city comes from danger of being caught in traps when he and his people search for food, and for the mouse from his not being able to procure food because the hermit from whom he takes it not only catches on to him but, joined by another hermit friend, he invades his fortress in the hole to steal his gold (Olivelle 86). There is irony first that the mouse is respected by his followers for owning gold, and then that it is ascetics who steal it, since an ascetic should not be greedy for gold. It is thus that the domicile of the crow on "the huge silk cotton tree" is abandoned for the "large lake in the middle of a dense forest" (Olivelle 71; 80). There is much discussion here, and in other stories, about why someone should or should not be forced to leave home. In "How the Sandpiper Defeated the Ocean" (Olivelle 50–54), for example, the crisis is activated by a care-system geared to nurture offspring, so that when the ocean washes away the sand-piper family's eggs, the wife wants to relocate, but the sandpiper decides to fight against the ocean rather than leave home. One of the sub-stories here is the well-known "A Tale of Three Fish," a famous story told by the wife to bolster her argument. In this sub-story, the foolish fish that trusts to fate and does nothing fails to survive. In the end the debate concludes with a consensus that home is where you have friends, and that only "small minded people make distinction between native and foreign lands" (Olivelle 99). This development not only addresses (in today's world) forced exile due to ethnic cleansing and voluntary migration of all sorts, but as a concomitant to these, children's anxiety about losing place attachments and friends when parents move.

Anchored to these concerns and anxieties, the motif of cross-species migration and friendship begins when the crow watches with amazement at how the dove king (Citragriva) guided his subjects to lift the fowler's trap (in which a large number of them were caught) and fly off, "soar high over a very rugged terrain." To the crow the hunter seems like Yama, the god of death, and the doves flying away along with the trap a won-drous sight (Olivelle 71–72). Seeing that the hunter is in pursuit, the dove-king, directs them to the kingdom of his friend, the mouse, Hiranyaka, who will cut their bonds (72). The crow is like a reader and observer, watching this spectacle, as, in contrast, the two jackals in Book I watched "a bloody drama" (Rajan 151). The innate abilities and skill sets of birds and animals are not used to establish a hegemonic order, but become resources for affiliation, alliance, reciprocity, commitment and attachment. In Book I, the story of the mouse maid is told by Damanaka to show that innate nature asserts itself over social learning; lion will always be a lion and bull a bull. In the context of Book II, on the other hand, the superiority of mice adds practical value to him as an ally. Briefly, the story centers on an ascetic, in some versions a famous Rishi, who saves an infant mouse and changes her to a girl. In the end she wants to marry a mouse and her father changes her back. During the proceedings, as the mouse-maid rejects one prospective groom after another (*No father, I will marry someone more powerful than [this]*), the sun testi-fies that the cloud is more powerful since it covers up the sun; the cloud testifies that the wind is more powerful because it scatters the clouds; and the wind testifies that the moun-tain is more powerful because it blocks the wind; finally, the mountain testifies that the mouse is more powerful because it can burrow holes in the mountain. The capitulation of the more powerful to less powerful undermines dominance hierarchy. Though Hiranyaka's name, meaning golden, is parodic because of his obsession with regaining his stolen gold, the mouse, as a species, is elevated in folklore and mythology. In the animated tale "There is Strength in Numbers," which is based on the doves' flight, the mouse king wears a golden crown. He does not cut the trap by himself, but is helped by his subject mice. Moreover, he resides in his kingdom by a gigantic mountain. This animated tale apparently combines the "Mouse Maid" story from Book I with the story of the melancholy, paranoid exile Hiranyaka, of Book II, who, but for the *care* of friends, would be lost.

Saliency of affiliation and attachment that cross barriers, with an understanding of limits, perils and possibilities is consistent in Book II. When the crow first approaches the mouse for friendship, the mouse says: "you are my enemy." Quoting scriptures, Hiranyaka refers to two kinds of enmity, "natural and incidental" (Olivelle 76). Incidental enmity has a "specific cause," which can be removed, but natural enmity cannot be obviated. Natural enmity he says is of two kinds, between animals who can cause harm to each other, as between elephants and lions. And, of course, many tales in Books I and II are instances of the lion king having to fight elephant(s) and be seriously injured in the process so that he cannot procure food for his retinue for a while. This causes some of the food crises that necessitate scapegoating of the non-flesh eating outsider. The second kind of enmity is unidirectional, when, for example one kills and eats another without provocation, whereas the other does not harm, injure or eat the first: "horses and buffaloes; cats and mice, snakes and the mongoose" (Olivelle 77). On these grounds, the mouse considers his friendship with the crow "an impossible alliance" (77). The crow's counter to this is: "All metals unite when they are melted down / Birds and beasts unite when there is cause" (Olivelle 78). Once the friendship pact is sealed, the crow comes across a wild buffalo that has been killed by a tiger, eats to his heart's content, and comes back to share some with his new-formed friend. The mouse, on his part, shares some grains ("husked millet kernels") and the friends eat "to show their affection for one another" (Olivelle 78). After this, they go to meet Mantharka, a turtle, who is the crow's "dear friend" and provides him with "fish and other delicious foods" (Olivelle 80). To his great admiration, Mantharka too is apprised of Hiranyaka's heroic ability to cut traps.

The process of forming alliances across species continues over the next few segments until what we would call a statistically significant mix of diversity is achieved. All the alliances have limitations and possibilities, and the practical principle of cooperation works around limitations, as it capitalizes on natural and learnt skill sets of each. One day they meet a frightened deer (Citranga) followed by a hunter. Though bigger than them, being a "grass eater" he is no threat to them, and they, being smaller than him also pose no threat. There are no innate barriers to friendship. When the deer does not come home one evening; the crow is sent in search since he can fly and he finds him "on a steep bank near a water's edge, tightly entangled in a leather snare tied to his neck" (Olivelle 97). To free him from the snare, the mouse (Hiranyaka) is quickly flown in, borne on swift wings of the crow. He snaps the cords and the deer is freed, and at this point shares his life story. As a baby, Citranga had learnt to sprint and not to jump. For this he got caught in a trap and became a prince's pet, living in luxury. However, palace life was prison and once in the rainy season he burst into song about his yearning to romp "in wind and rain" in the forest (Olivelle 97). The uncanny phenomenon of a speaking/singing animal scared the prince, even though a "noble man" told him, "all animals, my friend, do indeed talk, but not in front of people" (Olivelle 99). Well, our Citranga talked in front of the prince and this caused him to run for his life.

Human incomprehension of animal cognition and its appraisal as scary magic is a running theme across all parts of the the *Pañcatantra*. Friendship between humans and animals is rare, or non-existent. The *otherness* of animals to humans and threats posed by humans to animals is a recurrent motif. One iconic story that breaks this wall of otherness is the tragic story of the dove wife and her husband (Rajan 308–313). In the dense forest a fowler is caught in a storm, takes shelter under a tree, which is home to the dove couple. There, the husband is lamenting because his wife did not return home. The wife is caught in the same hunter's trap and lets her husband know, instructing him to treat the hunter as his guest. The dove lights a fire, and since there is nothing to eat, he throws himself into the fire to offer as food, following the *dharma* (ethical duty) of hospitality. The hunter is moved to compassion and releases the dove. When she sees what has happened she too throws herself into the fire. This couple, indeed, are a Romeo and his Juliet of the animal kingdom.

To our friends, Goldy, Swift, Slow, Gray Neck and Spot, to follow Ryder's re-naming of them, the hunter is the *enemy other*. The wall of otherness between animal species is broken, but not the wall between humans and animals. The final episode of their coordinated effort to sabotage hunters involves the turtle. We have seen that telling life stories plays a significant role in strengthening bonds of friendship as they join to break the bonds of entrapment. The turtle, though advised to stay put, takes a risk to be with his "loved ones" and hear the deer's story (Olivelle 100). Story telling for animals, as for humans, is a rite. As was feared, the hunter catches the turtle and ties him with rope. The "metals unite when melted down" analogy used for cross-species friendship (78) is demonstrated in its full efficacy in the ensuing combat of wit (and skill) between man and animal. As planned, the deer poses dead; the crow pretends to peck at this pretend corpse to convince the hunter and play upon his greed for a bigger catch. As expected the hunter throws down the turtle, runs towards the deer, who in the meantime has learnt to jump, and scampers away, while the mouse swiftly cuts the turtle's bonds (103). The hunter thinks the deer's fast disappearance was magic, then, seeing the turtle freed of bonds and gone, his magic thesis is confirmed, and "fearing for his own safety" rushes out of the forest (103). Before embarking on this guerilla tactic, Hiranyaka pays homage to the idea of friendship, embodied in the word *Mitra* (both friend and ally): a small word of two syllables refers to something precious that is "Shelter against sorrow, grief, and fear, / a vessel of love and trust" (103). In Book I, too, the love and trust was created between a carnivore and a herbivore that could, if allowed to flourish, have subverted social order from the top. Book II suggests a bottom-up change of social order. It is thus significant that Hiranyaka, possessor of gold, is advised by his friends to abandon the quest for his lost gold, also to abandon home and take refuge in a dynamic friendship with other species. Harmonious co-existence across differences—because of them, not in spite of them—is suggested in both books as a utopian fantasy.

Note

1 For this discussion I use Arthur Ryder, *The Panchatantra* (1956); Chandra Rajan, *Pancatantra* (1993, rpt. 2006); Patrick Olivelle, *The Pañcatantra* (1997), as well as references to the animated online Appuseries children's videos:

The Boy Who Was a Snake: www.youtube.com/watch?v=4QKJZd_Le_k
(in Telugu): www.youtube.com/watch?v=MqDvAnRhjMg
The Three Fish: www.youtube.com/watch?v=FfULzZGpbUM
The Mouse Maid: www.youtube.com/watch?v=GOssT9FJTTY
There is Strength in Numbers: www.youtube.com/watch?v=g88ngSotpJg

Bibliography

Baudrillard, Jean (2005) *The Intelligence of Evil or the Lucidity Pact.* Trans. Chris Turner. New York
  Berg Press.
Oatley, Keith (2004) *Emotions: A Brief History*, London: Blackwell.
Olivelle, Patrick. Trans. (1997) *The Pañcatantra: The Book of India's Folk Wisdom*, London: Oxford
  World's Classics.
Panksepp, Jaak, and Lucy Bevin (2012) *The Archeology of the Mind: Neuroevolutionary Origins of
  Human Emotion*, London: Norton.
Rajan, Chandra. Trans. (2006) *Visnu Sarman: The Pancatantra*, London: Penguin.
Ryder, Arthur W. Trans. (1956) *The Panchatantra*, Chicago: University of Chicago Press.

27

CHILD HANUMAN AND THE POLITICS OF BEING A SUPERHERO

Anuja Madan

Hanuman, India's first major commercial animated feature film,[1] was released by Percept Pictures in 2005. This Hindi film narrates the life story of Hanuman, the widely revered Hindu monkey-god (he is a *vanar*, an ape-like humanoid). Hanuman is the son of the wind-god, Vayu, which accounts for his supernatural abilities— he can fly faster than the wind, change shapes, vary his size, is immortal, and has enormous strength. The famous devotee of Rama is a central character of the Indian epic *Ramayana* in which he acts as an emissary between Rama and Sita, and plays a crucial role in the war against the demon king Ravana. A vast number of Hindu temples and shrines are dedicated to this highly popular god, and in the last couple of decades, many monumental icons of the protean god have been erected in different parts of India.

In his fascinating, wide-ranging book on the evolving representations of Hanuman across several media and time periods, Philip Lutgendorf (2007) classifies Hanuman as "the pan-Indian 'middle-class' god par excellence" since he is perceived as a powerful, energetic resourceful god who repeatedly delivers the help needed by his devotees in the face of difficult challenges (374). He notes that Hanuman is at the center of "a growing body of narrative that selectively edits, suggestively encompasses, and ambitiously expands on the Rama story to become…an emerging 'epic' in its own right" (28). The *Hanumayana*, as Lutgendorf calls it, contains a huge variety of stories in oral and written form, in different languages, that deal with various episodes in his life (122). Indian children's publishers have been issuing comics and picturebooks about Hanuman for many decades in several languages. Recently, Indian diasporic writers have published Hanuman picturebooks, testifying to the continuing appeal of mythological children's books outside of the borders of the country and to the popularity of this god. A few examples include U.S.-based Shailaja Joshi's *Hanuman and the Orange Sun*, and Singapore-based Bhakti Mathur's *Hanuman* trilogy in the "Amma, Tell Me" series on Hindu mythology. The film *Hanuman* is the first tale about the god told through the medium of animation. It narrates the eponymous character's legendary adventures in childhood, such as his attempt to seize the sun, and also highlights his role in the *Ramayana* as an adult.

Hanuman was a record-breaker on many counts. The 100-minute 2D film played across 200 screens in the country, and was successful commercially, reviving the Indian mythological genre. It also clocked the maximum VCD sales in the country that year, surpassing live-action hits. According to Yusuf Shaikh, Head of Distribution and IPR at Percept, *Hanuman* DVDs were in constant demand in the US and Australia as well (personal communication, May 12, 2015). A lot of this success can be attributed to iconographic innovation of chubby, fair-skinned Baby Hanuman (see Figures 1 and 2). The success of *Hanuman* led to a spate of mythological animation films and TV shows that revolved around the child personae of popular mythological heroes and gods such as Bheema, Arjuna, Krishna and Ganesha. Some animated content circulates primarily on YouTube (including films that imitated the concept of Baby Hanuman such as *Bal Hanuman* and *Pavan Putra Hanuman*), while other products were created mainly for TV. Producers saw in Hindu mythology the potential to counter the dominance of American and foreign content in the rapidly expanding children's entertainment sector.

Figure 27.1   Baby Hanuman defeating demons single-handedly (*Hanuman*).

Figure 27.2   Newly born blue-eyed Maruti manifests Hanuman's simian jaw coloration when he first looks at his mother (*Return of Hanuman*).

Though the film was Indian animator V.G. Samant's brainchild, Shailendra Singh, the Joint Managing Director of Percept Pictures, bought the rights to the franchise when the opportunity presented itself. He became interested in producing indigenous animation that would reflect a "belief in our own culture" after thinking about why Indian children only consumed Spider-Man and Superman rather than Krishna and Hanuman (personal communication, May 12, 2015). However, Hanuman was marketed in terms of Western cultural tropes; he was projected as the "original superhero," and the director claimed that his (historical) origin preceded that of Superman, Spider-Man and Batman by thousands of years (*Washington Post*, January 8, 2008). According to Singh, Hanuman "qualified on all parameters to be a superhero" since he has extraordinary qualities and is a savior. The use of the word "qualified" suggests the power of the predetermined "superhero" category which Hanuman could fortuitously be made to fit into. The fascination with casting Hanuman as a superhero isn't limited to animation films. It has recently been announced that Junglee Pictures will produce a big-budget Bollywood film, tentatively titled *Hanumaan*. According to the director, Anurag Singh, "it's a superhero film that marries mythology with modern technology." (*Mumbai Mirror*, December 19, 2016).

In a move influenced by the Hollywood business model and rather new to the Indian film industry, Percept launched a range of merchandise during the release of the film such as Baby Hanuman keychains, stickers, toys, mobile games, apparel, stationery, and so on, as part of an aggressive 360-degree branding exercise (*Rediff India Abroad*, February 2, 2006). A Hanuman comic book was simultaneously released in several Indian languages (*The Hindu*, May 24, 2006). Percept also built the brand of *Bal* ("child") Hanuman through other productions, including a 2D Hindi animation film *Return of Hanuman* (2007) that depicted the modern-day adventures of a fictional child called Maruti, who was Hanuman's alter-ego on earth (see Figure 3). Maruti, one of Hanuman's popular patronyms, means son of Marut, more commonly known as Vayu, the wind-god. This film was followed by a spin-off animated Hindi TV show, *The New Adventures of Hanuman* (2010–2011), which revolved around (a slightly older) Maruti, who repeatedly rescues his town and boarding school friends from aliens, demons and evil scientists (see Figure 4). *Hanuman* 3 is currently in production and also revolves around the toddler avatar of Hanuman, though the producers are non-committal about a release date because of problems in funding (Yusuf Shaikh, personal communication, May 12, 2015). However, the company has not been able to sustain the success of the first film. The 2007 sequel was a meandering film that failed to match the quality of the original, and also failed at the box office; the TV show was canceled after two seasons.

This essay focuses on the second film of the franchise, *Return of Hanuman* to address the following questions: What kind of a superhero is Hanuman cast as? How are the tensions between the national and global, and between cultural homogenization and indigenization negotiated through the figure of toddler Hanuman? What underlies the secularization and modernization of the mythic universe in the film? Before delving into textual analysis, I investigate the valences of the baby avatar of Hanuman. Scholars of mass culture have noted the "inter-ocularity" of the Indian public sphere (Breckenridge and Appadurai 1995, 12). The analytic of the "inter-ocular" foregrounds the intersecting, overlapping nature of images and different media in India, and recognizes that "no visual image is self-sufficient, bounded, insulated; instead it is open, porous, permeable, and ever available for appropriation" (Ramaswamy 2003, xvi). I use this paradigm to trace the overlaps between Indian calendar art (a ubiquitous form of popular culture in the country) and the animations.

Figure 27.3　Maruti manifests the simian blush (a product of strong emotion) as he prepares for his first day at school (*Return of Hanuman*).

Figure 27.4　Maruti and friends (*The New Adventures of Hanuman*).

Percept Pictures' Baby Hanuman doesn't resemble the god-posters of an adult (often muscular) Hanuman that are widely prevalent, but he shares with them the impetus towards humanizing Hanuman and making him furless (Lutgendorf 2007, 344). The hyper-masculine adult Hanuman in the 2005 film certainly shares the buff physique of many calendar art images of the deity. Furthermore, Hanuman's infantilization in the animation franchise must be discussed in relation to the preponderance of Hindu baby-gods in calendar art since the 1990s. Patricia Uberoi (2006, 99) observes that while *Bal Krishna* has widely been iconized in calendar art for many decades, the unprecedented proliferation of the baby forms of different deities such as Shiva, Ram, Vishnu and Hanuman or the "god-baby boom" is a new phenomenon (100).

Uberoi suggests that the child's sacredness and proximity to divinity in the country is an important factor for understanding Indian baby iconography (97). According to her, these iconographic innovations could be "another example of the ongoing cutification of Indian childhood, spearheaded by the booming advertising industry and the cable TV and cartoon channels" (100). Knut Jacobsen (2004) also links the popularity of the child god posters to sociological changes in India, such as rapid urbanization, increasing economic prosperity, as well as the growth of the middle class and television culture. He argues that "a child god is a god one approaches with paternal love," and that child gods represent urban, middle-class and family values (261). Uberoi and Jacobsen's astute observations about the factors behind the baby-god boom are applicable to animation films too. It is no surprise that several deity-centred mythological animation films and TV shows have chosen Hanuman, Ganesh and Krishna as their subjects, since they are highly popular gods among middle-class Hindus.

Percept's toddler Hanuman is visually very different from the Hanuman baby images in calendar art. Instead, he is modelled on Disney animations, reinforcing the impact of American cultural products on the Indian children's entertainment industry. His saucer eyes, round face, and pudgy body are traits that Disney characters like Mickey Mouse, Snow White and Bambi were endowed with in order to accentuate their cuteness or babyishness (Forgacs 1992, 365). Hanuman's sapphire blue eyes and fair complexion are in conformity with Caucasian standards of beauty, which have exercised such a major influence over the subcontinent. The hybridity of Baby Hanuman has had a key role to play in the appeal of this icon—branded on a Disneyfied body are traditional icono-graphic details associated with the god: the red loincloth, gold ornaments, golden mace, and "tilaka" on the forehead. Notably, even as a human child in *Return of Hanuman*, the eponymous character doesn't lose the characteristics that define him—his tail and simian jaw (often evident during the film).

Forgacs (1992) argues that the gradual shift towards "cutifying" Disney products is closely linked to the "myth of family togetherness" that underlies Disney's success as a provider of family entertainment. He writes:

> To see something as cute means to feel a nurturant affection for it as one does for a baby…To develop cuteness therefore means to develop a set of affective relays between adult and baby or child and baby…. The secret of Disney's current success lies largely in its skillful handling of these relays between past and present, adult, adolescent and child [which] depend primarily on the adult consumer as provider of revenue
>
> (362–364).

Since Hanuman is a beloved deity, his "cutified" toddler forms become especially adorable for Hindu adults. The affective relays between the animated boy-god and adults as well as child audiences take on a religious, devotional edge. Lutgendorf (2007 297) observes that the cute baby images of Hanuman in calendar art may be intended to evoke women's "maternal" devotion. Both *Hanuman* and *Return of Hanuman* rely on such a response, and foreground the relationship between son and mother, highlighting the latter's devotion to Hanuman and his dutiful affection for her. It is worth noting that in my interviews with Shailendra Singh and Yusuf Shaikh, they repeatedly used the word "cute" to describe this figure. Shailendra Singh expressed his intention of representing Hanuman as a "cute, fun, brattish and entertaining character" (personal communication, May 12, 2015). Shaikh capitalized on this "cuteness" to make merchandising a key part of the marketing strategy. Cuteness not only serves the purpose of evoking maternal feelings through its association with innocent babyhood, but also endears a young audience through its association with brattishness and mischievousness in the films.

Hanuman's brattishness is most evident in *Return of Hanuman* and the TV series *The New Adventures of Hanuman* (henceforth *ROH* and *TNAOH* respectively). Unlike the first film, *Hanuman*, these animations do not draw on traditional stories, and have a playful, irreverent tone. *ROH* starts with the adult Hanuman feeling bored in *swarg* (heaven), and using a Google maps-like software to zoom into a village called Bajrangpur, named after him. He witnesses a 4–5-year-old schoolboy being bullied by older boys. The mother of the distressed boy (Minku) prays for her son in front of her home's Hanuman idol and reassures her son (whose father is missing) that Hanuman will protect him. Back in heaven, Hanuman is resolved to intervene in a tangible way and requests Brahma (the god responsible for creation in the Hindu pantheon) to send him to Bajrangpur. Subsequently, he is born as a human baby to the wife of a priest who is the caretaker of the Hanuman temple in Bajrangpur. Maruti soon joins the local school and uses his exceptional strength to protect Minku from school bullies and take care of his own mother when his father is kidnapped. Towards the end of the film, Maruti transforms into *Bal* Hanuman in order to fight villains, rescue the kidnapped men and also save the planet from the doomsday effects of environmental pollution. Having revealed his true form to the community, he returns to heaven.

What does Hanuman/Maruti have in common with the archetype of the superhero? Coogan (2009, 77) defines American superheroes as characters that have "a selfless pro-social mission, who possess superpowers, advanced technology, mystical abilities, or highly developed physical and/or mental skills," a super-identity and an iconic costume. Maruti deviates from the archetype in several ways. He has superpowers and an iconic (albeit traditional) costume when he transforms into Baby Hanuman, but he does not possess advanced technology and does not operate from the metropolis. Nor is his real identity as Hanuman a well-kept secret—as mentioned earlier, he is born with his tail, and his parents know who he really is; his classmates too repeatedly reiterate that he is "different." Though Maruti has a pro-social mission insofar as he deals with a contemporary global problem (environmental pollution), he simultaneously wages a cosmological battle with evil *asuras*.[2]

The portrayal of Hanuman in *ROH* and *TNAOH* mirrors the impulse of Indian superhero comics towards cultural indigenization. In fact, Hanuman is not the first mythological hero who has been refashioned as a superhero; many Indian comic books (including the famous *Amar Chitra Katha* comics) have drawn on Hindu mythology to create uniquely Indian content that can compete with American comics. Indian comics adopted the superhero genre in the mid-1980s (Chandra 2012, 58). Suchitra Mathur (2010, 176) notes that the "distinctly indigenous superhero tradition" of Indian comic books was marked by "a self-conscious distancing from the Anglo-American comic tradition" but was also influenced by it. Nagraj, one of the first superheroes, has a divine origin that accounts for his superhuman powers, but "at the same time, he is proudly proclaimed as the Indian Spiderman" (Chandra 2012, 69). Shaktiman, the first Indian television superhero, who appeared in 1997, had mythological associations, as did the more recent Spider-Man India (Davé 2013: 134). Liquid Comics/Graphic India has created/refashioned several superheroes who have a basis in Hindu mythology.

In *ROH*, Hanuman is presented as a cosmopolitan, globe-trotting Indian superhero. In a playful song sequence at the beginning of the film, the god flies across the world, visiting the Statue of Liberty, Leaning Tower of Pisa, Eiffel Tower, Sidney Opera House and the Egyptian pyramids and other famous landmarks. In an instance that displays a self-conscious, playful subversion of American cultural and political dominance, Hanuman captures and hands over to brown policemen a group of people that includes Osama bin Laden and George Bush, while the lyrics identify the men as thieves and dacoits. Hanuman also replaces the sculptures of the four presidents on Mount Rushmore with those of Rama, Sita, Lakshmana and himself, and transposes his own facsimile onto the Statue of Liberty. In a meta-textual move that perhaps hints at the producers' fantasy of wish-fulfilment, Hanuman, as he flies across the cityscape, cuts Spider-Man's web and thus makes him fall from some tall buildings. While these moves may lead us to wonder whether Hanuman is projected as a subaltern superhero of the global south who contests the hegemony of the white, male, American superheroes who uphold American values and world order, neither the film nor the TV series offer revisionary narratives that could warrant such a reading.

ROH reinforces the dominant national imaginary of India as a liberalized nation. *Swarg* (heaven) is contemporized—the gods use touch screen technology, speak Hinglish (a mixture of Hindi and English) and obey traffic signals. Moreover, the language of capitalism permeates the mythological universe. Brahma, the Hindu god of creation, actively dissuades Hanuman from attempting to help humans by showing him bloodied and bandaged men who had been sent as emissaries to earth. One of these men requests the god to "transfer" him to another planet, even if it is at a reduced salary, since he doesn't want to go to earth again. When Hanuman persists in going to Bajrangpur, Brahma has him sign a lengthy contract and his powers are locked away to hold him to his end of the deal. There is an analogy here with what Nandini Chandra identifies in the earlier superhero comics: arguing that battlefields are equivalent to "reconstructed corporate boardrooms," she highlights the "coincidence of the superhero genre and the neoliberal state" since they share a "hyper-security consciousness" and everyone is a wage slave (2012, 70). Here too, the affinity of heaven to the neoliberal state is apparent—divine emissaries are mercenaries working in the business of rescuing humankind.

In this de-sacralized and commodified heaven, Brahma keeps his panoptical gaze on Maruti's adventures not through his divine sight, but through the computer. The eagle Garuda, lord Vishnu's mode of transport, has transformed into an airplane. Heavenly beings participate in a culture of consumption—Brahma enjoys cocktails on a sundeck brought to him by a curvaceous *apsara* (heavenly nymph) while his "secretary" Chitragupta is caught browsing the website of Menaka, the famously beautiful *apsara*, who is overtly sexualized.

In her reading of Indian advertisements as visual cultural texts, Leela Fernandes (2006, 53) argues that the "aesthetic of the commodity does not merely serve as a passive reflector of wider social and cultural processes but instead becomes a central site in which the Indian nation is reimagined." She observes that some advertisements employ religious imagery to suggest that the "the core of Indian tradition...can be retained even as the material context of that tradition is modernized and improved" (43). According to her, "the ability of multinational capital to combine the national and the global within a singular narrative of commodity fetishism" appeals to a new middle class that has become the "embodiment of the liberalizing nation-state" in dominant public representations (32).

Return of Hanuman goes a step further in modernizing the entire mythological universe to reinforce the values of consumerism. As many scholars have noted, Hindu mythology, especially the epic *Ramayana*,[3] has been crucial in establishing a nationalist imagination. By linking the mythic world with technological progress and material wealth, the film fetishizes hybridity between the traditional and the modern, the ancient and the contemporary, the sacred and the secular, the national and the global—a hybridity which serves the consumerist ethos. The secularization of the divine world entails making it more akin to the values of a consumer audience. Gods become consumers, and embody the idealized lifestyle that the new middle class symbolizes and aspires towards. The "sacrilegious" portrayal of gods may be one factor for the film's dismal performance at the box office, but the concept of contemporized consumerist gods has been adopted in other mythological animations such as the *My Friend Ganesha* trilogy and the TV series *Roll no. 21*. Moreover, *Return of Hanuman* has had almost 2.5 million views on YouTube as of December 2016, and the English, Tamil, Telugu and Malayalam versions of the film have also been viewed hundreds of thousands of times, testifying to its popularity in the digital realm.

Maruti's divine heroism is inextricably tied to the needs and prayers of his devotees, and the film thus reinforces Hanuman's status as a deity who embodies power and protection. But despite Hanuman's toddler persona, his role as protector is almost entirely cast within a masculinist paradigm of helping the "weak" women and children. Maruti compensates for the loss of patriarchal authority not only in the lives of his friends, but also in his mother's life. After his father is abducted and the villagers force his mother to leave the village, he carries away a house for them to live in. The main soundtrack of the film is the popular devotional hymn *Hanuman Chalisa* and is used often during the film. In *TNAOH*, the *Hanuman Chalisa* soundtrack is played whenever Maruti transforms to *Bal* Hanuman. In both the film and TV show, Hanuman's acts of bravery are met with refrains of *Jai Hanuman* (Hail Hanuman) from the community.

Shailendra Singh has said that Percept's presentation of Hanuman is that of a superhero rather than a religious figure (personal communication). Similarly, in a media report, a Percept Pictures executive mentioned: *"For all of us,* Hanuman is a remarkably special character and we have taken that into account. He will...[be] someone like superman, and he fights for the triumph of good over evil. We are not presenting him in a context based on any religion." (*The Hindu*, July 6, 2007; emphasis added). Yet the instances outlined above indicate that Hanuman is not in fact a secular superhero. *ROH* and *TNOH* quite deliberately showcase Hanuman as a god. The collapse between Indian and Hindu was evident in Shailendra Singh's statement that he was sure of the icon's success since "every Indian home is aware of Hanuman" (personal communication). The belief in Hanuman's universal appeal in a multi-religious society betrays the dominant construction of India as a Hindu nation-state.

The last few decades have witnessed the resurgence of Hindutva – the notion that India should be a Hindu nation, and that India's Hindu culture is its defining characteristic. Lutgendorf (2007, 367) notes that Hanuman was co-opted by Hindutva groups during the Ayodhya "liberation" movement.[4] A youth wing of the movement was named Bajrang Dal, loosely translated as "army of Hanuman"; it invoked Hanuman's folksy Hindi epithet of *Bajrangbali* or "iron-limbed hero." The Bajrang Dal's role in the violence and riots that accompanied the Ayodhya movement was widely noted in the press. According to Lutgendorf, the association of Hanuman with militant Hinduism rested on Hanuman's embodiment of some recurring tropes of Hindutva ideology:

> its glorification of physical and military strength, its insistence that Hindu men "prove" their manliness through violent encounters with the demonized members of minority communities, and its implicit agenda for the subordination of lower classes and religious minorities to … a primordial and monolithic Hindu nation-state ruled largely by upper-caste leaders
>
> (361).

Percept's child Hanuman is not a martial, muscular god, but he reaffirms the emphasis of Hindutva discourse on physical strength, and on the "sons of the land" needing to protect "an explicitly feminized familial and national body." (Bannerjee 2011, 125). At the end of *Return of Hanuman*, earth is not only feminized through the epithet "mother earth" but also Hinduized when she appears in the form of a sari-clad goddess and thanks Hanuman for saving her. Thus a potentially global, secular mission of saving the planet from the effects of pollution is laden with the symbolism of Hindu nationalism. *ROH* and *TNAOH* also enact the erasure of minorities—Bajrangpur is almost entirely composed of Hindus. Moreover, Maruti's high Brahmin caste is emphasized in the film on multiple occasions.

In her analysis of the trend of baby-gods in calendar art, Patricia Uberoi (2006, 100) postulates that the "recent multiplication" of baby-gods may be read as "a gesture of reconciliation in our communally polarized world, post Ayodhya" since, for example, "the sleeping baby-Ram is surely a benign image when compared to the militant adult Ram" [and] "the adorable baby Hanuman is a far cry from the aggressive, humanoid body-builder Hanuman iconography." While *Bal* Hanuman does not evoke militant Hinduism in the same way, the perpetuation of Hindu majoritarian ideologies in the franchise is insidious precisely because the "adorable" boy-god has a disarming effect on receptive spectators. The dynamics of identification for adult viewers are grounded in the sentimentalized, emotional bond between mother and son or devotee and deity, while the affective category of friendship becomes central to the child audience's identification with Hanuman. In *ROH*, Maruti's admiring friends transform into *Bal* Hanuman's devotees when the toddler reveals his true form. *TNAOH* reinforces this religious hero worship, which seems to model the desired relationship between the god and child viewers.

Lutgendorf (2015) observes that Indian public and political discourse has regularly struggled with the "foreignness" of the post-liberalization visual and consumption regime, and this unease is reflected in, for example, sometimes violent protests against Valentine's Day celebrations and multinational fast food outlets. He claims that the animated *Hanuman* must be read as a response to the "anxieties over the erosion and potential loss of "Indian" cultural identity, especially among the youth." (258). In a similar vein, John Lent observes that "Indian parents like these 'mytho-cartoons' because they introduce ancient tales to a generation they believe is losing touch with its 5000-year heritage, and because they supplant what existed before—U.S. animation and Japanese anime" (110–11). In his interviews with parents about mythological animation films Vamsee Juluri (2010, 67) found that they had expectations that these stories would reflect certain values. Most contemporary mythological animations and picturebooks cater to such expectations of religious didacticism (Madan 2010). Mythological animations such as the *Hanuman* franchise aim not only to inform children about the leonine deeds of mythological figures, but also attempt to impart values considered important for children to possess, such as bravery, honesty, hard work and obedience to parents.

Juluri (2010, 67) claims that "if, indeed, the new mythologies demand from viewers a discursive identification with definitions and labels (as Hindus, or as Hindu superheroes, for example)[,] then perhaps the political dangers are imminent. However, if these stories remain narrated in non-normative fashions, as ideals for values like 'devotion' and 'valor' as participants believe, then their use may remain politically unmotivated, and perhaps culturally desirable." Nevertheless, the producers/directors of these films do rely on, and actively encourage, viewers' religious identification with boy-gods, thus excluding the significant sub-set of the child population that is not Hindu, or does not identify as Hindu. One parent in Juluri's reception study had this to say about the Hanuman soft toy:

> I think it is rather cute. No problem with this…children adore Hanuman and I'm sure he is better to have as a security blanket than a teddy bear. My daughters, in any case, have a small god picture under their pillows when they sleep
>
> (67)

This statement suggests that Hindu middle-class parents may consume religious products uncritically, especially since producers play to their fears that their children are being alienated from their religious tradition in an increasingly globalized environment, and claim to redress this sense of deprivation through these products.

In the final analysis, Hanuman embodies discourses of Hindu majoritarianism, patriarchy and neoliberalism. The boy-god may be cute but is hardly harmless since he upholds hegemonic ideas of nation, gender relations and caste for an impressionable child audience.

Acknowledgements

I would like to thank Philip Lutgendorf and John Stephens for their insightful comments on an earlier draft of the essay. I would also like to thank Yusuf Shaikh and Shailendra Singh for giving me the opportunity to interview them.

Notes

1 Animation in India has a long history going back to the beginning of the twentieth century. John Lent notes that the 1990s saw a rapid liberalization-fueled expansion of the animation industry. In the last few years, many Indian media companies have partnered with American companies like Disney and Turner International to create local, indigenous animated content.

2 *Asuras* are loosely translated as evil and powerful supernatural creatures, frequently in conflict with heavenly deities. The TV series draws more on the American superhero tradition than does the film, especially in its choice of supervillain.

3 Much work has been done on the political appropriation of *Ramayana*. Purnima Mankekar (1999), Sheldon Pollock (1993), Arvind Rajagopal (2001) and Romila Thapar (1989) are a few scholars who have written on the role of exclusivist versions of *Ramayana* in reinforcing Hindu

nationalism and popularizing hegemonic forms of masculinity and femininity in both the domestic and public spheres.

4 This movement was geared to reclaiming what Hindu nationalists believe was Rama's birthplace in Ayodhya, on which a mosque had been built. The Hindu nationalists succeeded in destroying the mosque. The resulting religious riots led to the loss of scores of lives, especially those of Muslims.

References

Bannerjee, Anindita (2011) "A Higher Narrative in Pictures: Iconography, Intermediality and Contemporary Uses of the Epic in India," in Steven Shankman and Amiya Dev (eds.) *Epic and Other Higher Narratives: Essays in Intercultural Studies*, New Delhi: Pearson Education, pp. 112–127.

Breckenridge, Carol A. and Arjun Appadurai (1995) "Public Modernity in India," in Carol A. Breckenridge (ed.) *Consuming Modernity: Public Culture in a South Asian World*, Minneapolis, MN: University of Minnesota Press, pp. 1–20.

Chandra, Nandini (2012) "The Prehistory of the Superhero Comics in India (1976–1986)," *Thesis Eleven* 113(1): 57–77.

Coogan, Peter (2009) "The Definition of a Superhero," in Jeet Heer and Kent Worcester (eds.) *A Comic Studies Reader*, Jackson, MS: University of Mississippi Press, pp. 77–93.

Davé, Shilpa (2013) "Spiderman India: Comic Books and the Translating/Transcreating of American Cultural Narratives," in Shane Danson, Christina Meyer and Daniel Stein (eds.) *Transnational Perspectives on Graphic Narratives: Comics at the Crossroads*, London: Bloomsbury Academic, pp. 127–144.

Fernandes, Leela (2006) *India's New Middle Class: Democratic Politics in an Era of Economic Reform*, Minneapolis, MN: University of Minnesota Press.

Forgacs, David (1992) "Disney Animation and the Business of Childhood," *Screen* 33(4): 361–374.

Jacobsen, Knut A. (2004) "The Child Manifestation of Siva in Contemporary Hindu Popular Prints," *Numen* 51(3): 237–264.

Juluri, Vamsee (2010) "Reimagining Tradition: Globalization in India from MTV to Hanuman," in Youna Kim (ed.) *Media Consumption and Everyday Life in Asia*, New York, NY: Routledge, pp. 59–69.

Kashyap, Anurag (dir.) (2007) *Return of Hanuman*, Mumbai: Percept Pictures Company.

Lent, John (2009) "Animation in South Asia," *Studies in South Asian Film and Media* 1(1): 101–117.

Lutgendorf, Philip (2007) *Hanuman's Tale: The Messages of a Divine Monkey*, New York: Oxford University Press.

Lutgendorf, Philip (2015) "Bringing Up Hanuman: Hanuman and the Changing Imagination of Childhood," in Molly Kaushal, Alok Bhalla, Ramakar Pant (eds.) *Ramkatha in Narrative, Performance and Pictorial Traditions*, New Delhi: Indira Gandhi National Centre for the Arts, pp. 251–262.

Madan, Anuja (2010) "Construction of Morality in Contemporary English Adaptations of Mahabharata for Children," *The Journal of Children's Literature Studies* 7(3): 80–97.

Mathur, Suchitra (2010) "From Capes to Snakes: The Indianization of the American Superhero," in Mark Berninger, Jochen Ecke and Gideon Haberkorn (eds.) *Comics as a Nexus of Cultures: Essay on the Interplay of Media, Disciplines and International Perspectives*, London: McFarland and Company, pp. 175–186.

Ramaswamy, Sumathi (ed.) (2003) *Beyond Appearances? Visual Practices and Ideologies in Modern India*, New Delhi: Sage Publications.

Samant, V.G. and Milind Ulkey (dir.) (2005) *Hanuman*, Mumbai: Sahara Motion Pariwaar, Percept Pictures and Silvertoons.

The New Adventures of Hanuman, 2010. Season 1. TV, POGO.

The New Adventures of Hanuman, 2011. Season 2. TV, POGO.

Uberoi, Patricia (2006) *Freedom and Destiny: Gender, Family, and Popular Culture in India*, New Delhi: Oxford University Press.

28

WRITING ANIMAL NOVELS IN CHINESE CHILDREN'S LITERATURE[1]

Ying Hou
(Translated by Aiping Nie)

Animal images have always been common in children's literature. As research on animals deepens, and animal novels become rich and detailed, the realistic approach to animals in children's books has evolved as a popular genre. The genre can take several forms, but must always contend with the fact that any attempt to represent the nonhuman is mediated, and the nature and scope of the stories that can be told about animals will be shaped by these mediations. Children's animal fiction in China is relatively recent, and has evolved through three stages (Wang 2011: 11–14). In the first stage, during the 1980s, novels mainly explore the relationship between animals and humans, in which animals are usually hunted by people. The narrative techniques are based on those employed in folk tales, legends, and animal fables and stories. In general, narration does not adopt the point of view of the animals or attribute them with subject positions, but writes about them, as in Shen Shixi's *The Seventh Courser*, and *The Life of A Vulture*, Li Chuanfeng's *The Retired Army Dog Yellow Fox*, Zhu Xinwang's *The Little Fox Huabei*. The images of animals in these novels, quite symbolic and satiric, are the embodiment of an ethical pursuit that uses animals to "educate" people. In the second stage, animals become the protagonists in the novel, and their living environment and behavior have become the major concern in description. "The conflict, struggle and jungle law in the animal world are shown; complicated emotions related to death, love, hate, honor, disgrace, sorrow and joy in the animal-animal relationship have come into focus" (Wang: 11–14). Representative works are Shen Shixi's *The Dream of the Wolf King*, and *The Red Milch Goat*, Jin Zenghao's *The Gray Wolf*, Lin Jin's *The Death of the King of the Snow Mountain*, amongst others. The third stage starts from the beginning of the twenty-first century and more often takes an ecological approach and blends a variety of writing techniques. Animal novels now "try to probe deep into animals from the 'scientific' perspective of animal behaviorism, and render a true picture of the animal life" (Wang: 11–14). Books like Shen Shixi's *The Slave Bird*, Fang Min's *The Epic of Pandas*, Heihe's *Dark Flame* are of this category. On the other hand, if animal fiction is rather classified in terms of genres and representative writers and books, the following four categories become apparent.

Animal stories to inspire humans

Chang Xingang was best known in the 1980s for his teenage novels, but turned to animal stories in recent years. Novels like *The Cow Who Knows Art, Run! Rabbit!, The Outstanding Yellow-haired Tiger, The Adventures of a Free-range Cock, Be Happy, Piggy!* are classified as inspirational animal novels, centering on issues such as the relationships among animals, animals and people, and animals and the environment. Every novel relates a story about how a clearly defined animal challenges the living environment and strives to change its destiny, aiming to show unfamiliar aspects of the animals we are familiar with, such as their less known life and unique characteristics, through the combination of romantic fairytale imagination and realistic description.

Chang's novels are animal autobiographies, a genre which originated in Western children's literature in the second half of the nineteenth century (Dwyer 2015: 2). As Annie Dwyer points out, the animal autobiography represents animal interiority as analogous to human interiority and "endows animals with moral sense – the perception of the difference between right and wrong, the ability to understand the present in relation to past and future moments, and the recognition of the other as ontologically distinct from the self" (6). *The Cow Who Knows Art* tells the story through the mouth of a carefree calf incapable of work. While his father and elder brother work for people without complaint, his mind runs free and responds, for example, to the tree in the wild field which he hears call to him. One day, he is deafened by fireworks, but rescued by a red-headed bunting and its mother who brought him red petals of the wild lilies, which not only restored his hearing but also unexpectedly gave him superpowers. He could hear the voice of the crickets, who trained him to become a singing cow. While practicing, he was overheard by a talent scout from the theater and thus became a cow who performed on the stage. But disaster again struck, and he was deafened again during a performance by stereophonic waves, and was consequently driven out of the theater together with his "valet de chambre", a brown dog. Thereafter, he came to live in the wilderness, where the bunting and its mother again tried to cure his deafness.

The animals in the novel are highly personified. The calf was born different, capable of dreaming, rebellion, seeing trees others cannot see, hearing a special voice in his deafness, and finding a talent for singing when cured. The brown dog is grateful and conscientious; the little sparrow is energetic, kind, and helpful. These personified animals appear lively and vivid, making people feel strange and familiar at the same time. Some scholars dubbed Chang Xingang's animal novels "initiation fairytales", for their rich imagination, elegant thought and vivid, profound description.

Another major author in this genre is Zheng Yuanjie, sometimes referred to as "the King of Fairytales" (Zhu 2014: 12). His *Stories of the Twelve Animals of the Chinese Zodiac* have drawn on the cultural legends to present interesting and amusing stories about the animals, which also offer perspectives on people's daily lives.

Animal fantasy: between human-centeredness and animal-centeredness

When a writer recognizes that animal stories are dominated by anthropocentrism – the assumption that the world can only be perceived from a human perspective – it becomes possible to write against anthropocentrism and make it untenable. Jin Zenghao, especially through his animal novels, has exerted great influence on children's literature nationwide. The animals in Jin's books, based on his observations of animals in zoos, range from wild animals like wolves, lynxes, and foxes to others like dogs, turtles, snakes, and eagles. By adopting an animal-centered perspective, Jin attributes to these animals natural rights and wisdom, and hence, like people, they pursue freedom and happiness in life. If caught between freedom and confinement, the animals would rather choose to die instead of living a confined life.

Jin's *The Lone Wolf* (2013) recounts the story of a wolf, who after being captured and encaged by hunters, chooses to bite the steel cage every day. "Wolves do not fear death, and love freedom. To them, confinement is more terrible than death". In an earthquake, the wall falls down, and the wolf is able to return to the forest. There he meets a she-wolf and has his own cubs, accomplishing the task of carrying on the family line. The white horse Beibei in the novel *The Life of a White Horse* has an honorable history in horse-racing, but becomes blind in a disaster, and subsequently lives in confinement. Later, he gets rid of the chains and jumps off a cliff. His final choice is more a sign of incompetence than a pursuit of freedom in that the modern society which confines him is an institutionalized society with various rules and regulations. Even if he escapes from the cage, and goes back to nature, he cannot survive and only has to return to the human world. Jin Zenghao endeavored to depict the meeting point of the wild call and life instinct amid the gloomy city and poetic wilderness, and vehemently criticized the evil killing and harm people did to animals. Again, in *The Angry Foxes* and *Lynxes in the Vast Valley* Jin depicts an irreconcilable conflict between human-centered and animal-centered concerns which results in humans causing suffering to animals. The questions and issues raised in these books aim to arouse people from their numbness and greed and impress upon them that all sentient animals have rights and interests that are inherent to a sound moral view of the world.

Jin's animal novels try, in terms of the time, space, and techniques in narration, to minimize the influence of human culture, and offer readers access to the experience of a carefree and instinctual life. He strives to construct an ecological space in which people, animals, and plants are interrelated and mutually affected. In the rendition of the struggle for survival in nature, he never neglected the small, unimportant animals, and even wrote about the healing capacities of grass. A lively and rich nature will not disappear along with the disappearance of some animals. A sustainable living space gets activated in front of readers. The sky, land and ocean, with creatures living in them, comprise a complete ecological system, in which everything is interdependent. Their defense and struggle are equal in nature. His novels illustrate a broad view of the universe and life, which is really precious.

Animal fiction entails the description of the natural environment, which is not only the living space of animals, but the externalization and reproduction of the emotions and feelings attributed to them. Jin's animal novels abound in such descriptive passages. For example, *No. 66 Police Dog* (2013) tells how the sensitive, wise and responsible police dog Lala retires at the age of 13, after a productive career, but cannot settle into a life of idleness and comfort. He has been shown to have led a valuable life, so now goes to the wilderness to help guard medicinal herbs. There he finds peace at heart, especially as the valley at night evokes beautiful feelings: "The moonlight in the early autumn seems to rinse the valley with its pure, shiny water. Everything is white and moist, except the forest of black pines on the North Mountain. The water in the marshland gives off a silver shimmer. Viewed from the hill, the whole marshland is like a broken mirror. Several frogs croak now and then among the reeds and cattails. Against the rigid rippling pine forest, the croaking sounds weak and strange. A little snake is crossing the river, leaving its wake on the water. A many-legged insect swaggers on a piece of reed leaf". The charm of the writer's personality is reflected in his language, that is, a natural, unpolished language loaded with subtle emotions and capable of communicating with children without difficulty or obstacles. There is a huge cultural cohesive power and neat rhythm in Jin's animal novels, whether in artistic connotation or expressive forms, which are typical of the cultural temperament in South China. The plot employs a "bead string" structure which puts plants and medical herbs in an encounter with animals. This accidental meeting reveals the detailed description of the animal psychology. One can always find something extraordinary in the seeming plainness, together with the emotional control, profound philosophical thoughts and random emphasis. All these show the far-reaching cultural background behind the writer. It is very similar to the story-telling and ballad singing in Suzhou dialect, which may suddenly give you a big surprise amid its lighthearted poeticness and argument. It is also like the rich water and gray sky in South China, where the mystery of life is as charming as ever. Hence, it is easy to see how the profound cultural background helps him gain a deep understanding of life and humanity.

In addition, an animal-centered perspective is also evident in novels such as Xue Yifeng's *The Track of the Crocodile* (2011), Li Ziyu's *The Sea Wolf* (2011) and Li Di's *The Leopard Haqi*.

Animal legends: to see the world as an animal sees it

Case study: Shen Shixi

As Zhu Ziqiang points out, "The self-conscious creation of animal novels in China was launched in the 1980s" (2014: 165). The first animal novel in China to write only about animals without including human characters was Lin Jin's prize-winning *The Fierce Battle on the Icy River*, published in *Oriental Youth* in 1982. However, the writer who really made animal fiction well-known in China is Shen Shixi, also called "King of Animal Fiction". His thirty-year writing career has produced numerous novels, amongst which several have won literary awards: *The Seventh Courser, The Life of a Vulture, Red Milk Sheep, Holy Fire* and *The Dream of the Wolf King*, and *The Complaints of the Elephant Mother*. *Gorals Fly over the Sea* was included in the textbook list for seventh graders in China, and *The Last Embattled Elephant* was chosen for the sixth graders.

Shen Shixi's writing ideas and techniques are widely accepted by readers. Tragedy is common in his stories and tragedy is also what he is good at. The philosophy shown through his tragic arts, which pursue power and dignity in life, helps purify and elevate the essence of life in the furnace of tragic sadness. Therefore, nearly all the animals from the vulture, disabled wolf, the elephant king to the wolf king, and deer king have undergone a hard life and met their tragic end. The animals have taken on the significance imposed by human society and assert against it a sense of animals as subjects and agents to whom humans have moral obligations. "When the writer changes his artistic perspective, all of a sudden, the dwarfed and mean images of animals immediately appear human-like and take on shiny splendor in the jungle world. The shift of perspectives in animal fiction has contributed to the great progress in the writing of animal novels both in their ideas and in their artistic techniques" (Peng 2003: 43). Shen also said, "One may find something new and fresh when looking at society through animals' eyes. Modern animal fiction pays much attention to the new perspective, that is, to see and feel, to tell the story with animals' eyes" (1996: 53). What kind of components does Shen Shixi's tragic art include in order to engage such a large audience?

Most of the animals in his books are wild animals, who live mainly in the vast wilderness, the hot humid tropical rainforest, the freezing snow-covered mountain, or the surging Lantsang River. The unique landscape and settings in Xishuang Banna has given Shen ample room for creation, as well as material for an original taste of life in the forest. The life of animals in such environments is extremely hard. Danger from their natural enemies, competition among the same kind, shortage of food, and hunting by humans have always stood as great threats to their lives. No matter how smart, sly, and strong the animals are, they would eventually be killed by other animals or by people. There are thus numerous traps in Shen's jungles, and there is no happy ending or final closure. Even if an animal happened to escape from one crisis, it may never escape the next. His creation of animals like the goats, wolves, dogs, elephants, birds, cows, eagles, and so on all come from his long-time investigation in the virgin forest in Yunnan province, from his careful and penetrating understanding of animals' development, from his insightful thinking about life and destiny. The setting of the novel may be a barren mountain ridge, or a dark damp cave, or a dried water course, or a cliff. All those places are often frequented by Shen's animals. Although the animals there are free from human interference as they are rarely visited by people, the living conditions are extremely bad, where snowstorms, intense cold, rainstorms, or dust storms are quite common. The harsh conditions lead to their tragedies. He wrote at the very beginning of *The System of Jackals* that the Etis jackals marched ahead on the plain in the snowstorm. The jackals of about seventy or eighty in number are all listless, be it the old, the young, the male or the female. There is a thick layer of snow on their heads, and backs, making them look like mourners at a funeral. Every jackal is hungry as it can be seen that the stomach of each is so empty that it almost hits the backbone; their tails drag on the ground; their eyes glow dimly with greed and hunger. The group was disorganized, extending into the length of about two *li*. In such a harsh environment, the group is marching toward death. Then the writer describes how the starving head male jackal eats the dead jackal bodies at night, which quickly triggers the crisis and makes the members of the group fight against each other. In *The Eagle Jin Shanzi*, the harsh living conditions completely change the animal instinct. Eagles are sons of the sky. They are not gregarious, but on the contrary, quite territorial. If their own kind launches an attack, they will fight to the death in defense.

Shen's animal novels usually have fantastic plots, sharp conflicts, and are reminiscent of legends in form and atmosphere. His shaping of the animal characters also sheds light on their individualistic features. However, each animal is not only discernible in character, but also patterned on heroic experience and noble in thoughts and morals. Some scholars point out that his animal images are not based on actual animal behavior but are anthropomorphically endowed with noble moral thoughts and profound significance, and Shen himself in a 2015 interview agreed that, "The stories are actually about humans, but from a different angle …. Humans have the same struggle between good and evil, between fate, or basic instincts, and free will" (Lu n.p.). In *The Tomb of the Elephant* (2012), the she-elephant Baya chooses to help her son when the son challenges his father to abdicate the throne, and finally defeats the husband. But Baya in her prime of life decides to jump into the tomb and get buried together with the old elephant king, her husband. In *Gorals Fly Over the Sea*, the goral group are driven to the edge of a cliff by hunters and their hounds. The gorals divide themselves into two groups. And the old gorals choose to sacrifice themselves so as to let the young and strong ones safely jump onto the opposite cliff by stepping on them. Such plots are surprising, and do not reflect how animal groups are organized.

In his plotting of the tragedies, Shen not only focuses on animals' behavior, but also emphasizes their psychology, but this is typically highly personified. Rather than relying on description of external features and actions to evoke the feelings and emotions of animals, Shen Shixi goes directly into their inner world to show them. And the thinking reflected in these feelings is clearly based on the desires and responses of human psychology. Shen comments, "The reason why animal fiction is more attractive than other types is that its subject matter can easily penetrate through human culture and social formality, break the confinement of morality, as well as dismantle the falsehood in the civilized society, so as to reveal and show the original state of life, that is, a combination of beauty and ugliness. With the vicissitude of societies, culture may flourish or decline, social formality may be replaced, moral thoughts may get rectified, civilization may progress, but the cruel struggle for survival, the strong will to live and the pursuit of splendor will never change. So animal fiction has enough reasons to win readers, to attain immortality" (Shen 2010). Shen incorporates his understanding of life into his animal stories, and shows his thoughts on human existence, social development and national destiny. He adds social and anthropological meanings to his books by employing animals as a metaphor for people's social life, and by exploring the fate of animals as a reflection on the environment and an exposition of the change in the relationship between people and nature. He is good at describing the real, lively and dramatic scenes in the natural animal world and using them to insinuate similar events in human society.

Representing the inner life of animals

In the creation of animal novels in Chinese children's literature, Heihe, an Inner-Mongolian writer, is quite outstanding. Gerileqimuge Heihe, who was born in 1975 in the fringe area between the prairie and the rural villages in Inner Mongolia in the northeast of China, is the author of numerous novels, such as *Old Brother Ban*, *Return to the Prairie*, *The Kingdom of Reindeers*, *The Ghost Dog*, *Swan Pasture*, *Dark Flame*, *The Wolverine River*, *The Shepherd Dog on the Grassland*, and so on. He has been the recipient of many awards. He recaptures with his words the animals on the verge of losing the prairie and their wild nature. Between the lines flow his love, understanding and dedication to animals. Heihe's works are somewhat autobiographic accounts, closely related to his personal life experiences. In his childhood in Inner Mongolia, the blue sky, white clouds, grasslands, cattle, sheep and shepherd dogs gave him infinite happiness and freedom. That was also a period of social transformation in China from the primitive agricultural age to an industrial, commercial and informational age. On the one hand, the backward farming and pastoral life on the prairie was replaced by modern city life. High-rise buildings, factories, cars, motorways, and railways have eroded large areas of grasslands and farmlands. While there has been a great improvement in material life, new cultures, thoughts and values have clashed with people's old way of life. The transformation dealt a great blow to people's daily life, emotional world, spiritual pursuits, and moral judgment. With the passing of time and increasing age, Heihe's childhood on the grasslands faded away as he entered into the adult world, but the memories of his pastoral childhood never faded. "Ever since I left the prairie, I had been back so many times. I didn't know what I was looking for. … My dogs were there waiting for me". "I led them racing about in the sun in the wilderness. They were to me the age of gold rush that has never declined. That was where my childhood lay, the distant dream of a boy always cherishing a childish heart" (Heihe, *The Ghost Dog*, 6). However, nature is not always aesthetic and poetic. The seven-month-long winter and the freezing cold at forty degrees below zero in the northeast result in a shortage of food. Both the herbivores and carnivores have nothing to eat. Man, the omnivorous creature, highly appreciates the beauty of a body as strong and tough as the wild animals on the prairie, invalidating the aesthetic standard of the civilized world, and thus shaping their unyielding, optimistic, outgoing, humorous and straightforward cultural character. The geographical features of the tundra culture have propelled people to think and reflect in extreme cold. The prairie fosters an open mind and also brings about challenges. "Survival of the fittest" is quite true of the reality here, and the test is much tougher. *Caucasian Shepherd Dog* vividly tells the story of an inexperienced shepherd dog who gave birth to ten babies in cold weather, while only one survived in the end, quite a miracle of life in such bad weather conditions.

Since animals' actions and behaviors constitute the main plot of Heihe's animal novels, the animal characters are well rounded, while the human characters are usually two-dimensional. The first person narrator in Heihe's novels loves animals, while other people such as the old people, hunters, children, businessmen, and men who hurt animals are functional and flat characters in narrative terms. In contrast, the roles of animals reflect and remain true to their diverse, unique characters, such as the wild and intractable ghost dog, the loyal Dark Flame, the filial dog, the mischievous shepherd dog, and so on. They have a colorful inner world and a noble mind.

Heihe prefers a first person narrator who is the observer, companion, and friend of animals. This narrator – a self-portrait of the writer himself – is more than 190 centimeters high, loves grasslands and forests, and has a rich experience of surviving in the wild. He is also a person with rich spirit, sound psychology, and tender feelings, who shows respect and awe for the beauty and dignity of life, and can communicate with both children and animals. He is the owner of the dog.

Heihe's animal novels adamantly take the animals' side. They criticize the greed and wiliness of businessmen, and the foolishness and folly of simple-minded herdsmen who exchange the animals they love for two bottles of wine. They lash the hunting of the animals, while extolling the life force of animals themselves. They express guilt over the inconsiderate lack of protection which causes the accidental death of animals, and lament the unchangeable destiny of animals. They contemplate issues about "Great Nature" and "the Great Life", and still subtly depict "Little Life" and "Little Creatures". His works do not seek novel ways to recount the lives of animals, but seek to address contemporary issues such as disappearing grasslands, animals' life, natural ecology, free spiritedness, yearning for childhood, and so on. Heihe spent his childhood in the company of mother and son shepherd dogs. When he grew up, he went back to visit the prairie and forest every year, and established a solid friendship with the minority groups there. The blend and fusion of the subject into life has enabled his books to take on special meanings: "I endeavored to construct a utopian wild world filled with love, courage, freedom and loyalty" (*The Kingdom of Reindeers* 1). It exhibits his romantic thoughts and feelings about the harmony between man and nature, yet the worry and criticism underlying such thoughts can also be keenly felt. The scene of the dying Tibetan mastiff in *Dark Flame* is quite moving. "When a Tibetan mastiff realized his life was going to end, it always left the world quietly. ... The mother mastiff walks towards the snow mountain outlined against the first light of the day. ... When the dark form of the mother mastiff disappeared from the horizon, the daybreak came" (*Dark Flame* 1). The sun also rises. The whole picture is heroic yet tragic. Heihe's outlook on life is quite naturalistic. Man and animals are interdependent. Death is natural. All comes from dust and returns to dust. His works touch on wild nature, the essential qualities, and the future, while showing the vanity of attempts made to harness nature.

Another writer whose animal novels are mainly realistic is Liang Bo, who came to prominence before Heihe. In *The Last Wild Horse*, for example, Liang Bo spares no efforts in describing the hardship the wild horses are faced with in the wilderness. The unpredictable future and cruel competition between animals fully show his philosophy of "Survival of the fittest in natural selection". He puts animals and human beings in parallel lines, thus making the plot line coherent and close-knit. The ending whereby the mustang and Krym, a Uygur herdsman, get together to run after happiness not only extends the book's internal purport, but also naturally conveys the idea that every living creature is equal.

Finally, other writers whose animal novels faithfully represent the living conditions of animals and reflect on human conditions are Mu Ling (*The Fourth Miracle, Raging Waves, The Hard Return Journey, The King of the Wilderness*) and Fang Min (*The Great Struggle, The Great Destruction, The Great Perfection*). These novels all depict the hard struggle for survival against a harsh nature and violent attack from foes. The colorful animal images, the heart-rending emotional tie between people and animals, the soul-stirring legendary tales, and the wild, beautiful primitive life depicted will continue to attract readers one generation after another. This is the great power of animal novels on children's emotion and spirit, and also the importance and mission of animal fiction.

Conclusion

In recent years, the social transformation in China, the rise of the culture industry and the construction of ecological civilization have contributed to the flourishing of animal fiction in children's literature, which occupies an important place in the list of popular children's books every year and attracts well over one hundred million readers. Animal novels are not only important to the spiritual growth of children, but also inspire the creation of animal novels for adults, for example, Jiang Rong's internationally celebrated *Wolf Totem* (2004). This approaches the problems of humanity in the light of animal spirit. Its huge popularity with young readers prompted Jiang to produce a children's version, *Little Wolf, Little Wolf* (2005). Nowadays in China, more and more writers of adult literature have begun to write animal books for children. Accordingly, animal novels stand as a new growth point in the post-modern context with a positive cultural value. That the genre explores human emotions and spiritual return in culture from a specific perspective is of great literary significance. Animal novels abound in children's literature. They serve to arouse people through their aesthetic power to protect animals, but at the same time writing about humans and animals, whatever the approach, is always about the nature and survival of the human. Human beings on the one hand assume the power to conquer and exploit animals, while on the other hand cherish nature and seek to love and protect animals. Paradoxical as we are, we are forever struggling between the two sides. The history of the development of human relationships with animals is the history of human civilization. This history has witnessed so much blood, the blood of our animal neighbors as well as the blood of our own. Nonetheless, history still pushes human civilization forward, and romantic images of a pristine and more innocent world are images of a world few people would readily return to. The progress and development of human civilization should be highly valued. However, in some Chinese animal stories there seems to be an overemphasis on man's cruelty and killing of animals, and an intensification and exaggeration of the inferiority of human nature to that of animals. As a result, animals become deified while human beings are demonized. Famous writers and their books such as Shen Shixi's *Gorals Fly Over the Sea*, Yang Zhijun's *Tibetan Mastiff*, and Jiang Rong's *Wolf Totem*, on the one hand, downplay the human characters, while on the other, elevate animals into god-like perfect figures. In Shen Shixi's book, when the old gorals line up in the sky to form a springboard, so as to let the young gorals jump over the wide gap between mountains, the scene is undeniably impressive, but careful thinking would render this practically false and impossible. Any mathematical or physical calculation would deny such a scheme, but for the working of the theme, the writer chooses to ascribe to the animals any attributes that may facilitate the plot. Such a way is not objective, and has a quite clear educational implication, that is, these god-like animals should be role models and perfect teachers to teach and educate people. We should guard against such practice in children's literature.

Note

1 This paper was funded by the National Social Science Project On Animal Narratology: The Hidden Texts of Sense and Sensibility in the Human World (10BZW108).

Bibliography

Dwyer, Annie (2015) "Animal Autobiography and the Domestication of Human Freedom," *Arizona Quarterly* 71(2):1–30.
Heihe, Gerileqimuge (2010) *The Ghost Dog*, Beijing: China Children's Publishing House.
Heihe, Gerileqimuge (2010) *The Kingdom of Reindeers*, Beijing: China Children's Publishing House.
Heihe, Gerileqimuge (2008) *Dark Flame*, Guilin: Jieli Publishing House.
Jin, Zenghao (2013) *No.66 Police Dog*, Chengdu: Sichuan Publishing Group.
Jin, Zenghao (2013) *Lone Wolf*, Chengdu: Sichuan Publishing Group.
Lu, Feiran (2015) "Animal novelist sees parallels in human behaviour," Shanghai Daily, September 22 www.shanghaidaily.com/district/minhang/Animal-novelist-see-parallels-in-human-behavio-/shdaily.shtml (accessed 3/11/2016).
Peng, Siyuan (2003) "On Contemporary Chinese Animal Fiction," *The Journal of Chongqing Normal College* 3: 43.
Shen, Shixi (1996) "On Animal Fiction," *Yunnan Children's Literature Studies*, Kunming: Chenguang Publishing Press.
Shen, Shixi (2008) *Gorals Fly Over the Sea*, Hangzhou: Zhejiang Children's Publishing House.
Shen, Shixi (2010) *The Double-faced Hound*, Hangzhou: Zhejiang Children's Publishing House.
Shen, Shixi (2012) *The Tomb of the Elephant*, Hangzhou: Zhejiang Children's Publishing House.
Wang, Quangen (2011) "The Spiritual Weight and Multi-dimensional Construction of Animal Fiction," *Journal of Literature and Art*, 11–14.
Zhu, Ziqiang (2010) "To Search for the Spiritual Homeland with Homesickness," *The Journal of Suihua Teachers College* 3:43.
Zhu, Ziqiang (2014) *Chinese Children's Literature in the Golden Age*, Beijing: China Children's Press Publication Group.

29

THE CENTRALITY OF HAWAIIAN MYTHOLOGY IN THREE GENRES OF HAWAI'I'S CONTEMPORARY FOLK LITERATURE FOR CHILDREN

Stuart Ching and Jann Pataray-Ching

In this article, we categorize three trends in contemporary Hawai'i folk literature for children: literature that retells or adapts ancient Hawaiian mythology; literature that celebrates the *local* pan-ethnic identity that formed during Hawai'i's sugar plantation era; and literature that reproduces a paradisiacal Hawai'i, which is the central trope of Hawai'i's tourism industry. We use the above categories to contextualize the literature; to illustrate the literature's relationship to Hawai'i's economic, political, and cultural development; and, finally, to clarify the relationship between this literature and a Hawai'i that is sustainable for its children and for all.

Conceptualizing Hawai'i's folklore within histories of empire and globalization

According to David Russell, researchers traditionally agree that folklore comprises "all those stories handed down from generation to generation, from old to young, by word of mouth" (2000: 148). This folkloric tradition may entertain and captivate. In addition, it may function more deeply, as Russell summarizes: through folkloric traditions, societies wrestle with inexplicable natural phenomena, express collective public or repressed desires, and articulate reasons for being in the universe (2000: 149). Over time, the resulting world views – transmitted through story among generations – become embedded within culture. The significance of these stories and the world views that they communicate need no further explanation.

Hawai'i's folkloric tradition both affirms and complicates such collectivity, for since Western contact and then through the plantation era to the present, Hawai'i's native and multicultural folklores have been contested by narratives rooted in both indigenous and foreign desires. Said notes that while "stories are at the heart of what explorers and novelists say about strange regions of the world" (1993: xii), narratives additionally become the primary vehicle through which "people ... assert their own identity and the existence of their own history" against colonialism and imperialism. Said continues:

> The main battle in imperialism is over land, of course, but when it came to who owned the land, who had the right to settle and work on it, who kept it going, who won it back, and who now plans its future – these issues were reflected, contested, and even for a time decided in narrative. As one critic has suggested, nations themselves *are* narrations. The power to narrate, or to block other narratives from forming and emerging, is very important to culture and imperialism, and constitutes one of the main connections between them.
>
> (1993: xiii)

In relation to folk literature, Hawai'i's history affirms this connection between narration and land. That is, Hawai'i's folklore since Western contact has emerged within and evolved alongside control over Hawai'i's natural resources: from the *Māhele* (the 1848 division that dispossessed Hawaiians of their lands); through the sugar plantation era of the late 1800s and the early 1900s, which brought settlers from around the globe to Hawai'i; and during current times of globalization and transcontinental movement, in which tourism and global capitalism fuel Hawai'i's economy.

We briefly outline the major narratives of these eras as follows: we characterize the first narrative straightforwardly as Hawaiian mythology, which folklorist Martha Beckwith once called "the whole range of storytelling" (1970: 2) among the Hawaiians dating back to pre-Western contact and through which native Hawaiian scholar Lilikalā Kame'eleihiwa (1992) affirms Hawaiians' genealogies and connections to the *'āina*, or land. The second major narrative comprises accommodation themes, which scholars and artists have called the formation of a *local* (racially non-white, pan-ethnic) identity in response to the white late-nineteenth and early-twentieth century oligarchy of plantation paternalism (Sumida 1991; Chock 1996; Lum 1998; Romaine 1994; Kawamoto 1993).This accommodation metaphor often conflates local and native identities, for both locals and native Hawaiians have historically struggled for agency amid the whirlwind of capitalism. But while historians and artists have accurately documented the oppressive consequences of plantation paternalism, other scholars have argued that local identity appropriates the Hawaiian concept of sharing but neither fully realizes nor meaningfully supports native land tenure, which is necessary for the revival of native cultural practices and the reclamation of native sovereignty (Fujikane 2008; Okamura 1993, 1998; Trask 1993: 247–261; Morales 1998). Finally, the third narrative figures Hawai'i as paradise. Children's literature inspired by this narrative constructs an exotic, pastoral, and idyllic Hawai'i through tropes of paradise and Eden (Sumida 1991; Bacchilega 2007).

Hawaiian mythology and legends

Since the early Polynesians did not write their stories until Western missionaries introduced print, the early Hawaiians communicated, narrated, and retold culture orally. Many of these oral stories were lost when the last of the *kahuna* (roughly, shamans) died. However, as noted by Tachihata (1996) and Mower (2002), several scholars, most notably, Abraham Fornander, David Malo, and Samuel Kamakau, importantly recorded this body of folklore. Fornander's contributions include the *Fornander Collection of Hawaiian Antiquities and Folklore: The Hawaiian Account of the Formation of Their*

Islands and Origin of Their Race with the Traditions of Their Migrations, etc., as Gathered From Original Sources (1916) and *An Account of The Polynesian Race: Its Origin and Migrations and the Ancient History of the Hawaiian People to the Times of Kamehameha I* (1890). In 1898, native Hawaiian historian David Malo published the first version of *Hawaiian Antiquities: Mo'olelo Hawai'i* (1951), which describes Hawaiian culture before Christianity. Finally, native Hawaiian historian Samuel Kamakau documented other selections such as the "Story of the Three Lonos" (Kamakau, 1866–1871c), "The Story of Kapiolani" (Kamakau, 1866–1871d), "Legends of Waipi'o in Hawai'i and some of its Rulers who Died There" (Kamakau, 1866–1871a), and "Lore of the Kahuna Kilokilo and the Kahuna I ka papa huli honua aina" (Kamakau, 1866–1871b).

Martha Beckwith's seminal text, *Hawaiian Mythology* (1970), which was originally published in 1940, draws significantly from Kamakau, Fornander, and Malo, among many others, and her record of *The Kumulipo: A Hawaiian Creation Chant* (1972), originally published in 1951, collects and translates chants that chart the genealogy of the Hawaiian royal family.

One kind of Hawai'i children's literature connects young readers to such ancient myths. For example, as recorded by Beckwith (1972: 58) one of the earliest chants, *Kumulipo: A Hawaiian Creation Chant*, begins before creation:

O ke au I kahuli wela ka honua	At the time when the earth became hot
O ke au I kahuli lole ka lani	At the time when the heavens turned about
O ke au I kuka'iaka ka la	At the time when the sun was darkened
E ho'omalamala I ka malama	To cause the moon to shine
O Ke au o Makali'I ka po	The time of the rise of the Pleiades
O ka walewale ho'okumu honua ia	The slime, this was the source of the earth
O ke kumu o ka lipo, I lipo ai	The source of the darkness that made darkness
O ke kumu o ka Po, I po ai	The source of the night that made night
O ka lipolipo, o ka lipolipo	The intense darkness, the deep darkness
O ka lipo o ka la, o ka lipo o ka po	Darkness of the sun, darkness of the night
Po wale ho--'i	Nothing but night
Hanau ka po	The night gave birth
Hanau Kumulipo I ka po, he kane	Born was Kumulipo in the night, a male
Hanau Po'ele I ka po, he wahine	Born was Po'ele in the night, a female

This story expresses the genealogy of the Hawaiians and the origin of their Gods. The picture book *The Raven and the Sun: Echoing our Ancestors* (Kahanu 2007) connects this creation myth and the demi-god Māui, the legendary trickster who stops the sun from moving too quickly across the sky:

At the time when the earth was heated, at the time when the heavens turned about, born was Kumulipo in the night, a male; born was Pō'ele in the night, a female...

"Maui," his mother called, "look at my kapa. It is still damp! The sun is racing too fast across the sky and my bark cloth won't dry. Please slow him down for me. Go see your grandmother, and she will help you."...

The next morning as the Sun rose, Maui lassoed it with his rope. "Release me!" cried the sun. "Only if you promise to slow down," said Maui...

Māui legends figure significantly in Hawai'i children's literature. *Māui Goes Fishing* (Williams 1991) recounts Māui using his magic fishhook to pull up the Hawaiian islands. In *Māui and the Secret Fire* (Tune 1991), Māui tricks mud hens into disclosing the secret of fire-making. Other gods such as Lono, Pele, Hina, and Poli'ahu appear in children's books such as *Lono and the Magical Land Beneath the Sea* (Caren Loebel-Fried 2006), *Pele the Fire Goddess* (Varez and Kanahele 1991), *Pele and the Rivers of Fire* (Nordenstrom 2002), *Hina and the Sea of Stars* (Nordenstrom 2003), and *Pele and Poli'ahu: A Tale of Fire and Ice* (Collins 2005).

Other folktales in Hawai'i children's literature maintain indirect connections to ancient mythology. For example, *The Sleeping Giant: A Tale from Kaua'i* (Moran 2006) explains why the Kaua'i mountain range Nounou physically resembles a sleeping giant. This folktale loosely echoes the ancient myth of Kawelo (as recorded in Beckwith's *Hawaiian Mythology*), or the legendary warrior chief who slays the giant of Hanalei. Furthermore, *Uncle Kawaiola's Dream: A Hawaiian Story* (Pellegrino 2010), invokes spiritual connections to the land that are expressed in Hawaiian mythology.

Some authors are currently retelling ancient stories in both the Hawaiian and English languages. Caren Ke'ala Loebel-Fried, Nona Beamer, and Keola Beamer have collaborated on several projects: *Naupaka* (2008), *Legend of the Gourd* (2010), *Hawaiian Legends of the Guardian Spirits* (2002), *Lono and the Magical Land Beneath the Sea* (2006), *Hawaiian Legends of Dreams* (2005), *and Pua Polu: The Pretty Blue Hawaiian Flower* (2005). *Naupaka* (Beamer 2008) explains why the naupaka kahakai and naupaka kuahiwi, two plants of the same genus, grow in different places – the naupaka kahakai near the ocean and the naupaka kuahiwi in the mountains. The Hawaiian princess Naupaka falls in love with a commoner and, because of societal prohibitions, cannot marry him. As they part, Naupaka gives her lover half of a naupaka blossom and tells him that he will live near the sea and that she will live in the mountains. All naupaka blossoms today, whether growing near the shore or in the mountains, produce half a blossom.

Kawika Napolean's (2010) *'Ai'ai: A Bilingual Hawaiian Story* explains why the long, narrow rock formation in Leho'ulu, Hana on Maui differs strikingly from the scattered surrounding rock peaks. Long ago, Ko'ona, the giant eel, breaks through the rock wall that 'Ai'ai's father has built for the high chief. 'Ai'ai catches Ko'ona with a magic fishhook and brings the eel back to the giant fishpond where the eel rests and then turns into stone.

Finally, readers interested in folkloric Hawai'i children's literature should note that numerous bibliographies of myths and legends are available in various locations across Hawai'i, most notably in the special collections at the University of Hawai'i at Mānoa, but these are largely unpublished. Several publishing houses across the state of Hawai'i also focus on Hawaiian folklore for children. Among these presses are Beach House Publishing, Kamehameha Publishing, the University of Hawaii Press, and the Bishop Museum Press.

Local identity and stories

According to Takaki (1983), even as modern urban development erases Hawai'i's historic plantation era, that era's timeless character continues to shape Hawai'i's consciousness. Furthermore, Takaki (1983: 179) suggests that while the various ethnic groups of the plantation maintained their individuality, they simultaneously formed a collective "working class culture" that defined *local*-ness: "While Hawaiians, Chinese, Japanese, Koreans, Portuguese, Filipinos, and laborers of other nationalities retained their sense of ethnicity, many of them also felt a new class awareness" through their shared kinds of food, their shared language (a plantation pidgin that would become Hawai'i Creole English), and their shared struggle against oppressive labor conditions.

Contemporary *local* Hawai'i folk literature emerges from this history. Authors creating and working within this tradition of local folk literature predominantly appropriate Western fairytales or fairytale elements and design, and populate them with local characters, places, pastimes, and experiences. In this way, these stories make no claims to native/indigenous Hawaiian authenticity; rather, they foreground fantasy and *localize* or authenticate this fantastical universe by imbuing it with distinctly *local* flavor. Four picture books by Sandi Takayama exemplify this trend: *The Musubi Man* (1996), *The Musubi Man's New Friend* (2002), *Sumorella* (1997), and *The Prince and the Li Hing Mui* (1998). For example, *The Musubi Man*, an appropriation of the gingerbread man story, invokes elements central to local identity: first, the musubi man consists of popular local food. His body is a *musubi*, or rice ball. He wears a jacket of *nori*, or dried seaweed; his heart is an *umeboshi*, or pickled plum; his nose is an *ebi*, or shrimp; and his eyes are made of *takuan*, or pickled radish. Second, the elusive *musubi* man flees through the Hawai'i landscape, eluding hungry characters that collectively significantly figure the local imagination: a little old man and woman, a poi (or mixed breed) dog, a mongoose, a mynah bird, and a surfer. The other stories localize Western fairytales similarly: *The Musubi Man's New Friend*, in which the *musubi* man becomes enamored with a lovely Spam (or spiced ham) *musubi*; *Sumorella*, an adaption of Cinderella, which celebrates Hawai'i's local athletes who have relocated to Japan where they have become legendary sumo wrestlers; and *The Prince and the Li Hing Mui*, in which crack seed (dried or marinated fruit) – a kid-favorite in Hawai'i – becomes the story's central trope.

Picture books by Lisa Matsumoto also exemplify this genre: *How the B-52 Cockroach Learned to Fly* (1995), *Beyond 'Ohi'a Valley: Adventures in a Hawaiian Rainforest* (1996), and *The Christmas Gift of Aloha* (2004). The protagonists of these stories discover their inner heroism through traditional fairytale and high-fantasy plots of initiation, adventure, struggle, maturation, and return. However, a distinctly local milieu and local imagination color these fictive universes. For example, *How the B-52 Cockroach Learned to Fly* includes favorite local food, the Japanese bento box lunch; introduces termites, which are the nightmare of all Hawai'i homeowners; and exaggerates the greatest nightmare of all, the giant flying cockroach (stylishly wearing surfer board shorts) whose heroism elevates him from lowly outcast to legendary hero within the insect chain. The *Christmas Gift of Aloha* comprises a Hawai'i setting that replaces snowmen with sandmen and elves with *menehune* and that appropriates the Christmas holiday in order to convey the local concept of *aloha* spirit. And through quest narrative, *Beyond 'Ōhi'a Valley* teaches conservation of indigenous insects, animals, and flora in Hawaiian rainforests.

Finally, Hawai'i Creole English, or as locals affectionately say, pidgin, localizes and authenticates several of these stories. As Bill Teter notes (1998: 349), for locals pidgin is "fo' real" and the "the sound of 'home'". Validating pidgin and the local bodies that it enlivens and that likewise continue to breathe life into the language becomes Teter's primary motive for publishing (along with co-editors Eric Chock, Darrell H.Y. Lum, and James Harstad) the edited volume of stories and poems for and partly written by Hawai'i teens: *Growing Up Local: An Anthology of Poetry and Prose from Hawai'i* (1998). As novelist Milton Murayama reminds us in the title of his ground-breaking first novel, *All I Asking For is My Body* (1988; originally published for adults and now sometimes studied in some Hawai'i secondary classrooms), language *is* the local body. The two – language and body – are forever inextricable.

Touristic paradisiacal Hawai'i

The paradisiacal Hawai'i that both Sumida (1991) and Bacchilega (2007) challenge thrives in contemporary Hawai'i children's literature. Such works most often privilege Hawai'i as touristic, pristine, legendary, harmonious, and Edenic backdrop and de-emphasize cultural and historical authenticity (though sometimes they invoke and integrate characters and traditions that imply or implicitly make claims to a kind of authenticity). We characterize these works as folklore because, in folkloric fashion, they collectively generate and sustain perceptions that significantly shape and produce culture, in this case, the legendary Hawai'i that Sumida and Bachilegga challenge. Examples of these kinds of works are the following: *The Legend of the Laughing Gecko: A Hawaiian Fantasy* (1989), *Aloha Bear and Maui the Whale* (1989), *The Little Hawaiian Rainbow* (2004), *The Magic Sandman* (2000), and *Aloha Dolores* (2000). Another story, *The Gift of Aloha* (McBarnet, 1996), appropriates *The Little Drummer Boy* Christmas story and the American rags-to-riches tale, in which a young, poor girl, Leilani, has nothing of great value to give to the royal family visiting her island. Instead she strings flowers into a lei and serves as an island tour guide for the young prince. Enamored by Leilani, the prince professes his love through marriage.

Other works such as *How Six Little Ipu Got Their Names* (2005) and *Hula Lullaby* (2005) – both hula stories – are not so easily categorized. Both meaningfully affirm native Hawaiian cultural practices. However, we have categorized them here non-pejoratively for two reasons: first, their subject matter implies a kind of native authenticity. Second, despite this implication, both stories – through narrative and illustrations – derive their power from reproducing the master narrative of a harmonious, paradisiacal, and legendary Hawai'i rather than a narrative stance that authors native self-determination.

Issues of authenticity

As legends are re-told among generations, stories inevitably must change. Indeed, this is the nature of folklore. However, Mower argues that today's re-told legends must be shared with great care because children "know very little or nothing about the foreign culture ... [and have] no way of knowing if the literature they are reading or listening to trivializes or stereotypes the culture" (2002: 105). Some variations may be warranted depending on audience and context. For example, legends and myths once shared among villagers were not altered for children in the way that modern constructions of childhood might warrant. In relation to excerpts from the legend of *Kamapua'a*, one from Elbert's *Selections from Fornander's Hawaiian Antiquities and Folk-Lore* (Elbert, 1959) and the other from Buffet and Buffet's adaptation *Adventures of Kamapua'a* (1972), Tachihata (1996: 204) explains how societal assumptions of childhood might influence an author's decisions to alter content. Here Kamapua'a is backed against a mountain range with no apparent escape:

> But Kamapua'a uses his body to provide a means for his mother to climb over the mountain. He leans against the mountain and his body forms a groove to create the waterfall, Sacred Falls. In the Fornander version, the mother uses Kamapua'a's teats to climb over (*Selections* 202–203). In the Buffet version, the mother climbs using Kamapua'a's bristles (*Adventures* 50–54 and *Na Hana* 50–54). Probably, Buffet considered references to Kamapua'a's teats inappropriate for today's children.

However, other changes that raise questions of cultural authenticity are more concerning. For example, Mower critiques Wardlaw's adaptation *Punia and the King of the Sharks* (1997), in which she identifies numerous inaccuracies that are culturally inappropriate and possibly in "contempt" of Hawaiian culture (2002: 106). For example, son and mother are portrayed eating together; however, in ancient Hawai'i sons and mothers would have eaten separately. Sharks are portrayed as villains; however, for Hawaiians sharks are revered *'aumakua*, or family gods. Finally, the heads of villagers are elevated above the ruling *ali'i*, which ancient Hawaiian culture would not have allowed. Such inaccuracies along with narrative adaptations informed by "the Western cultural assumption that each story must have a tight unity – a beginning, middle, and end" are Mower's primary concerns (2002: 108).

Conclusion: the centrality of Hawaiian mythology

Bacchilega (2007) convincingly and ethically challenges those non-native/outsider retellings and translations of Hawaiian myths that construct an exotic, pastoral, and "legendary Hawai'i" rooted in and serving foreign desires so detrimental to native Hawaiian sovereignty. In contrast to such inauthentic appropriations and exploitations, native Hawaiian scholars continue to evoke mythology to imagine, articulate, and realize self-determination. Thus, in her critique of the 1848 *Māhele*, which severed Hawaiians from the land, Lilikalā Kame'eleihiwa invokes the Kumulipo – the origin myth – which realizes all natural and ethereal entities as one "indivisible lineage" (1992: 2). As Kame'eleihiwa explains, "land 'ownership' was not a part of the Hawaiian metaphor" at the time of the *Māhele* (1992: 9–10). Foreigners sought through the *Māhele* to divest Hawaiians of their access to the land and self-servingly to secure the land's foreign and private ownership. In contrast, according to Kame'eleihiwa, for Hawaiians the expression *māhele* denoted and connoted "sharing" the land through generosity rather than conquering and privatizing it through capitalism (1992: 19, 20–32). Within this context, legends such as the Kumulipo and Wākea and Papa reconnect contemporary Hawaiians to their genealogies; reinstate them as nurturers, cultivators, and caretakers of the land; and reconnect them as part of an "unbroken chain" to the spiritual energies, or *mana*, that have run through the land since "the beginning of the world". Similarly, Davianna Pomaika'i McGregor reminds us that the island of Kaho'olawe (desecrated by the U.S. military until 1990) was once named Kanaloa (Hawaiian god of the ocean) and Kohemālamalama o Kanaloa ("the shining birth canal of Kanaloa" or the "southern beacon of Kanaloa") (2002: 74–75). As McGregor notes, protesting against military use of the island enabled Hawaiians to rediscover both Kaho'olawe's sacredness and the concept of *aloha 'āina* – love and respect for the land. These examples affirm the ways in which mythology connects native Hawaiians through a shared genealogy and to a necessary land base, and affirms this mythology's centrality in native consciousness.

But this native narrative co-exists with others in island consciousness. The traditional definition of folklore – that is, stories created and then handed down from one generation to the next and, through this process, stories making and undergirding a culture – illuminates the process by which current Hawai'i children's literature composes three versions of the islands in both the child's and the popular imagination: indigenous Hawai'i, local Hawai'i, and legendary/paradisiacal Hawai'i. In presenting these categories, we insist that Hawai'i's cultural composition is not monolithic. In addition, we contend that these categories are never static. Instead, Hawai'i's cultural narratives – like Hawai'i's people who in all of their diversity struggle to get along within limited resources of land and amid an economy that relies so heavily on tourism and global capitalism – are always evolving, intersecting, and diverging dynamically. Hawai'i's children's literature mirrors these processes, for in this literature, we see both the intersection of and distinction among stories that attempt to author and reclaim traditional ways, that validate and accommodate the idea of the local, and that appeal to an imagined paradise.

Fully aware of these complexities, we have still attempted to categorize the production of kinds of contemporary folklore in Hawai'i in order to provide an ethical framework through which educators, scholars, everyday readers, and authors working and interested in this area may reflect on their perspectives, choices, and (if applicable) their teaching practices. Finally, we have chosen a subjective rather than objective approach, suggesting that the Hawai'i – and its youth – that we choose to narrate (through both readership and authorship) has significant ethical implications for native Hawaiians, for all others who reside in the islands, and for all who visit these shores.

Bibliography

Bacchilega, Cristina (2007) *Legendary Hawai'i and the Politics of Place: Tradition, Translation, and Tourism*, Philadephia: University of Pennsylvania Press.

Beckwith, Martha (1970) *Hawaiian Mythology*, Honolulu: University of Hawai'i Press.

Beckwith, Martha (1972) *The Kumulipo: A Hawaiian Creation Chant*, Honolulu: University Press of Hawaii.

Chock, Eric (1996) "The Neocolonialization of *Bamboo Ridge*: Repositioning *Bamboo Ridge* and Local Literature in the 1990s", *Bamboo Ridge: A Hawai'i Writer's Journal*, 69: 11–25.

Elbert Samuel H. (ed.) (1959) *Selections from Fornander's Hawaiian Antiquities and Folk-lore*, Honolulu: University of Hawai'i Press.

Fornander, Abraham (1890) *An Account of the Polynesian Race: Its Origin and Migrations and the Ancient History of the Hawaiian People to the Times of Kamehameha I.* Available from: Hathitrust http://hdl.handle.net/2027/uc2.ark:/13960/t04x57q4g (accessed 12 June 2014).

Fornander, Abraham (1916) *Fornander Collection of Hawaiian Antiquities and Folklore: The Hawaiian Account of the Formation of their Islands and Origin of their Race with the Traditions of their Migrations, etc., as Gathered from Original Sources.* Available from: Google Books http://books.google.com/books?id=tcQNAAAAQAAJ&printsec=frontcover&source=gbs_ge_summary_r&cad=0#v=onepage&q&f=false (accessed 20 June 2014).

Fujikane, Candace (2008) "Introduction: Asian settler colonialism in the U.S. colony of Hawai'i" in *Asian Settler Colonialism: From Local Governance to the Everyday Habits of Life in Hawai'i*, eds. Candace Fujikane & Jonathan Y. Okamura, Honolulu: University of Hawai'i Press, 1–42.

Kamakau, Samuel (1866–1871a) "Legends of Waipi'o in Hawai'i and some of its Rulers who Died There", *Ka Nupepa Kuokoa.* Available from: Hawaii Ethnographic Notes (HEN) http://data.bishopmuseum.org/HEN/browse2.php?stype=3&term=%20%20S.%20M.%20Kamakau (accessed 22 June 2014). Manuscript translation, HEN vol. 2: 691–696, held at Bishop Museum.

Kamakau, Samuel (1866–1871b) "Lore of the Kahuna Kilokilo and the Kahuna I ka papa huli honua aina", *Ka Nupepa Kuokoa*. Available from: Hawaii Ethnographic Notes (HEN) http://data.bishopmuseum.org/HEN/browse2.php?stype=3&term=%20%20S.%20M.%20 Kamakau (accessed 22 June 2014). Manuscript translation, HEN vol. 1: 708–710, held at Bishop Museum.

Kamakau, Samuel (1866–1871c) "Story of the Three Lonos", *Ka Nupepa Kuokoa*. Available from: Hawaiian Ethnographic Notes (HEN) http://data.bishopmuseum.org/HEN/browse2. php?stype=3&term=%20%20S.%20M.%20Kamakau (accessed 22 June 2014). Manuscript translation, HEN Thrum #257, held at Bishop Museum.

Kamakau, Samuel (1866–1871d) "The Story of Kapiolani", *Ka Nupepa Kuokoa*. Available from: Hawaiian Ethnographic Notes (HEN) http://data.bishopmuseum.org/HEN/browse2. php?stype=3&term=%20%20S.%20M.%20Kamakau (accessed 22 June 2014). Manuscript translation, HEN Thrum #171C, held at Bishop Museum.

Kameʻeleihiwa, Lilikala (1992) *Native Land and Foreign Desires/Ko Hawaiʻi Āʻina a me Nā Koi Puʻumake a ka poʻe Haole: Pehea lā e Pono ai?/ How Shall We Live in Harmony?* Honolulu: Bishop Museum Press.

Kawamoto, Kevin Y. (1993) "Hegemony and Language Politics in Hawaiʻi", *World Englishes*, 12(2): 193–207.

Lum, Darrel H. Y. (1998) "Local genealogy: what school you went?"in Eric Chock, James R. Harstad, Darrell H.Y. Lum, and Bill Teter (eds.), *Growing up Local: An Anthology of Poetry and Prose from Hawaiʻi*, Honolulu: Bamboo Ridge Press, 11–15.

Malo, David (1951) *Hawaiian Antiquities: Moʻolelo Hawaiʻi*, 2nd edn, Honolulu: Bishop Museum Press.

McGregor, Davianna Pomaikaʻi (2002) "Kahoʻolawe: Rebirth of the Sacred", *Amerasia Journal*, 28(3): 68–83.

Morales, Rodney (1998) "Literature" in Michael Haas (ed.) *Multicultural Hawaiʻi: The Fabric of a Multiethnic Society*, New York: Garland Publishing, Inc., 107–130.

Mower, Nancy Alpert (2002) "Retelling Hawaiian Legends: The Importance of Authenticity" in Suzanne Kosanke and Todd Sammons (eds.), *Literature and Hawaii's Children: A Gathering Place, Tenth Biennial Conference Proceedings*, Children's Literature Hawaiʻi, c/o Department of English, University of Hawaiʻi at Mānoa, Honolulu, 105–112.

Murayama, Milton Atsushi (1988) *All I Asking for is my Body*, Honolulu: University of Hawaiʻi Press.

Okamura, Jonathan Y. (1993) "Why There are no Asian Americans in Hawaiʻi: The Continuing Significance of Local Identity" in Peter Manicas (ed.) *Social Process in Hawaiʻi: A Reader*, 2nd edn, New York: McGraw-Hill, 243–260.

Okamura, Jonathan (1998) "Social Stratification" in Michael Haas (ed.) *Multicultural Hawaiʻi: The Fabric of a Multiethnic Society*, New York: Garland Publishing, Inc., 185–204.

Romaine, Suzanne (1994) "Hawaiʻi Creole English as a literary language", *Language in Society*, 23: 527–554.

Russell, David L. (2000) *Literature for Children: A Short Introduction*, 4th edn, New York: Longman.

Said, Edward (1993) *Culture and Imperialism*, New York: Knopf.

Sumida, Stephen. H. (1991) *And the View from the Shore: Literary Traditions of Hawaiʻi*, Seattle and London: University of Washington Press.

Tachihata, Chieko (1996) "Kamapuaa: Library Resources for this Retold Tale" in Suzanne Kosanke and Todd Sammons (eds.), *Literature and Hawaii's Children: Values and Traditions from Many Cultures: Children's Tales Told and Retold*, 1994, Proceedings, Literature and Hawaii's Children, c/o Department of English, University of Hawaiʻi at Mānoa, 202–205.

Takaki, Ronald T. (1983) *Pau Hana: Plantation Life and Labor in Hawaii 1835–1920*, Honolulu: University of Hawaiʻi Press.

Teter, Bill (1998) "Listening with an outsider's ear" in Eric Chock, James R. Harstad, Darrell H.Y. Lum, and Bill Teter (eds.) *Growing up Local: An Anthology of Poetry and Prose from Hawaiʻi*, Honolulu: Bamboo Ridge Press, 348–349.

Trask, Haunani-Kay (1993) *From a Native Daughter: Colonialism and Sovereignty in Hawaiʻi*, Monroe: Common Courage Press.

Bibliography of children's literature

Beamer, Nona (2005) *Pua Polu: The Pretty Blue Hawaiian Flower*, Honolulu: Bishop Museum Press

Beamer, Nona (2008) *Naupaka*, Honolulu: Bishop Museum Press.

Brimmer, Debi and Julie Coleson (2005) *How Six Little Ipu Got Their Names*, Honolulu: Bess Press

Buffet, Gy and Pam Buffet (1972) *Adventures of Kamapua'a*, Norfolk Island: Island Heritage.

Collins, Malia (2005) *Pele and Poli'ahu: A Tale of Fire and Ice*, Kaneohe: BeachHouse Publishing.

Kahanu, Noelle M.K.Y. (2007) *The Raven and the Sun: Echoing Our Ancestors*, Honolulu Kamahoi Press.

Kono, Erin Eitter (2005) *Hula Lullaby*, New York: Little, Brown and Company.

Loebel-Fried, Caren (2005) *Hawaiian Legends of Dreams*, Honolulu: University of Hawai'i Press.

Loebel-Fried, Caren (2006) *Lono and the Magical Land beneath the Sea*, Honolulu: Bishop Museum Press.

Loebel-Fried, Caren (2010) *Legend of the Gourd*, Honolulu: Bishop Museum Press.

Matsumoto, Lisa (1995) *How the B-52 Cockroach Learned to Fly*, Lehua, Inc., Honolulu.

Matsumoto, Lisa (1996) *Beyond 'Ōhi'a Valley: Adventures in a Hawaiian Rainforest* Honolulu: Lehua, Inc.

Matsumoto, Lisa (2004) *The Christmas Gift of Aloha*, Kaneohe: 'Ōhi'a Productions, Inc.

McBarnet, Gill (1996) *The Gift of Aloha*, Mililani: Booklines Hawaii Ltd.

Moran, Edna Cabcabin (2006) *The Sleeping Giant: A Tale from Kaua'i*, 'Ewa Beach: BeachHouse Publishing, LLC.

Napolean, Kawika (2010) *'Ai'ai: A Bilingual Hawaiian Story*, Honolulu: Kamehameha Publishing

Nordenstrom, Michael (2002) *Pele and the Rivers of Fire*, Honolulu: Bess Press.

Nordenstrom, Michael (2003) *Hina and the Sea of Stars*, Honolulu: Bess Press.

Pellegrino, Victor C. (2010) *Uncle Kawaiola's Dream: A Hawaiian Story*, Wailuku: Maui arThoughts Company.

Takayama, Sandi (1996) *The Musubi Man: Hawai'i's Ginger-bread Man*, Honolulu: Bess Press.

Takayama, Sandi (1997) *Sumorella: a Hawai'i Cinderella Story*, Honolulu: Bess Press.

Takayama, Sandi (1998) *The Prince and the Li Hing Mui*, Honolulu: Bess Press.

Takayama, Sandi (2002) *The Musubi Man's New Friend*, Honolulu: Bess Press.

Tune, Suelyn Ching (1991) *Māui and the Secret of Fire*, Honolulu: University of Hawai'i Press.

Varez, Dietrich, and Pua Kanaka'ole Kanahele (1991) *Pele the Fire Goddess*, Honolulu: Bishop Museum Press.

Wardlaw, Lee (1997) *Punia and the King of the Sharks*, New York: Dial.

Williams, Julie Stewart (1991) *Māui Goes Fishing*, Honolulu: University of Hawai'i Press.

30

FROM ORALITY TO PRINT

Construction of Nso identity in folk tales

Vivian Yenika-Agbaw

In his seminal work, *The African Quest for Freedom and Identity: Cameroonian Writing and the National Experience*, Richard Bjornson explains that, "In Africa, as elsewhere, people do not identify only with national communities. Many regard themselves privately as members of ethnic groups, whereas others insist that all Africans belong to the same community" (1991: xii). Most works of fiction from Anglophone Cameroon reflect this ethnic allegiance. While we may be hard pressed to find other explanations for this, in a multilingual nation such as Cameroon whose cultural identity is constantly shaped by forces that emanate from historical experiences of slavery, colonialism, and now globalization, clinging to one's ethnicity *may* seem like one way to remain centered from our hybrid multiple selves. Thus, there are works of fiction that reflect ethnic consciousness of the local writers and those that resound nationalistic views. To say that Anglophone literature in writing, as Bjornson observes, is still evolving is an understatement. Worse yet, there is very little literature in writing for Anglophone children. But there are oral narratives, which members of educated elites such as Samuel Akombi, Sarah Elive, Kenjo Wan Jumbam, Sankie Maimo, and Juliana Makuchi from different regions of Anglophone Cameroon have transmitted into print.

One other prolific author who clearly identifies with his ethnicity in Anglophone Cameroon is Dr. Daniel Noni Lantum. Though a medical doctor by training, and professor emeritus of Public Health, he is also noted within the Anglophone Cameroonian literary community for his classic folktale collection, *Folk Tales of Nso*, published twice in 1964 by Nooremac Press in Lagos, and reissued in 1969 by African Universities Press as part of the African Reader's Library series. Many Anglophone children of a certain generation, especially those who hailed from the North West region, may recall this collection. So would Nso children, for not only were many familiar with the tales, especially stories of Wanyeto, the anteater turned trickster and "*his*" antics, the chants remain popular and can be heard at cultural events in the diaspora (particularly at Bui Family Union-USA annual conventions). Lantum, living in Yaounde, the capital city of Cameroon, continues to uphold Nso traditions. A Nso title holder, Shuufaay wo Bastos, he is also a product of his hybrid Western education (British and American). He is thus like his peers "who became literate in European languages and worked in the cities [and] tended to maintain strong ties with their own ethnic groups" (Bjornson, 9). As one of the first elites from Nso to be educated in English, Lantum has ceaselessly promoted his cultural heritage not only through his medical practice [a pioneer in traditional medicine], but also through his literary works. His folktale collections for children and youth stand as evidence. In these he explains in the preface that the collections are to enable youth to "also participate in this wealth of our culture even in their class-rooms designed in Europe" (1964: iv); and that it is also an attempt by the Nso History Society to "preserve" the culture.

However, efforts at preserving cultures from extinction through art and the written word can be complicated. This paper thus explores the question: what happens to a people's culture when oral narratives are encoded in print with visual images? It could be said that narratives performed orally leave a lot to the imagination of the audience, whereas in print there is a deliberate attempt to impose certain images on the reader. Finnegan cautions about this constraint, noting that it "leaves uneasy questions about just what has and has not been captured and presented as 'the work'" (2007: 163).

Verbal and visual texts of traditional tales such as Lantum's therefore construct an image, albeit fictional, of a cultural group. This paper discusses the prevailing images "preserved" in the written versions of the classic Wanyeto [trickster] tales of the Nso people. Five of these tales appear in three published editions. I acutely remember my mother, aunty, and grandmother narrating Wanyeto tales to us in order to familiarize us with tales of their youth, and to "educate" us in Nso heritage. I examine this collection of "oral text" as *re*-presented by Lantum with the understanding that, "The formative role of such researchers in shaping the texts – and thus in representing and publicizing the oral arts of Africa – has received too little attention" (Finnegan 159). The idea is to get readers to think critically about the possible ideologies that may be embedded in oral narratives in print, a medium that offers opportunities for wider circulation. If nothing else, as Okpewho rightly observes about literary studies and Africa, "all knowledge aims at helping us understand who we are, the value of what we do, how we have reached the stage of civilization we have achieved, and what steps we can take to improve our condition" (1992: 18). This therefore adds urgency to the study of oral narratives in print that target children.

Orality and Africa

There is no doubt that folklore is a significant major component of African oral tradition. In every way, African oral narratives including folktales have continued to flourish and captivate the interest of Western intellectuals such as Abrahams, Bascom, Dundes, Finnegan, Roger, and more. Even if these folklorists do not agree on what to consider as subcategories of generic "oral texts," they recognize the performative nature of prose narratives within the different ethnic groups whose tales they each might have collected and tried to encode in print and/or have studied. The oral and performative nature of such tales can also pose significant challenges to researchers who transform them into creative works of art in printed forms. This is understandable as many folklorists have come to accept that each performance of a tale varies according to the performer, his/her purpose, the audience, and the context – social and physical etc.

The mid-twentieth century, when African countries began winning their independence from the West, brought more prospects for the educated elites to participate in the research and transmission into print of their indigenous tales. This was a step up from the past where "The processing into texts ha[d] often been under the control of non-native collectors" (Finnegan 2007: 158). However, like their Western counterparts, those who translated "African-language expression ... into a written European language" (158) in which they were educated faced a challenge: "Translators naturally formulate their products following the written convention familiar to themselves and their target readers" (Finnegan 2007: 171). African elites embarking on such translation projects are also implicated in such conventions. "Some" Okpewho postulates, "tried to be so 'fashionable'" but ended up sounding equally "un-African" (1992: 294). Lantum acknowledges this struggle, and since part of the agenda he states in his preface was to get students to learn about the Nso culture, there was the added challenge of how to *re*-present narratives originally told in Lamnso in accessible English that would convey the cultural significance to school children "in the lower forms of the Secondary School and the later years of the primary school" (1964: iii).

Folktales serve a variety of purposes, "although it is often said that they are told only for amusement" (Bascom 1965: 4). Lantum's collection may entertain and transmit aspects of Nso culture through the chants, which readers not familiar with Lamnso may elect to ignore in its printed form. However, this same audience listening to the tales as oral performance would be forced to participate. The pleasure appeal, which is heightened by the performer's ability "to meaningfully arrange the incidents and clearly relate them through his own extempore diction and mimesis" (Ukala 1992: 72), takes precedence in the oral form.

Though this paper recognizes Lantum's constructions as one version of Nso culture, albeit in three editions, because of the collection's canonical status in Anglophone Cameroon it has become something of a "standard text" (Finnegan 163). One may also argue that since many children in contemporary Cameroon and Africa now have a plethora of texts from which to choose for entertainment purposes, including the widely popular Nigerian movies, this collection no longer seems relevant. This may be so, but the relatively paucity of books in Anglophone Cameroon does not allow the luxury to ignore it (see Makuchi 2008 and Ashuntantang 2009).

Folktale conventions may vary depending on the culture. In terms of the structure, Denise Paulme identifies "seven structural types" of "African narrative" (cited in Ben-Amos 1975: 184), positing however that the structures themselves may be flawed. The Wanyeto tales with which this paper is concerned seem to fall under what is considered as Type 2: "Descendancy (Normal Situation – Deterioration – Lack). In these tales the deterioration is triggered by a violation of an interdiction; the sequence that follows results in a permanent negative condition" (184). Readers can observe this structural pattern in the first of the five Wanyeto tales, in which Wanyeto and Baa are constructed as friends whose relationship is compromised because of treachery. The decision to kill off their mothers creates a conflict that positions them as archenemies. Subsequent conflicts ensue until Wanyeto's demise. The five tales offer opportunities for Lantum to explore some aspects of Nso culture.

On the other hand, Dan Ben-Amos observes that:

> Folklore does not present the entire gamut of cultural ideas and actions of a society, but selected domains of themes which are deemed suitable for particular genres of expression ... Thus, the selection of themes for folklore depends upon their symbolic value in culture ... The incorporation of human and animal figures in prose and poetry transforms them into symbols for the culture, which are then repeated in traditional expressions with a constant meaning, creating a language of folklore for each culture
>
> (1975: 181–182).

This is understandable for, as acknowledged earlier, no one tale of a people, even of one family, can capture the entire experience.

Folk Tales of Nso and *Tales of Nso*: an analysis of Wanyeto tales

From the very first tale, it becomes obvious that the anteater, Wanyeto is a trickster. He is cunning, vicious, vindictive, and violent; and so his demise at the hands of a small bird comes as a relief in the last tale. Trickster tales are popular in Africa with Anansi, the spider, and Tortoise perhaps the most notable characters. Okpewho discusses the five functions of trickster tales as outlined in Dundes's study:

> This category of tales – mostly of animals but also of human characters – has to do with trickery and breach of faith. In his analysis of two of these tales from East Africa, Dundes finds there are basically five functions ... in the following order.
>
> 1. Friendship: The tale often assumes or specifies a situation of friendship or solidarity between the characters involved.
> 2. Contract: Next, there is frequently an agreement reached or some kind of appointment made which has the value or aim of testing the friendship.
> 3. Violation: One of the parties in the contract invariably does something that amounts to a breach of faith, e.g. by deceiving or cheating the other.
> 4. Discovery: The deceived or cheated party frequently discovers the trick played on it or the violation of the agreement reached. In many cases this is followed by a countertrick or counterviolation from the offended party.
> 5. End of Friendship: The final situation in the sequence is generally the termination of the cordial relationship between the parties, sometimes with the punishment or disgrace of the original culprit.
>
> (176–177).

The Wanyeto tales under study embody all these functions, with the trickster referred to in the verbal text as an anteater and Baa as a leopard, but both are portrayed as human beings in the visual text.

Cover design

The cover design of a work of fiction often creates expectations for what readers may encounter between the cover pages. The first two editions published in 1964 have two distinct cover designs, one with just borders of red/white/black and the book title centered; the second with a variety of images from crucial scenes. The four images on the front cover comprise: the king in the story "Wanyeto the Artist"; Baa chopping off Wanyeto's mother's head in "Wanyeto and Baa"; the hunter and his son fleeing from gorillas in "The hunter who tricked the gorillas," a story not part of the Wanyeto series; and Wanyeto carrying an antelope as a peace offering in "Wanyeto Reconciles with Baa." The back cover has a collage of images from different stories in the collection including "Wanyeto the Farmer" and "The End of Wanyeto." These illustrations provide an idea of how the characters appear, their activities, the settings, and the instances of violence that occur in the fictional community that is reconstructed.

The cover page of the 1969 edition has a black and white image of two half naked men rushing in the woods toward a hut superimposed on a pale orange background

Figure 30.1 From *Tales of Nso*, Daniel Lantum (1969).

(see Figure 30.1). This illustration is pivotal in the overall story plot in the series, since it captures the moment of deceit – when Baa finally realizes that Wanyeto's mother is still alive while he was tricked to kill his. It seems to project an adventure story, and so may be ironic, for one does not know whether the two characters are friends or foes. In this edition, the fourth tale is titled, "Wanyeto and Baa Meet Again" instead of "Wanyeto Reconciles with Baa." The back cover contains a list of titles in the African Reader's Library series, including Lantum's.

Verbal text: folk tales of Nso

The verbal texts in both editions of *Folk Tales of Nso* published in 1964 open with a dedication that reads: "To My People of Cameroon," followed by a verse by Lantum:

> The man of Nso'
> Though of savage look
> Was of noble soul
> Closer to nature
> In action and in word
>
> (n.p)

This echoes a "colonialist discourse" that constructs Africans as "savage, backward, and undeveloped" (Tyson 2006: 419). The verse sounds like an apology on behalf of the Nso people. This image seems problematic. More so, because it originates from a collaborative effort with the Nso History Society and one wonders about their endorsement of the projection of Nso people as "Noble Savage."

The collection comprises sixteen stories, including the five Wanyeto tales, a table of contents, a preface, eleven illustrations, an "invocation" by the editor, and a glossary of English words in both editions. The first tale, "Wanyeto and Baa" (1–13) introduces the two friends and the treachery that leads to their feud. Although he is smaller in size, Wanyeto, the anteater trickster, manipulates Baa, the leopard, into killing his mother. As the story opens readers are told that these animals are "old-time intimate friends," but in the time of famine survival instincts surface: "Wanyeto called his friend, Baa, one day and said, 'Look here old boy, is it wise that we should join our fathers in the grave when we are yet so young?'" (1). This problem sets the stage for the conflict: "I have an idea, if it will please you,' replied Wanyeto. 'Our mothers have enjoyed more days than we. Let us make food out of them.' … Baa accepted that they should kill and eat their parents' (1). The trickster devises a scheme that gets Baa to kill his mother while he protects his.

Cannibalism is central in this verbal text, although constructed as a necessity only in the time of famine, and the characters' dialogue establishes that it is not typical to "make food" out of one's mother. The text thus briefly humanizes these characters, making their conflict one of treachery. Because Wanyeto feels his mother is "priceless" (2), he tricks Baa into killing his. But when Baa uncovers this betrayal he "slew [Wanyeto's mother] with his axe" (8) according to their verbal contract to each kill his mother. The words are graphic but without the accompanying illustration it is left to the reader to imagine how these animal characters perform these acts of violence on their kin.

As the subsequent tales develop this conflict, further light is shed upon Wanyeto's character. He is sly with cannibalistic instincts as demonstrated in "Wanyeto the Artist" where he pretends to be a tattoo artist and eats the princesses in need of his services; and in "Wanyeto the Farmer" he pretends to be dead and captures the birds that have been feasting on his crops. His calculating and evil actions are consistent with African trickster tales, where the goal often is to outwit others, except that in Wanyeto's case he kills them for food. The fourth tale, "Wanyeto Reconciles with Baa" expands on his traits, as he feigns remorse to gain Baa's forgiveness and trust and then kills him. However, in the fifth tale, "The End of Wanyeto," a small bird outwits him by means of a comparable trick:

> One day he heard a bird singing away melodiously and advanced towards it. Before he was near enough to see the bird, it stopped singing and hid its head under its wings. However, Wanyeto came by it and picked it up. He examined this queer creature closely but found no head. He said silently, 'What a good creature worth eating! But how can I eat a thing without a head!'
>
> (41).

When he sees the bird's head, "Wanyeto walked up to it and said in admiration, 'What a beauty of a bird with hair so beautifully plaited! How do you do it? Who plaits it for you?'" (42). The small bird volunteers to plait Wanyeto's hair: "When all the braids had been tied to the branch," he asks Wanyeto to jump. "With happiness Wanyeto took a leap but remained hanging from the branch" and dies (43). The small bird becomes a hero in the "animal world," and is celebrated for killing a "great killer":

> *Ko – o la? – ko Sho'*
> *Ko – o la? – ko Sho'*
> Translated: Who caught? Sho' did
> Who caught? Sho' did.
> (44).

The verbal text projects animal figures acting out human behaviors, often vices that compromise relationships among friends and/or community members, perhaps as a cautionary tale on trust issues, or a cautionary tale about what could happen if people act on instincts as these animal characters do. Moreover, it raises concerns about the original Lamsno text and its emphasis on cannibalism and could get readers to ponder the intent. Was it to interrogate the colonial gaze of the Nso people as cannibals, a trope common in colonial literature that attempts to dehumanize Africans as the Other (Barnard 2005: 323)? Was it to caution listeners about the possibilities of cannibalism since the Nso people are "Closer to nature" (n.p)? However as constructed in print this message may be skewed. Thus, if a colonialist discourse is imposed upon a Lamnso narrative that integrates violence within a possible cautionary tale about trust and the violence that may emanate when it is breached, Wanyeto the trickster may become an archetype of the evil individual in society that takes advantage of others' vulnerabilities and tricks them sometimes to their death. The verbal construction of the Nso people interpreted in this way may problematize the cannibalistic elements of the narrative. It is plausible that the anthropomorphic qualities manifested in these characters, especially in their relationship dynamics, might have been of great concern to the Nso people of a certain period, but this remains a speculation. What does it mean that Wanyeto keeps seeing other members of *his* forest community as food? Some readers can rationalize that in the animal world every creature is food to the other, but it is the anthropomorphic aspects of the tales that make them disturbing in print.

Cannibalism is a common theme in oral narratives from Anglophone Cameroon. Another example is Makuchi's "King-of-Scabies," a tale from the Beba, where she points out that such stories raise questions about a cultural group "forc[ing] the (Beba) listener to ask such questions as: Does this mean that cannibalism was practiced among a people the Beba knew during their period of migration to their present location? … Did the Beba themselves practice cannibalism or did they so abhor it in others that they created this story to warn against it" (2008: 193)? Similar questions can be posed about Lantum's tales.

Verbal text: *Tales of Nso*

As part of the African Reader's Library series, the audience for the tale seems broader, since "Early titles were … supplementary readers for preadolescents in senior primary and Junior secondary school" (Dike 2005: 7). The edition's approach to the theme of cannibalism is to a slight extent subtley evident in the illustrations. By the late 1960s most countries in Africa had won their independence and the continent held a lot of promise for its inhabitants. Literacy was at the forefront of some of the cultural initiatives, and so African Universities Press was publishing more books for youth by African authors. Between 1962 and 1988 the series had thirty-eight titles. When Lantum's collection became part of the continental canon, African Reader's Library boasted seventeen books in the series with only one other from Anglophone Cameroon, Jedida Asheri's *Promise*.

Tales of Nso (1969) contains twelve of the original tales including the Wanyeto tales. Daniel Lantum is the sole author of the verbal texts, which are illustrated by J. Jarvies, about whom there is no information. There is no longer any front matter that discusses the background of the oral narratives as in the earlier editions. The writing style is slightly altered so that it is less colloquial. Overall, it could be said that in collaboration with the publishers the author privileges what Okpewho refers to as a more "literary than a sociological" approach in this edition. The first tale opens establishing the two characters as friends: "Wanyeto the Anteater and Baa the Leopard were old friends" (5), in contrast to the reference to "intimate friends" (1) in *Folk Tales of Nso*. It also problematizes the idea of matricide. The version sets up cannibalism as unnatural and presents Baa's discomfort with the idea of killing their mothers: "Baa did not like the idea. But Wanyeto argued and at last he agreed" (5). The text creates a distance from the notion of cannibalism and seems to ascribe more emotions to the characters. Thus, Baa and Wanyeto are constructed as loving their mothers equally even if Baa is persuaded to "cut off his mother's head" (6). The prose is more succinct with the five tales comprising 29 pages as opposed to 44. Cannibalism remains an integral part of the narratives as in the earlier versions. With no mention of the Nso people by name, readers of Nso origin can infer their culture primarily from the chants. They may choose to read with the text, interacting with Wanyeto tales as animal tales and hence fantasy, or engage with them as a commentary on the Nso people. In the second situation, there is then the need to rethink the significance of the custom of cannibalism attributed to the Nso people as constructed in the narrative. To other readers without the intimate knowledge on Lamnso represented by the songs, it remains a collection of tales from Africa. The notion of cannibalism is thus identified with the continent and not limited to a particular group.

Visual texts in all three editions

In the first two collections the illustrator is identified simply as a Nigerian, which insinuates otherness and difference. This could be interpreted as an attempt to caution readers about the possibilities of cultural misrepresentations or "flaws" in the visual construction of the images that complement the Wanyeto tales. But Lantum admits to posing in "*Kikum ke kom*" traditional attire, "to make a Nigerian artist understand what I meant ... by Cameroon costume" (iv). Lantum's nationalistic affiliation is highlighted here even as he poses as an Nso man for an African he perceived as clueless to the complex diversities that exist within Anglophone Cameroon.

In *Tales of Nso*, this is not the case. There is no mention of anyone posing for Jarvies, and there seems to be no need for cultural specificity. One image-type though of five illustrations and in shades of black/white/green/reddish prevails and it is of a generic half-naked native as was typical of the colonial times. The image is clean cut, one-dimensional and lacks some of the complexity and depth of those in the 1964 edition. Readers would notice that the cannibalistic acts mentioned in the verbal texts are absent from these visual texts. Thus, the illustrations do not seek to confirm or extend the texts; rather, they are there to reinforce the idea of the primitive African of which the Nso people are a part. These are archetypal stereotypical images of generic primitive Africa that have continued to haunt the African literary community since the nineteenth century, with little or no cultural markers that distinguish people from East, North, South or West Africa.

Illustrations in the 1964 editions often reproduce the violence in the text in ways that may shock some readers. The images are also stereotypical but there is an attempt to project a particular cultural group and to construct characters as individuals. While readers are unable to tell the difference between Wanyeto and Baa from the 1969 visual texts, we can certainly pick out Wanyeto in *Folk Tales of Nso*. The characters, both males and females, are half-naked humans, which echoes Lantum's perspective that Nso people are of "savage look ... / Closer to nature / In action and in word" (n.p). But the human behaviors constructed in the verbal texts, once transmitted visually contradict the point he makes, especially that they are of "noble soul" (n.p). Thus, with the visual construction of human beings acting out these vices, as for example Baa physically chopping off the head of Wanyeto's mother, the tales cease to be about animals and may translate more into a metaphor of the violence of the Nso man. These ambiguities prompt my ambivalence about animal tales that are transmitted into print form with visual images that depict human beings.

Finnegan offers this pertinent comment on primitivism and colonial discourses:

> Many oral tales have originated in cultures with colonial/ex colonial backgrounds and/or from groups pictured as in some way marginal or exotic (the stereotypical setting for "oral" practices). Unsurprisingly their translators have thus often reflected and reinforced contemporaneous stereotypes of "the primitive", "the African", and so on
>
> (Finnegan 2007: 170).

The images in the verbal and visual texts of *Folk Tales of Nso* may be shocking to some, but they were a product of a time when collectors, researchers, translators, and publishers attempted to preserve Nso oral narratives in print, as acknowledged in Lantum's front matter. They appear to be images of Nso people of a certain period as envisioned by the unidentified Nigerian illustrator. I agree with Okpewho (2008), that, "Our study of oral literature cannot be excused from the sorts of hard questions other intellectual disciplines have been asking for some time" (foreword, Makuchi 2008: xiii). My analysis of these tales is in this vein, as I ponder how oral narratives are adapted in print for a new audience. What has changed and what remains constant in the Nso culture that may continue to make the classic Wanyeto tales relevant? Trust remains vital in the sustainability of relationships and a community, but how does Lantum rethink the cannibalistic thread in these tales?

If we agree with Bascom that, "Folklore means folk learning" (1973: 254), Lantum's earlier collections seem to be driven by a desire for youth to learn about the Nso people. Does this make the collections more sociological than literary? Perhaps, but if we take into consideration his narrative style that retains some of its "oral style such as repetitions and exclamations" (Okpewho 2008: 11), including chants, there may be some evidence here that he attempts to strike some form of balance. His 1960s editions espouse a certain cultural ideal endorsed by the Nso History Society, the idea of trust and the consequences of breaching this trust. This remains a worthy goal even as readers may want to shy away from the heavy-handed cannibalistic tendencies ascribed to his "animal" characters, especially when visualized as humans in the printed text.

Conclusion

As Finnegan contends, "In approaching 'oral texts' we need to be aware of the layers of interpretation and human action that have brought them into the form in which they are now circulated" (2007: 177). *Folk Tales of Nso* and *Tales of Nso* are clear examples. That they were edited and authored by Lantum does not discount the fact that many people are behind these creations. Further, the historical context that shaped the product should be considered as readers revisit these narratives not simply with twenty-first century sensibilities. Translating oral narratives into print is worthwhile, but translators and authors should be mindful of the possibilities of distortion and how this can skew a reader's understanding of what the text might be trying to accomplish. "Translated oral texts thus need to be read with an awareness of the assumptions which underlie translators' renderings. This is not just something of past centuries or confined to 'coloniser'/ 'colonised' relationships" (Finnegan 172). It is a constant reality in a world where cultural circulation is now the norm. In this way, Lantum's twentieth-century take on Wanyeto tales *perhaps* may reflect a new global reality and its possible impact on the Nso people.

Bibliography

Ashuntantang, Joyce B. (2009) *Landscaping Postcoloniality: The Dissemination of Cameroon Anglophone Literature*, Bamenda: Langaa RPCIG.

Barnard, Debbie (2005) "Serving the Master: Cannibalism and Transoceanic Representations of Cultural Identity," *International Journal of Francophone Studies* 8(3): 321–339.

Bascom, William (1965) "The Forms of Folklore: Prose Narratives," *Journal of American Folklore*, 78(307): 3–20.

———— (1973) "Folklore and the Africanist," *Journal of American Folklore*, 86(341): 253–259.

Ben-Amos, Dan (1975) "Folklore in African Society," *Research in African Literature*, 6(2): 165–198.

Bjornson, Richard (1991) *The African Quest for Freedom and Identity: Cameroonian Writing and the National Experience*, Bloomington: Indiana University Press.

Dike, Virginia (2005) "Developing Fiction for Today's Nigerian Youth," *Sankofa: Journal of African Children's and Young Adult Literature*. 4: 6–17.

Finnegan, Ruth (2007) *The Oral and Beyond: Doing Things with Words in Africa*, Oxford: James Currey.

Lantum, Daniel (1969) *Tales of Nso*, Lagos, Nigeria: African Universities Press.

Lantum, Dan N. (1964) *Folk Tales of Nso*, Lagos, Nigeria: Nooremac Press.

Lantum, Daniel Noni (1964) *Folk Tales of Nso*, Bamenda: Nso Historical Society.

Makuchi, Juliana (2008) *The Sacred Door and Other Stories: Cameroon Folktales of the Beba*, Ohio: Ohio University Press.

Okpewho, Isidore (2008) "Foreword," in Makuchi, Juliana, *The Sacred Door and Other Stories: Cameroon Folktales of the Beba*, Ohio: Ohio University Press. IX–XV.

Okpewho, Isidore (1992) *African Oral Literature: Backgrounds, Character, and Continuity*, Bloomington: Indiana University Press.

Tyson, Lois (2006) *Critical Theory: A User Friendly Guide*. 2nd Edition. New York: Routledge.

Ukala, Sam (1992) "Plot and Conflict in African Folktales," in Eldred Durosimi Jones, Eustace Palmer and Marjorie Jones (eds.), *Orature in African Literature Today*, Trenton, NJ: African World Press. 62–72.

PART V

Picture books across the majority world

31

THE GRANDDAUGHTERS OF SCHEHERAZADE

Bahia Shehab

The most famous storyteller in the history of mankind is Scheherazade, an intelligent woman who courageously decided to save the lives of other young maidens in the kingdom by marrying the evil Sultan Shahrayr, and keeping him entertained every night by telling him a series of intertwined stories that refuse closure. Women have been, since the beginning of times the greatest storytellers because they have had to entertain life. However, for different tribal, social and economic reasons, the past 200 years have witnessed the silencing of feminine voices in countries where Arabic is spoken. In the past twenty years an increase in the production of children's literature spearheaded by different Arab women authors, illustrators, educators and publishers indicates that their voices are rising again.

This silence of half of Arab society can be attributed to several factors. Jennifer Zobair, for example, argues that, "Muslim apologists emphasize the rights given to women in the Qur'an, but Muslim religious spaces, interpretive tradition, and jurisprudence have been decidedly the province of men" (2015: 150). A chauvinist society was also the reason why many women in the Arab world do not have access to education. But the underlying factor remains the political turmoil that the Arab part of the world has experienced since the demise of the Ottoman empire and the consecutive division and colonization of its different regions by European countries. The plundering of the region's resources and more importantly its cultural heritage was not a productive context for culture to develop. The formation of the new post-colonial Arab world when different countries started gaining independence was also plagued by a series of wars, both international and internal. It is difficult for culture to thrive without political stability, but for the past century cannons have been speaking louder than words in the Arab world.

During each of these disasters a major migration of populations from affected areas takes place to various parts of the world, but mainly into nearby Arab countries. Palestinian settlements started in Lebanon, Syria, Jordan and Egypt amongst other Arab countries. The Lebanese community itself dispersed during the civil war. Then there were Iraqi settlements in Syria and Egypt after the American invasion of Iraq, and Syrian settlements in Lebanon, Jordan and Turkey, and other Arab countries. This consistent forced migration creates human connections and intermarriages between the people of different Arab countries that were divided after the colonization of the region but who were previously connected under the Ottomans. Lebanon, Jordan Palestine and Syria were one country with families and tribes inhabiting "Greater Syria," while Egypt and Sudan had one king. Arab populations have been apt to show sympathy towards each other whenever one of them faced adversity, but that sentiment was not necessarily reflected or supported by Arab governments. Lack of support at government level did not stop the formation of NGOs and other attempts by individuals, intellectuals and artists to incorporate the spilling of human tragedy into its new society. A clear reflection of this is the strong response of the Arab intellectual community towards the Palestinian cause, which continues today to varying degrees. This sympathy towards human suffering is possibly one of the reasons why storytelling started gaining momentum in the past twenty years across the Arab world It is due to the failure of governments to reflect the true sentiment of their citizens that sympathy amongst the nations of Arab countries has not crystallized into better human condition solutions.

Because governments in the Arab world have had bigger problems to solve, the development of children's literature has slowed, which in itself led to deterioration in educational standards and the soaring illiteracy rates. However, in spite of all these factors of political turmoil, governmental negligence and corrupt educational systems, in the past twenty years there has been a steady revival in the production of children's books in the Arab world due to a variety of reasons. The most important of these is the presence of women behind the steering wheel. Whether as writers, illustrators or publishers there is a generation of women who understand the need for developing children's literature and who have taken the lead in meeting this need. Some of these women studied or lived abroad, some of them have children of their own, some of them own their own publishing houses, all of them are very well educated with at least one or two university degrees, and they all understand the importance of telling stories.

After the events of 9/11, telling stories from and about the Arab world became an important tool for bridging perceptions and educating a younger generation that grew up into a world questioning their identity. These Arab women needed a story to tell other than the story of war. Because of the war they did not find many, and thus decided to write their own. This might have given them the reason to write, illustrate and publish new children's books in the hope of finding their voice and in the process creating a new identity and new ideas for a younger generation. Another reason could be the lack of interest in this business sector by men, who usually seek more lucrative business modules, because after all, how much money can you make by selling children's books in societies where reading is not socially supported and encouraged in schools by governments and their institutions?

Egypt has always had a leading role in the production of children's literature. Children's magazines were first to appear out of Cairo with publications such as *Sindbad* magazine published by Dar al-Ma'arif in 1952 and *Samir* published in 1956 by Dar al-Hilal. Both titles were targeted at Arab children in general but both titles are actually names of boys. Lebanon has also been a very fertile ground for the production of children's books. During the 1960s Beirut was a mecca of ideas for intellectuals and artists from all over the Arab world, including children's book illustrators. Egyptian artist Helmi el-Touni resided and worked in Beirut during that period, illustrating numerous children's books during his fourteen-year stay there. Dar al-fata al'arabi, the first Arab publishing house to specialize in publishing children's books, was founded in 1974 in Beirut. The titles of their publications varied from historic to scientific to a broad range of topics; they also targeted children of both sexes even though their name roughly translates as "The house of the young Arab boy." They commissioned hundreds of books from both male and female authors, but illustrators were mainly male. These included el-Touni and another prominent Egyptian designer, Mohieldine el-Labbad. The dominance of male illustrators for children's literature changed with the formation of professional graphic design programs at universities in post-war Lebanon in the early 1990s, which made available a pool of trained talent, the majority of whom were women, to illustrate and design an abundance of books, an advantage not found in other Arab countries. This variety of talent that was not available earlier or elsewhere helped writers and publishers alike produce more visually appealing books.

Several factors also helped boost children's book production across the region. Countries with booming economies in the Arabian Gulf region became aware of the importance of supporting the production of children's literature. Through yearly international book fairs and generous children's books awards, like the Etisalat one million dirham award established in 2009, these countries were able to encourage children's book production in all of the Arab world. Further, the hosting of high quality book fairs like the Abu Dhabi, Dubai and Sharjah book fairs gives authors and publishers world-class platforms to market their books and explore potentially new areas not explored before.

A final, rather indirect, reason for the recent surge in children's literature might be that publishing houses decided to translate successful international works. In a way, these translations were filling the void not provided by talent in the Arab market in terms of subject and target audience, specifically little girls. An example of needed topics is the translation of the Scholastic Inc. series of books about manners published in 2005 and translated by Dar al-Shorouk in Egypt in 2009. The series has titles like "A Book About Being Bossy" and "A Book About Whining" all of which tackle behavioral problems in children. The books not only highlight problems but provide children and care-givers with tips on how to deal with these problems. Another important translation project undertaken by Dar al-Shorouk is *Philozenfants*, or the "little philosopher," a series published in 2004 by the French publishing house Nathan. Titles like "Le bien et le mal, c'est quoi?" and others try to simplify philosophical questions so they are comprehensible to children and young adults. The books are nicely illustrated and try to deal with very big questions that occur to children as they are growing up, like what is freedom? what are emotions? and what is life?

While Dar al-Shorouk translated works for children on philosophical concepts and behavioral problems, the-Cairo based al-Balsam publishing house translated a book on psychological pressure that children face, a topic never tackled before in Arabic children's books. First published in English in 1996 by Macdonald books, "A Huge Bag of Worries" was translated into Arabic in 2004. It deals with the worries of a little girl that follow her like a big bag wherever she goes. The girl protagonist was a missing topic in Arab children's literature and for that reason al-Ma'arif publishing house in Beirut translated a whole series on the life of the little girl "Camille," first published by Hemma in Belgium in 2006. Camille is a cute little redhead who faces very common everyday problems, like wetting her bed, or going to the doctor, or dealing with her first day at school. The series provided a gateway for parents to discuss everyday problems with their daughters through Camille and her adventures.

Women as leaders and heroes appear in Natalie Maydell and Sep Riahi's *Extraordinary Women from the Muslim World* (2007), translated and published in Arabic by Dar al-Shorouk in 2011. This picture book features leading women from the Arab and Islamic world, such as Khadija bint Khuwaylid and Aisha bint Abi Bakr from Saudi Arabia, both wives of the prophet Mohamad, or Al-Khansa, a famous Arab poet also from Saudi Arabia, Rabi'a al-Adawiyya in Iraq, who was a woman saint, Arwa bint Ahmed al-Sulayhiyya, queen of Yemen, and all the way to India with Sultan Razia, the warrior queen of Delhi. Little girls in the Arab world were now given concrete examples from history of strong women who had leading roles in society. The book also features scholars and poets like Nana Asmau from Nigeria and a guerrilla leader, Tjut Njak Dien, from Indonesia. Women are documented as they are in reality and not as they are depicted in modern day media. Barbie was born in the 1950s and automatically became an object of desire for little girls in the Arab world, where blonde hair and a slim figure were marketed as the ultimate symbol of beauty. With colonization comes the loss of history and consequently of memory. *Extraordinary Women* came as a strong reminder of accomplishments by women in Islam from all walks of life and from all under-represented regions in the available and common perception and psyche of young Arab girls. The stories of the novelist and activist Halide Edib Adivar and the military pilot, Sabiha Gökçen, both from Turkey, or the Egyptian diva Umm Kulthum Egypt, the Morrocan painter Chaibia Tallal or the Nobel Peace Prize winner Shirin Ebadi from Iran, all created an alternative and more integral role for young women in Arab and Muslim countries. It did not highlight the physical beauty of these women but their role as agents of change in their societies.

Finally, Mark Alan Stamaty's *Alia's Mission: Saving the Books of Iraq* (2004) documented the real story of Alia, an Iraqi woman, who during the US invasion of Iraq saved the books of the Baghdad National Library by secretly smuggling them into a safe place. Previously marginalized and under-represented, little girls now had access to books that dealt with their everyday problems, behavioral and psychological, and were presented with heroic examples of Arab women, setting a new platform and a new set of role models not present or available on their shelves before.

These translations created the awareness of the need for original works by and about Arab women for a younger generation of girls who had been for decades absent from literature for children. The translations also highlighted the need for books on identity, because when publishers translated these works they could not translate the illustrations. Thus Camille kept her red hair and other illustrated children kept their blonde looks, thereby creating for the publishers a problem of a different kind. Even though the topics tackled in these books were important they did not fully reflect their audience in their visual illustration and representation of the problem.

A pioneering woman who has flipped the translation game on its head is Amira Abulmagd, who has spearheaded the children's section at Dar al-Shorouk publishing in Egypt. Her efforts to improve Arabic children's books have been recognized with national and international awards. Abulmagd has published more than 400 new titles to date, many of which have received numerous awards.[1] She is a great example of a visionary woman highlighting issues of identity and trying to address social problems through children's literature. She describes the challenges that face publishers in the Arab world from the market, the government and even writers and artists. Low literacy rates, non-existent reading habits and bad distribution channels are some of the main problems a publisher has to face. The most serious challenge is the deteriorating educational systems in most Arab countries, where learning is based on rote memorization that actually discourages reading. Although specifics vary from one country to another, the result is the same: most children are reluctant readers of Arabic.

Asala in Beirut was founded in 1998 as the children's section sister company of Dar Annahda Al'arabiya publishing. Asala's mission as stated on several online platforms is to encourage children's love for reading and learning in Arabic through using simplified language and beautiful attractive drawing and colors, aiming at keeping up with children's educational needs throughout different stages (www.annalindhfoundation. org/members/asala-publishers). They focus on producing original Arabic reading levels books, an endeavor that had been previously undertaken mainly through translation from English, as, for example, Ladybird's "Read it Yourself" series that had been translated by Maktabat Lubnan Nashirun since the late 1970s. What was particularly striking about "Ana aqraa" or the Read it Yourself series in Arabic was that their publisher commissioned a very famous Lebanese calligrapher, Albert Estphan, to write all of the text for the books, so artistically the books were illustrated by international artists and scribed by a local calligrapher, which yielded a series of beautifully designed books in relation to image and text.

Asala made it a priority to develop in large quantities locally written and illustrated reading books for all children in all age groups. It is clear from the artistic production that they were not very successful in their early years in finding the right talent to illustrate their books, a problem shared by most publishing houses in the region. Even though their books were important in terms of filling a market need for reading level books targeted at youngsters, their series "Kilma Kilma," targeted at a 4–6 age bracket, and their "Hourof fi qisas" and "Hourouf fi nashatat," targeted at children aged 7–10, both left a lot of room for improvement in their visual representation. There were signs of improvement with their "Silsilat iqraa bil'arab" that was published in 2010 and their "Es'ad ma' asala" series published in 2013, once they had begun to commission better illustrators. It is clear that Asala are keen to improve the quality of children books in the Arab world from the quantity of books they produce and their constant attempts to improve their products.

Another publishing house from Lebanon receiving global recognition and also headed by a woman is Dar Onboz. Nadine Touma, a multi-talented artist, has found an outlet for her creativity in developing books and events for children. Her desire for art to become anchored in the everyday life of children led Touma to found the publishing house Dar Onboz in 2005, together with Raya Khalaf and Sivine Ariss. In the same year they published their first title, *Ayna asabi'ie* (Where Did My Fingers Go?), the story of a child having to deal with losing her fingers, illustrated by the Lebanese artist Lena Merhej and written by Nadine Touma herself. The book contained a finger puppet, a CD of a musical composition with the reading of the story, and a Lebanese traditional children's folk song about fingers. *Ayna asabi'ie* tapped into the issue of disability with sign language symbols illustrated by Merhej, and thus another level of comprehension was added to the text. Touma has made sure her publishing house only deals with the best local and international talent to produce beautiful "art" books for children. Her house, since its foundation, has published some of the most beautifully illustrated and produced books for children to have come out of the Arab world in its modern history. Most of the artists the house deals with had studied graphic design or art at universities in Lebanon or are established international artists and/or designers. In 2011 Touma collaborated with artist

Eric Deniaud to produce *Noujoum*, a beautifully crafted book in which Deniaud utilized clay modeling for the characters combined with very colorful wool threads, culminating in a book that is a real work of art.

Dar Onboz's awareness of quality is not only limited to the visuals developed for their books, but also their typography. In 2010 Dar Onboz collaborated with the award winning designer Lara Assouad to develop two children's books, *Tabati* and *Aswat a. Abjadiyyah*, which were exhibited in Munich at the Haus Der Kunst in the fall of 2010 and at Agial Art Gallery in Beirut, also in 2010. In both books Assouad used the round shape of the circle to compose her modular font entitled "Tabati." The font was awarded a certificate of excellence in typography in 2011 from TDC New York. The Opera Prima Award at the Bologna Children's Book Fair in 2012 was received for the illustrations, type design and layout of *Tabati* the book.

The writing for the children's books published by Dar Onboz is always very creative. whether by Touma herself or other creative writers. The house strives to deliver high artistic quality in all areas of book production including experimenting with different types of art paper and special printing and even testing new formats. Every book produced is a total experience, not just a story. Touma is very concerned with the issue of reviving tradition, which can be noted from the plays she writes and performs and events she plans at different venues in Lebanon and the region, and also in the quality and diversity of the talents she collaborates with. She strives not merely to educate but to consciously revive the pleasure of consuming the Arabic language. On their website their mission statement is that: "The Onboz family wants to see children and youth enjoying the Arabic language and loving it, parents reading Arabic books to their children, teachers developing new methodologies for teaching Arabic, special books that will travel from the Arab world to the rest of the world. Writers, artists, and musicians who want to contribute in building their societies through a book, a drawing, a song, a photograph, a word or an animation Writers, artists and musicians who believe that culture and art are an amazing tool of growth and transformation." Through these collaborations Dar Onboz have been very successful in creating many books that are real works of art.

Another artist turned publisher in Lebanon is Rania Zaghir, who established the house al-Khayyat al-Saghir in 2007. Unlike the bigger publishing houses, Zaghir limits her production to two books per year. She has been the recipient of several awards, the Anna Lindh Foundation award for the children's book *Heya Huma Hunna* (She, The Two of Them, They) in 2010 and Assabil (friend of public libraries) Best Book Award for her children's book *Sissi Malaket talbasu kharufan wa dudatayn* (Sisi Malaket wears a sheep and two worms) in 2009. *Heya Huma Hunna* is a beautifully illustrated book by the designer Jana Traboulsi and written by Nahla Ghandour dealing with the topic of a physically disabled girl; it does not highlight the misery but merely states her disability as an obstacle that needs to be dealt with. A delightful read with delightful visuals, it can be used as a gateway to discuss disability with children. She is the only publisher to own her personal YouTube page and one of the few to embrace new digital platforms that could be the solution to many of the reading problems in the Arab world (www.youtube.com/user/ KhayyatSaghir). But her contribution to the field of children's literature does not stop at experimental children's books and technology, as she also organizes a bi-yearly conference on children's literature in Lebanon bringing together authors from the region and Europe. as well as illustrators and publishers. In her 2012 conference she had the controversial topic of politics in children's literature as a theme.[2] Zaghir is yet another example of how the contribution of one individual can make a difference even in a huge industry.

Balsam Saad founded Dar al-Balsam in Cairo in 2005 after realizing the market void concerning children's literature in the Arab world. Suffering from the same problems that all other publishers were suffering, such as lack of governmental support and lack of a proper marketing platform, Saad took a step previously reserved for bigger publishing houses and opened her own bookstore, which sold only children's books and possibly the only specialized children's books outlet in Egypt in 2010. Most bookstores in Cairo have a children's section or a children's corner, but Dar al-Balsam dedicated their store to catering only for children and utilized the space to organize workshops, weekly children's book readings and monthly book signing events. Dar al-Balsam releases their monthly event list via email announcing the reading events of two children's books at the weekend, offering children the option to buy the book during that reading at competitive prices. The bookstore is yet another move by a smaller independent publisher to push the circulation and development of children's books in Egypt and the region in the right direction.

The UAE eventually caught up on the children's publishing boom. Kalimat, a publishing house established in 2007 by Sheikha Bodour bint Sultan al-Qasimi, was a major game changer for children's book production in the Arabian Gulf region, as now children's books were produced for the first time with very high production values and that targeted mainly the Muslim majority and were specifically and culturally relevant. That is understandable since the founder and patron is a woman belonging to the ruling family and one of the driving forces of culture in her country. After reading a UN report that stated that less than 2 percent of the population in the Arab world read one book a year, Kalimat aimed to transform this picture, motivating children to read in Arabic by publishing entertaining and culturally relevant stories. "Topics and issues that Arab children everywhere face in daily life are deftly handled in 140 titles spanning a wide variety of genres, including activity books, fables, baby books, young adult books and audio CDs. In just four years, Kalimat has already won several prestigious prizes, including awards at the Beirut Book Fair in 2009 and 2010 and the Best Children's Book Award from the Riyadh-based International Forum on Children's Education and Development in 2011" (www.kalimat.ae/index.php?route=information/ information&information_id=216).

In the young adult section, the house had a great start with Fatima Sharafeddine's *Faten* that won the Beirut Book Fair Award in 2011. Since then the house has published several books for the same growing category. Their strategy was to wait for the market to develop a taste for similar books just as it had for Arabic children's books in the past decade, then they would have more manuscripts to choose from as writers develop a greater understanding of what readers in the teen and young adult group are looking for. Just as they moved from five books to seventy-five in the younger age group, they hoped that in the years to come they would look back and think that *Faten* was be the launchpad to their success in the young adult category. Like other publishing houses, they participate in book fairs on a regular basis and regularly organize readings, book signings, and illustration workshops designed to cultivate a love of reading in Arab children. They hold many activities around special occasions such as National Day, Mother's Day, or Father's Day. They had a launch party for their book *Hithaa Al Eid* that gave children an idea of what Eid festivities involve, with henna, sous and the traditional call for suhour. Their books try to highlight culturally relevant events and deal with daily problems children in the Arab world face. They are clearly targeting young girls in the Gulf in their books like *Sha'ir Mimi*, which discusses the problem of identity through hair. The story is of a young girl with long black hair who dreams of having blonde hair. Written by Fatima Sharafeddine and illustrated by Rasha Mounib Hakim, the book shows Mimi trying to resolve the problem of accepting her hair, which is the same as her mother's. Another book by the same team, also about the same character, Mimi, entitled *Mimi and her Busy Mother*, deals with Mimi's problem that her mother is very busy in her career as a pediatrician, illustrated by Mimi's mother wearing the classical khaliji abay, which is a long black cloak with a headscarf, to go to work. This was the first time such an illustration had appeared in an Arab children's book. When Sharafeddine was asked about the dictation of the illustration whether that came from her text, she clarified that it was dictated by the publishing house, a clear attempt by them to make their books address their local audience specifically (personal interview with Fatima Sharafeddine in 2012 at the American University in Cairo). They are also turning the translation game on its head by bringing Arab culture to the world by having several of their titles translated into other languages.

With all of these publishing houses lead by visionary and concerned women, there is a growing number of authors and illustrators joining this renaissance. Their number is too great to list in this article, but it is their voices, talent and hard work that is shaping the new identity of little Arab girls not just in the Arab world but all around the globe. They are conscious of the problems and all the limitations faced by the people in the Arab book world and in spite of that they are still trying to raise the bar and develop works that they hope will change their society and the way the world perceives it. They are writing and publishing books on all issues relevant to children, first experiences, fears, dreams, hopes, limitations and the future. The importance of what they are doing culminated in Queen Rania of Jordan writing a New York Times Best Seller *The Sandwich Swap*, a book that celebrates difference and understanding. It was published by Disney in 2010 and translated by Dar el Shourouk and published by them in the same year. It is a children's story about two young girls, Lily and Salma, who learn the value of diversity by exchanging food at school. Queen Rania is also the author of two other stories, *The King's Gift* and *Eternal Beauty*. The involvement of country leaders in the children's book production process helps bring it to the foreground of the media and facilitates other people in the industry to develop more work for children.

After 9/11 and the war on Iraq the need for dialogue between the Arab world and the Western world became an urgent necessity. Arabs realized that being silent in a global village meant being misunderstood and repeatedly misrepresented. No representation of Arabs on the global arena meant wrong representations by other people who have their own agendas, Arabs and non-Arabs alike. With Arab women already facing many social pressures it has become very important to give little girls an early start at knowledge since their presence in the workforce is essential for the development of a healthy balanced society. All of the above-mentioned initiatives, projects and campaigns, as well as many others like them, are slowly alleviating some of the problems resulting from poor education, as well as the challenges of bilingual schooling. In spite of the many problems there is a new generation of publishers devoting more enthusiasm and resources than ever before to the production of children's literature. This boom can only be credited to the women who have decided to become the new Scheherazades of the Arab world, telling stories to a younger generation of girls, and with these stories enlightening their minds and the minds of people all around the world on this region, its history and hopefully its bright future.

Notes

1 Awards received by Dar al-Shourouk for children's books include the Suzanne Mubarak Prize, the Bologna Book Fair's New Horizons, International Board on Books for Young People (IBBY), UNESCO and Etisalat's grand prize.
2 www.facebook.com/121101934571277/photos/a.160536170627853.43129.121101934571277/479187412096059/?type=1&theater

Bibliography

Maydell, Natalie and Sep Riahi (2007) *Extraordinary Women from the Muslim World*, illustrated by Heba Amin, Lancaster, PA: Global Content Ventures.

Sharafeddine, Fatima (2011) *Mimi and Her Busy Mother*, illustrated by Rasha Mounib Al Hakim, Sharjah: Kalimat.

Stamaty, Mark Alan (2004) *Alia's Mission: Saving the Books of Iraq*, New York: Random House (Dragonfly Books). Arabic translation, Dar al-Balsam, 2005.

Touma, Nadine, and Eric Deniaud (2011) *Noujoum*, Beirut: Dar Onboz.

Touma, Nadine, and Lena Merhej (2005) *Ayna Asabi'ie* (Where Did My Fingers Go?), Beirut: Dar Onboz.

Zobair, Jennifer (2015) "The Depth and Weight of Feminist Studies in Islam: A Response to 'The Evolution of Feminist Studies in Religion'" *Journal of Feminist Studies in Religion* 31(2): 149–154.

32

CHILDREN'S BOOK ILLUSTRATION IN COLOMBIA

Notes for a history

Silvia Castrillón

A significant production of illustrated books and picture books only emerged in Colombia in the last two decades of the twentieth century. Illustrated books had been published previously, and there were important examples of isolated cases of professional or amateur artists who illustrated works written for children (see the historical studies by Beatriz Helena Robledo and Zully Pardo), but it was not until the first years of the 1980s that, in a systematic way, children's books were published in which, as distinct from textbooks, illustration became an essential part of the book and not just a decorative element.

Illustrated books and picture books specially directed to child and juvenile audiences were first produced in Colombia in the context of certain material and non-material (or "spiritual") conditions: the material conditions were associated with the development of the market economy and the introduction of technologies that fostered the graphic arts field, and the non-material conditions were associated with the representation of childhood, ideas about education, and childhood culture. At the same time, it is necessary to place the national context in which children's book illustration is born within a broader international stage, which served as a model and accelerated this process in Colombia.

First, there was impetus from what has been called the "Reading crisis," responsibility for which was attributed to schools and led to proposals about "*deschooling* reading." Towards the middle of the 1970s, from a concern about the qualitative improvement of education emerged an improvement that, among other goals, should have enabled a solution to this crisis. This initiative led to the formulation of an educational remodeling, which emphasized the quality of education, which – it was claimed – had been affected by the expansion and democratization of the system. This program, carried out by the National Education Ministry, had as one of its main activities the creation of school libraries richly endowed with books for children and young people, available as never before in the country to large sectors of the population. Most of these books were acquired in Spain, since national production was almost exclusively limited to school textbooks and adaptations of the so-called children's classics.

As part of this school libraries program, the project "Laboratory of Literature for Children and Young People" was conceived and carried out as a mechanism to build a documentation center of books for children and youth. This center enabled, on one hand, the development of programs to train teachers about books, children's and youth literature, and the training of readers; and on the other hand, the development of evaluation and selection criteria for books in the libraries. The center included a good proportion of illustrated books, at that time produced abroad. This project was inspired in part by knowledge about the importance given in French-speaking Canada to books with a French origin for children and young people for training readers and thereby maintaining the French language, spoken by a minority in that country. This school libraries program, with its experimentation laboratory, was maintained until the end of the 1970s.

In parallel to what was happening in schools, a movement was initiated to create libraries and reading rooms for children. This movement considered, not only in Colombia but in other countries, that the pleasure of reading was created by offering attractive books in spaces and with methods and materials different from those used in schools.

At the beginning of the next decade, and in part as a response to the closing of the Program of School Libraries of the Education Ministry and its Laboratory, the Asociación Colombiana para el Libro Infantil y Juvenil, ACLIJ (Colombian Association for Books for Children and Young People) was created and constituted as the Colombian section of IBBY (the International Board on Books for Young People). Through ACLIJ, Colombia was able to establish close links with other countries, especially European countries and the United States and Canada, and hence identify the best books produced there, and have access to the analysis and reflection about these books as published in specialized books and journals. IBBY's biennial Honor Lists and Hans Christian Andersen Award have been a useful source of information about international children's books of high quality.

In 1978 Ediciones Ekaré was founded as the first publishing house established in a Latin American country with its origins in an organization dedicated to promoting reading, the Banco del Libro de Venezuela (Book Bank of Venezuela), which at the same time was the IBBY section in that country. This non-commercial origin, its autonomy under the pressures of the market economy, and its work through teams of specialists seriously trained in their country and abroad in the field of literature for children and young people, allowed this publisher to maintain a high quality level, which positively influenced some subsequent projects in Colombia, although these did not have the same good fortune and continuity.

With ACLIJ, Colombia started some activities that led to the consolidation of an illustration movement of children's books and to the professionalization of Colombian illustrators. Some training opportunities for illustrators were established, and groups for the study and analysis of children's books were formed, in which many of the current prominent and representative authors and illustrators participated, and the journals *El Libro Infantil* and *Las Hojas de ACLIJ* were also created as sites for reflection upon and analysis of books, literature and reading (see Figure 32.1). Likewise, the journals *La Lleva* and *La Barra* directed to children and juvenile audiences, respectively, were a means to draw attention to the best books that started to circulate in Colombia in the commercial sphere. This association also created an award for the Best Colombian Book for Children and Young People, as a way to foster national publishing. This award was granted between 1987 and 1990, but was unfortunately short-lived.[1]

At this time, the publishing house Carlos Valencia Editores began to publish children's books in which the design and illustration were one of their main concerns. Kapelusz

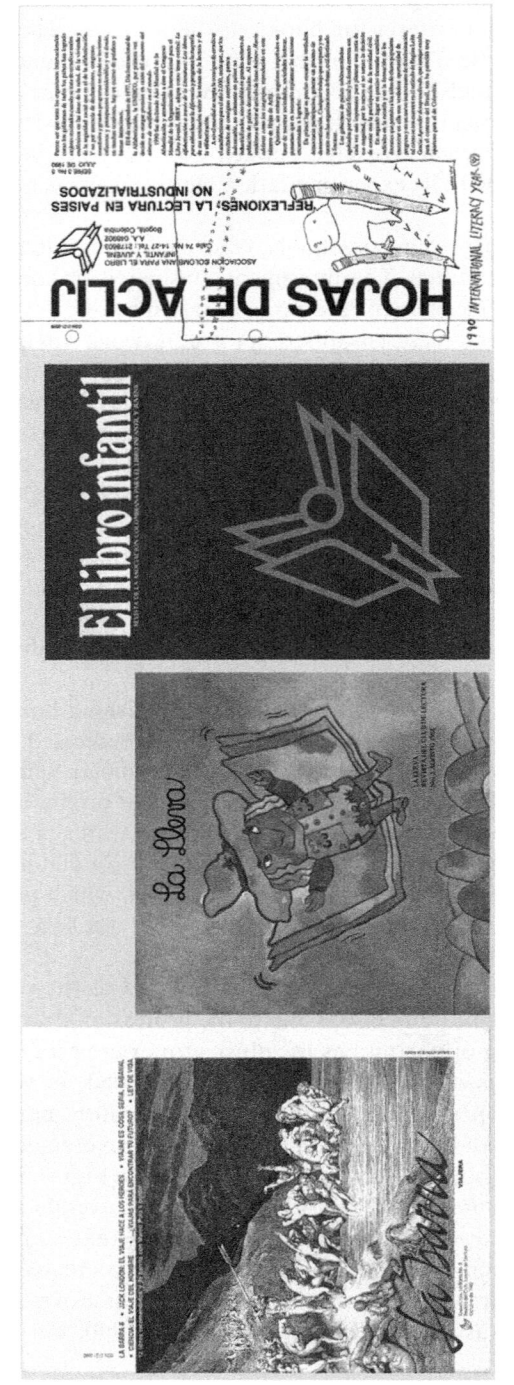

Figure 32.1   La Barra, La Lleva, El Libro Infantil and *Hojas de ACLIJ.*
Source: With permission of Silvia Castrillón on behalf of Asociación Colombiana para el Libro Infantil y Juvenil.

Colombiana produced the first books made in the country, with a dedicated and expert publishing team – on the model of Ediciones Ekaré – consisting of a publishing director, an art director, authors and illustrators. The Norma publishing house commenced its project of children's books published in Colombia with Colombian illustration. These three publishing houses initiated in the country the systematic production of picture books and illustrated books for children and youth.

As mentioned above, the emergence of children's illustration was shaped by both national motivations and international developments. According to the Spanish specialist Felicidad Orquín, the illustrated children's book underwent an important change between the 1960s and 1980s. In the IVth Symposium of the Foundation Germán Sánchez Ruipérez – "The Illustration as First Reading and Artistic Education" (1997) – she presented her study of great illustrators who emerged during those years and are still undeniable reference points in the field: "In the 60's emerges a new type of picture books that are radically different from those previously existing in the specialty of illustrated books for children. There is research on the image and new printing techniques make possible a different type of work. A new visual esthetics arises, a new language of images" (1998: 71). The illustrators mentioned by Orquín (herself a noted publisher in leading Spanish publishing houses) included, among others, Janosch, Tomi Ungerer, Maurice Sendak, Leo Lionni, Etienne Delessert, Arnold Lobel, Raymond Briggs, Roberto Innocenti and Quentin Blake.

All of these illustrators were part of the endowment of school libraries, of the collections of the Laboratory of Children's Literature, and the experimental collection of the ACLIJ, and source of inspiration for those who would become the new Colombian authors and illustrators and the publishing source of this first type of illustrated book, according to the characterization made by Felicidad Orquín. On the other hand, it does not seem risky to consider that the illustrated book is in debt to different coincident circumstances at this time.

First, research into the processes whereby children acquire written language had begun in Latin America at that time, under the leadership of Emilia Ferreiro, disciple of the psychogenesis or genetic psychology of Jean Piaget. This investigation displaces the beginning of reading learning from the first school years to the first years of life and, thus, recognizes these first years as a period of important discoveries and learning. These investigations generated as well the first suspicions about the abilities of text books as the only source and guide for learning.

In 1971, Etienne Delessert, one of the authors/illustrators mentioned by Felicidad Orquín, met Piaget and this meeting was decisive for him. Delessert commented in a newspaper interview in 2008:

> "I started to become deeply interested in children and children's literature when I met Piaget; I learned to ask questions, to pose problems, without trying to influence them. For me … it is very important to offer children stories that are not everyday stories and that impel them to ask questions, to ask themselves or their parents. A parallel world that is not the one in which they live everyday with their family, at school, etc. It is a way of fostering creativity".
>
> (*El País*, 11/ 03/2008, cited in Sánchez 2008)

A product of these reflections is his book *Comment le souris reçoit une pierre sur la tête et découvre le monde*, with a prologue by Piaget himself, which could be a paradigmatic example of how the new knowledge about learning influenced the conceptions about the nature of a good illustrated book. The text of the book itself is a metaphor about learning in the first years of life, when it describes how a mouse discovers the world when it leaves its cave.

The second circumstance could be those new ways of looking at childhood that value playing and transform child pedagogy, giving place to new cultural products distant from what is traditionally pedagogic, among them, books. The third circumstance is another perspective, that of the market economy that starts to see children as new potential consumers and recipients of new products especially manufactured for them, such as clothes food and, indeed, books.

In this context and with this background, books for children and youth began to be produced in Colombia: by the publishing house Carlos Valencia Editores, whose goal was oriented to offer a space for writers who were starting to direct their work to children and young readers; by Kapelusz Colombiana, an Argentinian company that became established in Colombia and began publishing children's books under the Barco de Papel imprint in 1982 (see Figure 32.2); and by Editorial Norma (which later acquired Kapelusz). According to some scholars these companies produced the first Colombian picture books and illustrated books.

But it wouldn't be fair if we do not mention in this inventory the collection about pre-Columbian ethnic groups supported by the Bank of the Republic, whose purpose was to rescue indigenous cultures. This production in the 1980s became so important that it transcended national boundaries when the Brazilian section of IBBY, the National Foundation for Children and Young People's Books, organized in that country the *Week of the Colombian Children's Book*, where ACLIJ took a sample of these first books to exhibit them at the National Library of Rio de Janeiro, along with six lectures. In this exhibition there were special guests, in addition to specialists, authors and illustrators and publishers, who recognized the publishing and graphic quality of the Colombian production, which then exceeded the Brazilian one, despite the long tradition in literary creation and illustration in that country.

Figure 32.2 Collection *Postre de Letras.*
Source: Reproduced with kind permission of Editorial Norma.

The collections of Editorial Norma

A notice in the journal *El Libro Infantil* 2 (1987): 14 announced the beginning of the first collections for children published in Colombia, produced by Editorial Norma:

> 18 titles will go out to the national market this year in three children's collections published by Norma. The books in the first series, *Mira qué es esto* (Look what this is), are directed to the little ones and were developed by a team of educators, designers and illustrators that have taken into account all the factors related to children's development and their ability to enjoy images. The second series, *Mira lo que hay a tu alrededor* (Look what is around you) [but finally titled *Un mundo de cosas para mirar* (A world of things to see)], is pursuing the same objectives as the fore mentioned, but it shows children different realities to those in the first series. The third collection, *Chigüiro* (Capybara), introduces a charming character typical of our wildlife, who recounts enjoyable and simple everyday life stories.

Further, this publishing project was based in the theoretical considerations briefly outlined at the beginning of this essay and in the theoretical and practical knowledge about books for children and young people in other parts of the world, especially those produced and circulated in France at that time. The purpose was to offer children, from the early months of life to adolescence and the early teen years, a broad range of possible practices for image and word reading in different manifestations and in diverse texts, some informative and others literary.

The first collection, *Mira qué es esto* (Look What This Is), came from the research by Paul Faucher, the creator and director of the *Albums du Père Castor* in France, into the ways by which a child grasps a two-dimensional representation of daily reality. It was about offering the possibility of progression from the closest objects of their surroundings to the ones that children could only access through images, such as the feeding bottle, the crib, a blanket, pets such as a dog and cat, plants, flies, wild animals, and so on. They were isolated realistic images without contexts, set against white backgrounds. The representation of a single object on a page accompanied by the letters which represent it was not intended to teach infants to decode writing, but was the foundation to indicate that objects could be represented by both images and words and that words could be written. The theory assumed that children, from early ages, are capable of complex intellectual elaborations, such as image identification in books, something that now nobody doubts, but back then the thought that babies can also "read" was a contradiction.

The second collection, *Un mundo de cosas para mirar* (*A World of Things to See*), following the same principles, invited readers to locate images in a crowded page, where there was not a unique way to enter and go over the image. The books were: *El mercado* (The Market), illustrated by Alekos, who had already illustrated the indigenous stories collected by Rosa Emilia Salamanca, *Las diversions* (The Pastimes), by Esperanza Vallejo, *La casa* (The House), by Cecilia Cáceres, *La escuela* (The School), by Stella Cardozo, *La ciudad* (The City), by Felipe Valderrama and *La granja* (The Farm), by Ivar Da Coll.

Ivar Da Coll responded in a brilliant way to the need formulated by the project to create a Colombian character whose characteristics made him lovable, cuddly, with all the conditions of a warm-blooded pet and whose furry skin warms up. This character, Chigüiro, was created for first readers who were offered the possibility of reading a story through images, adding to the previous collections – where the images were there only to be identified and to prompt dialogue even without words – the component of narrative time to create a reading that made it necessary to remember the previous image and anticipate the next. This character, who was then the protagonist of six stories, became perhaps with Rafael Pombo's Rin Rin renacuajo, one of the most important icons of Colombian Children's literature.

Traditional poetry and original poetry were also part of this publishing project. As in many countries, in Colombia it was mandatory to turn to adult and children's popular oral tradition and to collections of this tradition, some compiled by renowned anthropologists such as Guillermo Abadía. Apart from Rafael Pombo's work, there was not enough original poetry that was different from the moralizing, didactic and excessively sweet verse considered to be the only children's poems. The collection *Abra Palabra* was then designed, which in its first phase published almost simultaneously *Tope tope tun*, illustrated by Yesid Vergara, *Cúcuru mácara*, by Alekos, *Ensalada de animales* (Animal Salad), by Ivar Da Coll, *Palabras que me gustan* (Words I Like), by Esperanza Vallejo, *La casa que Juan construyó* (The House Juan Built) and *El mico y el loro* (The Monkey and the Parrot), by Diana Castellanos, *Poemas* by *Rafael Pombo, El Sapo y el cangrejo* (The Toad and the Crab) by Nicolás Lozano and *Adivíneme ésta* (Guess this One), by Ródez.

This collection, together with *Chigüiro*, started to offer an image of the country, with details of the Colombian Caribbean, the popular neighborhoods of Bogota, our colorful fauna and flora, without concessions or schematism; without aspirations of showing the image imposed upon us from abroad – exotic and "with local color" – and without idealization of childhood. These books were the result of a very serious investigation about our image, fostered by the Colombian illustrator Diana Castellanos and by the Brazilian illustrator Gian Calvi, who was in charge of the illustration workshops opened by the ACLIJ with the support of the Cerlalc, performed with the National Pedagogic University, in which was involved almost the whole group that participated in this project with Editorial Norma.

The entire project offered as well the possibility of informative reading, on one hand, and literary reading on the other; this means that it had fiction and non-fiction books according to the Anglo-Saxon nomenclature, maybe the most clear for this classification. The collections *Mira qué es esto* (Look What This Is) and *Un mundo de cosas para mirar* (A World of Things to See), were part of the information book category, and the collection *Abra Palabra* (Open Word) of the creative literature category, but only the poetry. A collection that allowed children to do things with their hands was missing. The collection *En casa* (At Home), which consisted of *En casa yo cocino* (At Home I Cook), *En casa cuido las plantas* (At Home I Take Care of the Plants) and *En casa cuido los animales* (At Home I Take Care of the Animals), offered illustrated books with a step by step method that allowed children to follow a process. The characteristic of its manufacture was the close work between the author and the illustrator starting from the sketches done by the authors.

The age cycle is complete – the different collections were thought to cover from small children, passing through the middle group to the older ones – and so is the diversity cycle in this project with the collection Torre de Papel (Paper Tower) conceived as the great collection of Colombian, Latin American and worldwide literature, with diverse styles, subjects, approaches, with renowned authors and with books for all ages. Its first titles were accompanied by illustrations mostly by Colombian artists.

Figure 32.3 The Collection *Abra Palabra*.
Source: Reproduced with kind permission of Editorial Norma.

Although some of these projects continued, most of them disappeared, not only because new titles were no longer produced, but because many that were memorable are not currently re-printed. Some were taken up by new publishing houses. Almost two decades passed before children's book illustration in Colombia began to regain the place it had back then.

This essay has presented an historical overview of picture books and illustration, and it is not its purpose to attempt a survey of the current situation, but it can be said in conclusion that the illustrated book in its different expressions – as the picture book with text accompanied by the illustration, and recently in the modality of graphic tale and novel – has recently gone through great development in the country. The major publishing houses and the multinationals have strengthened their lists of titles with Colombian illustrators; however, these lists pass from one publishing house to another due to the volatility of this market. But perhaps the recent most important phenomenon is the rise of new publishing houses. Some like Babel Libros (Babel Books) have had already ten years of constant work, consolidating a list of titles that remains active. Babel works with Colombian illustrators like Rafael Yochteng, Maria Paula Bolaños and the acclaimed Colombian author and illustrator Ivar Da Coll, already mentioned in this text as one of the pioneers of illustration in Colombia.

Note

1 This award, whose jury always comprised internationally well-known publishers and specialists, was made on the first occasion to the collection *Postre de Letras* (Kapelusz Colombiana); the second time, in 1988, two categories were awarded to children's and juvenile literature, the former to *Rin Rin, Simón y la viejecita*, by Rafael Pombo, illustrated by Santiago Correa (Medellín: Colina), and the latter to *Las cosas de la casa*, by Celso Román (Bogotá: Carlos Valencia Editores). In 1989, the award was made to *Pelea en el parque*, by Evelio Rosero (Magisterio); the final awards (1990) were made to *Tengo miedo*, by Ivar Da Coll (Carlos Valencia) in the children's category and to *Prisión de honor* by Lyll Becerra de Jenkins (Editorial Norma) in the juvenile category.

Bibliography

Delessert, Etienne (1998 [1971]) *Comment la souris reçoit une pierre sur la tête et découvre le monde* (How the Mouse Was Hit on the Head by a Stone and so Discovered the World), Paris: Gallimard Jeunesse; New York: Doubleday.

Orquín, Felicidad (1998) "Tendencias en los libros ilustrados para niños" (Trends in illustrated books for children), *Clij: Cuadernos de Literatura Infantil y Juvenil*, 102: 70–73.

Pardo, Zully (2007) "Panorama histórico del libro ilustrado de literatura infantil colombiana" (Historical Overview of the Illustrated Book in Colombian Children's Literature) Master's Degree Dissertation, GRETEL postgraduate studies, Banco del Libro de Venezuela and Universidad Autónoma de Barcelona (Autonomous University of Barcelona).

Robledo, Beatriz Helena (2012) *Todos los danzantes: Panorama histórico de la literatura infantil colombiana* (All the Dancers: An Historical Overview of Colombian Children's Literature), Bogota: Universidad del Rosario.

Salamanca, Rosa Emilia (1992) *El viaje al cielo del gallinazo y el sapo* (The trip to the sky of the vulture and the toad), Bogotá: ATI (Asociación de Trabajo Interdisciplinario).

Sánchez, Pedro Villar (2008) "Entrevista al ilustrador Etienne Delessert". http://pedrovillar.blogspot.com/2008/03/entrevista-al-ilustrador-etienne.html

33

THE *SHÔJO* (GIRL) AESTHETIC IN JAPANESE ILLUSTRATED AND PICTURE BOOKS

Helen Kilpatrick

Japanese picture books (*ehon*) are internationally recognized as artistically innovative, beautifully produced, and amongst the most outstanding in the world. Like Japanese art and culture, they are richly intertextual, heavily influenced by international philosophies, literature and art. Drawing on early twentieth century artistic experiments and new liberalist ideas introduced from the west, these books blend traditional Japanese and European aesthetics. Many Japanese picture books thus instantiate and deconstruct complex intercultural ideologies and subjectivities. The motif of the "girl" (*shôjo*), for instance, recurs throughout modern Japanese illustrated books, and often subverts gendered constructions in ways that are not always well understood outside (or inside) Japan. The "girl" is often unfairly criticized as childish or "cute" (*kawaii*). Although often found in *manga*, *anime* and "girls' novels" (*shôjo shôsetsu*) in Japan and internationally, the girl motif has rarely been associated with picture books (Kilpatrick 2010: 149; 2012), and remains an under-examined aspect of illustrated Japanese books.

This paper employs the concept of "girl consciousness" (*shôjo ishiki*) to shed light on the *shôjo* image in some less internationally prominent but nonetheless major Japanese illustrated and picture books while also demonstrating some of the richness, history and diversity behind them. "Girl consciousness", introduced by Takahara Eiri (1999: 9), develops Honda Masuko's earlier (1988; 1992) concepts of a "fluttering" (*hirahira*) aesthetic and "girl collective" to help dispel ideas of the unthinking or submissive girl.[1] Both Takahara and Honda acknowledge the peripheral position of the *shôjo* and see the imagination as a form of potential resistance to real social confines. Takahara maintains that reading *shôjo* fiction with "girl consciousness" can inspire an imaginative "freedom" (*jiyû*) and "arrogance" (*kôman*), which in turn release a critical resistance and creative power. While cautioning that this "freedom" and "arrogance" are *imagined*, non-concrete faculties, he asserts that any such "girlishness" is open to both males and females who seek to reject societal norms and restrictions (1999: 10). That is, any "girl conscious" reader can use the power of the imagination to satisfy desires not possible in the actual world. Honda (1992; 2010) argues that girl-signifying frills, ribbons, flowers and wide open spaces in art and literature express a "fluttering" movement and lightness through which time can be suspended. This liminality represents the girl's imaginative, if momentary, respite from and resistance to the restrictions of her daily life. My examination of the *shôjo* image focuses on two enduring "girl" figures from Hans Christian Andersen's *Little Mermaid* and Lewis Carroll's *Alice in Wonderland* which often resonate with this kind of resistant "girl". The first is the sad, contemplative mermaid as depicted in two re-visionings of *The Red Candles and the Mermaid* (Akai rôsoku to ningyô) by Ôgawa Mimei (1882–1961), illustrated respectively by Iwasaki Chihiro (1918–1974) and Sakai Komako (b. 1966); and the second is a recent, more transgressive Alice figure as portrayed by well-known (male) *shôjo* artist Uno Akira (b. 1934) in Minagawa Hiroko's picture book *Maimai and Naina* (Maimai to Nainai).

While cultural transformations have helped shape the Japanese female image over time, the innovations of earlier authors and artists, both Japanese and international, have also influenced the representation of gendered subjectivities in Japanese picture books and the development of the resistant *shôjo* figure. The production of illustrated books flourished in two historical phases, first in the early 1900s and then following World War II (Masaki and Miyake 2001: 17–19). In both periods there was much experimentation with the image of the child and, in particular, the "beautiful girl" (*bishôjo*), which has come to be characterized by an aesthetic of intense inner emotions through a blend of beauty and sorrow.

The *shôjo* holds a special status in Japan, not as a demographic, but as a prepubescent, "not-quite-female-female" (Robertson 2002: 158), or "neither and both [mature/ infantile; man/woman]" (Honda 1988: 10; Aoyama 2010: 40) who yearns for the faraway sky (Honda 1992: 182; 2010: 35). This aesthetic coincides with changing ideals of beauty, which represent broader cultural ideas and important transitional periods. Japan's first cultural contact with the outside world for over 200 years in the mid-1800s impacted upon social attitudes to women and girls. The female transformed, for example, from an object of (male) sexual desire in the Neo-Confucianist Edo period (1603–1867) (Kami 2006: 118), through the more demure, obedient daughter (*musume*) of late Meiji (1868–1912), towards a more independent *shôjo* in the "modern" Taishô era (1912–1926) (Shamoon 2012). Woodblock images of beautiful women in the late Edo period by artists such as Kitagawa Utamaro (1753–1806) depicted courtesans with narrow eyes, large heads, and elongated faces, necks and bodies. While these images continued to form the basis for ideals of female beauty through the 1800s, standards were gradually challenged by the huge, sparkling eyes and pale-skinned "cuteness" found in the art of the 1910s. Subversive images of the androgynous beautiful girl/boy (*bishôjo* and *bishônen*), the schoolgirl, and the modern girl (*moga*) with her masculine, bobbed hairstyle, also became popular at this time (Seaman 2006: 157). This change represents part of the challenge to the earlier Neo-Confucianist patriarchy and the 1890s' concept of "good wife, wise mother" (*ryôsai kenbo*) promulgated by a male-dominated Ministry of Education (Sievers 1983: 22). As the Japanese state embraced modernity and aimed to build a rational and internationally competitive (imperialist) nation, the concept (re-) defined the "modern" woman as a devoted wife and mother (and obedient daughter) in order to benefit the state. As a construct, it emphasized modesty, chastity and compliance as female virtues (Uno 1993: 303). The concept was promulgated through mass media and schools in an effort to have Japanese households (women and girls in particular) emulate both earlier Confucian virtues and "modern" Victorian ideals of the family. The term *shôjo* emerged in contrast with the term *shônen*, a previously non-gendered term for all children: the first "official" use of *shôjo* was in Meiji, with the New Educational Law of 1887 (Kume 1997: 195–226), and thereafter it became a dominant image (Kan and Fujimoto 2008: 6). Along with the "good wife, wise mother" concept then, the *shôjo* came to be defined and controlled as part of the state's imperial ambitions, but new images also arose.

In art and literature, the new decorative, tragic, and emotional "girl" came to contrast with the roles prescribed by the earlier "good wife" model. This inward-looking and melancholic *shôjo* subverted models of "propriety" such as the virtuous daughter. As Kami Shôichiro suggests (1981: 72), solitary girls with sad downcast looks expressed a feeling of dislike and rejection of the real world. Their limpid eyes gazing into the far-off distance also signalled their secret yearnings and desire for affection. Two particular artistic styles were established: sentimental, lyrical line drawings and detailed, descriptive miniatures (Kami 1995: 94). These became mixed and continue today, but Japanese lyrical art originated with this (pre-war) "*shôjo* period" and had three main characteristics: the *shôjo* as the main subject of the picture; the expression of sentimental feelings particular to the transitional *shôjo* phase; and the expression of sentimental feelings through flowing, elegant art and line (Kami 2006: 107). According to Kami, Japanese lyricism expressed the artist's imaginative view of life and nature rather than merely illustrating the contents of a novel or story, and contrasted with European love and eroticism by expressing the beauty of "sorrow" (*aishû*), which came with the modern *shôjo* (2006: 109).

Moreover, the transition to the sorrowful *shôjo* coincides with the "democratic" Taishô era when fresh concepts of childhood independence saw the foundations of a new Japanese children's literature. In accordance with new child-centred theories, which eschewed didacticism (Kami 1995: 93), specialized literary picture magazines for children proliferated. These magazines were soon divided according to gender, with new role models for the "girl" visible throughout the numerous publications with *shôjo* in the title: the first was *Shôjokai* (Girl's World) in 1902. The terms *shôjo* and *shôjo shosetsu* (girls' novels) also came to apply to Anglo-American translations (Kan and Fujimoto 2008: 6), which helped transform imaginative representations of young female protagonists at this time. Translations of works like *The Little Mermaid* (c. 1904) and *Alice in Wonderland* (c. 1908; see Kinoshita (2007) for the historical reception of *Alice* in Japan) had a huge impact in literary and artistic circles, and both the mermaid and Alice figures still inspire new creative works. The literary and aesthetic images of the Romantic, glassy-eyed beauty found in the early literary magazines also extended into the visual art for later works such as L. M. Montgomery's *Anne of Green Gables* (first translated in 1952).

The subversive *shôjo* is simultaneously associated with the Taishô Romanticism (Taishô Roman), which was disseminated by many children's artists and literary figures during the artistic developments of the early 1900s. *Shôjo* visual images can be traced from the Romantic European landscapes and pre-Raphaelite beauties like Jane Burden. Japanese artists were influenced by the "modern" art and philosophies of Pre-Raphaelites like William Morris (1834–1896) and Aubrey Beardsley (1872–1898) (Hariu 1998:149), and the French symbolist Odilon Redon (1840–1916). Artists like Takehisa Yumeji (1884–1934) and Nakahara Jun'ichi (1913–1988) depicted lithe, long-limbed women and wide-eyed "girls" and others such as Hatsuyama Shigeru (1897–1973) sometimes followed their lead. Both Yumeji and Jun'ichi (known by these given names) became leaders of the Taishô Romantic movement; renowned respectively for their lyrical "Yumeji beauties" (Yumeji *bijinga*) and "Jun'ichi style" ribbon fashion (Honda 2010: 21–22, 28). Watanabe Shûko (2008: 106) suggests that it was Yumeji who initiated the huge eyes of the Japanese girl, and that many artists learnt to use the "single eye" (*hitotsu no me*) image from Odilon. She cites Takabatake Kashô (1888–1966, known for his "beautiful boys") as suggesting that Yumeji moved from communicating emotion through personification to expressing deeper human sentiment through the eye. Watanabe further suggests that whereas Yumeji used the shadows of long lower lashes to express the *shôjo's* complicated inner feelings, his more frontal, outward-looking beauties constituted a deliberate rejection of the Edo period Utamaro-like beauty while expressing the girl's desire to enter society. All of these Taishô Romantics depicted variations of the delicately iconoclastic, "modern" *shôjo* crying into her sleeves or looking off into the distance in the now-iconic images that are disseminated widely throughout Japan in postcards, art catalogues and magazines.

The origin of the Romantic, emotionally intense *shôjo* in fiction has been traced to Yoshiya Nobuko's *Flower Tales* (Hanamonogatari), each of which was entitled with the name of a bloom (Honda 1992: 171–202; 2010: 20–21). Jun'ichi also illustrated *Flower Tales*, which was first serialized in *Girls' Illustrated* (Shôjo Gahô) in 1916. The narratives depicted romantic friendships, mostly between girls, with unhappy endings. As Watanabe suggests, protagonists often staked their lives on unrequited or hopeless affection, and died after their (same sex) love was thwarted. One of the reasons for the popularity of these stories was that, in contrast with Meiji fiction in which girls were chaste and heterosexual love was taboo, they expressed girls' profound feelings and affection for each other (2008: 105). Such tragically romantic imaginings were often the only form of resistance open to the girl.

There was a revival of sorrowful, Yumeji-like lyricism around the 1970s when, despite the promise of equal rights in the 1947 constitution, the aspirations of girls and women were still being thwarted by the patriarchal system (Kami 1981: 69–74). Many of the Taishô artists had become active again from the 1950s, simultaneously with Tezuka Osamu's *manga* and *anime* featuring doe-eyed characters. In the 1970s, *shôjo manga* by the likes of Moto Hagio and Takemiya Keiko featured blonde-haired, sparkling-eyed androgynous figures against Romantic, bucolic settings. The "beautiful women" of the pre-modern woodblock prints had transformed into the "beautiful girl and boy" in *manga* and other visual art. Moreover, the *shôjo* image is still prevalent in the literary and visual spheres, as evident throughout the 2014 exhibition, "Bishojo: Young and Pretty Girls in Art History" (Aomori Museum).

A variety of images of the contemplative and tragic "girl" are also found in many modern books but two particular artistic interpretations of Ôgawa's *Red Candles and the Mermaid* exemplify Kami's "revival" of the beautiful, marginal *shôjo* whose social choices are limited. Inspired by Andersen's *Little Mermaid*, the *Red Candles'* narrative first appeared in the Tokyo-Asahi Newspaper in 1921. More recently, the delicate artwork of Iwasaki Chihiro and Sakai Komako, for publications in 1975 and 2002 respectively, brings the narrative into the broader community of the "girl." Both artists foreground aspects of the tragic girl by drawing on earlier *shôjo* conventions from visual art and literature.

Although Ôgawa's narrative can be read as a proletarian work, it is replete with all the accoutrements of the *shôjo* – the loneliness, melancholia, and unfulfilled dreams of both mother and daughter mermaids who suppress their suffering as they selflessly give love and yearn for affection. Their suffering partially derives from their liminal positions. They remain un-named, at the verge of motherhood and womanhood, between land and sea, and as part-human part-fish. The mermaid-mother's pain is manifest as she contemplates relinquishing her as-yet-unborn daughter to a better life in the "kinder" human world than would be possible in the harsh and lonely sea. After the mermaid-daughter is born then left near a seaside temple, she leads a peripheral existence on land where she feels the pain of separation and growing up as an outsider. The daughter's suffering is amplified by her precarious position as step-daughter to an elderly couple who run a chandlery. After she has worked hard to create beautiful candles and earn her foster-parents' love, they force her into another heart-rending separation and more severe form of confinement by selling her to a travelling showman who cages her with his other beasts. The story ends with her escape back into the sea, from where she watches the chandlery go up in flames, with the implication that she has wrought supernatural revenge upon an oppressive human world. While the mother suffers from relinquishing her daughter, the daughter is confined indoors on land, silently tormented by the separation from her mother and sea-home while working for the couple or the showman, all within the limitations imposed by the commercial and patriarchal social system. Their sorrow and yearning are apparent through both sets of pictures, but Chihiro (her given name) and Sakai draw out different aspects of the beautiful, solitary *shôjo*.

Chihiro was a major Japanese children's artist whose delicate images of flowers and birds (both girl signifiers) and solitary and pensive young children show an affinity with the *shôjo* genre. She blends western watercolor with India-ink to produce a lyrical, flowing style reminiscent of the girl. Chihiro was also impressed with earlier *shôjo*-inspired Romantic images: art by Hatsuyama Shigeru, who depicted images of Alice and the mermaid; Marie Laurencin's modernist paintings of delicate, pensive women; and the Romanticism of writers like Miyazawa Kenji and Ôgawa, both of whom were inspired by Andersen's and Carroll's girls. Chihiro created many illustrations for Andersen's *Little Mermaid*, publishing it as a picture-board story (*kamishibai*) in 1960.

The pathos of Chihiro's mermaid in *Red Candles* is evident throughout the images which make up over a third of the illustrations for the book (Matsumoto 1974: 51). The gaze of the young long-haired daughter figure on the cover immediately recalls the yearning *shôjo*. Her dark eyes gaze out past the viewing space to express her melancholy and evoke compassion for her oncoming troubles. The book's internal images confirm an ominous forecast, beginning with the introductory picture of the isolated mother, barely discernible against the expanse of a roaring night sea (Figure 33.1). The mother's tiny,

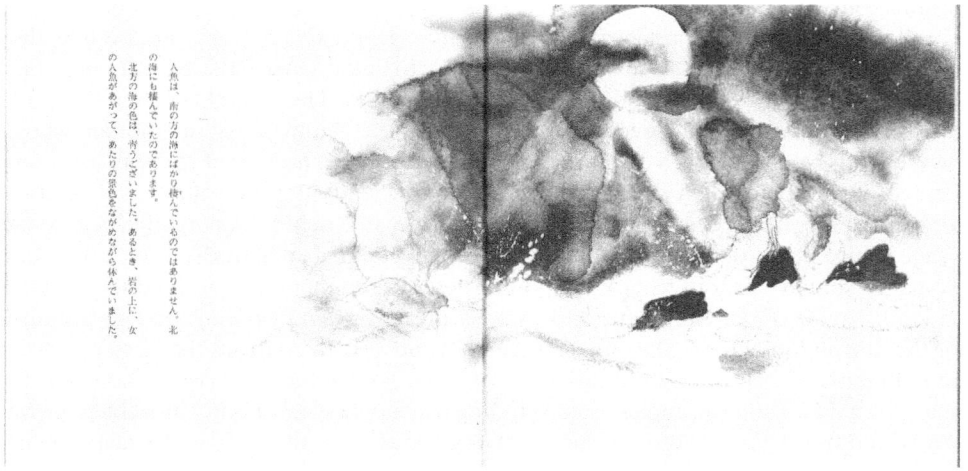

Figure 33.1   Ôgawa Mimei and Iwasaki Chihiro (1975) *Akai Rôsoku to Ningyô*.
Source: Reproduced with permission of the Iwasaki Chihiro Museum.

far-off figure atop a black rock appears forlorn and diminutive under the dark looming clouds and swirling waves which engulf her. All the tragic beauty of mermaid liminality is encapsulated in her distant placement between the viewer and the sea, with her long *shôjo*-like hair and curvaceous tail hanging languidly along the rock. The contrast with the proximity of the figure on the cover is not only prescient of their separation, but also emphasizes their precarity and the bleakness of their life choices.

The empty backgrounds and India-ink blurs against wide expanses follow a traditional Japanese aesthetic, which favours suggestion over realism (Hokkaidôritsu kindai bijutsukan 1991: 60–63) to engender a whimsy and transience that underscores the tragedy of the story. In a dramatic frontispiece, for example, evocative black swirls and runs suggest a sea-scape of stormy clouds and waves. Devoid of any figures, this scene envisions the loneliness and pathos of both mermaids' lives. Other spare images without background detail provide a space for an imaginatively "girlish" resistance. Such voids are particularly evident in backdrops for the yearning *shôjo* daughter. They create room to imagine her suffering and loneliness as she constantly longs for the sea while dejectedly fulfilling her duties on land, in the real world, where she is without family, oppressed and poorly treated. Moreover, the final image of small shells which sprawl forth from under the final line of the narrative across the empty page opposite imply all the exquisite pathos of the eternally lonely and yearning girl.

In comparison with Chihiro's spare monochromes, Sakai positions a sumptuously seductive mermaid in acrylic washes against jet-black to resonate with the sensory qualities of Honda's "fluttering" aesthetic (1992: 165). The luminous translucence against the profound blackness conjures the vertiginous girl who seeks escape from the absolute darkness of her social confines. Luscious washes of color run unrestrainedly over charcoal outlines to evoke the complexity of both mermaids' internal imaginings. In one early picture, for example, the mermaid-mother imagines her daughter playing with friends amidst a shadowy ring of more luminous, girl-signifying birds and flowers. Her imagination offers her both maternal solace and longing as she watches from outside the sphere, immersed in her solitary daydream, her forlornness and beauty visible as the lines and flow of her hair seep through the dark depths, which also symbolize a kind of death – another "girl" trope.

Like Chihiro, Sakai characterizes both mermaids with *shôjo* reverie, but even as they gaze into the distance, the close viewing proximity to Sakai's mermaids exposes their brilliant beauty and nakedness, and their embodied fragility. They are also facing the world and their problems more directly than, for example, Chihiro's distant mother who is viewed from behind. Sakai's opening picture introduces the mother at mid-range, in profile, looking and moving forward (in the direction of reading, right to left) as if ready to confront her troubles, despite being bound in the oceanic depths. A magnification of her visage brings her closer towards viewing space two pictures later, in the book's sole double-paged spread (without text) at the point where she has made up her mind to give birth on land (Figure 33.2). Her beautiful facial features are magnified and her eyes are open for the first and only time. She looks out and beyond as if to confront the viewer with her inner dreams of her daughter's anticipated future. As she moves forward, however, the rising air bubbles and the angles of two circling fish indicate her surging movement downwards, and thus her sense of reticence at having her as-yet-unborn daughter abandon her home in the sea. Both fish surround her from different directions to connote the binds on her freedom as her curvaceous undulating tail and hair "flutter" in synchronicity upwards behind. The picture expresses all the pathos of the bitter-sweet separation.

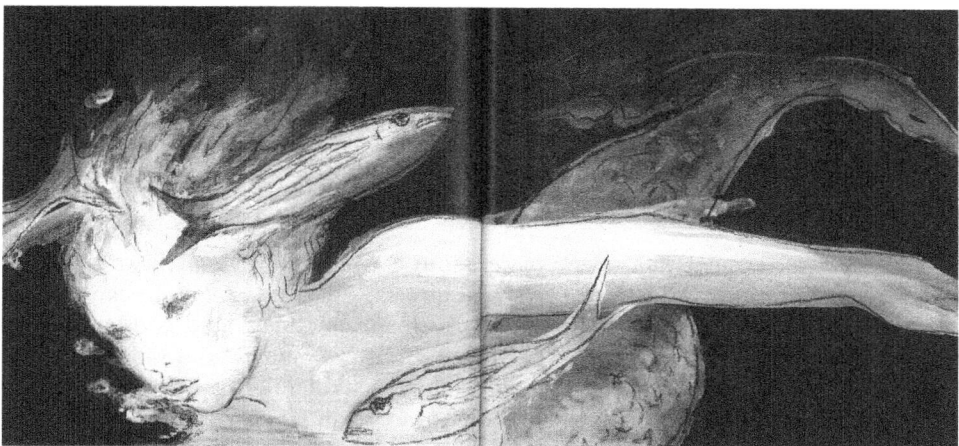

Figure 33.2   Ôgawa Mimei and Sakai Komako (2002) *Akai Rôsoku to Ningyô*.
Source: Reproduced with permission of Kaisei-sha Publishing Co., Tokyo. ©. Komako Sakai.

While the isolation of both mother and daughter is emphasized in both books, each artist posits a different perspective on the daughter's marginality in the human world, when she is separated from the sea and her mother. Whereas Chihiro's daughter is visibly more human than her always-"mermaid" mother to emphasize their separation, Sakai foregrounds both figures' "mermaid-ness" to emphasize the tragedy and sensuousness of their liminality. The constant sight of their mermaid-tails accentuates their half-humanity, but especially that of the daughter who is prevented from fitting into her new world whether as foster-daughter or as caged animal. Moreover, Sakai's daughter is always set against domestic or familial scenes, and her ever-downward-looking visage indicates her yearning and lack of solace, thus her internal resistance to the unwelcoming spaces of the land.

In these ways, both Chihiro's and Sakai's art offers today's readers different tastes of the girl. Both artists nevertheless engender a "girl consciousness" that resists the social confines of, for example, the "wise mother" or obedient daughter whose only available resistance is through her imagination, the only place where her desires can be momentarily fulfilled. While Chihiro's 1970s' girl is resistant to patriarchal binds through her sad and distant rejection of the real world, Sakai's twenty-first century beauty yearns but nonetheless confronts her chains in a more proximal and challenging defiance of her obvious marginality. Even as she remains perpetually bound in blackness, her determination is dazzlingly apparent against the deathly darkness.

While these mermaid figures express the subjectivity of the sad and resistant girl who cannot escape her real-world fate, the Alice figure's adventurous spirit is synonymous with the highly imaginative, and offers a more conspicuously independent *shôjo*. In contrast with Chihiro's and Sakai's yearning beauties, the story of *Maimai and Nainai* (*Maimai to Nainai* 2011) takes up this more iconoclastic Alice figure. The book is part of a series of "uncanny" (kaidan) picture books, and is written by award-winning fantasy-mystery author Minagawa Hiroko (b. 1930), with whom artist Uno Akira has previously collaborated. Although the narrative does not directly refer to *Alice in Wonderland*, Uno's signature *shôjo* illustrations and long association with the Alice image bring her to mind (see Kodai 2005: 41–87). In 2012, for instance, Uno curated an "Alice" exhibition which, together with his own art, featured Jun'ichi's and Yumeji's 1920s' lyrical girls (Nakahara 2012). Uno was originally inspired by these artists and many "girl" symbols through his younger sister's magazines. As he puts it, he loved the "stories of the Takarazuka [the 1920s' all-female theatre group which continues today], curtain frills, flower corsages and bouquets, appliqués and fringes petticoats, girl's hairdos, dolls and the literature of Kawabata Yasunari [and others]" (Uno 2000: 56–57). Uno's Maimai, for example, has 1960s'-style big eyes and flowing Pre-Raphaelite hair.

The *Maimai* narrative is a poetic piece about a young girl, Maimai, who finds an imaginary little brother, Nainai, and puts him into a walnut shell. Only she can see him. "Nainai" can mean "secret", "nothing", or "to hide something" and is often used by infants. The word "maimai" can be a pet-name or mean "snail," and a snail features in most pictures. Maimai is also the name of a children's studies' journal in which Honda's "Genealogy of *hirahira*" was first published (Aoyama and Hartley 2010: 14 n. 8). Both meanings remain ambiguous in the story because the children's names are not written in kanji ideographs, but in the katakana script usually used for non-Japanese words or for emphasis. As Maimai is out in the forest one day, a horse rears up and kicks out her right eye, so she puts the shell into her empty eye socket. Nainai often opens this eye secretly while she is sleeping. As her night dreams spread through the room, Nainai drags them into the shell, and they float around in Maimai's mind. Maimai pleads with Nainai to get rid of the dreams but he instead closes up the walnut-eye, and she is stuck with these dreams until she can find someone to release her. The last line has her hailing the reader with: "Hey you, please help me!"

There are many *shōjo* elements in the narrative such as the dreams, mystery, and the girl's secret desire for friendship (with the boy). Although Maimai finds a playmate, Nainai disappoints her by leading her into restless dreams and failing to console or save her. In typical *shōjo* style, she dreams of finding everlasting affection and is pained by Nainai's ambivalence. In a tragic reminder of the limits of the girl's secret inner life, she ultimately becomes ensnared by her own dreams. In so doing, however, she will remain an eternal girl, without the social restriction imposed by wifedom or motherhood. Moreover, even though she is caught up by her dreams and by caring for the boy, both her voice and visual countenance ultimately demand attention.

Uno's surrealistic images challenge the idea of simplistic outward cuteness and underline the depths and ambiguities surrounding the inner *shōjo*. Uno is a master of the in-between (and half-animal) *shōjo*, as the cover suggests (Figure 33.3. For a sequenced slide-show of the first three pictures of the book, see: Kaidan ehon, n.d.). Maimai is holding a colorful swirling lollipop, which simultaneously signals her "girlishness" and echoes the shape of the background snail on which Nainai sits. While the narrative does not specify gender, Uno presents Maimai as his immediately-recognizable Alice figure, with prominent eyes, small Yumeji-like rosy lips, long wavy hair, flowing white lacy-fringed dress, all signaling her *shōjo*-ness. Conversely, her sense of adventure, her rebellious nature, and her raucous inner life are evident here and in the first picture in which she is striding forth in contrastingly heavy boots. Her colorful figure on the cover is framed by a monotonal natural environment to emphasize her prominence outside the ordinary and at the edge of the imaginary where she finds her new friend (Nainai). Her petite body, clothing, striped socks, and lollipop suggest her youth and naiveté, but also contrast with her oversized head, hair, face and eyes, which suggest a more worldly

Figure 33.3 Minagawa Hiroko and Uno Akira (2011) *Maimai to Nainai.*
Source: Reproduced with permission of Iwasaki Shoten, Tokyo.

or knowing girl in the vein of the Pre-Raphaelite image, or even John Tenniel's adult-like Alice (Waki 2013: 145). Maimai's unruly pink hair further contrasts with the often blonde-haired *shôjo* and recalls Jane Burden's flowing auburn hair to signal her rebellious nature. Together with Maimai's side-tilting head and secretively concealed hand, the unnatural pink suggests a subversive attitude, which coincides with her imaginative powers, her concealment of the tiny boy from her parents, and his secretion into her dreams.

Maimai's gaze further indicates her bid for independence in resisting parental or societal authority and in catering to her internal needs by keeping and caring for her invisible friend. While her dreamy gaze looks out beyond the viewer, her large eyes are also "demanding". As Watanabe indicates, big eyes can imply an adaptation of Descartes' famous aphorism as, "I see, therefore I am" (2008: 106). Her unyielding full-frontal stance further signals her more defiant *shôjo* spirit than, for example, Chihiro's or even Sakai's mermaids. Forward-facing Maimai's gaze, stance and clothing demonstrate a more openly resistant demand to be noticed, which goes beyond the starry-eyed yearning of Yumeji, Chihiro or Sakai girls.

Although Chihiro's, Sakai's and Uno's artwork cannot be considered representative of the full range of "girl" images in illustrated or picture books, it nonetheless demonstrates the endurance of the tragic, liminal *shôjo* motif. The three books illustrate ways in which authors and artists can create an imaginative space for the "girl" to contemplate and resist her social and cultural binds. Whereas Chihiro and Sakai access the contemplatively resistant girl through sad longing gazes, Uno's Alice-Maimai, even though she does not succeed in attaining independence, boldly rejects the chains of the real world by living out her defiance through keeping the boy and demanding attention through both her verbal and visual appeals.

Even though a variety of influences have helped lay the foundations for the beautiful, sorrowful *shôjo*, the mermaid and Alice figures continue to inspire literary and visual girl images, both sombre and playful. Even in modern Japanese picture books, where the *shôjo* is less readily acknowledged or recognized, she is a dominant yet shifting figure. As demonstrated, Japanese authors and artists often transform and play with the image. Such "play" with *shôjo* traits and motifs in turn helps engender and strengthen the community of the "girl" who, within Japan's stubbornly rigid patriarchy, has few other avenues besides the imagination to resist prescribed limitations. Nuanced *shôjo* images in Japanese illustrated and picture books continue to construct and transform complex subjectivities and challenge prescribed gendered roles within the binds of established cultural hegemonies.

Note

1 All Japanese names appear in the order of family name followed by given name, apart from artists such as Takehisa Yumeji or Iwasaki Chihiro who are so renowned that they are usually referred to by their given names.

Bibliography

Aomori Museum (n.d.) "Bishôjo no bijutsu shi" www.aomori-museum.jp/exhibition/60/pamphlet. pdf [in English: "Bishojo: Young Pretty Girls in Art History – 16 Perspectives for Studying the Idea of the bishojo" www.aomori-museum.jp/en/exhibition/60/index.html] (accessed 3 April 2015).

Aoyama, Tomoko (2010) "The Genealogy of the 'girl' Critic Reading Girl," *Girl Reading Girl in Japan*, T. Aoyama and B. Hartley (eds.), London and New York, Routledge, 38–49.

Aoyama, Tomoko and Barbara Hartley (2010) "Introduction," *Girl Reading Girl in Japan*, T. Aoyama and B. Hartley (eds), London and New York, Routledge, 1–14.

Hariu, Ichiro (1998) "Illustrations from Kodomo no Tomo," *The World of Original Illustrations for Children's Books Exhibition: Pictorial Expression from Kodomo no Tomo, 1956–1997*, Robert Reed (trans.), Tokyo: The Committee of the Exhibition of the World of Original Illustrations for Children's Books, 149–152.

Hokkaidôritsu kindai bijutsukan (1991) *Kaiga nyûmon kodomo to oya no bijutsukan* [An Introductory Picture Gallery for Parents and Children], Hokkaidô, Shinchôsha.

Honda, Masuko (1988) *Shôjoron* [Treatise on the Girl], Tokyo, Seikyûsha.

———— (1992) *Ibunka toshite no kodomo* [The Child as Another Culture], Tokyo, Chikuma Shobô.

———— (2010) "Hirahira no keifu" [The Genealogy of Hirahira: Liminality and the Girl], in *Girl Reading Girl in Japan*, T. Aoyama and B. Hartley (eds. and trans.). London and New York, Routledge, 19–37.

Kaidan ehon (n.d.) www.iwasakishoten.co.jp/special/kaidan/07952/ (accessed 6 April 2015).

Kami, Shôichiro (1981) "Joryû dôga no sekai to Motai Takeshi: Iwasaki Chihiro, Ajito Keiko, Motai Takeshi," in *Nihon no dôga (Dai 7 maki): Iwasaki Chihiro, Ajito Keiko, Motai Takeshi*, Tokyo, Daiichihôki, 69–74.

———— (1995) "Kenji dôwa sashie no hyakka ryôran" [The Riot of Blooms in Illustrations of Kenji's Tales], in *Miyazawa Kenji kaiga-kan: Gakatachi ga kaita Kenji no sekai*, Tokyo, Aputo Intânashonaru, 92–95.

———— (2006) *Nihon no dôgatachi* [Japanese Children's Illustrators], Heibonsha, Tokyo.

Kan, Satoko and Fujimoto Megumi (2008) "'Shôjo shôsetsu' no rekishi o furikaeru," in *Shôjo shôsetsu' wandārando* [A Wonderland of Girls' Novels]: *Meiji kara heisei made*, Kan Satoko (ed.), Tokyo: Meiji Shoin, 5–23.

Kilpatrick, Helen (2010) "Transcending gender in pictorial representations of Miyazawa Kenji's 'Marivuron and the Girl'", *Girl Reading Girl in Japan*, T. Aoyama and B. Hartley (eds.), London and New York, Routledge, 145–159.

———— (2012) "Envisioning the Shôjo Aesthetic in Miyazawa Kenji's 'The Twin Stars' and 'Night of the Milky Way Railway'", *PORTAL Journal of Multidisciplinary International Studies*, 9(3): 1–26.

Kinoshita, Shin'ichi (2007) "The Acceptance of Two Visual Versions of Alice in Japan" www.hp-alice.com/lcj/ronbun/handout_IRSCL2007.pdf (accessed 3 May 2015).

Kodai, Nariko (2005) *Hon to onna no ko: Omoide no 1960–70 nendai* [Girls and Books: Remembering the 1960s and 70s], Tokyo, Kawade Shobô Shinsha, 41–87.

Kume, Yoriko (1997) "*Shôjo shosetsu sai to kihan no gensetsu sochi*" [Shôjo Fiction: the discursive devices of difference and regulation], in *Mejia hyôshô ideorogii: Meiji sanjunendai no bunkakenkyû* [Media, Representations, and Ideologies: Cultural Studies of the Third Decade of Meiji Era], Komori Yoichi (ed.), Tokyo: Ozawa Shoten, 195–226.

Masaki, Tomoko and Miyake Okiko (2001) "A Short History of the Japanese Picture Book," in *Through Eastern Eyes: The Art of the Japanese Picture Book*, London, The National Centre for Research in Children's Literature.

Matsumoto, Takeshi (1974) "Mikan e no omoi" [Thoughts on an Unfinished Work], in *Akai rôsoku to ningyô, Ôgawa Mimei and Iwasaki Chihiro*, Tokyo, Dôshinsha, 47–53.

Minagawa, Hiroko and Uno Akira (2011) *Maimai to Nainai*, Tokyo, Iwasaki Shoten.

Nakahara, Jun'ichi (2012) "Uno Akira-san purodyûsu: shôjo gaten ni genga shuppin!" [Uno Akira-san's Produce: Exhibition of original shôjo images] at: www.junichi-nakahara.com/archives/2070 (accessed 19 April 2015).

Ôgawa, Mimei and Iwasaki Chihiro (1975) *Akai rôsoku to ningyô*, Tokyo, Dôshinsha.

———— and Sakai Komako (2002) *Akai rôsoku to ningyô*, Tokyo, Kaiseisha.

Robertson, Jennifer (2002) "Yoshiya Nobuko: Out and Outspoken in Practice and Prose," in *The Human Tradition in Modern Japan*, Walthall, Anne (ed.), Wilmington, Scholarly Resources Books.

Seaman, Amanda (2006) "Women Writers and Alternative Critiques," *Woman Critiqued: Translated Essays on Japanese Women's Writing*, R. L. Copeland (ed.), Honolulu, University of Hawai'i Press.

Shamoon, Debra (2012) *Passionate Friendship: The Aesthetics of Girls' Culture in Japan*, Honolulu, University of Hawai'i Press.

Sievers, Sharon (1983) *Flowers in Salt: The Beginnings of a Feminist Consciousness in Modern Japan*, Stanford, Stanford University Press.

Takahara, Eiri (1999) *Shôjo ryôiki* [The Territory of the Girl], Tokyo, Kokusho Kankôkai.

Uno, Akira (2000) "Uno Akira zen essai 1968–2000: bara no kioku" [Essays by Uno Akira from 1968 to 2000: Recollections of Roses], Tokyo, Tokyo Shoseki, http://d.hatena.ne.jp/syncrokun/20110908 (accessed 9 April 2015).

Uno, Kathleen (1993) "The Death of 'Good Wife, Wise Mother'?" in *Postwar Japan as History*, Andrew Gordon (ed.), Berkeley, University of California Press, 293–322.

Waki, Akiko (2013) *Shôjotachi no 19 seiki: ningyôhime kara Arisu made* [Ninteenth Cenutury Girls: From *The Little Mermaid* to *Alice*], Tokyo, Iwanami Shoten.

Watanabe, Shûko (2008) "Saffo no manazashi: hanamonogatari to sashie" [Sappho's Gaze: Hanamonogatari and its illustrations], in '*Shôjo Shôsetsu*' *wandârando: Meiji kara heisei made* [A Wonderland of Girls' Novels: From Meiji to Heisei], Kan Satoko (ed.), Tokyo, Meiji Shoin. 104–113.

34

"LIGHT LIKE A BIRD, NOT A FEATHER"

Science picture books from China and the USA

Fengxia Tan

Both in the East and the West, the picture book market is dominated by story picture books, while science picture books are relatively marginalized, and widely acknowledged masterpieces are rare. Science picture books take scientific knowledge as their subject matter, and differ from illustrated handbooks of scientific knowledge in their imaginative and often complex interaction of verbal information and illustrations that aspire to be both artistic and scientifically accurate. Drawing on books from mainland China, Hong Kong, Macao, and Taiwan, China's biennial Feng Zikai Picture Book Award, first presented in 2009, has recognized the importance of science picture books. In 2009, Qiu Chengzong's *Above and Beneath the Pond* (2008) was nominated for the Excellent Book Award in the first Feng Zikai Illustrated Book Award. In 2013, Liu Bole's *I Saw a Bird* (2011) won the first prize in the third Feng Zikai Picture Book Award. These two ingenious award-winning picture books display the high quality that science picture books can attain, and provoke the question of what is the full potential of this specific picture book type and its disciplinary orientation? Are science picture books confined to the artistic representation of scientific knowledge? How extensive is the aesthetic space that science picture books, as art books in the full sense, can open, and how rich is the domain of meaning it can generate? This essay carries out case studies by probing into typical science picture books in China and in the United States. Distinctive science picture books in other countries are also included for supplementary comparison.

Intertwined multiple spectra

As art has its exciting attractiveness, so does science. Rabindranath Tagore, the first winner of the Nobel Prize for Literature in the East, excelled in literature and art. Nevertheless he praised science highly. Once, he told Mrs. Devi, a Bangladeshi poet, "I really like science, but you like romance. These whispering leaves in the sun absorb sunlight in every swing and manufacture many chemical ingredients. Through countless vessels of nature, there's a certain kind of miracle going on… people are literally stunned." Excellent science picture books should be able to show the wonders of the scientific world in a way that is both scientific and artistic, which is a great challenge for creators.

Science picture books are responsible for the transfer of scientific knowledge, but exactly how much knowledge should a picture book contain? And how should the knowledge be organized, connected, and transmitted in an interesting way? Creators of science picture books must find ways that can subtly transmit scientific knowledge in order to attract readers. In *How to Create Good Picture Books*, Hao Guangcai asks whether a picture book is a tree or a forest, and avers that a picture book should be a tree, not the whole forest. This theory is applicable to story picture books, and science picture books are no exception. Story picture books are so constructed that the text and pictures complement each other by omitting information, with neither telling the whole story. However, science picture books usually incorporate a lot of knowledge and information, which indicates accretion. But there is both accretion and omission: a creator needs to ponder and screen what and how he/she should add and omit, so as to make the picture book an integrated "big tree" with leaves and branches flourishing, but not cumbersome.

Scientific knowledge in science picture books usually unfolds organically, consistent with a narrative line. While creating *Above and Beneath the Pond*, Qiu Chengzong not only observed and kept records of the ecology of the pond over many years to accumulate scientific knowledge, but also took pains to prepare for the artistic conception, and edited his records constantly. Finally he chose to take the life cycle of the dragonfly *Anax panybeus* as the main line, complemented by bio-information about the groups above and beneath the pond, showing the ecosystem of the whole pond. This picture book is simple, yet rich; it highlights the life cycle of the protagonist, anax panybeus, and reveals the dependencies among different species and between species and the environment. The text of the picture book consists of three spectra: the first spectrum is the overall narration in the main pictures, which describes in a highly literary tone the growth and changes in the pond from one spring to the next; the second is the observation records of anax panybeus displayed under the main illustrations, which is arranged chronologically in a detailed, genuine, and meticulous way. The first two spectra run through the whole book, while the third, the specified description of the biological structure in the minor pictures, appears occasionally. The three spectra with their respective orientations toward knowledge comprise a three-dimensional text, which conveys to readers poetical pleasure in combination with clear and specific scientific cognition.

In *I Saw a Bird*, another ecological picture book, Liu Bole adopts a different approach in the transmission of scientific knowledge. Liu Bole has been engaged in the painting of birds for years. His careful observation and elaborate paintings have brought birds in the book to life. The text begins with an observation note of a bird written and drawn by a child, consisting of the salient figures of birds and a brief note about birds' characteristics or habits. For the Chinese characters unknown to young children, he uses the phonetic symbols instead, which suggests the age of the character and also adds a playful childlike humor. What's more, the title of the note is followed by a smiley face logo. The bird observation note implies the speaker observes birds in nature, gathering a lot of information and never feeling bored. However, this picture book is not a rambling collection of knowledge about birds. Instead, taking the unfolding of a realistic story as its thread, the book shows the intuitive cognition of birds. In the book, the process of a little girl looking for a "strange bird" with her mother serves as the major focus, and the speech bubbles formed by the dialogue between the mother and the daughter are an extension of the content. In addition to the text, knowledge about birds is conveyed through a trail map in the Dakeng Scenic Area on the front endpaper and a bird-watching map in the Chiang Kai-Shek Camp Site on the back endpaper, which show what the child has seen. The two echo each other and serve as the "prelude" and the "epilogue" of the book, respectively. The creator has not aimed to introduce specific knowledge about birds, but focuses on the vivid representation of the birds' visual images with his fine brushwork.

Most American science picture books have given a very prominent position to the presentation of scientific knowledge, seeking for rich contents as well as ingenious ideas. One of the classical science picture books is Virginia Lee Burton's *Life Story* (1962), a book that took the creator eight years to complete. She tells about the course of life on Earth with a multivolume five-act play. The narrators in the book are an astronomer, a geologist, a paleontologist, a historian, a grandmother, and Virginia Lee Burton, the author herself. Each narrates scenes and acts in turn. The main actors include animal actors, plant actors, and so on, and the knowledge spectra are extensive and diversified. With an epic sweep, the 72-page science picture book depicts Earth from its very beginning to the author's homeland and the immediate moment; the knowledge about the vast temporal changes is carefully selected and briefly presented. On the left pages, a few small stick figures are depicted to summarize the developmental trajectories of life, while the right pages reproduce the scenes with splendid and gorgeous colored paintings and vivid narration, as well as funny and vivid details. Another set of the world's best-selling American science picture books is *The Magic School Bus* series (twelve volumes, 1986–2010), written by Joanna Cole and illustrated by Bruce Degen. Many books in this series have won non-fictional Magic Reading Awards from the American *Education Magazine*. The success is attributed to the novelty of the story line: taking Ms. Frizzle's magic school bus, the students travel in the mysterious world of science. Each of the works is a multiple vocal ensemble. For example, there are four parts in *Lost in the Solar System* (1990): the main story line, the characters' dialog boxes, questions about science on students' note pages, and a brief description of objects or phenomena. In *The Magic School Bus*, fascinating stories are interspersed with a wealth of scientific knowledge, and personalized children's images are well-shaped, which make the series attractive and appealing. Peter Sis has created two science picture books with distinctive personal styles: *Starry Messenger: Galileo Galileo* (1996) and *The Tree of Life* (2003). The two picture books ground their narratives in the life trajectories of the two scientists, namely Galileo and Darwin, and insert relevant people and events of their times, as well as their scientific discoveries. The two works are characterized by broad vision, pictures of intricate sizes and detailed knowledge. The size and shape of picture composition correspond to the textual content of different spectra with distinct rhythm and in good order. They have managed to present in limited space the social life and scientific world of the scientists to the utmost.

Numerous other high quality science picture books are listed in the review journal *Science Books & Films (SB&F)*, especially in their announcements of the annual AAAS/Subaru SB&F Prizes for Excellence in Science Books (see, e.g., Young 2012, for a substantial annotated list). The 2015 recipient – *Tiny Creatures: The World of Microbes* (2014), by Nicola Davies, illustrated by Emily Sutton – demonstrates a welcome capacity to make a difficult concept accessible through playful and inventive text and illustrations, and is an excellent example of how the distinction between a creative and a fact-based picture book can be erased. As Young observes, the capacity for disseminating knowledge in science picture books is enhanced by the relationship between texts and pictures. Not all the texts explain scientific knowledge. They can be flexible, and the forms can be rich and varied, and form diverse spectra by interaction with the pictures, but, as Perry Nodelman argues, "Words can provide a cognitive map, a schema that we can apply to inherently unassertive pictures in order to determine the varying significance we might find in their details" (1988: 213). Nodelman points out in addition that, "Words can also act as visual objects that create relationships *within* the image" (56). In Peter Sis's *Starry Messenger*, for example, a narrative about the life and discoveries of Galileo is juxtaposed with text in cursive script – sometimes Galileo's words – and these cursive passages may face different directions, so readers need to turn the book and engage with it from a different angle, horizontally, vertically and in a circular motion, thereby attaining an interesting "three-dimensional" reading effect and expanding the meaning of the text itself. There are also surprising details, such as a spiral around a compass, a fan reflecting characters' multi-ideologies, and so on. An ingenious touch is the shape of eyes composed of words, which shows that although Galileo became blind, he could still see a lot of truth.

Science picture books are committed to the presentation of a wealth of scientific knowledge. Generally speaking, science picture books in China usually employ omission, attaching importance to the whole rather than to the parts, to clarity rather than to close texture, to freehand brushwork rather than to details, which are related to Chinese aesthetics and a preference for traditional painting techniques. In contrast, illustrated books in the United States prefer accretion, increasing knowledge spectra in texts and diversified details in pictures, which may have something to do with Westerners' rigorous scientific method. Furthermore, it is in the same strain with traditional Western painting techniques which attach importance to appearance, details, and density. Due to its multiple spectra, a science picture book will emphasize the integration of points, lines, surface, and body, and strive to achieve harmony at different levels of content.

The infiltration of humanistic feelings

When Paul Hazard talks about "books of knowledge" in *Books, Children, and Men*, he expresses this preference: "My favorite thing is to put forward the most difficult yet the most necessary knowledge from a wide range of knowledge, that is, the books of knowledge which are about human minds" (1944: 44). If science picture books only serve the purpose of promoting popular science, they are likely to be monotonous and dull. Some science picture books are impressive, not because the knowledge transferred is novel or profound, but because they contain humanistic feelings about "human minds" and are intriguing and thought-provoking.

Behind the depiction of the morphology of birds in the illustrated ecological book *I Saw a Bird* lies the author's spiritual wisdom. In the center of the cover, there is a five-colored bird, with its eyes directed at the two red Chinese characters "看见" (kanjian) (meaning look at and see). It is obvious that the two characters are the "eyes" of this book. The story begins with a little girl having seen a "strange bird" while taking bird watching notes in the forest. Based on her own experience, the mother denies the child's discovery and believes that the child must have made a mistake or drawn incorrectly. Then the girl, feeling deeply wronged, asks, "I will take you to look for it and you will believe what I have noted when you see it in person." Seeking and proving become the clues to push the story forward. At first the mother does not take it seriously, but with the observation of birds of various shapes, gradually she becomes curious and finally sees the "strange bird," which also solves the previous mystery. The rose-ringed parakeet is not local, but must have been raised by someone and then escaped from the cage and flew to the wild. Behind the story there lies a simple philosophy: "look" and then you can "see." The keyword in the title, namely the two Chinese characters "kanjian", can be broken down into two words, "look" and "see" of sequential order and causal relationship. The character "kan" emphasizes the action, meaning "to make eye contact with people or things," and the equivalent in English is "look;" the character "jian" emphasizes the result of this behavior, and the equivalent in English is "see." Only after exploring while "looking" can we "see" the truth.

The painting style of this science picture book also reflects the author's attitude toward life. He mainly uses eco-painting to vividly display various postures of birds, most of which are close-ups or close shots, with even the feathers being meticulously presented. The style is fresh and fine. Deliberately putting these birds among verdant foliage and fruits, the author depicts the beauty of the woods with rich translucent watercolors. In a study of the relationship between perception and connotation, with a particular focus on the question of whether there are "general connotative dimensions along which colors are described, and if these dimensions are to some extent consistent from person to person and from culture to culture" (1962: 89), Benjamin Wright and Lee Rainwater concluded that greater color saturation produces greater "warmth," "forcefulness," and "showiness," and hence saturation "manifests itself most powerfully in this analysis of the relations between connotations and perceptions" (98). Yellow, blue, and green employed in this book to describe the birds' feathers reflect a higher saturation; the main color in the woods is green, with well-arranged shades and ethereal beauty, revealing both a world full of vigor and the creator's love. The author claims that "I am, I think, I write, I draw" encapsulates his pursuit of life. The birds he draws embody his thoughts and inspiration about nature and life, looking at the world with clear eyes. Although the illustrated book is entitled *I Saw a Bird*, it in fact contains the mutual looking at and seeing between humans and birds. The birds in almost every painting are looking: looking at the mother and the daughter who are looking at them or looking at the world around themselves, and the readers of the book too. The attractiveness of birds in the book is reflected in the quiet, tranquil, composed meditation of the author. The painter is committed to the artistic expression of the external appearances of birds and atmosphere, for, as Nodelman explains, "surface appearances [not only] create feelings and attitudes but [...] they *mirror* interior feelings and attitudes; and therefore [...] the way things look is highly evocative of what they mean. In their very existence, then, picture books express our assumption of the metaphorical relationships between appearance and meaning" (49). The last close-up picture displays the calm posture of the parrot at large in the green leaves, with a feeling of serenity, conveying the author's salute to the beauty of freedom. In the pictures where people coexist with birds, the changes of their respective positions also indicate the development of internal relationships. Cartoonish figures are mostly placed at the corners of the pictures while birds and flowers occupy the main screen. At first, birds and people exist independently, but they integrate into a harmonious whole in the woods at last, which signifies the convergence of birds and humans. The presentation of the convergence of humans and nature in this science picture book guides readers to appreciate the beauty of nature through ethereal and delicate brushwork. The consistent pursuit of humanity in the narrative and the artistry of the illustrations have opened rich implications apart from knowledge acquisition.

Even science picture books that focus on in-depth popularization of scientific knowledge contain humanistic feelings almost without exception. The book *Above and Beneath the Pond* implies intellectual thoughts while transferring knowledge of the existence of various creatures above and beneath the pond: to express the state of vitality and harmony through the changes in the pond all through the year and to reveal the mysteries and beauty of life through the four stages of the protagonist anax panybeus' life cycle: egg, larva, pupa, and adult. *Above and Beneath the Pond* focuses on a small pond at a microscopic level to show the light and enchanting life psalm, whereas *Life Story* by Virginia Lee Burton shows magnificent poetry through the macroscopic evolution of the Earth's history, from the vastness and remoteness of space and time to the author's homeland. In the last picture, the time changes helically from the ancient Phanerozoic Eon to a certain minute one day to greet a sunrise outside the window, with increasing human interest. The book's closing remarks well reveal the gist of the book, "Now, it's your turn to tell your life story. You are the protagonist and the stage is ready. The time is now and the place is where you are. Every second passing is like a new link in the endless chain of time. The story of life is like a drama that will never end, constantly changing and renewing, always joyous and amazing." This is the thought and call of human life extended from the evolution of the universe. Another example is Peter Sis' *Starry Messenger*. The humanistic feelings are as distinct as the profound knowledge of astronomy. The continuously emerging star image has metaphorical meaning, which demonstrates Galileo's tireless pursuit of truth and the creator's respect for the great scientist.

It is the infiltration of human feelings that makes science picture books shine, not only because of the knowledge they transmit, but also because of their intrinsic quality, adding glamour to the outward artistic brilliance. When we fully appreciate the world of science represented in science picture books, we will also move closer to the real world, which is full of emotions and experiences. Only when we look with our hearts, can we see the bright and shining images in our life evoked by the pictures. Excellent science picture books can display science artistically by using humanistic feelings as the intrinsic context. It is also through art that the scientific world and the realm of life achieve harmony with each other.

Fun in exploration

Different from story picture books, which are apt to cultivate domestic settings, science picture books are responsible for inspiring children's desires to explore the universe. However, both types are most effective when the interaction of texts and pictures requires readers to make connections and perceive meanings that emerge from the interaction. *I Saw a Bird* works hard at artistic design, which is especially reflected in the relationship between the front cover, the title page, and the back cover. On the cover there is a meticulously depicted colored bird, while on the title page is a parrot in stick figure, which causes a mismatch that leads to suspense. "What bird exactly have 'I' seen?" Similarly, the extremely humorous guessing game design of the front and back covers also shows subtlety and ingenuity in the content and the artistic design. However, as to each specific page of the text, it seems that the creator has not wholly pursued the principle that pictures in picture books should be interactive rather than fine art. As a result, though the pictures are beautiful, they are not challenging and can't invoke a reader's desire to explore the story further through imaginative engagement.

Although science picture books intend to popularize knowledge and reflect a rigorous attitude to scientific research, most important is to stimulate children's curiosity and to attach importance to the cultivation of the imagination. Einstein considered that intelligence resided not merely in knowledge, but demanded imagination: "Imagination is more important than knowledge. For knowledge is limited, whereas imagination embraces the entire world, stimulating progress, giving birth to evolution. It is, strictly speaking, a real factor in scientific research." Science picture books also need some imaginative gaps while transferring objective knowledge, and the gaps that exist between pictures and texts in science picture books can enable readers to engage in discovery through imaginative fun. To think highly of the element of imagination and to express it intensively also reflects a strong and deep spirit of exploration by the creators, which can resonate with readers. In this regard, Peter Sis, with his imaginative originality, has made science picture books reach an extraordinary height. His often surreal approach helps to transfer knowledge while fostering speculation and imagination in the readers. For example, when Galileo was tried in court in *Starry Messenger*, the interrogators in red hats and red clothes form a dense circle at the top, suppressing Galileo, who is at the bottom. The place where he stands is not the real court, but the universe, to which he is committed. His tiny figure is surrounded by many constellations of animals, which truly embody the oppression and solitude that the scientist is subjected to. And in that memorable map of Europe, Peter Sis uses various animal images with distinct temperaments (such as bears, cranes, fish, and lions) to represent the territories of different countries and demonstrate their respective military matters, history, cultural identities, and national characters. The work embodies the beauty of genuine knowledge, thoughts, and imagination, and has created aesthetic space full of inspiration and challenges.

The popularity of the *Magic School Bus* series is mainly due to its fun in exploration: the details in the pictures are varied and exotic. Even the teacher's earrings, clothing, and shoe patterns imply clues of secret scientific exploration. The British science picture book series, the *Fast Forward* books, written by Nicholas Harris and illustrated by Peter Dennis, provides another paradigm of using a realistic approach to create fun in exploration. Different from the *Magic School Bus* series, which takes characters' adventure stories as a clue, this series unfolds pictures about the evolution of human history, culture, science, nature, and daily life in the context of vertical historical development. The text is concise, whereas the illustrations are magnificent and detailed. In each picture there is an enormous amount of information with many cleverly arranged points of interest. Readers not only learn about historical knowledge, but also imagine stories of all sorts with the help of varied details. For example, *The Story of a City* integrates history with ordinary people's lives, adding a delightful texture of life to generalized knowledge. This illustrated book has also incorporated some interactive games for readers. In each book, there are thumb indexes to help readers travel across time quickly, so as to have a before-and-after comparison and motivate readers to active exploration.

Unlike story picture books, science picture books do not win children's hearts with thrilling stories or delicate and moving emotions. Therefore, they need to be more creative and interesting when spreading knowledge, so as to engage readers; ingenious details and gaps are undoubtedly effective strategies, because they can create a sense of fun, give birth to imagination, inspire interest in exploration, and enhance interactivity, which is the best gift that science picture books bring to children. When talking about "books of knowledge," Lillian H. Smith states, "Life without the cultivation of endless interest in the universe and spiritual strength of constant exploration is rather boring. ... What buds in a child's heart first of all is the feeling revealed when literary tastes and his mind contact one another. Consequently, the child will yearn for issues about reality, nature, and human coexistence" (1999: 383). This insight into the relationship between children's literature and children can also be applied to the literature of science. Science picture books should deliberately cultivate children's "endless interest in the universe and spiritual strength of constant exploration." The strength of science picture books is to inspire children to explore the secrets of science, as well as of life, with curiosity and motivation.

While Western picture books prefer the approach of achieving fun by using numerous ingenious details to set up gaps and express imagination, Oriental picture books generally follow the style of evoking imagination through leaving space, a technique used in Oriental paintings. Tadashi Matsui, a well-known Japanese theorist of picture books, once said, "The large area of white space in pictures is to leave psychological and poetic space for readers' imagination ... How important space is for imagination! Both the application and the trade-off of space deserve extra attention and meditation" (2009: 170).Oriental paintings emphasize the importance of white space, and consequently the illustrations in picture books put emphasis on the formation of artistic conception, whereas Western picture books attach importance to weaving intricate images. Thus, although the surface-level function of science picture books is to transfer objective scientific knowledge, Eastern and Western picture books differ from each other in subjective temperaments concerning the overall style of artistic expression. Oriental science picture books are mostly quiet and distant, emphasizing realistic representation and displaying their content with a gentle rhythm and in a clear way. Ecological picture books such as *Above and Beneath the Pond* and *I Saw a Bird* call more for appreciation and rumination of the beauty of life and nature. Both of the books consist of double spread openings, and the pictures have no set borders. There is a lot of white space, which conveys a feeling of openness, visual peace, and harmony. What William Moebius refers to as "the codes of the frame" (1986: 150) are an important element of how a picture book is read: "The code of the frame enables the reader to identify with a world inside and outside the story. Framed, the illustration provides a limited glimpse 'into' a world. Unframed, the illustration constitutes a total experience, the view from 'within'" (150). In Western science picture books such as *Life Story* and *Starry Messenger*, as with information books more generally, most illustrations are framed to represent the world outside themselves in a fine and complicated way. With undulating rhythm and multiple fantastic images, science picture books in the West achieve truth in a witty, exaggerated, undulating, and humorous style. While adhering to their own styles, science picture books of different countries may also refer to and blend with some exotic styles, so as to develop vaster and more vivid aesthetic space.

Conclusion

In summary, science picture books are an organic unity of science and art, with particular emphasis on the harmony of the various parts. Calvino, who analyzes literature from a scientific point of view, thinks highly of the form of "crystals." He believes that the "crystal" is one of the perfect forms that we should gaze upon. "The crystal, with its precise faceting and its ability to refract light, is the model of perfection that I have always cherished as an emblem, and this predilection has become even more meaningful since we have learned that certain properties of the birth and growth of crystals resemble those of the most rudimentary biological creatures, forming a kind of bridge between the mineral world and living matter" (1988: 70). As for science picture books, there are distances among contents of different levels, but a clever creator will strive to "build bridges" between information of different orientations, and integrate them into a sparkling "crystal" with the belief that young readers have the ability to appreciate numerous lights refracted by the "crystal." Burton, the creator of *Life Story*, said in her Caldecott Award acceptance speech, "I have learned a few things during the co-creation with kids. First of all, we must not 'underestimate' children while writing for them… In addition, as children's thinking is clear and sharp, every detail, no matter how small, must have its own interest and meaning and comply with the overall design of the book." A good science picture book is the blending of multiple factors, namely, science, humanity, and arts skills, and this blending needs to have the sense of "being light" with ease: "One should be light as a bird, not like a feather," as the poet Paul Valéry put it. Birds enjoy life when they can fly freely, while feathers, no matter how delicately and closely woven, are lifeless and fragmented parts of existence. A science picture book should be as ample and brisk as a bird, and in its "flying" will lead children to explore a world that is so amazing and fantastic.

Bibliography

Calvino, Italo (1988) *Six Memos for the Next Millennium*, Cambridge, MA: Harvard University Press.

Cole, Joanna, and Bruce Degen (1990) *Lost in the Solar System*, New York: Scholastic Press.

Davies, Nicola, and Emma Sutton (2016) *Tiny Creatures: The World of Microbes*, Somerville, MA: Candlewick Press.

Hao, Guangcai (2006) *How to Create Good Picture Books*, Taipei: Gelin Press.

Harris, Nicholas, and Peter Dennis (2005) *The Story of a City*, London: Pavilion Books.

Hazard, Paul (1944) *Books, Children & Men*. Trans. Marguerite Mitchell. Boston: The Horn Book, Inc.

Liu, Bole (2011) *Text & Illustrations: I Saw a Bird*, Taipei: Qinglin International Publishing Co Ltd; Jinan: Tomorrow Publishing House (2014).

Matsui, Tadashi (2009) *On Picture Books*, Shanghai: Shanghai People's Fine Arts Publishing House.

Moebius, William (1986) "Introduction to Picturebook Codes," *Word & Image* 2(2): 141–58.

Nodelman, Perry (1988) *Words about Pictures: The Narrative Art of Children's Picture Books*, Athens and London: The University of Georgia Press.

Qiu, Chengzong (2008) *Text & Illustrations: Above and Beneath the Pond*, Taipei: Commonwealth Publishing; Shanghai: Hope Publishing House (2015).

Sís, Peter (1996) *Starry Messenger: A Book Depicting the Life of a Famous Scientist, Mathematician, Astronomer, Philosopher, Physicist: Galileo Galilei*, New York, NY: Farrar, Straus and Giroux.

Sís, Peter (2003) *The Tree of Life: A Book Depicting the Life of Charles Darwin- Naturalist, Geologist & Thinker*, New York: Farrar, Straus and Giroux.

Smith, Lillian H. (1999) *Happy Times – Lilian H. Smith's Views on Children's Literature*. Trans. Fu Lintong. Taipei: Fuchun Culture Publishing Co Ltd.

Tagore, Rabindranath (2012) Preface to *We Have Already Met the Love – The Tagore Classic Anthology*. Trans. Zheng Zhenduo. Preface by Ji Xianlin. Beijing: New World Press.

Wright, Benjamin, and Lee Rainwater (1962) "The Meanings of Color," *Journal of General Psychology* 67(1): 89–99.

Young, Terrence E., Jr. (2012) "November is Science Picture Book Month," Science Books & Films (SB&F) November, 296–302.

35

ILLUSTRATED BOOKS IN THAILAND

From *Mana-Manee* to the eighty picture books project

Salinee Antarasena

There has been a resurgence in 1990s' nostalgia in Thailand since 2001, epitomized by a huge comeback made by *Mana-Manee* in *A Day Magazine*. The *Mana-Manee* books were written in the late 1970s by Ratchanee Sripaiwan, at the head of a team from the Thai Ministry of Education. Although there are no statistics on how many people have been involved in this phenomenon, anecdotal evidence for the nostalgia upsurge appears in the announcement in early 2016 by PUBAT (The Publishers and Booksellers Association of Thailand) that the selling price of original copies of *Mana-Manee* has risen from 5.50 THB to 600–700 THB per copy, and at that time the *Mana-Manee* official reprint of 135,000 hard copies had sold out.

As one of the nation's foremost children's books between 1978 and 1995, the *Mana-Manee* series was used in compulsory education nationwide as an interdisciplinary approach to inculcate desirable attitudes, beliefs and behaviors in children and youth, and was often referred to as *Tam Narn Dek Dee, or* literally, the Legend of Good Children (Chainarongsingha 2001, January). Probably the longest story in the mandatory curriculum for Grade 1 to Grade 6, *Mana-Manee* revolves around the life of five central child characters who are the same age as the target readers (children studying Grade 1 to Grade 6), which makes it easier for the children to identify themselves with the main characters and relate to the events in the story.

With simple illustrations for children to synthesize text and remember the learned letter sounds of familiar words and simple concepts, the story for Grade 1 students (a total of forty chapters) develops their early literacy by introducing the family members of the central child characters and their family pets, along with the concept of maintaining the cleanliness of public places, such as in their own school, and the polite form of basic greetings and daily conversation. Then, the thirty chapters in Grade 2 further connects the children with what they would observe about how things around them work, such as rainbows, the moon, transportation, traffic rules, home appliances, and some popular cultural events, such as the sand-carry into a monastery on Songkran Period (Thai New Year) for good fortune and blessings. In Grade 3 to Grade 6, some narrative legends and tales are inserted as parallel narratives—retold from the perspective of the child characters of the series. The story ends with the graduation of the child characters. In 1995, this series was removed from the curriculum because it was deemed to contain outdated stereotypes, unsuitable for the complexity of contemporary world society (PUBAT 2016, Feb 2).

A major step in the development of an official national character had already been taken a couple of years before the *Mana-Manee* series was introduced into the compulsory education system. Between 1976 and 1977, Prime Minister Tanin Kraivixien launched the Thai Identity project in order to promote pride in being Thai, particularly among children and youth, and four desirable qualities for children were introduced at that time, comprising Discipline, Responsibility, Generosity and Honesty (Tiranasar 2004: n.p.).

The effort was followed closely by the blooming of children's illustrated books in Thailand—a period dating from the International Year of the Child in 1977, to its peak in 1979, and a subsequent decline in 1997, during the Asian Financial Turmoil. National characters again became a topic of serious discussion in 1998 and the Office of the National Primary Education Commission stressed the importance of desirable character formation at an early age, and the benefits of desirable character formation among young readers were then subsequently broadly and academically confirmed.

After the removal of the *Mana-Manee* series from the education system, the demand for the representation of desirable characters for Thai children shifted to reappear in major children's book competitions, such as those organized by the Foundation For Children (FFC), which has stipulated in their submission guidelines that the desirable characters of Thai children should be a central theme of the plot. Nanmeebooks Publishing Company has augmented the number of desirable characters, adding Diligence, Thriftiness, Politeness, Unity, Gratitude, and so on, as additional central components of the plot.

Nevertheless, although the effectiveness of the formation of desirable characters for children is judged by the process by which such characters have been formulated and then fully appraised by the relevant public, the national characters for Thai children were not officially tailored until the following decade after an economic recovery from the financial crisis of 1997. In order to commemorate His Majesty King Bhumibol's 80th Birthday Anniversary in 2007, the Ministry of Education, acting through the Non-Formal and Informal Education Commission, initiated a nationwide project to distribute eighty picture books, proposing that thirteen characteristics selected from the stories are desirable traits for the young to emulate. These traits are: Discipline and Responsibility, Generosity, Honesty, Diligence, Thriftiness, Politeness, Unity, Gratitude, Cleanliness (of Public Places), Bravery, Modesty, Rationality, and Emotional Intelligence.

The stories selected for this project share a simple narrative structure, with obvious scenes depicting the push and pull of moral forces. However, unlike the control of conduct by law in actual society, which is accomplished primarily through the threat of sanctions imposed as a result of legislation, the consequence of undesirable behavior in the stories results in guilt and disapprobation of the characters who offend, whereas desirable behavior merits praise. For example, one story adapts a traditional tale, "Juntakorop," which tells of a young prince named Juntakorop, who left his palace and headed into a deep magical jungle where he learnt magical spells from a powerful hermit. When the long period of his study ended and the prince prepared to go home, the hermit gave him a small decorated box and told him not to open it until he reached the palace. However, because of his growing curiosity, he opened it on the way home and inside found a beautiful maiden. The prince became infatuated with her, to the extent that as he brought her along the way with him he cut off his own flesh to satisfy her hunger and gave her his blood to slake her thirst. The story ends with the maiden's change of mind, so that she fell in love with a bandit and colluded with him to kill the prince. The moral of this story associates fear and violence with one of the target desirable characteristics, Discipline— that is, if the prince had obeyed his master, the hermit, he would not have experienced all the misfortunes, the torture of his body and eventually his untimely death.

Initial criticism of such content in the selected stories could focus on how the overt representations of desirable/undesirable characters in the narrative structure of the stories is over-simplified, so that the violent punishment meted out to those who lack desirable characteristics—in the case of "Juntakorop," the failure to practice self-discipline— seems arbitrary. However, the overt representations of such enforcement of desirable/ undesirable characters in the narrative structure of the stories could be viewed as appropriate in that the push-and-pull forces in the stories are intended to be inculcated among young readers nationwide, so the representation can be absorbed by young readers across a wide spectrum of understanding with ease, and can be used as a regulator of conduct. Kasem Wattanachai, Secretary of Office of the Education Council, and former Minister of Education, also supports story-reading for young children, and points out that the situations in the stories could be used to teach children and can create positive influences in children's lives (2004).

If it is assumed that the content in the stories contains nothing harmful, at least to the Thai children and their future behavior, it is still important to examine the basis for predicting the consequences of the desirable/undesirable characteristics. A helpful analogy can be derived from the continuing political crisis that began in Thailand in September 2008 with the military coup that deposed Prime Minister Thaksin Shinawatra. The importance of selecting ethical persons for public positions and imposing harsh punishment for the absence of good morals has often been cited in the so-called Clashes of Colours, and Buddhist morals have been invoked as a means to help the country out of the ongoing political turmoil, which at times has been simplified into a crisis caused by a lack of ethical politicians, or lack of *Dhammapibarn* (Buddhist ethics) in particular (Promkerd 2015: 90).

Nevertheless, the imposition of Buddhist teaching as the basis for justifying the action of the violator is an effective potential tactic, as debates about Buddhism can very quickly turn sensational and emotional, and the violator could thereby escape from further controversy. Thailand's successive constitutions have affirmed total freedom of religion, allowing all Thai citizens to choose their own faith and requiring only the king to be Buddhist, so that a variety of religions are found in Thailand: Islam, Christianity, Hinduism, and other faiths including animist practices. However, in practice, even though Buddhism does not have the status of official national religion, Thailand has always allocated a larger proportion of funding to Buddhism in comparison to other religions. At ground level, the great majority of people in Thailand are Buddhist and develop a close tie with Buddhism from birth to death. It is practised and taught in public schools in their younger days. Then, as they go through successive stages of their life cycle, they experience Buddhist rites and ceremonies—the only religious public holidays indicated in the official calendar. At state level, Buddhist values also provide justification for the country's position on sensitive issues, such as alcohol, abortion, and censorship. For such reasons, Thailand can therefore be described as a de facto Buddhist nation, and regardless of religious or cultural background, the justification of desirable/undesirable characteristics is officially grounded in Buddhist ideology and Buddhist teaching.

The versions of popular Thai literature that have been selected and adapted for the eighty picture books project, along with original stories also included, are heavily influenced by the Buddhist beliefs and values of Thai writers. As Robyn McCallum and John Stephens have argued more generally, "all aspects of textual discourse, from story outcomes to the expressive forms of language, are informed and shaped by ideology, [that is,] a system of beliefs which a society shares and uses to make sense of the world and which are therefore immanent in the texts produced by that society" (2011: 360). They further argue that ideologies, whether overt or implicit, perform the social function of defining and sustaining group values and the cognitive function of supplying a meaningful organization of the social attitudes and relationships which constitute narrative plots (360). These processes are very evident in the overt didacticism apparent in the eighty picture books' adaptations of familiar stories such as *Juntakorop, Phikul Thong, Utaithevi, Krai Thong, Sangthong, Nang sibsong, Pra Suton-Manohra, Holvichai-Kavee,* and *Pla bu tong.* At the end of each story, the insights on the nature of moral obligation are stated in order to help young readers encapsulate the representations of moral goodness and remind them of their duty to the nation, giving them hope that, eventually, good triumphs over evil.

The process of extracting a moral from a traditional tale is apt to be selective, if not reductive, as can be seen in the retelling of other popular tales, such as *Utaithevee, Krai Thong,* and *Phikul Thong.* In *Utaithevee,* a tale type widely known across East and Southeast Asia, a beautiful maiden called Utaithevee (daughter of a handsome forest spirit and a female Thai mythical naga) was adopted by a couple—old and very poor. The maiden hid herself in a frog's corpse and would only come outside when the couple went out to work. From that time, when they came home, they would always find the house thoroughly cleaned, and well prepared food awaiting them. One day, the maiden begged to accompany them to a temple and came out of the corpse. There, a young prince met her and immediately fell in love with her. The old couple then became greedy. They told the prince to build a golden bridge from his palace to their house; otherwise, they would let the maiden marry someone else. In the evening, soldiers visited the old couple's house and informed them that the prince had agreed to build a golden bridge on condition that they must build a grand golden palace corresponding to the golden bridge; otherwise, all of them would be beheaded on the following day. After the soldiers left, the couple reproached the maiden, blaming her for bringing them misfortune. However, she was beyond ordinary so after nightfall, she sneaked out of the house and magically built the grand golden palace. The story ends happily for Utaithevee and the prince, and with the moral that cleanliness is a great merit.

In *Krai Thong* (cf. Chadchaidee 2011: 29–32), the story is set in a peaceful riverside village, where a rich man had two beautiful daughters, Tapaothong and Tapaogaew. There was also a river monster named Chalawan, the king of crocodiles, who lived in a nearby underwater cave with his two wives. He had an iron-clad body and he was always on the lookout for fresh human victims to eat, especially young maidens. One day, when Tapaothong and Tapaogaew were bathing in the river, Chalawan appeared and took Tapaothong down to his isolated underwater lair, where he made her his third wife. Her parents in fear and desperation turned to many warrior monks and all the hunters in the village—seeking someone to fight with the fierce, frenzied beast and bring back their beloved daughter. The father offered his second daughter and part of his estate as a reward. However, it turned out that every day they would send more men down into the water to feed the hungry monster. Eventually, Krai Thong, the hero of the story, was their last hope. He was summoned to destroy the monster. The story ends with the death of the monster and the happy life of Krai Thong with both Tapaothong and Tapaogaew as his wives and the wealth bestowed upon him by their father. The moral of the story is that bravery is a great merit.

The final example is *Phikul Thong* (cf. Chadchaidee 2011: 5–7), which, like *Utaithevee* is a widely familiar international tale type ("The Kind and the Unkind Girls," Aarne-Thompson-480), which exists in over a thousand variants (Roberts 1994). Phikul is a beautiful young orphan who has been reduced to a servant's role by her step-mother and step-sister. One day while fetching water she is approached by an old crone who asks for a drink, which Phikul gladly gives her. She is rewarded with a magic gift that golden flowers would fall from her mouth whenever she spoke while feeling sympathy for another. When her step-mother sends her daughter in quest of a comparable gift, the girl responds abusively to the elegant woman she instead meets, and receives a curse that whenever she spoke in anger worms would fall from her mouth. Phikul was blamed for this misfortune and driven away, but while wandering in the forest encountered a prince who was captivated by her person and her story, and took her as his wife. The moral of the story is that merit is earned by compassion and kindness, and that in human relations one should not speak in anger. While this conclusion is not unlike the morals appended to Charles Perrault's variant, "Les Fées" ["Diamonds and Toads" in English versions], which contends that kind words are more precious than material riches, and kindness may bring unexpected rewards, *Phikul Thong* develops a particular Buddhist perspective through the idea that extending compassion earns merit, as compassion is a major tenet in the Buddha's teaching.

Because the historical and cultural contribution of Buddhism to Thainess is as old as Thailand itself, the justification of desirable/undesirable characteristics based on Buddhist teachings has then constructed the "mainstream Thainess."

A key person who profoundly and widely dominated Thai thinking from the 1950s onward is M.R. Kukrit Pramoj, the thirteenth Prime Minister of Thailand from 1975 to 1976 and a prominent scholar who "communicated so actively with the Thai society that he had the greatest influence on its thinking in the past fifty years" (Sattayanurak 2007). Sattayanurak argues that the focus of Kukrit's ideology, which belonged in the same intellectual wave that inherited the ideology of "Thainess" from the absolute monarchy period, enabled "Thainess" to powerfully respond to social situations of post-1932 revolution and post-World War II politics, and to offer resistance to competing ideologies such as liberalism and socialism. His ideology of "Thainess" asserts that the royal institution and the kingship are indispensable to the "Thai nation" and draws a close link between Buddhism and "kingship" and "nation," with Buddhism as a source of ethics that allows the "king" to be a righteous ruler, and allows Thai who relate to each other in a "know-thy-place" manner to co-exist peacefully without exploiting each other.

Drawing away from some frightening scenes in the stories and from the fact that Buddhist principles could have been employed to ground the assimilation of desirable characteristics in younger generations, the real question is whether Buddhism in mainstream Thainess is comprehensive enough to substitute for Thai citizens as a whole. In fact, Thailand has never consisted of one monolithic group, but has been the home of over fifty other ethnic minorities varying in history, language, religion, appearance, and patterns of livelihood. The largest of these groups is the Karen; others include the Hmong, the Lahu, the Lawa, the Mon, the Phuthai, and the Shan. More specifically, the northern Thai are heirs to the heritage of the Lanna kingdom in Chiang Mai. The southern

Thai, living on the peninsula, have been influenced by living close to the Malay. The other group of Thai people are the Isaan; they are almost as numerous as the central Thai, and are descendants from Lao people flocking into Northeast Thailand, and many still call themselves Lao. People outside central Thai speak their dialect, and, roughly, the country has around 85 spoken languages as distinct from the standard Thai. Because of such a large diversity in race and languages, it is fairly true to say that the kingdom of Thailand comprises a heterogeneous population with diverse spoken languages, united under a nationalist Buddhist ideology and it is not possible to construct the conception of Thainess using a given genetic-linguistic grouping. In addition to ethnic diversity, the insurgency in Thailand's Deep South throws doubt on any assumption that the mainstream Thai can really provide moral grounds that are appropriate for contemporary Thailand.

These circumstances could explain why the time was ripe for the advent of the *Mana-Manee* nostalgia craze. The series re-emerged at a time of heightened political divisiveness, after almost two decades of internal conflict and social division. *Mana-Manee* has taken the majority of Thai people (those born in and around the 1990s) back to a time of innocence—a pre-1992 Black May before the divisive politics of the twenty-first century.

Thailand is the only Southeast Asian nation that has never been colonized, but the country has changed much of its social structure during its modernization era. The term Thainess was defined, developed, and inculcated by means of a state-led process that was so effective that the disparate small groups populating the kingdom have been mandated, if not pressured, by the "becoming Thai" promulgation, to immerse themselves into the mainstream of the conception of Thainess as defined by the intellectuals and leaders of their time.

Even in the early twenty-first century, the images of ethnic minority groups in Thailand have not yet been improved; such promulgations have become increasingly intense in the past decades, perhaps to counter political unrest as well as the mounting scale and sophistication of the South insurgency, when the government was prompted to recognize that there was a serious issue of uniting the nation, and as a result the National Identity Board mandated that mainstream Thainess be a compulsory feature of the Thai educational system and be disseminated through mass media and cultural institutions.

On the other hand, one may argue that in actual social discourse and daily interaction the use of legal rules as a means of control of conduct is applied, and any violations of the regulations entail monetary sanctions, or legal expenses or imprisonment. If this argument is true, the representation of minority groups other than the mainstream Thai in children's stories—and the increasing likelihood of imitation from the moral practice derived from Buddhist teachings—can be considered a trivial issue, given the notion that everyone must be treated equally under the law. However, there is a caution that in many circumstances, legal rules and the "internal incentives" can work together to control a vast range of behavior or conduct, but a number of crimes and torts are not legally sanctionable but are nevertheless considered immoral. This makes the redefinition to acknowledge an ethnically diverse population vital, and thus demands serious consideration instead of being taken as a trivial matter.

Also, the evolution of the moral grounds in the selected stories for children might also demand some further consideration: it should not be overlooked that, for instance, *Mana-Manee*, The Legend of Good Children series, was totally removed from the system because it was considered outdated for contemporary Thai society. In the same way, the interpretation of Buddhist teaching is always a sensitive issue in Thailand and by dismissing challenges, the teachings have always been absolute, so well preserved that they perhaps have never been up-to-date for contemporary Thailand.

Conclusion

In practice, Thainess cannot be pinned down as one ideology. However, the mainstream conception of Thainess has been consistently cultivated in Thailand through a complex process of learning and inculcation since childhood. Through selected stories, the child learns to reproach and to approve certain behaviors.

Perhaps, instead of the constant efforts to instill any conception over the years of childhood, the minority cultures and religions should also be treated as components of a unified national identity, or as "many features" of Thainess. This could make the newer generations see a more refined image of ethnic characteristics and benefit from the development of a conscious ethnic identity, when multicultural frameworks are used in their learning environments.

Bibliography

Chadchaidee, Thanapol (Lamduan) (2011) Fascinating Folktales of Thailand, e-book, www.bangkokbooks.com

Chainarongsingha, W. (2001) "Mana Manee Piti Chujai Our Good Old Friends," *A Day Magazine*, January, Volume 5.

McCallum, Robyn, and John Stephens (2011) "Ideology and Children's Books" in Shelby Wolf, Karen Coats, Patricia Enciso, and Christine Jenkins (eds), *Handbook of Research on Children's and Young Adult Literature*, New York: Routledge, 359–71.

Non-Formal and Informal Education Commission Center (2007) "Guidelines to Promote Moral Reasoning Through the Reading of Selected Tales," Bangkok: Rungsrikarnpim.

Promkerd, P. (2015) "Going Beyond the Thai Democratic Development Trap Through the Development of Democratic Political Culture: Towards a More Sustainable New Path," *KKU Research Journal*, 32(3): 90.

PUBAT (2016, Feb 2) "Nostalia Market Boom." Retrieved from http://bit.ly/2bTUnk0

Roberts, Warren (1994) *Tale of the Kind and Unkind Girls: AA-TH 480 and Related Tales*, Detroit, MI: Wayne State University Press.

Sattayanurak, S. (2002) *Development of Thai Nationalism and Thainess by Luang Vichitvatakarn*, Bangkok: Matichon.

Sattayanurak, S. (2003) *Somdet Kromphraya Damrong Rajanubhap: Kansang attalak 'muang Thai' lae 'shan' khong shao Siam* [Prince Damrong Rajanubhap: The Construction of Identities of "muang Thai" and "Classes" of the Siamese], Bangkok: Matichon Press.

Sattayanurak, S. (2007) *Kanmuang lae kansang kuam pen thai doi momrajawong Kukrit Pramoj* [Politics and the Construction of Thainess by M. R. Kukrit Pramoj], Bangkok: Matichon Press.

Sattayanurak, S. (2005) The Construction of Mainstream Thought on "Thainess" and the "Truth" Constructed by "Thainess." *Faa-Diew-Kan* (Same Sky Books) 3(4): 68–81.

Tiranasar, A. (2004) "Cultural Identity and Art Education in Thailand," Paper presented at the 2nd Asia-Pacific Art Education Conference, 28–30 December. Retrieved from: http://pioneer.netserv.chula.ac.th/~tampai1/hk2004.htm

Wattanachai, Kasem (2004) "How to Make Thai People Love Reading" (interview), *Matichon Newspaper*, Jan 9: 4.

36

EARLY CHILDHOOD LITERATURE IN BRAZIL AND MEXICO

Illustrated books for children aged 0 to 3

Alma Carrasco and Mônica Correia Baptista

The recognition that babies can be readers is fairly recent in Brazil and Mexico. For a long time, it was believed that the ability to understand complex relationships between sounds and graphic symbols was almost indispensable for reading. From this perspective, the story of the reader would start once she/he became proficient in understanding the basic rules of this representational system. Reading is a social practice, however, a practice embedded in a cultural process that has been historically constructed, and more recently it has been understood that the story of the reader begins as soon as the child arrives into the world as a listening participant (cf. Imhof, 2013). Hence, to read is to develop the ability to symbolize, to construct meaning from written texts, to resort to the symbolic tools created by humankind, to appropriate the knowledge and practices that have been developed and transmitted by previous generations, and to create new forms to interact with what has been written. Understood as such, the act of reading begins as soon as the baby arrives into the world, immersed already in a symbolic universe.

This new perspective has begun to modify the practices of several actors of these societies. Although book production has traditionally focused on school-age children (4–6 for kindergarten and 6–12 for elementary), since the 2000s there has been a growing body of literature for babies and the first *bebetecas* (baby libraries) have appeared, offering a meeting point for babies and books.

In the last few decades Brazil and Mexico have supported programs to encourage reading and equip kindergarten, elementary and secondary schools with a high-quality, universal book collection. These programs are *Programa Nacional Biblioteca da Escola* (PNBE, or National School Library Program, launched in 1997) in Brazil and *Programa Nacional de Lectura* (PNL, or National Reading Program, launched in 2001) in Mexico. The collections, which are distributed every year to school and classroom libraries, offer options for individual and collective reading, whilst being both supplementary to and different from the readings found in textbooks. These are innovative national projects that promote the development of readers and writers (cf. Bonilla Rius, 2007).[1]

The impact that such national initiatives have had on the publishing industry is evident in the development of guilds of authors, illustrators and publishers specializing in books for early childhood. It is also clear that the population of children aged 0 to 3 has yet to receive adequate attention in Mexico. Although there was a similar situation in Brazil, in 2010 an important adjustment was made to the PNBE: within the Childhood Education category, a new stage called *creche* ("day care center" in Portuguese) was created for children 0 to 3 years of age.[2] Two important differences among the experiences of our countries need to be highlighted. First, and as already mentioned, the 0 to 3 years stage has been included as a target of cultural initiatives in Brazil, but not in Mexico. Second, the policies for book collection acquisition in Mexico include informational texts besides literary texts. This is not the case for Brazil.

Our discussion analyses children's literature books that have been explicitly produced (or destined) in our countries for children 0 to 3 years of age. Our analysis takes into account the literary genres of such books, their figuration and frequency, their aesthetic and literary quality, the subjects they address and their graphic project—that is, a plan that defines the visual characteristics of a graphic design (in this case, a book). We examine a set of illustrated books and picture books[3] for early childhood, comprised mainly of narratives and songs related to the everyday life of small children. Works of poetry, local oral traditions, and classic tales re-narrated in either their Mexican or Brazilian versions are also included.

Analysed corpus

In the case of Brazil, the book selection analysed is that of the PNBE's collection. The Mexican case took into account both pre-school books included in the PNL[4] and books available at *Lee Antonia*, the children's room of the library at Consejo Puebla de Lectura, a local non-profit institution.[5] The analysis takes into account the literary genres of the sample, their figuration and frequency; as well as their aesthetic and literary quality, the subject addressed and their graphic project.

Quality has been the fundamental selection criterion for this analysis. The determination of such quality revolves around two main axes: the multi-cultural features in the early childhood literary books, and the main subjects used to narrate the life of young children: their needs, their fears, their socialization challenges, and their experience of being young children.

Within the distribution of narrative genres in the Brazilian collection more than half of the selected books are written in prose. Two of Mexico's PNL categories specifically require texts containing poetry, rhymes, songs and word games. Nevertheless, the national publishing offering of rhymed texts is still insufficient in both countries, in spite of the rich oral tradition that they both enjoy.

Characteristics of the literary collections for early childhood in Brazil and Mexico

Prose texts

A salient feature of the narratives that compose the collections analysed is that, in general, they appear to privilege or be closer to the universe of children above two years of age. Very few narratives refer to babies and their surroundings, or invite interactive engagement, the identification of relationships, the emergence of questions, the request for explanations, or the representation of what has been read through dioramas, maps, dialogs and performances for hand puppets, as suggested by Chapela (2010).

In Brazil, books such as *Como é bonito o pé do Igor* [How pretty is Igor's foot!] and *Lá vai o Rui* [There goes Rui], written by Sônia Regina Rosa de Oliveira Dias de Jesus and illustrated by Luna, are exceptions that seem to fulfill these goals since they address subjects and contain illustrations that refer to everyday situations for children under 2, especially infants that still don't talk or walk. Also *Gildo*, by Silvana Rando, besides offering a format that allows babies to handle the book, refers to fear in a way that is very relatable to the feelings of babies.

In Mexico, *Hic, hic, hic* (2014), by Mercedes García Besném with illustrations by Alejandra Estrada, depicts an extended family lovingly devoted to take care of a baby girl that has the hiccups. Also *Sinfonía natural* [Natural Symphony] (2004), written by Leticia Herrera Álvarez and illustrated by Gabriel Pacheco, and *El otro lado* [The Other Side] (1993), written by Alejandro Aura and illustrated by Marcos Límenes are examples of this. Both are 40-page books printed in bond paper that are enjoyed by younger readers but unfortunately do not allow for infants to handle them.

Besides the subjects and images depicted in these stories, the publishing production decisions for these works also seem to have considered younger readers: they are shaped like a square, are smaller in size and both their cover and inner pages are made of a stronger paper. They are books that facilitate being handled.

In both Brazil and Mexico there are examples of books that invite viewers to play games that are particularly attractive to babies, such as peek-a-boo, or that stimulate babies' curiosity regarding their bodies and their willingness to name its parts, such as *Pedrinho, cadê você* [Where are you, Little Peter?], by Sônia Marta Junqueira, and *¿Que te picó la hormiga de los pies a la barriga?* [Did the ant bite you from your feet to your belly?], a rhymed narrative by Isaías Isabel.

A couple of texts that are singularly enjoyed by both younger and older children are *Quem soltou o Pum?* [Who let Pum out?] by Brazilian author Blandina de Almeida Prado Franco, and *La peor señora del mundo* [The worst lady in the world] by Mexican author Francisco Hinojosa and illustrated – as are many of this author's works – by Rafael Barajas, known as El Fisgón. Both texts are particularly interesting because they address everyday life subjects in a smart way, resort to a refined sense of humor and manage language in such a way that allows for the construction of multiple meanings.

Poetry texts

Poetry texts written by contemporary authors are in Mexico as plentiful as local traditional stories, but less so in Brazil. Poetry texts written by Brazilian authors are, perhaps, one of the most effective literary experiences offered by PNBE's collection for children 0 to 3 years of age. For instance, the books written and illustrated by Eva Furnari, such as *Assim Assado* [Like this, like that] and *Você troca* [Would you change...?], share some common characteristics such as short, rhymed phrases with unexpected questions. Also, they are accompanied by illustrations that expand the possibilities for constructing new and humorous meanings from what is being read and seen. For instance, in *Você troca* [Would you change...?], the use of anaphora and the unusual presentation of subjects and situations involve the readers in a game in such a way that they continue to enjoy the author's proposals and may even want to engage in a game of their own: "Would you change a happy cat for a toothless duck?" *Cadê* [Where is it?], written and illustrated by José Augusto Brandão Estellita Lins, is a rhyme that, due to its textual and metrical selection stimulates memorization and the desire to discover the upcoming scene. The title *Gabriel* by Ilan Brenman is also a good example of a book with artistic qualities and aim, considering its aesthetic references. It is a major benchmark for literary and graphic esthetics. The text employs rhymes and repetitions along with unusual questions about improbable and funny topics. In the image, Gabriel has climbed a tree and is sawing off one of its branches, unaware that an open mouthed crocodile is awaiting right under him

As to the written text, the author resorts to rhymes and repetitions based on an introductory text that goes like this: "Just like any other kid, Gabriel likes to touch everything he sees, but would he be able to touch..." From that point on, questions start defining the rhythm of the text: "a crocodile in a swamp?" "Or a horse that's colossal." Illustrations have a plethora of small details that enable attentive readers to explore certain meanings that could be overlooked if approached with a quick, careless glance. For instance, the illustration accompanying the aforementioned text includes a little bird (which appears in all of the book's illustrations and is not referenced in the text) pulling the Superman cape that Gabriel wears while cutting a tree branch over a lake in which the crocodile awaits with his open mouth, showing multiple teeth.

In Mexico, María Baranda has created two notable board books expressly for younger children: *Arrullo* [Lull] (2008), illustrated by Margarita Sada and *Un abrazo* [A hug] (2009), illustrated by Cecilia Varela. Other poetry works by Mexican authors appear in the CIDCLI collection for younger readers, also produced as board books, and combining songs, rhymes, word games and innovative illustrations in order to present informative texts. Books in this category by Alfonso Núñez include *Buen provecho, animales al acecho* [Bon appetite! Animals on the Lookout] with illustrations by Juan Gedovius; and *Y la luna siempre es una* [And the moon is always one], illustrated by Antonio Castellanos. Also *Me parezco, me parezco* [I look like... I look like...], written by Édgar Román and illustrated by Ana Sanfelippo, is a rhymed text that sets out to start a dialogue about resemblances that exist among family members, a recurring subject amongst children.

Particularly noteworthy amongst Mexican illustrated books are *El rey que se equivocó de cuento* [The king that got into the wrong story] written by Antonio Granados and illustrated by Alain Espinoza; *El canario y el sabueso* [The canary and the bloodhound], written by Silvia Molina and illustrated by Erika Martínez; and *¿A dónde fue el ciempiés?* [Where did the centipede go?] written by Coral Bracho and illustrated by Rafael Barajas (El Fisgón). These are texts with distinct artistic features – the first, for instance, works with monochrome illustrations. Although these books were not explicitly created for younger children, their relevance for this age bracket has become apparent during reading promotion activities.

Among poetry texts, the works containing Brazilian and Mexican literary traditions stand out. In the Brazilian case, it is worth mentioning a verse narration of the classic *Chapeuzinho Vermelho* [Little Red Riding Hood], created by Braguinha, a Brazilian singer and composer born in 1907 whose songs—written for this specific tale—marked the childhood of several generations. In Mexico, songs by Cri-Cri, born also in 1907, have had a major impact on several generations of Mexicans.

Folk lyric and tradition

Oral tradition has been the main linguistic resource for sharing old songs, tales and games with children. In Mexico, the publishing industry of the 20th and 21st centuries has transformed such songs, tales and games into illustrated books with varying formats, which have had an uneven distribution across the country. Vicente Mendoza

(1983) has compiled an outstanding collection of lullabies, rhyming couplets, games and never-ending stories that have been published by several Mexican publishing houses as books for younger children. Examples of these are: *Los Changuitos* [The little monkeys] (1989), illustrated by Claudia de Teresa; and *El Torito* [The little bull] (1994), illustrated by Norma Patiño, published by Conafe within its program for reading promotion in rural areas. Other compilations are: *Riquirririn y Riquirrirrán* [Riquirrín and Riquirrirrán] (1990), by Trino; *Amapolita* [Little Poppy] (2003), by Luz María Chapela; and *Naranja dulce, limón partido* [Sweet orange, cut lemon] by Mercedes Díaz Roig and Maria Teresa Miaja de la Peña (1981).

In 1999, the publishing house Clío launched the complete works of Francisco Gabilondo Soler – Cri-Cri (1907–1990) – composer of over 210 songs for children. Through the radio, his work was "a constant presence in Mexican childhood since the 1930s" (Gatti, 2010). Every Mexican knows at least one song by "Cri-Cri the singing cricket," a character that, according to Gatti, wanted to be more audible than visible. Cri-Cri's production can be situated between oral tradition and contemporary production of children's poetry.

In Brazil, *Cantigas, Adivinhas e Outros Versos* [Songs, riddles and other verses], compiled by Ana Claudia Rocha in two volumes, is notable for its high literary quality, as are *Borboletinha* [Little butterfly] and *Samba Lelê*, both compiled by Andreia Sanchez Moroni. *Brinque-Book Canta e Dança* [Sing and dance playbook] includes a CD to accompany the lyrics of traditional songs from several Brazilian regions used in sing-along games.

Of poetry created for younger children, María Baranda offers two anthologies: *Digo de Noche un Gato y otros poemas* [I say at night a cat and other poems] (2006), and *Sol de amigos* [Sun of friends] (2010). *Deja un rastro de luz* [Leave a trace of light], by Gilda Rincón presents an anthology of songs, verses and rhymes made popular through the recordings of The Rincón Brothers in the 1980s. Strictly speaking, this is not a book for children, but is nevertheless a compilation that offers singularly creative songs that left an imprint on a generation of urban youth in Mexico City.

In the early 1990s, Mexican poets like Coral Bracho, Alberto Blanco, Elsa Cros and Alberto Forcada published poetry books written for children through CIDCLI's collection *Reloj de Versos* [A Clock of Poems]. Consejo Nacional para la Cultura y las Artes also published this collection. The CONACULTA introduction says: "The books in these series, made by adults for children, offer much more than traditional songs and rhymes: these are the joyous and sensitive expressions of several of our poets" (CONACULTA's Catalogue, pp.94).

Stories narrated with images

Along with poetry, picture books constitute an innovation in literary language. Picture books present stories full of humor and laughter, as well as sad and emotional situations. In the Brazilian production, the title *Poá* by Marcelo de Assis Moreira offers a very rich illustration work with traces that escape stereotypes. With an exquisite sense of humor, the book narrates the story of a guinea fowl that sees triangles, rectangles and flowers in the back of her peers instead of their characteristic round spots. Then, the guinea fowl "leaves" the story to come back with glasses that help her regain a normal vision. Humor is also present in the already classic books of Eva Furnari and her unusual characters, *Zuza e Arquimedes* [Zuza and Arquimedes] and *Bruxinha Zuzu y su gato Miú*

[Little Witch Zuzu and her cat Miu]. On the other hand, books such as *Coração de Ganso* [Goose heart] by Regina Coeli Rennó, and *A Flor do Lado de Lá* [The flower on that side] by Roger Mello, use very delicate and well-manicured illustrations to tell stories of characters going through difficult times or displaying attitudes of solidarity.

In Mexico, there is a growing editorial production of wordless picture books. Telling stories through images requires a language and graphic repertoire that babies are just starting to develop. Picture books entail the opportunity for babies to become familiar with the semiotic codes of the culture. Hence, picture books leave the image interpretation and narration in the hands of whoever reads the story to a baby, arriving at very uneven results as to the richness of the language and the construction of interesting stories that go beyond the sequential description of images. Picture books certainly constitute an expanding genre for the publishing industry and emerge in a context of growing production targeted to early childhood. However, it is more likely that these works are targeted towards pre-school and older children, and not necessarily babies.

On a brief analysis of book formats, only a few of them offer some sort of innovation. A clear example of innovation is the Brazilian book *Eu vi!* [I saw!] by Fernando Vilela, with an extraordinary structure—also seen in other works—in which odd numbered pages spread out as if they were some sort of folder. It is also important to mention that none of the books analysed have hard covers; neither are their pages made of more resistant paper. Both aspects are extremely necessary if they are intended to be used on a daily basis by babies and smaller children.

A change of perspective on children

Colomer (2010) points out that there is a difference between the moral values portrayed in children's books of the second half of the 20th century. In the first half of the century, "democracy, equal rights, personal independence, and the capacity to relate" (44) used to be promoted, whereas in the latter prevails "a perception of people as 'individuals' with their own opinions, will, and actions. The social representation of childhood evolved towards the inclusion of individual rights for children, which led to questioning the absolute authority of adults and blurring the boundaries between traditional ways of behaving and of enjoying oneself at different stages of life" (43).

Early childhood books written by Mexican and Brazilian authors are mainly literary fiction, written mostly in poetry in Mexico and mostly in prose in Brazil. Also, traditional songs and tales tend to be revived more strongly by Mexican publishing houses than by their Brazilian counterparts. Among illustrated books for early childhood, picture books are a minority. This might be explained because of the need to characterize these works, which demand a greater involvement on behalf of the reader. A book of tales, according to Shulevitz, emphasizes anecdotes while the illustrations, which may be included or not, tell the same story again. Conversely, in a picture book, readers "see and listen directly" to the story, as if it was a direct, touching theatrical experience. (2005: 11). Nevertheless, it is important to avoid an over-simplistic view of what children's literature is. With reference to picture books produced in the last decades of the twentieth century, in which the interaction between text and image creates layers of meaning and opens a book to different interpretations, Evelyn Arizpe and Morag Styles observe that such books "diverge from any concept of children's books as 'simple', if by simple we are referring to such aspects as clear-cut narrative structures, a chronological order of events, an unambiguous narrative voice and, not least, clearly delineated and fixed borders between fantasy and reality."

Based on data from the PNBE program, it may be concluded that books for children under 6 years are still not a priority in Brazil. Books for children of 0 to 3 years are even less of a priority, as per the registrations of publishing houses in the selection process. Hence, in the three selection processes in which the 0 to 3 age bracket has been included (2010, 2012 and 2014), the percentage distribution was approximately the following: 53 percent of all books for the early years of elementary, 27 percent for youth and adults, 17 percent for children age 4 to 5 and only 3 percent for children of 0 to 3 (Pereira, 2014).

In Mexico, cultural initiatives related to school libraries for children only started in the 1980s. They are targeted at pre-school children, not at 0 to 3 children. As to literary production in itself, books explicitly targeted at children would only appear in the 18th century, such as the fables written by Fernández de Lizardi (1776–1827). According to Gatti (2010), the 19th century provided the best environment for the creation of children's books. It must be noted that the Mexican publishing sector, quite heterogeneously, still faces the challenge of building collections targeted at younger children, particularly babies.

In conclusion, both in Mexico and Brazil, younger children that are not included in compulsory education are underrepresented or bluntly absent from cultural initiatives and still have not reached a significant figuration in the publishing market. This may be because our societies, in spite of looking at early childhood from a new perspective, still doubt that babies are truly capable of interacting and constructing meaning from what they see and experience. On the other hand, the growing competition among national authors leads us to believe that soon Mexico and Brazil will grant our children an increasing number of books that could expand their experiences and help them develop as readers and individuals.

Notes

1 Available at http://lectura.dgme.sep.gob.mx/coleccion/caracteristica.php (Accessed on 27 October 2014).
2 In Brazil, the 1988 Federal Constitution defines childhood education as the first stage of basic education, and it is comprised of *creche*, for children 0–3 and *pré-escola*, for children 4–5.
3 According to Banco del Libro (2001), every book that contains illustrations, regardless of their proportion to the text, can be considered as an illustrated book. An image book is a mainly illustrated book with little or no text. A picture book combines images and words where neither prevails over the other. Both illustration and text have a narrative function and therefore it is not possible to construct meaning if they are read separately.
4 The 2013–2014 catalogue is available at: http://basica.sep.gob.mx/Catalogo_LR_2013-2014.pdf
5 www.consejopuebladelectura.org

Bibliography

Anonymous (1989). *Los Changuitos* [The little monkeys], Mexico City: Consejo Nacional de Fomento Educativo.
Anonymous (1994). *El Torito* [The little bull], Mexico City: Consejo Nacional de Fomento Educativo.
Arizpe, Evelyn, and Styles, Morag (2003). *Children Reading Pictures: Interpreting Visual Texts*, London: RoutledgeFalmer.
Aura, Alejandro (1993). *El otro lado* [The other side], Mexico City: Fondo de Cultura Económica.

Baranda, María (2006). *Arrullo* [Lull], Mexico City: El Naranjo.

Baranda, María (2006). *Digo de Noche un Gato y otros poemas* [I say at night a cat and other poems], Mexico City: El Naranjo.

Baranda, María (2009). *Un abrazo* [A hug], Mexico City: El Naranjo.

Baranda, María (2010). *Sol de amigos* [Sun of friends]. Mexico City: Ediciones El Naranjo.

Bonilla Rius, Elisa (2007). La experiencia de seleccionar libros para Bibliotecas Escolares y de Aula en México: un proceso de aprendizaje riguroso y transparente, *Pensar el libro* [The Experience of Selecting Books for School and Classroom Libraries in Mexico: A Rigurous and Transparent Learning Process, Reflecting on the Book], Num 5, Cerlalc-UNESCO. www.cerlalc.org/revista_enero/pdf/06.pdf9 (accessed 27 October 2014).

Bracho, Coral (2007). *¿A dónde fue el ciempiés?* [Where did the centipede go?], México City: Era.

Brenman, Ilan (2008). *Gabriel*. São Paulo: Brinque-Book.

Chapela, Luz María (2003). *Amapolita* [Little Poppy], Mexico City: Trillas.

Chapela, Luz María (2010), *Dime, diré y dirás. Los menores de siete años como lectores y autores.* [Tell me, I'll Tell, You'll Tell. Children Under Seven as Readers and Authors]. Serie Lectura y Escritura, Colección SomosMaestros, Mexico: SM.

Colomer, Teresa (2010). "Picturebooks and Changing Values at the Turn of the Century," in Colomer, Teresa; Kûmmerling-Meibauer, Bettina; Silva-díaz, María Cecilia (eds.). *New Directions in Picturebook Research*, New York: Routledge.

Conaculta (1993). *Catálogo de la Dirección General de Publicaciones del Consejo Nacional para la Cultura y las Artes. Infantiles y Juveniles, 1993. I* [Catalog for Children and Youth of the Directorate-General for Publishing, National Council for Culture and Arts, 1993. I], Mexico City, Dirección General de Publicaciones.

Díaz Roig, Mercedes; Miaja, María Teresa (comp) (1981). *Naranja Dulce, limón partido* [Sweet orange, cut lemon], Mexico City: El Colegio de México.

Franco, Blandina de Almeida Prado (2013). *Quem soltou o Pum?* [Who let Pum out?], São Paulo: Claro Enigma LTDA.

Furnari, Eva (1994). *Você troca?* [Would you change...?], São Paulo: Editora Moderna.

Furnari, Eva (2007). *Zuzu e Arquimedes* [Zuzu and Arquimedes], São Paulo: Pia Sociedade Filhas De São Paulo.

Furnari, Eva (2009). *Assim Assado* [Like this, like that], São Paulo: Pia Sociedade Filhas De São Paulo.

Furnari, Eva (2010). *Bruxinha Zuzu e Gato Miú* [Little Witch Zuzu and the cat Miu], São Paulo: Editora Moderna.

García Besném, Mercedes (2014). *Hic, hic, hic*, Mexico City: Fondo de Cultura Económica.

Gatti, Sebastián (2010). "Orígenes de la LIJ en Latinoamérica" [Origins of Children and Youth Literature in Latin America], in Jaime García Padrino (ed.) *Gran diccionario de autores latinoamericanos de literatura infantil y juvenil* [Grand Dictionary of Latin American Authors of Children's and Youth Literature], Madrid: Fundación SM, 24–25

Granados, Antonio (1995). *El rey que se equivocó de cuento* [The King that got into the wrong story], Mexico City: Fondo de Cultura Económica.

Herrera Álvarez, Leticia (2004). *Sinfonía natural* [Natural symphony], Mexico City: Alfaguara.

Hinojosa, Francisco (1992). *La peor señora del mundo* [The worst lady in the world], Mexico City: Fondo de Cultura Económica.

Imhof, M. (2013). "The Point of Departure: Listening as the Basis for Literacy Development," in J. F. Maas, S. C. Ehmig, C. Seelmann (eds.) *Prepare for life! Raising Awareness for Early Literacy Education*, Wiesbaden Germany: Federal Ministry of Education and Research, 45–52.

Jesus, Sônia R. R. de Oliveira Dias (2009). *Lá vai o Rui...*[There goes Rui], São Paulo: Frase Efeito Estúdio.

Jesus, Sônia R. R. de Oliveira Dias (2009). *Como é bonito o pé do Igor.* [How pretty is Igor's foot!], São Paulo: Frase Efeito Estúdio.

Junqueira, Sônia Marta (2010). *Pedrinho, cadê você?* [Where are you, little Peter?], Belo Horizonte: Gutemberg Comércio e Representação.

Lins, José Augusto Brandão Estellita (2009). *Cadê* [Where is it?], Brazil: Globo Livros LTDA.

Mateos, José Manuel AKA Isaías Isabel (2003). *¿Que te picó la hormiga de los pies a labarriga?* [Did the ant bite you from your feet to your belly?], Mexico City: CIDCLI.

Mello, José Roger Soares de (2011). *A flor do lado de lá* [The flower on that side]. São Paulo: Gaia LTDA.

Mendoza, Vicente, T. (1983). *Lírica infantil de México* [Mexican Lyrics for Children] Colección Lecturas Mexicanas, Mexico City: FCE, First Edition (El Colegio de México), 1951.

Molina, Silvia (2006). *El canario y el sabueso* [The canary and the bloodhound], Mexico City: Norma.

Moreira, Marcelo de Assis (2009). *Poá* [Poá], São Paulo: Casa Amarela.

Moroni, Andreia Sanches (2013). *Borboletinha* [Little butterfly], São Paulo: Estudio da Carochinha Produção Editorial EPP LTDA.

Moroni, Andreia Sanches (2013). *Samba Lelê*, São Paulo: Estudio da Carochinha Produção Editorial EPP LTDA

Núñez, Alfonso (2007). *Buen provecho, animales al acecho* [Bon appetite! Animals on the lookout], Mexico City: CIDCLI.

Núñez, Alfonso (2007). *Y la luna siempre es una* [And the moon is always one], Mexico City: CIDCLI.

Pereira, Fernanda Rohlfs (2014). "Práticas de leitura literária na educação infantil: como elas ocorrem em turmas de uma UMEI de Belo Horizonte?" [Literary reading practices in early childhood education: how do they occur in classes at UMEI in Belo Horizonte?]. Master's Thesis, Department of Education–Federal University of Minas Gerais, Belo Horizonte.

Raymundo, Silvana Albertini Rando (2010). *Gildo*, São Paulo: Brinque-Book.

Rennó, Regina Coeli (2007). *Coração de Ganso* [Goose heart], São Paulo: Mercuryo.

Rincón, Gilda (2008). *Deja un rastro de luz* [Leave a trace of light], Mexico City: Nostra.

Rocha, Ana Cláudia (org.) (2010). *Cantigas, Adivinhas e outros versos* [Songs, riddles and other verses], Volumes 1 and 2, São Paulo: Melhoramentos.

Román, Édgar (2007). *Me parezco, me parezco* [I look like... I look like...], Mexico City: CIDCLI.

Sanson, Suzana Taves Dadid de (2003). *Brinque-Book canta e dança* [Sing and dance play book], São Paulo: Brinque-Book.

Shulevitz, Uri (2005) "Qué es un libro álbum" [What is a Picture Book], in Bellorín, Brenda (ed.) *El libro álbum. Invención y evolución de un género para niños* [The Picturebook: Invention and Evolution of a Genre for Children], Colección Parapara Clave, Caracas: Banco del Libro, 8–13.

Silva, Fernando Vilela de Moura (2013). *Eu vi!* [I saw!], São Paulo: SDS Editora de Livros EIRELI.

Trino (1990). *Riquirrirín y Riquirrirrán* [Riquirrín and Riquirrirrán], Zapopan, Mexico: Petra.

37

CONCEPTION AND TRENDS OF IRANIAN PICTURE BOOKS

Morteza Khosronejad, Atiyeh Firouzmand and Fatemeh Farnia

Whereas western children's literature was produced over time by its milieu, it cannot be assumed that this process pertains also to "developing" countries, where, as well as drawing on folktales, classics, and religious tales, children's literature has also encountered the challenge of a well-established and hegemonic discourse of modernity. In addition to different internal criteria, therefore, external factors, though sometimes paradoxical, have also been very influential in the construction of Iranian children's literature. This influence is evident in two ways: first, the ideal modern pattern has proved to be very alluring; second, because of its monist nature, modernity has challenged Iranian national identity and has promoted resistance and returning to self. So the internal movements of developing countries assume a new form through the dynamics of "attraction and repulsion." The development and growth of picture books in Iran seems to have mirrored this phenomenon.

Major trends in the verbal narratives of Iranian picture books

Most theorizing about picture books begins with the assumption that they are a multi-modal form in which meaning is produced by the interaction of verbal and visual media. Perry Nodelman, for example, remarked that pictures and words engage with each other in a unique way in order to communicate information and tell stories (1988, viii–ix). This section of the article focuses, however, more on the narrative aspect of picture books. In general, in Iranian picture books the meaning of the verbal narrative is not necessarily incomplete if read without reference to the pictures. Rather, these books can be located on a spectrum which at one extreme features a few books that lose their meaning if their pictures are removed and at the other features illustrated books where pictures are merely ornamental. As we move from the first extreme toward the other, the verbal text increases until it dominates the pictures, although there is still a dynamic interaction between them, hence pictures change or influence the audience's interpretation of the verbal text. Accordingly, this study focuses on the majority of Iranian picture books located midway through this imagined continuum.

The verbal narratives of these books can be classified into three broad categories. The first includes rewriting and recreation of literary classics, Qur'ānic stories, and especially folktales. Rewriting itself includes two forms: simple rewriting and adaptation. In rewriting the tales are simplified, sometimes abridged, and modified to contemporary prose style. Rewritings usually seek to faithfully transmit the cultural heritage to younger generations. For example, a retelling from Ferdowsi's *Shahnama*, Mostafa Rahmandoust's *Zāl and Sīmurgh* (2013, Zal and the Phoenix), the tale of a baby abandoned on a mountain and raised by the *Sīmurgh* (a mythical phoenix-like bird), is a distinguished instance of rewriting among contemporary picture books. Adaptations attempt to purge traditional folktales from acts of violence or any other elements considered inappropriate for the child audience. Naser Yusefi is among the proponents of this trend. As Foroughozaman Jamali observes,

> In his rewritings, Yusefi depicts children as intelligent, kind, and caring who stand by kind adults in confronting their difficulties. And even bad and unkind adults can also be reformed. It is as if folktales are not good enough in their original versions, and they should be purged of their violent contents in the adapted version.[1]
>
> (2011: 67)

Yusefi utilizes various techniques like modifying the characters of dīvs (demons) and ghouls, eliminating the term "stepmother," and softening harsh language. Therefore, he follows an educational-romantic approach, which seeks to represent to children an ideal picture of a peaceful world and safe life.

Adaptations, however, take a different stance by employing a creative attitude toward cultural heritage. Here, the writer attempts to reinvest the tradition with a novel form and signification that render very different versions of the original stories and invite a creative response from audiences, as exemplified by *Nice and Wise Stories* (2009) a five-volume series by Ali Asghar Seidabadi and *Tales, Games, and Joys* (2011) a ten-volume series by Morteza Khosronejad. Seidabadi opens each book with a question that simultaneously functions as its title, too. Then, three possibilities are proffered to answer this question and a fourth possibility also allows readers to come up with their own choice in an open-ending. Through borrowing famous characters from folktales and appealing to postmodern techniques, the verbal narratives allow the illustrator and the graphic designer to create novel and different works. In the fable *Who Did Khālih Sūskih Marry?*, for instance, an old folktale is recreated but given a postmodern appearance. The book is distinguished from similar picture books by various paratextual devices, by typographical experimentations such as the use of bold-face and italic characters and different font sizes, and by the way the text breaks the frame of the page margins. In the original folktale, Khālih Sūskih (a beetle) is sent by her father to marry a wealthy husband, Mash Ramiẕūn, who already has several wives. On her way to her arranged marriage, she meets some people who also ask for her hand, but she invariably declines them all when they give a harsh answer to her question "How will you beat me if we have domestic troubles?" She finally accepts the proposal of Āqā Mūshih, that is, Mr. Mouse, when he replies "I will beat you with my soft and delicate tail." Seidabadi, however, sets out to subvert this stereotypical understanding of marriage so that Khālih Sūskih marries anyone but Āqā Mūshih. The first possibility is that while traveling on a bus she meets and marries Mash Ramiẕūn. According to the more conventional second possibility, she stays at her father's home waiting for suitors to appear, and Āqā Mūshih is her first suitor, whom she actually marries. In this way, the character is subjected to the stereotypical and closed ending of a story that she dislikes. In the third option she leaves home, refuses all the suitors, and arrives at a school.

There, she meets a teacher who advocates equality for men and women and she marries him. Confronted with her question about domestic violence against women, the teacher replies that "men and women are equal and should mutually respect each other." The book closes with a page dedicated to the ending that the reader is supposed to write for the story. A critical outlook toward tradition, satiric tone, and reader's involvement in this book are prone to attract an audience who is already familiar with the original version of the tale.

The second major trend in the verbal narratives of Iranian picture books seeks to create original works similar to those of western writers and illustrators, especially Anglophone examples, and ignores or marginalizes any dialogue with the native tradition. Navid Seyyed Ali-Akbar, Hadis Lezargholami, and Ahmad Akbarpour are among these writers. They (especially the first two) belong to the new generation of Iranian children's literature and have created significant works in collaboration with creative illustrators. In Akbarpour's *The Giant and The Bicycle* (2009), a first-person narrator tells a story to his daughter, Dursā, who wishes to have a bicycle. He has already promised to buy her a bicycle and the story he narrates is about a boy who is caught while stealing one. Dursā, who herself reported the boy to the police, regrets her decision and asks her father to change the story. Later on, Dursā and her father help the boy break from prison, and she then again intervenes in the plot line and makes her father replace an incident in which she and the thief are shot by the police with an escape to a jungle. There, they meet a young ghoul who loves bicycles and promises he will not devour them if they bring him one. The boy (thief) who has already befriended the ghoul stays with him while Dursā and her father return home where they realize the dream of a bicycle for the boy and ghoul by writing it. Asking "Daddy, when will you buy me a bicycle?" Dursā falls asleep.

The third major trend vacillates between the previous two and creates a new continuum of works which neither rewrite/recreate Iranian traditional tales nor purely follow the western tradition. It utilizes western thematic and stylistic patterns while it also makes intertextual references to Iranian native tradition as well as other contemporary works. Mohammad Reza Shams' *The Madman and the Well* (2008) and *I, I The Big Skull* (2010) are examples that offer a synthesis of the traditional and modern, native and western, and that thus can be considered clear examples of "global thinking and domestic acting" in Iranian children's literature. In *I, I The Big Skull*, Shams creates intertextual relations amongst Iranian folktales, and modern and postmodern western writers. Although this work is far from children's understanding it could be interesting for intellectual and well-versed young adults who enjoy challenging fictions. The narrative incorporates three sub-plots (see Figure 37.1). The first reiterates a well-known nonsense story that opens, "A king had three sons two of whom were dead and the third had no head." The second sub-plot is based on the subversion of a play and later links to another nonsense story while finally recreating it. The last, which apparently seems to be the main plot, is a longer and episodic original story. Using poetic style and satiric tone, each episode is narrated through the perspective of a man who is sitting on a bench in a park and watching what occurs around him before involving himself. The first episode depicts the man watching a large pool lit with variegated lights with clear water where different kinds of fish swim around in agitation. The man, fish, and lights are deeply annoyed that the pool lacks fountains. The man then decides to become a fountain himself, so he takes off his clothes and climbs the stone in the middle of the pool. While the fish, water, lights, and children are all happy, the sentries make the man retreat from his

Figure 37.1   The three sub-plots in *I, I The Big Skull* by Mohammad Reza Shams. Text ©
Mohammad Reza Shams, 2010; illustrations © Golmohammad Khodaverdi, 2010.
Source: Reprinted with kind permission of Ofoq.

position. Each episode is filled with nonsense and extraordinary incidents which make
sense if considered in the context of the whole episode.

The first two sub-plots appear on some pages as well as on page margins with different text directions while the third is usually printed on the page center following normal
right-to-left text direction. The graphic designer also contributes to the verbal text by
more typographical experimentations like splitting, extending, or reversing letters. In the
end, the first sub-plot concludes as its original version, but the second unexpectedly is
joined to the writer's actual life, which is united with the story's main plot (third subplot).
But there is still one more surprise to come: in the end of the book, there is another section, "Instead of a Biography" (top and right-hand side of recto), and "I, Borges, Kafka,
and the rest" on the bottom and left-hand side of verso. So we might be misled into
thinking that we are reading the closing of the book, only to find that this is the opening
of the last part of the book.

This section reveals that the narrator is Shams who is striving to create a story that can
compete (or at least be comparable with) those of Kafka and Borges. Shams, Kafka, and
Borges are sitting on a bench in a park, and Shams is staring at the pool while repeating
the opening line of the first episode of the last sub-plot, that is, "What is the use of a pool
without a fountain?", which motivates him to strip off his clothes, climb the stone, and
become a fountain. The book closes with this remark: "Kafka is sitting beside Borges.
They look at each other. Kafka says, 'Now, this is something' and they both laugh." So
in a circular movement, the opening episode of the book also closes it. Shams reveals
his inclination toward modern and postmodern styles by bringing Borges and Kafka in
his story.

Major trends in the illustrations of Iranian picture books

Similar trends can be discerned in the illustrations of Iranian picture books. Firouzeh
Golmohammadi is a rare instance of an illustrator who resorts to Iranian styles when

adapting versions of Persian classics such as Rumi. Golmohammadi insists that Iranian illustrators and writers should turn to their native heritage and adapt it to their contemporary epoch and language. This can be interpreted as an attempt to return to a purist Iranian national identity (cited in Ghaeni, 2009: 143).

Other illustrators, like Farshid Mesghali, a pioneer picture book illustrator, who can be considered a modernist, and illustrators of later generations, who simultaneously manifest both modern and postmodern tendencies, are hardly influenced by traditional Iranian styles while they follow western styles. Ghaeni contends that Iranian illustrators are inclined toward the west and proposes two reasons to account for this. First this tendency is encouraged by global conditions and international festivals: "Previous generations attempted to localize the works of foreign illustrators, or sought their lost identity in picture books. But the 2000s generation ...mostly tries to follow the trends set by international markets in order to secure a position for themselves there" (2009: 146). She continues: "They have failed to produce any book that addresses a large audience in Iran and responds to local psychological and aesthetic needs, while they have participated in international fairs to introduce Iran's illustrative art to the world – the art which was famous in the world in 1970s too" (146). Second, Ghaeni maintains that the western orientation is caused by the illustrators' detachment from their contemporary society and its concerns, and deems the relationship between illustrators, publishers, critics, librarians, and the audience to be defective – a situation caused, in its turn, by the Iranian centralized system of education, which is merely confined to pre-set textbooks and does not prepare the ground for the introduction and reception of children's literature. Accordingly, as Ghaeni says, Iranian illustrators' participation in international fairs has detached Iranian illustration from its national identity, tradition, and heritage. While an emerging stream of picture book writers creates a dynamic dialogue between the modern and the traditional, for most illustrators international accomplishments take priority over establishing a meaningful dialogue between words and pictures. Largely, they are confined to the illustration art, rather than to words and audience, and attempt to pique the taste of western art juries. While most distinguished western illustrators are deeply committed to interaction with both the verbal narrative and their audience, Iranian illustrators, despite their mastery in their art, ignore their audience. Nevertheless, the dialogic attitude does seem to be gaining recent momentum among Iranian illustrators.

Child-centered and adult-centered attitudes

The two globally known trends can also be noticed in contemporary Iranian picture books: child-centered and adult-centered orientations. As picture books take both children and adults as their audience, there is not always a symmetrical attention to both in their power relations. In other words, some books aim to empower children while others reinforce adult authority over children. So some books might appeal to the needs and aesthetic values of adults while others tend toward prioritizing children. Having these two attitudes in mind, Jamali writes:

> [C]hildhood studies convey that the establishment of childhood as an institution has led societies to consider the child as an autonomous being with specific needs, like adults. This outlook is discernable in recreations by Seidabadi and Khosronejad. The autonomy and dignity of the child goes so far as to reach a level where he/she

is allowed to participate in the creative act of writing the story and its meaning, and becomes the writer's confidante about the mysteries of writing fiction.

(2011: 74).

Iranian picture books nowadays tend to entertain children and give them pleasure besides granting them an active role as an agent who consciously decides and acts. They acknowledge the complexity of children's cognition and aesthetic perception, and cover a wide variety of themes including philosophy, religion, family, society, psychology, recognition, and tolerance of difference. Some publishers invest as much time and energy in publishing high-quality children's books as they do on their adult market products.

There is still a long way to go: as recent studies have also indicated, ethnic, racial and religious minorities, immigrants, and the disabled are still under-represented. As content analysis of picture books has disclosed, issues like anger, fear, single parenthood, war, culture, and social matters are ignored (Mansoureh Sedaghat, 2011).

Word-centered, picture-centered and holistic attitudes

Verbal, pictorial, and holistic approaches are the three major trends in the structure of picture books in Iran. During the 1980s and 1990s, writers' main concern was with the verbal narrative, but this attitude has faded in the 2000s. Word-centered writers seem to forget that they are connected with a pictorial medium as a powerful signifying system that can contribute to the creation of books. Accordingly, they envisage illustration as mere embellishment and assume its purpose is to explicate the verbal content. This approach seems to be rooted in the dominance of words over pictures in Iranian literature. Illustrators had no other choice than to depend on texts that had already gained the consent of the State, because attempts at autonomy and initiation might have been interpreted as ideological transgression.

On the other hand, there are a few illustrators who also feel subjected to the verbal narrative and merely reproduce the content in another medium, whereas most illustrators favor picture-centered attitudes and utilize the words merely for ostentatious display of their artistic abilities, which inevitably leads to a similar attitude toward their audience and children. As Seidabadi (2013) mentions:

[T]he illustrations of Iranian children's books are successful only when they are dissociated from the verbal text and are considered on their own. This is why the Iranian books that are sold in international markets either receive a totally new verbal narrative concordant with the pictures or are drastically modified to create an accordance between text and pictures.

(2)

In contrast, the third approach (the holistic approach) considers the picture book as a unified and organic entity and insists that words and pictures are inseparable. Sometimes an illustrator succeeds in establishing such a constructive dialogue with the work of a writer, who might even tend toward prioritizing words, that the end result offers a totally different reading from the one that the verbal narrative implies. The holistic approach to picture books is becoming more prevalent these days. Some successful examples include *There is Nothing Wrong with It!* by Fariba Kalhor (2009), *Cock-a-Doodle-Doo* by Hadis Lezargholami (2010), and *The Black Dīv (Demon) with a Tail on His Head* by Tahereh Eibod (2011).

In *The Black Dīv with a Tail on His Head*, the verbal narrative tells the story of an old woman who, while sitting on the beach, falls into the sea. In a spontaneous answer to the octopus, the whale, and the shark who appear one by one to eat her up, she claims to be the mother of the Black Dīv with a Tail on His Head. These three animals spread a report of her claim, and consequently the Black Dīv learns about the story and warmly welcomes his god-sent mother and invites her to his home where they live together for a time until she returns to her own house. Up to this point we might consider the old woman to be the protagonist of the story, but the illustrator's emphasis on Dīv on the closing page makes an alternative reading possible. The last page of the book, which is devoid of any words, depicts Dīv's large eyes over the water surface sadly watching the old woman's departure. The verbal narrative invites the reader to accompany the old woman who has finally come out of the sea, while the anxious Dīv's close-up engages the viewer's eye, mind, and heart (see Figure 37.2). Words take the old woman to be the protagonist of the story while, in a subversive alternative reading, Mahkameh Sha'bani, the illustrator, foregrounds the Dīv.

There is Nothing Wrong with It! also succeeds in establishing a significant dialogue between the words and pictures. On a moonlit night, a ghoul visits a woman named

Figure 37.2   Close-up of Dīv from *The Black Dīv with a Tail on His Head* by Tahereh Eibod. Illustration copyright © Mahkameh Sha'bani, 2011.
Source: Reprinted by permission of Amirkabir Publishing House.

Figure 37.3   Illustration from *There's Nothing Wrong With It!*, Fariba Kalhor. Text © Fariba Kalhor, 2011; illustration © Sahar Haghgoo, 2011.
Source: Reprinted with permission of Beh-Nashr.

Moon and devours her. Then he goes to an old man named Haj Baba, but since he does not open the door, the ghoul devours the whole house. The old man and woman marry in the ghoul's belly and live there. The writer, Fariba Kalhor, who has previously proved her ability to explicate philosophical themes in literary form in her *Rhinoceros's Trips* (2011), adopts a satiric tone toward death in *There is Nothing Wrong with It!* She is very succinct and leaves various gaps in the verbal narrative, especially up to page 20, which provides ample possibilities for creativity on the part of the illustrator. Sahar Haghgoo's elegant, clear, and interpretative illustrations open a dialogue with Kalhor's words to create a very interesting text for a young audience. Haghgoo proves that an illustrator can create his/her own pictorial narrative out of the verbal narrative in a way that adds to the suspense, beauty, and pleasure of the verbal narrative and opens new vistas for the active engagement of the audience in the creative process. If we overlook the illustrator's shortcomings in the last three pages, where the writer also falls into the trap of verbosity, Haghgoo functions as a film director who has created a movie based on an available scenario which gives repeated pleasure to its audience (see Figure 37.3).

Major critical and theoretical trends in studies of Iranian picture books

The Institute for the Intellectual Development of Children and Young Adults (IIDCYA) and the Children's Book Council of Iran (CBCI), both founded in the early 1960s, have had prominent roles in establishing children's literature in Iran (Khosronejad 2004, 1906); the former has published picture books and the latter has promoted reading and evaluating them. Early in its career, IIDCYA first invited well-known Iranian writers, and illustrators to create the first artistic picture books. *The Little Black Fish* by Samad Behrangi is one of the best examples of such works and of course the only Hans Christian Andersen Award winner for its illustrations so far. After IIDCYA, there have been several successful publishers in the domain of children's literature including Ofoq, Beh-Nashr, and others.

The 2000s witnessed the establishment of children's literature as an academic discipline and its institutionalization in Iran. The establishment of the Shiraz University Center for Children's Literature Studies (SUCCLS) and M.A. programs in children's literature, as well as the biannual publication of the journal *Iranian Children's Literature Studies* mark a turning point in this realm. Succeeding other individual attempts in translation like those of Razi Hirmandi (translator of Shel Silverstein and Dr. Seuss), Nasrin Vakili, Tahereh Adinehpour, and Farmehr Monjazi, SUCCLS have translated a series that includes picture books by Maurice Sendak, Anthony Browne, Leo Lioni, Shaun Tan and others. The M.A. program includes a course on picture books which explores various examples from around the world, and the program produces a substantial number of theses which explore the significance of interactions between pictures and words as well as the holistic approach to picture books. *Iranian Children and Adult Youth's Book Review and Informational Journal, The Research Quarterly of Children and Youth's Literature* and *Roshanan Quarterly* have also dedicated special issues to picture books.

While the interactions between words and pictures have been previously emphasized by, for example, Soraya Ghezelayagh (2004) and Ghaeni (2011), the holistic approach to picture books is quite recent and is not dominant in the criticism. Rather, analysis of picture books remains mostly asymmetrical, with an emphasis on either words or pictures rather than a more evenly holistic approach.

Conclusion

What is the relationship between polarities such as modern *and* traditional, child-centered *and* adult-centered, picture-centered *and* word-centered? Whereas child-centrism is a modern inclination, picture-centered illustrators do not usually attempt to meet the needs and tastes of children. Rather, they mostly seek their own adult goals. On the other hand, word-centrism seems to imply adult-centrism and many word-centered writers do not leave enough space for the illustrator to contribute to the artistic creation as a whole, and this might point to the general problem of accomplished editing in Iran. Accordingly, they seem to ignore children's demand for imagination and pictures. However, these very writers attempt to empower the child by granting him/her agency, hence they realize child-centrism. Besides the complexity and multi-layered nature of reality, the fractured state of artists and critics in the age of globalization can also explain this tension. Seemingly many artists have neither a deep understanding of their native traditions nor of modernity. Similarly their understanding of the essence of picture books and children is deficient. Thus they simultaneously tend toward the traditional, modern, and even postmodern. To overcome this, Iranian writers and illustrators should establish a creative dialogue with 1) their native traditions, 2) their addressees and their contemporary writers and illustrators at national level, and 3) the modern and postmodern world (Khosronejad, 2011).

"[C]hildren's literature is becoming more and more national and isolated," Nikolajeva (1996) claims, "[a]lthough the general exchange of information in the world is growing," (43). Similarly, in her investigation of Chinese picture books, Fengxia Tan (2013) agrees that Nikolajeva's claim holds true in the context of China. She writes, "As far as the nationalization of Chinese indigenous picture books is concerned, this pursuit in the new millennium can be considered as a kind of cultural self-defense in globalization as well as a strategy to propel native cultures toward the world" (84). Such general claims, however, should be accompanied by a note of caution, as the situations in Iran and China are quite disparate, arguably because of their cultural, social, and political differences. In the age of globalization any country's children's literature can be considered to be positioned somewhere on a continuum between the global and the local. The place of each country on this spectrum is thus determined not only by its own cultural, social, and political conditions but also by its attitude toward the west.

The tension between the traditional and the modern is manifested in all aspects of Iranian picture books. The question, "Do we have Iranian picture books as they exist in the west?" was the topic of a forum in 2013 (Seidabadi et al, 2013). Both the formulation of the question and the ensuing discussion assume an endorsement of the western definition of picture books and hence further assume that the failure to produce such books in Iran is a deficiency. Kianoosh Gharibpour, an art director and graphic designer, confesses that he has attempted to organize Iranian writers and illustrators to create a definitive example of a picture book as it is known in the west, but in vain. He speculates that this can never be achieved, due to the word-centric attitudes of writers and picture-centric attitudes of illustrators. Seidabadi, a well known writer and critic, concludes:

> We are in a situation in which our previous experiences do not seem to suffice. A new entity, i.e. picture book, is introduced that engages our children… We have not produced a native version of it and are simply consuming the translated foreign ones on the market … I think we can neither argue that the Iranian version of picture books should be ignored, nor can we disregard what is imposed on us from abroad. Now, how are we supposed to react?
>
> (18)

Seidabadi's stance clearly shows the tension between the traditional and the modern in Iran. This tension leads to a new ambivalence that might not be a serious concern for the child reader, but is nevertheless a great challenge for the adult reader and, on a larger scale, for all those living in countries where national identity is under strain in an age of globalized identities.

Notes

1 All translations are our own.
2 Dates for Iranian publications are dual, referencing both the Iranian and Western calendar.

Bibliography[2]

Akbarpour, Ahmad. 1388Š/2009. *Ghūl va dūcharkhih* [The Giant and The Bicycle]. Tehran: Ofoq. [Persian].
Behrangi, Samad. 1346Š/1967. *Māhī sīāh-i kūchūlū* [The Little Black Fish]. Tehran: The Institute for Research on the History of Children's Literature in Iran. [Persian].

Eibod, Tahereh. 1390Š/2011. *Dīv-i sīāh-i dum bi sar* [The Black Dīv with a Tail on His Head]. Tehran: Amirkabir Publishing House. [Persian].

Ghaeni, Zohreh. 1388Š/2009. "Az Franklin tā Shabāvīz: taṣvīrgarī-i īrān dar chishmandāzī tārīkhī" ["From Franklin to Shabaviz: A Historical Survey on Iranian Illustrations"]. *Herfeh Honarmand,* 30: 136–156. [Persian].

Ghaeni, Zohreh. 1390Š/2011. *Taṣvīrgarī-i kitāb'hāyi kūdakān, tārīkh, ta'rīf'hā va gūni'hā* [Children's Books Illustration, History, Definitions and Genre]. Tehran: The Institute for Research on the History of Children's Literature in Iran. [Persian].

Ghezelayagh, Soraya. 1383Š/2004. *Adabīyāt-i kūdakān va nūjavānān va tarvīj-i khvāndan* [Children's Literature and the Promotion of Reading]. Tehran: Samt. [Persian].

Jamali, Foroughozaman. 1390Š/2011. "Chihriy-i kūdak dar afsāni'hāy-i bāznivīsī va bāzāfarīnī'shudi" ["Child's Image in Rewritten and Recreated Folktales"]. *Roshanan Quarterly* 11: 54–76. [Persian].

Kalhor, Fariba. 1388Š/2009. *Chi 'ībī dārih!* [There is Nothing Wrong with It!]. Mashad: Beh-Nashr. [Persian].

Kalhor, Fariba. 1390Š/2011. *Safarhā-ī kargadan* [Rhinoceros's Trips]. Tehran: Amirkabir Publishing House. [Persian].

Khosronejad, Morteza. 2004. "Iran." In *International Companion Encyclopedia of Children's Literature*, Second Edition, Volume 2, Edited by Peter Hunt: 1095–1098.

Khosronejad, Morteza. 1390Š/2011. *Qiṣṣih, bāzī, shādī* [Tales, Games, and Joys]. Mashad: Beh-Nashr. [Persian].

Khosronejad, Morteza. 2011. "Iranian picture books: the picture and the story of national identity formation in Iran." Paper presented at *The Child and the Book Conference.* Oslo, April 8–10. [Unpublished paper].

Lezargholami, Hadis. 1389Š/2010. *Qūqūlī ghūghūl* [Cock-a-Doodle-Doo]. Tehran: Ofoq. [Persian].

Nikolajeva, Maria. 1996. *Children's Literature Comes of Age: Towards a New Aesthetics.* New York: Garland.

Nodelman, Perry. 1988. *Words about Pictures.* Athens and London: University of Georgia Press.

Rahmandoust, Mostafa. 1392Š/2013. *Zāl va Sīmurgh* [Zāl and Sīmurgh]. Tehran: IIDCYA.

Sedaghat, Mansoureh. 1390Š/2011. "Barrasy-i darūnmāyi'hā-i āshkār, pinhān va tuhī dar dāstān'hāyi kūdak" ["A Study of the Overt, Covert and Null Themes in Iranian Children's Fiction"]. M.A. thesis in History and Philosophy of Education, Shiraz University. [Persian].

Seidabadi, Ali Asghar. 1388Š/2009. *Qiṣṣihā-i shīrīn-i maghzdār* [Nice and Wise Stories]. Tehran: Ofoq. [Persian].

Seidabadi, Ali Asghar. 1388Š/2009. *Khālih Sūskih bā kī izdivāj kard?* [Who Did Khālih Sūskih Marry?]. Tehran: Ofoq. [Persian].

Seidabadi, Ali Asghar, Kianoosh Gharibpour, Sahar Tarhandeh, Farshid Shafiei. 1392Š/2013. "Guftu'gūyi gurūhī: az matn tā taṣvīr" ["A Forum on Picture books: From Text to Pictures"]. *The Research Quarterly of Children and Youth's Literature* 7 (58): 6–30. [Persian].

Shams, Mohammad Reza. 1387Š/2008. *Dīvānih va chāh* [The Madman and the Well]. Tehran: Ofoq. [Persian].

Shams, Mohammad Reza. 1389Š/2010. *Man mani kal-i gūndih* [I, I The Big Skull]. Tehran: Ofoq. [Persian].

Tan, Fengxia. 2013. "Breakout and Bondage: the Nationalization of Chinese Picture books." In *Looking Out and Looking In: National Identity in Picture books of the New Millennium*, edited by Åse Marie Ommundsen, 75–87. Oslo: Novus Press.

Further reading

Khosronejad, Morteza. 1387Š/2008. "Naghd va naẓarīyih-i adabīyāt-i kūdak dar īrān: mugh'īyat, vīzhigī'hā, ẓarūrat'hā" ["Children's Literature Theory and Criticism in Iran: Situation, Characteristics and Necessities."] In *In Quest for the Centre: Greats of Children's Literature Theory and Criticism*, edited by Morteza Khosronejad, 41–67. Tehran: IIDCYA. [Persian].

38

MULTIMODAL CHILDREN'S BOOKS IN TURKEY

Illustrated books and picture books

Ilgım Veryeri Alaca

Picturebooks represent an underdeveloped potential in Turkey, given the depth and richness of the country's literary and visual heritage. Turkish—a part of the Turkish language family and linked with languages such as Tatar, Uzbek and Kazakh, to name a few—is used widely across Europe and Asia (Göksel and Kerslake 2005). Turkish children's books overall are nourished from a large and diverse number of sources, mostly European, Anatolian, Central Asian, Persian and Arabic. The ancient land of Anatolia has for centuries been a literary wellspring for important writers, poets and storytellers including Homer, Aesop, Nasreddin, Yunus Emre and Rumi. In terms of visual heritage, the history from which Turkish children's books might draw extends from the Hittites to the Sumerians, from Byzantine mosaics to Ottoman miniatures. Yet in terms of the production of children's literature, most books so far have consisted of illustrated children's books, where a focus on the development of cognitive and linguistic abilities has rested on the text, with the illustrations themselves little more than an afterthought. Access to children's literature in Turkey is largely tied to affordability: the wealthiest families spend fourteen times more on educational expenditures than the poorest (Alonso et al. 2011), and premium picturebooks, priced higher than illustrated books, remain a luxury for the few. Most children who are not enrolled in preschool education, 70.8 percent in 2011 (Eurostat 2014), might have no access to picturebooks at all. While there are constant attempts to promote reading, bookstart projects and picturebooks in libraries are not common.[1] Enriched Libraries Project (Z-Kütüphane) run by the Ministry of National Education (MoNE) is an attempt launched in 2011 to jumpstart school libraries including preschools which will gradually increase the access of children to quality picturebooks.

In 2014, over a million copies of a newly designed workbook *My Cotton Candy 1–2* was printed and distributed nationwide for free to children enrolled in preschool. This was carried out as a part of the project, "Supporting Preschool Education" run by MoNE and supported by the European Union and UNICEF. The visual component of these books is more functional than imaginative, however, and the verbal text is dominant. This is in line with the generic emphasis on the verbal text in most children's books produced in Turkey. While literature for children, including that of oral storytelling, has been a research area in Turkey, innovative book design geared towards children that pays close attention to visual aspects of children's literature has not yet been a key priority. A quest for high quality picturebooks that can trigger the joy of reading especially in the informal education environment of the home accords with the urgency towards improving early and primary childhood education qualitatively in Turkey, which, according to the 2009 Program for International Student Achievement (PISA) scores, is ranked thirty-two out of thirty-four OECD countries (Blanchy and Şaşmaz 2011). The research associates skills tested in PISA with preschool exposure to books and shared reading (OECD 2012), and picturebooks are thus particularly important as a resource for early childhood development. At a point in their development when children cannot yet read, thinking via images should be prioritized, triggering visual learning and problem-solving skills (Nodelman 1988).

The growth of children's books in Turkey with almost 14 percent market share among other publications faces numerous challenges, some of which are faced by children's literature overall. Translated books, from Europe, for instance, continue to dominate the market, although local major publishers have gained momentum since 2000, with noteworthy publications of Can Çocuk, Elma, Günışığı, İletişim, Marsık, Mavibulut Redhouse Kidz, Remzi, Tudem, and Yapı Kredi (Turkish Publishers Association n.d. Kozikoğlu 2013). Publishers such as Alef, Desen and Ithaki are printing works by Shaun Tan and Peter Sis, thereby expanding the concept of picturebooks into crossover literature. Private publishers, as well as publishers with government support from institutions like Tübitak and İşbank, tend to publish a variety of children's books such as information books, storybooks, picturebooks, and alphabet books, introducing a rich array of books to the readers. A qualitative gap, however, continues to remain between most local and translated books, and this impedes development of a local children's literature. Only a small number of picturebooks are translated from Turkish to other languages some under the auspices of the Translation and Publication Grant Program of Turkey (TEDA), an effort to support foreign publishers to translate Turkish books that express the cultural heritage of the country as well as its artistic and literary resonances.

While picturebooks influence aesthetic, linguistic and cognitive processes of the child (Colomer et al. 2010), and have the potential to go beyond didacticism via innovative image and text relations, enhancing creative and divergent thinking, there is currently an insufficient platform to build high quality picturebooks through support for illustrators themselves; a course on children's books illustration is not offered in most universities, publishers give most illustrators a limited amount of time and resources to work on a picturebook, thus precluding the requisite for long hours of contemplation and craftsmanship essential for a fully achieved visual page. The fruitful cooperation of the publisher, writer and illustrator is a work in progress as well. A final challenge for children's publishing is that e-books from Turkey are not yet developed widely partly due to emerging standards for the distribution of electronic information. Furthermore, factors such as family, social pressure, economy and tradition inhibit creativity in Turkey, as Oral has argued (Oral 2006). Yet forays by determined individuals have started to lay the groundwork for a picturebook tradition worthy of Turkey's rich visual and literary heritage, and which can enhance literacy across Turkey's young population. Mustafa Delioğlu has been celebrated for his illustrations in watercolour at times reminiscent of characters from the traditional shadow play Karagöz. Can Göknil and Behiç Ak have written and illustrated stories. Their work cultural heritage in a modern and personalized way. Among a new generation of illustrators, Deniz Üçbaşaran's lyric aesthetics integrating ornaments and Ayşe İnan Alican's detailed imagery in acrylics have been awarded by

IBBY Turkey and praised by parents and children at large. Sadi Güran's pensive figures, Sedat Girgin's witty characters and Reha Barış's dynamic compositions introduced a new type of aesthetics with their uncommon color palette. Author Yekta Kopan's international collaboration with Cuban illustrator Alex Pelayo on "The Nose" resulted in a unique book and picturebook aesthetics. Complementary relations of chaotic imagery with a simple story line sustain the child's search for the "nose", that is lost throughout the pages, reminiscent of Nikolai Gogol's story. The overall design makes this book much superior to forays into international collaboration in the earlier 20th century and constitutes a new direction in children's books publishing.

The role of institutions in making picturebooks

Institutions in Turkey have historically played a role in the development of children's literature, including picturebooks. İbrahim Mütefferrika initiated the first printing house during the Ottoman Empire in the 18th century, printing a book in Turkish in 1729 (Watson 1968). The influence of institutions has been double-edged, serving both to promote the visual aspects of literature and to set key limitations. Illustrated books dominated the 20th century in children's books from Turkey during processes of modernization and westernization. The foundation of the Republic in 1923 brought with it reforms such as the change from the Arabic to the Latin alphabet (1928), which had a profound effect on children's books and literacy. Such changes also required an adaptation period. The prominence of illustrated books in comparison with picturebooks is not only the result of economy or education but also of the place of visuality in Turkish society over several centuries. The painting tradition in Turkey emerged mainly after the 18th century. Miniatures in Ottoman books were executed for the Ottoman upper class, mainly the sultan. The general public were accustomed to oral traditions, poetry and riddles. Folk tales illustrated with lithography technique in 19th century revealed a different taste flourishing from folk aesthetics (Derman 1988). Drawing and painting lessons in the western sense emerged first in the army in the 18th century. Through this time, thus, visuality in art and literacy was limited in its circulation to very specific subsets of the population. Subsequently, the pioneers of Turkish painting were pashas. The first higher education institution teaching fine arts, the Sanayi-i Nefise School (currently called Mimar Sinan University) was founded in 1882 (Arsal 2000). During the early Republican Period, texts with illustrations became more widespread, but the common practice was to integrate foreign graphics into texts, a practice that had a coarse impact on the changing visual culture. In the text geared towards students, for example, printed in 1928 and called *An Enjoyable Reader for Republican Children*, it is suggested that the didactic hodja figure is to be replaced by a modern teacher with a suit, fedora and a smiling face. The students are illustrated as relaxed and in casual conversation with the teacher. The illustration in this case was signed by a foreign artist (Fortna 2011). Only later did such works come to be composed with more fluidly associated text and image relations.

An alphabet book cover in 1937 illustrated by graphic designer İhap Hulusi Görey signified an emerging professional input in book design by local artists (Bassa and Ural 2002). The *Clever Ali* series of 1968 (see Figure 38.1), written by a primary school teacher Rasim Kaygusuz, was illustrated by Selçuk Seymen. The simple drawing, a characteristic of the series, became extremely popular among children and teachers in the context of the first year of reading. Yet the scarceness of paper and materials limited prosperous book publication activity until the 1970s. Most books were printed in small format with only

Baba   Cin Ali   At

Cin Ali, bak! At.
Bak, Cin Ali, bak. Bu at.
- Baba, o atı bana al.

— 1 —

Figure 38.1 From *Cin Ali'nin Atı* (The Horse of Cin Ali), Rasim Kaygusuz.
Source: Reprinted with kind permission of Cin Ali Publications.

the cover in colour and remaining imagery in black and white. In 1980, the military coup created a further disruption in the production of literature (Alpöge 2002, Erdoğan 2004).

The role of institutions in the rise of an emergent group of picturebook artists and academic specialists such as Nazan Erkmen was critical, particularly the role of fine arts universities like Mimar Sinan, Marmara and Gazi. Children's books illustration is often taught as a part of graphic design courses and children's literature is offered as a course in most education departments as a part of teacher training. Yet, a program solely dedicated to illustration of children's books still does not exist. Apart from institutions with resources such as the MoNE and National Library of Turkey, there is no major centre with holdings of national as well as international picturebooks or an extensive archive of older, out-of print-books, original illustrations that children's book illustrators, researchers, publishers and writers can draw upon. Existing children's books collections are quite fragmentary. The Vehbi Koç and Ankara Research Center (VEKAM) holds educational documents such as children's literature along with textbooks, curricula, and yearbooks, mostly from the period 1923–1945. UNICEF and the Mother and Child Education Foundation (AÇEV) work with children and introduce children's books yet do not prioritize their collection or production. Bosphorus University was instrumental in promoting children's books and housing the international The Child and The Book Conference in 2007. The IBBY Turkey, known as the Child and Youth Publishers Association (ÇGYD), gives annual awards for children's books. Other associations that exist in relation to children's books include Writers of Children's and Youth Literature Association, the Child Foundation and Ankara University Child and Youth Literature Center (ÇOGEM). Personal initiatives also exist; children's book author Gülten Dayıoğlu has established a foundation and an award, for example, that supports the growth of children's literature. *Birdolapkitap* is a web-based forum of children's literature in Turkey run by volunteers. Publishers such as TUDEM and Günışığı also play a role, both bodies organizing small conferences and competitions about children's literature. Newspapers such as Cumhuriyet, Radikal, Birgün and Aydınlık review children's books weekly, as does the print and open access online magazine İyi Kitap.

The frontiers of children's books in Turkey

The expansion in the children's books market is visible especially at the International İstanbul Book Fair. Children's books in general in Turkey are as yet tentative about handling diverse aesthetics such as a predominantly dark or black-and-white palette, as well as certain issues such as violence, death, diversity, and multiculturalism. Postmodern picturebooks are a novel phenomenon within traditions that do not necessarily embrace profound image and text relations. Picturebooks are not often considered as crossover literature geared towards both children and adults.

In a study that investigates children's rights as represented in the 100 Basic Literary Works (100 Temel Eser), the major reading list recommended for primary education by MoNE, Karaman-Kepenekçi wrote that statements not necessarily prioritizing children's rights were apparent. This is thought to be linked to the fact that the books in this list were written before the United Nations adopted the Convention on the Rights of the Child (CRC) in 1989 (Karaman-Kepenekçi 2010). Turkey undersigned the CRC in 1990 as the 43rd country. Adaptations of these works are at times mass printed in low-quality volumes and are only minimally illustrated, affordable especially by families of low socio-economic status. These books are read alongside the textbooks that are distributed for free by the MoNE. Children outside the big cities in particular have a low chance of seeing a premium selection of picturebooks since the policy of free textbook distribution has an unintended effect of decreasing sales in many small bookstores, leaving print runs of children's books in the one or two thousands (Turkish Publishers Association n.d.). There is thus a uniformity of books to which most children are exposed, which leads to conservatism and a threat against the production and translation of a diversity of books.

There are a number of books that have confronted the restrictive boundaries set by this pervasive conservatism. Making a point about children's rights, *Letters to Havva* (Figure 38.2) is a book that is at the threshold of artist's books, emphasizing a call for a change in children's narratives. The short story *Havva* (Bener 1952) triggered a debate in a Turkish children's literature class in 2005 such that children were impelled to respond via letter writing and drawing to its protagonist. Their work was later collected as *Letters to Havva* consisting of visual and verbal reflections of children towards the book's stepchild

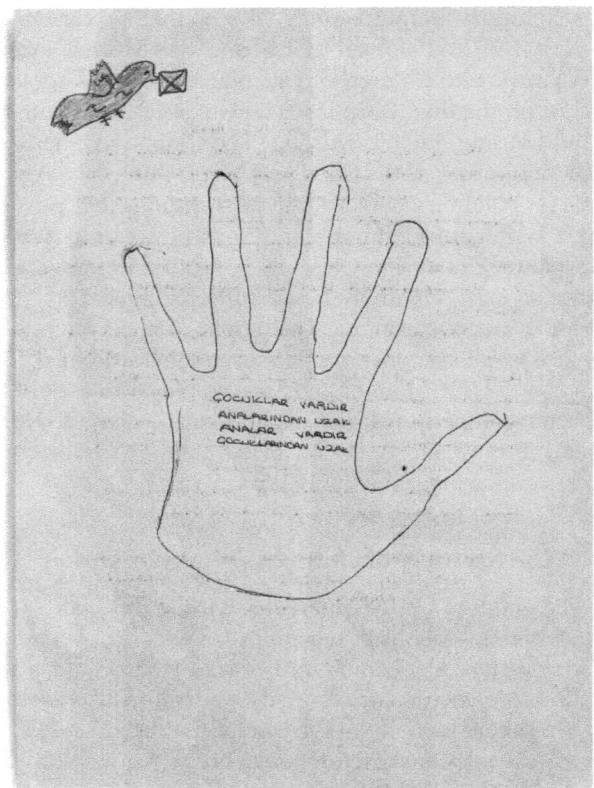

Figure 38.2   Gültekin, A.O. and Gültekin, A. (eds.) (2005) *Havva'ya Mektuplar* (Letters to Havva).
Source: Reproduced with kind permission of Norgunk Publications, Istanbul.

protagonist who has been mistreated by her host family. Children's responses reflect an emerging sense of children's rights as they empathize, communicate with Havva via drawing and writing. Likewise, the "Children's Rights Children's Books Project" that involved children's input was carried out by Anadolu Kultur. Asa Lind's story *Biliam and I While Thinking* was illustrated by children from Turkey during a series of workshops and printed as a picturebook.

Betül Sayın's *5 Children, 5 İstanbuls* is a particularly notable effort to create a picturebook that is faithful to the layered cultural heritage of İstanbul. Depicting İstanbul as a hub of universal culture, the book presents a playful story arc which involves five child protagonists starting with Mert, an inhabitant of contemporary İstanbul and going back in time to the girl-with-a-bone-hairpin. The protagonist embraces the heritage of the previous generation each time after noticing a curious object kept in a corner such as a fez, a mirror, a sack with bronze coins and a hairpin made out of bone. This book bridges diverse eras in a simple-to-understand chronology represented visually, and with an art historical consciousness. The illustrator and writer Sayın transforms the color palette, architecture and urban setting while introducing culture-specific artistic acts such as pottery making as a change occurs in the timeline. She also makes use of colour symbolism such as using purple for the page of Helen of Byzantium, the colour that the royals of that era preferred.

Adaptation as genre and the European influence: *Who would be Afraid of Red Riding Hood?*

Given that Turkish children's literature has in recent times been dominated by translated books from Europe, it is not a surprise that local production of picturebooks has found success in building on bonds with the widely distributed story of Red Riding Hood. The national award winner *Who would be Afraid of Red Riding Hood?* (see Figure 38.3) is a metafictional retelling of the Riding Hood story with a focus on the wolf, who in this case wears the red hood. This picturebook is initially the result of an extensive collaboration between the writer Sara Şahinkanat, illustrator Ayşe İnan Alican and the editor of Kırçiçeği Publications, Aslı Motchane. There is a textual and a pictorial play in the book (Beckett 2002) where details, including toys, books, and a family portrait, familiarize the reader with the wolf's secluded life in the forest.

The theme of the picturebook develops as the mother wolf directs questions to the little wolf who wants to go out to play in the forest. On each opening page they go over the potential dangers to make sure the young wolf can take precautions and avoid a close encounter with the real Red Riding Hood, the grandmother and ultimately the hunter, to elude the presumed ending. In Figure 38.3, the third-person text translates, "The mother looked at her child with love, and took the child on her lap, hiding away her worries she

Figure 38.3 From *Kim Korkar Kırmızı Başlıklı Kız'dan?* (Who would be Afraid of Red Riding Hood?). Sara Şahinkanat and Ayşe İnan Alican, YKY, 2014.
Source: Reproduced with kind permission of Yapi Kredi Cultural Activities, Art and Publishing Ltd.

whispered…" They decide to make a poster that the young wolf can hang in case he needs to take a nap saying that he only eats pasta with broccoli and that wolves no longer like being demeaned as negative figures in fairy tales.

Further intertextuality is introduced by the collection of books that belong to the little wolf and his mother: the mother's books are *My Name is Red* by Orhan Pamuk, *Animal Farm* by George Orwell, as well as a book entitled *Development of a Child Wolf*. For the child, two children's books have been re-titled as *Today's Wolves are Wonderful* and *The Booted Wolf* (original titles, *Today's Children are Wonderful* by Aziz Nesin, and *The Puss in Boots*). The arching depiction of the walls of the room supported with the use of curves and curvilinear objects give the space a cosy feeling. While aspects of the characters and setting are European, Turkish aesthetics nonetheless predominate in the book. The romanticized placidity of the house as central to life features strongly, with the corollary that public space is not necessarily a favoured haven. The segregation of an idealized interior space from the outside world just like the snow globe in the background hints at a metanarrative intersecting the western one (Stephens and McCallum 2013) in Turkish literature evident in texts such as Yakup Kadri Karaosmanoğlu's *The Rented Mansion* (Bertram 2008) or Orhan Pamuk's *The Museum of Innocence* (which has a spatial counterpart in the form of a museum housed in an old wooden Turkish house, also called the Museum of Innocence).

Folk tales, riddles and rhymes

A major source of adaptions in Turkey is the cycle of tales concerning Nasreddin Hodja, a satirical Sufi figure who both dispenses wisdom and is a figure of fun. He is perhaps best known internationally by Demi's picturebook *A Tale from Turkey: The Hungry Coat* (2004), but there have been numerous adaptations within Turkey. Of particular interest is a compilation of stories printed in 1961, accompanied by the remarkable line drawings of Abidin Dino, although with its few illustrations and dense text the book targets adults rather than children. Another notable example is by Serap Deliorman, illustrator of *Learning How to Reason with Nasreddin Hodja*, a collection of stories accompanied by questions that enhance critical thinking skills. The illustrations of Deliorman are especially significant for composing scenes in which today's children appear with Nasreddin, whereas most books do not represent present-day scenes.

Whereas Perrault and Grimm stories have been adapted by many artists, writers and publishers internationally, children's books featuring the legendary sage Dede Korkut and Turkish rhymes, riddles or folktales have not been commonly circulated outside their native, Turkish-speaking communities. *The Book of Dede Korkut* is a collection of epic stories of the Oghuz Turks and represents the oral storytelling tradition and heritage of pre-Islamic Turks especially. These stories remain obscure for children outside of Turkey and possibly certain Turkic countries since there has not been a constant adaptation, modernization and interpretation of them in different languages with current aesthetic sensibilities. While the Dede Korkut stories built the foundations of stories for children in Turkey, their initial transfer to the written format took place in the 15th century, then becoming widely distributed in the 20th century as illustrated books (Sarıyüce 2012, Şimşek 2006).

A significant part of oral literature was riddling and riddle contests, a part of daily life for adults and children in the form of a game, a ritual at weddings, a form of instruction or a way to show aptitude. In many of these instances the oral narrative was improvised and acted out. At times obscure and loaded with metaphors, riddles were actively used until the early 20th century (Başgöz 1965). Rhymes on the other hand have been a hodge-podge component of Turkish tales, usually repeated at the beginning, middle and end of stories according to the improvisation of the storyteller (Boratav 2013). İlhan Başgöz draws connections with performance art and Turkish folk romances, in which the story-teller – variously called *ozan* "poet", *aşık* "lover", or *meddah* "storyteller" – plays a key role at times as a mystic or a performer, and sometimes plays the saz, a string instrument. The 19th century involved a turn from eastern tale traditions to western traditions in Turkey, yet the first half of the 20th century still bore significant traces of transition.

An interest in documenting and retelling Turkish tales emerged in the 19th century, starting with the attempts of Hungarian turcologist and linguist Ignacz Kunos (1860–1945). Friedrich Wilhelm Radloff (1837–1918) studied the languages of Central Asian Turks and collected epic, lyric and prose tales. Following these studies, Ziya Gökalp (1879–1924) also studied and documented Turkish tales. A prominent scholar in the field of folk literature was Pertev Naili Boratav (1907–1998). Eflatun Cem Güney (1896–1981) and Tahir Alangu (1915–1973) adapted Turkish tales for children. The transfer of oral stories and rhymes from Turkey into children's books continued throughout the twentieth century and some are translated to English (Walker 1990). The Uysal-Walker Archive of Turkish Oral Narrative at Texas Tech University is prominent for offering an open access resource.

A major picturebook that utilizes the cultural heritage of Turkish tales and rhymes is *Lunatic Hasan* by artist and writer Can Göknil. Göknil makes use of Pertev Naili Boratav's research to create an amusing picturebook which introduces ancient oral story traditions and folklore accompanied with rhyming dialogue (Figure 38.4). *Lunatic Hasan* is a surreal

Figure 38.4   Göknil, *Lunatic Hasan.*
Source: Reproduced with kind permission of Can Children's Publications, Istanbul.

tale located in a liminal space – "the neighbourhood that does not exist". The protagonist leaves this space in search of a wife. He leaves behind his friends, animals such as the mosquito king, owl judge, tailor bird, and flower seller donkey. The book makes use of exaggeration, as when the protagonist purchases a cup of yogurt, blends it with ninety-nine glasses of water and prepares *ayran*, a Turkish drink, for the road or when the protagonist needs to move a mountain. Absurd compositions introduce such nonsense as men losing a camel train in a watermelon. Among other strange things that happen is a windmill grinding roasted chickpeas, a local variant of an international folktale (Aarne-Thompson type 565, the Magic Mill). Behind its entertaining tone, literary nonsense bridges the book-form and the rhyme/riddle traditions. At the same time, *Lunatic Hasan* encompasses social commentary, as its parody comments on ethics at many levels, as when the coffee shop owner deceives Hasan in order to marry him to his daughter. Hasan, at his wedding, sees the bride, who is bizarre and grotesque, and gets so scared that he escapes on two horses through a key hole, a playful evocation of absurdity and tradition. The protagonist at last becomes a storyteller, highlighting the ranking of oral storytellers as poets/mystics/lovers, a status gained traditionally only after a certain maturation period.

Conclusion

Despite the rich sources and cultural heritage in Turkey, children's books over the last few decades have left the visual language of the works mostly as a supplement, as illustrated, small format books dominated the market. Some inspiring experiments in picturebook production have marked a recent direction in Turkish children's books, but illustrations are generally still literal accounts of things mentioned in the text, rather than engaging interactively with the story. Sophisticated arrangements of image and text in picturebooks have the capacity to enhance dialogue and problem solving skills, as well as activate imaginations and a sense of irony. Unfortunately, little research on picturebooks is available in Turkish, and the absence of a major international children's library and media center hinders publishers, writers and illustrators from being able to fully absorb contemporary trends in picturebooks. Didactic books exist in Turkey, and the tradition of giving advice in books (Şimşek, 2006) and animations – a continuation of an older literary tradition – are to some extent still alive. The government-funded television channel TRT Çocuk geared towards children attracts more attention than books. The adaptations of traditional stories such as of Egghead (Keloğlan) are common and popular on this TV channel.

Turkish children's literature, which is essentially an art form on the one hand, and on the other a body of scholarly work, can grow by studying recently created picturebooks and ongoing research. This can be supported by policies to enhance reading in the early years. More and more didacticism can lead the way to playful books, linking tradition to innovation, local to global, encouraging an international dialogue. Turkey's cultural heritage introduces a hybrid imaginative realm for a child. In this regard, children's picturebooks from Turkey promise a flourishing production period, one of the outcomes of which should be a fascinating addition to the field of international picturebook and children's media research.

Note

1 There are nearly 23 million children between the ages 0 to 17 in Turkey. Approximately ten million child users checked out three and a half million books from 1,073 public libraries and 47 children's libraries in 2013. (TUIK 2014)

Bibliography

Alonso, J. D., McLaughlin, M. and Oral, I. (2011) "Improving the Quality and Equity of Basic Education in Turkey, Challenges and Options," World Bank Report No 54131-TR, http://siteresources.worldbank.org/TURKEYEXTN/Resources/361711-1216301653427/5218036-1326807255367/EducationQualityReport2011-en.pdf (accessed 7 September 2014).

Alpöge, G. (2002) "New Trends in Children's Literature in Turkey Today," *Bookbird: A Journal of International Children's Literature*, 40(1): 27–30.

Arsal, O. (2000) *The Sociology of Modern Ottoman Painting, 1838–1924* (Modern Osmanlı Resminin Sosyolojisi-1838–1924), İstanbul: Yapı Kredi Publications.

Başgöz, İ. (1965) "The Function of Turkish Riddles," *Journal of the Folklore Institute*, 2(2): 132–147.

Bassa, Z. and Ural, S. (2002) "Children's Book Illustrations in Turkey Today," *Bookbird: A Journal of International Children's Literature*, 2: 32–34.

Beckett, S. (2002) *Recycling Red Riding Hood*, New York: Routledge.

Bener, V. O. (1952) *Dost Hikayeler*, Ankara, Seçilmiş Hikayeler Dergisi Kitapları.

Bertram, C. (2008) *Imagining the Turkish House: Collective Visions of Home*, Austin: University of Texas Press.

Blanchy, N. K. and Şaşmaz, A. (2011) "PISA 2009: Where does Turkey stand?" *Turkish Policy Quarterly*, 10(2): 125–135.

Boratav, P. N. (2013) *Az Gittik Uz Gittik* (Travel a little, Travel far), Ankara: İmge Publications.

Brenifier, O. and Millon, I. (2000) *Learning How to Think with Nasreddin Hodja* (Nasreddin Hoca ile Düşünmeyi Öğrenmek), illustrated by Serap Deliorman, İzmir: Tudem Publications.

Colomer, T., Kümmerling-Meibauer, B. and Silva-Diaz, C. (eds.) (2010) *New Directions in Picturebook Research*, New York: Routledge.

Demi, M. K. (2004) *A Tale from Turkey: The Hungry Coat*, New York: McElderry Books.

Derman, G. (1988) *Resimli Taş Baskısı Halk Hikayeleri* (Folk Stories Illustrated by Lithography), T.C. Atatürk Cultural Center Publication, No: 24.

Erdoğan, F. (2004) "Turkey," in Peter Hunt (ed.) *International Companion Encyclopaedia of Children's Literature*, Vol. 1, 2nd ed., London: Routledge, 1246–52.

Eurostat (2014) Eurostat: The EU in the world 2014: A statistical portrait, Luxemburg, Publications Office of the European Union.

Fortna, B. (2011) *Learning to Read in the late Ottoman Empire and the early Turkish Republic*, New York: Palgrave Macmillan.

Göknil, C. (2010) *Çatlak Hasan* (Lunatic Hasan), İstanbul: Can Children's Publications.

Göksel, A. and Kerslake C. (2005) *Turkish: A Comprehensive Grammar*, New York: Routledge.

Gölpınarlı, A. (1961) *Nasreddin Hodja* (Nasreddin Hoca), illustrated by Abidin Dino, İstanbul: Remzi Publications.

Gültekin, A. O. and Güktekin, A. (eds.) (2005) *Havva'ya Mektuplar* (Letters to Havva), İstanbul: Norgunk Publications.

Karaman-Kepenekçi, Y. (2010) "An analysis on children's rights in stories recommended for children in Turkey," *Journal of Peace Education*, 7(1): 65–83.

Kaygusuz, R. (2013) *Cin Ali'nin Atı* (The Horse of Clever Ali), illustrated by Selçuk Seymen, Ankara: Cin Ali Publications.

Kopan, Y. (2012) *Burun* (The Nose), illustrated by Alex Pelayo, İstanbul: Marsık Publications.

Kozikoğlu, T. (2013) "Turkish Delight: Sweet or Sour? The Double Face of the Turkish Children's Book Market," *Bookbird: A Journal of International Children's Literature*, 51(2): 71–75.

Lind, A. (2011) *Biliam ve Ben Düşünürken* (Biliam and I While Thinking), İstanbul: Ayrıntı Children's Publications.

Nodelman, P. (1988) *Words About Pictures: The Narrative Art of Children's Picture Books*, London: The University of Georgia Press.

OECD (2012) http://data.oecd.org/pisa/reading-performance-pisa.htm (accessed 8 August 2014).

Oral, G. (2006) "Creativity in Turkey and Turkish-Speaking Countries", in J. C. Kaufman and R. J. Sternberg (eds.), *The International Handbook of Creativity*, New York: Cambridge University Press, 337–373.

Sarıyüce, H. L. (2012) *Türk Çocuk and Gençlik Edebiyatı Ansiklopedisi* (Encyclopedia of Turkish Children and Youth Literature), İstanbul: Nar Publications.

Şahinkanat, S. (2014) *Kim Korkar Kırmızı Başlıklı Kız'dan?* (Who would be Afraid of Red Riding Hood?), illustrated by Ayşe İnan Alican, İstanbul: YKY Publications.

Sayın, B. (2005) *5 Çocuk 5 İstanbul* (5 Children 5 İstanbuls), İstanbul: Günışığı Publications. Also as: *Mert und der wundersame Fes: Eine Reise durch die Zeit in Istanbul* (2008), transl. Reinhard Fischer (bilingual German-Turkish edition.

Şimşek, T. (2006) "Çocuk Edebiyatı" (Children's Literature), in T. S. Halman and O. Horata (eds.) *Türk Edebiyat Tarihi* (History of Turkish Literature), Vol. 4, İstanbul: Ministry of Culture and Tourism Publications, 543–565.

Stephens, J. and McCallum, R. (ed.) (2013) *Retelling Stories, Framing Culture, Traditional Story and Metanarratives in Children's Literature*, New York: Routledge.

TUIK (2014), Statistics on Child 2013, Turkish Statistical Institute, Printing Division, Ankara (accessed 12 December 2014).

Turkish Publishers Association (n.d.) 2014 Book Market in Turkey Report, http://turkyaybir.org.tr/research-statistics/2014-book-market-in-turkey-report/515 (accessed 12 March 2015).

Walker, Barbara K. (ed.) (1990) *The Art of the Turkish Tale*, Vol. 1, Texas: Texas Tech University Publications.

Watson, W. J. (1968) "İbrahim Müteferrika and Turkish Incunabula," *Journal of the American Oriental Society*, 88(3): 435–441.

PART VI

Trends in children's and young adult literatures

39

RECENT TRENDS AND THEMES IN REALIST CHINESE CHILDREN'S FICTION

Li Lifang

Since the implementation of the reform and opening-up policy in 1978, China has been changing rapidly. This development has comprehensively influenced and changed the values and daily life of the people, and has also renewed the education model and maturation experiences of children from generation to generation. On one hand, what society has achieved has gradually afforded an unprecedented social condition in terms of both material and spiritual life for our children. On the other hand, a bunch of social problems, brought by the transformation stage of social development, has impacted upon the everyday life of children, bringing them new survival and living problems. This situation pertains across the whole domain of school and family education.

Colorful everyday life in itself is a great resource for the writing of contemporary realistic fiction and offers infinite possibilities for a children's literature author to choose a realistic topic to work on. With thirty years' development under the reform and opening-up policy, what Chinese children's literature itself accumulated and achieved has proved an important ground for the development of contemporary realistic fiction.

On the basis of what realist fiction has achieved, it is possible to discern two development tendencies. The first is realist fiction that reflects or reflects upon the school life of children and, set in a background in which traditional Chinese educational ideas and their containing system are inverted and criticized, aims to enhance the subjectivity of children. Such works are enthusiastically welcomed by child readers for their happy mode, aesthetic qualities of playfulness and humor, and their positive representations of children's mental and physical lives. The second strand in realist fiction is "problem" writing that focuses on the problems that restrict the life quality of children. These works depict a complicated social background and are apt to concentrate on a particular range of social issues. The style is usually serious and emotional, and the purpose is to draw social attention to the problems faced by children. These two modes interpret the realist aesthetic from two different perspectives. At the same time, there is more than one side to each in their own exploration of art, as demonstrated in the following discussion of specific examples.

Realist writing – universally acknowledged by children.

For eleven of the first twelve years of the twenty-first century, Chinese children's publishing enjoyed double-digit growth each year. The rate has gone beyond China's national economic growth rate and the whole Chinese publishing growth rate. At present, children's literature accounts for one-third of the entire children's book market. This is closely tied up with the new century's fast development of original children's literature which is mainly supported by the emergence of contemporary realist fiction that closely reflects the real life of children. A key writer is Yang Hongying, the first author since the beginning of the century to write realist fiction well received by children.

Yang Hongying was writing fairy tales before she published her fiction *Girl's Diary* in 2000. *Girl's Diary* was written for her daughter in sixth grade. As her daughter grew into adolescence, Yang came up with a plan to record her growth in a realist novel. Her fiction in the form of a private diary highlights the real life of children and directly describes their inner feelings, avoiding a conventional story line in which adults ignore the real world of children. When published, *Girl's Diary* was very popular amongst readers and became the first original children's book to remain a best seller in the market.

As realistic fiction closely following the real life of children, the appearance of *Girl's Diary* was of great significance for Chinese children's literature. The success of this book encouraged Yang to write more fiction, such as *Bad Boy of Class 3, 5th Grade* in 2001, *Boy's Diary* in 2002, *Fairy Teacher and Bad Boy* in 2003. These works have achieved great attention and success, and led up to an unprecedented climax in the history of children's literature with the publication of *Naughty Boy Ma Xiaotiao* in 2003, the most popular of all books among child readers. Henceforth the sluggish market for original children's literature in the Chinese children's book market was transformed.

In the fierce children's book market competition, these works have shown the value and the potential of Chinese original children's literature. Zheng Zhong, the vice director of a children's publishing house of Zhengjiang province, points out that the introduction of *Harry Potter* transformed the market, and the introduced children's literature began to be popular with the publication of the *Goosebumps* series by R. L. Stine in 2001 and the *Tiger Team* series by Thomas Brezina in 2002. These three imported super best sellers had been at the top of the Chinese children's book charts for a long time and took an almost 80 percent share of the whole children's literature market. At a time when the market was dominated by imported works, Chinese original children's literature began to enjoy a boom, fueled by Yang's works, and the "Chinese weak, West strong" publishing structure was finally changed.

The example of Yang Hongying demonstrates what great vitality a literary work may have if it is close to children's real lives. In fact, what Yang has achieved in the new century depends not only on her experiences during the preceding quarter of a century, but also her positive thinking about issues like Chinese traditional education, the spiritual state of children and the nurturance of modern children's values.

Yang Hongying finds that in the school and family education model pertaining in China the subjectivity of children has always been ignored, suppressed and disregarded, and children have always been required to conform to and be judged by adult society in accordance with the existing values. Therefore, many "adult" children are produced artificially, who are clever and glad to do whatever they are bade instead of having a real disposition of a child. With her deep understanding of child psychology and education, Yang has successfully shaped a cohort of educators, including teachers, parents and principals, who now embrace educational ideas that refuse the single relationship between "children restrained" and "teacher manipulating" of traditional education. They are also willing to treat every child as a respected individual subject, to live with them equally, to find their advantages with understanding and compassion, and to judge a child's mind without applying traditional standards of value.

The significance of Yang's breakthrough is that she has initiated a writing practice in Chinese children's literature that brings the literature into line with the life and mind of Chinese children. She has gained a well-deserved reputation as a spokesperson for childhood innocence, a position which is actually marked by the publication of her *Naughty Boy Ma Xiaotiao* series. In this series, she has created different types of images both of children and teachers that can be observed in the contemporary Chinese education system, and vividly depict the reality of Chinese education and ways children experience it. In doing so, she endows Ma Xiaotiao's life with ideal, future possibility, so that he embodies a modern image of children, an innocent and healthy child who fully expresses the beauty and rhythm of life, a modern child who signifies that the values associated with Chinese children have entered into a new historic era.

The issue of the development of Chinese children expounded in Yang's realist fiction is actually a serious and wide-ranging topic. She is laying a basic groundwork for the mental health of Chinese children. Whether using children's peer groups or adult society as a setting, she has blazed a trail in the representation of the subjectivity of children. But she does this between the lines, as it were, dealing with a significant cultural and literary issue by inviting readers to think about the gaps between Ma Xiaotiao's interpretations of his world and their own more informed understanding. Readers thus expect that Ma Xiaotiao's behaviour will in some way be transgressive, since his role throughout these books is to test the boundaries of adult authority, and even when his schemes fail readers can see that transgression questions the models used to explain the world. In this way, society changes and moves forward. Yang's simple and straightforward writing style and humorous situations make the books' intricate plots easily accessible to children and guarantee the widest possible audience.

The huge success of Yang Hongying's style and her enormous sales inevitably lead to a great number of imitations. Therefore numerous "Naughty boy" stories suddenly appeared. However, many young writers don't have rich life experiences and enough literary knowledge to draw upon, and nor do they have a consciousness of social problems and insight into possible solutions. What they have done is just simply imitate existing works and invent funny stories around school life. This directly results in a chaotic children's book market with different levels of quality, inviting criticism from outside the field. And Yang Hongying is also blamed for this undesirable situation.

But undoubtedly, an important literary miracle in Chinese children's literature history has been wrought by Yang Hongying in the new century. Since 2006 the *Smiling Cat Diary*, a fairy-tale series retaining an essence of realism and connected to *Naughty Boy Ma Xiaotiao*, has been produced by Yang. It remains popular among child readers, with a circulation of more than thirty million. Yang Hongying's literary experience has greatly advanced the original creation of children's literature by following the principle she explained in an interview with the author of this article: "children of each time need their own realistic works." This idea explains the "epochal character" of Yang's literary creation and profoundly implies that children's lived experiences and realistic problems are still the key issues for the development of Chinese children's literature in the future.

Realist "problem" fiction

The second stream of realist fiction, a counterpart of the realist style represented by Yang Hongying, tends to be more "realistic." Such works often focus on vulnerable children or children in special living conditions, and the mental health problems caused by these bad situations. The purpose of this fiction is to promote social concern for the children facing these issues. The urbanization and industrialization of recent decades has been responsible for a mass migration of labor from rural to urban areas, and this movement of people has resulted in a huge increase in two groups of often disadvantaged children: the so-called "left-behind children" and migrant children. In 2008 there were approximately 27.3 million migrant children, or 9.8 percent of China's child population, and approximately 55.1 million left-behind children, or 19.8 percent of China's child population (Lu et al. 2016: 59).

A prominent contemporary social problem that has attracted much concern in Chinese realist problem writing is that of children left behind in a rural area when their farmer parents migrate to the city, and who are raised by grandparents or relatives. The main problems facing these children are that there are no formal custodial provisions, no guaranteed nine years' compulsory education, and little necessary affection, so that their physical and mental health is alarming. Therefore it is very easy for them to develop anti-social attitudes and values, and consequently an abnormal personality and psyche, which in turn leads to an increased tendency toward criminal behavior (Jiang 2005).

Given that there is such a huge group of vulnerable children, it is no surprise that children's literature authors have addressed it. Of twenty awarded works in the eighth National Excellent Children's Literature Prize in 2010, for example, two books deal with "left-behind children": *Twelve Months of Empty Nest* (2015) by Qiu Yidong and *Across the Sorrow Flower Season* (2008) by Wang Jucheng.

Twelve Months of Empty Nest is a rewriting of documented life experiences. Its author, Qiu Yidong, comes from Sichuan province where there is a large number of "left-behind children." He gathered a great deal of first-hand material by interviewing more than 1,000 left-behind children. The novel is organized as four thematic structures with differing aesthetic effects. Its themes are "experience of loneliness; resilient self-development; growth of sympathetic understanding; and positive social integration," which imply an attainment of agentic subjectivity despite the challenges faced and a message of hope for the life of "left-behind" children. Qiu Yingdong's objective was to write a book that "left-behind" children themselves would enjoy reading and that might offer them comfort and inspiration. Feedback from his readers has been strong and positive.

Qiu Yidong's writing practice further suggests that we should reconsider the question of the function of children's literature. In accord with contemporary social development, the thematic focus of children's literature could also change. Since the inception of the opening-up policy, the concept of the liberation of children in Chinese children's literature has focused on freeing their subjectivity from the chains of the "education" theory. Thus after thirty years of social transformation, the representation of relaxed playfulness has finally become a trend in children's literature, and the literature is more aligned with the lives of children and their tastes. The change in the conception of the literature has been revolutionary.

Nevertheless, reconceptualization of children's literature has always been a concrete historical issue and its development has never been an isolated and static matter. When we take an overview of the problems facing Chinese children, we will find that the main contemporary social problems are still those of the 1980s. There are more complicated and varied living realities of children, so that children's literature's aesthetic pursuit must transcend "games" to produce a more varied aesthetic style which addresses the spiritual demands of children in different states.

During the 1990s, there was a movement away from the realism that had been dominating children's literature towards an emphasis on imagination (Louie and Louie 2012: 180). In 1993, for example, Fan asserted that Chinese children's literature should not be a stark representation of reality, but should depict a world "not as concrete as the real world, [but a] better place to satisfy children's imagination, children's love, children's passion, children's purity, and children's active imagination" (cited and translated in Louie and Louie 2012: 178). In contrast, it is arguable that realist literature should be closely aligned with everyday experiences, since the internal reality of children involves problems that a writer may seek to deal with on the basis of an understanding and service view of what children need during their mental growth and maturation. The depiction of "left-behind" children in Qiu Yidong's fiction employs such a realist style.

Other realist writers also deal with "left-behind" children: Wang Jucheng's *Across the Sorrow Flower Season* explores the life of children in a rural area by using extended, affective stories to narrate the living conditions and sorrows of two "left-behind" children. *A Flurry of Golden Leaves* (2009) by Lu Mei employs fictional characters and poly-form narrative structure to build an aesthetic effect that derives from the combination of the perspective of the feelings of the "left-behind" children and that of a supportive outsider, a reporter who is writing a story to try to help a girl who has fallen into juvenile prison because she has been "left behind."

Another social group produced by internal migration comprises children who accompany their parents to the city. As a special group of inhabitants in the city, these children often feel themselves mismatched with city culture and their living situation is marked by a sense of alienation. *Sapphire Summer* (2006), by Li Xuebin, was awarded the seventh National Excellent Children's Literature Prize, an award that has much to do with its realist narration about the personal growth of children of migrant workers. The urban experience of these children is also an important realist subject because it deals with conflict between two kinds of values. Wang Jucheng's *Smiles in the Sun* (2011) also reflects on this experience, but in contrast to Li Xuebin's depiction of the experiences of two children in one family, Wang Jucheng ranges more widely to include more diverse children, the differing choices of route that might be pursued to integrate into urban life, and the changes of attitudes of urban youths towards them. His primary concerns are to guide the rural children to develop self-worth and to show how rural and urban children can gain mutual recognition.

Nowadays due to a significant proportion of migrant workers in Chinese cities, all social problems related to the migrant workers have been without exception inherited by their children. Stamped automatically by the cultural identity "migrant worker's children," they are destined to endure an additional mental burden in the growing progress even though they are staying with their parents in the city. It is a socially noteworthy problem that, beset by anxiety about cultural identity, these children struggle to acquire a sense of self-fulfillment within the prosperous society in which they live.

Sapphire Summer begins with the happy rural life of the two principal characters, brothers Le Xiao and Le Kai. When they later move to the city with their parents the completely unfamiliar environment poses new undertakings and challenges for them. Thus it is a hard realistic question for these two children to discover how to work together to reconstruct their own value and dignity. In narrating his story, Li Xuebin explores how will and spirit work in reality. Although they suffer a lot, Le Xiao, Le Kai and their parents have not given up. They remain determined and preserve their faith, good and true personalities, and the tolerance and understanding of society. Their efforts finally pay off.

Another representative writer who pays attention to children of migrant workers is Xu Ling. *Flowing Flowers* (2011), a novel which describes the process of realization of the life dream of migrants' children, was recipient of the National "Five-one project" Prize awarded by the Publicity Department of the Central Committee of the CPC. The creation of the book is based on the reality of the migrant children's cry that "I want to be local in the future" and on the situation of suffering that some Chinese children now experience, and which cannot be ignored. When facing it, no one can escape from it but accept it and change himself. Xu Ling depicts a realistic possibility for those children, affording survival power for their growth in a practical and timely way.

Following a successful career as an elementary school teacher, Xu Ling turned to writing for children. She has always persisted with the realist concept of grounding her writing in a local place. Her *My Love* series also employs realist fiction to show the heavy burden of children's life, focused now on the deep relationship between children and parents. This is a topic endowed with a new modernity in contemporary China. In *I Will Love You with All My Heart* (2012), a story about an eleven-year-old girl looking for her father, separation of child and parent because of employment in a distant city progresses to the death of the father. Xiong Miaomiao's family has protected her from the truth, so that her quest-journey to find him transforms into a need to face the hardship of death and absorb it into the process of maturation. A theme that emerges from Xu Ling's writing is that if ordinary people maintain their original childhood capacity for love they will be able to overcome difficulties and solve crises, and thus face an unstable internal reality with courage.

In contrast to *I Will Love You with All My Heart*, *The War between Me and my Dad* (2013) focuses on the achievement of wholeness, instead of gaps due to death. After his mother's death, Zhao Ziniu, a 12-year-old boy, has to live with his father who has just got out of jail. From that moment a long war between the two men starts.

A major aspect of Xu Ling's art and her sense of writing for children is her ability to sustain child-centered writing. In her books, the pure emotional experience and limited self-judgment of the child are mixed together, producing an immature form of children with a strong subjectivity. Once these things meet with a dysfunctional family, potentially serious problems develop between child and adult. This situation is inescapable for both children and adults because it rends personality and is painfully integrated into everyday life. The only thing they can do is fight that reality and work together to resolve conflict. Xu Ling's work expresses a strong optimism which enables her to understand life's tough side and make it meaningful. It does not shy away from the suffering in life because everyone is seen to have the capacity to resist it, except for complete suffering due to meaninglessness. The realism of Xu Ling seems cold but has a warmer aspect, which suggests that in her works a deep inner meaning exists beyond the superficial sufferings of life. Finally, meaning is available to remove sorrow, and initiate understanding and dialogue between children and grown-ups.

Another theme in contemporary realist fiction grounded in the relationships of parents and children concerns the children of single-parent families. The main reason for the problem of children in single-parent families is the rising divorce rate in China in recent years, so that since 2000 there has been a steady increase in fiction about this theme. Yang

Hongying's *Diary of a School Boy* (2002), for example, features a protagonist who is a child from a single-parent family. But the writer depicts the child, Wu Mian, as a mature idealist who handles the situation of his family with a positive attitude. This best-seller indicates that Yang Hongying prefers to set an active upward example for those who live in a single-parent family. A harsher perspective was later offered in Yao Emei's *Tilting Sky* (2004), which was serialized in *Children's Literature*, an influential national magazine founded in 1963 with a circulation in the millions. The story is about Bai Jian, a boy who has a tough time as he grows up. He has been moving around with his free, unpolished father since he was 8 years old, when his mother divorced his father. For a long time he hasn't enjoyed the caring that a child should have, even a comfortable and secure home. Instead, he has to worry about his father and face everyday reality on his own, which is a daunting challenge for him. As a primarily adult literature author, Yao Emei's writing is different from that of most children's literature writers, as she realistically describes the frustrating emotional living state of adult society and the material and spiritual suffering of innocent children within that society.

Representation of the mental and physical health problems of children in single-parent families will be a main agenda of Chinese children's literature for quite a long time in the future. Indications are that authors will face and challenge this difficult problem with a reasonable attitude based in a reasonable and realistic view.

In realist writing about social problems, authors specifically address Chinese children's increasing anxiety, sorrow and depression, which lead to confrontation with school, family and society. The main reason for this is the school education system and the management model. Since the 1980s, the Chinese education concept and education system has been gradually transformed from exam-oriented education to EQO (essential-quality-oriented) education. The education process emphasizes the development of a rounded human being and focuses on socialist morality, personality and the fostering of ability, and physical and mental health enhancement.

Although the transformation has achieved a lot, it is still in the middle of development and under construction. Therefore all kinds of problems exist for both the educator and the students, and even the relationship between them. It is still very common that a score-oriented assessment system prevails in schools most of the time. The teacher judges and treats a student merely according to his/her superficial test results, and this leads to an unhealthy mental problem for both the high-scoring students and low-scoring students.

Some children's literature writers were originally school teachers, so they are familiar with the real situation and write realistically in order to rethink and criticize school education. *Every Child is an Angel* (2011) by Wang Jucheng is an example. Due to the improper education activities of the teacher, the character and behavior of two children have been seriously damaged during a period when they transition into middle high school from elementary school. The writer goes deeply into the detailed daily life of the children, depicting the inner feeling of teacher and students in a calm and objective language. In an age with diversified values and when money determines everything, the author is crying out for a more personal education that could make a beautiful campus purer and cleaner, and so offers the reminder that, "every child is an angel. And it is the teacher who leads the angel to be a human."

The psychological counseling fiction by Yu Liji has been developed as a distinctive style in contemporary children's literature with a focus on children's mental health problems. With the aim of addressing the mental disabilities of young children, he offers the example of Xin Lan, who lost her legs in a traffic accident, as the main character.

Educated and guided by her father who is a psychologist, the young disabled girl not only keeps on living positively but also helps her classmates to deal with their mental problems. When Yu writes books, he often includes a large amount of medical knowledge, along with excellent case studies. His latest book, *Beautiful Mind* (2014), has been very well received by child readers.

Realist fiction enjoys a central position in the current development of the Chinese children's literature, and it has and will continue to have a close relationship with changes in China's social reality. However, children's literature still has a long way to go in the exploration of reality, and it is probable that the exploration of naturalness in art performance and multimodal forms of art will be central activities.

Bibliography

Christensen, Samantha (2014) "Hongying Yang: China ★ Author," *Bookbird: A Journal of International Children's Literature*, 52(2): 14.

Jiang, P. (2005) "The absence of home education and its strategies of rural children left behind," *Theoretic Observation*, 4:79–81. (In Chinese)

Li, Xuebin (2006) *Sapphire Summer*, Wuhan: Changjiang Juvenile & Children's Publishing House

Louie, Belinda Yun-Ying and Douglas Louie (2012) "Children's Literature in the People's Republic of China: Its Purposes and Genres," in Wenling Li, Janet Gaffney, J. Packard (eds) *Chinese Children's Reading Acquisition: Theoretical and Pedagogical Issues*, New York: Springer Science & Business Media, 175–194.

Lu, Shuang, Yi-Ting Lin, Juliann H.Vikse, Chien-Chung Huang (2016) "Well-being of migrant and left-behind children in China: Education, health, parenting, and personal values," *International Journal of Social Welfare*, 25(1): 58–68.

Qiu, Yidong (2015) *Twelve Months of Empty Nest*, Chengdu: Sichuan Children's Publishing House.

Wang, Jucheng (n.d.) *Across the Sorrow Flower Season*, Chongqing: Chongqing Press.

Wang, Jucheng (2011) *Smiles in the Sun*, Wuhan: Hubei Children's Press.

Wang, Jucheng (2011) *Every Child is an Angel*, Beijing: China Children's Publishing House.

Wang, X., L. Ling, H. Su, J. Cheng, L. Jin, Y-H. Sun (2015) "Self-concept of left-behind children in China: a systematic review of the literature," *Child: Care, Health & Development*, 41(3): 346–355.

Xu, Ling (2011) *Flowing Flowers*, Taiyuan: Hope Publishing House.

Xu, Ling (2012) *I will Love you with All my Heart*, Beijing: China Children's Publishing House.

Xu, Ling (2013) *The War between me and My Dad*, Beijing: China Children's Publishing House.

Yang, Hongying (2000) *Girl's Diary*, Beijing: China Writers Publishing House.

Yang, Hongying (2011) *Naughty Boy Ma Xiaotiao Book Series* (20 books), Nanning: Jieli Publishing House.

Yang, Hongying (2006–) *Smiling Cats Diary*, Jinan: Tomorrow Publishing House.

Yao, Emei (2004) *Tilting Sky*, Beijing: China Children's Publishing House.

40

THE *MORIBITO* SERIES AND ITS RELATION TO TRENDS IN JAPANESE CHILDREN'S LITERATURE[1]

Yasuko Doi

The work of Nahoko Uehashi is illustrative of the present situation of Japanese literature for young adults and children. Uehashi is a highly popular fantasy writer for young adults (YA), winner of the International Andersen Prize in 2014, and has had several works adapted to animation, manga and fan fiction. Uehashi's *Moribito* series (1996–2012, twelve volumes) is one of the high points of the genre of fantasy writing for YA and children in Japan. Because of its multicultural mix of characters and values, the series has also been well received in other countries. Its themes of family values, friendship, work, sex and gender mean that the *Moribito* series reflects issues in present-day Japanese society which are also prevalent in YA literature fictional realism. That *Moribito* has also been published in an adult's edition illustrates the phenomenon in which the border between adult, YA and children's literature is becoming blurred. Further, the adaptations of the *Moribito* series to other media demonstrates how children enjoy stories in a variety of forms.

The *Moribito* series as part of Japanese YA and children's literature

The *Moribito* series is a fantasy involving both the political intrigue of various neighboring countries and direct interaction with a number of other dimensional worlds (Kilpatrick and Muta 2013; 81). The genre of fantasy for YA and children, which originally came from the west and has long been an object of interest and exploration in Japan, was established in that country by the Moribito series. The two main protagonists are Balsa, a thirty-year-old female bodyguard who is originally from Kanbal and now living in New-Yogo, and Chagum who is the prince of New-Yogo. Over the series, Chagum grows up amid political strife and war between New-Yogo and its neighbors and the interventions of worlds from different dimensions to his own. While Balsa protects Chagum and some other gifted children through political conflict and war, she discovers more about her childhood and finds love with Tanda, a shaman healer. Thus the typical sword hero and mage hero roles common in mid-twentieth-century western fantasy are reversed.

Japanese fantasy writers

Japanese fantasy effectively began with Kenji Miyazawa, who first introduced the genre with *Night of the Milky Way Railway* (Ginga Tetsudô no Yoru) in 1934. His now renowned works describe a unique world view, exploring human nature in a poetic style that evokes the power of the Japanese language and they have had a strong influence on subsequent Japanese fantasy. New fantasy works appeared after World War II. They were written by authors who had read *Alice in Wonderland* and the *Narnia* series and wanted to establish the fantasy genre in Japan. Among these were Tomiko Inui's *Yuri and the Little People* (Kokage no ie no kobitotchi) and Satoru Sato's *The Tiny Country That Nobody Knows* (Daremo shiranai chisana kuni), both published in 1959, and Toshiko Kanzawa's *The Adventures of Little Kamu* (Chibikko Kamu no bôken) in 1961. The former are about the manifestation of the extraordinary in everyday life and the latter is an adventure story set in a fantasy world. These books provided the framework for fantasy for children as a genre. In particular, *Yuri and the Little People* and *The Adventures of Little Kamu* were the pioneer works of everyday magic and other-world fantasies respectively, in spite of the clumsiness with which they borrowed the framing devices found in western fantasy. Similarly, *The Tiny Country That Nobody Knows* established a fantasy genre about Borrower-like little people living in our world. Subsequently, the idea of the irruption of the extraordinary into everyday life was notably extended by Eiko Kadono in her eight volume series *Kiki's Delivery Service* (Majo no takkyubin; 1985–2016).

The 1970s saw the emergence of short story writers such as Naoko Awa and Kimiko Aman, whose fantasies deal with the entry of the uncanny into everyday life. Saito Atsuo's novel-length *Adventures* (Bokensha-tachi) appeared in 1972. It is an animal fantasy about a rat named Ganba who fights against evil weasels, and it was subsequently adapted as a popular TV series and a film. In 1973, Taijiro Amazawa, a poet and eminent researcher of Kenji Miyazawa's works and medieval French literature, published a long fantasy called *Spin, Lightwheel!* (Hikariguruma yo maware), the first volume of his *Three Magic* trilogy (completed in 2011). The story, set in the real world, is about the battle between a group of children and the forces of evil, and draws parallels with the problems of modern Japanese society such as environmental degradation, divisions in society and between individuals. It is notable for the way in which the children try to change the world by themselves. The underlying scheme of this fight between good and evil can be traced back to the stories that emerged from Japan's ancient animistic belief systems, and the books explore deep moral and philosophical issues, perhaps at a level beyond their readers.

Japanese fantasy was taken to a new level by Noriko Ogiwara's 1988 novel, *Dragon Sword and Wind Child* (Sorairo Magatama), which has now become the first part of the *Magatama* trilogy. The series uses ancient legend to explore issues of identity and independence for a female protagonist who is openly involved in the politics and religion of her society. Other fantasy writers who are now playing an active part in children's literature began to appear in the 1990s: Yoko Tomiyasu adapts characters from Japanese folktales and legends for works such as *Zawazawa House in the Oak Woods* (Kunigi bayashi no zawazawa so; 1990) and *Summer Holiday at Fox Mountain* (Kitsune yama no natsuyasumi; 1994) (which are mainly aimed at children around the age of 10). Notable works in other sub-genres of fantasy are Jun Okada's *Tales of the Kosoado Forest* (Kosoado no mori no monogatari; 1994–2017), set in a miniature imaginary world about a community living in the Kosoado Forest; Hiroshi Saito's *Tales of a White Magical Fox* (Shirakomaki; 1996–2012) is time-travel fantasy; and Yu Ito's *A Bridge to the Other*

World (Oni no hashi; 1998) is time-slip historical fantasy, set in the Heian period (late eighth to twelfth century). These authors are using the fantasy genre in order to create their own worlds, which in turn reflect Japanese society.

Nahoko Uehashi emerged from this renaissance of the new fantasy era and has become one of the most eminent and prolific Japanese fantasy writers, with books such as *O God of the Moon Forest, Sleep* (Tsuki no mori ni kami yo nemure; 1991) and the four volume *Beast Player* series (Kemono no sôja; 2006–2009). The popularity of the latter, in particular, has been extended by manga and anime adaptations. Her *Moribito* series is an otherworld fantasy as well as an adventure fantasy which, while exploring the characters' identities, describes the politics, economics and religions of five fictional countries. Although the *Moribito* series built on the past achievements of Japanese fantasies, it broke new ground in terms of scale, complexity, and the appeal of its characters.

The description of the five countries and the extra-dimensional world are especially unique. Uehashi's research and teaching as an anthropologist inform her depiction of the five countries, their differing geographical features, politics and religions, and the ethnic divisions of their various tribes. The minority tribes have their own languages, religions and legends, which often help to solve the problems in the country. The tribes are also portrayed as being more in touch with the other worlds which, again, stems from Uehashi's anthropological studies of aboriginal Australian and Okinawans as well as her love for the work of Rosemary Sutcliffe (Kodama and Uehashi 2009: 41). Political ideas are clearly espoused in the *Moribito* series. In the last volume for example, Chagum, the young prince who is now king, expresses his desire for a country where individuals, rather than autocratic government or organized religion, define their own fates (Kilpatrick and Muta 2013; 92). The extra-dimensional world in the series exists in a time and space of its own. There are people and mysterious creatures who can cross the border between these worlds, allowing for a consideration of differing perspectives on our world and its values. The books are not only about political intrigue, however. The lives of ordinary people are described in detail, especially the food of each country (including recipes). There has even been a spin-off cookery book, *Balsa's Dining Table* (Barusa no shokutaku).

The two principal characters grow and develop as the series continues. Balsa is an itinerant warrior who protects the defenseless with her skill with the short spear. The events of her childhood, portrayed in *Moribito II: Guardian of the Darkness*, in part explain why she became a bodyguard. She struggles with the contradiction between fighting and possibly killing people in order to protect others. The other main character, Chagum, whose father, the king, attempts to murder him at the beginning of the story, follows a path to maturity which involves nurturing something from another world, travelling to other countries, becoming a hostage in one of those countries, and trying to end a war between them by engaging in diplomacy with their politicians. Both Balsa and Chagum have a strong sense of justice and responsibility, which appeals to readers. The series also gains in richness through the use of secondary characters to illustrate past conflicts and their resultant problems. Thus Uehashi creates a fantasy work that has universal themes and that could be appreciated around the world.

YA literature, fictional realism and the *Moribito* series

As well as sharing a primarily teenage audience, the *Moribito* series has many themes in common with YA works of fictional realism. YA literature is a relatively new genre that has gradually penetrated the market since the late 1980s. It flourished in the 2000s partly as a response to the government's concerns about the diminishing numbers of active teenage readers. Many original Japanese YA titles have been published as well as titles translated from English and German. The realist genre for younger children follows similar trends, but does not include the theme of romantic love.

Family values and friendship are by far the most common themes in YA literature. Family values are thematized in the *Moribito* series, in that the parentless Balsa and Chagum, who came close to being a victim of infanticide, can both be described as "orphans". As well as stories about foster homes and neglected and abused children like Rie Muranaka's *The Moon in a Ramen Bowl* (Châshû no tsuki; 2012), there are many YA titles in Japan that deal with psychologically orphaned or somehow isolated children (Griswold 1992: 5). One possible reason for this is that the breakdown in societal consensus regarding values has left many adults feeling insecure, and their children find themselves having to deal both with troubled parents and the need to chart a course for their own lives. For example, Mutsumi Ishii's *Alice in the City* (Tokai no Arisu; 2013) describes the process by which a 13-year-old girl, Sachiko, begins to understand her mother, a business woman who embarks on a sudden journey to "find herself" after leaving the girl's father, a struggling actor, to do all the parenting. Sachiko calls herself Alice and plays in an imaginary world based on *Alice in Wonderland*, which somehow enables her to see the family situation objectively.

The *Moribito* series illustrates the bonds of love and trust between people, perhaps best exemplified in Chagum's belief in Tarusan, the second prince of Sangal, and Chagum's attempts to save Tarusan life. This theme is very important for children in Japan where there are serious problems involving bullying and truancy. Bullying is a major theme in Maruha Nakamatsu's *School Quest* (Gakko kuesto; 2010), in which an internet game is used to punish five children whose bullying had driven another child to suicide. Children who have difficulties in communicating are described in Yoko Saso's *Iemoto Detective, Masuno* (Iemoto tantei Masuno-kun; 2010).

In addition to family values and friendship, the *Moribito* series shares other themes with realist YA literature, such as romantic love, work, sex, gender, and war. The love between Balsa and her longtime friend Tanda involves both risking their lives to save the other on numerous, dramatically described occasions. In contrast, apart from Jôko Iwase's *Cloudy, and Sometimes Fine* (Kumori tokidoki hareru; 2014) and Nao Kosaka's *Strawberry Blue* (Sutoroberi buru; 2010), which describe the thrills of teenage love, realistic YA novels in Japan do not deal with love much, even though it is an important topic for teenagers, who enjoy the love stories (often merely stereotypical wish-fulfillment fantasies) in manga, TV and animation films.

Perhaps in response to the social problem of "*Hikikomori*" or "social withdrawal" in Japan, in which young people eschew all contact with the outside world, including never having a job (Zielenziger 2006: 9–12), the number of books published relating to the world of work is increasing. In the *Moribito* series, Balsa's vocation as a bodyguard and Chagum's preparation for his role of emperor are dealt with in some detail. The importance of taking on the responsibility of work, of doing it with a passion for self-improvement can be seen in everything they do. The world of work is the focus of the protagonist's attention in YA fiction such as Sumiko Yatsuka's *For Our Tomorrow* (Oretachi no asu ni mukatte; 2012) and Akira Yokozawa's *Swing* (Suingu; 2011). A challenge to assumptions about gendered occupations is implicit in various roles performed in the *Moribito* series, from Balsa's occupation as a bodyguard, to Tanda's enjoyment of cooking, to Chagum's "giving birth" to an "egg" from another world. The powerful role women play in Sangal's politics is an obvious contrast to the actual small participation by women in Japanese politics, which is still largely categorized as a male domain (Sheel, 2003: 4097). Comparable challenges are posed in YA fiction, as in Mito Mahara's *Spray of Iron Splashes* (Tetsu no shibuki ga haneru; 2011), in which a high school girl competes against boys in a metalworking contest. Stereotypical ideas about gender are slowly being changed in YA and children's books, perhaps best exemplified by the female turner in *Spray of Iron Splashes* and the father who does all the housework in *Alice in the City*.

The porous border between children's literature and adult fiction

The increased activity in the crossover market between YA and children's literature and other media indicates that the border between children's literature and adult literature is becoming less clear. The "light novel" genre, which is very popular with teenagers, is also providing frequent examples of "crossovers". Reception of these adaptations is not merely passive: readers produce their own related fan-fiction in the form of manga, artwork and even spin-off novels. The *Moribito* series is part of this trend. There are hardcover, paperback and soft-cover editions of the series and it is clear that adults are the target for the latter because of the use of more sophisticated *kanji*, or Chinese characters. This crossover phenomenon is quite common in Japan and there are, for example, adult editions of both Fuyumi Ono's *Twelve Kingdoms'* series (Jûni kokki; 1992–2001) and Saso's *Iemoto Detective, Masuno*. Novels originally written for adults are also published in children's versions. For example, *Stepfather Step* (Suteppu fâzâ suteppu; 2005) written by the highly popular mystery novelist, Miyuki Miyabe, has been put into a series for children called *Kodansha Blue Bird Books* (Kodansha aoi tori bunko). Moreover, many authors write both for adults and children. Atsuko Asano, Eto Mori, Mitsuyo Kakuta, Mizuki Tsujimura, Kaori Ekuni, Ira Ishida, Kiyoshi Shigematsu, Takami Ito, and Risa Wataya have written for both adults and children and many of them have won prestigious literary honors, such as the Akutagawa and the Naoki awards.

It could be said that these developments can be traced to the gradual blurring of the border between adulthood and childhood and perhaps the breaking down of the distinctions between author and reader. They might also be explained by the rise in the quality of YA and children's literature (Nogami 2009: 192), and the way that some literature for adults is also aiming for a certain narrative simplicity. It would seem that this is a time when the definition of what constitutes literature is changing, especially as it responds to changes in the concepts of childhood and authorship.

One of the main attractions of the *Moribito* series is the strength of its characters, and this quality accords with the "light novel" genre, in which the characters are by far the most important element of the story. This genre, which sells enormously well,[2] is said to have had its inception on Science Fiction (SF) forums on the internet around 1990 (Shinjo 2006: 17) and the books in this genre have some common features. Some people use the word "light" to suggest narrative simplicity or lack of depth. These books are usually first published as paperbacks and the cover and frontispiece illustrations feature the characters' faces in an anime style. This is because the characters are considered to be the most important element of the light novel, a phenomenon from which derives the term "*chara moe*" or "character crush". The characters are usually 14–17 year old boys and girls who are good-looking in the extreme. The stories are usually set in heterotopias, places closed to the outside world, like schools or dormitories.

Many of these books are serialized, but usually the protagonist does not grow up or develop. Instead readers focus their enjoyment purely on what happens to the protagonist. Politics, social problems and conflicts between the characters are not welcome in this genre. Its form is chiefly composed of dialogue and descriptions of the characters' actions rather than attempts at psychological or descriptive depth. The writers are roughly the same generation as their readers and there is a feeling of comradeship between them. The reason for the flourishing of this genre can be explained as the desire of the readers to immerse themselves in a story world with the characters they love.

The light novel has had some influence on YA and children's literature, which sometimes mimics the style of its dialogue and its use of illustrations. As an example of the latter point, on the cover of *The New Translation of Alice in Wonderland* (Fushigi no kun no Arisu shinyaku; 2010), Alice looks like an anime character (see Figure 40.1). Some light novels in which scenes of sex or violence have been excised are also published as children's books. The difference between the characters in the *Moribito* series and those in the light novel is that those in the former grow through conflict, and exist in a world where politics and social problems are described in detail. The *Moribito* series also attempts to imbue its characters with psychological depth, and includes vivid descriptive passages.

Fan fiction and other media

The *Moribito* Series has also provided the basis for a great deal of fan-fiction, both on the internet and in print. Some are only illustrations of "sexy Balsa", "transvestite Chagum", or "love scenes between Chagum and Shuga" (an astrologist in the narrative's modern Japan). Such illustrations are usually drawn by and for girls, and while they depict homosexuality between males, their tenor is to suggest "pure love" in that pregnancy is not an issue. Other creative fan writing appears as manga and novels that develop the *Moribito* stories or make up new ones by using the characters from the series. This fan fiction phenomenon (Yamakawa 2009: 88) originally developed through manga, games, anime and the light novel form, and especially, via "Comike" (an abbreviation of comic market), a convention for fan-fiction magazines since 1975. At the Comike, the participants dress up in their favorite character's costume, which is called Cosplay (an abbreviation of costume play).

The *Moribito* series was adapted for an anime series and broadcast on the NHK satellite broadcast channel in 2007. These animated stories were subsequently converted to manga. The order of the adaptations varies but the result is a constantly occurring media mix of some complexity. In order to illustrate how this media mix relates to YA and children's literature, I offer a brief discussion of how the *Moribito* series has been adapted for anime and manga and the differences in those forms.

The anime series, was directed by Kenji Kamiyama, who had directed *Ghost in the Shell Stand Alone Complex* (Kokaku Kido Tai; 1995). The *Moribito* anime consists of 28 episodes, which were later released in DVD format as well as being shown in, amongst other countries, Korea, France and Germany. Kamiyama said that the reason he decided to direct this anime was that the characters were realistic and that the world it was set in was very solid and consistent (Kamiyama 2007: 102). Kamiyama depicted New-Yogo as similar in appearance to mid-Edo period Japan (Kamiyama 2007: 102). Balsa looks voluptuous rather than muscular and her action scenes are presented theatrically, placing them in the historical context of beautiful girl soldier animation (Tanaka 2011: 229), such as *Sailor Moon*. Kamiyama inserted some original episodes in order to better illustrate

Figure 40.1 From *Fushigi no Kuni no Arisu Shinyaku.*
Source: With permission of Ascii Media Works, Tokyo.

Chagum's growth and the ersatz mother-child relationship between Balsa and Chagum, thus enabling the audience to empathize more deeply with the characters.

Some of the influences on animated YA and children's literature in Japan have come from Disney animation as well as that of Osamu Tezuka, Studio Ghibli, and Katsuhiro Otomo (who animated *Akira* (1988)), amongst others. In turn, Japanese YA and children's literature has provided the basis for animations such as *Adventures of Ganba*, *Kiki's Delivery Service*, and Fuyumi Ono's *Twelve Kingdoms*, which became highly popular.

The manga of the *Moribito* series by Kamui Fujiwara was adapted from the anime but both start with the same scene from the written work:

> At the moment the royal procession reached the Yamakage Bridge, Balsa's destiny took an unexpected turn. She was crossing the commoners' bridge downstream, the Aoyumi River visible through gaps between the planks.
>
> (Uehashi 2008: 1)

Thus we begin with the name of the protagonist and are primed to expect an encounter between people from different classes, a feeling heightened by the image of the bridge that links the two worlds. And in the phrase "Balsa's destiny took an unexpected turn" there is a brief foretelling of what is to come.

In the manga version, the first two title pages show a landscape of mountains and rice fields, a nameless figure with a short spear, and words from a folk song later revealed as "Chagum's life is saved". After this setting, the biggest frame on the first picture of the first page is an upper body image of Balsa (see Figure 40.2). The spear she holds runs in a diagonal from the bottom right to top left and the low angle of view conveys the

Figure 40.2 Moribito: Guardian of the Spirit "GANGAN COMICS", Square Enix Co., Ltd (2007). © Nahoko Uehashi/KAISEI-SHA/*Guardian* of the Spirit Committee. © 2007 Kamui Fujiwara/Square Enix.
Source: Reprinted with permission of Square Enix Co., LTD.

impression that Balsa is a tough woman and someone to be admired. When Balsa says "Yogo is as nice as I had imagined. I feel relaxed", the readers understand she comes from somewhere else and likes this new place. Then, at the bridge, a resting man who is watching Balsa, remarks upon her status as a woman and a foreigner, to which she does not reply, indicating an element of mystery or enigma about her. The last frame of the page is the bridge seen from downstream, presaging danger. Thus, in the manga form, from the first page, Balsa is in the center of the pictures although her name has not yet been mentioned, intriguing the reader and making them want to know more about her. Although this is just one example, one can see that whereas the book invites the readers into the story, the manga, with its shifting angles, frames and dialogues, invites them to meet Balsa, the character.

It is said that now that manga is used in Japanese textbooks it is moving from an outsider cultural form to an insider cultural form. The number of manga read by the Japanese is huge and we cannot talk about YA and children's reading without talking about manga.[3] Many YA and children's literature titles have been adapted into manga, just as many manga have been novelized. Many writers of YA and children's literature, including Uehashi, read manga in their childhood, so that aspects of the form – especially in the dialogue and the descriptions of action – can sometimes be detected in their works.

Conclusion

The world of the constantly mixing popular modern forms of light novels, manga, and anime can be seen in the treatment of the *Moribito* series, which has been animated and adapted for manga, media where the characters are seen as the most important elements, a mindset which in turn has had an influence on YA and children's literature in Japan. Out of this high identification with characters, the forms of fan-fiction and "Cosplay" have become highly popular among the young.

Although the characters of the *Moribito* series are indeed attractive, in their written form they struggle, change and grow as people. The books also present a richer blend of elements, notably race, politics, philosophy, religion and geography. Although there is not sufficient space in this article to discuss themes such as developmentally challenged children and the mystery genre, neither of which are relevant to the *Moribito* series, it should be noted that contemporary Japanese authors such as Kae Arisawa, Tomoko Ida and Kaoru Hayamine are tackling these themes.

The folktales and legends the characters encounter in the *Moribito* series actually help save its world, showing the importance of the search for the meanings of those stories and the need to hand them on to future generations. No doubt the media mix and its focus on "characters" will go on, but what the *Moribito* series shows is that if YA and children's literature continue to use the power of the written word to express the feelings, conflicts, and growth inherent in present-day society, they will help children and young adults in their struggles with everyday life and communication.

Notes

1 For translations of the Japanese book titles, I have referred to: *J'Lit Books from Japan* (www.booksfromjapan.jp/) and *One Hundred Japanese Books for Children* 1946–1979 (www.iiclo.or.jp/100books-e1946.htm) (Accessed 31 August 2014.)
2 The representative light novel, *Suzumiya Haruhi* Series (11 vols., 2003–11) has sold 800,000 copies and the 11th volume sold 51,000 copies in its first edition as well as being translated

and sold in Asia and Europe at the same time. Hiwatari, Takahiro. *"Tekusuto no Rekishisei"*
Ichiyanagi, Takahiro and Kume, Yoriko. Eds. (2013) *Light Novel Studies*, 249.

3 A weekly manga magazine, *Shonen Jump* (Boys' Jump) sells about 270,000 copies, but was
averaging about 630,000 copies in 1995. Shinoda, Hiroyuki. "Manga shijo no gekihen" (Rapid
Changes of Manga Market) *Tsukuru*. 44–5, April, 2014.

Bibliography

Amazawa, Taijiro (1973) *Hikariguruma yo maware*, Tokyo: Chikuma-shobo.

Arisawa, Kae (2013) *Kasanechan ni kitemina*, Tokyo: Kodansha.

Carroll, Lewis (2010) *Fushigi no kuni no Arisu shinyaku*. Translated by Shoichiro Kawai. Illustrated
by Okama. Tokyo: Ascii Media Works, 100–107.

Fujiwara, Kamui (2007–2008) *Seirei no Moribito*, 3 vols. Tokyo: Square Enix.

Griswold, Jerry (1992) *Audacious Kids*, New York: Oxford University Press.

Hayamine, Kaoru (2003–2017) *Machi no Tomu & Soya*, 14 vols. Tokyo: Kodansha.

Ida, Tomoko (2012) *Omake-dori*, Tokyo: Shin-nihon-shuppansha.

Inui, Tomiko (1959) *Kokage no ie no kobitotachi*, Tokyo: Chuo-koronsha.

Ishii, Mutsumi (2013) *Tokai no Arisu*, Tokyo: Iwasaki Shoten.

Ito, Yu (1998) *Oni no hashi*, Tokyo: Fukuinkan Shoten.

Iwase, Jôko (2014) *Kumori tokidoki hareru*, Tokyo: Rironsha.

Kadono, Eiko (1985–2016) *Majo no takkyubin*, 8 vols. Tokyo: Fukuinkan Shoten.

Kanzawa, Toshiko (1961) *Chibikko Kamu no bôken*, Tokyo: Rironsha.

Kamiyama, Kenji (2007) "Kamiyama Kenji interview," *Otona Anime*, Vol. 4 (May). Tokyo:
Yosensha.

Kilpatrick, Helen and Muta, Orie (2013) "Deconstructions of the (Japanese) Nation-State in
Uehashi Nahoko's *Moribito* (Guardian) Series," in Kit Kelen and Björn Sundmark (eds.) *The
Nation in Children's Literature: Nations of Childhood*, New York: Routledge, 81–95.

Kodama, Kiyoshi and Uehashi, Nahoko (2009) "Monogatari ga tachinoboru shunkan ni Tachiau
Yorokobi" [The Pleasure of the Moment When the Story Takes on a Life of its Own], in
Kodama Kiyoshi no Ano Sakka ni Aitai [Writers Kodama Kiyoshi Wants to Meet], Tokyo: PHP
Kenkyusho, 39–46.

Kosaka, Nao (2010) *Sutoroberi buru*, Tokyo: Kadokawa Shoten.

Mahara, Mito (2011) *Tetsu no shibuki ga haneru*, Tokyo: Kodansha.

Miyabe, Miyuki (2005) *Suteppu fâzâ suteppu*, Tokyo: Kodansha.

Miyazawa, Kenji (1991) *Night of the Milky Way Railway*. Translated by Sarah M. Strong. New
York: M.E. Sharpe.

Muranaka, Rie (2012) *Châshû no tsuki*, Tokyo: Komine-shoten.

Nakamatsu, Maruha (2010) *Gakko kuesuto*, Tokyo: Doshinsha.

Nogami, Akira (2009) *Ekkyô suru jidô bungaku* [Children's Literature is Crossing the Border],
Tokyo: Nagasaki-shuppan.

Ogiwara, Noriko (1993 [1988]) *Dragon Sword and Wind Child*. Translated by Cathy Hirano.
New York: Farrar, Straus and Giroux.

Okada, Jun (1994–2017) *Kosoado no Mori* series, 12 vols. Tokyo: Rironsha.

Ono, Fuyumi (1992–2001) *Jûni kokki* series, Tokyo: Kodansha.

Saito, Atsuo (1975) *Bôkenshatachi*, Tokyo: Maki shoten.

Saito, Hiroshi (1996–2012). *Shirakomaki*, 6 vols. Tokyo: Kaiseisha.

Saso, Yoko (2010) *Iemoto tantei Masuno-kun*, Tokyo: Kodansha.

Sato, Satoru (1959) *Dare mo shiranai chiisana kuni*, Tokyo: Kodansha.

Sheel, Ranjana (2003) "Women in Politics in Japan," *Economic and Political Weekly*, 38(39):
4097–4101.

Shinjô, Kazuma (2006) *Raito Noberu chô nyûmon* [Super Guide to Light Novels], Tokyo: Softbank
Creative.

Tanaka, Hiko (2011) *Fushigina fushigina kodomo no monogatari* [Extremely Strange Children's
Stories], Tokyo: Kobunsha.

Tomiyasu, Yoko (1990) *Kunugi bayashi no zawazawa-so*, Tokyo: Akane Shobo.

Tomiyasu, Yoko (1994) *Kitsune yama no natsuyasumi*, Tokyo: Ajabe Shobo.

Uehashi, Nahoko (1991) *Tsuki no mori ni kami yo nemure*, Tokyo: Kaiseisha.

Uehashi, Nahoko (1996–2012) *Moribito* series, 12 vols. Tokyo: Kaiseisha.

Uehashi, Nahoko (2008) *Moribito I: Guardian of the Spirit*. Translated by Cathy Hirano. New York: Scholastic.

Uehashi, Nahoko (2009) *Moribito II: Guardian of the Darkness*. Translated by Cathy Hirano. New York: Arthur Levine.

Uehashi, Nahoko (2006–2009) *Kemono no sôja* series, 4 vols. Tokyo: Kodansha.

Uehashi, Nahoko and Team Hokkaido (2009) *Barusa no shokutaku*, Tokyo: Shinchosha.

Uehashi, Nahoko (2011) *Moribito no subete: Moribito shiriizu kanzen gaido* [The Complete Guide to the *Moribito* Series]. Ed. by Kaiseisha. Tokyo: Kaiseisha.

Yamakawa, Tomoharu (2009) "Characters" in Eds. Ichiyanagi, Hirotaka and Kume, Yoriko. *Light Novel Kenkyu Josetsu* [Introduction to the Study of Light Novels], Tokyo: Seikyusha.

Yatsuka, Sumiko (2012) *Oretachi no asu ni mukatte*, Tokyo: Poplarsha.

Yokozawa, Akira (2011) *Suingu*, Tokyo: Doshinsha.

Zielenziger, Michael (2006) *Shutting Out the Sun. How Japan Created Its Own Lost Generation*, New York: Doubleday.

41

RECENT TRENDS AND THEMES IN MALAYSIAN CHILDREN'S FICTION

Sharifah A. Osman, Lai Suat Yan and Siti Rohaini Kassim

This essay examines some of the recent trends and themes in Malaysian children's fiction through a discussion of not only canonical texts of Malaysian literature for children such as classic folktales and legends like *Puteri Santubong, Bawang Merah, Bawang Putih* and *Mahsuri* (among those that reflect and perpetuate an inherently conservative patriarchal ideology) but also revisionary tales like *Puteri Pucuk Kelumpang* and *Dewi Laba Kundur*, among others, that illustrate a more inclusive rendering of gender, class and race in Malaysian society. The essay aims to trace the evolution of these literary texts as aesthetic and cultural forms within the context of Malaysia as a former British colony, to its current status as a postcolonial nation reflecting upon its own identity in the face of modernization and globalization. The essay is in three parts. Part 1 presents a historical overview of children's literature in Malaysia, with a particular emphasis on the influence of the English literary canon in the formation of the Malaysian school syllabus, from colonial to present times. Part 2 discusses the significance of popular folktales, myths and legends in Malaysian culture and society in the transmission of feudalistic or patriarchal values through the analysis of three representative tales: *Puteri Santubong* (Princess Santubong); *Bawang Merah, Bawang Putih*; and *Mahsuri*. Part 3 covers various folktales that feature a more progressive outlook in the representation of female characters and/or marginalized societies. Ultimately, these literary texts highlight the diversity of voices in the contemporary production (and reproduction) of Malaysian children's fiction published in English, and the viability of such stories for the promotion of cross-cultural understanding among young readers, not only in Malaysia but also globally.

A historical overview of children's literature in Malaysia

A glimpse into the literature for children available in the Malaysian market reveals that there is no dearth in the supply of material for improvement of literacy for children, particularly children's books. However, these books and sundry material collectively fall short of showing a definite "Malaysian-ness" in content. Because Malaysia is multiracial and multicultural, and each racial component has a cultural tradition of its own, how do we even begin to recognize a Malaysian tradition in children's literature? What colors should go onto the palette of Malaysian children's literature to enable a true representation?

And how far has literature for children in English been part of the literary tradition of Malaysian children? These are pertinent issues to consider if ever a single identity in literature for Malaysian children and young adults is to be realized. This section shares some observations on the kinds of literary texts that have had a part in contributing towards the development of children's literature in Malaysia. It will also indirectly comment on the direction of Malaysian children's literature in its efforts towards developing its own identity.

Children's literature in Malay

The beginnings of literature for children in the Malay language were in the oral tradition—narratives in the form of tales and folklore such as *Angan Mat Jenin, Pak Pandir*, and *Sang Kancil* that were told to children to inculcate moral and religious values. Some of the most original stories are found in *Sejarah Melayu* (the Malay Annals), which includes *Hikayat Hang Tuah*, the tale of the legendary Malay Muslim warrior Hang Tuah, and the saga of *Princess Hang Li Po*, the Emperor of China's daughter offered as a bride to the Sultan of Malacca. Originally meant for older audiences, these tales have also fascinated children of all ages.

A brief survey of the literature demonstrates that children's books in the Malay language have had a much earlier beginning compared to those in English. Similar to the tradition in the west, these early books were written to develop reading and writing skills. Many such books were written by Christian missionaries who came to Malaya to spread the faith, but realizing that the problem of illiteracy had first to be resolved, produced such titles as *Menolong Segala Anak* (Helping All Children, 1818), *Buku Pelajaran Bahasa Melayu* (Malay Language Textbook. 1838, 1847), and *Budak Hampir Tenggelam* (A Child Almost Drowned, 1844) alongside books that directly or indirectly propagated Christian religious teachings (Ishak 2005: 25–45).

At the end of the nineteenth century, with the direct involvement of the British colonial government in the education of the local people, school texts and readers flooded the market through publishing houses responsible for supplying recommended texts and readers. The contents of these books were mainly translations and adaptations of English classics, but also contained stories from the Quran and well-known Malay *hikayat* (stories, often about national heroes) and *syair* (stanzaic poetry, usually narrative or didactic) such as *Hikayat Amir Hamzah, Syair Siti Zubaidah*, and *Hikayat Hang Tuah* (Ishak 2005: 25–45).

Local publishing houses, particularly Dewan Bahasa dan Pustaka (DBP), played and continue to play a crucial part in developing literature for children and young adults in the Malay language. A survey of books for children and young adults published by DBP shows clear evidence of the support it gave and still gives to local writers, which directly helps to build an enriched collection of quality works by writers, to the point that Malay literature for children has developed into a local canonical tradition in itself.

Children's literature in English

Based on requests for teaching material made to the Colonial Office in London by British officers serving in the Federation of Malaya in the late 1940s (documented in the National Archives, Kew), it can be deduced that Malaysian children's literature in English had its beginnings with the setting up of the British colonial government in Malaya in the first half of the twentieth century. Before this, literature for public consumption was mainly written in the vernacular or Arabic. Through the education system reorganized by the colonial government, English language and literature became a significant component of Malaysia's colonial heritage. To a certain extent the selected texts brought in by the British colonial government and used in schools formed the beginnings of the shape and nature of literature in English in subsequently independent Malaysia.

Early books in English for children were published mainly to introduce the English language into Malaya, as part of the British government's colonizing program. Letters and notes from serving officers to the Colonial Office indicate that part of the British colonial government's agenda was to introduce English into the existing education system without disrupting the local education system, particularly since vernacular schools already existed then, with the eventual purpose to make English the medium of instruction in government-aided schools. The syllabus introduced was the English school syllabus, with the teaching of poetry, drama, short stories or novels geared towards preparing students for the English assessment system—the Junior or Senior Cambridge examinations. Books were initially brought in from England, and the contents of these were naturally Eurocentric in essence. Literature in English was introduced as part of the teaching of the English language. Typical English lessons involved reading excerpts from prose versions of Shakespeare, and poems such as Wordsworth's "Daffodils" or Noyes' "The Highwayman". These texts were often so removed from the Malaysian cultural context that many students found the lessons difficult, simply because they could neither visualize what a daffodil looked like, nor imagine who or what a highwayman was. Nevertheless, these problems notwithstanding, this move by the British colonial government paved the way for the development of literacy through an education system in which English was significant, which has now developed into not only an important second language for intercultural and interethnic communication for Malaysians in general but also a valuable language for global communication.

After independence in 1957, Malaysia developed its own selection of texts to help in nation building, with concerted efforts to make English materials more accessible to local children. Malaysian writers were and are encouraged to produce works that portray a consciously Malaysian cultural background. Hence as far as books and other print material are concerned, these have also provided a rich source for literacy development in general. As part of the endeavor to create and develop a unified Malaysia, amidst its characteristically multicultural attributes, children's literature in English plays an important role in the nurturing processes of young Malaysians. Children's literature is now readily available in various forms, both print and multimedia. There is also stronger support from the general public and the government for the teaching of literature in schools, specifically in the use of children's and young adult literature as a tool in language teaching. Adjustments have also been made to include literature in English as a separate elective in the curriculum (Syllabus (revised) for the Subjects English Language and Literature for Secondary Schools, 2007).

Literature in English that has been available for Malaysian children may be broadly categorized into either traditional "imports" or local publications. The former include works for young and preadolescent children, directly brought in from Europe, or local reprints or re-presentations of traditional European and British folk and fairy tales, such as those by Hans Christian Andersen and the Grimm Brothers as well as popular nursery rhymes. Novels for older age groups include *The Wonderful Wizard of Oz, Alice in Wonderland, Little Women, Robinson Crusoe, Black Beauty*, and *Bambi*, all distinctly

European in origin and essence, but given the Malaysian touch through illustrations, as represented by Malaysian publishers. Various versions of such tales are readily available, including those translated into Bahasa Melayu. One advantage in having this category of children's books is that they provide excellent models of idiomatic use of English, and are therefore popular among parents who wish their children to develop a high standard in English.

Alongside "imported" children's literature, a proliferation of works produced by local writers and publishers now exists. These materials are clearly Malaysian based, and in a multitude of formats—picture books, board books, novels, nursery rhymes, and so on. Many still show influences from western traditions, as is common in most postcolonial writings, but there is a clear sense of works developing a Malaysian identity, as in examples such as Daphne Lee's *1 Red Flower* (2007) and *Sweet Pink Posies* (2007), or collections of local folk tales such as those in *Malaysian Children's Favourite Stories* (2004), *Timeless Tales of Malaysia* (2009), and *Legendary Princesses of Malaysia* (2013). The continued production of both groups reflects the directions in which children's literature is developing in Malaysia.

Children's literature in English has been enriched by its historical and cultural background, both being relevant influences on its growth, either as a genre or as support material for enhancing literacy among children in Malaysia. As a consequence of Malaysia's colonial past, children's literature in English cannot escape from traces of its Eurocentric character, but with growing awareness as well as concerted efforts from various quarters, a Malaysian identity in literature for children and young adults is very much a possibility. Further investigation could be done on how far we have moved towards developing a Malaysian identity in children's literature in English, to ensure that children's literature in both Bahasa Melayu and English run on par, which would have broader implications for Malaysian children and their future, to enable them to thrive in a world becoming figuratively smaller through globalization.

Popular folktales, myths and legends in Malaysian children's literature in English: three case studies

A survey of various Malaysian folktales and legends in locally published literature in English for children reveals stories that share common elements with those in similar genres in the traditional western canon. Like readers who grew up with fairy tales such as *Cinderella* and *Sleeping Beauty*, many Malaysian readers retain fond memories of Malay folktales like *Puteri Santubong* and *Mahsuri* from their childhood. As Jack Zipes argues, fairy tales "[communicate] the values and the various preoccupations of different nations", and were "cultivated for children as part of the civilizing process", to educate them about morality, charity, virtue, manners and good conduct (2006: x-xi). However, fairy tales also function as "sites for the construction of appropriate gendered behaviour" and play a crucial role in the reproduction of patriarchal values (Parsons 2004: 135–137).

The gender stereotyping seen in many traditional Malay folk tales written for children mirrors a similar trend in European fairy tales in that both reflect and perpetuate patriarchal and feudalistic values by emphasizing female virtue and moral behavior. Based on the discussion of three Malaysian legends, *Puteri Santubong, Bawang Merah, Bawang Putih* and *Mahsuri*, this section demonstrates how the definition of "feminine" qualities in such tales is influenced by an inherently patriarchal ideology, where women appear either as passive "damsels in distress" or dysfunctional figures in conflict with each other, awaiting "rescue" by the hero. Exemplary heroines are often physically attractive, chaste, filial, and rewarded for their submissiveness by marriage to a rich and/or powerful man. Conversely, female villains appear as wicked stepmothers or sisters: they are obstacles/ rivals in the heroine's quest for the love of a worthy man, and consequently punished through death or marginalization.

Puteri Santubong (Salmi 2010), from Sarawak, East Malaysia, tells of Puteri (Princess) Santubong and Puteri Sejinjang, sent down to Earth by their father, the King of Kayangan (the land of fairie) to end the feud between the villagers of Pasir Putih and Pasir Kuning. They are warned not to fight with each other or to be influenced by human folly. However, conflict arises when both sisters fall for Prince Serapi, a mortal. Unable to decide whom to wed, he proposes to both, leading to a bitter quarrel between the sisters. Such selfishness and lack of filial piety incurs the King's wrath, who punishes both daughters by turning them into two mountains, Mount Santubong and Mount Sejinjang, which dominate the landscape of Sarawak until today.

As a cautionary tale, *Puteri Santubong* illustrates the role of gender stereotyping in emphasizing desirable "feminine" traits like docility and filial piety over rivalry and the disobedience of patriarchal law. Despite being emissaries of peace, the princesses are admired not for their leadership traits but their beauty and domestic talents (Santubong for weaving, and Sejinjang for threshing paddy). With Prince Serapi as a common object of desire, they reveal their frailties as women and are thus literally petrified into silence and submission. The King's dramatic punishment meted out to his daughters thus warns the generations after of the deadly consequences of defying patriarchal authority.

Similarly, the tale of *Bawang Merah, Bawang Putih* (Salmi 2011) highlights the virtues of female docility and sacrifice in the face of persecution and injustice. The hardworking Bawang Merah, daughter of Pak Ali and the kindly Mak Labu, is pitted against the spoilt Bawang Putih, daughter of the wicked second wife Mak Kundur. After Pak Ali's death, Mak Kundur forces Mak Labu and Bawang Merah to do all the household chores while she and Bawang Putih laze about. This culminates in Mak Kundur pushing Mak Labu into the river, where she drowns but magically turns into a fish. Mak Kundur serves this fish to Bawang Merah, who realizes with horror that she has eaten her own mother, but bears this grief and hardship with patience. Based on a dream she has of her mother, Bawang Merah finds a magical swing under a banyan tree and enchants the Sultan with her beautiful voice. Intrigued, the Sultan follows her home. Mak Kundur tries to deceive him by passing Bawang Putih off as the singer but fails as she is unable to make the magical swing move or sing beautifully for the Sultan. This angers the Sultan who feels cheated. Upon searching their house, the Sultan discovers Bawang Merah, falls in love with her, and they marry and live happily ever after.

Like *Puteri Santubong*, *Bawang Merah, Bawang Putih* highlights the theme of female rivalry over a man, first between Mak Kundur and Mak Labu for Pak Ali, and later between Bawang Putih and Bawang Merah for the Sultan. Significantly, the orphaned Bawang Merah, like Cinderella, is rewarded for her sufferings through a singular power (her alluring voice) and is thus noticed and "rescued" by the Sultan. As Zipes asserts, the fairy tale heroine "must be passive until the right man comes along to recognize her virtues and marry her" (1979: 25). Through the distinct oppositional qualities between Bawang Merah and Bawang Putih, the narrative reproduces a familiar trope that reinforces the subsidiary role of women in a patriarchal society, by suggesting that female desirability lies in the balance between sacrifice and the stoic display of virtue in the face of injustice and oppression.

If the tale of *Bawang Merah, Bawang Putih* idealizes female passivity and sacrifice, then the legend of *Mahsuri* (Salmi 2010) from Langkawi, Kedah, complicates and challenges such notions. In Salmi's retelling, the beautiful Mahsuri is born under mysterious circumstances after an elderly wife becomes pregnant after eating a crust of rice found in their paddy field (the state of Kedah is also known as "the rice bowl of Malaysia"). Mahsuri attracts many suitors, including the village Chieftain, Datuk Karma Jaya, who already has a wife, Mahura, and several grown children. Humiliated by her husband's intention to marry Mahsuri, Mahura bears a grudge against her. Although Mahsuri marries their son Mat Deris, Mahura remains jealous of Mahsuri and vows revenge. When Mat Deris is called to war, Mahura spreads rumors about Mahsuri's apparent infidelity, and convinces Datuk Karma Jaya and the entire village of Mahsuri's affair with a poet, Deraman. Both Mahsuri and Deraman are sentenced to death despite their pleas of innocence. The executioner attempts to stab Mahsuri but fails; she confesses that she can only be killed with a sacred *keris* (dagger). When the executioner finally kills Mahsuri, white blood gushes from her wound and white mist surrounds her, proving her innocence and supernatural powers. Before she dies, Mahsuri curses the villagers with seven generations of bad luck for the senseless accusations and injustice inflicted upon her. Langkawi is invaded by the Siamese and left desolate and barren for many generations, proving Mahsuri's curse.

As a means for the transmission of cultural values, characters in the tale conform to gendered roles within Malay feudalistic society: the wronged heroine Mahsuri who bears the injustice against her with fortitude; the evil Mahura who slanders Mahsuri; the vain Datuk Karma Jaya who falls for his wife's deceit; the pawn Deraman, who fails to save Mahsuri, and is thus silenced and emasculated. Furthermore, the potency of Mahsuri's curse affects not only those who directly betrayed her, but all of Langkawi for seven generations, a message that warns against envy, rumor-mongering and cruelty toward the innocent. Mahsuri's supernatural power, combined with the poignancy of her status as a victim of slander, elevates her curse beyond the expression of female anger, vengeance and bitterness, manifesting itself instead as a profound reality with terrible consequences. Although aptly glorified as a symbol of feminine innocence and purity, the legend of Mahsuri also serves as a stark reminder of the power of female agency in the face of societal injustice and patriarchal oppression.

As case studies of how Malaysian folktales reflect "the aspirations, needs, dreams and wishes of the people, either affirming the dominant social values or revealing the necessity to change them" (Zipes 2006: 5), these legends demonstrate how children's literature is crucial not only to the propagation of patriarchal and feudalistic ideology but also highlight moral and cultural values essential to nation-building like hard work, fortitude, benevolence and justice. Other stories in the *Asian Legends* series can also be read using a similar approach, especially *Dang Anum, Puteri Gunung Ledang*, and *Batu Belah, Batu Bertangkup*. While the emphasis on female virtue in *Puteri Santubong, Bawang Merah, Bawang Putih*, and *Mahsuri* appears didactic, even incongruous, to contemporary readers inclined to more progressive views of femininity, the conservative depictions of the protagonists in these legends (both male and female) do not have to dilute the enjoyment of such tales nor the absorption of their moral values. Indeed, the understanding of the limited freedom of women in the past only enhances the appreciation of current young readers of the genre, regardless of gender, of a journey towards progress, modernity and independence that cannot, and should not, be taken for granted.

Revisionary tales of feminine identity of the Malays from Perak and the indigenous peoples from Sabah and Sarawak

This section highlights the diversity and empowerment underlying the revisionary feminine identities in Malaysian children's fiction through the analysis of four stories: *Puteri Pucuk Kelumpang* (The Kelumpang Tree Child) from the Malays of Perak (Dutta 2009), *Dewi Labu Kundur* (Dutta 2009) and *Frog Princess* from Sabah, and *How the World was Formed* from Sarawak. *Frog Princess* and *How the World was Formed* are the work of the Women's Development Collective (WDC), a feminist organization in Malaysia formed in 1987.[1] Such depictions reflect the aims of the WDC to promote "values...towards building a gender-sensitive, just, equitable and humane future generation of Malaysia" through the retelling of folktales (foreword). Significantly, the female protagonists portrayed in these tales challenge the stereotypical identity of women as damsels in distress for they are neither defined by nor made to serve the hero as seen in many traditional Western folktales as well as those from Malaysia discussed above.

These revisionary feminine identities are delineated into three main themes: women's assertion of their autonomy; the expansion of the female subject position in non-traditional domains; and the power and agency of the wise and respected female figure. However, these are not rigid delineations, as some values such as mutuality, co-existence and the sharing of household tasks can be found in more than one tale. The stereotypical and binary role of not only women but also men are challenged and reconstructed in these folktales. Nevertheless, at times, this co-exists with patriarchal values.

On woman's terms

The heroines in *Puteri Pucuk Kelumpang* and *Frog Princess* are not docile damsels in distress awaiting rescue but instead assert their autonomy by standing up to the unreasonable demands of their husbands. In *Puteri Pucuk Kelumpang*, Mudalara goes against the wishes of her husband, Sampar, to abandon their baby daughter Puteri. For him, only sons are important. The story contrasts Sampar's selfishness, arrogance and devaluing of the female child with Mudalara's revaluing of their daughter and her privileging of family and communal bonds. In the end, Sampar seeks forgiveness from Mudalara and rejoices over his daughter. Through the emphasis on maternal care, the folktale highlights the civilizing effects of female influence over male authority. Read through a feminist lens, the folktale is revisionary as the heroine deviates from the usual trope of Malay folktales that focuses on female docility. Instead, wise, resourceful and courageous Mudalara asserts her autonomy to protect her daughter from her husband's unjust authoritarian rule. Significantly, while maternal love is celebrated as is typical of Malay folktales, there is simultaneously an emphasis on the revaluation of the female child.

Similarly, in *Frog Princess*, Lingkut defies her husband's wish to "disown" her parents. He is embarrassed by them, given his much higher status as a prince. Lingkut decides this after she realizes "they [her parents] loved her and took care of her even when she was only an ugly frog girl", (WDC, n.d., 15) in contrast to the prince who has only seen the beautiful version of her. As a feminist text, the folktale challenges the conventional emphasis on external beauty by drawing attention to the internal beauty of the brave and discerning heroine.

While the tale highlights the theme of filial piety common in Asian societies, it also sets it against the trope of the Malay patriarchal folktale whereby the heroine's ultimate aim is to be happily married. Initially Lingkut obeys her husband's wish not to see her parents but finally returns to their home and erects a barrier to prevent him from pursuing her. Instead of subscribing to the stereotypical submissiveness of patriarchal folklore (Craven 2002: 124), Lingkut asserts her agency as a woman by forgoing her marriage when she decides to stay with her parents and uses her magical powers for herself and her community.

Expansion of the female subject position in non-traditional domains

The folktale *How the World was Formed* from the indigenous peoples of Sarawak expands feminine roles into domains traditionally associated with male spiritual power such as being a co-creator of the world. In this story, Grandma Eti narrates to the village children that a woman has creative powers similar to that of a man, as they both co-create the world. This contrasts with the often powerful and spiritual position of the creator as male identified in the patriarchal worldview. Metaphorically, baking—typically associated with women—is used to depict the creation of human figures. The process is described thus: "They [Rigih and Sunang] took some rice flour, mixed them with water and put in some sugar. They rolled them flat! And rolled them thin! And they made them into human figures" (WDC, n.d. 10). Although the humans created have different names and physical appearances, they all love one another. Rather than equating cooking as solely women's province, the husband Sunang is shown involved in both cooking and childcare. Indeed, during the Gawai (Harvest) festival, both Rigih and Sunang cook, just as they co-created humans through the metaphor of baking.

This tale as a feminist text illustrates progressive ideas about family values as the "subject position" for women is expanded through their role as co-creators of the world, while those for men expand to include their involvement in domestic tasks as they cook and care for children. This depiction of the family institution in terms of the co-sharing of domestic duties opposes Menon's assertion that folktales like *Bawang Merah, Bawang Putih* reflect the constraints of traditional Asian culture in which "the father is the bread-winner of the family, whilst the mother is the nurturer who looks after the home, spends time with the children and instils good values in them" (2009: 38). The characterization of Rigih and Sunang illustrates how their "subject positions" are expanded as there is no fixed set of characteristics to which either gender must adhere, challenging the binary notions of masculinity and femininity. The folktale thus highlights the theme of co-existence and mutuality between man and woman, which serves to critique patriarchal culture.

The power and agency of the wise and respected female figure

The tale of *Dewi Labu Kundur* (The Gift of the Winter Melon) from Sabah highlights the agency of the wise, respected female figure, who in her role as a *bobohizan* (spiritual healer) wields the power to reward or punish in the tale. The domestic tasks she sets for Anak and Bongkoron as young men overturn the conventional roles associated with masculinity and femininity. In the absence of the *bobohizan*, Anak is instructed to care for her children, tend to her farm, and feed her family; he achieves these through kindness, hard work and good judgment, and is rewarded by the bobohizan with the gift of a winter melon that transforms magically into a lovely maiden. Her approval of Anak's behavior demonstrates the endorsement of family values: punctuality, respect, wisdom, diligence and patience. In contrast, the *bobohizan's* "punishment" of Bongkoron (whose gift of winter melon turns into a "hideous old hag") reflects the rejection of the values he represents: laziness, impatience, selfishness and greed, all negative traits that hinder the progress of civilization. In highlighting these opposing versions of male behavior, the tale suggests that Anak's virtues are admired not only by the *bobohizan* and the community but also universally, thus indicating how the folk tale functions as the reflection and reproduction of desirable social values (Parsons 2004, 139).

However, there is a patriarchal twist to the tale as Anak's hard work, kindness and wisdom is rewarded with a "lovely maiden", while Bongkoron's laziness, selfishness and greed is repaid with a "hideous old hag". The tale suggests that a beautiful, young woman is still the trophy wife to be won by deserving men even if bequeathed by a respected female figure, an act that displays how the tale remains confined in its conformity to patriarchal ideology. Nevertheless, while heroines in folktales such as Mahsuri in the *Mahsuri* legend and Sita in *Ramayana* are typically idealized for their innocence, purity and fidelity to the hero, here Anak is glorified for his wisdom, care for the children and the farm—all of which can be symbolically read as traits of a good provider and reliable husband. In short, despite its patriarchal undertones, *Dewi Labu Kundur* does reflect progressive ideas of gender in highlighting female agency through the figure of the powerful *bobohizan* who rewards Anak for his ability to provide and care for the family, thus earning his reward.

While the tale of *Dewi Labu Kundur* overturns gender stereotypes on the care and management of the family and household, it is still replete with patriarchal values and hence falls short of its emancipatory potential. Or, read differently, this tale reflects the contradictions within a person or society in which one can be feminist in certain ways and patriarchal in others. In comparison, *How the World was Formed* is devoid of patriarchal values as it primarily emphasizes how both men and women should collaborate in the spirit of mutual respect in tasks both big and small such as co-creating the world and in sharing domestic duties. Different from traditional folktales where the hero is in a position of power, one that is "often exercised to dominate and rule others", this folktale illustrates how the heroine "assumes a position of power to attain independence and to forge mutual respect", with the aim of "self-discovery and personal development rather than domination over others" and where "human interdependency, rather than competition" is stressed (Parsons 2004: 140).

As beings "[s]till in the process of being shaped by ideological beliefs," children's minds "can go in multiple directions" (Baecker 2006: 200). As part of children's literature in Malaysia, folktales need to offer a range of subject positions that includes a revisionary perspective of femininity. Emphasizing that the identity of characters should not be stereotyped and oversimplified, Nair and Talif argue that "attention must be paid to messages about gender construction […] because they affect identity construction in young children" (2010: 139). Children who read such revisionary folk tales can thus be empowered by the depiction of such heroines in roles not defined in opposition to the male, and to view power and agency in terms of interdependency rather than domination over others. As Nair notes, numerous studies of Malaysian children's literature "show that the majority of books are dominated by male figures, and girls are portrayed as acted upon rather than active" (2005: 54). Thus, these folktales, while still within a hetero-normative framework like most patriarchal legends, are inspiring as they provide alternative views of womanhood: wise, courageous and autonomous women, rather than passive, suffering objects of beauty who are frequently acted upon.

Conclusion

In charting the trends and themes in Malaysian children's literature in English, the most distinctive feature appears to be the dynamic growth of the genre, given the volume, diversity and availability of works currently produced by local writers and publishing houses. As a relatively young nation at the crossroads of tradition and modernity, Malaysia and its literary scene provide fertile ground for exploring the vast potential in catering to a young audience eager to understand its place in the world. As the discussion above hopes to have shown, the consumption of such classical tales serves a dual purpose and historical relevance for its intended demographic: as didactic emblems and repositories of its literary and cultural heritage, but also to assess its attitudes towards its people in its journey to becoming a progressive and developed nation. Through the analysis of such tales, children can be nurtured to participate in discussions of the roles of both men and women in society ("traditional" and "modern", past and present) as well as to develop a genuine understanding and appreciation of the cultural and political dynamics that influence their lives as maturing citizens, whether of Malaysia or the world.

Acknowledgments

This essay is the collaborative output of a research project funded by the University of Malaya Research Grant UMRG410-12HNE from Nov 2012–April 2014. We also wish to thank Grace Chin (University of Brunei Darussalam) for her constructive feedback and contribution to our reading of *Mahsuri* on the role of the curse as an example of female agency in the traditional Malay folk tale.

Note

1 For details on the formation of WDC and the arrest of its members for their social activism see Lai 2003, 62 and 202 endnote 13, and for its advocacy work during the 1999 General Election see Lai 2004, 129–133. For a summary of its activities see www.hati.my/women/womens-development-collective-wdc/ [Accessed 13 October 2014].

Bibliography

Baecker, Diann L. (2006) "Surviving rescue: A Feminist Reading of Scott O'Dell's *Island of the Blue Dolphins*," *Children's Literature in Education*, 38(3): 195–206.

Craven, Allison (2002) "Beauty and the Belles: Discourses of Feminism and Femininity in Disneyland," *European Journal of Women's Studies*, 9(2): 123–142.

Desai, Christina M. (2006) "National Identity in a Multicultural Society: Malaysian Children's Literature in English," *Children's Literature in Education*, 37(2): 163–184.

Dutta, Tutu (2009) *Timeless Tales of Malaysia*, Subang: Marshall Cavendish.

Ishak, Md. Sidin Ahmad (2005) *Perkembangan Sastera Kanak-kanak dan Remaja di Malaysia: Buku Melayu Mencari Nafas Baru*, Shah Alam: Cerdik Publications.

Lai, Suat Yan (2003) "The Women's Movement in Peninsular Malaysia, 1900–99: A Historical Analysis," in Meredith L. Weiss and Saliha Hassan (eds.) *Social Movements in Malaysia*, London and New York: RoutledgeCurzon.

Lai, Suat Yan (2004) "Participation of the Women's Movement in Malaysia: The 1999 General Election," in Hock Guan Lee (ed.) *Social Movements in Malaysia*, Singapore: Institute of Southeast Asian Studies.

Menon, J. Yasodhara (2009) "A Study of Archetypal Patterns in Selected Malaysian Folk Tales," *Jurnal Sarjana*, 24(1): 27–42.

Nair, Ramesh (2005) "Recognizing Sexist Language through Children's Literature," *The English Teacher*, 34: 51–59.

Nair, Ramesh and Rosli Talif (2010) "Lexical Choices and the Construction of Gender in Malaysian Children's Literature," *Kajian Malaysia: Journal of Malaysian Studies*, 28(2): 137–159.

Parsons, Linda T. (2004) "Ella Evolving: Cinderella Stories and the Construction of Gender-Appropriate Behaviour," *Children's Literature in Education*, 35(2): 135–154.

Salmi, Mohamad (2010) *Asian Legends (Malaysia): The Curse of Mahsuri*, Petaling Jaya: MPH Group Publishing Sdn. Bhd.

Salmi, Mohamad (2010) *Asian Legends (Malaysia): The Legend of the Two Princesses (Puteri Santubong)*, Petaling Jaya: MPH Group Publishing Sdn. Bhd.

Salmi, Mohamad (2011) *Asian Legends (Malaysia): Bawang Merah, Bawang Putih*, Petaling Jaya: MPH Group Publishing Sdn. Bhd.

Women's Development Collective, n.d. *Frog Princess* (in English and Malay), Petaling Jaya: Women's Development Collective.

Women's Development Collective, n.d. *How the World Was Formed* (in English and Malay), Petaling Jaya: Women's Development Collective.

Women's Development Collective, www.hati.my/women/womens-development-collective-wdc/ (accessed 13 October 2014).

Zipes, Jack (1979) *Breaking the Magic Spell: Radical Theories of Folk and Fairy Tales*, London: Heinemann.

Zipes, Jack (2006) *Fairy Tales and the Art of Subversion: The Classical Genre for Children and the Process of Civilization*, London and New York: Routledge.

42

BRAZILIAN LITERATURE FOR CHILDREN AND YOUTH

Between the reader and the market

Regina Zilberman

The state of literature for children and youth in Brazil in the second decade of the twenty-first century is encapsulated in the figures reproduced in Table 42.1:

The number of books for children and youth in Brazil is a fraction of the number of available textbooks, as shown in Table 42.2:

Censo da educação básica (The School Census of Basic Education) released in 2012 by the National Institute of Educational Studies and Research (INEP) indicated that the student population of Brazil consists of approximately fifty million people, extending from primary to high school and including segments dedicated to Special Education and Education of Youth and Adults. Considering the quantity of volumes written for children and youth and printed in each year, it may be assumed that each of the enrolled students was expected to consume at least one copy. The average is higher, when compared with the number of schoolbooks produced. Continuing print production for the student audience constitutes significant figures: the percentage of books classified as youth and children's literature reaches, and at times exceeds, 10 percent of consumers; this percentage is surpassed only by textbooks, which represent around 50 percent of the market.

Table 42.3 summarizes the global annual turnover of book production in Brazil, and demonstrates the quantity of books printed:

This market, however, does not depend on individuals acquiring books spontaneously or because of the encouragement of school, as the main client is rather the Brazilian State, at the federal, state, and municipal levels. The federal government is the major purchaser, by means of programs promoted by the Ministry of Education, such as the National Library Program in School (PNBE) and the Textbook National Program (PNLD). The PNBE is directed towards the purchase of books for children and youth, even though the annual acquisitions do not always choose titles intended for that audience, as the selection also includes works that respond to teachers' classroom needs. Table 42.4 shows the PNBE's acquisitions from Brazilian publishers:

The annual lists of books acquired through the budget of the Ministry of Education include novels, short stories, poetry, dramaturgy, adaptations, graphic novels, and proceed, mainly, from Brazilian authors, both canonical and emerging names.

On one hand, the State interference has a perverse effect because it induces the production of titles with subjects and for age ranges determined by public and governmental

421

Table 42.1 Brazilian youth and children's literature

	2010	2011	2012
Total books printed	70,291,036	30,911,591	47,413,402
Printed titles	[not available]	[not available]	11,011
Market participation	14.27%	6.19%	9.74%

Source: Brazilian Publishing Sector's Production and Sales – Base 2012[1]

Table 42.2 Production of textbooks

	2011	2012
Total books printed	282,827,709	214,250,244
Printed titles	[not available]	10,276
Market participation	56.59%	44.04%

Source: Brazilian Publishing Sector's Production and Sales – Base 2012

Table 42.3 Global turnover and copies sold

Year	Turnover in GBP	Copies
2010	1,184,766,489.04	437,945,286
2011	1,271,935,141.26	469,468,840
2012	1,310,632,353.57	434,920,064

Source: Brazilian Publishing Sector's Production and Sales – Base 2012

Table 42.4 PNBE: turnover and copies sold

Year	Turnover in GBP	Copies
2010	18,675,945.12	13,376,477
2011	20,641,386.15	10,086,824
2012	18,700,084.36	11,353,211

Source: Brazilian Publishing Sector's Production and Sales – Base 2012

guidelines. On the other, such a course of action strengthens the publishing industry and, above all, professionalizes authors and illustrators, giving the country's youth and children's literature an enviable position, if compared to their peers in terms of general fiction and poetry. A review of the historical trajectory of children's and youth literature in Brazil will show what determined the growth of trust in the genre, which has never before experienced such a propitious market position.

The first century

One of the first books for children to circulate in Brazil must have been *Tesouro dos Meninos* (The Children's Treasure). Judging by the observation of John Luccock, a British tradesman who lived in the then-Portuguese colony between 1808 and 1818, the book dealt with "ethics, virtues, and manners" (1975: 379). From 1818 that role was filled by *Leitura para Meninos* (Readings for Children), which comprised "a collection of moral stories related to ordinary defects faced by the young and a dialogue about the geography, chronology, and history of Portugal and natural history" (Cabral 1881).

Leitura para Meninos shared with *Tesouro dos Meninos* an educational, mainly moralizing, purpose, and the presentation of fictional tales to be read to children. It was many times reprinted, and not long after its first edition, suggesting that the book reached its audience, perhaps among adults who desired tools that teach children to read and to behave. Rubens Borba de Morais considers it the founder of Brazilian youth literature: "Youth literature arises, in 1818, with a title that was successful, as it was reprinted in 1821, 1822 and 1824. It is a 'reading book', as was said previously: *Leitura para Meninos*..." (1993: xxix).

That the youth audience began to take shape in the beginning of the nineteenth century is indicated by the translation, in 1814, of *Aventuras Pasmosas do Célebre Barão de Munkausen* (The Amazing Adventures of the Famous Baron Munchausen). In 1847, the book is included in the catalog of Laemmert, a major publisher in Rio de Janeiro, indicating the permanence of its attraction.

In spite of an auspicious start, there were frequent complaints of lack of variety in books intended for children, especially for school. In 1850, *Tesouro dos Meninos* was still in circulation, alongside *Simão de Nântua* (Simon from Nantua), probably the most widely read book among Brazilian youth in the 1800s. That there were few adequate titles intended for children does not mean that the market lacked potential. Schools required printed materials, and the government helped to meet the demand. Primitivo Moacyr tells of the books distributed in 1866 among primary schools in Rio de Janeiro, among them 652 copies of *Contos de Schmid* (Schmid's Tales). He also reproduces the values, in the currency of the time, spent for the acquisition of the books: "2:000$000 réis assigned in the [governmental] budget" (approximately US$ 85,400), and, available for the following year, "4:000$000" (approximately US$ 170,700), to be spent on the purchase of "titles about history of Brazil, which are missing, and the metric system and the Coruja arithmetic" (240).

Alongside the popularity driven by the government purchases of Schmid's tales were fables adapted for the Portuguese language and the Brazilian reader by authors born in Brazil. Justiniano José da Rocha, in 1852, launched the *Coleção de Fábulas Imitadas de Esopo e de La Fontaine* (Collection of Fables Imitating Aesop and La Fontaine), reedited in 1863 and 1873. The Baron of Paranapiacaba also translated La Fontaine, publishing in 1883 *O Primeiro Livro das Fábulas (...) para Uso das Escolas de Instrução Primária* (The First Book of Fables (...) for Use in Schools of Primary Instruction), reedited in 1886. Beside books whose titles highlight that they are designed for the school market are books oriented by declared audience. *Contos Infantis* (Children's Tales), by Adelina Lopes Vieira and Júlia Lopes de Almeida, was launched in 1886 and adopted for use in primary schools, according to the determination by the Public Primary and Secondary Instruction of the federal government.

The editorial breakthrough, however, was the launch of the Biblioteca Infantil (Children's Library), sponsored by Livraria Quaresma, whose owner in 1894 commissioned Figueiredo Pimentel to produce a selection of fairytales, entitled *Contos da Carochinha* (Old Wives' Tales). Once again, the consumer market showed itself responsive: the (unattributed) preface to the 24th edition of *Contos da Carochinha* (1958) recalls the book's success since inception, as the first edition "sold out completely, in less than a month" (8–9).

The business of books for children, incipient in the era of *Tesouro dos Meninos* and *Livro de Leitura*, prospered at the end of the 1800s. While there were not enough Brazilian authors and subjects at that time, these began to manifest themselves in the beginning of the next century, when the following titles were published: *Porque Me Ufano de Meu País* (Why I Am Proud of My County), by Afonso Celso (1901); *Contos Pátrios* (Patriotic Tales), by Olavo Bilac and Coelho Neto (1904); *Histórias da Nossa Terra* (Tales of our Land), by Júlia Lopes de Almeida (1907); and *Através do Brasil* (Through Brazil), by Olavo Bilac and Manuel Bonfim (1910). The titles are enough to indicate a preference for nationalism, as if children's literature was only able to succeed in the country if, at the same time, it affirmed the country itself. Thanks to this choice, Brazilian children's literature maintained its ties to the school, guaranteeing a result that had already pertained for almost a century: a captive audience and an assured consumer market.

The modernization of the book and the modernity of children's literature

In 1919, Thales de Andrade published *Saudade* (Nostalgia), a very successful book that until at least 2002 continued figuring in the catalog of a Brazilian publisher. The beginning of its auspicious career is due to an action of the government of São Paulo, which sponsored the initial imprint of 15,000 copies, and then another 20,000 were printed by the *Jornal de Piracicaba*, a newspaper from the author's native town. These circumstances do not make Thales de Andrade's book less important, because the dependence on the state dated back to the time of the emperor and lasted until the present day. What gave *Saudade* the condition of inaugural milestone is that the plot was a product of the author's imagination, breaking the cycle of adaptations that, since *Aventuras Pasmosas do Célebre Barão de Munkausen*, passed through the hands of Figueiredo Pimentel, and were practiced before by Carlos Jansen, and, after, by Arnaldo de Oliveira Barreto.

Andrade, like Jansen, was a teacher; like Barreto, he graduated from the Pedagogical School and wrote books aimed at teaching. His ties to the school linked him to the system put into practice until that time, according to which a text was written and edited to be read by students, even when that action would occur outside the classroom. To break this vicious cycle, Monteiro Lobato introduced his business vision and outperformed the pioneer role carried out by Thales de Andrade. *A Menina do Narizinho Arrebitado* (The Girl with the Snub Little Nose), with which, in 1920, Lobato debuted as a children's author, started his trajectory in the steps of *Saudade*. However, soon after, he exceeded the limits there established, opening new horizons for the genre in which he participated.

A Menina do Narizinho Arrebitado was first published in the format of 29 x 22 cm, with an illustrated cartoon cover. The drawings, by Voltolino, were colored, and the volume, of 43 pages, attempted to resemble books sold near Christmas, given as children's gifts. In 1921, Lobato reedited the story, added new episodes, simplified the name to *Narizinho Arrebitado* (Snub Little Nose) and extended the book to 181 pages. The format, now in 18.5 x 13.5 cm, also changed to appear more like textbooks of the period. The illustrations were still by Voltolino, but, in this version, they were printed in black and white. More important than these modifications was the increase of the quantity of copies, which surpassed 50,500. This extraordinary number, even today, is due to the purchase of the book by the government of São Paulo, which chose it for the school audience.

In his debut, Lobato repeated the two strategies then in vogue: the publication of tales intended for children as Christmas albums; and a partnership with the State, a client upon whom he could rely. For this reason, it is not surprising that, one year later, Lobato published *Fábulas* (Fables), a book approved by the Board of Public Instruction of São Paulo for educational use, following the precedent set by Justiniano José da Rocha and Paranapiacaba during the monarchy.

Monteiro Lobato, however, was not a teacher. He did not work for educational institutions, did not write textbooks, and nor did he organize collections for a youth audience. He had already been a public prosecutor in Areias, a small town in the state of São Paulo, owner of a farm and a writer of fiction. None of these professions and tasks pushed him toward the field of education; on the contrary, he preferred to invest the funds made from the sale of his land in the printing of books, and so founded a publishing house to which he gave his own name: Monteiro Lobato & Cia., in 1920. He was, after all, a business man, and this change in position determines transformations in his conception about the production and circulation of books. From the production perspective, he would take into account not only the invention of plots and of the characters, but also the physical form that supports the written word; from the circulation perspective, his profound consciousness that he has to convince an anonymous, random, and distant audience to buy the object that he offers and not another one determines the adoption of specific sales strategies, beyond dependence on the government and the purposes of education.

The tactics Lobato employed proved themselves to be efficient, even though he passed through a series of ups and downs during his 25 years dedicated to writing for children. He helped the literary genre he chose to progress, not only because he created a literary universe with a great impact on Brazilian culture, but also because he showed the business angle of all products, both aesthetic and pragmatic, aimed for consumption. Monteiro Lobato's trajectory seems to give the impression that he was a one-man band. However, he was not alone, although he appears to have synthesized what was occurring at the time. Since the end of the nineteenth century, São Paulo led the economic growth of Brazil. As a result of enrichment arising from the production and exportation of coffee, it experienced an industrial expansion that favored urban development and strengthened not only the middle class, but also the working class, who had jobs in the factories situated on the city's periphery.

The economic and social frame repeated itself, on a smaller scale, in other urban centers, including Rio de Janeiro, the Federal Capital, where workers, civil servants, liberal professionals, and merchants swelled the consumer population of industrialized goods, including the book. The publishing industry surpassed the boundaries that limited it to the school market, stimulating the production not only of translations of foreign writers, but also the spread of national authors, especially those of the generation committed to the modernist movements.

Monteiro Lobato, in the 1920s, integrated an environment that enabled him to act not only as a creator and an artist, but also as an enterpreneur. Throughout the twenties, he discontinued this function, but he left behind a legacy inherited by the publishing houses that he founded, such as the Nacional, in 1925, and by those that followed in his footsteps, such as José Olympio, in Rio de Janeiro, or Globo, in Porto Alegre, that began consolidating in the 1930s and whose activities continued until the 1970s. Lobato thus shaped the paths for the production of Brazilian books, and, within this process, he included literature for youth and children. Moreover, if the process of production was new, it follows that its result – literature – should also be original. Therefore, even though with the first books he may have sought to reproduce what had been done in the initial decades of the twentieth century, from the first book that inaugurated his career as author for children and young people he introduces novelty, enhanced during his creative trajectory.

A Menina do Narizinho Arrebitado and its successor, *Narizinho Arrebitado*, synthesized, then, the two times – that of the past and that of the future. From the past, the production system was incorporated: a Christmas album, later, a schoolbook. The setting of the book's plot also matters – the farm of Dona Benta, an idyllic rural space, is perhaps reminiscent of the author's childhood, as he was raised on his grandfather's estate, but it was also the landscape of Thales de Andrade's already popular *Saudade*. However, the author was not satisfied with this, and he designed for the future a set of possibilities that established his works.

First, he disdained the nostalgia in which Andrade's book is rooted. Even if the site of Picapau Amarelo does not present itself as a progressive place which is transformed after *O Poço do Visconde* (Visconde's Well) (1937), the characters that inhabit the farm demonstrate initiative and new ideas. Additionally, they are in tune with the modernity of the 1920s, represented by the movies and translated, in the book, by the presence of Tom Mix in the middle of Narizinho's adventures. Furthermore, in *O Gato Félix* (Felix the Cat, 1928), the hero of the then popular comic cartoon interacts with residents of the farm.

An admirer of manifestations of mass culture and conscious that it would be fruitless to confront them, Lobato preferred to combat the traditional characters from fairytales. In *Cara de Coruja* (Owl Face, 1928), the narrator reports the reception, by Dona Benta, of the princesses of European tales who desire to escape from the slavery imposed by Dona Carochinha. In other episodes, characters of remodeled European children's literature, such as Pinocchio and Peter Pan, indirectly appear as protagonists in Lobato's fictitious universe, in, respectively, *O Irmão de Pinóquio* (Pinocchio's Brother, 1929) and *Pena de Papagaio* (Parrot Feather, 1930).

The literary strategies adopted are processes of renewal: the author carnivalizes the tradition, while at the same time integrates, through intertextuality, artistic procedures with which he agrees and with which he seeks to associate his work. At the same time, he employs the resources of metafiction to discuss the creative process utilized, without falling into the sins of didacticism and indoctrination. On the contrary, if there is something that Lobato prizes, it is independence – an attitude that he associates with intelligence, embodied by the doll Emilia, the character that expresses his vision of the world from the very beginning of her fictitious existence. His books are, then, basically transgressive, since they contradict the tendency to reinforce socially acceptable behaviors and thus to please parents and teachers, whereby a book was guaranteed a positive reception by schools and, as a consequence, book sales to the government. By inverting the model, Lobato proposed rebelliousness, the questioning of established ideas, and the commitment to social and economic progress. He preferred to take the side of youth and children, instead of appealing to adults, and not infrequently, in his narratives, the characters that embody youth disempower the older ones, represented initially by Dona Benta and Aunt Nastácia, afterwards by institutions like the state and government.

The resolution to represent the perspective of his young readers, and even then not to speak on their behalf, cost Lobato dearly. While he lived, his books (except for the first) were not acquired by government agencies. *História do Mundo para Crianças* (The History of the World for Children, 1933), for example, was censored in Brazil and prohibited in Salazar's Portugal. In the 1950s, the author, already deceased, was accused of promoting communism, and his books were banned from many Catholic schools.

This does not mean, however, that they did not sell well: sales records, dated 1941 and sent to the author by Octales Marcondes Ferreira, owner of the National Publishing Company, indicate that, until that date, 1,029,500 copies of his books (children's, adults', adaptations and translations) had been sold, earning 5,785,000 000 réis (approximately US$ 96,000) in the currency of the time (CEDAE MLb 3.2.00407cx8).

Beside Lobato, other authors promoted literature written for children and youth. Viriato Correia, Erico Verissimo, Thales de Andrade, Ofélia and Narbal Fontes, Malba Tahan, Orígenes Lessa, and later Maria José Dupré, Lúcia Machado de Almeida, Jerônimo Monteiro and Francisco Marins were contemporaries and successors to the creator of the Picapau Amarelo farm, sharing his literary findings and the audience that he attracted. However, they did not develop new ways of dealing with the market, which continued to grow and which, because of a lack of innovation, leaned towards mass culture, represented most strongly by comics. Ignoring Monteiro Lobato's solution that instead of going against the mass media literary production should find an alliance with it, they ended up by establishing a rivalry, a position incorporated by the educational system. Production and public walked on different and, at times, completely opposite paths. Hence arose the regression of youth literature, as well as the anachronism found in a good portion of the works by authors active mostly between 1950 and 1970.

A new start, a post-modern end

The industrial development in the first decades of the twentieth century, in a rhythm that did not fade until the 1950s, determined the relocation of contingents of people from the countryside to the city, and from the Northeast to the South. The change of the Federal Capital, from Rio de Janeiro to Brasília, also encouraged the mobilization of people, first from workers involved in the building of the city, and, after its opening, in 1960, of civil servants, liberal professionals, politicians, and members of the government staff. The economic and political changes explain the new composition of society. Whereas in the early twentieth century the economic base came from the countryside, now factory production, oriented towards the domestic market, moves the financial world. On the other hand, Brazil has not been released from the ties of dependence, no longer upon the colonial metropolis Portugal or British imperialism, as had been the situation until autonomy in 1822 and during the nineteenth century, but to North America capitalism, owner of the means of industrial production installed in Brazil, especially after the end of World War II.

In the middle of the twentieth century, Brazil experienced conflict between the ideologies of the political left, with a strong nationalist leaning, and of the authoritarian oriented right. The latter, in 1964, occupied the state with a coup d'état supported by the army; in 1985, power returned to the civil sector, and the democratic system was slowly regularized and the interests of different economic and social sectors accommodated.

Culture, especially literature – books written for children and youth included – followed the crossing from democracy to dictatorship and back again, but did not stop manifesting its aspirations for freedom of expression, even in critical moments of repression and censorship. And it benefitted from two factors that characterize contemporary Brazil: the growth of the urban population, followed by the increase of literate people. The developmentalist policy, present since the 1950s and intensified by the military government, was supported, on the one hand, by the building of large-scale public works (roads, dams, public housing), and on the other hand, by the welcoming of international capital, represented by industries and multinational banks. Brazil modernized its infrastructure, but, at the same time, the country maintained its dependence on foreign economic power. This policy, to achieve the desired success, required trained workers, an aim to be accomplished through schooling.

The 1970s witnessed a comprehensive reform of the education system that made elementary school mandatory, with a duration of eight years. Illiteracy, still high during this period, compromised the modernization project of the State, which, being authoritarian, could impose it in all regions of Brazil. The book industry, also in an increasing process of denationalization, was mobilized to respond positively to the new demand, which greatly favored the textbook sector.

Children's literature also benefitted, as the new legislation enforced the use of books for children in the classroom. The necessity to provide literary material for students led, at first, to the recycling of books launched in previous decades. Between 1970 and 1980, the books of Maria José Dupré, Lúcia Machado de Almeida and Orígenes Lessa were reprinted with great success. Soon, however, a new generation was introduced: that of Ziraldo, in the 1960s, of Fernanda Lopes de Almeida, Lygia Bojunga, Ana Maria Machado, Ruth Rocha, Marina Colasanti, João Carlos Marinho, Bartolomeu Campos Queirós, Joel Rufino dos Santos, in the 1980s, and of Pedro Bandeira, Ricardo Azevedo, and Marcos Rey in the following decade.

The participation of the State in the process of the expansion and diversification of literature for children and youth was not restricted to intervention at a distance. Complaints that schools did not fulfil their functions in a satisfactory way, and were apparently incapable of developing proficient readers, and the demand that the access to books be democratized required the government to take initiatives to solve these needs. From 1970 to 1990, the measures adopted primarily involved the acquisition and distribution of textbooks. However, already in 1984, the program Reading Rooms sought to reorient this practice, valuing the books intended for a youth audience. It was followed in 1997 by the National Program Library in School (PNBE), whose consistency and continuity were guaranteed by a Resolution promulgated by the National Education Development Fund (FNDE).

Thanks mainly to the action of the PNBE, the Brazilian publishing sector for youth literature presents the robust numbers reproduced in Tables 42.1 to 42.4. For the same reason, the number of publishing houses of literary production for children, adolescents, and young adults has increased enormously in the past decades. Another result has been the transfer of Brazilian editors to foreign companies, following a process of aggregation on the international scale.

The Brazilian children's book market does not move in a voluntarist way, as many of its actions are induced by the public power. This prompting is also noticeable when the literary works have to be adjusted to the criteria of annual purchases by the Ministry of Education, or when it has favored subjects valued in school, in the wake of the educational system's pedagogical demands. Individual literary creations, however, were not yoked to the state's demands. The freedom to write and manifest personal ideas, to adhere to vanguard poetics and to provide artistic experiences is exercised by each one of the authors that composes the current patrimony of Brazilian youth literature. In addition, authors seem dedicated to an ideal that harks back to the literary practice of Monteiro Lobato — they desire to interact with their readers and to represent their yearnings and aspirations.

This process assumes different forms and is constantly changing, tuning itself to the post-modern aesthetics, to which it is a legitimate witness. One of its expressions is metalinguistic experimentation, motivating a dialogue with the repertoires and culture canon of young readers, as noticeable, for example, in *Um Homem no Sótão* (A Man in the Attic), by Ricardo Azevedo, or *O Fantástico Mistério de Feiurinha* (The Fantastic Mystery of Feiurinha), by Pedro Bandeira. Other procedures are the use of hypertextuality and the breaking with the boundaries of the printed support materials, as in the work of Sergio Capparelli, Angela Lago, Roger Mello, Luís Dill and Leo Cunha.

The numbers reproduced in Tables 42.1 to 42.4 suggest that Brazilian youth literature celebrates its second century as an independent and solid system. It constitutes a system because it has its own channels of production, distribution and circulation, authors devoted to the genre, and varied and peculiar lines of creation. The books are offered to the market, divided into distinct themes, designed for defined age ranges and written according to specific techniques, which are modified in consonance with the public for which they are intended. The beneficiaries are both the authors and the readers, the former because they can professionalize, without necessarily having to supplement their income with non-literary activities. Therefore, authors such as Ziraldo, Pedro Bandeira and Ana Maria Machado have for many years surpassed the mark of the first million books sold. The industry benefits young readers because they can enjoy a range of literature rich in diversity and quality, embracing many books chosen through public purchase, and even non-canonical genres, such as fantasy fiction, are frequently consumed by the youth readership.

In 1984, Pedro Bandeira published *A Droga da Obediência* (The Drug of Obedience), a novel reprinted with slight changes in 2003, in which he depicts the resistance of the novel's heroes, young students at an elite school, against the authoritarian system adopted by the institution in which they are enrolled. The principal characters, both male and female, succeed in supplanting the authoritarian director, who wanted to submit them to a chemical drug that would ensure their subjugation and dependence. Instead of obedience, they propose rebelliousness and freedom. Nothing is more representative of the production of books for children and youth in the present day. The "drug of obedience" is not consumed by society, nor by national literature, and the current Brazilian catalog for children, adolescence, and youth is an example of this unsubmissive position, in its permanent quest for new paths.

Note

1 Produção e Vendas do Setor Editorial Brasileiro – Base 2012. Câmara Brasileira do Livro; Sindicato Nacional de Editores de Livro; Fundação Instituto de Pesquisas Econômicas [Brazilian Publishing Sector's Production and Sales – Base 2012. Brazilian Book Chamber; National Syndicate of Book Publishers; Economic Research Institute Foundation]. In: www.snel.org.br/dados-do-setor/producao-e-vendas-do-setor-editorial-brasileiro. Accessed on May 26, 2014.

Bibliography

Cabral, Alfredo do Vale (1881) *Anais da Imprensa Nacional do Rio de Janeiro de 1808 a 1822* [Proceedings of the National Press of Rio de Janeiro from 1808 to 1822]. Rio de Janeiro: Tipografia Nacional.

CEDAE: Centro de Documentação Cultural (2013) "Alexandre Eulalio" [Cultural Documentation Centre "Alexandre Eulalio"]. *Censo da educação básica: 2012* [Census on basic education: 2012]. Brasília: INEP.

Luccock, John (1975) *Notas sobre o Rio de Janeiro e partes meridionais do Brasil* [Notes on Rio de Janeiro and southern parts of Brazil]. Belo Horizonte: Itatiaia; São Paulo: EDUSP.

Moacyr, Primitivo (1939) *A instrução e as províncias* [The instruction and the provinces]. Volume 2, São Paulo: Nacional.

Moraes, Rubens Borba de (1993) "A Impressão Régia do Rio de Janeiro: origens e produção" [The Royal Printing of Rio de Janeiro: origins and production], in *Bibliografia da Impressão Régia de Rio de Janeiro* [Bibliography of the Royal Printing of Rio de Janeiro], Vol.1. São Paulo: EDUSP Kosmos.

Pimentel, Alberto Figueiredo (1958) *Contos da Carochinha* [Old Wives' Tales], 24th edition. Rio de Janeiro: Quaresma.

43

DEVELOPMENT OF LITERATURE FOR CHILDREN AND YOUNG PEOPLE IN CHILE

Manuel Peña Muñoz
(Translated by Helen Satchwell)

In recent years, there has been a great development in Chilean literature for young people, with the emergence of authors with new styles. The accompanying illustrations are of superb quality, and have become recognized internationally. New publishers with creative ideas have emerged. Conferences, seminars, courses, workshops and book fairs dedicated to children's and young peoples' literature are occurring continually. Specialized magazines have emerged, as have institutions dedicated to promoting the field. Foreign writers and specialists have come to Chile to share their experiences. Children's Literature has appeared in academic curricula, including various universities offering a Master's degree in Children's and Young People's Literature. It appears that academics, publishers, teachers, librarians and parents have come to understand that it is during childhood that people develop a love of reading. As such, it is necessary to produce popular, high-quality books that help children's appreciation and a sense of self-fulfillment.

In a technological world, it seems contradictory that books are making a comeback into the home, and more and more, publishers are paying close attention to the details and illustrations as they are aware that to educate children and young adults, the books must be aesthetically pleasing.

Classics of Chilean children's literature

However, children's literature has not always been this way. During the 19th century, children's literature was used didactically or for religious purposes, as children's books were used as tools for teaching morals and for their educational content, and books with artistic quality were not produced until the 20th century. The first literary manifestation was the magazine *El Peneca* (1908–1960), which featured the European classics, and opened their publication to Chilean writers not only as narrators and poets, but also as illustrators. *Coré*, the pseudonym of Mario Silva Ossa, was the precursor in Chile of the illustrating children's books.

During the first part of the 20th century, there are four milestones in the development of Chilean literature for children: Gabriela Mistral's *Ternura, Canciones de niños* (Tenderness, Songs for Children, 1924; 1945); Hernán del Solar's *La Porota* (The Little

Bean, 1946); *Papelucho* (1947) by Marcela Paz (Ester Huneeus de Claro); and Alicia Morel's *La Hormiguita Cantora y el duende Melodía* (The Little Singing Ant and Melodía the Elf, 1957).

Though Chilean by birth, Gabriela Mistral wrote books of a more global ("Hispano-American") nature, evident in the fact that many of her books were initially published outside of Chile. Of all her books, *Ternura* most closely resembles her childhood. Mistral's inspiration for writing poetry was deeply rooted in folkloric origins, from which she re-created the oral poetry for children circulating in Hispano-American countries, and thus connected readers to authentic literature of the oral tradition. She was a pioneer in the re-creation of rounds and nursery rhymes from popular oral tradition, charting a new path followed by other Latin American poets. A strong advocate of the social position of children, she wrote about motherhood, education, women, nature, and indigenous native culture, but was concerned primarily with childhood. She was awarded the 1945 Nobel Prize in Literature.

Hernán del Solar, the author of *La Porota* (1946) stimulated interest in children's literature in Chile by creating the first publishing house specializing in this area, between 1946 and 1950. It was called Rapa Nui (the native name for Easter Island, which belongs to Chile), and included the best authors and illustrators of the period. *La Porota* tells the story of a little girl who loses her doll. The author uses a dream to introduce and entice the reader through fantastic events, which serve to comment on the distressful reality of that time, as the atomic bomb had just been dropped on Hiroshima in 1945. The doll is a witness to the Second World War, and serves as a nexus between the real and imaginary worlds. Finally, *La Porota* discovers that in reality there are enemies that seek to destroy the world, as do the bats in the kingdom of the dolls in the story, which destroy the toys. The book switches between fantasy and reality, creating a beautiful biblical parable in literary fiction.

In contrast to the serious themes of *La Porota*, *Papelucho* (1947) by Marcela Paz, depicts its eponymous protagonist as a rebellious, spontaneous and fun-loving child, typical of the Chilean middle-class. The book was well received as children felt connected to this rebellious boy who was critical of his elders. Perhaps this sense of connection was enhanced because the book is a diary written from a first-person perspective in language that is accessible and easy to understand and contains scenes of sparkling imagination and humor. Further, young readers were able to identify with a well-written book that does not have a moral or is trying to educate them. It has nothing to do with school. It creates a convincing impression that it is a real diary, reflecting real life. Today it continues to be published as a long series, and continues to enrich the imagination of children through its spontaneity. In addition, *Papelucho* has been translated into many languages and has remained relevant to several generations of children until today. The author fully deserved the National Literature Prize, awarded in 1982, for *Papelucho*'s innovative representation of its protagonist's personality.

Finally, Alicia Morel's collection of stories, *La Hormiguita Cantora y el duende Melodía* (1957), explores the hidden truth in the garden world inhabited by snails, fireflies, spiders, ladybirds, caterpillars, bees, butterflies and all of the small insects that dance and converse, if children can decipher their mysteries. The stories combine narrative and lyric genres, embedding short poems within the stories, which are meant to be sung as the story is read aloud. With many re-issues, the book remains a classic within Chilean children's literature because of its clever mixture of fantasy and reality.

Recent trends

During the 1960s and 1970s literature for children in Chile suffered a decline, partly due to the advent of television in 1964, and later from the military dictatorship, which commenced in 1973. This political situation created a climate of instability and brought on the closure of publishing houses such as Quimantú, which specialized in children's literature written for all socio-economic groups. However, in the 1980s there was a publishing renaissance, which coincided with the same awakening that occurred in other Latin American countries. The Chilean publishing companies that compete on an international level are Andrés Bello and Universitaria. In addition, foreign publishers such as SM, Norma and Alfaguara are active in this area. In this climate, new authors appear who refresh the genre with new themes and forms of expression. Saúl Schkolnik, for example, has written many books for children within three main areas: science and ecology, fantastic inventions, and the re-creation and adaptation of Chilean or Latin American oral myths. Schkolnik began writing for children with *Un cazador de cuentos* (A Hunter of Stories, 1979). He then published *Cuentos para adolescentes románticos* (Stories for Romantic Adolescents, 1979), *Cuentos de Tío Juan, el zorro culpeo* (Stories of Uncle Juan, the Fox, 1982), *Breve noticia de mi infancia* (Brief News of my Childhood, 1984), *Antai, la historia del príncipe de los Licanantai* (Antai, the Prince of Licanantai (an indigenous group from the north of Chile), 1986) and *Tres príncipes* (Three Princes, 1993) among others. Within his own publishing house, Alicanto (the name of a mythical bird from the north of Chile), Schkolnik has published over 100 books and stories and continues to encourage children's literacy by making visits to schools.

A significant author of fantasy literature is Jacqueline Balcells, whose first book for children was *El niño que se fue en un árbol* (The Boy who was in a Tree, 1986), a collection of seven stories. She later published *El polizón de la Santa María* (The Stowaway of the Santa Maria, 1988), named on the IBBY Honour List 1990, *La Hacedora de Claros y otros sueños* (The Maker of Light Rays and Other Dreams, 1988), *Cuentos de los reinos inquietos* (Tales of Restless Kingdoms, 1993) and *Siete cuentos rápidos y cinco no tanto* (Seven Quick Tales, and Five not so Quick Ones, 1993) among many others. Distinguished fantasy novels were also produced by Ana María Güiraldes: *Un embrujo de cinco siglos* (A Spell of Five Centuries, 1990), *El castillo negro en el desierto* (The Black Castle in the Desert, 1992) and *El violinista de los brazos largos* (The Violinist with Long Arms, 1994). Güiraldes is also author of a series of books that incorporate word-play, particularly in books for small children, in which playful, and onomatopoeic rhymes appear. Psychological narratives are the special province of Cecilia Beuchat, notably in such books as *Cuentos con algo de mermelada* (Tales with a bit of Marmalade, 1987), *Cuentos con olor a fruta* (Tales Smelling of Fruit, 1989) and *Cuentos de perros, gatos y canarios* (Tales of Cats, Dogs and Canaries, 1993). These stories feature children who find solutions to problems through affection and understanding. In recent years, she wrote and translated, together with Carolina Valdivieso, *Cuentos de otros lugares de la tierra* (Tales from Other Parts of the Earth, 1998) and *Cuentos sobre el origen del hombre y del mundo* (Tales of the Origin of Man and the World, 2001).

Social realism

In the 1980s Victor Carvajal, who came from a theater background, performed his work in Germany during his political exile from Chile. While preparing the arguments in his books, he realized that he had an ability to narrate, and used that ability to create his plots. It was in this way that he wrote his first stories, subsequently compiled in *Cuentatrapos* (Rag Tales, 1984), for which he was awarded the Barco de Vapor (Steam ship) Prize in Spain in 1984. After his time in Germany, he decided to return to Chile where he dedicated himself to writing children's literature of a realistic and social nature. In Santiago, he founded Sol y Luna (Sun and Moon), the first bookshop in Chile dedicated to children's books. He later created his own publishing house with the same name.

Cuentatrapos gained recognition in the Spanish-speaking world, and also in other countries, and was translated into various languages. His stories, which take place in lower-income neighborhoods of Santiago, Chile, highlight the stark truth of the conditions in which children live in these under-privileged communities. Eschewing an accusatory tone, Carvajal throws a fresh light on the children of these neighborhoods, limiting himself only to an honest recount of what he had observed. In this respect, his narratives are similar to those of the Brazilian writer, Mauro Vasconcelos, whose book *Mi planta de naranja lima* (My Sweet Orange Tree) depicts children according to their social circumstances.

The majority of his books generate social awareness marked by profound humanism, and their direct and poetic language connects readers with the child protagonists and flows on to larger universal themes. His stories take place in lower-income communities and in rural areas of Chile where the children still live in critical situations. Carvajal creates realistic scenarios, highlighting anthropological, ecological and cultural issues. He has also written books about indigenous cultures, and about the childhood of Chilean writers, such as the novelist Maria Luisa Bombal. In *Sakanusoyin, El Cazador de Tierra del Fuego* (Sakanusoyin, the Hunter of Tierra del Fuego, 1990), he attempted to re-construct a cultural world that has been lost: set in Patagonia, the region located in the southern tip of Chile, the novel imagines the lives of a group of boys from the *yaganes* indigenous tribe, which is now extinct. In a similar way, *Mamire, el último niño* (Mamire, the Last Child, 1996) describes the life of a child in the north of Chile, inland from the port of Iquique, an area that has become depopulated as the residents have left the community. One of his bestselling books is *Como un salto de campana* (a Spanish idiom for "a radical change", 1992), in which he mixes rich mythology from the island of Chiloé with the more mundane knowledge brought by a child educated in Europe. All of his work emphasizes a profound reflection on the human race, its origins and the idiosyncrasies of Chileans.

Politics, society and children's literature

At the beginning of the 21st century, *La Composición* (The Composition, 2001), by Antonio Skarmeta, received the UNESCO Prize for Children's and Young People's Literature in the Service of Tolerance, awarded in 2003 (awarded biennially from 1997–2003). *La Composición* was illustrated by the Spanish artist Alfonso Ruano and published by Ekaré of Venezuela. The jury panel, which was unanimous in its choice, appreciated the story's message about freedom, the quality of its language, its literary style and the sense of humor with which the author portrays a dramatic historic event. In its depiction of how a child goes about his daily life while living under military rule, the novel emphasizes the intelligence and maturity of a child who is conscious of the historical moment in which he lives. It also draws attention to how a child helps his family in this difficult time thanks to a "composition", a product of his imagination, demonstrating the power of the imagination. The saving power of the book, coming from the hand of a child, makes this a much more interesting approach. At the same time, it shows that on many occasions children are more aware of what is going on around them than adults realize.

New authors

At the beginning of the 21st century, several outstanding new authors have emerged thanks to the encouragement from the publisher Editorial SM, which has created the Premio El Barco de Vapor Prize in Chile. Several distinguished authors have received this award, among them Felipe Jordán, author of *Gallito Jazz* (The Little Cockerel Jazz, 2006), Sergio Gómez, author of *El Canario Polaco* (The Polish Canary, 2008), Esteban Cabezas, author of *María la dura, no quiero ser Ninja* (Hard Maria, I Don't Want to be a Ninja, 2009), and Camila Valenzuela, author of *Nieve negra* (*Black Snow*, 2013). Esteban Cabezas is the creator of the Julito Cabello series, very popular with Chilean children. His books include *Julito Cabello contra la lata tóxica* (Julito Cabello Against the Toxic Can, 2004), *Las descabelladas aventuras de Julito Cabello* (The Crazy Adventures of Julito Cabello, 2004) and *Julito Cabello contra los zombies enamorados* (Julito Cabello Against the Zombies in Love, 2008). In 2016 *La Tortulenta* (The Slow Turtle), illustrated by Pato Mena, won the Medalla Colibrí.

Two female authors who have become prominent in the early 21st century are Sara Bertrand and Camila Valenzuela. Bertrand's first novel was *Antonio y el tesoro de Juan Fernández* (Antonio and the Treasure of Juan Fernández, 2007), and she became very popular for works such as *Otelo, y el hombre de piel azul* (Otelo and the Blue-skinned Man, 2010), *La casa del ahorcado* (The House of the Hanged Man, 2011) and *La momia del salar* (The Mummy from the Salt Lake, 2011). Camila Valenzuela, a writer and academic, began her writing career in young adult fantasy with the *Zahorí* trilogy (2013–2015) and *Nieve negra*, an adaptation of the fairytale of "Snow White". In 2016 she turned to young adult realism with *La espera* (The Wait), an intricate representation of a girl's subjectivity through the perceptions of her family.

Children's poetry

There are many books of poetry for children, as well as nursery rhymes, tongue-twisters, guessing-games, rounds, rhymes, and skipping-rope songs, all originating from a rich folklore for children in Chile. Children's poetry at its best is exemplified by the work of María José Ferrada, who has received many prizes in Spain and Chile. As a student and teacher of Japanese culture and literature, she has been immersed in things Japanese, and as a result her poetry is characterized by a certain delicacy and economy of expression, inspired by eastern culture. Her poetry employs short verses reminiscent of the Japanese lyrical style of *haiku*. María José Ferrada writes with a great beauty of form. Her most important books are: *Un Mundo Raro* (A Strange World, 2009), *El Lenguaje de las cosas* (The Language of Things, 2011), *El Idioma Secreto* (The Secret Language, 2013), *Notas al Margen* (Notes in the Margin, 2013) and *Niños* (Children, 2013). All of these books have received critical acclaim. *Niños* has been recognized by an important award from the Academy of Language in Chile. In *Niños* Ferrada presents intensely moving, lyrical poems about 34 children executed during the Chilean military dictatorship.

Children's poetry and digital animation

An innovative approach to nursery rhymes is evident in the work of Chilean writer María de la Luz Uribe. Living and working in Barcelona, she demonstrated in her writing the need for children to connect with their Latin American cultural identity. This connection is expressed in a DVD entitled *Tikiticlip*, which integrates music, handcrafted puppets and digital animation. The title of the piece combines the word *Tikití*, which is used in Chile to commence the *cueca*, the national dance, with the word *clip*, used to describe the short, musical-film clip format.

The DVD has 12 of the author's poems, which were inspired by Chilean culture. The production presents a novel and creative approach within the field of contemporary nursery rhymes, putting forth an original idea within the most creative approaches to contemporary children's literature. Although it is inspired by national roots, it places them in a more playful and humorous light. The segment titled *La señorita aseñorada* (*The Lady-like-Lady*) portrays a brief history depicting such absurd humor, which is acted out by handcrafted puppets from Chile, knitted with horse-hair. In *El rey de papel* (The King of Paper), the protagonist is portrayed by a Mapuche girl (the Mapuche are an indigenous tribe in Chile), who finds herself in the middle of an enchanted world dressed in traditional Mapuche costume. *Arrorró* (Lullaby) depicts a mother singing to her child. Models carved from volcanic ash typical of the craftsmanship of Northern Chile were brought to life through digital animation, proving nursery rhymes traditional to Chile can be modern.

Historical reconstruction

Fiction can eloquently evoke the past, as in an historical novel, written by Felipe Jordán Jiménez entitled *El misterio de la Cañada* (The Mystery of Cañada Street, 2012). In this precise and rigorous work, based in Santiago in the late 18th century, the author reconstructs the Colonial period, and includes a map of Santiago, Chile, so that young readers can see how the city in this period was laid out, as the lights were lit and carriages slipped through the cobblestone streets. Using meticulous language, the author takes us through the interiors of houses and unravels the ways of peaceful colonial life in Chile as seen through the eyes of a young and curious observer. His name is Manolo, and he has seen a carriage of dead bodies pass by, and he decides to solve the mystery of "la Cañada", as the street La Alameda (the main street in Central Santiago) was known in those times, when Puente de Cal y Canto (Cal and Canto bridge) existed across the Mapocho River.

Humor

One of the literary types that children most enjoy is humor. In this area Mauricio Paredes stands out, a follower of the unconventional humor of Roald Dahl, whom Paredes greatly admires. It is a humor that moves between a parody and a criticism of adults. Among his outstanding books are included *La cama mágica de Bartolo* (Bartolo's Magic Bed, 2002),

Ay, cuanto me quiero (Oh, How I love myself, 2003), *Verónica la niña biónica* (Veronica, the Bionic Girl, 2005), and many others.

The epic fantasy

The epic fantasy genre has sparked the interest of children and young readers through series such as *The Chronicles of Narnia* by C. S. Lewis, and the *Harry Potter* series by J. K. Rowling. This literary movement has inspired Chilean authors to write young adult novels in this style. Camila Valenzuela's *Zahorí* trilogy (2013–2015), mentioned above, locates the story's origins in Ireland and continues in a remote village in the south of Chile. The series features four sisters who try to discover the legacy they inherited. The best-known exponent of this genre outside Chile is expatriate author Isabel Allende, who entered young adult literature with her magical realist epic trilogy *La Ciudad de los Bestias* (City of the Beasts, 2002), *El Reino del Dragón de Oro* (Kingdom of the Golden Dragon, 2003), and *El Bosque de los Pigmeos* (Forest of the Pygmies, 2004). The series blends adventure story with ecological and social justice themes.

The graphic novel

One of the recent trends in Chilean literature for children is the graphic novel, which has received a great development in the hands of its creators. A notable example is *Mochadick, La Leyenda de la ballena blanca* (Mochadick, the Legend of the White Whale, 2013) by journalist and writer Francisco Ortega, illustrated in black and white by architect and draftsman Gonzalo Martínez. Martínez is a prolific illustrator of graphic novels, also known for *Quique Hache, Detective* (2009), with text by Sergio Gómez, and *Celeste Buenaventura: La Hija del Trauko* (Celeste Buenaventura, Daughter of Trauko, 2010), with text by Marco Rauch. *Mochadick* received the Marta Brunet Prize in Literature for Children and Young People from the Cultural Council of Chile. The story is related to other novels about whale hunting, such as the legendary *Moby Dick* by Herman Melville, and other works of world literature. It also contains references to the view of the world found in the original villages in the south of Chile, and the culture of the island of Mocha. It is a presentation of characters that embody adventure, honor, and the solidarity of friendship. A glossary helps the young reader to achieve a deeper understanding of the boats used to hunt whales, and the geographical locations where these activities take place. At the same time, there is a bibliography that invites the reader to expand his or her knowledge.

Development of children's literature

In recent years, there has been a growing interest amongst teachers and librarians to expand their knowledge, and hence there has been a rise in the number of professionals, including writers, researchers, teachers, illustrators and librarians, who have become interested in internships available at international institutions. Some of these include the German Sánchez Ruipérez of Salamanca Foundation, the International Youth Library in Munich, the Fundalectura of Colombia and other foundations that promote literacy in Mexico, Colombia, Argentina and other countries. In turn, Mexico, Colombia and Argentina have sent experts to Chile to give guest lectures and workshops. The development of children's literature has also seen a boost through the practice of storytelling.

Another positive aspect brought by the creation of new institutions that sponsor children's literacy has been the Consejo Nacional de la Cultura (National Cultural Assembly). Their initiatives have been spread throughout Chile through the Seminar for Children's Literature, the building of libraries for children, and the support of the distribution of children's books and the creation of literary awards and other initiatives. In addition, new organizations such as Lectura Viva (Reading Alive) have developed stimulating projects made specifically to promote literacy to infants, the blind, as well as to those in prison or who live in economically disadvantaged areas (more information can be found at their website www.lecturaviva.cl). The Internet has allowed for a connection between international institutions and access to digital magazines such as the *Fundación Cuatrogatos* (Four Cats Foundation, www.cuatrogatos.org), the *Vuelan, vuelan* (Fly, Fly) newsletter published by the Bolivian Academy of Children's Literature (www.ablig.com) and *Imaginaria* (Imaginary) magazine in Argentina (www.imaginaria.com.ar). This also includes access to magazines retrievable online and dedicated to promoting children's literature. The Chilean section of IBBY (International Board on Books for Young People, www.ibbychile.cl) has developed initiatives to promote children's literature through having its members participate in conferences, literacy panels, school visits and publishing in anthologies and writing articles for magazines and other publications. IBBY brings together Chilean writers and other specialists in children's literature. In recent years, IBBY has created the Medalla Colibrí (Hummingbird Prize) that is awarded to the best children's books of the year according to distinct categories.

The Center for the Selection of Children's Literature has also been created within Chile's National Library to help guide professionals who engage in reading to children and young adults. These professionals read and recommend age-appropriate, quality texts by publishing online reports useful for those purchasing materials for libraries. The Center for Learning Resources creates classroom libraries throughout Chile, and participates in various activities that encourage children to read. Also noteworthy is the *Había una vez (Once Upon a Time) Foundation*, which has an excellent selection of books and a comprehensive program of activities that encourage reading throughout Chile. The foundation publishes an online magazine, which is an outstanding source for those who specialize in children's literature (http://fhuv.cl/revista-habia-una-vez/numeros-rhuv/#).

Specialized libraries have also emerged in Chile such as the Santiago Library, Puente Alto Reading Center, Lo Barnechea and Osorno Reading Centers, among others. Their employees work to give children individual attention as well as aid in the program selection of children's text and specialized courses. Several foundations have created children's libraries, such as the Mustakis and Lafuente Foundations. The latter stands out as a novel project involving the integration of libraries in shopping centers around Santiago.

Another important development that has recently emerged has been the appearance of professional illustrators, who have renewed the genre. Paloma Valdivia is an illustrator who has received national and international awards. Other illustrators are Alberto Montt, Francisco Javier Olea, Raquel Echeñique and Soledad Sebastián, among many others. The Siete Rayas (Seven Stripes) Group integrates the best illustrators (www.sieterayas.cl). The *Galería Plop* (Plop Gallery, www.plopgaleria.blogspot.com) is dedicated to giving illustrators of children's books a platform to show their art. It has also taken part in the exhibition of high-quality children's literature, specifically picture-books.

Specialized publishers

Several specialized publishers of children's literature are active in Chile. Pehuén, for example, has innovatively presented a collection of bilingual children's books in Spanish and the languages of the indigenous people in Chile, including *rapa nui* (the language of Easter Island) and *mapadungún* (the language of the Mapuches). This has started a trend of valuing the language of Chile's ancestors. Very important is Ekare Sur (www.ekaresur. cl), with many books very well edited. Also, Amanuta has published a collection of myths and legends that include native stories of the first Chilean settlements and are carefully and aesthetically prepared books.

One of the contributions of Amanuta has been the publication of four unpublished stories in verse written by Gabriela Mistral over 90 years ago. These stories comprise her own version of the classic fairytales "Little Red Riding Hood", "Sleeping Beauty", "Cinderella" and "Snow White and the Seven Dwarves". Mistral wrote these stories in the 1920s while living in Mexico where they were published in school textbooks, as well as in Colombian cultural supplements. For the first time, these stories appear as individual books, illustrated by well-known illustrators in Chile, and in an original format, bound in rustic cardboard. The books were highly acclaimed and won major awards in both Chile and abroad. They received Santiago's Municipal Prize for best publication, Mention New Horizons, Bologna Ragazzi Award, 2014. "Little Red Riding Hood" illustrated by Paloma Valdivia received the "White Ravens label" from the International Youth Library in Munich, a designation given to books that deserve worldwide attention because of their innovative artistic and literary style and design. The collection of four stories was awarded Most Beautiful Book of 2014 by the Comision Alemana (German Commission) of UNESCO, which was presented to the publisher at the Frankfurt Book Fair.

Conclusion

As seen in recent years, Chilean children's books have stood out as examples of careful and aesthetic publishing. The volume of books published has been impressive; illustrating has become a growing specialty. Some of the prominent trends generally seen in children and young adult readers have been in the genres of fantasy, science fiction, ecological narrative, social realism, children's poetry, epic fantasy, the graphic novel, picture books, and spoken nursery rhymes. The traditional fairytales of the past, following the European pattern, have been replaced by new trends connected with Chilean culture. This reflects a general interest in recovering Chile's own identity.

Bibliography

Beuchat, Cecilia (2006) *Narración oral y niños. Una alegría para siempre* (Oral Storytelling and Children, A Joy to Share), Santiago: Universidad Católica de Chile.

Edwards, María Angélica (1985) *La Hora del Cuento* (Story Time), Volume 1, Santiago: Universitaria.

Edwards, María Angélica (1991) *La Hora del Cuento* (Story Time), Volume 2, Santiago: Universitaria.

García Padrino, Jaime (2009) *Gran diccionario de autores latinoamericanos de Literatura infantil y Juvenil* (Dictionary of Latin-American Authors of Children and Young People's Literature) Fundación SM: Madrid.

Peña Muñoz, Manuel (2009) *Historia de la Literatura Infantil en América Latina* (History of Children's Literature in Latin America). Fundación SM: Madrid.

Peña Muñoz, Manuel (2009) *Historia de la Literatura Infantil Chilena* (History of Children's Literature in Chile). Editorial Andrés Bello: Santiago de Chile.

44

CHILDREN'S AND YOUNG ADULT LITERATURE IN GUATEMALA

A mirror turned over to face the wall

Frieda Liliana Morales Barco

Reading and the national education system

During the period 1821–1847, the capital of the ancient Kingdom of Guatemala began a process of transformation from a federal sociopolitical organization towards a Republic, which, finally, was consolidated in 1871. A revolutionary movement followed, which helped set the economic, social and cultural foundations of the country on liberal and positivist pillars. The intention was to create a coherent discourse that bound the people together within a homogeneous culture, with a sense of unity and identity, and enabled the establishment of national symbols like the flag, the *Himno Nacional* (national anthem), the Coat of Arms, and so on. In other words, in this way the imagined community of the country called Guatemala became a real one.[1]

Within this model of social organization, the implementation of the educational system was a key factor that ensured the development of children, and contributed to the entry into the power framework of a particular social group of the Guatemalan population: the ladino or mestizo.[2] The school thus played an essential role in demonstrating good models for future citizens, encouraging social trust and conveying social values. For these purposes, the national education system was structured. The laws and regulations were created, primary schooling was declared secular, free and compulsory,[3] a Ministry of Education was established under the aegis of the Ministry of Foreign Relations (1872), schools for children were established from 1875, and, finally, a range of methods and teaching materials were developed to be employed within local public institutions.

In the case of reading practices, the first book used in public schools was the *Constitutional Political Catechism of the Mexican Republic* written by Nicolás Pizarro Suárez (1861), a text widely used in Mexico during the government of Benito Juárez. Republished in Guatemala, it replaced the religious textbooks in public schools. This book dealt with the rights and duties of man, his guarantees, property, family and individual freedom. Many of the articles of the new Guatemalan Constitution were explained through it. Because the book was written from a declared liberal and anticlerical position, the author upholds individual freedom of petition, association, press, religion and education (Traffano, 2007: 1052). In other words, through the book the image of the modern state was outlined and disseminated to the children, the republican institutions were explained, and organization and expression of power were legitimized (Traffano, 2011: 1049). From this perspective, Suárez's book fulfilled the objectives of civic education that were being implemented in the country because of the Liberal Revolution of 1871, and well suited the purpose of making education the best vehicle for transmitting an ideal of freedom, norms, attitudes, skills, and civic and moral values. At the same time, it helped to form the basis of a "Guatemalan identity," in accordance with the national project of modernization. The *Catechism* thus reinforced the objectives of the new Republic; subsequently, it was hoped that a political revolution could be followed by cultural and social revolution.

During the last quarter of the nineteenth century, there was a sense that these revolutions could be made possible by means of the diffusion and dissemination of diverse ideas, especially in Guatemala City, through literary societies and education conferences. Prominent educators such as José María Vela Irisarri, Santos Toruño, Sóstenes Esponda, Rafaela del Águila, Natalia Górriz de Morales and Concepción Saravia de Zirión promoted reflection and discussion of pedagogical work in the country, and their ideas influenced the structure of the rising national education system.

The *Catechism* was replaced in 1884 by a collection of literacy books written by Vela Irisarri, along with the *Elements of Spanish Grammar* (1885), as they met the requirements of adaptation to the cultural identity of Guatemala (Hernández, 1984: 34) required by the Minister Antonio Bátres in 1887. These books remained in use until 1930.

Later, during the government of José María Reyna Barrios (1892–1898), despite the economic downturn that the country faced in the last five years of the century, there appeared two collections of important books: 1) Central American literature anthologies called *Libros de premio* (1–4); and, 2) *Libros de lectura* (2–6) published between 1895 and 1896 for use in public elementary schools. The intention of these collections was to use literature to foster the spirit of Central American union from early childhood, an ideal pursued by liberals. From the literary point of view, the texts included here formed a real canon of eighteenth- and nineteenth-century Isthmus literature. However, the texts relate to the customs, traditions and written culture of Central America, and especially of Guatemala, which emerged after independence, but not those of the previous period, or of its Mayan population. Projecting the tradition of the young republics born from 1821 on, these were formative books, which, by creating their own narrative voices, sought to build a national identity. From this perspective, the time of origin of this proto narrative did not take into account more remote time, because there were no sources that pointed to that origin. Neither the oral or popular traditions, Spanish and indigenous, served as bases for this. The only possibility envisaged was to start building the "promised land" from a discernible presence in history, that is, events such as the discovery and conquest of America, the founding of cities, description of physical and geographical space, and through heroic songs, hymns, odes, and so on.

That is, a kind of creation myth was developed, which represented a whole image of the newborn country: it belonged to us and such possession consequently gives us the right to inherit and pass it from generation to generation so it will be preserved, not forgotten. For this reason, there was no desire to adapt or import books from outside to facilitate the understanding and learning of children. Instead, the classical literary texts of Central American writers were chosen to construct identity, because in their stories and poems citizenship breathed and patriotic ideals were pursued.

At the same time, cultural products independent of the school context appeared, such as the first children's newspaper, *Los Niños* (1892), which was sold by subscription or single copies, every Sunday; and the first children's theater company organized by Justo Soret and Argimiro Valdivieso in 1897, with national amateur actors. This company remained active until the 1920s.

During the administration of the dictator Manuel Estrada Cabrera (1898–1920) his staff introduced changes in the liberal project, mainly related to a search for other ways to construct identity through the national education system and teaching methods. To do this, his political needs were sustained by the slogan "order for progress," which in practice supported the dictatorship. The model of the Nation was reinforced through a form of moral education with the introduction of the text, *Moral razonada y lecturas escogidas* (Rational Morality and Selected Readings) written by Rafael Spinola (1900), advisor to the president. This book, in the author's words, "is not just a compendium enclosing universal moral precepts, but is also a READING BOOK, and as such, could not consist of a small number of pages, given the diversity of verse and prose pieces collected within it" (xxii). The purpose behind this statement is clear: first, because the project embarked on the creation of a Central American identity, the formation of a Guatemalan identity through literature was interrupted; now the guidelines of this formation would be grounded on norms, standards and principles governed by a morality whose models were sought in the Greco-Roman classics. Second, the concept of "reading" in this work has a different meaning, in that the purpose of reading is now to explain the meaning of words, to recite, to help memorize the moral lesson and hold it "forever in the heart, as verses learned in childhood, that sometimes are not readily forgotten, or are never forgotten" (xxv). From here on, the concept of reading indicates only practical features: it is utilitarian, and puts aside those emancipatory, critical, significant and/or reflective qualities proposed by literature.

Reading practices and books for children were, thus, shaped by the positivist state project of modernization and progress as planned. The teaching of literature was also subject to the same pattern, which resulted in the creation of books with historical and moralizing focus but devoid of recreational aspects and aesthetic originality. Further, because literacy education no longer had the objective of creating better reading habits, especially amongst children, its teaching created only functional literates who could respond to the national liberal and economic project.

New models and the emergence of children's literature

During the 1920s there were major social and cultural changes that favored the development of educational reforms and creative writing in general, due to a crisis of the liberal project as a model to produce a homogeneous Guatemalan society in which all had a place, and in addition to achieve the ideal of citizenship previously aspired to. At this time, the quest for a new model was based in the "social-Catholic doctrine and agnostic spiritualism, which was a confluence of theosophy and heliosophy" (Casaús Arzú, 2005: 292). The gaze of intellectuals also focused on indigenous roots and oral and popular traditional sources to try to regenerate Guatemalan society. The intellectuals in education thought that, through art and education, in some way, a social regeneration could be possible. Juan José Arévalo Bermejo, for example, who became president of Guatemala in 1944, published *Método nacional (para aprender simultáneamente dibujo, escritura y lectura)* (1927), which was well received by teachers. Professor Daniel Armas published a similar work to Arévalo's, entitled *Indohispano, método global silábico* (1928). Then, the Nobel Prize winner Miguel Ángel Asturias, editor of the newspaper *El Imparcial*

Collection, a series of paperbacks, published an anthology of Hans Christian Andersen tales (1928). The writer Rafael Arévalo Martínez, wrote articles alluding to the tercentenary of birth of Perrault, and Luis Martínez Montt gained a scholarship to Switzerland where he worked with Jean Piaget.

The emergence of a children's literature is heralded in this period with the publication of *Mi niño, por el hogar, por la escuela* by Daniel Armas (1929), illustrated by M. Mazariegos Rosal. The author met the entire cost of the publication. Then, in 1932, the book was honored by the municipal corporation of Quetzaltenango, and also affirmed as a guide in elementary school by the Ministry of Education. Armas said that this book was born due to the urgent need to provide parents and teachers with an instrument of initiation into the field of literature, especially poetry, because they had no suitable literary material to provide their children. Moreover, few writers were concerning themselves with the genre of children's literature. Armas subsequently published *Pepe y Polita* (1939), *Barbuchín* (1940) and *Cascabel* (1947), because he felt that early readers needed stronger knowledge of the alphabet, and through these books he offered teachers better tools with which to engage children's imagination and creativity. It also gave them the opportunity to have good experiences with their learning and the creation of better reading and writing habits. For all of these reasons, he became, formally, the first precursor of Guatemalan children's and young adult literature (CYAL). His publications make it possible to begin to outline the history of children's literature, because from that moment children's books began to appear, most of them funded and distributed by their own authors in small print runs.

Guatemala's "Democratic Spring"

In the middle of the twentieth century, another sociopolitical fact affected the development of Guatemalan CYAL: the Revolution of October 20, 1944, known as the Democratic Spring (1944–1954). With this movement, a dictatorial period ends and a time of numerous reforms begins. The priorities of the civil government led by Arévalo (1945–1951) were to establish internal organizational bases and create entities and institutions to protect the citizenry as a preamble to building a just, united and democratic society. In that sense, the first step was to enact a Constitution in which for the first time the guarantees and fundamental rights of Guatemalan citizens were recognized, including the independence of state agencies: Legislative, Executive and Judicial; and the indigenous community was inserted into this framework. Acceptance of these actions created dialogic conditions whereby it might be possible to make a better diagnosis of the Guatemalan reality in order to facilitate the construction of a democratic political project, and to establish, among other things, the entrance of the nation into the international economic environment with more competence. As a result a number of development programs were implemented, especially education and culture aspects. To achieve this, an invitation was extended to all social sectors to become involved and participate in this process, but it all ended up with a return to the system of repression and control that previous governments had established.

This situation created conditions that enabled a deeper reflection and discussion of the importance of literacy, reading and Guatemalan CYAL in the construction of citizenship and a strong identity basis from childhood on. Within this context, some national writers began to produce children's books that attended to recreational elements, aesthetic language, illustration and graphic format. The best example was the children's magazine

Alegría, which was created in 1946 by Marilena López and published until 1962. The first four numbers were issued with funds provided by her, but from the fifth number the magazine was funded by a contract with the Ministry of Public Education. It was an innovative proposal to introduce literature to children, as well as other elements of general culture. In its structure, López privileged playfulness and left to the end the para-didactic elements. All of its sections had as a major component an emphasis on national identity, which was consistent with the environment of modernization and democratization of the state that was taking place at that historical moment.

López not only helped with the editing and publication of the children's magazine, but also worked to revive and modernize the Puppet Theater in Guatemala and to encourage the publication of children's literature and theoretical works. Thus, she exerted influence on subsequent national writers, who contributed to the formation of the CYAL system in the country.

However, this state of progress changed abruptly on June 27, 1954, when a putsch demanded the resignation of the Guatemalan president. This situation suddenly put an end to the progress already achieved in just ten years with respect to social security, health, education, economy and politics in the country. From this date began a new chapter in national history and in particular an increased U.S. government intervention in the politics of Guatemala. In relation to the children's magazine *Alegría*, fifteen days after the ousting of Colonel Jacobo Arbenz Guzmán (1951–1954), the new president, Colonel Carlos Castillo Armas, issued a decree whereby the publication of *Alegría* was suspended, based on an assertion that it was transmitting communist ideas to the children. Later, after a thorough review of the illustrations and contents, decree 72 was repealed on October 29, 1955. The magazine was authorized to be published again, with the proviso that the Ministry of Public Education should control the material to be published thereafter, in order that its contents did not harm children morally and intellectually, through the commission created for monitoring children's publications attached to the General Direction of Fine Arts and Cultural Extension. This control over children's publications endures until today.

Other important texts, which appeared during this period, were the first theoretical CYAL books: *Prontuario de literatura infantil*, by Daniel Armas (1950) and *Literatura infantil: condiciones y posibilidades* by Rubén Villagrán Paul (1954). In addition, the first press for children's books and educational materials named Popol Vuh (1953) was created; the course in Children's Literature at the Faculty of Humanities of the University of San Carlos of Guatemala (1955–1969) was introduced; and also, many articles and essays related to the books, reading, library and CYAL were written and published. However, as mentioned before, the process was cut short by the coup. Children's books published after this date were projects that were compelled to combine pedagogy with literary elements. Meanwhile, a few books devoted primarily to aesthetic features were published and funded entirely by their own authors and in small print runs, which were marketed mainly outside the school system. This situation made it possible for the Guatemalan CYAL to survive in disguise.

In this context, the work of Professor Mario Álvarez Vásquez holds a prominent place. He insisted, like Armas, on the value of literary reading in early childhood, especially the reading of fiction and anthologies. His first works were consistent with what President Castillo Armas had advocated in his speech inaugurating the First National Congress of Education in 1955, which launched another educational reform. Castillo Armas said that developed works and teaching materials had to be offered in the native language, not copied from other latitudes, and that it was necessary to embark upon a program of research in the field of teaching, and thereby to construct an authentic Guatemalan school. Álvarez Vásquez then published reading books like *Ema, Milo y yo* (1961), *Ema y yo* (1962) and *Senderos de luz* (1965), accompanied by a teacher's guide designed for first, second and third grade levels respectively. The structure of these books is by thematic sections and, in order to respond to the national requirements, they include a section dealing with popular folklore and oral tradition. Simultaneously, he published two important anthologies: *Poesía para niños* (1963) and *Poesías y rondas para los niños de América* (1964). With these, he brought to public attention a group of Guatemalan and Latin American authors and books unknown in the country and provided a possible canon for Guatemalan nursery rhyme.

Following the same nationalist spirit, new books appeared reflecting all aspects of CYAL: poetry, narrative, theatre, oral and popular tradition, music and traditional games that gradually were shaping the Guatemalan canon of this literature, especially through the 1960s. A notable moment was the founding of the Children's Theater Company in September 1962, which achieved great popularity with young audiences and is still active. Editing and publishing were carried out with more responsibility and an ethical commitment to young readers, and there was more openness in the literary circuit composed of the writers, readers, illustrators, designers, editors, librarians, teachers, parents. Finally, reviews and articles were published in local newspapers. Children's libraries were also established. However, this state of things passed away quickly and by that time it had not been sufficient to situate publication and related activity outside the school walls, and, moreover, definitely not enough to consolidate the Guatemalan CYAL.

The situation was greatly impacted by the beginning of the civil war in Guatemala on November 13, 1960, which lasted until the signing of the Peace Accord on December 29, 1996. This was a time of socio-political instability in the country where "one of the objectives was to extend the process of *ladinización*[4] ['miscegenation'] of the indigenous population, and to do this, the army proceeded to break the sustaining basis of traditional popular culture, rooted mainly in indigenous communities in the highlands of the country. The cultural dimension of war was evidenced in the 'Operation ashes' (military offensive of 1981–1983), which can be called ethnocide" (Cuevas Molina, 1992: 29). This cultural policy of the Army spread fear to exercise any cultural activity throughout the population, as terror was used as the main mechanism of coercion and subjugation of the population. This circumstance has not changed at all since the signing of the peace accord in 1996 because the culture of fear remains strong nowadays.

Consequences of this policy are reflected in the official information that Guatemala is deemed to have the highest illiteracy rates in the region, low education, absenteeism, poverty, hunger and, more recently, the phenomenon of the exodus of unaccompanied migrant children to the U.S. to escape the prevailing conditions. All of these had not allowed the development of the educational project nor constructed a strong citizenry and identity in the Guatemalan population. Instead, they have created a fragmented and divided society. On the other hand, neoliberal ideas had been strengthened in relation to culture and education and had served to form a pool of cheap labor rather than a sense of citizenship. Mario Roberto Morales further argues, that "the cultural logic of this globalizing transnational capitalism is called postmodernism, and has meant an audiovisual culture of whimsy and hedonist entertainment, that provokes in the youngest people the incapacity to read and manage the literate code, and as a consequence an unwillingness to study and an addiction to videogames and to the new virtual entertainment forms" (2014: 110).

For these reasons, even though non-governmental institutions had organized many initiatives, campaigns, projects and programs, including many seminars, workshops and training programs, focusing on the creation of reading habits throughout the country to consolidate CYAL, most of them had been isolated efforts that have not produced any long-term impact.

Their outcomes described could not be demonstrated because there is no systematization or validation of these experiences, and there is a lack of formal research programs to investigate the status of the genre or the extent of influence achieved in the country because of various initiatives and programs. Despite all of these efforts, people constantly reiterate that there is as yet no Guatemalan CYAL, that there are no writers working in the genres, and many other misconceptions of a similar kind.

Conclusion

The last educational reform in Guatemala was launched in 1996, and since that date there have been five presidents, each of whom has implemented his own Reading National Program using different strategies to combat the illiteracy and the lack of reading habits of most of the Guatemalan population. Some examples are the establishment of public and scholarly libraries, which are provided with literature and reference books; kits of activities intended to promote interaction amongst teachers, students, families, librarians and other reading mediators; and the development of diverse methodologies and strategies to increase better reading habits. So far, however, the outcome has not been positive, reading proficiency amongst students remains low, and children do not meet the standards needed to become culturally and economically proactive in Guatemalan society in the near future.

Although reading proficiency also relates to the publication of CYAL in Guatemala, this is an aspect that has not been studied adequately. There are no real and formal statistics, and there is no specific selection committee for CYAL. Further, no national CYAL collection exists anywhere in the public or the private sphere and there is no legal deposit system in place. As a result, libraries hold only a few books, which do not give an overview of this genre in the country. Because of all this, it is said that most Guatemalan CYAL books are invisible ("elf books"): this image reinforces the myth that they do not exist, that there are no Guatemalan writers and, there is no literature at all directed to Guatemalan childhood. In effect, this situation could be considered a kind of censorship that does not allow us to see and reflect upon others and ourselves through literature, and hence we cannot construct identity and citizenship from the diverse gazes and the symbolic imaginary that could be provided by Mayan, Xinca, Garífuna or mestizo peoples.

In this context, the first three communities mentioned above had been excluded from the national imaginary since the publication of the first books in the nineteenth century. When these indigenous literatures appeared, they were used to fulfill political objectives, to teach manners or health habits; other publications were commissioned to describe the indigenous people from fields like archeology, anthropology, ethnology or linguistics, that is to say, to inform about their worldviews instead of creating symbolic worlds expressed by them. This state of things demonstrates how society has rendered them dysfunctional and created many barriers that prevent a consolidated awareness in Guatemala of children's and young adult literature, reading habits and the literary system in general.

Paradoxically, for all that has been described above, it could be possible to design a map of the Guatemalan CYAL system, which evidences its existence, and to reinforce this map by adducing recent studies, investigations and theoretical publications in the field undertaken outside the official system. However, everything described here is more like a tale of fiction than reality itself, because this literature and its beneficiaries remain invisible for most people. The state of things will not change significantly until a way is found to make the genre more visible and to encourage others to develop a real interest in supporting Guatemalan CYAL and its children. But, until these days arrive, the mirror will remain turned over to face the wall and Guatemalan children's and young adult literature will continue its growth in silence.

Notes

1 The Constitutional Republic of Guatemala is characterized as a multi-ethnic nation (four communities: ladino or mestizo, Maya, Garifuna and Xinca), multicultural and multilingual (25 languages are spoken, including 22 indigenous Mayan, Garifuna and Xinca). These features define it as a country with a unique heterogeneous culture. The above-mentioned ethnic groups make up a completely Guatemalan nationality and from the legal point of view, this national identity is supported by the fact they all live in a limited geographical area and under the governance of a constitutional democracy and a Constitution.
2 Ladino, the product of a mixing of Creoles and Indians, originally occupied a peripheral status in the Kingdom of Guatemala, as both social groups rejected them. There were no laws to protect them and soon they became the kingdom's "gypsies," a mass moving aimlessly within the realm providing their services to the highest bidder. This situation was favorable for property owners, because it was a way to get cheap labor and to evade paying taxes to the Crown. Hence, when this social group assumes the reins of power they reject the other two, Creoles and Indians, and build their own universe (Martínez Peláez, 1994).
3 The first primary school was declared secular, free and compulsory by the State under President Mariano Gálvez (1832).
4 *Ladinización* is a term used specifically in Guatemala to mean "miscegenation" ("mestizaje").

Bibliography

Armas, Daniel (1950) *Prontuario de literatura infantile*. Guatemala: Piedra Santa, 1980.
Casaús Arzú, Marta Elena, and Teresa García Giráldez (2005) *The Central American Intellectual Networks: A Century of National Imaginary (1820–1920)*. Guatemala: F&G.
Cuevas Molina, Rafael (1992) "State and Culture in Guatemala and Costa Rica," *Yearbook of Central American Studies, Costa Rica, Central American University*, 18 (2): 25–39. http://revistas.ucr.ac.cr/index.php/anuario/article/viewFile/2274/2233
González Orellana, Carlos (1970) *History of Education in Guatemala*. Guatemala: José de Pineda Ibarra.
Hernández, Manolo (1984) *History of Ministry of Education of Guatemala*. Guatemala: CENALTEX.
Ministerio de Educación Pública (1955) *Memoria del primer congreso nacional de educación (Report of the First National Educational System)*. Guatemala: Ministerio de Educación.
Morales, Mario Roberto (2014) *Brief Intercultural History of Guatemala*. Guatemala: Cultura.
Morales Barco, Frieda Liliana (2004) *Once upon a time… Guatemalan Children's Literature, a proposal in a Multicultural Society*. Guatemala: Letra Negra.
——— *"Alegría"*. Children's electronic magazine www.cuatrogatos.org
Morales Barco, Frieda Liliana; Henry Gioovanni Sipaque Chavarría; Rolando Gabriel Masaya Gamboa (2012) *Catálogo enciclopédico en línea de la literatura infantil y juvenil de Guatemala* (Encyclopedic Catalog of Children's Literature in Guatemala). Guatemala: Universidad de San Carlos de Guatemala, Faculty of Humanities, Institute of Studies of the National Literature.
Spínola, Rafael (1900) *Moral razonada y lecturas escogidas: Primer curso*. Guatemala: Tipografia nacional.

Traffano, Daniela (2007) "Educación, civismo y catecismos políticos: Oaxaca, segunda mitad del siglo XIX" ("Education, citizenship and political catechisms: Oaxaca, second half of the nineteenth century") *Revista Mexicana de Investigación Educativa*, 12(34): 1043–1063. Available at: www.redalyc.org/articulo.oa?id=14003411 (accessed on November 29, 2011).

Villagrán Paúl, Rubén (1954) *Children's Literature: conditions and possibilities*. Guatemala: Popol Vuh.

Zilberman, Regina, and Ligia Magalhães Cademartori (1987) *Children's Literature: authoritarianism or emancipation*. São Paulo: Ática.

45

BREAKING ILLUSIONS

Contradictory representations of
African childhood

Shalini Nadaswaran

In recent years, there has been a great rise in scholarly work on African children's literature. Finding its roots in folklore and oral tradition, children's literature in Africa not only promotes literary and cultural appreciation to children and young adults but at the same time development of moral values. This chapter will discuss the rise of African children's literature as key to African scholarly attention and then further explore how literary perceptions created within children's psyche or imagination by African children's literature tend to serve aesthetic purposes, creating tensions with and contradictions to the representations of the figure of the child. There is a troubling inconsistency between, on the one hand, the fictional and scholarly work intent on representing or dismantling former stereotypes in African children's literature and, on the other, a continuous misrepresentation of conditions and social relations in Africa.

My argument about the tensions between African children's literature and representations of African childhood depends upon an understanding of the background and purpose of African children's literature. African children's literature finds it roots in oral literary tradition. It was common in precolonial, agrarian African communities for members to gather at dusk after a long day's work to listen to folktales, myths and legends being narrated beside the fire. Adults as well as children in the community listened intently to the orator who regaled them with stories of legends, traditions and values. These stories were meant to develop communal spirit, concurrently infusing moral propriety, "stimulat[ing] children's interest in listening and nurtur[ing] their imagination" (Osa 1987: 318). The storyteller was highly respected within the community, playing a key role in "the stimulation of the child's world of imagination and story" (317). While children listened to this form of oratory and played in the moonlight, they also sang "in praise of legendary African heroes", which fused activities of leisure and socialization (317). It was understood that "twilight is story time in [Africa]. After the sun has set, darkness comes in a few minutes but in those last rays of light, village children gather round the feet of the story-teller begging him for a story ... they all want a story before bedtime, and they take their places on mats on the floor while the story-teller sits on his stool in the middle" (317). Yet, with the advent of colonialism and postcolonialism, the orator became a less important part of a narrative tradition, replaced only much later by print as a means of retrieving oral heritage.

In the meantime, before the bridge between African orality and written literature was built, children who attended colonial schools were exposed to mostly British literature. According to Chinua Achebe, "before 1960 the Nigerian child read nothing but British literature ... bleak and chilly mid-winter, snowflakes, men who gallop by whenever the moon and stars are out" (quoted in Ngugi 64). However, realizing the importance of written literature as a vehicle for preserving oral literature, African writers began to slowly fill the bookshelves and minds of African children with "suitable reading material for [African] schoolchildren", creating a vital avenue for children to "[read] their folktales in school instead of listening to them at home" (Osa 1987: 318). While this intent was focused on reinstating the importance of African literature, culture and heritage to young children, instead of unfamiliar, unseen "mid-winter" settings, the recurrent themes in these literatures were from local stories, adventure narratives and historical tales, similar to those stories found in African oral literature. Hence, African children's literature was meant to fill African children with their heritage, close cultural and social "gaps with stories of African childhood" that were relevant to their cultural and social experiences (Yenika-Agbaw xvi).

The African Universities Press Series and the Macmillan Winners series were the early publishing series that disseminated early African children's literature. Some of the titles included Nkem Nwanko's *Tales Out of School*, Anezi Okoro's *The Village School*, Chinua Achebe's *Chike and the River*, Ifeoma Okoye's *Village Boy*, Nana Wilson-Tagboe's *Efiok Begins Again*, Bayo Adebiyi's *Sparing the Rod* among others. These books were meant to sustain children's interest, so that "the African child can identify with at least one character in each of them" and "inculcate in children those ideas and ideals which will make them grow into good citizens, create an awareness of their cultural heritage, and promote friendship, peace and understanding among children throughout the continent and thus promote unity" (Osa 320). Ifeoma Onyefulu's *The Girl Who Married a Ghost and Other Tales from Nigeria* clearly demarcates in her introduction that children's stories were "all about moral values. They were certainly not about happy endings, although some were funny ... all the stories had important messages ... taught [children] about obedience ... how greed will get you into trouble ... how wrong it was to steal and ... [the] futility of envy" (Onyefulu 6–7). Thus it is apt to surmise that "most of these novels for African children bluntly or subtly extol the virtues of courage, honesty, and hard work, and bluntly or subtly condemn dishonesty and other vices. In its didactic bent, African children's fiction hits at the core of traditional African character education ...novels offer a cultural and intellectual service" (Osa 1984: 596). Apart from education and entertainment, African children's literature was also meant to "create possibilities for children" (Yenika-Agbaw 11). These forms of written or illustrated stories were part of a process of image-making that would enable children to expect, believe and work towards such futures for themselves.

Following this socio-moral stance, contemporary criticism in African children's literature on the other hand has attempted to redress the depictions of Africa. Vivian Yenika-Agbaw (2008) posits that writings after the 1960s tended to present Africa in a certain neo-colonial, stereotypical image of primitive and barbaric and she attempts to redress this imbalance. Yenika-Agbaw urges readers to be socially conscious, to responsibly question and subvert preexisting stereotypical images. Likewise, "teaching children to 'consciously subvert signs' enables them to read varying kinds of books in an empowering manner. Rather than accept these signs as absolute truths, children ask questions to uncover the different layers of meanings that are undergirded by specific ideologies" (Yenika-Agbaw 15). Yenika-Agbaw states that

> [Her] concern now, though, is the plight of African children. Who will tell their stories? Who will capture their joys and pains in books for them in particular to read? Who will help them develop their own voices, so they can actually participate in the literary debate at the child level? I ask these questions because while most children in the West can take reading, books, and literature for granted, African children do not have this luxury

> (111)

Yenika-Agbaw's apprehension is not unfounded. As she questions stereotypical representations of Africa, she also expresses the importance of content in children's literary fiction. While writers and scholars have attempted to represent African tradition, culture and values in children's literature, most prescribed works in African children's literature for children's reading at home by parents or in the school syllabus continue to misrepresent conditions and social relations in Africa. While it is important to represent African values, traditions and culture in children's literature, representations seem to be in contradiction to present socio-economic realities in Africa. How then do we negotiate this difference? Are these representations of childhood in works of adult and young adult African fiction something that should also be included in works that children should be exposed to, or do we continue to create "illusive" illustrations? How will children be empowered to "subvert" and question social ideologies while representations of childhood are contextualized in oppressive and subjugated circumstances?

There are many works in African literature that give us troubling representations of childhood. As noted by Adebayo Williams (1996), "the crisis of governance and democratization in Africa has left a profound mark in literature ... African writers have played a crucial role in the political evolution of the continent", and this is also seen in their depiction of the effects of political democratization on children in Africa (49). The child in African society was regarded as "wealth" to families, symbols of a hopeful, better future, their birth and presence in society celebrated and valued. Yet in contemporary times, the African child's value has been corrupted and misused, boys and girls subjected to unspeakable horrors. Exposed to their nation's neo-liberal policies, structural adjustment programs (SAPs), corruption, embezzlement, war, poverty and socio-economic inequality, children face atrocities as a repercussion of mismanagement and misgovernance. Ironically, "[their] leaders are therefore responsible for the malaise and stasis of the continent. Regression has replaced progress ... those who are closer to power belong to the system while those who are not are marginalized into subjection" (Pangmeshi 122). An analysis of a symptomatic range of texts illustrates the ways in which the children depicted are more often than not marginalized into oppressive circumstances. Each of the works I discuss here addresses particular issues faced by children in Africa, while distorting the image of the child. I do not claim that these are the only situations faced by children in Africa or these are the only texts that represent these problems, but they are samplings that allow us a platform from which to scrutinize the troubling subversion of childhood in Africa by exploring issues of the commodification of children through trafficking and children as victims of war.

Children as commodities

Abidemi Sanusi's young adult novel *Eyo* (2009) is a poignant text that addresses the horrors of child sex trafficking in Africa. A novel that depicts the life of its main protagonist, Eyo, whose name – paradoxical to her situation – bears the meaning "African flower", this narrative is not an easy read as it plunges the reader into a world of unspeakable horrors of sex trafficking. The epigraph to Sanusi's novel – "Don't you see that children are GOD's best gift? The fruit of the womb, his generous legacy? Like a warrior's fistful of arrows are the children of a vigorous youth. Oh, how blessed are you parents with your quivers full of children! *Psalms* 127:3–4 (The Message)" announces that there is something that has gone wrong in the way children are valued in Africa, so that their presence as gifts in families has turned into commodification. Poverty and desperation are one of the main reasons why the transnational business of human trafficking exists, as "the intersection of the socioeconomic bedlam promoted by economic globalization and a historic, deeply rooted bias against females" through "socioeconomic disenfranchisement" (Kara 30). African families who face economic hardship like Eyo's often send their eldest daughters to work. The novel opens with Eyo hawking ice: "Iced water! Ice water! ... the girl couldn't have been more than ten years old ... underweight, with thinner arms that looked like reeds" (Sanusi 3). When her trade proves insufficient to feed her family, Eyo is sent to England to "take care of someone else's children and get paid for it in pound sterling and get free education" (20).

This is where her life of trafficking begins, first as free labor to the family she lives with, who do not send her to school as promised nor pay her family in Nigeria, and then to be raped by the father of the family, Sam Balogun, who eventually turns his toilet into a brothel, making Eyo service friends who were willing to pay for sex, "he had to find a way of getting Eyo out of the flat into another location and where she could service clients without interruption and without arousing interest ... Eyo's services were performed in the bathroom. There were four regular clients, each of whom came twice a week at pre-arranged times" (115). Eyo's tragedy does not end there, as she is then sold to Big Madame and then retrafficked to Johnny whose horrendous acts of violence included "[making] her have sex with two men and an animal, filmed it and later, made her watch it to punish her" (254). Also, "Johnny who made sure her insides were so damaged that she suffered from crippling stomach cramps and intense migraines. He also took out her womb without her permission" (253). Sanusi's representation of Eyo shatters our illusions of children and young adult's life in Africa. For Sanusi, *Eyo* was her "attempt to draw attention to the twin issues of child trafficking and sex slavery ... Whilst it is true that this is a work of fiction, any African child trafficked to [foreign countries] will encounter, at some point or other, some or all of Eyo's experiences ... There are thousands of Eyos in Europe". *Eyo* (2009) is Sanusi's way of using literature as a social discourse to comment on child sex trafficking in Africa since "the best defense against modern-day slavery is a vigilant public" (Bales 255). It is significant that in the novel Sanusi depicts how Eyo's strength to "endure" her circumstances is linked to the mother's words, words she remembers throughout her abuse by Sam and Johnny:

> Your uncle has paid a lot of money to do this for you; money that we will never have or hope to repay. You understand? You must endure.
>
> (Sanusi 30)

It was her mother's face she clung to when she heard the sitting room door open silently as it did most nights and Sam started fumbling with her underwear.

(96)

She would wait a while, find a way, any way, to make money … and Mama would be proud of her for having done well in the UK, for having *endured*, and not bring shame on the family's head.

(235)

You should've thought of that before you decided to come back and lumber us with an extra mouth to feed …what happened to you is no more or no less than what other girls go through … You should have endured in London. Sade still has a chance to live the life she ought to live … but you … whatever hope there was for you … There is a guy … he sends people to London … think about it.

(332–33)

These extracts reflect Eyo's psychology of survival, her endurance because it was the "right" behavior she was firmly warned to have by her mother. The final extract is particularly heart-wrenching as her mother is oblivious to her pain and suffering in London, overlooking one daughter's suffering, pushing her towards a life of being trafficked again so she can save the other daughter from a similar fate that poverty and destitution offer. The novel presents a narrative that questions the validity of parental counsel and the reality faced by African children, when Olufunmi insists that Eyo endure in spite of her circumstances.

Another form of trafficking, the trafficking of children for forced labor, is disclosed in Mende Nazer's *Slave: My True Story* (2003). Sudanese Mende Nazer was kidnapped from her Nuba village in 1993 by Arab raiders. A happy child at 12 years old, Nazer was "studying hard because [she] wanted to be a doctor when she grew up" (Nazer 1). Sold to a wealthy Arab family who live in Sudan's capital, Mende's life as a slave begins with "masters" who own her and called her "Yebit", which means "black slave". Mende came from a hunter-gatherer tribe and "loved all her family dearly" but she spends the following years until adulthood as a slave to an Arab family (Nazer 2). As a slave, she is subjected to terrible mental and physical abuse, forced to sleep in a shed and eat scraps of food left over by the family. Like Eyo's life of entrapment, Mende too had no rights or freedom. Her narrative informs us how the Nuba people and their culture are being obliterated by the kidnapping and modern day trade of their children. In her narrative, Nazer questions, "how many other slave girls like us were there … Hundreds probably. How many would have stories just like us – of being beaten, abused, exploited and lonely? So many broken hearts, stolen childhoods and wrecked lives" (221–22). Mende's stolen childhood includes "[forgetting her] own family … [her] memories just began to fade" (190).

The novel expresses a profound critique of individuals who believe that children are commodities and of families who have children themselves enslaving other children into a life of servitude. Mende's "master" Rahab is proud of her ownership of Mende: "every day she cleans the house, does the washing up and washing out clothes too … Anytime you need her, she's here … No days off, no holiday, no wages. She's always here. She belongs to me" (157). The exploitation of Mende Nazer who is forced to live and work in such inhumane conditions with no pay testifies to the manner in which the African child is abused. While Mende Nazer escaped her captors and today is an activist speaking out against these injustices, there are still many children (from Sudan and other countries of Africa) who are kidnapped and enslaved.

Children as victims of war

As Alcinda Honwana (2006) observes, the recruitment and deployment of child soldiers "demonstrates the inability of governmental and international programs to deal with the serious problems of poverty and under-development that are at the origin of child soldiering and children's victimization by war" (164). Whereas, as Jill E. Korbin (2003) observes, "conventional wisdom holds that children are to be treated with solicitousness and care, to be nurtured and protected", the reality is that children are not immune from violence (432), and the violence of war experienced by children in Africa affords another example of how the suffering of children is represented. Ishmael Beah's autobiography *A Long Way Gone* (2008) relates his childhood story as a war-affected child, a child soldier conscripted into the army after he fled from rebels attacking his village, and his loss of innocence as a child when he carried out terrible acts of violence with his AK-47. Margaret Angucia posits that "African children [establish] social identity and position through contribution to the household and community" (79). This involvement in daily chores, cultivation and communal activities creates their sense of purpose and belonging as well as understanding of culture and identity. However, "many children in the world today are growing up in families and communities in armed conflict ...the spaces where childhood is lived and experienced – become the battleground" (Angucia 82) – the same familiar ground that gathered laughing children now abuses children as combatants in the battlefronts. Thus, these conditions rob them of the opportunity to develop their social identity, replaced instead by the practice and familiarity of violence. Beah recollects that as he escaped the rebels, "[Junior's] hands didn't swing as they used to when he strolled across the yard on his way back to school ... I thought about where my family was, whether I would be able to see them again, and wished that they were safe" (26). Beah's story is compelling and disturbing, as familiar faces and places become a blur in his new childhood. Even as he tries "to hold on to the memories of [his] family ... [he] has trouble conjuring up these thoughts" because his thoughts were now embedded in the regular violence he carries out (Beah 71–2).

Representations of children are prevalent in African wars: "That children have been used in armed conflict and have made their contribution to the political end results of these conflicts in Africa is no longer a disputed fact. In the past decades, civil wars, in Sierra Leone, Angola, and Sudan among others, heavily relied on the abuse of children in the battlefronts" (Angucia 82). As a child soldier, Beah is forced to consume drugs and kill with his AK-47: "they looked like white capsules ... the corporal said it will boost your energy ... I raised my gun and pulled the trigger, and I killed a man. Suddenly, as if someone was shooting them inside my brain, all the massacres I had seen since the day I was touched by war began flashing in my head" (116–19). Likewise, Mariatu Kamara in her autobiography *The Bite of the Mango* (2008) shares a similar experience of being attacked by child soldiers who "looked no older than [she] was" (30). The cruelty exhibited by child soldiers is shocking: "one of the boys pointed his long rifle at the man's back. Two others forced the man into a kneeling position on the ground facing his wife. In front of us all, an in front of her husband, they killed her and the baby she is carrying" (34). While we focus on the corruption of childhood innocence through war that turns boys into mercenaries, Beah and Kamara's narratives also show us what Angucia refers to as children's involvement to create political end results. Mariatu Kamara was a child victim caught in the political crossfire of the war in Sierra Leone. When she loses her hands to rebels who cut them off, this reflects the duality of the victimization of children in war, how children are used in battlefront and how they suffer as casualties in war conditions. Kamara is

> forced to choose a punishment before she leaves … Which hand do you want to lose first? …Why would you want to hurt someone … Because I don't want you to vote … We are not going to kill you …We want you to go to the president and show him what we did to you. You won't be able to vote for him now. Ask the president to give you new hands … As the machete came down, things went silent
> (39–40).

Kamara too is a war-affected child, left to die by other war-affected children, after having to witness and suffer the dismemberment of her limbs: "my hand flew from the rock onto the ground. The nerves kept it alive for a few seconds, and it leapt from side to side, as trout did when we caught them from the river … It took them three attempts to cut off my left hand" (41). This reveals how "children are both victims of war and combatants" (Korbin 440).

Society, tradition and culture are destabilized in war, and affected children are left in the consequent vacuum. War-affected children not only have their childhoods disrupted but also their futures impinged on. As Ertl et al. argue, not only do these children frequently suffer from Post-Traumatic Stress Disorder and depression, but disadvantages resulting from missed education impede their prospects of achieving self-sufficiency and reintegration (2014 10). What increases the reader's revulsion and at the same time evokes heartrending emotions is that, as Mariatu Kamara loses consciousness, "[she remembered] asking herself: 'What is a president?'" (41). This quotation explicitly shows us how children neither understand corruption in the adult world nor the politics of war and are merely a means to an end. Similarly, as Ishmael Beah attempts to rebuild his life by trying to recall his childhood days he finds it impossible (160). His thoughts are tormented by "flashbacks of the first time [he] slit a man's throat. The scene kept surfacing in [his] memory … and each time it happened, I heard a sharp cry in my head that made my spine hurt" (Beah 160). Both Mariatu Kamara and Ishmael Beah live with the repercussions of war. Their accounts lead us to examine the representations of children in war, their physical as well as psychological vulnerability and the reality that children live in a morally incomprehensible world.

Conclusion

The texts analyzed are either young adult fiction or autobiographical fiction. They were published between 2003 and 2009, a sample of works that reflects third-generation writing focused on a realist agenda, questions the legitimacy of crimes against children in Africa, and portrays the effects of extreme economic deprivation, brutal and inhumane civil wars and trafficking. These works also bring insight and historical accuracy to African conflicts, allowing us to rethink the effects of these injustices on children as well as the image of the African child. While these texts are categorized as young adult fiction, they may not necessarily be prescribed reading for African children and African young adults. In many ways, Sanusi, Beah and Kamara's texts are "fictional trajectories of justice" (Nadaswaran 382). These trajectories issue a clarion call by African writers to end appalling activities that continue to rob Africans of their socio-economic wealth and peaceful well-being (Nadaswaran 394). Therefore, representations of children in these fictions inform us of the vital need to depict these reprehensible conditions and social relations in Africa. These writers are not deluded that change will happen immediately, but they do set the basis for us to consider the existing subversions of the image of childhood and think of ways to attain social justice and recognize children's rights. This also allows us to consider whether the content in children's literature prescribed for children's reading should merely create a world of culture, tradition and values, which is often in direct contradiction with present socio-economic and political situations in Africa.

Bibliography

Achebe, Chinua (1960) *Chike and the River*, London: Cambridge University Press.

Adebiyi, Bayo (1981) *Sparing the Rod*, Ibadan: Macmillan.

Angucia, Margaret (2009) "Children and War in Africa: The Crisis Continues in Northern Uganda." *International Journal on World Peace* 26(3): 77–95.

Bales, Kevin and Ron Soodalter (2009) *The Slave Next Door: Human Trafficking and Slavery in America Today*, Berkeley: University of California Press.

Beah, Ishmael (2007) *A Long Way Gone: Memoirs of a Boy Soldier*, New York: Farrar, Straus and Giroux.

Ertl, Verena, Anett Pfeiffer, Elisabeth Schauer-Kaiser, Thomas Elbert, Frank Neuner (2014) "The Challenge of Living On: Psychopathology and Its Mediating Influence on the Readjustment of Former Child Soldiers," *PLoS ONE* 9(7): 1–11.

Honwana, Alcinda (2006) *Child Soldiers in Africa*, Philadelphia: University of Pennsylvania Press.

Kamara, Mariatu (2008) *The Bite of the Mango*, Toronto: Annick Press.

Kara, Siddharth (2009) *Sex Trafficking: The Inside Business of Modern Slavery*, New York: Columbia University Press.

Korbin, Jill K. (2003) "Children, Childhoods, and Violence," *Annual Review of Anthropology* 32: 431–446.

Maddy, Yulisa Amadu and Donnarae MacCann (2008) *Neo-Imperialism in Children's Literature about Africa*, New York: Routledge.

Nadaswaran, Shalini (2014) "Motif(ve)s of Justice in Writings by Third-Generation Nigerian Women," *Tradition and Change in Contemporary West and East African Fiction. Matatu* 45: 381–395.

Nazer, Mende and Damien Lewis (2003) *Slave: My True Story*, New York: Public Affairs.

Ngugi, Pamela Y (2012) "Children's Literature Research in Kenyan Universities: Where are we now?" *International Journal of Arts and Commerce* 1(2): 60–77.

Nwankwo, Nkem (1963) *Tales Out of School*, Lagos: African Universities Press.

Okoro, Anezi (1966) *The Village School*, Lagos: African Universities Press.

Okoye, Ifeoma (1980) *Village Boy*, Ibadan: Macmillan.

Onyefulu, Ifeoma (2010) *The Girl Who Married a Ghost and Other Tales from Nigeria*, London: Frances Lincoln Children's Bks.

Osa, Osayimwense (1996) "Review," *Research in African Literatures* 27(1): 221–225.

Osa, Osayimwense (1987) "The Growth of African Children's Literature," *The Reading Teacher* 41(3): 316–322.

Osa, Osayimwense (1984) "Contemporary Nigerian Children's Literature," *The Reading Teacher* 37(7): 594–597.

Pangmeshi, Adamu (2014) "Mirror Writing, Social Realism and the Interrogation of the Postcolonial Nation: Alobwed'epie's *The Death Certificate* and *The Day God Blinked*," *Matatu: Journal for African Culture & Society* 45(1): 117–129.

Peek, Lori (2008) "Children and Disaster: Understanding Vulnerability, Developing Capacities, and Promoting Resilience – An Introduction," *Children, Youth and Environments* (18)1: 1–29

Sanusi, Abidemi (2009) *Eyo*, Nairobi: WordAlive Publishers Limited.

Schmidt, Nancy J, "Children's Literature about Africa," *African Studies Bulletin* 8(3) (December 1965): 65–70.

Schmidt, Nancy J. (1970) "Children's Literature about Africa: A Reassessment," *African Studies Review* 13(3): 469–488.

The Message New Testament with Psalms and Proverbs (1993). Trans. Eugene H. Peterson. Colorado Springs: Navpress.

Williams, Adebayo (1996) "Literature in the Time of Tyranny: African Writers and the Crisis of Governance," *Third World Quarterly* 17(2): 349–366.

Wilson-Tagboe, Nana (1982) *Efiok Begins Again*, Ibadan: Macmillan.

Yenika-Agbaw, Vivian (2008) *Representing Africa in Children's Literature: Old and New Ways of Seeing*, New York: Routledge.

46

FACING UP TO REALITY

Recent developments in South Africa's English literature for the young

Sandra Stadler

The demise of apartheid was a watershed experience for every South African. That the early 1990s breathed change and hope was the notion that characterised private and public lives of that era. For many South Africans, the inauguration of Nelson Mandela as the first black President of the Republic of South Africa presaged the imminent realisation of a "rainbow nation." Moreover, the whole world had followed South Africa's peaceful transition and had watched when the country's people were allowed to vote for the first time in 1994. The implementation of the world's most democratic and egalitarian constitution two years later was as much understood as the tombstone of apartheid as the birth announcement of "the new South Africa."

The coming-of-age of the South African country was, however, subsequently marked by many regressions and twenty years later the atmosphere of hope had given way to one of desolation and frustration. Vast political and private transformations as well as measures to restructure the spatial outline of the country followed the implementation of the new constitution. These processes not only affected public bodies but forced South African individuals of whatever ethnic descent to redefine their notion of the country and what they considered home. The social impact of political programmes such as the Black Empowerment Movement or the Spatial Development Plan, which have been in practice for the last twenty years, can be felt in the countryside, in cityscapes, and in everyday life spaces such as the workplace or the home.

In retrospect, these massive transformative processes on both the public and the private level had an invigorating effect on art and culture, such that South Africa's literature is as much in a phase of transition as the country itself, so that it is now possible to speak of a new era of literary emancipation of the formerly overpowering past. In particular, the development of contemporary English literature for young adults mirrors the development of the South African nation. The genre has gained new momentum since the mid-1990s, effectively reinventing itself on two levels: content and publishing format.

New contents

With its focus on the generation that is currently coming of age, young adult literature addresses those themes and issues with which its contemporary audience struggles on a daily basis. Due to political circumstances, this has not always been the case. The early developments of the genre in English have been authoritatively documented by Elwyn Jenkins (1993, 2002, 2006, 2012), who concludes that "[a]fter [an] illustrious start [in the early nineteenth century], English South African children's literature did not raise questions of rights again until the 1960s" (Jenkins 2012: 7). A new era was eventually triggered by the Soweto uprising of school children in 1976: "Writers [now] found it possible to write novels about young people coming to grips with the great socio-political issues of apartheid" (Jenkins 2012: 10). Despite this progressiveness, many youth books containing liberal content could still only be published abroad and books about "dissident" topics were still in danger of being banned; Beverly Naidoo's *Journey to Jo'burg* ([1984] 1985) and *The Sound of the Gora* (1980) by Anne Harries (cf. Jenkins 2012: 10) are well known examples of books banned in the 1980s. Nevertheless, since the 1980s, more and more of those "liberal" youth novels made it also to the shelves of South African bookstores. During that time academia began to take notice of the field of children's and young adult literature and a few years later two conference proceedings appeared, *Towards Understanding* (1988) and *Towards More Understanding* (1993) (Jenkins 2012: 196). A reading of these essay collections makes it clear that the earlier claim of a progressive South African children's and youth literature is not new. Andreé-Jeanne Tötemeyer stated already in 1988 that literature for teenagers had "become quite progressive in recent years [i.e. the 1980s] and tackled themes such as drug abuse, juvenile delinquency, parental rejection, illegitimacy, alcoholism and so on" (87). On the other hand, she pointed out that "these themes concentrate mainly on conflict-management at an inter-personal (micro-social) level, i.e. in the family, school and peer group," and hence "it has however become imperative for authors to broaden their perspective to include conflict management on the macro-social level, i.e. towards peace and understanding between groups in society at large" (Tötemeyer, 1988: 87).

Contemporary literature for young South Africans appears to have answered Tötemeyer's call (Inggs 2000; Lehman, et al. 2014). A recent assessment of more than 300 South African youth novels – which were written in English by South Africans and published in South Africa between the years 2000 and 2013 – has shown that on the content level the literature written for the "born free" generation has its finger on the pulse of the time (Stadler 2015). In this study, I analysed the content of these youth novels according to four categories – setting, gender, ethnicity, and social economics – and found that Tötemeyer's desiderata were now being met: "the comparatively high number of novels with characters of mixed backgrounds and multiple ethnicities are a promising result, as these novels are in themselves heterogeneous and have the greatest potential to promote diversity" (Stadler 2015).

In so far as the literary medium has become a vehicle of delivery, since the end of apartheid local authors have predominantly written "socially committed novels" (Pinsent, 2005) and teenage problem novels (Stadler 2015). They have used the realistic mode to address key issues of contemporary South African society, such as crime, violence (e.g. Zachariah Rapola, *Stanza on the Edge*, 2001), drug abuse (e.g. Dianne Case and Yvonne Hart, *Katy of Sky Road*, 2007), the dangers of social media and online communities (e.g. S. A. Partridge, *Dark Poppy's Demise*, 2011), and (im)migration – that is, topics that were formerly considered unacceptable for young readers. Authors no longer avoid issues debated in day-to-day politics but discuss them openly in young-adult literature. Topics such as xenophobia (e.g. Jayne Bauling, *E Eights*, 2009; and Patricia Schonstein Pinnock, *Skyline*, 2000), the lack of parental role models and father figures (e.g. S. A. Partridge,

Fuse, 2009; and Gail Smith, *Someone Called Lindiwe*, 2003), the persistence of patri-archy in vast parts of society and the ever-lurking danger of sexually transmitted dis-eases and the stigma connected with them (e.g. Margie Orford, *Dancing Queen*, 2004; and Jenny Robson, *Praise Song*, 2006) dominate twenty-first-century teenage novels of South Africa. Also the persisting (mental) separations between the different ethnic groups are addressed. Today, frictions between different groups persist mainly for socio-economic reasons and no longer necessarily due to racism or the legally fixed spatial confinement of people. Youth novels, such as Ian Fritz's *Taking the Rap* (2004), present new perspectives and fresh approaches to how the (mental) divide between different milieus can be over-come. In these novels, youth are empowered and obtain a mediator position between old traditions and new developments. The more general message is that with this empower-ment comes a responsibility to take an active part in the (re)construction of present-day South Africa.

A further reason for the heterogeneity in the representation of topics is the ever-wider group of authors who write for young adults. Although still more whites are writing English youth novels, the number of celebrated young black and colored voices is mount-ing. Sello Mahapeletsa (*When Lions Smile*, 2003; *Tears of an Angel*, 2007), Sifiso Mzobe (*Young Blood*, 2010), Kopano Matlwa (*Coconut*, 2007) and Kgebetli Moele (*Untitled*, 2013) are only four of these celebrated new voices. They have already been awarded a number of prizes for their narratives: Matlwa received the European Union Literary Award and the Wole Soyinka Prize for African Literature for *Coconut* (2007), Mzobe was awarded the Sunday Times Fiction Prize, the Herman Charles Bosman Prize and also the Wole Soyinka Prize for *Young Blood* (2010), for instance. In their stories these young authors break fresh ground in the way they address controversial topics (Stadler 2014). Kgebetli Moele, for example, wrote *Untitled* in the form of a diary, and while this is not a new format within the South African context, what is innovative about this novel is Moele's raw and undisguised approach to the topic he tackles in his book, namely rape. The female protagonist narrates her story with all the immediacy of the first-person nar-rator pointing the reader to the incredible and thus thought-provoking fact that her rape had always been inevitable.

Only a minority of twenty-first-century texts address an area that still causes political outcry, acts of violence, and denial in present day South Africa, namely homosexuality and transsexuality. *My Funny Brother* (2012) by Robin Malan, *The Hidden Life of Hanna Why* (2007) by Marita van der Vyver, *This Book Betrays my Brother* (2013) by Kagiso Molope are some of those rare examples. In both van der Vyver's and Molope's novels the homosexual characters remain secondary characters. *My Funny Brother* (2012) is the most didactic text of the three as it not only contains actual lessons of biology but clearly speaks out for a more inclusive society. It has to be noted that although there are only a small number of texts in that field their publication is a major achievement and docu-ments a slow emancipation of authors and publishers. Nevertheless, the relative scar-city of such texts reflects the persisting gender conservatism in teenage fiction (Grobler 1988: 132–141; Jenkins 2012; Stadler 2015).

The beginning of the twenty-first century saw another innovation, a turn towards speculative fiction. The emergence of this field happens on various platforms and through different media: there is an online spec-fic magazine, *Something Wicked* and in 2012 the *AfroSF: Science Fiction by African Writers Anthology* appeared in print. Significantly, the emergence of the South African sub-genre coincides with a more global turn toward the fantastical: the *Twilight* series (2005–2008) by Stephenie Meyer, which is responsible for an international hype about vampire stories, the *Percy Jackson* series (2005–2009) by Rick Riordan with its mix of Greek mythology and present-day American culture, *The Hunger Games Trilogy* (2008–2010) by Suzanne Collins and the *Divergent* series (2011–2013) by Veronica Roth, which create dystopian realities, are but some examples of this international phenomenon. In South Africa, Lily Herne's *Mall Rats* trilogy (*Deadlands*, 2011; *Death of a Saint*, 2012; *The Army of the Lost*, 2014), Lesley Beake's *Remembering Green* (2010), Jenny Robson's *Savannah 2116 AD* (2004) and Cat Hellisen's *When the Sea is Rising Red* (2012) and its sequel, *The House of Sand and Secrets* (2014), are some of the most prominent examples of the past years.

Speculative fiction is one of the most inclusive sub-genres in contemporary South African fiction. First of all, there are almost as many spec-fic publications for a young adult audience as for an adult audience. Second, the classification of the books into the categories of either adult or young adult novel is not always clearly possible. Hence, the differences between the two literary categories are least visible in this sub-genre. This is because many authors write for both age groups. Moreover, the decision how to market a book is made by the publishers and not the writers themselves. Sarah Lotz, for instance, writes under different pseudonyms and in different collaborations. As Lily Herne, she writes together with her daughter, Savannah Lotz, for a young adult audience; together with Louis Greenberg she produces speculative fiction for adult readers under the pseudonym S.L. Grey (*Downside* trilogy: *The Mall, 2013*; *The Ward*, 2012; *The New Girl*, 2013; the latter was longlisted for the Sunday Times Prize 2014). Another celebrated writer, who was one of the first to successfully write speculative fiction in South Africa, is Lauren Beukes (*Moxyland*, 2008; *Zoo City*, 2010; *The Shining Girls*, 2013; *Broken Monsters*, 2014). By 2014 she had gained international fame, with her books republished in the United States, Australia, and the United Kingdom, amongst others. The advent of a South African specific genre underlines the more general urge to re-write the present condition of the rainbow nation. In addition, the all-inclusiveness of the sub-genre is symptomatic of the new mindsets that permeate the new South Africa.

A familiar international genre, school stories, are also being written in South Africa. These include novels set in a boarding school or college context (e.g. Fiona Snyckers, *Team Trinity* (2013), and *Trinity Rising* (2008)) and stories that have their main content carried out on school grounds but the protagonists live with their families (e.g. Edyth Bulbring, *The Club*, 2011). The genre has witnessed a revival after the tremendous success of John van de Ruit's boarding-school novel, *Spud* (2005), and its three sequels (*Spud – The Madness Continues…*, 2007; *Spud – Learning to Fly*, 2009; *Spud – Exit, Pursued by a Bear*, 2012). Due to its success, the *Spud* series has partly been made into film starring local actors as well as the internationally famous John Cleese. In 2014, South African librarians voted the series amongst the best and most important books of the country since the end of apartheid. This notion coincides with the reception of the books by the public, which has been compared to the *Harry Potter* phenomenon of the early 2000s – with the exception that van de Ruit's novels do not contain any magic. No other novels have sold more copies in South Africa than the *Spud* series, which is read by both teenagers and adults. Written in diary format, the story is set at a boys-only boarding school in rural KwaZulu-Natal in the early 1990s. The books tell the story of John "Spud" Milton, a white, lower-middle-class boy, and how being a boarder shaped his coming-of-age. Van de Ruit's key ingredients in the books are humour and bluntness. His choice of the perspective of the young adult growing up in those times of transition further supported his notion to address the end of apartheid from a different angle. The teenage narrator allows for a fresh, ironic and amusing approach to a period in South Africa's history that still haunts the present. Van de Ruit used the efficacy of comic discourse to open a space where new debates and opinions about the past are possible (Stadler 2014).

A further genre within new contents in South Africa's contemporary youth literature is the book series. This format, which is characteristic of speculative fiction, has also become more prominent for teenage problem novels and socially committed novels in recent years (e.g. Edyth Bulbring, *April-May Books*, 2011–2013). Two important series are the *Siyagruva* series, which was published in the late 1990s and early 2000s, and the *Harmony High* series, published by Cover2Cover since 2010. The two series are the most explicit expression of an ideology advocated in the novels of the new South Africa: diversity. The explicit voicing of persisting stereotypes between the different ethnic groups makes the youth novels in these series such a valuable contribution to the contemporary corpus (e.g. Ros Haden, *Broken Promises*, 2010; Sivuyile Mazantsi and Sam Roth, *Too Young to Die*, 2012; Mteto Mzongwana, Onele Mfeketo, and Orbin Lamna, *Mom's Taxi*, 2003; Russell H. Kaschula, *Divine Dump Dancer*, 2003). These texts have undeniably didactic intentions. In all of the novels, the teenage protagonists are empowered and detect new ways of living in the multifaceted South African society. The fictional characters are able to overcome their prejudices and the great majority of stories end hopefully. The didacticism of twenty-first-century literature is thus to promote cultural diversity and acceptance without making it sound condescending (Hunt 1994). The series format is favorable for the transmission of these notions, as readers can follow different developments in the lives of the same set of characters in different settings over various novels. The publication of books in the series format is clearly also a decision influenced by the profit-oriented publishing industry. This leads us to the second area of discussion, the new politics of publishing in South Africa.

(New) politics of publishing

When freedom of press and expression were inscribed in Section 16 of South Africa's constitution, it was generally believed that the threat of censorship, which was omnipresent during apartheid, was over. However, debates about these constitutional rights have continually resurfaced subsequently. The most recent example is the public outcry caused by the Media Appeals Tribunal and the Protection of State Information Bill in 2010. Both were seen as a threat to the freedom of expression and the media as such, leading two of the country's most eminent and celebrated writers, Nadine Gordimer and André Brink, to draw up a petition against the passing of the bill. Despite their efforts, the law was enacted in 2011. Three years later, around the time of the twentieth anniversary of the founding of the Republic of South Africa and as a consequence of her disillusionment with present developments in South Africa, Nadine Gordimer, a declared voice of the anti-apartheid movement, announced her retirement from writing fiction in an interview conducted by Michael Skafidas, which was first published in *The Huffington Post* in April 2014. Gordimer's conclusion regarding the present state of South Africa is a bitter one: "I am afraid that we have not done with our freedom what we said we were going to do. And that makes it now the worst of times because it is a great disillusion, having emerged from a terrible past while we are making in many ways a mess of the present."

Connected to the discussions about the freedom of press are the politics of publishing literature in South Africa. The democracy recognises eleven official languages and aims to provide literary texts in all of these. Yet intention and reality continue to clash in this respect. The number of books available in the different languages is not even remotely similar. Equal representation of literature in the official languages will not be achieved in the near future, and there remains a question about the status of English in relation to the other ten official languages. English is the language of the business world, the media, and politics in present-day South Africa and can be considered the lingua franca of the country even though only roughly 10 percent of South Africans name it as their mother tongue. The *Annual Book Industry Survey 2011* provides detailed insights in the book market: in terms of book sales and the number of books published, English publications rank second after Afrikaans publications. Indeed, the majority of children's and youth literature is still produced and sold in the Afrikaans sector (turnover R33.8 million). The English market for children's and young adult literature made R6.4 million profit in 2011. Publications in any of the nine indigenous languages continue to play a minor role; interestingly however, in 2011 every book published in the indigenous languages was a children's or young adult book, not adult literature (Stadler 2015).

To date, the print runs of literary publications remain considerably smaller and vary between 500 and 2,000 titles. High prices for printed books (R50 to R300) are an important factor in why the establishment of a reading culture has been so difficult in this country. Many South Africans simply cannot afford to buy a book. Small print runs and the low profit connected to them are reasons why many authors of children's and youth literature write texts that are potentially attractive for the school market, as this is the most profitable market. Others turn to overseas publishing houses, as has been a popular custom in the 1970s and 1980s (e.g. Fanie Viljoen, *Scarred Lion*, 2011; Joanne Hitchens, *Stained*, 2008; Suzanne van Rooyen, *The Other Me*, 2013). Edyth Bulbring's novels have been republished in the United Kingdom with a new title: *The Summer of Toffie and Grummer*, first published by Oxford University Press South Africa in 2008, was retitled *I Heart Beat* (2014) by the UK-based publisher Hot Key Books, for instance. Still, the reception of South Africa's children's and youth literature outside of the country is rather limited, due to the small print runs and the difficulty in purchasing the printed book version abroad. A further reason why only a few of South Africa's children's books are known abroad is that only a minority of them are translated into languages other than English. Examples are Kopano Matlwa's *Coconut* (2007), which was translated into Italian, and novels by Lutz van Dijk (e.g. *Themba*, 2006), Kagiso Lesego Molope (*The Mending Season*, 2005), Michael Williams (*The Billion Dollar Soccer Ball*, 2009), and Linzi Glass (e.g. *The Year the Gypsies Came*, 2007), which were translated into German. A number of award-winning Afrikaans teenage fictions, such as Marita van der Vyver's *The Hidden Life of Hannah Why* (2007) or Fanie Viljoen's *Mindf**k* (2011), have been translated into English. Generally, national prize competitions, such as the Percy FitzPatrick Award for best children's literature in English or the Sanlam Prize for Youth Literature, still play an important role also with regard to what kind of topics authors choose to deal with in their children's books.

Significantly, contemporary politics of publishing South African literature do not only concern the previously debated issues of language and questions of availability of printed books. In fact, the postmillennial years have given rise to new concepts and forms of book publishing for the younger generation, which have changed the reception of South Africa's children's literature altogether. By making use of new technologies and electronic devices organizations such as FunDza or Paperight have effectively sparked a reading revolution over the past few years. This is a big claim to make in a country that is said to have had no reading culture so far. With the rise of the new media, a new era of accessibility of South African children's and youth literature has begun. As the printed book is only available in restricted numbers for a reasonably short period of time new book formats such as e-books or mobile phone novels have become significant alternatives. Theirs is a durable and cheaper format, which is moreover accessible from even remote areas. Thus, it is a format that responds to three key issues regarding the literary market: price, availability and accessibility. Mobile phone novels, a genre that has its origins in Japan, are particularly well received by the young adult audience, as the success of a South African non-profit organization, FunDza, demonstrates. FunDza recognized the problems that high prices for printed books cause and targeted them from a different angle. As the cell phone is one of the most accessible technological devices in South Africa and many (young) South Africans use it to go online, FunDza saw the electronic device as their point of access. They created mobile phone novels, short stories, plays and poetry with a specifically South African content. Furthermore, they reintroduced the serial format, most popular and best known during the nineteenth century in Britain. Thus, only one chapter of a story is released per day. At the end of each chapter they ask their readership whether they liked or disliked the character's development and how the story would (or should) proceed. Their mobile books are available from R1,35 and are therefore considerably cheaper than printed books, which cost at least R50. Readers can access the stories not only on their mobile phone but also via social media platforms or on the organization's web page. In 2014 their "Growing Communities of Readers" program recorded over 300,000 readers who accessed a total of 15,624,187 pages. An evaluation of the program by the University of Cape Town's Monitoring and Evaluation Unit concluded that the more participants read, the more likely they were to engage in independent reading, indicate that they enjoyed reading outside of school, perceive themselves as good readers, and read for longer periods (*FunDza Annual Report* 2014: 9, 13). These findings show that the project has not only revolutionized the literary market for young South Africans but has achieved what many before them did not: the gradual establishment of a reading culture. Significantly, it is not technology and the use of new media alone that lead to the tremendous accomplishments of the project. It is above all the stories that are told and the fictional worlds created that draw the target audience in.

Conclusion

In order to get young South Africans to read, publishers have "faced up to reality" and now meet the teenagers where they are – the blog, on social media sites, via their smart phones and in the actual book shop. Next to changes in the book format, the topics addressed in twenty-first century youth novels are closer to reality and simultaneously further away from it than ever. On the one hand, the majority of South Africa's young adult novels (70 percent) have been a mix of *Bildungsroman*, coming-of-age story and social novel since the turn of the century (Stadler 2015). The texts are socially committed and give a realistic representation of contemporary South Africa. Thus, the country's authors have reinterpreted established genres, such as the realist novel, by adapting them to their specific cultural context. On the other hand, the emergence of a distinctly South African speculative fiction underlines a broader social phenomenon, namely the interest in other-worldly experiences, the search for alternative readings of reality, the urge to escape from this world to another while reading and the necessity to redefine traditional literary categories such as teenage fiction and adult fiction. Today, South Africa's literature for children and youth is vibrant and actively engages in processes that shape the future of the country. It is due to both new and established voices that literature – both in print and in the digital format – continues to be one of the crucial media through which pragmatic, social, and socio-economic changes are processed and (didactically) mediated in South Africa. In addition to the books mentioned above, the following are especially notable: Troy Blacklaws (*Karoo Boy*, 2005), Joanne Bloch (*A Few Little Lies*, 2009), Helen Brain (*No More Secrets*, 2009), Sarah Britten (*The Worst Year of My Life So Far*, 2000), John Coetzee (*Dance of the Freaky Green Gold*, 2008), K. Sello Duiker (*The Hidden Star*, 2006), Judy Froman (*Solomon's Story*, 2011), Joanne Macgregor (*Jesse's Story*, 2008), Thiathu Nemutanzhela (*Bua, Comrade!*, 2007), Russell Kaschula (*Take Me to the River*, 2006), Henrietta Rose-Innes (*Shark's Egg*, 2001; *Rock Alphabet*, 2007), and many more (Appendix, Stadler, 2015).

Bibliography

FunDza Annual Report 2014. www.fundza.co.za/about-fundza/our-annual-reports/annual-report-2014/

Grobler, Hilda (1988) "Me Tarzan – You Jane: Sex Stereotyping in Children's Books," in Isabel Chilliers (ed.) *Towards Understanding: Children's Literature for Southern Africa*, Cape Town: Maskew Miller Longman, 126–141.

Hunt, Peter (1994) *An Introduction to Children's Literature*, Oxford: Oxford University Press.

Inggs, Judith (2000) "Character, Culture and Identity in a Contemporary South African Youth Novel," in Jean Webb (ed.) *Text, Culture and National Identity in Children's Literature. International Seminar on Children's Literature: Pure and Applied*, Helsinki: Nordinfo, 46–55.

Jenkins, Elwyn (1993) *Children of the Sun: Selected Writers and Themes in South African Children's Literature*, Johannesburg: Ravan.

——— (2002) *South Africa in English-language Children's Literature, 1814–1912*, Jefferson, N.C.: McFarland.

——— (2006) *National Character in South African English Children's Literature*, New York: Routledge.

——— (2012) *Seedlings: English Children's Reading and Writers in South Africa*, Pretoria: University of South Africa Press.

Lehman, Barbara A., Jay Heale, Anne Hill, Thomas van der Walt, and Magdel Vorster (eds.) (2014) *Creating Books for the Young in the New South Africa: Essays on Authors and Illustrators of Children's and Young Adult Literature*, Jefferson: McFarland.

Pinsent, Pat (2005) "Language, Genres and Issues: the Socially Committed Novel," in Kimberley Reynolds (ed.) *Modern Children's Literature: An Introduction*, New York: Palgrave, 191–208.

Skafidas, Michael (2014) "Nadine Gordimer: The Great Post-Mandela Disillusion," *The Huffington Post*, 14 April. www.huffingtonpost.com/michael-skafidas/nadine-gordimer-mandela_b_5143759.html (accessed 17 June 2014).

Stadler, Sandra (2014) "Generation Z und der Beginn einer Leserevolution," *Africa Süd*, 43(3): 16–17.

——— (2015) "Debating Equal Representation in South African Youth Literature Written in English (2000–2013) – A Statistical Assessment," *Bookbird*, 53(2): 46–58.

Tötemeyer, Andreé-Jeanne (1988) "Towards Interracial Understanding through South African Children's and Youth Literature," in Isabel Chilliers (ed.) *Towards Understanding: Children's Literature for Southern Africa*, Cape Town: Maskew Miller Longman, 80–88.

47

"I DO YEARN FOR CHANGE, BUT I AM AFRAID AS WELL"

An analysis of Iranian contemporary young adult novels

Morteza Khosronejad, Fatemeh Farnia
and Soudabeh Shokrollahzadeh

I was left alone. I stood in front of the mirror. There was no one else in the mirror. Yet I did not identify with my own image. My aunt had told me that I was shedding skin just like a snake. I searched every day but could not find any skin except my own covered with horrible red acne. I looked at my profile. Right, left, back of my head and neck. Where were these changes, these sheddings leading me to? I was afraid. I did yearn for change, but I was afraid as well.

(*Hasti*, Hasanzadeh, 2010: 182) [1]

When Hooshang Moradi Kermani was writing *The Tales of Majid* for radio broadcast in 1974, he could have not imagined that his script would not only serve as the scenario of a successful television series but also anticipate the direction of young adult (YA) discourse in Iran. The radio program proved to be a success for some children, many adolescents and even some adults, and twenty years later *The Tales of Majid* was adapted for television in post-1979-Revolution cultural, social and political circumstances. It had also been repeatedly reissued as a book, with the most recent edition, the 24th, appearing in 2012. It is the story of an orphan who, living a meagre life with his grandmother, struggles to meet his most basic needs and desires. The characteristics of Majid, the protagonist, are symptomatic of later YA discourse: a critical mind, creativity, valor, determination, and good humor. He confronts and successfully overcomes his challenges and difficulties, while simultaneously growing in maturity through these rites of passage and initiation. The constant appeal of *The Tales of Majid* shows that this discourse has remained relatively stable over the past four decades. Adolescents' hope for the future, well-being and self-actualization is why they attempt to break from the past while facing various challenges and making critical choices. These very choices mold their selves through different crises and contribute to their development toward adulthood. Various elements of this thematic discourse persisted after Kermani, while others disappeared.

Subjects and themes of Iranian YA novels

Some of Kermani's subjects and themes are struggles with cultural and societal traditions, self-actualization and self-establishment, poverty, love, autonomy and attempts to be accepted by adult society. Ali Ashraf Darvishian before the Revolution, and Mohammad Reza Bayrami and Fereydon Amoozadeh Khalili after the Revolution were also concerned with similar themes in their fiction. In *The Mountain Called Me* (2012), Bayrami tells the story of a boy who struggles against both societal and natural impediments to prove his acceptance in adult community. Amoozadeh Khalili's short story "Two Unripe Dates" (2000) artfully merges domination by poverty and the pains of love. With the outbreak of the Iran-Iraq War (1980–1987), YA novels are dominated by patriotism and attempts to encourage their readers to join the army and fight for the cause of Iran and Islam. Later, however, new themes emerge that promise the writers' increasing attention to the needs of their audience. However, while poverty remains a constant theme, it is coupled with issues such as cultural destitution, war and migration to other cities. Iranian YA novels also manifest other thematic concerns.

Mythical and epic themes

Mohammad Reza Yusefi pioneered the introduction of mythical and epic themes through his creative retellings, and today he is followed by the young writer, Arman Arian. As Ja'fari Ghanavati (2007) observes, in contrast to the west, "Appropriating, rewriting, recreating, and being inspired by classical literature has not attracted Iranian writers' attention during the last decades, with the exception of very rare cases" (127). However, Arian's creation of successful novels based on his knowledge of epics represents a turning point in the 2000s. He recreates parts of Ferdowsi's *Shahnameh*, or *The Epic of the Kings*, as well as stories of kings and princes in his trilogy *Persians and I* (2003–2005). The first title, *Azh Dahak Fortress* (2003), features a modern adolescent named Ardeshir who flees to an underground shelter when the security forces invade their home. He miraculously takes part in the epic stories his father has written. They are about the fights between Zahhak, the Dragon King, an oppressive ruler on whose shoulders there are two snakes, and Kaveh the Blacksmith and Fereydun who fight for liberty against him. Following the success of this trilogy Arian wrote another trilogy, *Ashvazdangheh* (2008–2014), based on the name of a pious man of Ancient Iran whose name is repeated in some Yashts of *Avesta*. Having drunk an elixir made by his master, Ashvazdangheh gains immortality and thus lives for 6,000 years. Besides magical capabilities, he has also gained metaphysical knowledge due to his extensive travels around the world. He can read and manipulate others' minds and defeat demonic forces, although he believes it is not his mission to conquer Ahriman (the "destructive spirit" in Zoroastrianism).

Ashvazdangheh is a modern and traditional Iranian superman through whom Arian links historical Iran and the contemporary world. This modern myth entertains, empowers and enlightens its audience, as Arian does not merely repeat epic and heroic themes for the new generation, but extends them to the contemporary era and updates them by actively engaging in their creation.

War themes

War is another recurrent theme in Iranian YA novels. Three broad approaches can be discerned in novels about the war between Iran and Iraq. First is an advocative approach, which encourages the audience to enlist as a soldier and fight in the war. Works that emphasize the significance and value of victory and martyrdom were especially popular at the outset and during the war (all who die in defense of Iran are designated martyrs). Bayrami's *The Eagles of the Sixtieth Hill* (2011) represents an example of this attitude.

Second is a critical approach that became dominant in the first decade of the twenty-first century. *Wake Me Up, when War is Done* (2011) by Abbas Jahangirian, *Hasti* by Farhad Hasanzadeh, *The Night That Crickets Don't Sing* (2006), and *Romances of Jonah in the Fish's Belly* (2010) by Jamshid Khanian are among the most distinguished examples. These novels reverse some of the values of the previous approach and underscore the atrocities of war and its aftermath: migration, displacement, depression, death and destitution. Whereas being a war victim and a martyr's son is highly valued in the former approach, a martyr's immigrant son in *Wake Me up, when War is Done* is the target of his fellow students' sarcasm in Qum, the most religious city in Iran. While provocative novels aim to depict the sorrows of defeat in war and of war migrants due to the destruction of their cities and their zeal to be killed in defending their country and becoming a martyr, yet, the protagonist of *Romances of Jonah in the Fish's Belly* is merely concerned about saving her piano as her sole source of comfort. In other words, for the family that the novel depicts, music, that is an emblem of peace, is valued over war and even defending one's country.

The third approach, the situational, takes war only as its setting, not its theme. In Ahmad Akbarpour's *Moments of Hiccup* (2013), the adolescent narrator and his peer are keen rivals even though they are on friendly terms. The narrator enlists in the army and is engaged in war as the result of his jealous rivalry. In the end, they conclude that it is not important who does what, that what is important should be done anyway. So their friendship and its development is the subject of this novel. Although it is possible to find some traces of this attitude in the critical approach, its pure representation is actualized in recent war novels.

Theme of love

Besides poverty, epic, myth and war, love is yet another recurrent theme in Iranian YA novels. Most war novels that take war as either central or peripheral also feature love; it is as if war and love are coterminous. Of course, the first post-war novels that concern love do not feature anything about war. Here, love is symbolic. Kermani in *Not Wet, and Not Dry* (2003), features love in a symbolic sense within the socio-political structure and employs a satiric tone toward it. Jahangirian's *Hamoon and Darya* (2009) narrates the story of a boy named Hamoon (meaning desert) who dearly loves his cousin, Darya (meaning the sea). But she has five more suitors and her parents do not give their consent for her marriage with Hamoon. She has an attack of jaundice and the physician prescribes that she should swallow some fish alive that live in Ahovaan Pond (Pond of Deer). All suitors leave for the pond but the perils they encounter on their way dissuade them one after another from fulfilling their mission. Only Hamoon successfully undertakes the challenge and brings her the fish, and in the end he dies so that his beloved can continue living. Jahangirian, however, takes a much more down-to-earth attitude toward love in the following decade when he returns to it in his *Wake Me up, when War is Done*. He even goes so far as to delineate the physical features of the beloved including her hands, eyes, hair and breath. Relationships between boys and girls are a formidable taboo in fiction, however, and that is why partial transgressions from these taboos reveal certain hidden relationships. A suppressed love leads to elopement in hope of marriage in Khanian's *Babor's Beautiful Heart* (2003). The girl's brother deems love to be "defamation" and "nonsense" in *Wake Me up, when War is Done* (54, 55), while her grandmother believes that love and even speaking with a male stranger is a sin. The protagonist, a boy, on the other hand, wavers between a conventionally religious standpoint with regard to his relationship to stranger girls and his yearning to express his love to his beloved:

> I will buy Houri [i.e. the girl's name denoting a female heavenly creature] a ring. It looks like silver but I know the glittering color will fade soon. But it can anyway make us husband and wife, and save me from hell. Grandma has smelled a rat and frequently warns me against talking to stranger girls. She daily preaches about the horrors of hell. And I am left in purgatory, unable to decide whether I would go to heaven or hell. Whenever I talk to Houri, I visit a holy shrine afterwards to repent.
>
> (52–53)

Resorting to violence, Darya's brother, who equates love with dishonor, attempts to cut her relationship with Hamoon in *Hamoon and Darya*. In Khanian's *The Night That Crickets Don't Sing*, love can only be allowed through traditional marriage. Yusefi's *Gūātī* (One who Suffers from Goitre, 2003) also depicts unfulfilled love and arranged marriage. Although Zargol's love for Abdulrahman is never fulfilled, she can never forget him even after her arranged marriage (or actually after she is sold) to Hajbaba.

Arian's trilogy, *Persians and I* seems to be the only novel that has been successful in circumventing Iranian strict censorship and explicitly touching upon physical relationships between the two sexes. In "Romance in the Woods," a chapter in the second part of the trilogy *The Secret of the Bird Mountain* (2004), the main characters stealthily watch three pretty girls swimming, while the narrator openly describes the scene and talks about their feelings. The three girls lead the main characters to their lodging and warmly receive them, but the next day it is disclosed that they are actually entrapped by three witches. It seems that this novel could only gain the required publication permit because of its genre (fantasy) and the unhappy outcome of this scene.

Girls' and women's roles

Critical reflections on women and the feminine role as well as attempts to break gender stereotypes are among the most significant themes of enlightened YA novels in Iran. Underprivileged women, like those who belong to lower social strata and poor districts, are shown to be doubly repressed. Yet Hasanzadeh proffers a different picture of women and the underprivileged classes in his recent novel, *Hasti*. Hasti, whose father favors boys over girls, feels dejected and isolated. She even goes so far as thinking that she is an abandoned child later adopted by this family. Sometimes, she thinks of her father as a step-father and imagines how her actual father would someday find her. Her mother and her aunt, a university student, support Hasti, but she is so disheartened that she totally denies her femininity and manifests male inclinations: she takes karate lessons during their displacement in war, fights boys and rides a motorbike. She finally defeats her father when she manages to save him in war. Hasti meets a robust and well-mannered young man, who joins the battlefield; she falls in love with him and regains a modified version of her modern, agentic femininity.

Furthermore, the depiction of urban life and the middle class gives an alternative view of women in Iranian society. The adolescent girl in *Romances of Jonah in the Fish's Belly* plays the piano and listens to Beethoven. However, middle class girls are not necessarily like her. Sometimes they read and reflect, but at other times they are left alone while their parents do not understand them. Khanian depicts the fragile atmosphere of a family in the strange incidents they encounter in their new house in *A Box of Pizza for Roasted Trapezoid* (2012), and Hamid Reza Shahabadi in *A Lullaby for A Dead Girl* (2011) links economic poverty during the Constitutional Revolution (1905–1907), which led to girls being sold to wealthy men, with the emotional poverty of contemporary middle class life, and underlines the historical process and the way girls have been ignored in Iranian society. Zohreh, one of the narrators, has four brothers much older than herself and no sisters. She feels lonely and alienated from her parents in their new house in the suburbs of Tehran:

> It were as if [my father] did not know me … as if we were strangers. I wonder if he ever embraced me when I was young. For years we had little to talk about except for trite remarks. He left home early in the morning and returned at night; then he had his dinner and slept. And all my fat mother … did was to cook, wash, and clean. She would have disposed of me in her cleaning, if she could.
>
> (22)

In this novel as well as his next, *When Moji Was Lost* (2012), Shahabadi shows that alienation and isolation are the causes of adolescent girls' flight from home.

Subjects, themes and issues of the middle class

Middle class adolescents and their issues are other themes of Iranian YA novels. The middle class seldom occupied a prominent role in children's literature due to the prevalence of leftist ideologies (including both Marxist and Islamic) both before and after the 1979 Revolution and because of the suppressive and provocative atmosphere of the Iran-Iraq war years. Economic growth, prospering of the private sector, post-war peace, and rapid expansion of metropolises like Tehran during the 1990s and 2000s provided an opportunity for the middle class to gain relative prominence both in society and in children's literature. This development was evident in the production and consumption of fantasy and thriller genres. Besides the extraordinary sale of the *Harry Potter* series in translation, *Persians and I* has been reissued ten times and even thrillers are among the best sellers. This trend indicates that the audience, especially those who can afford and are willing to buy books and have enough time to read them, mostly seek to satisfy their desires. Therefore, the role of the middle classes has become more significant in the development of children's literature. Ali Asghar Seidabadi (2011) also underlines the determining role of this class when he writes:

> Writing about urban middle classes inevitably changes the stories drastically. Their value system is more similar to the global one and it offers the writer a wide variety of life styles that might be at odds with the official outlook. Interestingly enough, this very class has been very active and has even shaped many social changes during the last decades.
>
> (87)

"Null" subjects and themes

It does not suffice to explicate the extant themes of YA novels (Khosronejad 2004); in other words, it is never enough just to illustrate what these works say in ideological investigations. Following Elliot W. Eisner (2001) who believes that the learners' behavior is formed not only by what they learn but also by what they do not learn (107), and borrowing the concept of "null curriculum," Khosronejad explores the null theme in a collection of Iranian YA novels. He concludes that issues like critical thinking, love, environment, satire, peace, friendship, individual identity, work, death, and tolerance are absent in these novels (Khosronejad, 2004). After a decade, some of these issues—like love, satire, promotion of peace, critical and philosophical thinking—have found their way into recent works. Maryam Omidinia, Leila Maktabifard, and Esmat Mo'meni (2013) deem the Iranian YA novels of the 2000s to be appropriate to the study of critical thinking skills. Similarly, Hossein Sheikhrezaie (2010) conveys how Khanian's novels include ethical issues useful for philosophical inquiry. However, having Alice Trupe's *Thematic Guide* (2006) in mind, we can take the following subjects as "null" in Iranian YA fiction: abuse, sexual violence, accepting difference, suicide, dating's challenges, emotional problems confronted, pregnancy, parenthood and abortion, sexual desire, multiculturalism, and queer themes. Generally speaking, otherness has been among the gaps of this literature. One of the most evident proofs for this claim is the absence of child and adolescent immigrants, especially Afghans. Similarly, Iranians in diaspora who left Iran as the result of the 1979 Revolution or war between Iran and Iraq are also excluded. In his study, Amin Izadpanah shows that Iranian children's literature allots neither an audible voice nor a highlighted presence to the other. Although the other is restricted in his/her relations with the dominant by his/her alterity, some instances of constructive, and sympathetic negotiation and relationship can also be discerned (Izadpanah, 2012).

Genres

Realistic fiction is the most common in Iranian YA fiction, though many styles are employed in its creation. Hasanzadeh, for instance, is inclined toward a classic style, while Akbarpour and Khanian favor the postmodern. Fantasy that was once popular through the works of Mohammad Hadi Mohammadi has been rejuvenated by Arman Arian and other novelists, including Siamak Golshiri and Mehdi Rajabi. Furthermore, despite the criticism aimed at thrillers in Iran (Ghoreyshinejad, 2011), these novels are also well-received. Shadi Khoshkar (2013) reports that Golshiri's *Dracula Series* (2008–2013) has been the only title originally published in Persian that has been among the best sellers in Iran (32, 34, 36). As the main character of this series is Dracula, Golshiri's position is affirmed because "Characters like Dracula and Frankenstein no longer belong to any specific country" (Moosavian 2011, 24); they belong to all thriller-lovers around the world.

Science-fiction has not been very successful. *Rustam in the Twenty-Second Century* (1934) was the only sci-fi written between 1921 and 1974 in Iran (Honarmand, 2014). Besides being a pioneer, this novel is important because it employs the famous mythical figure of Rustam. However, despite this promising start, it seems that Iran's social, cultural, economic and scientific circumstances have not promoted the development of sci-fi novels.

Statistics prove the financial success of satire, and writers have created noteworthy satiric works; however, satire has not yet secured an autonomous position for itself. Razi Hirmandi (2012) notes,

> Defying taboos and authority, including linguistic authority, are among the characteristics of satire addressed to children and adolescents. Iranian satire is flourishing, but due to certain considerations and limitations, we still face difficulties in satire, especially for young adults.
>
> (15)

Historical novels have also been disregarded, although Mohsen Hejri's *Eagle's Eye* (2011) has attracted some attention.

Stylistic techniques

Most Iranian novelists favor classic styles, although there are some writers who employ modern and postmodern stylistic techniques such as intertextuality, metafiction, and polyphony. Intertextuality is manifested in a novel's connections with native or foreign folklore, contemporary stories, arts (cinema, music), scientific theories and concepts and historical events. Shahabadi's *A Lullaby for A Dead Girl*, for instance, employs many such intertextualities. He refers to famous Iranian and world novelists like Fahimeh Rahimi (a writer of popular novels), Moradi Kermani, John Christopher, and Erich Kästner among others. This novel focuses on women's suppression, which also creates historical intertextuality. A girl who had been sold and cruelly suppressed only to die during the Constitutional Revolution (1905–1907) is revived in the daydreams of a contemporary girl. As one of the characters is a researcher conducting a study on the topic of women sold during the period of Constitutional Revolution, time travel is realistically feasible. This also creates a dialogue between two different historical periods as well as between science and art, research and novel. The novel is also linked to folklore through a folktale (*The Tale of Nokhodi*) that mentions the imprint of the ruling class's suppressive acts in the Iranian collective unconscious. Accordingly, this novel acts as a site for the meeting of the past and present, traditional and modern cultures, eastern and western literatures, science and art, as well as two generations (young and old) who are struggling in the intersection of all these dialogues. Examples of the use of metafiction in Iranian YA novels include Akbarbour's *Emperor of Words* (2007), *A Thousand and One Years* (2003) by Mandanipour, and *Babor's Beautiful Heart*. The adolescent narrator of *Babor's Beautiful Heart* directly and implicitly talks about employing narration and other literary devices as elements of fiction.

While metafiction and intertextuality are manifestations of polyphony in novels, polyphony is even more evident in the plurivocality of narratives and characters. Khanian achieves this in *Romances of Jonah in the Fish's Belly* through separating the narrator from the focalizer, and in *A Box of Pizza for Roasted Trapezoid* by employing an impartial narrator. Shahabadi and Akbarpour, in *A Lullaby for A Dead Girl* and *I am not My Dad's Servant* (2014), respectively, achieve polyphony by letting all characters narrate a part of the story.

Pitfalls and concerns

Different factors have been said to hinder the growth of YA novels in Iran: novelists' inadequate understanding of their audience and their expectations; thriving of populist commercial books; state organizations' intervention that promotes solicitation and uses its economic power and influence to create a false market for its favored books, which do not necessarily excel according to literary standards; writers' distance both from their own adolescence and from their young adult audience due to the deficiencies of the educational system and public libraries; and their scant knowledge about recent theories, criticism and international masterpieces (see Kafeili, 2010).

Furthermore, Ensiyeh Moosavian (2010) explains why foreign novels are preferred by Iranian adolescents: they are not restricted by cultural and religious considerations, so they can handle the themes adolescents favor. In other words, they respond to their needs for love, satire, and sensation seeking. This is especially because these writers update themselves as their audiences do, and they are orientated toward recent science and technologies. Moreover, their structure and other literary elements are of higher quality. Finally, publishers are more interested in multi-volume series (Moosavian 2010, 172–173).

Hejri (2010), a novelist and critic, also observes that "The authority and dominance that ideological narratives seek to impose on [our] audience especially during the last three decades [i.e. since the 1979 Revolution] is among the reasons why our native fiction has failed to attract adolescents" (127). Khosro Aghayari, the editor of *Roshanan Quarterly*, who promotes a religious approach to children's literature, also maintains that theoretical shortcomings are the reason behind the inadequacy of Iranian YA novels. However, he believes the only way out is to resort to theorizations based on Islam and the values of Revolution; in an interview with SUCCLS, November 5, 2014, he says:

The main problem of literature and children's literature in Iran is the opposition between the secular theories and rationalism and religious rationalism. Unless the Revolution can establish its own rational system as a basis to answer the need for theorization in social, economic, cultural, artistic and literary domains, this literature can never reach an autonomous theory based on Iranian and Islamic culture. Accordingly, it cannot have its own system of literary criticism. Such circumstances will lead to nothing but imitation and following the western lead.

(n.p.)

In contrast, Shahabadi (2013), the manager for Series of Today's YA Novels project at IIDCYA (Institute for the Intellectual Development of Children and Young Adults), argues that the reason behind the vacuum in indigenous novels is the novelists' low motivation as the result of their economic problems (16–17).

Conclusion

Investigating the Iranian situation confirms Emer O'Sullivan's (2005) claim that, "the special literature actually addressed to young adults ... focuses on teenagers' search for identity and autonomy, their struggle against adult authorities in order to develop their own set of values" (43). There is no great difference in this regard between novels that feature a boy as their protagonist and those featuring a girl. As O'Sullivan also notes, "If the dominant theme in the traditional adolescent novel with a male protagonist is his search for identity, with a usually autonomous finale, novels with female protagonists often have different narrative patterns, more often bearing greater resemblance to the family novel and the love story" (43–44). The adolescent girl in *Hasti*, as mentioned before, has been successful in attracting female audiences through her towering subjectivity and subversive inclinations. Therefore, the Iranian YA novel can be said to yearn to surpass its preliminary primary traditional stage. This similarly coincides with O'Sullivan's contention that, "Adolescence is recognized as having a central function within the ethno-psychoanalytical discussion of social change" (42), and Mario Erdheim's (1984) claim that "only in and from adolescence can those impulses come that alter a society which is fundamentally inclined to preserve the status quo" (quoted in O'Sullivan 2005, 42). Discourses of adolescence have moved towards imagining young adults as real, rather than ideal human beings, as progressive, constructive, agentic, plural, inquisitive sensation seekers. It also seeks to hear the voice of adolescents while it simultaneously encourages them to listen to other voices. This inclination is evident in the endorsement of new styles that make polyphony possible. However, these novels cannot yet attract their audience and are often aesthetically lacking. The Iranian YA novel thus has far to go before it is fully established. There are no well-funded awards for YA novels comparable to those for adult novels in Iran. No Iranian novel has avid fans like those of the translations of *Harry Potter* that proved to be instant hits in the market. Though adolescent voices are heard in these novels, even polyphonic novels have not succeeded in fully representing these voices, and sometimes they are so impersonalized that one can easily substitute a boy for the heroine. Finally, even though the young generation has been successful in making adults hear their voice even in their silence, their articulate voice has not been fully reflected in novels as a representative of their personalities and needs. YA literature should be a revolutionary literature as the nature of its audience demands. To realize this cause, however, novelists, publishers, critics, teachers and adults should have a deeper understanding, a stronger will and more courage. Though fearing these changes, adolescents have achieved much more than their adult fellows. What the heroine of *Hasti* says, as quoted in the epigraph to this essay, actually seems to reflect the contemporary situation of many Iranian adults: they are aware of the inevitability of change; they yearn for change, but they are afraid even more than young adults who are on the threshold of a new life.

Notes

1 All translations from novels and of the titles of research items are our own.
2 Dates for Iranian publications are dual, referencing both the Iranian and Western calendar.

Bibliography[2]

Akbarpour, A. 1384Š/2007. *Impirāṭūr-i kalamāt* [Emperor of Words]. Tehran: Peydayesh. [Persian].

Akbarpour, A. 1392Š/2013. *Lahẓi'hā-yi siksikih* [Moments of Hiccup]. (From Series of Today's YA Novels), Tehran: IIDCYA. [Persian].

Akbarpour, A. 1393Š/2014. *Man nukar-i bābā nīstam* [I Am Not My Dad's Servant]. 8th ed. Tehran: Ofoq. [Persian].

Amoozadeh Khalili, F. 1379Š/2000. *Dū khurmā-yi nāras* [Two Unripe Dates]. Tehran: Ghadyani, Banafshe Books. [Persian].

Arian, A. 1382–1384Š/2003–2005. *Pārsīān va man* [Persians and I]. Tehran: Moaj. [Persian].

Arian, A. 1382Š/2003. *Kākh-i izhdihā* [Azh Dahak Fortress]. Vol. 1 of *Persians and I*. Tehran: Moaj. [Persian].

Arian, A. 1383Š/2004. *Rāz-i kūh-i parandi* [The Secret of the Bird Mountain]. Vol. 2 of *Persians and I*. Tehran: Moaj. [Persian].

Arian, A. 1385–1393Š/2008–2014. *Ashvazdangheh*. 3 Vols. Tehran: Moaj. [Persian].

Bayrami, M.R. 1390Š/2011. *Uqāb'hā'yi tapi-yi shaṣt* [The Eagles of the Sixtieth Hill]. Tehran: Sureye Mehr. [Persian].

Bayrami, M. 1391Š/2012. *Kūh ma rā ṣidā zad* [The Mountain Called Me]. Tehran: Sureye Mehr. [Persian].

Eisner, E. W. 2001. *The Educational Imagination: On the Design and Evaluation of School Programs.* 3rd ed. New York: Pearson.

Ghoreyshinejad, N. 1390Š/2011. "Ta'ṣṣīr-i adabīyāt-i vaḥshat bar nūjavānān: nūjavānān chi mīgūyand?" ["The Impacts of Gothic Literature on Adolescents: What do Adolescents Say about it?"]. *The Research Quarterly of Children and Youth's Literature* 1 (52): 112–116. [Persian].

Golshiri, S. 1387Š/2008-1392Š/2013. *Majmū-i'yi khūnāshām* [Dracula Series]. 5 Vols. Tehran: Ofoq. [Persian].

Hasanzadeh, F. 1389Š/2010. *Hastī* [Hasti]. (From Series of Today's YA Novels), Tehran: IIDCYA. [Persian].

Hejri, M. 1389Š/2010. "Mukhātab-i dar hāl-i 'bur: buḥrān-i mukhātab dar rumān-i nūjavān" ["The Passing Addressee: the Crisis of the Addressee in YA Novels"]. In *Proceedings of the Fourteenth Festival of Children and YA Books: Children and YA Novels: Ideas and Difficulties*, 120–129. Tehran: IIDCYA. [Persian].

Hejri, M. 1390Š/2011. *Chishm-i uqāb* [Eagle's Eye]. (From Series of Today's YA Novels), Tehran: IIDCYA. [Persian].

Hirmandi, R.; Shafiee, Sh.; Sadr, R. 1391Š/2012. "Guftu'gūyī darbāriy-i imkānāt va maḥdūdyat'hāy-i ṭanz-i kūdakān-i: ṭanz-i kūdakān-i, nigāh-i kūdakān-i" ["A Forum on Facilities and Limitations of Children Satire: Children's View."] *The Research Quarterly of Children and Youth's Literature* 5 (56): 6–22. [Persian].

Honarmand, M. J. 1392Š/2014. "Barrasy-i tawṣīfīy-i ketāb'hāy-i 'lmī-takhayulī dar īrān va maqāli'hā va naqd'hāyi muntashirshudi dar īn bāri" ["A Descriptive Study of Science Fiction Books in Iran, and Articles, and Reviews Published on Them."] MA thesis in Children's Literature, Shiraz University. [Persian].

Izadpanah, A. 1391Š/2012. "Barrasy-i jilvi'hāyi dīgarānigy dar adabīyāt-i kūdak va nūjavān" ["A Study of the Representations of Otherness in Iranian Children's and YA Literature"] MA thesis in History and Philosophy of Education, Shiraz University. [Persian].

Ja'fari Ghanavati, M. 1386Š/2007. "Asāṭīr-i īrān dar qālib-i rumān" ["Iranian Myths in Genre of Novel"] *Roshanan Quarterly* 6: 126–135. [Persian].

Jahangirian, A. 1388Š/2009. *Hāmūn-u daryā* [Hamoon and Darya]. Tehran: Monadi-e Tarbiyat. [Persian].

Jahangirian, A. 1389Š/2010, 1390Š/2011. *Jang ki tamām shud bīdāram kun* [Wake Me up, when War is Done]. Tehran: Ofoq. [Persian].

Kafeili, F. 1389Š/2010. "Barrasy-i vaẓīyat-i rumān-i nūjavān dar nishasti takhaṣuṣy: bī angīzigy va takhaṣuṣzudāyī-i nivīsandigān yā raqībī bi nām-i rasānih?!" ["A Report of the Status of YA Novels in a Professional Assembly: Writers' Lack of Motivation and their Despecialization or a Rival Named Media?!"] *Iranian Children and Adult Youth's Book Review and Informational Journal*, 160: 97–100. [Persian].

Khanian, J. 1382Š/2003. *Qalb-i Zībā-yi Bābur* [Babor's Beautiful Heart]. Tehran: IIDCYA. [Persian].

Khanian, J. 1385Š/2006. *Shabī ki jarvāsak nakhānad* [The Night that Crickets Don't Sing]. Tehran: IIDCYA. [Persian].

Khanian, J. 1389Š/2010. *Āshiqānihāy-i Yūnus dar shikam-i māhī* [Romances of Jonah in the Fish's Belly]. (From Series of Today's YA Novels), Tehran: IIDCYA. [Persian].

Khanian, J. 1391Š/2012. *Yik ja'bi pītzā barāyi ẕūzanaqi-yi kabābshudih* [A Box of Pizza for Roasted Trapezoid]. Tehran: IIDCYA. [Persian].

Khoshkar, Sh. 1392Š/2013. "Guzārishī taḥlīlī darbāriy-i mīzān-i furūsh-i kitāb'hāyi kūdak va nūjavān: purfurūsh'hā va rumān'hā" ["An Analytic Report on the Marketing of Children and Young Adults' Books: The Best Sellers and Novels."] *The Research Quarterly of Children and Youth's Literature* 8: 31–36. [Persian].

Khosronejad, M. 2004. "Null Theme and its Role in Imaging Childhood in Young Adults Fiction." Paper presented at ACLAR Conference. Sydney, July 17–18. [Unpublished paper].

Mandanipour, Sh. 1382Š/2003. *Hizāru yik sāl* [A Thousand and One Years]. Tehran: Afaringan. [Persian].

Moosavian, E. 1389Š/2010. "Chirāgh-i kamsūy-i t'līf" ["The Dim Light of Authorship"]. In *Proceedings of the Fourteenth Festival of Children and YA Books: Children and YA Novels: Ideas and Difficulties*, 170–177.Tehran: IIDCYA. [Persian].

Moosavian, E. 1390Š/2011. "Guftu'gū bā Sīyāmak Gulshīrī: joz'īyāt bi jāyi mūsīqī va gul-i ābī" ["An Interview with Siamak Golshiri: Details Instead of Music and Blue Lights."] *The Research Quarterly of Children and Youth's Literature* 1(52): 22–25. [Persian].

Moradi Kermani, H. 1382Š/2003. *Na tar, va na khushk* [Not Wet, and Not Dry]. 2nd ed. Tehran: Moeen. [Persian].

Moradi Kermani, H. 1391Š/2012. *Qiṣṣihā-i Majīd* [The Tales of Majid]. 24th ed. Tehran: Moeen. [Persian].

Omidinia, M., L. Maktabifard, and A. Momeni. 1392Š/2013 "Barrasy-i mahārat'hāyi tafahur-i intiqādī dar rumān'hāyi barguzīdiy-i nūjavān-i fārsī dahiy-i hashtād bar asās-i fihrist-i Peter Facione" ["A Study of Critical Thinking Skills in Selected Persian YA Novels in the 2000s Based on Peter Facione's List"] *Thinking and Children* 4 (1): 1–26. [Persian].

O'Sullivan, E. 2005. *Comparative Children's Literature*. U.S.A: Routledge.

Sanatizadeh Kermani, A. H. 1313Š/1934. *Rustam dar qarn-i bīst-u duvvum* [Rustam in the Twenty-Second Century]. Tehran: Etehadiye Printing House. [Persian].

Seidabadi, A.A. 1390Š/2011. "Chand nukti darbāriyi dunyāyi munsajim-i dāstānīy-i yīk nivīsandih: ḥikāyatnivīs mabāsh!" ["Some Points about the Coherent Fictive World of a Writer: Don't be a Mere Story-Writer!"] *The Research Quarterly of Children and Youth's Literature* 1 (52): 82–88. [Persian].

Shahabadi, H.R. 1390Š/2011. *Lālāī barāyi dukhtar-i murdi* [A Lullaby for A Dead Girl]. 3rd ed. Tehran: Ofoq. [Persian].

Shahabadi, H.R. 1391Š/2012. *Vaqtī Muzhī gum shud* [When Moji was Lost]. (From Series of Today's YA Novels), Tehran: IIDCYA. [Persian].

Shahabadi, H.R., Sh. Hariri, L. Maktabifard. 1392Š/2013. "Guftu'gūy-i guruhī: dar qīyāb-i zindigīy-i imrūz" ["A Forum: In the Absence of Today's Life"] *The Research Quarterly of Children and Youth's Literature* 8: 16–30. [Persian].

Sheikhrezaie, H. 1389Š/2010. "Rushd-i akhlāqīy-i kūdak va adabīyāt'i dāstānī bi hamrāhi barrasy'i āsāri dāstānī-i Jamshīd Khānīān az manẓar-i rushd-i akhlāqī" ["Moral Development of Children and Fictions and A Study of Jamshid Khanian's Fiction from Moral Development Point of View"] *Thinking and Children*, 1(1): 37–67. [Persian].

Trupe, A. 2006. *Thematic Guide to Young Adult Literature*. Westport: Greenwood Press.

Yusefi, M. R. 1382Š/2003. *Gūātī* [One who suffers from Goitre]. Tehran: Andishe Sho'le. [Persian].

INDEX

477